A HISTORY OF PRIVATE LIFE

III · Passions of the Renaissance

Roger Chartier, Editor

Arthur Goldhammer, Translator

The Belknap Press of
Harvard University Press
CAMBRIDGE, MASSACHUSETTS
AND LONDON, ENGLAND
1989

This book was willed, conceived, and prepared by Philippe Ariès. Death prevented him from seeing it through to completion. We, the contributors, have written it with his goals and thoughts of his friendship in our minds.

Originally published as Histoire de la vie Privée, vol. 3 De la Renaissance aux Lumières, © Editions de Seuil, 1986.

This book is printed on acid-free paper, and its binding materials have been chosen for strength and durability.

Library of Congress Cataloging in Publication Data (Revised for volume 3)

A history of private life.

Translation of: Histoire de la vie privée.
Includes bibliographies and indexes.
Contents: v. 1. From pagan Rome to Byzantium / Paul Veyne, editor   — v. 3. Passions of the Renaissance / Roger Chartier, editor; Arthur Goldhammer, translator.
  1. Manners and customs—Collected works. 2. Family—History—Collected works. 3. Civilization—History—Collected works. 4. Europe—Social conditions—Collected works. I. Ariès, Philippe. II. Duby, Georges.
GT2400.H5713 1987   390'.009   86-18286

ISBN 0-674-39975-7 (v. 1 : alk. paper)
ISBN 0-674-39976-5 (v. 2 : alk. paper)
ISBN 0-674-39977-3 (v. 3 : alk. paper)

A HISTORY OF PRIVATE LIFE

Philippe Ariès and Georges Duby
General Editors

III · Passions of the Renaissance

Contents

A HISTORY OF
PRIVATE LIFE

Passions of the
Renaissance

Introduction

Philippe Ariès

*I*S IT possible to write a history of private life? Or does the notion "private" refer in different periods to such different states and values that relations of continuity and difference among them cannot be established? That is the question which I hope will be answered.

Let us begin by comparing two periods whose characteristic features I will simplify for the sake of argument. In the late Middle Ages we find the individual enmeshed in feudal and communal solidarities, incorporated into a more or less functioning system. As part of a seigneurial community or a clan or bound by ties of vassalage, he (or she) and his family moved within the limits of a world that was neither public nor private as those terms are understood today or were understood at other times in the modern era.

Simply stated, private was confounded with public, "chamber" with exchequer. What did this mean? First, and crucially, it meant that, as Norbert Elias has shown, many acts of daily life were, and for a long time would continue to be, performed in public. Let me correct this broad statement by appending two remarks. First, the community that defined the boundaries within which the individual moved—whether rural village, town, or urban neighborhood—was a familiar world in which everyone knew and kept an eye on everyone else. Outside lay a *terra incognita* peopled by figures of legend. The only inhabited space, the only space subject to the rule of law, was communal space.

Second, even in periods of relatively dense population, there were places in the community where a precarious intimacy flourished. These were recognized and to some extent protected: a corner by a window or in a hallway, a quiet spot beyond the orchard, a forest clearing or hut.

Compare this medieval situation to the situation as we find it in the nineteenth century. Society is far vaster and more anonymous.

People no longer know one another. Work, leisure, and home life are separate, compartmentalized activities. Men and women seek privacy. To obtain it, they insist on greater freedom to choose (or to feel that they are choosing) their own way of life, and they withdraw into the family, which becomes a refuge, a focus of private life.

As late as the beginning of the twentieth century, however, old forms of collective and communal sociability persist, particularly among the urban working class and peasantry: for men, the cabaret; for women, the public washhouse; and for both, the street.

How was the transition between these two historical periods made? Several ways of approaching the problem suggest themselves. One possible approach is evolutionary. According to this view, the history of Western society since the Middle Ages was foreordained; progress toward modernity was steady and uninterrupted, with perhaps an occasional pause, an abrupt reversal, or even a momentary regression. Such a model obscures the diversity and complexity that must be counted among the leading characteristics of Western society in the sixteenth, seventeenth, and eighteenth centuries. It is hard to distinguish between the innovations and the survivals (or between what we take to be innovations and survivals).

A second approach is more attractive, and closer, I think, to the reality of the situation. It requires us to modify the usual periodization, arguing instead that from the central Middle Ages to the end of the seventeenth century there was no real change in people's fundamental attitudes (*mentalités*). I reached this conclusion through my work on the history of attitudes toward death. In other words, a periodization that is appropriate for doing political, social, economic, and even cultural history is not appropriate for the history of *mentalités*. There were so many changes in material and spiritual life, in relations between the individual and the state, and in the family that we must treat the early modern period as something autonomous and original, even bearing in mind all that it owed to the Middle Ages (seen of course in a new light). Nor was the early modern era merely a precursor of the modern: it was something unique, neither a continuation of the Middle Ages nor an adumbration of the future.

The Evolution of the Modern Age

What events changed people's attitudes, in particular their ideas of the individual and his role in daily life? Three external events, belonging to the realm of political-cultural history, played a part. The most important of these probably was the change in the role of the state, which from the fifteenth century on steadily established itself in a variety of forms and guises. The state and its system of justice increasingly intervened, at least in name and, in the eighteenth century, also in fact, in the social space that had previously been left to the communities.

One of the individual's primary missions was still to acquire, defend, or increase his or her social role within the limits of the community's toleration. As communities gained new wealth in the fifteenth and sixteenth centuries, and as the inequalities between people in different walks of life grew more pronounced, there was greater room to maneuver within those communal boundaries. People sought to win the approval or incite the envy of others, or at least to secure toleration of their difference, by means of show, or *honor*, as this particular form of appearance was called. To protect and defend one's honor was to save face before the eyes of the community.

What mattered was no longer what an individual was but what he appeared to be, or, rather, what he could successfully pass himself off as being. To ensure such success, no effort was spared: lavish expenditure, generosity (in judiciously chosen moments at least), insolence, ostentation. In defense of honor words and blows were exchanged publicly and duels were fought, unleashing a cycle of vengeance (since recourse to the courts or other state institutions was ruled out).

From at least the time of Louis XIII the state did what it could to establish some semblance of order in this world of appearances. Under Richelieu, for example, dueling was prohibited on pain of death, and sumptuary laws regulated ostentation in dress (and the use of such ostentation to usurp a position to which the wearer was not entitled). The lists of the nobility were revised to eliminate interlopers. The state increasingly intervened in what we consider the very heart of private life, the family, by means of the so-called *lettres de cachet*. More precisely, the state placed its power at the disposal of one member of the family to be used against others. This enabled family heads to avoid recourse to normal government institutions, which was considered demeaning to family honor.

This strategy had important consequences. The state and its system of justice viewed society as a composite of three elements. First was the king's court, a veritable forum, which perpetuated in a modern form an archaic mixture of political action, festivity, personal commitment, service, and hierarchy, many elements of which already existed in the Middle Ages. At the other end of the social ladder we find the urban lower class and the peasantry, among which the traditional mix of work and celebration, ostentation and prestige persisted for a long time. Social relations were extensive, variable, and constantly changing. This was the world of the street, the tavern, the mall, the church square. Finally, between the common people and the court was an intermediate zone, populated for the most part by people of culture, the minor nobility of office and the church, the middling sort of notables who in unprecedented fashion enjoyed staying at home and engaging in agreeable relations with a select "society" (the very word that was used at the time) of friends.

The second major event that changed attitudes was the progress of literacy and the increased availability of books, thanks largely to printing. The increasingly common practice of silent reading did not entirely eliminate what had long been the only way of reading: out loud; in rural *veillées* we find passages from broadsides and blue books—inexpensive pamphlets distributed throughout the country by hawkers. Nevertheless, silent reading allowed more than one person to form his own idea of the world and to acquire empirical knowledge. It made possible, outside convents and hermitages designed with the needs of pious solitude in mind, a solitary reflection that otherwise would have been far more difficult.

Not unrelated to the changed role of the state and the spread of literacy was the development of new forms of religion in the sixteenth and seventeenth centuries. The new religions, while fostering inward piety, by no means discouraged more collective forms of parish life. They also encouraged individuals to examine their consciences—Catholics through confession, Puritans through keeping private diaries. Among laymen, prayer most commonly took the form of solitary meditation in a private chapel or even a corner of the bedroom, using an item of furniture specially designed for the purpose: the prie-dieu.

Measures of Privacy

How did these changes affect people's attitudes? I shall examine this in six distinct areas.

(1) The literature of civility reveals how the chivalric customs of the Middle Ages were transformed into rules of conduct and etiquette. Norbert Elias has found evidence in this literature to support his idea that the gestation of modernity was a long, slow process. More recently, Roger Chartier has taken a fresh look at the subject, and Jacques Revel reviews current thinking on the question in his contribution to this volume.

Between 1500 and 1800 people developed new attitudes toward their own bodies and toward the bodies of others. Where earlier literature on civility emphasized, say, the proper way for a young man to serve food at table, later treatises stress the impropriety of touching or looking at other diners, thereby creating a protected zone around the body. People stopped embracing with wide-open arms; they no longer kissed the hand or foot of a woman they wished to honor, and men stopped prostrating themselves before their ladies. These histrionic demonstrations gave way to discreet, understated gestures. People no longer attempted to cut a figure, to create an appearance, to assert themselves; they behaved properly in order to discourage attention, to pass almost unnoticed. A new modesty emerged, a new concern with hiding certain parts of the body and certain acts. "Cover this breast, which I do not like to see," says Tartuffe. Gone was the sixteenth-century practice of covering the male organ with a codpiece that simulated an erection. Newlyweds were no longer put to bed by a crowd of onlookers who returned to greet them the following morning. The new modesty, in conjunction with ancient taboos, even made it difficult for a male surgeon to gain access to the bed of a woman in labor—a place reserved "by nature" for women.

(2) Private diaries, letters, confessions, and autobiographies revealed the determination of some people to set themselves apart. They wrote in order to know themselves, but not necessarily to communicate that knowledge to anyone except perhaps their own children, who, it was hoped, would keep their memory alive. Heirs were often instructed to destroy such writings, the variety of which indicates the new relation that existed between reading, writing, and self-understanding.

People did not necessarily write only *about* themselves, but often they wrote *for* themselves and no one else. Few sought to publish what they wrote. Written purely for pleasure, such works survived, if at all, only by chance, stored away perhaps in a forgotten trunk or attic. Autobiography met a need, and met it so well that it became a literary genre (like the medieval will) and a means of literary and philosophical expression, from Maine de Biran to Amiel.

It is no accident that in England, the birthplace of privacy, diaries were widely kept from the late 1500s. In France there is nothing comparable, although *livres de raison*, kept by growing numbers of people, were perhaps more detailed than ever before.

(3) In the past it had been thought improper for a man of quality to be alone, except for prayer, and this attitude persisted for a long time. The humblest folk needed company as much as the great. Loneliness was the worst form of poverty, hence it was deliberately sought out by ascetic eremites. Solitude, which causes boredom, is contrary to the human condition. By the end of the seventeenth century, however, these traditional beliefs had fallen out of fashion, and a taste for solitude developed. Mme de Sévigné, never alone in Paris, wrote later in life of the pleasure that she experienced in Brittany, where she was able to spend three or four hours by herself, walking with a book among the trees in her park. The wooded park had already taken on some aspects of what Rousseau would later hail as "nature."

(4) People became so fond of being alone that they wished to share their solitude with a dear friend, a teacher, relative, servant, or neighbor—a second self. Friendship of this sort had little to do with the

brotherhood of arms of the medieval knight, which largely survived in the military camaraderie of a period when war was the occupation of the noble male from a very early age. Great friendships like those found in Shakespeare's plays or in the life of Michelangelo were probably quite rare. Friendship was usually a more civil sentiment, a gentle commerce, a tranquil fidelity, which existed in a wide range of varieties and intensities.

(5) All these changes, and many others, contributed to a new conception of daily life and a new way of organizing it. The primary determinants no longer were chance, utility, architecture and art. Living became a matter of externalizing one's inner life and private values. Hence a great deal of attention was paid to what went on in routine home life and daily intercourse. Sophistication, requiring time and interest, came to be prized, and taste became a real value.

In the past little had been done to decorate the home. Tapestries might be hung on walls or tables provided for the display of precious objects. Other furniture—such as beds, chests, benches—was simple, capable of being taken apart and transported from place to place as the owner required. But now people began to reserve a special place for the marriage bed. The storage chest became an objet d'art or, still more significant, was replaced by an armoire or commode. No longer did armchairs signify and dramatize the social eminence of their occupants. Mme de Sévigné straddles the divide between two eras, and her letters contain examples of both attitudes. On her first journey to Les Rochers, she took her bed with her, and though still relatively indifferent to the minor art of furniture, she admired her daughter's taste.

The minor art of interior decoration inspired the high art of painting. Seventeenth-century Dutch painters often portrayed domestic interiors, which represented a new ideal, a new concept of how people ought to live. At the same time there developed an art of food and drink, which required an initiation, a cultivation, a critical spirit—all aspects of what we still refer to as "taste." Not only did grand cuisine become an art; but ordinary cooking took on a new sophistication, requiring perhaps greater skill than ever before. Crude, rustic dishes were transformed into the traditional recipes of the *potagers*, carefully and often subtly prepared. Similar observations could be made about dress, especially home attire.

(6) The various psychological changes that took place may be most fully revealed by the history of housing. After remaining fairly stable from 1100 to 1400, housing began to undergo a complex series of changes that have continued up to the present day. The size of rooms was reduced. Small rooms first appeared as annexes to main rooms, as offices or alcoves, but soon most activity was concentrated in them and

they took on a life of their own. Private stairways, halls, corridors, and vestibules were provided to allow rooms to be entered without the need to pass through other rooms. Rooms acquired specialized functions. (Samuel Pepys had a nursery, a bedroom for himself, another for his wife, and a living room; Mme de Sévigné had nothing comparable at either the Hôtel de Carnavalet in Paris or Les Rochers.) In many places rooms were reserved for a particular kind of work rather than a particular form of intimacy. The history of the fireplace, which was used for both heating and cooking, is particularly important. Monumental fireplaces, once a key architectural component, gave way to smaller fireplaces equipped with conduits and blowers, possibly a Western adaptation of the Central European stove.

The Individual, the Group, and the Family

How were these various elements brought together to form coherent and highly unified structures of daily life, and how did those structures evolve? The sixteenth and seventeenth centuries saw the triumph of individualism in daily life (though not in ideology, where there was a time lag). The social "space" liberated by the rise of the state and the decline of communal forms of sociability was occupied by the individual, who established himself—in the state's shadow, as it were—in a variety of settings, none of them very functional. Consider that legacy of the Middle Ages, the window:

> Beautiful Doette sits by the windows
> Reading a book her heart is not in,
> For it belongs to her friend Daon,
> Who has gone away to far-off Laurion.

Often the need for privacy was associated with the pursuit of love. A new bedroom arrangement created useful space for private intercourse. The bed was moved from the center of the room toward the wall, creating a ruelle, or space between bed and wall, where lovers could exchange confidences and where politics and business could be discussed in private, even when the bedroom was full of people. In the late seventeenth century young Jamerey-Duval, aged seven or eight, fled his stepmother and for a while found refuge among shepherds, who taught him to read. He later became a domestic servant in a community of eremites, who gave him a corner of his own in which he was able to acquire his autodidact's erudition. Much later, the glazier Jacques-Louis Ménétra had a room of his own, but he used it to receive mistresses, much like a nineteenth-century bourgeois!

After 1800 individualism declined as the family took on new importance. The family became the focus of the concerns of even its more recalcitrant members. Solitary pursuits were still possible, but they were largely confined within the home.

Between 1500 and 1800 there was change among the "middling sort," people who stood below the court but above the common folk. Here a new culture developed, a social life that revolved around conversation, correspondence, and reading aloud. People met in intimate, private rooms or around a lady's bed—for the ladies played an important role in these "little societies," at least in France and Italy. When the possibilities of conversation and reading were exhausted, people sometimes joined in "society games" (the term is significant), sang or played music, or engaged in debate (the English "country parties").

In the eighteenth century some of these groups adopted formal rules and organized as clubs, intellectual societies, or academies, losing some of their spontaneity in the process. They became public institutions. Other circles shed some of their gravity and turned into literary salons. In the nineteenth century prominent ladies set aside certain days for receiving visitors, days that became one of the diversions of the cultivated bourgeoisie. Tentatively I would argue that "conviviality," as the term was understood in the seventeenth century, had ceased to be a major factor in society by the end of the nineteenth century.

Ultimately the family became the focus of private life. Its significance changed. No longer was it merely an economic unit for the sake of whose reproduction everything had to be sacrificed. No longer was it a restraint on individual freedom, a place in which power was wielded by women. It became something it had never been: a refuge, to which people fled in order to escape the scrutiny of outsiders; an emotional center; and a place where, for better or for worse, children were the focus of attention.

In developing these new functions, the family became a haven, a defense against outsiders. It separated itself more sharply from the public realm. It extended its influence at the expense of the anonymous sociability of street and square. The family head became a figure of morality, a prominent fixture on the local scene.

This was only the beginning of an evolution that would culminate in the nineteenth and twentieth centuries. Resistance to change remained quite strong, and little seemed to be occurring except in certain social classes in certain regions and cities. Anonymous forms of sociability persisted in old guises (as in the street) as well as new, derived perhaps from the conviviality of the preceding period (country parties, clubs, academies, cafés). These changes that slowly took place within the family came about within a relatively stable community and in competition with new forms of conviviality. The result was a mixed culture, which would continue to evolve throughout the nineteenth century.[1]

The Dual Definition of the Public

As I see it,[2] the entire history of private life comes down to a change in the forms of sociability: from the anonymous social life of the street, castle court, square, or village to a more restricted sociability centered on the family or even the individual. The problem then becomes: How did the transition take place from a form of sociability in which private and public are confounded to one in which they are distinct, and in which the private may even subsume or curtail the public? I am here using the word "public" as it is used in "public park" or "public place," to denote a place where people who do not know each other can meet and enjoy each other's company.

The history and scope of this important change is well worth tracing. I soon discovered, however, that, although my friends and colleagues did not entirely disagree with my thesis, neither did they fully accept it.[3] They conceived of the public/private dichotomy differently. The seminar on the History of Private Space and the conversations that followed it helped me to realize that the problem was not as monolithic as I had imagined.

A second aspect of the public/private opposition had escaped me because I have been alienated from political history. The word "public" also refers to the state, and to service of the state, whereas "private" (or *particulier*, as one used to say in French) referred to everything outside the state's purview. For me, this was a new and most rewarding way of looking at the question.

In the Middle Ages, as in many societies in which the state is weak or plays only a symbolic role, the individual depended for protection upon a community or patron. A person had nothing that he or she could call his or her own—not even his or her own body. Everything was in jeopardy, and only willingness to accept dependency ensured survival. Under such conditions public and private were not clearly distinguished. No one had a private life, and anyone could play a public role, if only that of victim. This approach, centered on the state, is not without parallels to the other, centered on sociability, for the same conditions encourage a confusion between public and private forms of sociability.

An important first step was the appearance of what Norbert Elias has called "court government." The king's court assumed responsibility for certain governmental functions that had previously been decentralized, such as maintaining law and order, courts of law, the army, and so on. Space and time thus became available for activities without public significance: private activities.

The change did not come about simply. In the sixteenth century and the first half of the seventeenth century the state did not actually perform all the functions it claimed as its right. The void was filled by client networks, which exercised both public functions and private ones. Henri de Campion did not hesitate to leave the king's service and join the princes in rebellion against him. In fact, he insisted that he was serving the king no matter which side he fought on. Those who exercised real power (military, judicial, or police) in the king's name did so, moreover, with their own money and were quite pleased if from time to time the king, through generous gifts, allowed them to recoup their costs and more. Under such conditions, the home of a provincial governor or *premier président* [chief judge in the court of law known as the *parlement*] came to be identified with his office. Mme de Sévigné, for example, complains of the extravagant expenditures of M. de Grignan, the king's lieutenant-general in Provence; but Grignan was acting as stand-in for the king in his court. It was impossible to bring a lawsuit without entering into dealings with the judges of a sort that to our modern way of thinking seem unethical but without which the judges would not have been informed about the facts of the case. Litigants were actually dealing with the state, and were perfectly well aware of the differences between a government official and a private individual, but the state was still administered as though it were family property.

This attitude toward public affairs and public service corresponds, chronologically at any rate but perhaps in deeper ways as well, to the different forms of sociability that I have distinguished. Human relations were important as a means of transmitting information and shaping and carrying out decisions, and groups in this period tended to be defined by affinities, which determined the nature of conviviality. Contacts made in the course of "public" life encouraged "private" friendships which were indispensable for creating trust.

Things changed when the state finally succeeded in discharging the functions that it had long claimed rightfully belonged to it. In France the government of Louis XIV, with its *intendants* and its minister Louvois, replaced clientele networks with clerks and "bureaus" and substituted a public payroll for private expenditure. Other states, such as England, followed a different course: the local nobility (service clientele, we would call them) played the role of the intendants, while agreeing to accept and obey the laws and orders of the state.

We thus reach the end of the seventeenth century and the beginning of the eighteenth. The public realm is by now quite "deprivatized." Public affairs are no longer confounded with private interests. Hence it became possible to create a closed private preserve, or at any rate a private realm totally divorced from the public service and completely autonomous. This liberated zone would be filled by the family. But the men who inhabited this private realm without participating in public life (unlike the nobles and notables of the sixteenth and seventeenth centuries) felt frustrated, and from this frustration were born a way of thinking about politics and a set of political demands. Thus we come full circle.

The problem of private life in the modern era must be approached from two directions. One approach should focus on the opposition between the public servant and the private individual and the relations between the state and what would ultimately become the domestic preserve. The other should focus on the transition from an anonymous form of sociability, in which notions of public and private were confounded, to a more fragmented sociability that combines remnants of the old anonymous form with relations based on professional affinities and with the equally private relations born of domestic life.

Pieter de Hooch, *Farewell in front of a Country House*. (Amsterdam, P. de Zoer Gallery.)

❦ 1 ❧

Figures of Modernity

Yves Castan
François Lebrun
Roger Chartier

Introduction

by Roger Chartier

I N ORDER to understand the new way in which a boundary was traced between the private realm and the purview of public and communal authorities in the sixteenth, seventeenth, and eighteenth centuries, Philippe Ariès suggested that we look at three fundamental changes occurring at that time in Western society: the new role of the state, which was increasingly taking a hand in matters that had long remained beyond its reach; the Protestant Reformation and the Catholic Counter-Reformation, which demanded of believers greater inward piety and more intimate forms of religious devotion; and the spread of literacy, which enabled individuals to emancipate themselves from the old bonds that had attached them to the community in a culture based on speech and gesture. In this section we have followed Ariès's advice and tried to understand how the modern state, post-Reformation religion, and spread of literacy redrew the dividing line between public and private in three centuries' time. In so doing, we touched on, and engaged in dialogue with, many other subjects of active historical research.

It is generally agreed that the limits of the private sphere depend primarily on the way public authority is constituted both in doctrine and in fact, and in the first place on the authority claimed and exercised by the state. (This is true whether social life is "private" virtually in its entirety or the private sphere is limited to the family and household.) Thus the gradual construction of the modern state—not necessarily absolutist but always administrative and bureaucratic—is a necessary precondition for defining a private sphere as distinct from a clearly identifiable public one.

The connection between the consolidation of the state and the process of privatization can be understood in several different ways. That proposed by Norbert Elias in his now classic book *The Civilizing Process* establishes a close relation between the fashioning of the absolutist state, most fully achieved under Louis XIV, and the various emotional and psychological changes that led to the relegation of once-public acts to the private sphere. The new type of state that developed in Europe between the end of the Middle Ages and the seventeenth century aimed to establish social peace, hence punished all unsanctioned violence; it strengthened and regulated the bonds that existed between individuals; and it yielded a new social formation—the court—distinguished by a code of conduct that became more and more constraining as it gradually came to be imitated by other social strata. For all these reasons the new type of state instituted a new way of being in society, characterized by strict control of the instincts, firmer mastery of the emotions, and a heightened sense of modesty.

These changes in the social environment (*habitus*) first affected the court, then gradually spread, whether by appropriation or inculcation, to the whole of society, thereby creating the private sphere. Henceforth, two types of behavior were sharply differentiated: that which was permissible in public without embarrassment or scandal, and that which had to be hidden from view, including (with differences in time or degree according to the social class) exhibition of the naked or sleeping body, satisfaction of natural needs, and the sexual act. The taboo applied not only to actions but also to words, to the naming of functions that ought to be kept secret or parts of the body that had become shameful. This external distinction between types of behavior appropriate in public and private was also inscribed within individuals themselves. Psychic conditioning to control the instincts and inculcate the proper distinctions between appropriate public and private behavior disciplined individuals by forcing them to internalize social norms. External constraints imposed by the authorities or the community were transformed into internal inhibitions.

Elias portrays changes in the state, and the effects of those changes on society, as the decisive factor in explaining how the new classification of behavior came into being. The state determined, in more or less peremptory fashion, which activities were permissible and which were illicit, which were to be visible and which hidden, which were public and which private. He also focuses our attention on the historicity of man's psychic makeup, which, he argues, is by no means universal or immutable. Thus he relates the progress of privacy, which over the centuries affected a growing range of behavior and social strata, to changes in the structure of the personality, which was reshaped in the modern era owing to the increased tension between instincts and social controls, emotions and repressive forces.

Seen in the light of Elias' interpretation of the evolution of Western society and civilization, the history of France, in this sense paradigmatic, can be viewed as a transition from a relatively weak state to a powerful administrative monarchy, which, using resources previously monopolized by families and private *corps*, began to redefine the boundaries of private life. The public authorities proposed to regulate and, if need be, to defend private interests in such a way as to maintain an autonomy that served its own ends. These private interests (regional governments, professional groups, families) were rivals, enough so to make an alliance against the sovereign impossible, yet dependent enough on one another that none was sufficiently powerful by itself to threaten the social equilibrium.

Yet if the "private" is a product of the modern state, the "public" is by no means a state monopoly. In England by the end of the seventeenth century and in France during the eighteenth, a public space began to develop outside of government. It grew out of the private sphere, a consequence of what Jürgen Habermas has called the public use of reason by private individuals. The public social life of the Enlightenment took many forms, only some of which were institutionalized. Discussion and criticism gradually came to focus on the authority of the state itself. In literary societies, Masonic lodges, clubs, and cafés, people learned to associate as intellectuals, recognizing all participants, regardless of status, as equals. The demand for rational critique was extended to areas hitherto exempt from public debate, as intellectuals claimed the right to speak in the public's name against the policies of the prince.

This led to a startling reversal in the meaning of the words public and private, as is illustrated by Kant's article "What Is Enlightenment," published in the *Berlinsiche Monatsschrift* in 1784: "The *public* use of our reason must always be free, and it alone can bring enlightenment to man. But the *private use* of reason can be severely limited without noticeably impeding the progress of enlightenment. By public use of reason I mean the use that one makes of reason as a *scholar* before the *reading* public. I call private the use that one is entitled to make of one's reason in a *civil post* or office." As an example of the private use of reason, Kant cites the case of an officer in the army or a minister in church; such private use can and perhaps even should be limited, he argues, for the sake of discipline and obedience. But the individual's right to the public use of reason is inalienable. The public sphere is the place where private individuals address other private individuals in full freedom and in their own name, whereas the private sphere is associated, in Kant's view, with the holding of a civil or ecclesiastical office. This semantic inversion reveals a new division in which public and private are no longer opposed as they were in the seventeenth century. Instead, practices once characterized as private define the realm of public reflection and political affirmation.

The new affirmation of personal piety in the Reformation may have been the result of a similar process of definition, a similar insistence on private discipline by the public—in this case, the ecclesiastic—authorities. Personal piety was not limited exclusively to Protestants, nor was it a solely private affair. In the Catholic Church personal religious practices were incorporated into the heart of collective devotions conducted under the auspices of a priest. Silent prayer in the vernacular during mass, the duty to make individual confession during the Easter season, and the pilgrim's private vow were all ways of encouraging introspection and intimacy with the sacred. By contrast, domestic piety was practiced outside consecrated places and without clerical discipline, raising the possibility of heresy. Private devotion in its various forms, whether that of the worshiper in the privacy of his soul or that of the small group gathered for the purpose of prayer, became an important part of the Church's efforts to establish a Catholic (etymologically, a universal and communitarian) religion. Following a symmetrical path, the Protestant churches, based on individual faith and personal knowledge of Scripture, soon enmeshed the individual in a web of teachings and practices intended to ensure a proper reading of the Bible, spiritual conformity, and a communitarian spirit. Despite their differences and confrontations, churches on both sides of the Christian divide pursued the same goal: to articulate, within the context of a revitalized Christianity, the disciplines necessary to the faith, coupled with a credo invariably uttered in the first-person singular.

The development of the modern state, like that of a more individual religion, depended crucially on the written and printed word. Increasingly, and in the face of resistance, the will of the authorities was transmitted in written form, and it was the written word that sustained the more intimate forms of piety. For those who did not yet have access to the supreme experience—purely mental prayer and direct conversation with God—the book was a necessary prop, as Teresa of Avila points out in the *Way of Perfection*: "I spent more than fourteen years unable to meditate except with a book. Many people are no doubt still in that position." To which she adds: "Others are even incapable of meditating upon what they read; they can only pray out loud." This suggests a hierarchy of spiritual exercise, in which devotional reading (which of course presupposes an ability to read) is an obligatory stage on the way to communion in God. In the Protestant sects, where (although the development may have come later than is generally believed) each member was expected to read the Bible in its entirety several times during his lifetime, reading was the keystone of the new faith, establishing a close connection between religion and literacy.

The state too, with its courts and its exchequer, born in the late Middle Ages and consolidated in the first two centuries of the modern era, required a growing number of people capable of reading and writing. Writing in its various forms (judicial, administrative, polemical, and so on) did much to undermine the old values associated with the spoken word, which had long been the primary means of enunciating the law, pronouncing sentence, uttering commands, and, in a word, wielding power. That these changes did not come without hesitation and opposition is beyond doubt, but in the end they profoundly transformed relations between the individual and the state at the same moment in history when the relation between the individual and God was also being reconsidered. The spread of literacy is important, therefore, not only because it opened new possibilities for solitary, gregarious, and family activities to a growing number of people but even more because it was an essential ingredient in the major political and religious changes that occurred in the West between 1500 and 1800, redefining, alongside of or even within public space, a sphere of existence that was held to be private.

School of Charles Le Brun, *Etablissement de l'Académie des sciences*. Measurement of the earth was one of the primary concerns of the Academy of Sciences. In this scene the globe is turned in such a way as to give prominence to Europe and the Atlantic, the objects of France's ambitions. (Château de Versailles.)

ᶜᵛ Politics and Private Life

Yves Castan

WHEN Etienne de La Boétie attempted to explain that most incomprehensible perversion of the social bond, the "voluntary servitude" that made possible the tyranny of one over all, he did not attack the principle of delegation of authority.[1] For him, the peril stemmed from showing excessive confidence in, or even feeling a proper gratitude toward, the sovereign, on the model of private friendship. "Our nature is such," he wrote, "that the common duties of friendship consume a good portion of our lives. It is reasonable to love virtue, respect noble deeds, feel gratitude for the boons we have received, and often to diminish our own comfort in order to increase the honor and advantage of the one we love and who is worthy of it."

PRIVATE CONNECTIONS AND PUBLIC AUTHORITY

Although Renaissance jurists reserved the bulk of their praise for republican government, seeing the common good as incontrovertible justification for domination and tribute, more worldly men clung to the habit and need to dedicate their ardor and their service to superiors whom they knew well and to whom they committed themselves voluntarily. Even in quite literary circles, where men manifested a concern to measure the value and the cost of the subordination to which they assented, Henri de Campion, a Norman gentleman who composed his *Memoirs* early in the seventeenth century, discovered without scandal but not without some resentment how difficult it was to reconcile the obligations of the noble client with the duties of the loyal subject.[2] No doubt we should see Campion's adherence to the princes' party—the party of his protectors, the Count of Soissons and the Vendômes—as a sign of his approval of a just effort to combat tyranny, an effort with which the political conscience of this honest and lucid gentleman was perfectly at ease. Yet even Campion records periods of tension during which he was obliged to think hard and make moderate use of casuistical skill in order to find an honorable way out of his predicament.

| *Political Adventure and Clientage* | A needy gentleman and younger son who, out of tact, felt bound to offer his loyalty only to a prince prepared to accept it, Campion carefully notes the elective affinity at work in his choice of the Duke of Beaufort, who "lived with me at that time and ever after in a most obliging fashion and with greater civility than princes ordinarily show to those who have given themselves to them; so that I immediately felt a zeal and an affection for him that no ill treatment has been able to make me lose." At the beginning of his career, however, in 1634, when he was in his twentieth year, he had been less cautious. As an ensign in a royal border regiment, he was invited to improve his position by joining the forces that the Duke of Orléans, following a private pact with Spain, had begun to levy in preparation for a bellicose return from exile. At that time the problem was not a political one: "I was in truth only a poor cadet seeking to make his fortune. But I wished to achieve my end by none but honorable means, and, since I was currently serving with the king's troops and in a place that belonged to him, it seemed to me that it was not appropriate for me to engage myself until I had returned my commission to my adjutant." In other words, Campion merely wished to resign his commission in the proper manner so that later no one could accuse him of desertion. As for leaving the king's service to join a prince allied with his enemy and bent on subverting the realm, "I would have a valid reason to exonerate me, in that I would not have acted as a deserter and, Monsieur [as the Duke of Orléans was called] being the brother of the king and heir apparent to the throne, no one could accuse me of treason, especially . . . since this prince, claiming no lapse in the obedience he owed H[is] M[ajesty], had no quarrel but with his enemy the Cardinal [Richelieu]." The whole argument is couched in terms of private honesty, the goal being self-advancement: Campion is recruited by a relative for "the purpose of putting me, too, on the road to fortune." Who can blame a soldier in a mediocre position, |

The Duke of Beaufort, whose style was too agitated for Campion's taste, here pays "just tribute" to the king. Note the amused or self-satisfied looks of these willing participants in the ceremonial of power. The legitimate authorities were never overtly rejected, but merely flouted, often with the greatest of ease. (Paris, Bibliothèque Nationale.)

without prospects, who resigns of his own free will in order, as he frankly avows, to curry favor with the heir to the throne? We have a clear sense that thirty years later Campion is still proud of his most considerate decision, which unfortunately he is unable to carry out as planned because, obliged to flee for his life along with two comrades, "we dispensed with the ceremony of returning our commissions to the adjutant." At the beginning of his memoirs he states that he is writing to instruct his progeny, so we must assume that in recounting this minor and rather fruitless adventure he is commending the practice of scrupulously discharging one's duties even when making the most radical change in one's loyalties. At issue was nothing more than a personal decision, with nothing at stake beyond one officer's availability to one camp rather than another.

A more perplexing dilemma was posed in 1643 by the Duke of Beaufort's plot to assassinate Mazarin. Campion did not approve, for in his eyes the minister was exempt from so violent a judgment, for which he, gentle soul, did not wish to bear the blame. Furthermore, he believed that success in this murder would not prove advantageous to the party that carried it out. Nevertheless, he agreed to keep the secret, and, if it was decided to proceed with the plans, engaged himself to do as Beaufort wished, provided only that he was not required to deliver the blow against the cardinal personally. His private ties with Beaufort were thus reaffirmed: "I had resolved to follow him come what may and never to abandon him whatever decision he might take." If the prince was determined to be present at the scene, he, Campion, would overcome his repugnance and stand "without scruple at his side . . . my employment with him and my affection equally obliging me to do so." This time he plainly rejected the political pretext and understood that he was taking part in an unjust, capricious, and outrageous act; he even said as much to the duke. Yet he was obliged "to serve him loyally and as a man of honor," that is, according to the norms of private devotion to which he had assented and which outweighed his scruples as a citizen and his conciliatory caution. Much progress in comprehending the reasons for men's actions had been made by this studious man, who never departed for battle without books as "part of the wagon's load." But as for direct motives, honesty and loyalty, those two guarantees of honor, though sufficient to cause change, are in themselves invariable. They are part of the reservoir of affection, which is so powerful a force in Campion's life once he has accepted the accident upon which his friendship, love, or paternal amazement is built.

Private Ambitions and the Capture of the State

This generation of Frenchmen, which was born and attained maturity during the period of crisis associated with the growth of the monarchical state, faced a paradoxical situation, in which the state was obliged to reward its clients with liberal favors in much the same way as the leaders of sedition rewarded theirs. Once again Campion clearly saw how things stood, thanks to the example of his prestigious elder brother Alexander, who had preceded him down ambition's road: "His long familiarity with the factious . . . had inspired in him, against his penchant, a desire to see the court of State always in turmoil; he has since given several other signs of this inclination, more acquired than innate." Logically enough, Campion also hoped that the causes he espoused one after another would bring him a good deal of renown. What we see in these attempts to capture the political realm by means of private intrigue is therefore not a simple matter of greed and avarice.

Those who served the seditious princes usually lived on emoluments offered by the regiments entrusted to their protectors. They made it a point of honor to discharge their duties with distinction, even panache in battle, and with ingenuity in council. They lived and died at the king's expense, or, when victory allowed, at the expense of his enemies. A man had to learn when to quit his lieutenancy and his company: in bleak periods of inactivity, for instance, or when—sure sign of disfavor or neglect—no promotion followed after scenes of human carnage had been witnessed at close quarters. Should a man in such a position accept the subsidies that generous princes did not fail to offer? Campion's attitude was that such gifts should be refused. He preferred to gamble, and excelled at it, once he abandoned the hazards of dice for backgammon and various card games; for, although games of chance were nobler, they were also riskier, and honest skill, maintained through fortune and misfortune, eventually reaped its reward.

But to a man obliged to flee his country, past favor and employment were of no avail, and gambling was useful only for a limited time. Only in exile, therefore, was it permissible

Dirk Hals, *Game of Trictrac.* The pleasure and the spectacle of gambling. (Lille, Museum of Fine Arts.)

Not a call to military duty but an image of pride in mastery of an art. (Paris, Bibliothèque Nationale.)

Anonymous, *Soldiers in a Guardroom.* 17th century. Campion had other interests besides gambling, but he did not disdain either the profits or the risk. (Béziers, Museum of Fine Arts.)

to live at the expense of a patron, provided that zeal in service was responsible for the exile in the first place. Liberality might also be authorized by a faction's success: "I told [the Duke of Vendôme] that when his side's situation had changed, he could pay me in accordance with my service." Although he later found cause to complain of the family's ingratitude, Campion readily acknowledged the correctness of the pension he was offered, limiting his grievance to the charge that he was treated more distantly and less openhandedly than in the past. It was probably in a spirit of derision rather than amusement that Tallemant des Réaux exaggerated to the point of caricature the subjection of belonging: "A gentleman of the count of Lude, on the point of death and urged to confess, said: 'It has been my wish never to do anything without Monsieur's consent; I must find out whether he approves.'"[3] Even as he prepares to shed his last ties to this world, the *fidèle* is said to be as blind as the miser who refuses to make restitution of his ill-gotten gains; one anecdote does for both, and the naïveté of the one could be mistaken for that of the other.

What was this sense of "belonging" that directed toward a person and the group he headed all the feelings of devotion

and affection normally reserved for a man's family and "fatherland"? It was more potent, it seems, than a mere sense of duty. Henri de Campion, just as he shamelessly confesses his love of gambling and of winning, also avows that, though not himself of a quarrelsome nature, he was always tempted to join in the quarrels of his friends. "I liked my friends to become involved in disputes so that I might serve them, with the idea that, according to the custom of those times, I might distinguish myself by dueling and in the ceremonies that surrounded it." As always, he shows no compunction in acknowledging concern for his own "fortune." Dueling, like war, offered an opportunity to display valor, but with much greater certainty of obtaining advantage by attracting the excited attention of a man's peers, who admired spontaneity and courageous initiative. Serving as a client, binding oneself by what can only be called a private contract, offered the greatest opportunity for advancement in a society predicated on devotion of a familial type and esprit de corps.

How does such private thought and action assume, on its periphery, a public aspect? Beyond his Christian attitudes, Henri de Campion exhibits a humanity capable of according to all, even to the troops of the enemy—that vile herd slaughtered after battle by order of the victor—a compassion he regards as their due. He is able to judge the political action in which he is engaged from the standpoint of the public good, the only standpoint he deems appropriate. In his account, however, it is as if these broad views were of no avail, as if the real forces could act only within the concentric spheres of private life: the need to maintain self-discipline at the cost of harsh sacrifice; the duty to seek one's fortune, at times staking one's life in the endeavor; and the fascination with the fate of the great men behind whom one advanced or perished, in the hearty comradeship of others who had given of themselves without reservation.

Such are the attitudes of the subjective center toward the social surround, attitudes which, through a sense of dignity, honor, distinction by deeds, and devotion to the prince as embodiment of the state, invigorated the political virtues. The sketch of those virtues, flattering but by no means contaminated by an entire century's ethnic reveries, which the viscount de Bonald would much later supply in his *Tomb of the Nobility*, incorporates most of these features but ascribes to them an entirely public purpose. Privilege, favor, and quality are, for Bonald, mere corollaries of the nobility's distinctive station, which establishes its vocation as one of public service by freeing it from the need to amass wealth and conserve life's resources.[4] An arresting paradox: an entire class, constantly reproduced by commerce, by the passion to get and to get ahead, by reverence for ancestors and profitable marriages, is subordinated to a political purpose and portrayed as avid for the annual rites of spring that preceded its galloping off to battle and consuming at each new stage of growth the advances so generously offered one stage earlier.

A monarch is too generous to make selfish use of his allies. Generosity is a royal virtue par excellence. (Paris, Bibliothèque Nationale.)

The trappings of military life were despised, but the bourgeoisie liked a parade. Here as usual the wealthiest are most in evidence. (Bourges, Hôtel Jacques-Coeur.)

Two generations after Campion, in the period between the last of the wars of Louis XIV and the beginning of the Seven Years' War, we find in these same lower ranks gentlemen under no illusion as to the limits of fortune, men who traveled much greater distances to serve in much larger armies and without benefit of powerful protectors. All that saves them from anonymity is the brotherhood of arms and the possibility of serving under a colonel with enough influence at Versailles to promote their careers or at any rate to win recognition of their merits. The correspondence of officers—unpublished letters of Gascon noblemen—reveals a concern for useful contacts but in more reserved and courtly terms; letter-writers invoke relatives with supposed influence and recall former comrades promoted to better positions.[5] There is little enthusiasm for the narration of martial exploits; at

Serving the King

Distant and severe, the king is not only protector of the arts but a redoubtable warrior. Beneath medallions depicting the works of the monarchy and surrounded by courtiers frozen in gestures of deference, he assumes the pose of a hero whose collaborators are gods. (Paris, Bibliothèque Nationale.)

A drawing of lots to choose men for military service, which was feared not so much for its dangers as for its duration. (Paris, Bibliothèque Nationale.)

most, discreet allusion is made to well attested merits. Letters are filled with news of the court and of battle, anxiously heeded but for practical reasons; with talk of supplies; with the movement of troops; with precautions to be taken by individuals and families; and with professional matters, there being a constant need for advice and a friendly hand in dealing with the thousand and one details of forage, livestock, discipline, subsistence, uniforms, and equipment. For these officers the discipline of a regimented public service is coupled with the free and familiar manners of men accustomed to living at close quarters with other men. Theirs is a rather temperate spirit of tolerance, which must be maintained even when an impromptu inspection requires feverish preparation. The bureaucratic organization easily and perhaps profitably accommodates this ability to maintain a private life in the midst of a common effort, but it is clear that there are no more private designs, no ambitions that reach beyond the promotions and honors planned for these subalterns, who after thirty years of service, should they be lucky enough to live so long, were entitled to a Cross of Saint Louis and a pension of 500 livres. Professional soldiers, they owed little to the contacts and patrons who at most secured their commissions for them at a time when the king had need of his military nobility. Poor families contributed enough to give their man a start and make sure that he would never return home: 300 livres for equipment, twice that to tide the man over until he received his first pay. Thereafter soldiers helped one another, circulating information, some in the bivouacs, others in the upper reaches of the general staff—two separate worlds, whose paths rarely crossed. Between field and staff officers there existed feelings of vigilant affection, made tender by distance and not compromised or threatened by any confusion of interests.

These men were no longer, like Campion, soldiers of fortune who, to advance themselves, pledged to follow patrons whom they served loyally, not distinguishing between private ambitions, honors, and service and what, by anticipation of usurpation, counted as public. For the lower-ranking officers of the bureaucratic monarchy, military service was one of the few ways to live and die in dignity. Their lives were absorbed by their work, as they moved from garrison to garrison, battlefield to battlefield, allowed an occasional leave but almost never permitted even to think that they could live in any other way. Their letters, filled with details of projects not of their own devising, never suggest devotion to

Troops were used not only in war. The imposing palace guard underscored the presence of the prince and his army. (Paris, Bibliothèque Nationale.)

Georges de La Tour, *Dice Players*. A pure game of chance, except where there was cheating. (Middlesborough, Teesside Museum.)

some great public purpose; instead they manifest a resigned submission to higher purposes translated at this level into abuse. These subalterns take their public roles seriously but not conscientiously; their daily labors are a routine from which amusements provide a respite that sometimes seems more like a duty. Gambling, which for Campion was an absorbing possibility, is now no more than an unavoidable occasion to risk scarce funds with little hope of success. These settled warriors scornfully viewed duels of honor as mere games indulged in by young knaves still wet behind the ears and simpleminded dragoons fond of the adventure of attacking the king's tax collectors with saber and sword.

It is tempting to characterize the condition of the professional military as one of servitude rather than service; no longer was the officer free to quit when his mediocre position no longer held out promise of glory. Campion, in his avid youth, would not have tolerated the long periods of boredom

Jean-Baptiste Pater, *Troops on the March*. Military life was not yet cut off from the people. Manners were observed even in the field, and the entourage was not entirely military. (Caen, Museum of Fine Arts.)

in which the military machine became mired when obliged to stand still. But if discipline and hierarchy eliminated the last vestige of personal ambition from the military, officers now lived in an atmosphere not of rivalry but of familiar, almost familial, affection. When friends cast their eyes back over their years in the field, they recite the names of the dead, not with an eye to positions opened and promotions made available but with a tone of pious and fraternal commemoration, recalling close, cordial, and trusting friendships through years of virtual exile.

Nicolas de Largillière, *The Aldermen of Paris* (detail). Symbol of the Arts joining their prestige to the dignity of Commerce. Honest pursuit of profit served the glory of the state. (Amiens, Picardy Museum.)

For Campion, who in public life never distinguished between political and private goals, an exemplary loyalty, warmed by feelings of gratitude and hopes of fortune, served a variety of purposes: it assuaged his conscience, renewed his zeal, and gave evidence of partisan commitment. Having declared himself to be a man full of sympathy and emotion, he needs an intimate stage on which to display his feelings life-size. He can neither fully enjoy his private happiness nor fully

A Close and Absolute Superior

The natural order is an extension of the political order, which promotes knowledge of the laws of nature in the general interest and as a means of enhancing the sovereign's power. (Paris, Bibliothèque Nationale.)

The king heeds counsel, but intuition is his only master. His decisions are received as the revelation of his will, of general significance. (Paris, Bibliothèque Nationale.)

drain his cup of sorrows except in the domestic setting, again
with relationships so exclusive that, when his favorite daughter dies, he finds it his duty to show no more than unenthu-
siastic concern for his remaining children. Apart from
emotions associated with love, he seems susceptible only to
that bitter disappointment that ever since the Middle Ages had
been an inevitable part of the vassal's commitment. Toward
one's superior it was still necessary to feel a mixture of respect,
gratitude, and love, to say nothing of righteous fear, as seventeenth-century treatises on moral theology recall.[6]

The word "superior," with its connotations independent
of the type of superior concerned (whether husband, master,
priest, officer, magistrate, or lord), goes a long way toward
explaining why it was so difficult to separate the notion of
beneficent and lifegiving power from that of cringing affection, the ultimate fear being one of banishment from the
source of benevolence and nourishment. Since it was not, at
every level of society, necessary for every individual to have
a direct relation with every conceivable superior, it was considered praiseworthy, indeed parsimonious, to limit one's
homage to one's immediate superiors. A woman in the temporal order could claim to recognize no superior other than
her husband, and a servant went beyond legitimate bounds if

Gabriel Metsu, *Soldier Visiting a Young Woman*. Respectful solicitude like Campion's was a far cry from soldierly impudence. (Paris, Louvre.)

FIDE ET OBSEQUIO.

NIL SINE TE.

"Chancellor Séguier," *The Entry of Maria Theresa into Paris* (detail). Pomp and reverence surround a high servant, satellite of the great star. More than any other official, the chancellor was enveloped in symbols of royal majesty, for it was he who made the king's acts explicit. (Stockholm Museum.)

Loyalty and submission were crucial words for the clients of the king and the nobility. High-ranking ministers were great personages, but as servants of their master. (Paris, Bibliothèque Nationale.)

he or she appealed to an authority higher than the master's, to, say, a political authority. Transgression of these boundaries would have called their very meaning into question and raised a host of other problems. As it was, a valet could be as confident of the excuse that he was just following orders as Campion was that the Duke of Orléans would feel duty-bound to include in his treaty with the king mention of those subalterns whose only crime was to follow the orders of their prince. Even as late as the Enlightenment the charge, leveled against people of modest station, of being "republican" was in no way intended to impugn their loyalty to the monarchy. If they were seen as "bad subjects," it was not as subjects of the king, of whom they had no opportunity to speak; in question usually was their insubordination toward masters and other notables, the rector or the lord, or perhaps simply a lack of alacrity and obligingness or a presumption to judge the actions of the curate or the consuls by the standard of public utility.

This limiting of acknowledged authority to those closest at hand did not prevent people from attaching an often prestigious symbolic value to authorities whose exercise of power had consequences—such as taxes—but which entailed no real contact and brooked no conceivable opposition. People readily hailed as "Our Lords" remote authorities such as the Parlement or the royal court; in Languedoc the title was even accorded to the deputies of the Estates General of 1789, much as it had been granted in the past to the deputies of the provincial estates. The term almost always connoted distant respect for the power that validates and authorizes rather than that which is exercised directly.

In these customs of speech and action, legitimacy was regularly recognized but rarely effective, yet the question of the legality of obedience was almost never raised, so utterly did the reality of the superior impress the imagination or govern the habits of his subjects. Abnormal situations did arise on occasion, however, demanding specific responses that reveal something about the nature of authority.

The heroic sign of power transmitted from the prince to the assembly. Sovereign power penetrates the body of the virtuous, heroic, generous assembly. (Private collection.)

A *Community in Disarray*

An example from the early years of the eighteenth century concerns a case of rabies in a small community in the *bailliage* of Gévaudan.[7] Everyone—the afflicted man, his family, and all the parishioners, peasants from the surrounding countryside—turned to the curé of Pierrefiche to cope with the emergency. Pierre Marcou, the victim, relied on the priest not for medical care (having himself done what was necessary at the appropriate time and having touched the miraculous holy keys) but because he felt death approaching and, aware that his malady posed a threat to the general public, wanted protection in his final days. While the doctors and neighbors, alarmed by his outbursts of rage, debated possible ways of putting an end to his life or abandoning him, the priest offered reassurance, taking into account the victim's spiritual as well as physical interests, rejecting the idea of deliberate murder (by opening four veins), and refusing to countenance abandonment of the dying man, which would have caused him to abandon hope.

Marcou's relations with the priest had not been good, the curé having pressed him for the payment of certain debts. Nevertheless, under the circumstances he felt he could count on the priest's protection, which he demanded in the name of "loyalty." He demanded the same loyalty of the apothecary who did the bleeding, which he accepted as treatment yet feared might be used as an unobtrusive method of taking his life. Noticing that his vein remained open, he wondered whether it was wise to close it and turned to the curé for advice: he "relied on him [to know] whether it would be wrong to leave his vein open in order to die sooner, for if it was wrong he did not want to do it."

Following the priest's advice, he closed the vein but took note of the fact that this legitimate authority, whose loyalty was guaranteed by his duties as minister, was not the only person with control over his fate. The neighbors who were called upon to stand guard over him were afraid to tie him up; instead they placed a screen around his bed to confine him. But in a fit of rage he tore it down, shouting that he wanted to bite everyone and burn everything. The guards were forced to flee the house and to extinguish the flames with water poured into the house through a wooden conduit placed in a window; they were then obliged to surround the house and keep it under siege through a long December night at an altitude of more than 3,300 feet, fearful lest they fall asleep and be awakened by a fatal bite. Earlier, Marcou, well aware of what inevitably came to pass in cases such as his, had anticipated that the townspeople would want to kill him. After making confession, ordering restitution, and asking for prayers, he refused extreme unction because he thought that his best protection against the impatience and panic of his guards was to leave the preparations for his death incomplete. Strangely enough, he seems to have paid little attention to the temporal authorities, represented in the admittedly unimpressive person of the lord's bailiff. It was the guards who hit upon this expedient. Because the priest who had organized the guard was paralyzed by a sense of duty, someone was needed who, in the name of public safety, would dare to hasten Marcou's death. The bailiff accepted the role that was thrust upon him and dispatched his son to shoot Marcou with a rifle.

In the minds of these peasants, nearly all of them illiterate (as is shown by the fact that only one of the witnesses signed the affidavit), the danger and difficulty of this pathetic situation made action imperative. There was wide agreement, however, that only the family, the close relatives of the afflicted man, had the right to make decisions, in this case when to abandon hope in medical treatment. A priest from a nearby parish advised the priest of Pierrefiche to do nothing more than administer the sacraments and otherwise to stay out of the affair. The failure of the family to assume its responsibility in a sense forced the hand of those who, in one way or another, believed they bore official responsibility. Marcou had no one on his side but his young wife, terrified by his sudden illness and soon driven by fear and by her husband's orders to seek refuge with the priest, where she cried, begged, and sought help in vain. Afraid of his own rages, astonished by his horror of whatever came into view, Marcou had sent the rest of his family away. He had no close friends. Although the term friend, or good friend, was widely used, it was in the sense of good neighbor, a person with whom one enjoyed cordial relations. Neither Marcou nor those who surrounded and for the most part liked him gave any thought to a friendship that might go beyond relations of habit, familiarity, and loyalty.

Before long the common good became the paramount concern: since Marcou was suffering the tortures of the damned, and since his madness drove him to do terrible things, why not do away with him? Had he not cried out to be torn limb from limb, so that he might merge his suffering with that of Christ in his Passion? Had he not screamed that

he wanted prayers sung around his corpse? Had he not tried
to hide in the pile of wood chips in front of the warm oven
to stop his shivering, even though he could no longer bear
the sight of fire? Had his family been present, they would
surely have assented to a fate of which Marcou himself whispered: after the last rites, let him be suffocated or bled to
death.

The evidence that public security was at risk in this case
of violent execution was not well received. The murderers
loudly proclaimed their horror of an action that they under-
took only with the greatest reluctance. The witnesses, when
compelled to speak, expressed the bitterness of people who,
eager to see the drama end and be relieved of their guard,
wanted simply to make way for the proper officials to do their
job, to deal with the calamity properly and without scandal.
Those who did not take sides were unashamed to say that the
important thing was to contain the victim's destructive frenzy
by restraining or confining him after the last sacraments had
been administered and enough food had been provided to see
him through to the end. It would have been preferable to have
left any irreversible decisions to the family and its private sense
of honor, but, failing that, the community had been obliged
to do what prudence and decency required. The problem was
that there had been no official prestigious enough to see to it
that the afflicted man was treated firmly but without violence.
Most people had resigned themselves to abandoning the dying
man to his fate, partly because they had notified the responsible officials and partly because there was nothing they could
do to alter the inevitable. Neither the bailiff nor the apothecary
could offer any solace beyond a quick and violent death. The
latter, because he was the only one who knew much about
the horrors of the disease, was also the only one who dared
admit that he was glad to have put his patient out of his misery.

The attitudes and behavior revealed by this case can be
analyzed thanks to the care taken in the interrogation of witnesses and the patience of the "official," or ecclesiastical
judge—who is almost always more thorough than the ordinary judge with whom he collaborated—for this was a criminal case in which a priest was implicated. It would have been
easy to conclude on the basis of a more summary investigation
that the community wished to deal on its own, according to
its tried and true traditions, with a problem in which the curé
had been invited to play a limited preliminary role. In fact,
however, the community did not act as an autonomous col-

lectivity. Initially, it was the priest who took in the family, organized the guard, and offered or ordered whatever assistance he deemed necessary. His behavior may be judged ambiguous, in that it anticipated the more cruelly decisive second phase of whose inevitability the priest was aware. Still, when the neighbors discovered that their siege was useless and in the absence of a response that could truly be termed "private," that is, from the family, they did turn to a person whom they were able to regard as the representative of public authority. At this modest level, the hesitation of the populace seems to indicate not an extension of private solidarity but an anxious quest for a public authority capable of dealing reliably but according to its own norms with a case for which tradition provided no norms at all.

What strikes the modern observer of this drama is that the atmosphere is not one of anonymity and indifference. At first the response is private: the neighbors rush to assist. Then the secular authorities are called upon, and their orders are rigid and brutal but clear and probably reasonable, justified by the purpose of confining the disease. The only truly private party involved, the man's wife, lacked the strength to influence

Hope of a miracle fervently maintained at the end of the Enlightenment. Private gratification combines with public amazement. (Paris, Carnavalet Museum.)

events directly. She lacked the support of a public authority that could have represented her interests, as the priest did within the confines of his religious domain, to work out a compromise acceptable to the family in distress. The lonely victim's only success had been to remove from the scene all who might have been moved by pity or loyalty toward him; his rage and his impassioned threats had put them in an impossible position. The outcome was a foregone conclusion, since there was no family prepared to assume full and effective responsibility and since the private individuals pressed into service to protect the public interest had no rules to guide their conduct in such an emergency.

Long-Term Justice

The very fact that such a complex investigation was carried out four years after the incident shows that the courts had a substantial role to play and were capable of uncovering facts and punishing offenses. Did the wheels of justice grind so slowly that the courts intervened only belatedly, in time to provide the drama with its epilogue? Yes, but this failure is not the important point, since the fact that the court did intervene was the first step in establishing rules to ensure that such situations would in the future be dealt with in more orderly fashion. The most serious flaw in the operation of justice is that the crime would have remained buried along with its victim beneath the frozen winter soil had it not been for a private grudge that the prior of the commandery nursed against the curé of Pierrefiche. The case of Pierre Marcou, like the fate of the man himself, was decided by outside forces.

Remote as these poor peasants were from the world of politics, their malaise stemmed from causes not unlike those responsible for Henri de Campion's scruples. When public authority is not organized, or in any case not wrapped in the mantle of legal obligation, it is difficult for modest and humble folk to defend their privacy or even to establish its boundaries. The extended family, the parish, the community, and the patron appear to offer protection until they become the means by which social imperatives are transmitted to the individual, and transmitted with all the more bluntness and coercive force because they are so close, and obliged to make do with limited means. The witnesses to Marcou's murder reflected upon their experience with a bitterness not unlike that occasioned in Campion by his disappointments. They had observed a man who wished to die of natural causes but who had been unable to forestall the obvious preparations for a deliberate crime. Campion, once an ambitious man, had seen himself reduced to the state of a penniless exile with no hope of obtaining a settled position.

It would be wrong to generalize from such examples by saying that the sovereign power worked to obtain greater freedom for its subjects. It is more accurate to say that, in the early modern period, the sovereign tended to back the authority of subordinates too weak to offer rivalry or resistance but strong enough to transmit its orders and to serve as instruments of its action. States, cities, corps, communities, and families were exhorted to make themselves useful; in return they were guaranteed certain privileges in their restricted domains. Two antagonistic but complementary meanings of the word "privacy" emerged. One referred to the authorized defense of the civil liberty of each individual insofar as that individual's behavior was not governed by law or the duties of office. The other, more active interpretation of private authority was to specify the legitimate scope of the authority of the superior over individual members of a group, that is, his right to govern their work, their leisure, and the use they made of their property, positions, and even, in the case of the family, their bodies. This authority was justified on simple grounds: exact reciprocity in the case of marriage; in the case of a group, a concern for maintaining order, without which the group risked disintegration; or, in the case of the weak, the need to obtain the protection of the strong. The model of all authority, that of God over his creatures, implicitly precluded any hasty defense of individual rights. The superior by right showed solicitude to, and therefore supervised the behavior of, the inferior.

A political order also makes its influence felt in the way it distributes powers, positions, jurisdictions, responsibilities, and honors. Each official seeks to ensure that he will have a free hand to exercise those powers for which he must answer to higher authority. Many people prided themselves on cheating the tax collector, often a well-known neighbor, of his peremptory exactions, or depriving a creditor, scarcely more indulgent than the king's agent, of his due. Even the most commonplace supplies such as lard and grain were hidden from prying eyes in safe storage, and although the dinner menu varied little from house to house, it was considered secret enough to preclude visiting during the hours when dinner was being prepared. Records of investigations and hear-

Many people wished to keep private accounts; in the absence of convenient means of calculation, tables of sums enjoyed considerable success. Aptitude for mental arithmetic, developed by youthful practice, was less cumbersome, but it was easier to resort to the ready-reckoner. (Paris, Bibliothèque Nationale.)

ings generally reveal the uselessness of such precautions, since the truth could rarely be hidden from the sharp eyes of watchful neighbors. Attempts to preserve the secrets of daily life had a more subtle purpose: people were not obliged to speak of what they did not see, and neighbors, even if they knew, could feign ignorance and avoid making public what proximity made perceptible. For relatively poor families, private life depended less on their ability to isolate or hide themselves than on the convention—partly sincere—of seeing and hearing only what was deliberately divulged and reporting only what was deliberately made manifest. This explains why a neighborhood or family dispute would draw crowds of indiscreet onlookers: in the heat of argument people said things that they ordinarily would have concealed from third parties. When a disreputable person was accused of a fairly serious crime with a strong likelihood of family complicity, the family's version of each member's role was generally accepted by the authorities, as long as someone was willing to make a plausible acknowledgment of guilt. It was considered the family's right to conceal the details of the plot that had brought its members together! Through this presumption of ignorance as to relations between husband and wife, parents and children, the authorities were able to economize on punishment. At any rate general opprobrium and discredit attached to the entire family, and people cast a suspicious eye on the possible machinations of the bad seed. Allowance was made, however, for secrecy in family relations when the entire family was not involved in criminal activity, in which case the right to secrecy was consecrated by custom. But a crime committed against another family member could outweigh this scruple.

A Limited Emancipation

Certain limits were more firmly respected once their legal standing had been tested.[8] Take the case of a peasant who defended his "land" against an alleged easement guaranteeing passage. As long as the case remained in dispute, the man took it as a test of his neighbors' discretion: did they spy on him as they came and went? Once he had the court's judgment in hand, however, he repelled all intruders with truly military determination. The neutrality of public space could be invoked to protect its use for leisure activities or games which injured no one, occasioned no criticism, and suffered no prohibition. A hunter who leans against a tree on "the king's road" will not countenance a protest from the owner of the adjoining

property, who demands to know "whose land he pretends to be hunting on." Youths sitting on the steps of a covered market discussing plans for a future celebration will not allow an unwelcome intruder to sit beside them: "We are discussing our own business. Leave us alone. You would be better off over there." Teasing, always especially lively in the country-side, turned malicious rather than insolent. There were fewer brawls in cabarets, fewer flagons and goblets swept from the table with the back of the hand, fewer humiliations of the enemy, but more shrewd or insidious manipulations designed to aggravate the other fellow and force him to make the crude gesture or aggressive move. To treat any person as a man with no will of his own, infinitely malleable, became unacceptable. The stranger who, while watching a heated card game, made ironic jibes against one of the players went too far when he grabbed the man's purse and dumped the few small coins it contained onto the table. He thereby violated boundaries of privacy that everyone considered inviolable. It was permissible to force the gambler himself to prove that he had sufficient resources to play in a high-stakes game, but it

Jan Josef Horemans, *Cabaret Interior*. Drinkers, smokers, and onlookers surround cardplayers absorbed in their calculations. Gambling was a favorite recreation, for it made talk largely unnecessary and lent unusual gravity to action. (Cambrai, Municipal Museum.)

was highly offensive to lay hands on his money for the purpose of an indecent display. A gentleman whose purse has been pilfered and who, riding crop in hand, insists on taking the thief back to the scene of the crime to be identified is begged by onlookers either to forgive the man or turn him over to the authorities but in any case to leave him to his work, since there is no danger that he will flee.

Attitudes in this regard had changed considerably, as can be seen from records of trials in the second half of the seventeenth century which involved, beyond disputes over property (which often were mere pretexts), abusive or brutal attitudes that public opinion increasingly refused to tolerate, at least outside the domestic redoubt. No longer could a gentleman without warning seize the first peasant who happened by and set him some task, which the peasant was supposed to perform happily and even enthusiastically in the hope of being rewarded by the generosity of his better. No longer could a

Grevenbroeck, *Visits to the Usurer and the Fortuneteller.* Two ways of coping with the future: a cash advance and knowledge foretold. (Venice, Correr Museum.)

nobleman invade a peasant's home on the pretext of getting out of the sun, there to order the man's servants about, to rest in the man's chair and drink his wine. Even sharecroppers, who could not refuse the visits of the lord who controlled the way they worked their land, attempted to maintain a professional tone in their exchanges, precluding idle curiosity. Valets and maids, however, imprisoned in a home that was not their own, remained subject to arbitrary intrusions. This, it can be argued, was a problem of cohabitation, always difficult to resolve in any family. But debt, even when contracted for a limited term only, sometimes created a deliberate servitude, subjecting the unpunctual debtor to taxation, forced labor, and the whim of his creditor. The debtor understood quite well that his best hope of avoiding the worst—seizure of his property by the creditor—was to make the debt agreeable and even profitable. Thus he freely offered his services, allowed his creditor to gather fruit from his orchard, vineyard, or garden, and willingly submitted to various controls on his expenditures. Many patient lenders, by no means inclined to seize the property of their victims in arrears, were quite adept at taking despotic and unscrupulous advantage of the private power that their credit secured.

Wherever the legal guarantee of independence was nullified, whether in domestic servitude or alienation through debt, an uncontrolled appetite to absorb the private domain of others emerged. The change of attitude, at least in the middle classes vulnerable to the actions of the courts, no doubt had to do with the protection that the law was felt to afford to property and person. Although verbal insults were still freely exchanged outside the distinguished classes of society, the slightest physical assault, the least attempt to appropriate or embezzle property, could be punished, provided the plaintiff took the precaution of having the facts of the offense verified. And even if one did not face a powerful opponent, who could be sure that a malevolent adversary would not be glad of an opportunity to annoy and exploit a penniless wretch at little cost to himself?

Surveillance and Security

The aim of justice, upon which the government insisted most firmly at the precise moment when the king's exchequer needed to ensure the solvency of his most humble subjects, was surely not to guarantee that every man would enjoy peace and quiet in his own home. The need was to guarantee proper and profitable use of property and talents, so potential aggressors had to be taught that to attack even the most modest of homes, possessions, and persons was fraught with peril. A poor wretch whom some hardy predator had thought to harass with impunity might receive assistance from a personal enemy of the plaintiff. Given the necessary subsidies to pursue the case by appeal to a higher court, the defendant's resolve might be stiffened. Once deprived of the possible protection of the local magistrate, the presumptuous village luminary might find himself faced with a heavy judgment damaging to both his fortune and his prestige.

"Secret parties" increasingly involved themselves in court proceedings, and people soon learned that it was prudent to abstain from provocation or intrusion. In the 1660s youthful revelers in Toulouse broke down the doors of the poor, especially poor widows unable to defend their daughters' virtue; a century later young gentlemen were obliged to offer consideration and gifts in exchange for the clandestine concessions of women "of the lowest rank" but apparently decent. Indeed, respectability was so easily offended that honest pretexts had to be found for visits that might otherwise alarm neighbors and provoke complaints. People who lived in want knew that they owed their survival to their betters, who recommended them for jobs and charity. Such favors went to those who were "interesting" not only for their poverty but also for their innocence, hard-working determination, and pure morals, to say nothing of their zeal in gratitude. Undeniably this encouraged certain domestic virtues such as cleanliness, not to mention a certain ostentatious prudishness that discouraged the often unwanted familiarities of neighbors.

The new rules brought some measure of decency and privacy to the lives of the least fortunate, the poor and the fallen, who lived without visible or regular means of support. The deserving poor adjusted their behavior as instructed, to avoid being seen, heard, or in any way attracting attention. Officious neighbors who came to satisfy themselves that a proper standard of decency was being maintained had to be welcomed. It is always difficult to be sure whether compulsory decency promoted private life or undermined it. During working hours one room was expected to be kept clean and neat for visitors, and necessary chores were to be hidden from view. Women had work to do at home, and custom provided few legitimate occasions for them to go out. They were truly free only in the hidden recesses of the house. Hours of sleep and work were strictly regulated, as were the much rarer hours of leisure. Shabby housing held all sorts of surprises for its tenants: blood dripped through the ceiling of one apartment located beneath a butcher shop; ash and plaster rained down when the room above was used for storage; abominable odors wafted in when it was used for drying hides.

In the workers' quarters, where visits were frequent and doors were kept open, respectability seems to have been less strenuous than in more middle-class neighborhoods, where except for the occasional ceremonial visit people mostly stayed at home. Those who closed their doors, drew their curtains, and refrained from gossip became the focus of suspicion. Not that people expected free access to their neighbors' homes at any time of day or night. Even children were taught to respect the threshold and to call to friends from street or landing. Doors were closed at mealtimes and at nightfall. Behind them people spoke freely and loudly and laughed or cried without restraint; relations, good or bad, were intense. Usually this is considered a sign of emotional vitality rather than want of privacy.

The variety of private life is not so great as to suggest a corresponding variety of conditions in public life. The very ease of access offered to thieves and intruders and the openness with which private quarrels were pursued in public suggests not that the lower orders were fatalistic but that they had confidence in "the public faith." Ordinarily there was nothing to fear, because the good folk behaved as they always do: if by chance some good-for-nothing appeared in the neighborhood, there were plenty of eyes to survey his movements. Frank and frequent communication among neighbors guaranteed security. Yet privacy was no problem, for the clock dictated when visits were and were not acceptable. The occasional noisy celebration was easily tolerated. Already many prided themselves on keeping up appearances. Wealth, which made the task easy, is not a useful discriminant. Ambitions most often exceeded means, hence security required a wall of discretion. There was nothing to fear from neighbors' actions, but much to fear from their curiosity, which, if unsatisfied, exposed its object to risk, especially if he was a stranger or newcomer to the neighborhood. There were few accusations of dishonesty as such, but many charges of disreputable background, dubious character, and bad habits, born of a desire to get rid of a troublesome or scandalous neighbor by making allegations to the *dizenier* or priest, the secular authorities being less ready to take offense. This too reflects substantial confidence in the public order, which in normal circumstances could tolerate, without undue alarm and little more than moral concern, a family's withdrawal behind private walls. What of the temptation to destroy, for frivolous or malicious reasons, a social facade constructed with the utmost difficulty? And what of indignation, real or feigned, against those who might hide their debauch behind an irreproachable front? Clearly no private life was possible unless publicly sanctioned. Securing privacy required little effort, only firm determination. Because everyone knew at once virtually everything that everyone else did, any perceptible and verifiable offense brought quick response to which no culpable party could remain indifferent, since the lure of damages and the support of interested rivals could easily overcome the timidity of the most humble.

Surely the first to avail themselves of the sanctions guaranteeing privacy were those strata of society that had most to gain from good reputation and from the orderly home life and morals on which reputation rested. The cost of maintaining order was considerable, especially for those who did not directly profit from it. Keeping up appearances was crucial, and to do so people did not hesitate to make sacrifices including death. Privacy manifested itself primarily as discipline, but it could also be nourishing and life-sustaining. Without it, people with a bare minimum of resources could not have risen to the daily challenge of surviving with dignity. It is hard to say whether the exhausting struggle for survival aroused enough enthusiasm, pride, and camaraderie to permit, in the face of all the obstacles, pleasure in the delights of private life and family tenderness.

In Praise of "Countenance"

Even if the political authorities were only seeking subordinates capable of extending their control to the most humble of subjects and taxpayers, they shored up their authority with guarantees and warnings reinforcing the moral significance of the "countenance" recommended by manuals of etiquette. The ability to keep one's countenance was a virtue of prodigious importance, capable of disconcerting demons, which, being of angelic nature, were incapable of penetrating a man's conscience but clever at interpreting the emotions betrayed by his features and gestures. The secret man, Baltasar Gracián's *el Discreto*, was more than just a model for magistrates and courtiers who concealed their designs beneath a reassuring outward mask; he set for all an example of retirement, aloofness, and freedom of maneuver, qualities that enabled him to maintain his rectitude without either immobilizing or exposing his countenance. Once violence became unavailing as a means of thwarting organized plots, ascetic vocations, and ambitions of all sorts, then prudence, whether natural or assumed, and the need to anticipate the course of events in the near or more distant future required a discretion in manners and language of a nature to forestall any possible challenge.

It is hardly surprising, therefore, that the longing to retire to private life is a constant theme of picaresque adventure. The rewards of privacy are pursued by social outcasts who at first seem highly unlikely to succeed. Whatever the underlying motive of *Jean l'an prés*, whose dramatic aspect Emmanuel Le Roy Ladurie sought to discover beneath Abbé Fabre's sunny southern style, the plot hinges on the need, for one whose start in life has been fraught with difficulty, to secure prosperity by making a "good" or at any rate a reasonable marriage.[9] The hero, son of Truquette, a thief who ended on the gallows, endures a childhood which, despite its reality of wretched poverty, is wreathed in mythical language by a grandmother who has never given up her dreams of grandeur. She wants her grandson to acquire education and manners, but he sees the foolishness of her plans and prefers the life of the petty thief roaming fields and orchards, surviving by dint of strength and cunning—a rural Ulysses, who draws a new and useful lesson from every episode along the way to his goal.

In the end he reaps the reward of the legitimate heir, for he recovers his grandmother's secret hoard, the remains of his father's booty. Truquette's accomplices, spared his sad end, remember him as a generous fool, for which reason Sestier, the wealthiest and most settled of the group, agrees to hire the son as a jack-of-all-trades. The young man conceals his game well, gets Sestier's daughter with child, and finally, in a speech addressed to the lord but in the manner of a soliloquy, reveals his modest pride at being received as son-in-law in a rich man's home. There is nothing miraculous in this rather vulgarly realistic tale, yet the grandson of a woman who sells matches and the son of a hanged man grows up to be a gentleman worth 40,000 écus, a goodly fortune for a country boy, much of it in measures of grain whose price knows no limit.

An optimistic outcome—or an immoral one if, like the lord in the tale, you prefer to observe the proprieties—and a conclusion all but unimaginable in the Spanish picaresque of the seventeenth century, conceived before the social order had attained such a peak of perfection. That a new order has been established is plainly indicated by the fact that wealth is justified not by history but by the mere appearance of legality. No one is concerned to trace the origins of the hero's fortunes back to its legitimate roots, or to wax indignant if no such roots can be found. Truquette's treasure is ill-gotten, to be sure, but at what price! No matter, since Jean l'an prés [the name is dialect for "John took it"] is the legitimate heir. Sestier's trust is abused, but he who is deceived is himself a would-be deceiver. His daughter Babeau is as eager as her seducer, whose intentions are as pure as his motives are just. Those who know the true story have least to gain by telling it, and in all likelihood the heir whose birth is imminent will never know. Old Sestier with his powdered wig had already obtained respectability and patronage. Babeau is a charming child, radiantly naive. Jean will be what he always wanted to be, a good landlord, alert to the realities of life. After three generations of debauched women, "gibbet's prey," thieves and scoundrels, the cradle is ready to receive an honest man, who will be lavished with affection, carefully educated, and prepared to take his place in good society.

The point to notice is that the family, whatever its inclinations, never lacked "countenance," that indispensable component of private demeanor. Masculine honor and feminine tenacity preserved its essential qualities, resorting as necessary to absurd pretension and strict secrecy, stubborn deception and heroic endurance. To pretend to such a degree, to conceal even the realization of one's true purpose, is to protect one's privacy. Such an attitude is credible only as long as success remains plausible. The vices of Jean l'an prés and his grandmother are presented without the slightest hesitation in this minor morality tale: from Truquette's ridiculous wedding meal to the burial of the Huguenot grandmother, everything is exposed in the most wretched detail, even the undignified private quarrels that no sense of propriety conceals. In the end, however, the peculiar private project succeeds. Nurtured in solitude, its vigor remains undiminished and its existence unknown, and the wealthy, securely ensconced in privilege, are outwitted and outmaneuvered by the agile and determined poor. In this world of at least temporary poverty, where it is almost impossible to escape the neighbors' scrutiny, where the door cannot be slammed in anyone's face and probably has no lock, individuals must protect their privacy by more secretive means. They must conceive their plans in secret and carry them out surreptitiously, calling upon whatever assistance and credit they can muster. Even before achieving comfort, respect, and security, they can work their will, but at the price of aloofness and secrecy.

Jean l'an prés tested his mettle in a world in which it was still permissible to compel an impudent upstart to atone for his audacity by ordering him beaten at the hands of lackeys and valets. But such methods were of little avail against an ambitious man who knew how to harden himself. To the man who knew what to make of ambition, the law provided strong enough guarantees to dispel fatal fears and give hope of success.

The law did not create the cells within which ties of work and kinship were supposed to form, but in the civil sphere it did provide guarantees of cohesion that encouraged what might be called a "solidarity of proximity," coupled at times with a warmth of emotion. Private behavior became more determined, even if that determination resulted from repressive constraints, as can be seen in judicial archives concerning various kinds of domestic and business relations. At Toulouse, for example, in the final years of Louis XV's reign, the widow of a master craftsman accused one of the journeymen employed in the shop of stealing tools. The charge was quite plausible, since a locksmith's kit of tools was expensive to acquire, to say nothing of the cost of equipping the shop itself, and a workman whose position was precarious after the death of the master might well aspire to go into business for himself. In this case, however, abundant testimony indicated that it was not true.

Within a guild it was easy to obtain restitution without pressing formal charges of theft, which, if they resulted in conviction, could entail the death penalty. Hence it seems likely that the gravity of the charge was intended as a threat, and that the case was motivated by either hatred or blackmail. The answer appears to lie in the widow's distress. In the hope of finding a successor for her late husband, she had cast her eyes on the intelligent and hard-working journeyman, even though he was much younger than she. She had hoped that

Legal Chicanery

the lure of promotion in a trade where it was all but impossible to obtain the status of master craftsman except through inheritance would overcome any reluctance caused by the disparity in age. When the man hesitated, the widow brought pressure to bear by accusing him of theft, a charge that was easy to substantiate since the locksmith used the master's tools every day as though they were his own. The mistress left herself room for negotiation, for she could later concede that she had misinterpreted the journeyman's actions. Cynics often said that the best way to ensure a servant's loyalty was to possess proof that he had committed some offense. In this case the mistress wanted not only a good servant but a husband, whose loyalty would subsequently be enforced by a common interest in the business.

Another case involved a theft of wool. A confession is heard by hidden witnesses, and to settle the affair the thief is forced to acknowledge an enormous debt that can be repaid only by a lifetime of indentured servitude. The witnesses and the thief became confederates, to whom the secrets and misdeeds of the business could safely be revealed.

These foci of solidarity, secrecy, and, ultimately, privacy were not created by common accord or natural cohesion. The guarantees and threats of the law were used to create and

Law and order were slow to take hold. The legend, which reads "Tax collector who pays straightaway the proceeds of his collections," suggests an ironic appreciation of the brigand's act. (Paris, Bibliothèque Nationale.)

strengthen bonds among people who shared neither friendship nor affinity. Such relations were unintended and no doubt unforeseen consequences of the law itself, of the logic of delegating authority primarily in order to foster responsibility. Since each family, each business, and each community was assigned primary responsibility for maintaining its own order and exacting its own price, an esprit de corps, born of anxiety over the risks of mismanagement and sometimes inspired by the honor implicit in responsibility, served to maintain close relations even among people who felt no sympathy for one another.

When a chimney fire threatens to burn the tax collector's house, all the village inhabitants hasten with buckets and ladders to extinguish the blaze, as neighbors should—but not out of a spirit of charity. Everyone knows that the collector's property will, as a regular precaution, be sequestered in order to guarantee the king his due. Nothing saved from the fire will remain for his own use. "Provided enough remains!" the people think; otherwise the community will still be liable for the tax, having paid their taxes already for nought. Such was the system of joint responsibility, to which people were subject by custom, not choice. Often the only way out was to name the individual who was to bear the burden in case of a legal claim, so that, for example, only the head of the family could be dunned, or the master craftsman of the shop, or the consul or syndic of a town.

The Troubled Gaze of Justice

The social fabric was sturdy enough to be manhandled without tearing, but everyone was aware of the damage. Agencies were called "private" not only to distinguish them from what was public but also because, although they might fulfill a strictly public function, their resources and motivations were private. The art of politics was to exert control over a vast network of such agencies with the smallest possible means. It was no small feat to integrate forces that rarely pulled together. The term *affidé* (confederate), which etymologically suggests confidence, still carried a pejorative connotation.

Criminal trials in the lower courts provide a window into otherwise closed milieus, revealing certain ambiguities in the attitudes of public authorities toward their private rivals. Family feeling, clan spirit, and local and domestic loyalties are plain to see in court documents. Parties worked out their story in private, taking prudent liberties with the truth in order to

A crime is attested, a judge hears the case, and cruel torture is endured. The truth was extracted either under oath or by torture. No greater violence could be done to the individual. (Paris, Bibliothèque Nationale.)

present a plausible version of the case. Witnesses performed loyally but under duress. Deals were made of course, and witnesses sometimes tripped themselves up by not daring to tell the crucial lie. When the several depositions were finally read and compared in open court, the more timid witnesses liked to leave themselves some means of escape in case they were caught in a lie. Appeals to higher courts were seldom futile, for the appeals judge could easily divine the witnesses' hesitations and doubts from the transcript and therefore tended to discount their testimony. Not even fearful servants could readily be compelled to fully support their masters with their testimony, and even the poorest of debtors could discredit such malleable witnesses. Private conspiracies regularly succeeded, probably owing to the influence of family and hierarchy, but frequently they yielded only partial success or even crushing defeat. Thus the courts aroused bitterness and suspicion, suggesting that people were made uneasy by the unpleasant facts of collusion and coercion.

The discomfort was increased by rampant hypocrisy: witnesses, if not actually asked to lie, were asked to swear to things of which they had no knowledge. There was nothing to fear. They did not risk damnation, for the cause in which they were enlisted as coconspirators was legitimate. For some, however, the tension was too great. Although they might willingly repeat hearsay, they could not in good conscience make their version of the truth coincide exactly with that of their master or benefactor. In thousands of cases it is rare to find an instance in which another person's words are repeated exactly (and when it does happen it is usually because the witness is feebleminded). Between husband and wife or parents and children, communication, especially in isolated rural families, was so thorough and complete that agreement as to the facts does not necessarily prove deliberate collusion. Even in the kinds of cases most likely to engender myths, such as fear of brigands or obsession with witchcraft (which, incidentally, became less common in the eighteenth century), we do not find stories so consistent as to enforce general conviction. When identical versions do occur, with all witnesses repeating a lesson learned by heart, it may be taken for granted that the story was invented and agreed to in advance. What the witnesses believed in their heart of hearts is another matter.

These observations do not suggest a significant decline in private solidarities. The delegation of authority actually increased the power to command private allegiance. A more pertinent question is whether individuals learned to weigh one allegiance against another and refused to go along automatically, mimicking or feigning conviction instead. The religious enthusiasms of the Reformation and Counter-Reformation enforced adherence to a new kind of community. The Huguenots of southern France quickly and effectively created a disciplined minority community, and the Jesuits similarly sought to stiffen the resolve of the larger Catholic community. Both developments convey the urgency of the situation. Lacking anything better, the power of the state, naked and triumphant, needed the support of intermediate societies. But these, with the exception of the family, turned out to have no soul, to be in themselves inert, simple cogs driven by outside forces.

It does not follow, however, that Enlightenment society was no more than a vast, undifferentiated mob. Common attitudes emerge in tranquil and lawful affirmations of community, but only in highly self-conscious bodies or in the general assemblies of rural parishes. Increasingly the virtual activity of society took place in associations defined, symbolically at any rate, by shared purposes—societies of thought, lodges, and clubs—that is, in associations in which individuals joined with others whom they did not necessarily know beforehand but who were impelled by similar tastes or ideas to participate in common causes or activities. These associations were the heirs and in some respects the continuators of the sociability of the confraternities. But the confraternities usually drew their members from a single parish and as such were a mere embodiment of preexisting private ties, if not representatives of a professional or occupational group. There was something ambiguous in these associations born of familiarity, opportunity, and proximity; they fostered hostility as well as neighborliness. That hostility was largely quelled by the effective prohibition of serious violence, albeit with the undesirable consequence of encouraging litigiousness. But litigation was too costly for many pocketbooks.

FAMILY AND COMMUNITY LIFE

Did the disarming of warring parties encourage warm and trusting relations, widening the circle of security, fostering freedom in manners and speech, and nurturing attitudes of helpfulness and devotion? Eighteenth-century court records from Languedoc reveal considerable tolerance of vigorous speech and by no means uncordial familiarities in both the lower and the upper classes. This ease of social intercourse was warmly esteemed, and any departure from the norm, any display of anger or contempt, called for explanation. It was permissible to test a person's readiness to help, for there was no false shame when it came to setting limits, and everyone knew more or less what he could expect from others. Helpfulness was a clear and rather generous measure of benevo-

Emanuel de Witte, *Woman at the Clavecin.* Music was a presence at social gatherings and in the most intimate settings. (Rotterdam, Boymans-van-Beuningen Museum.)

lence, but prudence remained a consideration. It was not wise to tell all to "strangers," and children were warned at an early age about the dangers of indiscretion. Nor was it wise to be truly importunate or to seem impoverished or incapable, hungry or thirsty—unless of course one was truly penniless. Finally, it was a good idea to remain on guard against unexpected, disturbing, or alarming events, hence not to reveal too much and not to risk being caught unprepared. Outside the family good humor, a decent fancy, and a light tone were valued qualities. Relations were informal and governed by tradition.

It was essential to be tight-lipped with outsiders concerning family matters: money and property, ambition, marriage, and work were none of their business. This does not mean that the family debated such matters in plenary session. Every decision was governed by a set of interdependent factors, simple in some cases, complex in others. The father, or sometimes, in the case of a daughter's marriage, the mother, disclosed the family's intentions to interested parties and agents. Threats were rarely necessary; consent was taken for granted. When only one family member was involved, he or she was asked to keep the decision secret until the time was right for a public announcement. A family might rent or buy a piece of land for a younger son to work, so he would have some-

The young ladies gather in small groups around their teachers, each studying on her own in accordance with the Italian pedagogical maxim that "another person's rule is valid only for him." (Saint-Omer, Henri Dupuis Museum.)

thing useful to do at home, but there was no need to inform him of the details of the agreement or the ultimate fate of the property. Such things were more properly discussed with the woman of the house or the eldest son. Or, better yet, not discussed at all: absolutism arouses opposition when it goes looking for approval. A man could act like a paterfamilias of Roman Law without knowing it. Mme de Maintenon explained to "her girls" at Saint-Cyr that a patrimony, regardless of its legal status, was not something that its owner could dispose of freely, being bound by duties of management, conservation, and devolution. Absolutism avoided complicating those duties further with a need for justification.

Private Life, Ordered Life

Within the family an atmosphere of intimacy (in which people later placed great hopes) was kept from developing, not by the loosening of family ties, contempt for women and children, or insensitivity, but by the concentration of authority and responsibility in paternal hands. On this point too Mme de Maintenon took a severe tone with her girls, much given to dreaming of husbands who would accord them idyllic freedom: "You will have, Mademoiselle, your husband to look after, and then you will have a master . . . You may displease him; he may displease you. It is virtually impossible that your tastes will be similar. He may be of a mind to ruin you; he may be greedy and deny you everything. I would be tedious if I told you what marriage was like."[10]

The letters, opinions, and conversations of this most august teacher show that her constant concern was to prepare young ladies for domestic life, for managing relatively humble households whose lack of wealth enforced modesty without dampening pride. Families living in such conditions were not likely to spend much time mingling in high society; with proper instruction they should have had ample opportunity to foster a private life at home. Yet the most frequent warnings are against the illusory comforts of uninhibited privacy. Compared with life at boarding school, with its myriad rules and regulations, family life was even more demanding. Once married, a girl might as well bid farewell to sheltered youth and the affectionate companionship of mistresses and friends. Her life became one of toil and struggle, of coping with necessities, sustaining life, husbanding resources, sacrificing her hours of leisure and even the time she might have liked to devote to piety and charity. She was supposed to serve her family with

Private tutors went beyond primers in preparing students for secondary school. Here the students work independently, but are quizzed by the master. (Paris, Bibliothèque Nationale.)

prayer in her mind, knowing that she might have no other time for religion. She even had to overcome her desire to give to the needy, for the first imperative was to meet the needs of family and servants.

To girls who believed that no discipline could be more severe than that of their school, Mme de Maintenon affirmed that the rule of family life was far harsher. A married woman could count on no rest, no secrecy, no privacy of her own, for her services were continually and urgently in demand by husband, children, dependents, and servants. She had no more private life than "a sergeant traveling from skirmish to skirmish" in the thick of battle—and battles were relatively infrequent, whereas the married woman was constantly under fire.

Such a prospect should seem daunting, Mme de Maintenon told her pupils, only to the lazy and willful. Resignation, submission, even subjugation were virtues of the finest sort. We can now see why the state was able to recognize and even encourage private life organized in accordance with such norms. There was no mystery about privacy. Everyone did some things in private. Publicity would have been pointless and possibly indecent. The relation between public and private was a question of honor. Proper demeanor within the home made people more capable of behaving honorably outside it;

nothing must ever be done to forfeit esteem. In private, in an atmosphere of mutual trust (but not connivance), motives best hidden from public view could be discreetly avowed. What was forbidden and what was permitted were clearly defined, and religious teaching made matters even more explicit. When not under orders from higher authority, a person's first concern was unabashedly for his family. A solid family structure formed the foundation of the state, and the education offered the girls of Saint-Cyr shows that this was a matter of great concern to the king. More dramatically, the conclusion of Molière's *Tartuffe* shows the sword of justice ready to strike at any perversity, however devout, that threatens the household of a loyal subject.

The Public Spirit: Mme Roland

The eighteenth century does not seem to have achieved such a satisfactory compromise between public and private authority. It is as though the citizen is no longer free to choose a career of state service. The man who would advance his family's fortunes as he might plot a political strategy can no longer find full satisfaction in the range of choices open to him; he must painfully repress his most natural emotions.

When Turgot, in the final days of the ancien régime, observed that France had declined into what he called an "indiscriminate society" (*société générale*), he was expressing outrage at the withering of family feeling.[11] No longer did anyone express affection for or indulgence toward women and children, unless somehow they managed to make their presence felt in the enlightened conversation of the salons. Normally they had no part in those circles where the broader interests of the nation were discussed, far beyond their modest horizons. Were children at least cared for as they deserved? Child-rearing by parents seems to have become obsolete, or at least it was no longer considered to be in good taste. Children were entrusted to servants, who everyone pretended to believe were zealous in their duties. Adolescents were sent away to boarding schools or convents, whose usefulness as educational institutions would later be challenged. As young people grew to adulthood in the care of paid retainers, some fared better than others. Society required a new tone, a new candor, which could, among others of their own class, disqualify those who were educated at home. Such an education was fit only to create "private" citizens, comfortable in their own homes and among those with whom they came into contact in the course of daily life but not fit to participate in "higher" society.

What had caused this disturbing turn of events, against which new educational theories protested vehemently, as did the new theater of sentiment, with its "simple and natural" characters, and the new painting, with its moralistic and sentimental subjects? Manon Phlipon, who became Mme Roland, was an exceptional woman in many ways. Yet it is interesting to consider her as a specimen: one who, though gifted in expressing her emotions, stubbornly insisted and no doubt believed that she never abandoned her wifely role, even as she succumbed to the fatal attractions of high politics and high society. [The wife of Jean-Marie Roland de La Platrière, a revolutionary statesman, she kept a salon in Paris that was the headquarters of Republicans and Girondins; she was executed during the Terror.] In her prison writings, although she does not entirely forget about her courageous husband Roland or the touching little daughter who would be left an orphan in a storm by a mother determined to sacrifice herself, she is mainly concerned with offering an impassioned justification of Girondist policies and heaping calumny upon the "monsters of the Mountain" (her political enemies). She makes no real attempt to save her life for the sake of her family. The republican heroine has no need to complain about the perversion of the revolutionary regime, which is simply a part of the tumult of the times that the revolutionary soul must overcome. For her to think nostalgically about individual happiness means recalling the time before she entered the world, when the affection of relatives and the friendship of other girls at the convent filled her heart with the charm of private life. All that belongs to her childhood, to the time before she became involved in the shaping of events. It is a far cry from her new life as the wife of the Minister of the Interior, giving dinners and soirées which she considered public because the guests were her husband's collaborators, who naturally continued over dinner the debates that animated their working hours. "His colleagues of every description, along with a few friends and acquaintances, gathered at his table once a week. There, in very public conversations, they openly discussed matters that interested everyone." The ambiguity in this text is shrewd: it was essential to avoid any suggestion that this was a small clique meeting to hatch some sort of plot. To be sure, Mme Roland draws a clear distinction between political life, whose attractions she recognizes, and private friends, people with whom she "was on terms of friendship independent of any political consideration." Immediately, however, she adds that friendship means a sharing of feelings and opinions: "I admit it openly and rejoice in such conformity." Is this not proof, she asks, of her and her friends' utter devotion to the public good, since they choose one another on the basis of their shared conception of the common goal? Not all the revolutionaries are her friends, but her friends share a common view of republican righteousness. It is the cause that defines affinities and friendships; private relations merely reflect the accidents of birth and profession. To internalize, along with one's comrades, the general will means giving up much of the autonomy of privacy.

The Real Issue: Private Life

The old order had its tensions and imbalances, but with little effort the sovereign was able to settle the minor differences that arose. Under the new political order, however, the wills of individual citizens were simultaneously mobilized to create an irresistible general will. If a Saint-Just made steadfastness in friendship a test of republican virtue, it was simply to promote solidarity in the ranks of the citizenry. Roger Chartier, analyzing the monarchy's strategy of reproduction, cites a key passage from Norbert Elias' *The Civilizing Process*: "The equilibrium among the various social groups of roughly equal strength and the resulting ambivalent attitude of each group toward the central ruler were certainly not the creation of any one king. But when interdependence and social tension produce a situation of this type, it is of vital interest to the central ruler to perpetuate the instability."[12] The king did this by limiting the power of authorities internal to each group, thereby encouraging the group to develop some measure of autonomy; at the same time the emulation of other groups introduced dynamism and resolve. Conformity was encouraged, individualism discouraged, and internal discipline recommended by moral and political authorities.

Consolidated by administrative pacification, the ancien régime strengthened its subaltern agencies, built around narrow sympathies and confident of their survival, which combined, at least symbolically, duties of love, fear, and solidarity. This encouraged despotisms, in the proper sense of absolute domestic authorities, or repelled disappointed sensibilities, for emotions overflow naturally in families not pressed by neces-

Wedding Meal. A sumptuous wedding feast. (Paris, Louvre.)

sity. Well-to-do bourgeois and noble families had begun to taste the delights of comfort and leisure. Authority began to be relaxed, although it could be suddenly reasserted when a son was ordered to remain celibate or a daughter to marry a man she did not love. Disappointments and resentments undermined family order and revealed the absurdity of sacrifice in so petty a cause. The only great causes, ones worthy of individual adherence, were public, as the Ancients had insisted. For young people there was scarcely any other educational or emotional model, for the Counter-Reformation had run its course and no longer could attract an audience with the charms of piety.

Hence the groundwork was laid for the illusion that Benjamin Constant would denounce once it became possible to reflect upon the results of the Revolution, upon whether or not it had answered the true aspirations of people in the final years of the monarchy. In his foreword to Constant's *De la liberté chez les Modernes* (On the Modern Idea of Liberty), Marcel Gauchet calls attention to Constant's horror of that "almost limitless empire over human existence," which, from Mably to Rousseau and Filangieri, late-eighteenth-century political philosophy attributed to a new kind of power, conceived without sin, a power that would entail no corruption but rather would drain the abcesses that selfish private interests had created in the body social.[13]

The law, Mably wrote, "ought to seize hold of us in the first moments of life, hedging us about with examples, pretexts, rewards, and punishments. It ought to direct and improve that numerous and ignorant class which, having no time to examine things for itself, is condemned to receive truths on faith and as if prejudged. Whatever time the law leaves to us is time left to the passions to tempt, seduce, and subjugate us." Because the indvidual is emancipated, freedom seems assured, but now society is held together only by the coercion of the state, which alone must create the universal social bond. There is no further need for intermediate social cells; although the family, it is generally conceded, is still required for reproduction, any other intermediate cells merely serve as screens, blocking out the organizing light of reason. The family must be freed from all the private associations that cluster about it in the local community. Private life is reduced to nothing more than an agency for providing indispensable care to relatives enfeebled by dint of age, sex, or physical or mental constitution.

Constant takes a very different view of the subject. The revolutionaries, he says, wanted to limit the arbitrariness of the political authorities, which endangered customary liberties, but they never intended for people to be made subject to an omnipotent and unquestionable law. To be sure, "arbitrary rule is the enemy of domestic bonds," to be combated by insisting on strict adherence to the forms of justice. The law is harsh not in order to make citizens vigilant but in order to punish where necessary; it respects "the generosity that leads men to pity the weak when attacked by the strong and to offer their assistance without hesitation." The people's profound wish was that private life be delivered from arbitrary rule, from the abuses and excesses of authority; but the two regimes engendered by the Revolution failed to see that the people by no means wanted authority over families and communities to be handed over intact to the new, purified power of the general will. Nevertheless, Constant's analysis, more penetrating than most in this period of transition, foresaw the development of new "private" needs in an era of economic growth and argued that it was reasonable for citizens to look to the authorities for help in matters of education, health, and relief of the poor. As a liberal critic of the Revolution, he was uneasy about the state's encroachment on private prerogatives, but he anticipated desires that would arise when the comforts of private life became available to all.

This painting by Pietro Longhi shows a priest hearing a woman's confession in a Venetian church. The rudimentary confessional separates the confessor from the penitent. (Venice, Querini Stampalia Gallery.)

The Two Reformations: Communal Devotion and Personal Piety

François Lebrun

FROM its inception, Christianity has been torn by two apparently irreconcilable tendencies. It is an eminently personal religion, calling upon each person individually to convert, find faith, and seek salvation: "Daughter, thy faith hath made thee whole" (Mark 5:34). It is also a communal religion dependent upon a church: "Thou art Peter, and upon this rock I will build my church" (Matt. 16:18); "That they may be one, even as we are one" (John 17:22). The quintessential religious act is prayer, and Christ prescribes that prayer be individual: "But thou, when thou prayest, enter into thy closet, and when thou hast shut thy door, pray to thy Father which is in secret" (Matt. 6:6). A few days later, however, he seems to recommend collective prayer: "For where two or three are gathered together in my name, there am I in the midst of them" (Matt. 18:20). This contradiction lies at the heart of Christianity, along with that between contemplation and action and between the church as institution and the church as mystical body. But did not Christ define himself as a sign of contradiction?

The history of Christianity begins with the community of the twelve apostles, who, on the night of the Ascension, gathered in "an upper room" and "all continued with one accord in prayer and supplication" (Acts 1:13-14). Idealized, perhaps, by the writer of the Acts, these early Christian communities, or churches, would later serve as a model for those displeased by the obtrusive power of the institutionalized church—an ambiguous model, since the early church, though egalitarian in its practices, was also highly collectivized and by no means individualistic. Gradually the Church took on a hierarchical structure, with local churches headed by bishops,

Service at the parish church of Saint-André in Lille. Water-color from F.-C. Pourchez, *Description of the Celebrations in the City of Lille, 29 September 1729, in Honor of the Birth of Monseigneur le Dauphin.* (Lille, Municipal Library.)

first among whom was Peter's successor, the bishop of Rome. As early as the third century, however, Christians seeking total perfection fled the world for the desert, where, in solitude, they hoped to find God through prayer and mortification. Soon these desert anchorites were joined by communities of cenobites, who also led an ascetic life, but not alone. Though highly structured, these monastic communities fostered intense personal piety and even mysticism.

To a degree the dialectical tension between personal and communal religion has shaped the entire history of Christianity. The tension between these two contradictory vocations has been constant. A hierarchical institution, the Church has always been wary of what it considered to be excesses of personal piety. It often appears to have been satisfied with a communal religion whose apparent unanimity may have indicated more of docile conformism than of sincere, deliberate commitment.

This background should be kept in mind as we examine the role of Christianity in the emergence of private and inner life. We begin with the Reformation in the sixteenth century. To what extent did the Protestant sects and the Roman Catholic Church encourage or hinder private worship? There can be no doubt that Christians of all persuasions agreed that, because individual salvation is the crux of Christian life, personal piety is of paramount importance. But while Catholics reaffirmed the value of the seven sacraments and reinforced the role of the clergy as obligatory intercessors and guardians of orthodoxy, Protestants insisted on a direct relation between the individual believer and God, yet without eliminating the role of the family and the ecclesial community.

THE CATHOLIC VIEW

In response to Protestant attacks, the Catholic Church after the Council of Trent sought to reemphasize the importance of collective piety. Closely supervised by the clergy, communal religious practices were thought to express the reality of the universal church. At the same time, however, the influence of sixteenth-century Spanish and seventeenth-century French mystics led the Church to pay greater attention to various forms of personal piety. In the seventeenth and eighteenth centuries many compulsory as well as optional religious practices were affected by these apparently contradictory but in fact complementary tendencies.

Attendance at mass on Sundays and holy days was the sine qua non of Catholicism. In areas bordering on non-Catholic countries, failure to observe this obligation aroused suspicion that a person belonged to a reformed sect. Mass, though a collective rite, was for a long time less a communal devotion than a conjunction of individual prayers. During the sixteenth and much of the seventeenth century the faithful formed a passive audience, many of whom could not even see what was going on at the altar because they were seated in a side chapel or behind a rood screen. This state of affairs does not seem to have offended religious writers. In 1635 Jean Huchon, curé of Saint-Sauveur in Lille, wrote in his *Flambeau des chrétiens*: "Anyone who is present in body and attention during the celebration of the mass, even if he is far from the altar but provided he attends to the entire mass, fulfills the commandment; it is not necessary to see the celebrant or to hear his voice."

Catholics were exhorted to pass the time as devoutly as possible, by reciting the rosary. In 1610 Saint Francis de Sales wrote to one of his penitents: "At mass I advise you to recite your rosary in preference to any other vocal prayer." Father Suffren recommended the following prayers during the time spent at mass: "Vocal orisons, rosary, litanies, the seven

Participation in the Mass

Jean Lepautre, engraving: a Roman-style altar of the late 17th century. The altar, previously in the apse, was now placed at the crossing of the transept, closer to the faithful in the nave. (Paris, Bibliothèque Nationale.)

psalms, and the hours of the Cross, the Holy Spirit, or the Virgin." In 1642 Saint Jean Eudes recommended "reciting one's hours or rosary."

Only the sermon interrupted this passive participation. It was preceded by prayers recited in unison by the entire congregation, in response to the priest: these included prayers for the dead, the pope, the king, and the local seigneur, followed by the Pater, Ave Maria, Credo, and commandments of God and the Church. Then came the sermon proper (a "familiar explanation of the gospel of the day or of some point of Christian ethics for the instruction and edification of the congregation"), followed by notices of holy days, fasts, the offices of the week, and possibly marriage bans or the reading of an episcopal letter. In other words, the congregation actually participated only in those parts of the service that did not belong to the mass proper.

The situation evolved considerably in the second half of the seventeenth century. Change had been urged by various religious writers, especially the priests of the Oratory, who agreed that the mass ought to be something more than an exercise in individual devotion, indeed that it was the essential act of the Catholic faith and as such required the participation of the entire community. At the beginning of the century Saint Francis de Sales had wondered openly whether the mass as then practiced was really superior to "prayer at home." In 1651 the Archbishop of Rouen, François de Harlay de Champvallon, published *On the Proper Manner of Hearing Mass*, which met with great success. In it he wrote: "All prayer must cease when the priest prays and when he offers the sacrifice for all. You must pay attention to the prayer that he makes on your behalf and on behalf of the entire congregation, and you must think about the sacrifice, offering it and yourself through the priest in the spirit and union of the Church." Numerous other works on the subject express similar sentiments. In 1676 a writer from Lille produced *Method for All the Faithful to Celebrate the Mass Usefully along with the Priest*. This treatise states: "It is a mistake to think that it is better to recite one's hours or rosary or other devotions during mass than to join one's spirit and intention with that of the priest. The Church also makes us sacrificers along with the celebrant." This is a far cry from what Jean Huchon had said just forty years earlier. In the preface to the *Missal of Paris in Latin and French* (1701) we read: "Although those who, inspired by devotion, pray silently or out loud during the divine sacrifice are not to be condemned, we nevertheless remain convinced that the best way to hear the mass is to join with the priest so as to enter into the spirit of the words he utters."

These recommendations led to certain concrete measures intended to encourage real communal participation in the celebration of the mass. Toward the end of the century rood screens were removed and choirs altered in many churches, particularly in large cities. To be sure, these renovations also reflect a new taste for orderly, uncluttered, and well-lighted designs, which can be characterized as neoclassical. Primarily, however, they reveal a desire to make religion more vital and communal by bringing the congregation closer to the altar, the theater of the sacrifice in the mass. In this, the design of Saint Peter's Basilica in Rome was very influential, and new churches were said to be "in the Roman style." In 1698–1700 at Angers, for example, the canons of Saint-Maurice cathedral led the way: the old rood screen was removed and the main altar was moved from the apse to the transept. Similar changes were made in five other churches in the city between 1706 and 1722.

Another way of involving the congregation was through the use of missals in which French and Latin texts were printed side by side. Catholics were urged to buy such missals and use them in church. Worshipers could follow the celebrant and recite the prayers along with him. Thus, rather paradoxically, the bilingual missal, an instrument of private devotion, became a primary means of involving the congregants in the mystical communion of holy sacrifice. But this communion was the opposite of a communal religious practice, for the prayers were not recited out loud but murmured quietly by each individual. Bilingual missals were distributed widely at the end of the seventeenth century in the hope that they would be used to convert Protestants. To that end, Pelisson in 1679 ordered that a *Latin-French Missal* be printed and distributed in France. In 1685, the year of the Revocation of the Edict of Nantes, the Archbishop of Paris caused to be printed, on orders from Louis XIV, 100,000 copies of *Catholic Hours*, preceded by the ordinary of the mass in French.

There was vigorous opposition to such translations, which were characterized as Jansenist. Detractors feared, or pretended to fear, that lay Catholics would imagine that "they are priests in the same sense as the priest." The battle grew even fiercer after publication of the papal bull *Unigenitus* (1713); but this did not prevent the publication of new missals

This book, published in 1681 at the behest of François de Harlay de Champvallon, Archbishop of Paris, contained most of the prayers for Sunday mass. In 1651, while still Archbishop of Rouen, Harlay de Champvallon published *La Manière de bien entendre la messe* (On the Proper Way of Hearing Mass). (Paris, Bibliothèque Nationale.)

in which a literal French translation or paraphrase appeared alongside the Latin text of the ordinary. Also published were various *Exercises for the Holy Mass*, anthologies of prayers and meditations for use in various parts of the service. The purpose of such books was, as one author put it, "to enter into the sense of what the priest is saying without following his words exactly."

How widely were these missals and other works distributed, and exactly what role did they play? Illiteracy of course limited their impact. Between 1686 and 1690, 71 percent of grooms and 86 percent of brides did not sign their marriage certificates. There were regional variations: if we draw a line across France from Saint Malo to Geneva, the area below that line, comprising most of southern and western France, was more illiterate than the area above. But the figures are misleading; more men and certainly more women knew how to read than these statistics indicate. Yet even among the minority who knew how to read (larger in the city than in the countryside), probably only a small number owned and used missals and books of spiritual exercises. That is why certain priests with Jansenist leanings recommended that the celebrant read all the prayers of the mass aloud, including the canon. Still, as Henri Bremond wonders, What good did it do laymen to hear the prayers of the canon recited in a language they did not understand? No one, not even the most out-and-out Jansenists, called for the mass to be celebrated in French. Some, however, did go so far as to ask that, after the gospel was recited in Latin, it be read again in French translation.

In fact, apart from private use of missals, which remained rare (except possibly in some urban parishes and in the chapels of religious communities open to laypersons), all attempts to involve the congregation in the prayers of the liturgy recited at the altar ended in failure. The most perceptive priests, especially those who officiated in rural parishes, would have agreed with the prior-curate of Roissy-en-France, who said, in 1687: "It is not necessary for every individual who attends the service to hear every word that is said. The devotion with which they accept, in a spirit of charity and communion, the wishes and duties of the Church will suffice to permit them to share in the grace and bounty that God provides."

Things changed little over the next century. Priests were content as long as their parishioners attended Sunday mass. (In the diocese of Strasbourg, a verger in each parish inspected houses during the hour of mass to make sure that no more

The Office of the Virgin, published in Paris in 1651, is a collection of prayers and ceremonies for celebrating the feasts of the Virgin. The book is a typical product of a movement that attempted to provide books of prayers to Christians in French without Latin. (Paris, Bibliothèque Nationale.)

than one person stayed home to stand guard, as was deemed indispensable.) They required little more of their parishioners than respectful attention during the service and perhaps participation in the singing of the canticles in French, German, Breton, or Occitan. While the priest celebrated the holy sacrifice, the most devout of the congregation recited their prayers, usually the rosary. I therefore find it difficult to agree with Henri-Jean Martin that in the second half of the seventeenth century a veritable revolution in religious practice occurred, as attendance at mass ceased to be merely one of many forms of worship and participation in the divine sacrifice assumed a central place in a person's spiritual life. Admittedly this was the goal proposed by many French religious writers, but it is far from certain that this goal was attained to any significant degree.

Although attendance at Sunday vespers was not compulsory, in the eighteenth century many parishioners seem to have acceded to pressure from the clergy to participate in this service as well. But even more than during morning mass, participation was passive. Only the devout recited prayers, while in the choir the clergy chanted psalms in Latin. Parishioners attended mass and vespers not only on the fifty-two Sundays of the year but also on obligatory holy days. The number of holy days, which varied from parish to parish, was reduced from between forty and sixty in 1650 to about thirty in 1780 by bishops concerned about the fate of the poorest workers, for whom every holy day was a day without work, hence without pay. Of even greater concern to the bishops was the "profanation" of these holy days, which, instead of being observed as days of rest and prayer, were all too often given over to pleasure and recreation.

Another obligation incumbent upon every Catholic was confession and communion at Eastertime. In the early seventeenth century communal confession and general absolution, widely practiced in the fifteenth and sixteenth centuries, were still in effect in many dioceses in northern France (but not in the south, in parishes where the *langue d'oc* was spoken and the Roman custom observed). Communal confession took place at the end of Lent, in some dioceses on Holy Thursday but more frequently on Easter Sunday. The ceremony, which followed the offertory, began with the recital, out loud and in French, of the first part of the Confiteor. This was followed

Individual Confession and Frequent Communion

by a detailed enumeration of sins, the list of which varied from diocese to diocese, probably modified by each priest based on his knowledge of his parishioners and the kinds of sins they committed most often. This was followed by recital of the second part of the Confiteor, which included an admission of guilt, a promise not to repeat the sin, and a plea for intercession and absolution. Finally, the celebrant granted collective absolution, employing one of several formulas, and the parishioners approached the holy altar to receive communion.

The value of communal confession was limited, however. Remission could be granted for venial and forgotten sins, but mortal sins could be effaced only by individual confession followed by absolution granted by a priest (who uttered the words *ego te absolvo*) and private penance. A fifteenth-century diocesan manual states the Church's position: "No one should think that [communal confession] is valid for absolution of any mortal sin of which he has memory, unless it is confessed secretly and with true repentance." Despite such warnings, the practice lent itself to misinterpretations. Over the course of the seventeenth century it was gradually eliminated, owing partly to questions raised by Protestants, partly to the substitution of the Roman liturgy for northern French practices, and partly to the growing importance of clerical examination and direction of the individual Catholic's conscience.

Seventeenth-century catechisms stress the idea that examination of one's conscience, in the sense of a "diligent search for the sins that one has committed," was the "primary prerequisite for properly receiving the sacrament of penance." The *Catechism of Agen* (1677) insists that examination of the conscience is a highly personal matter, a question of stringent introspection: "Question: What must I do in order to examine my conscience well? Answer: First, you must retire to a private place; second, you must kneel down and beg God to bestow upon you the light necessary to know your sins . . . Question: How diligent must this examination be? Answer: You must take as much care as you would with an important matter of business, since our salvation is the most important business of all."

For a minority of the devout, regular self-examination and confession led to what was called the direction of conscience or the "cure of souls." Some men and even more women not only went monthly or even weekly to confession, but chose confessors with whom they kept track of their progress toward perfection, recording every lapse. The con-

Giuseppe Maria Crespi, one of the series of *Seven Sacraments*, supposed to illustrate a central episode in the life of Saint John of Nepomuk (1330–1393), confessor to the Queen of Hungary. The confessional, a type in common use for several centuries, has a place for the priest in the center and two small windows giving access to penitents kneeling on either side. (Turin, Sabauda Gallery.)

fessor offered advice, warnings, and encouragement. Most spiritual directors belonged to an order such as the Jesuits, the Oratorians, or the Dominicans. In his *Familiar Conversations between a Penitent and His Spiritual Father* (1627), the Jesuit Antoine de Balinghem praised those "men of religion, much in vogue in the sacred ministry of hearing confessions and highly renowned on account of their great dexterity in calming agitated and troubled consciences."

There were several reasons why the regular clergy played such an important role in the direction of consciences. In the absence of a major impediment, Easter confession was compulsory and had to be made to the parish priest. Other confessions, however, could be made to any priest with the permission of the local bishop. Unlike the parish priest, the regular clergy had time to spare. Confession was also fashion-

Bernard Picart, engraving (1733), showing a more theatrical confessional scene. (Paris, Bibliothèque Nationale.)

able, and the reputation of certain orders, such as the Jesuits, attracted many of the devout or those who would seem devout, the hypocrites mocked by La Bruyère in the 1694 edition of his *Caractères*: "Choose a director more widely heeded than the Gospel. Derive all your sanctity and all your prominence from the reputation of your director. Disdain those whose director is less in vogue and set little store by their salvation. Love only those words of God that your director preaches. Prefer his mass to other masses and the sacraments given by his hand to those less suitable." Although the direction of consciences inevitably encouraged laxity and hypocrisy, the practice increased markedly in the seventeenth century and contributed greatly to the development of internalized, personal forms of privacy among the lay population.

But for most of the faithful, particularly in rural parishes, individual confession, required at least once a year, was the most reluctantly accepted of all the compulsory practices of the faith. Many Catholics were reluctant to confess their sins to a priest, not only because they were ashamed but also because they feared that he would not respect the secrecy of the confessional. In 1700 Christophe Sauvageon, prior-curate of the parish of Sennely in the Sologne, described the situation in candid terms that no doubt apply to other parishes as well:

"There is an entrenched but deplorable custom in this parish of going to confession without the slightest preparation. People approach the confessional without having examined their consciences in any way. They rush to church, hasten to the confessional, and practically fight one another to be the first to enter. But once at the priest's feet, they scarcely even cross themselves, unless they've been told to do so. They almost never remember when they made their last confession. Most of them have not completed their last penance. They have done nothing and accuse themselves of nothing. They laugh and talk about their wretchedness and poverty. If the priest reproaches them for some sin that he has seen them commit, they give alibis and plead their case, they blame their neighbors and accuse everyone but themselves. In short, they do everything in the confessional but what they are supposed to do, which is to state their sins with sincere contrition. They praise evil as well as good, minimize their faults, and whisper their most serious sins between clenched teeth for fear that the priest might **hear** what they are saying. Seeking to deceive him, they deceive themselves. There are very few good confessions, especially on the part of those whose lives are not upright and Christian."

The attitude of most confessors encouraged such reluctance on the part of their parishioners. Thanks to the influence of Charles Borromeo's widely used *Instructions to Confessors*, almost an "official manual" for the French clergy, confession became one of the primary instruments of religious indoctrination. In the confessional (which came into wide use in the sixteenth century), the priest, alone with the penitent, asked specific questions intended to explore the conscience of the sinner who had not already done so; he then reminded his charge of the magnitude of his or her sins and the punishments they entailed, before imposing penance and pronouncing absolution. Hence annual confession was usually seen as a distasteful obligation to be completed as painlessly as possible.

Only in unusual circumstances was confession honest and aboveboard, leading in some cases to personal conversion. Missionaries went to villages and preached intensively for three to five weeks in order to prepare the villagers for a "general confession of their entire past life." Another exception was the deathbed confession. This too was supposed to be a general confession, as recommended in one *Guide for the Sick and Dying* (1706) used by the clergy: "According to Saint Francis de Sales, it is appropriate as death approaches to make

Philippe de Champaigne, *Portrait of Saint Charles Borromeo.* Charles Borromeo, nephew of Pope Pius IV, was named Archbishop of Milan in 1564. His efforts to improve Christian education and moral training helped bring about the success of the Catholic Counter-Reformation. He became the model of the post-Tridentine bishop for all of Europe. (Orleans, Museum of Fine Arts.)

a general confession, covering in at least summary fashion the various situations in which the patient found himself during the course of his life." At such times everyone left the sick-room, leaving the priest alone with his penitent.

Easter communion, even when not preceded by a general confession, was one of the high points of the liturgical calendar, expressing the unity of the parish in communion with the resurrected Christ. In the words of Christophe Sauvageon, "Easter is the high holy day of priests, at which time they eat the Lamb along with the disciples." Few people failed to observe this essential obligation of the faith. Those who refused were officially denounced as public sinners; if they persisted unto death, they were buried outside the consecrated ground of the cemetery. Increasing numbers of the faithful went beyond mere Easter communion. By confessing more often, they were able to participate more often in the sacrament of the Eucharist. After the Council of Trent, it became customary for pious Catholics to receive communion monthly—if not weekly or even daily; frequent communion became the hallmark of personal piety. Even the Jansenists recommended it, regardless of what their adversaries said. The *Catechism of Nantes*, which was accused of Jansenist sympathies, was quite explicit: "Question: Should a Christian be content to confess once a year and to receive communion on the holy day of Easter? Answer: No, piety should lead him to participate in these two sacraments far more often, on every one of the holy days of Our Lord and the Holy Virgin, say, or once a month, or even every Sunday, in order to lead a holier and more Christian life in proportion as he approaches the holy mysteries more often."

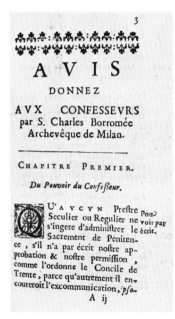

Charles Borromeo's *Instructions to Confessors* was soon translated into French. The saint recommends among other things that the curé or his vicar keep a chart describing the state of the soul (*status animarum*) of each parishioner. Here, a dagger signifies an affirmative answer, a zero a negative answer. (Paris, Bibliothèque Nationale.)

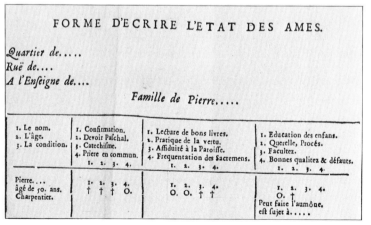

Apart from the events of the liturgical calendar, individuals participated in a variety of acts that were not only religious but also rites of passage: the sacraments of baptism, communion, marriage, and last rites concerned the individual's personal relation to God, but the associated ceremonies expressed his membership not only in the parish community but also in the invisible community of the universal church. Salvation, every Catholic was reminded, is the major concern of each person's life: "For what shall it profit a man, if he shall gain the whole world, and lose his own soul?" (Mark 8:36). And salvation was not possible outside the communion of saints.

Baptism, celebrated on the day of birth or the day after, marked the newborn's entry into Christian life. Washing away original sin, baptism made the infant a Christian. If, as was only too common, the child died in the days or weeks that followed, he or she would be assured of eternal beatitude. When a name was bestowed by the godfather or godmother, the child received a patron saint who served as both model and intercessor. The godparents also pledged to assume re-

The Sacraments: The Ritual and the Intimate

Bernard Picart, engraving (1733). Emergency baptism was performed when there was danger of a newborn's dying without benefit of baptism. The midwife or father or priest poured water over the child, uttering the words, "I baptize thee." (Paris, Bibliothèque Nationale.)

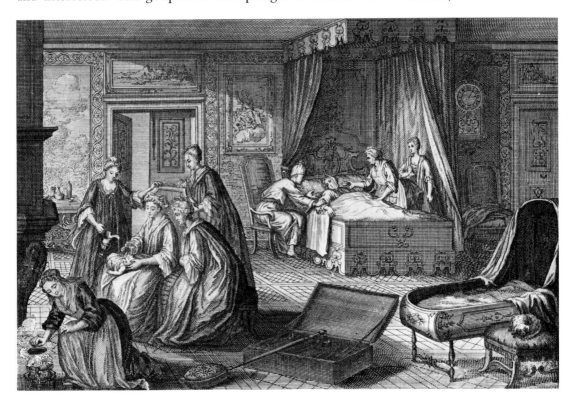

The Church also authorized home baptism when the parents wished to delay the formal baptism ceremony. Here the Duke of Brittany is baptized on the day of his birth, 25 June 1704. (Paris, Bibliothèque Nationale.)

Pietro Longhi. More commonly, the child was brought to the church "as soon as possible." There, the godfather and godmother, who gave the child its name, presented it to the priest, who then baptized it. (Venice, Querini Stampalia.)

sponsibility for their godchild: "You have become his guardians in the eyes of the Church. It is your duty to ensure that he faithfully executes the promises he has made through your words. It is your duty to remind him of his great obligations and urge him to live up to them just as soon as he is old enough to understand and to lift his heart up to God." Generally only a few persons attended the baptism (the father, the godparents, the infant's brothers and sisters), but the ringing of the church bells involved everyone in the parish.

Upon completing catechism class (at age twelve, thirteen, or fourteen, depending on the parish), the child received communion for the first time. In the sixteenth and seventeenth centuries there was no special first-communion ceremony; on Easter Sunday each child simply received communion along with its parents. Toward the end of the seventeenth century some parishes established a special ceremony, generally on the Monday or Tuesday after Easter or on one of the following Sundays: the children, especially well dressed for the occasion and carrying lighted candles, received communion together, boys on one side, girls on the other, in the presence of the assembled parishioners. In some places they then "renewed the promises made at baptism." By the late eighteenth century first-communion rites were a firmly established custom, al-

Giuseppe Maria Crespi, another
of the series of *Seven Sacraments*, this one illustrating communion. The priest, wearing
surplice and stole and holding a
ciborium, distributes the host
to those kneeling before him.
(Dresden, Gemäldegalerie.)

Bernard Picart, engraving
(1733): a more common form
of communion. The communicants receive the eucharist from
the hand of the priest, who
takes the host from the ciborium. Behind him, the door of
the tabernacle is open. The
priest will close it after returning the ciborium to its place. In
the background, other worshipers deposit their offerings
in plates. On the table are a
crucifix and reliquaries. (Paris,
Bibliothèque Nationale.)

though they had yet to assume the importance that they would take on in the following century.

Marriage was not only a sacrament but also a commitment by husband and wife to fulfill the primary purpose of their union: to bring a child into the world and baptize it as a Christian. However much they might desire each other, marriage was more than a joining of two individuals. The *Catechism of Nantes* is quite specific on the point: "Beyond the joining of a man and a woman, marriage implies what is greatest in religion, namely, the union of Jesus Christ with his Church . . . The grace of the sacrament of marriage is its fecundity, but a fecundity which gives children to God. The benediction of marriage is not to have children who are born only unto the world." A marriage involved the whole parish, and much of the community participated in the ceremony.

The final sacraments, too, had both an individual and a communal meaning. Penance, communion, and extreme unction made a "good death" possible. Whereas many Catholics seem to have resented the obligation to confess annually, they looked upon the priest's presence at the deathbed as a grace and a necessity, and upon his absence as the worst of misfortunes. Priests were conscious of their responsibilities in this regard. In 1653 Henri Arnauld, Bishop of Angers, addressed his clergy: "What will God's priest answer on Judgment Day, what will he say to a soul which, having been lost for eternity usually because of want of assistance at the end of his life, asks God, in the midst of eternal flames, that justice be done to him who left that soul in such wretched abandonment?" Of all the obligations incumbent on Catholics, baptism and last rites were the only ones the seventeenth- and eighteenth-century clergy did not have to remind their parishioners about. People looked upon both as necessities, the stakes being eternal salvation. Both birth and death were wrapped in ritual expressing the idea that no one can hope to achieve salvation on his own. Except during final confession, a dying man or woman was surrounded by priest, family members, perhaps even "brothers" of a confraternity. All present prayed ardently to help the dying person repel the devil's final assaults, confess past sins, and obtain God's mercy.

The pomp of the funeral depended on the social rank of the deceased. The observance included transfer of the body from the mortuary to the church, a religious ceremony, and burial in the church or cemetery. In the lower classes it was all rather simple: the family and a few friends followed the

Pietro Longhi, *The Final Moments.* After administering extreme unction to the dying man, the priest, in surplice and stole, accompanied by members of the family, recites the prayers for the dying. (Venice, Querini Stampalia Gallery.)

Bernard Picart, drawing of a funeral procession, 18th century. Two caparisoned horses draw the funeral coach with the coffin draped in black cloth. The coach is surrounded by prominent personages; a cortege follows in the rear.

casket, carried by a few pallbearers. Among the wealthy and the nobility, however, funerals were occasionally far grander. Numerous priests from the parish and religious communities preceded the casket, which was carried in a hearse drawn by caparisoned horses. The hearse was followed by paupers from the general hospital, dressed in black and carrying candles; next came family and friends and finally members of the deceased's confraternity, corps, or community. In the church, draped in black, a funeral mass was said around a catafalque bristling with lighted candles. To be sure, there were degrees of ostentation, and not all funerals of the wealthy exhibited such baroque profusion. But the laying to rest of the deceased was always, even in the most modest cases, conceived as a spectacle, in which the entire parish was invited to participate as actor or spectator.

Public Devotion:
Confraternities

In addition to the compulsory practices of the faith, there were various optional devotional practices, some of them, such as confraternities and pilgrimages, collective. Created or recreated in the seventeenth century, usually at the behest and always under the control of the clergy, confraternities were intended to be primarily religious organizations. Listen to the statutes of the Confraternity of the Holy Sacrament in the

parish of Coësmes, diocese of Rennes (1653): "Woe unto him who is alone, for should he stumble, no one is there to help him up. Better two than one, for there is profit in society and company." Later the same statutes offer nothing less than an apology for the concept: "The confraternity joins us together in such a way that all our affections, which without it would be isolated, are through it mingled and reunited in bonds of brotherly love, stronger even than the love between natural brothers because it is based on something nobler and more solid than nature, which is Jesus Christ in the beloved sacrament of the Eucharist."

Confraternities bore a variety of names. Scattered throughout France were Confraternities of the Agonisants, which as the name implies were intended to solace people in the throes of death. Rather similar were the confraternities of Charité found in most Norman parishes, whose members, known as *charitons*, cared for the sick and dying and helped with funeral arrangements. There were Confraternities of Souls in Purgatory, especially numerous in Provence; Confraternities of Saint Joseph, patron of the good death; of the Sacred Heart of Jesus, whose numbers increased between 1720 and 1760; and of various saints, differing from diocese to diocese. In southern France, Confraternities of Penitents spread from the cities to the countryside. Typical of the ancient

Popular image, Paris, 17th century. The Confraternity of Saint-Cloud served the master nailmakers, tinsmiths, and ironsmiths of the city of Paris. (Paris, Bibliothèque Nationale.)

and ostentatious religion of Languedoc and Provence, on numerous occasions these groups attracted the suspicion of the clergy. Penitents, wearing hoods and robes, gathered in public for brothers' funerals as well as for the procession of the Passion. Most widespread of all were the Confraternity of the Holy Sacrament and that of the Rosary. Confraternities of the Holy Sacrament proliferated in every diocese in France during the seventeenth and early eighteenth centuries; by 1720 one-third of the parishes in the diocese of Aix had one. They encouraged their members to take part in the sacrament of the Eucharist, especially the Benediction of the Blessed Sacrament. The Confraternities of the Rosary, created at the behest of the Dominicans, stressed worship of the Virgin and recitation of the rosary.

Apart from whatever religious practices confraternities may have encouraged, all served as mutual-aid societies, offering primarily spiritual but in some cases also material assistance to their members. Looking beyond the fine rhetoric of their statutes to the rights and duties of members and, where possible, to what they actually did, we find that all shared the goal of seeing to it that their members would die a good death. To that end they required members to do various things. As a group, members took part in masses, processions, and benedictions of the Blessed Sacrament on prescribed days of the year. Oddly, however, confraternity members were required as individuals to perform certain religious exercises, in exchange for which they received indulgences according to an

Flemish school, 17th century. Parade, in arms, of the members of the Guild of Saint Barbe, patron saint of the cannon- and crossbow-makers of Dunkirk, 10 May 1633. (Dunkirk Museum.)

established schedule. In 1733 the Confraternity of the Rosary established in the Dominican monastery known as Bonne Nouvelle at Rennes received a papal grant: "One hundred days' indulgence for each silent prayer lasting a quarter of an hour; for two quarters of an hour in succession, seven years of the same indulgence; and for two quarters of an hour in succession [*sic*], or at least a quarter of an hour every day for a month, we shall grant them, once a month, plenary indulgence and remission of all their sins." Similarly, bulls of indulgence delivered to members in the form of membership certificates or cards stressed the major concern of every Christian: "Considering the fragility of our mortal nature and the severity of the Last Judgment, we hope with all our might that the faithful prevent that final judgment by good works and devout prayers, so that, by effacing the stain of their sins, they can easily achieve eternal happiness." When a member lay mortally ill, his brothers stood by at his bedside; when death came, they helped with funeral and burial arrangements and prayed for the repose of his soul.

When all is said and done, however, joining a confraternity was a calculated move; it cost money, which people were willing to pay not out of disinterested love of God or their neighbor but in order to secure salvation for themselves.

Pilgrimages

Not all Christians belonged to confraternities, even though they could be found in nearly every parish. But all or nearly all Christians made a pilgrimage at least once in their lives. Of ancient origin, the practice remained extremely popular. To be sure, lengthy pilgrimages were less common than they had been in the Middle Ages or the sixteenth century. Trips to Jerusalem and Rome increasingly became a privilege of the wealthy, although penitents of every class continued to wend their way to Compostela.

Within France, however, various sites attracted a steady stream of pilgrims: Mont-Saint-Michel, Saint-Martin of Tours, Sainte-Baume, and, for devotees of Mary, Chartres, Le Puy, and Rocamadour. Even greater numbers of pilgrims set out for lesser-known regional or local shrines in honor of the Virgin or a saint, some ancient, others quite recent. In the diocese of Saint-Malo, for instance, two sites stood fairly close together. The shrine of Saint Méen (or Mewan) dated from the seventh century. The saint, a companion of Saint Samson, was the founder of the abbey that bore his name. The other

EGO
DILIGENTES ME
DILIGO

REVERENDO ADMODUM DOMINO D GERARDO SERGEANT PRÆPOSITO DIGNISSIMO CÆTERISQUE VENERABILIBUS
CONGREGATIONIS ORATORII IN ASPERO COLLE CONSTITUTI PATRIBUS IN MARIANO CULTU CHARISMATA
MELIORA ÆMULANTIBUS HANC QUAM IN DELITIIS HABENT UT IN OCULIS ETIAM HABEANT GLORIOSA
VIRGINIS IMAGINEM FRED HOVIUS D D CONSECRATQUE

site, the Shrine of Our Lady at Plancoët, dated from October 1644, when two villagers saw an "image of Our Lady" in a fountain. Pilgrims immediately flocked to the site, and the first miracles soon followed. In December 1644 the Bishop of Saint-Malo dispatched his vicar-general and his *promoteur* to investigate and gather testimony. He then authorized pilgrimages to the site under the supervision first of the Oratorians and, from 1647 on, the Dominicans. The whole story conforms to the classic pattern of the "invention" (in the Latin sense), of which there were many examples in France in the first half of the seventeenth century: a discovery by a shepherd or peasant in the woods or near a fountain; arrival of the first pilgrims; miracles; resistance on the part of suspicious ecclesiastical authorities; followed, after brief investigation, by surrender before the enthusiasm of the populace.

Most saints venerated in this way were thought to have healing powers. They were invoked not only to cure the diseases of men but also to preserve livestock and protect harvests. Each saint had his or her particular specialty. Some were thought to have the power to cause certain diseases, known or evoked by the saint's name, hence also the power to cure those same maladies. For example, scabies, which often affects the hands, was called Saint Méen's disease, according to the learned Dom Lobineau (1725), "because of the relation between hand (*main*) and Méen, just as there is a relation between Eutrope and dropsy (*hydrope*) or between Louis and hearing (*ouie*)." The Virgin, considered the most powerful of all intercessors, was invoked in all circumstances against all kinds of diseases. Each province and locality had its own shrines dedicated to the Virgin and the various protective and healing saints.

Pilgrims were obliged to follow precise rules in order to obtain the favor they were seeking. The sufferer (or, if he could not make the journey, his proxy) had to go to the consecrated spot, which might be the altar of a parish church or an isolated chapel near a fountain. There he repeated the ritual prayers before kissing the saint's statue or reliquary or immersing himself in the fountain (or, in the case of a proxy, dipping a piece of cloth in the fountain so that, upon his return, it might be placed upon the absent sufferer's body).

A pilgrimage could be either an act of personal piety or of communal devotion. People were free to set out at any time of the year to pray for immediate grace, to fulfill a vow, or to offer thanks that a prayer had been granted. These were

The True Portrait of the Miraculous Image of Our Lady of Valcourt. (Paris, Bibliothèque Nationale.)

Pilgrimage to Our Lady of Montaigu in Brabant (northeast of Louvain), 17th century. In the foreground, a legless man gives thanks to the Virgin for saving his life. Beyond, a possessed man has his demon exorcised. In the background, a procession led by the clergy wends its way to the church, having passed by the tree with the image and two chapels. (Paris, Bibliothèque Nationale.)

personal acts, attesting to the individual's profound confidence in the saint's intercession. At the major pilgrimage sites one found numerous pilgrims, many of whom had walked alone for long days or even weeks. Before leaving, they obtained a certificate from their local priest, an indispensable passport which entitled them to lodging in hospices along the way. Women and children were accompanied by one or more family members. On the final legs of the journey, pilgrims sometimes joined other travelers whom they met on the road or at hospices where they passed the night. Of the 2,500 pilgrims who stopped at the Hospice of Saint Yves in Rennes in 1650 prior to embarking upon the final day's journey to Saint Méen's tomb, 40 percent were traveling alone (almost all of them young men between the ages of twenty and thirty), 50 percent were accompanied by a family member, and 10 percent belonged to groups that had formed en route.

Another 17th-century image of a pilgrimage to Our Lady of Banelle, near Gannat in Auvergne. Once again, miraculous images are found in a tree, one of Mary with the dead Christ, the other of the crucifixion. Crutches and replicas of arms and legs hang from the branches, attesting to the miracles obtained. (Paris, Bibliothèque Nationale.)

IMAGE DE NOSTRE DAME DE PITIÉ TROVVEE A BANELLES, QVI FAIT PLVSIEVRS MIRACLES.

IMAGE DV CRVCIFIX TROVVEE A L'OPPOSITE DE LADITE NOSTRE DAME DE BANELLES.

Some pilgrimages were demonstrations of collective piety. On their saint's feast day, whole parishes set out under the leadership of their priest. Such mass pilgrimages were not only religious events but also popular revels; at night the pilgrims stopped to drink, gamble, and dance. This explains why the practice was so popular. It allowed people to escape the routine of the parish's institutionalized religion and participate in another kind of religion, combining the extraordinary and the irrational, in a communion in which peasants and city dwellers, rich and poor, men and women all mingled. It is not hard to understand why the church hierarchy attempted to impose discipline and eliminate "abuses," including belief in the magical healing powers of certain saints, indiscriminate claims of "miracles," and debasement of religious celebrations into profane revels, reprehensible in themselves but particularly scandalous on a holy day.

Popular image (detail), Orleans, late 18th century. This frieze, which might have decorated the front of a fireplace, depicts, on the left, the four evangelists, John and the eagle, Matthew and the ox, Luke and the angel, and Mark and the lion. On the right are the doctors of the Church: Augustine (shown), along with Gregory the Great and Jerome (not visible). (Paris, Musée des Arts et Traditions populaires.)

Missions and Works of Charity

Missions too were manifestations of collective piety, their purpose being, in the words of Louis-Marie Grignion de Montfort (1700), to "renew the spirit of Christianity among Christians." To that end, missionaries—Capuchins, Lazarists, Jesuits, Montfortians—organized their missions as though they were dramatic productions, with themselves as the directors and the parishioners as both actors and spectators.

This description applies not only to the assemblies and processions that marked the opening and closing of the mission but also to the preaching that constituted its reason for being. Sermons addressed to different segments of the populace (children, women and girls, men and boys, servants, and so on.) were delivered one after another according to a care-

Abraham Bosse illustrates one of the seven works of mercy: "giving drink to those who are thirsty." This is a good pretext for a realistic portrayal of the contrast between rich and poor. (Paris, Bibliothèque Nationale.)

fully prepared schedule. Preachers addressed their audience in a very direct manner, aiming not to persuade but to impress and move the audience in such a way as to bring about "conversion," which manifested itself concretely in restitutions, foundations, offerings, and other pious works, as well as in confession and communion.

The clergy looked upon pious works as unambiguous signs of piety and love of one's neighbor. Whether done collectively in a confraternity or, as was more common, individually, the works of charity and misery traditionally numbered seven: giving food to the hungry; giving drink to the thirsty; giving lodging to pilgrims; visiting prisoners; visiting the ill; clothing the naked; and burying the dead. Not only was charity a theme treated by many seventeenth-century artists such as Abraham Bosse, it was a daily reality in the lives of many Christians. True, after 1680 the state attempted to intern paupers and beggars in the general hospitals, hoping that henceforth they would be viewed not as Christlike figures but as dangerous individuals best dealt with through confinement and forced labor. Despite all the official proclamations, however, the "great confinement" ended in failure. The "eminent dignity of the poor" remained firmly rooted in the Christian conscience. An economic necessity, charity in the form of household assistance and alms remained the most common embodiment of the commandment to "love thy neighbor."

A less common manifestation of personal piety and religious fervor was the practice of foundations. By "founding" a mass, a sermon, a mission, or a school, a Christian could participate in the prayers of the Church or help in its apostolic works. The financial sacrifice required could be fairly substantial, but usually it was posthumous, most foundations being endowed by will. Drawing up one's last testament was considered nothing less than a religious duty, and writers on spiritual subjects advised that it not be "put off until a time of illness, when the mind is too agitated to do as one should." Preparations for a "good death" included signing a will, which involved more than just settling worldly affairs. Wills dealt with conditions of burial, repaired wrongs done during the lifetime of the deceased, and through legacies and foundations sought to ensure that prayers would be said for the soul as long as possible after the death of the body. Wills opened with an invocation of the Trinity ("In the name of the Father, of the Son, and of the Holy Ghost") and with a pious thought ("Since nothing is more certain than death and nothing less certain than the hour of its occurrence"). Always included was a clause in which the testator "commends his soul to God Almighty, to his Only Son Jesus Christ, to the blessed Virgin Mary, to Saint Michael Archangel, Saint John the Baptist, Saints Peter and Paul, and all the saints in heaven." He then indicated in general terms how he wished to be buried, including the location, the number of priests and monks to be included in the ceremony, and the nature of that ceremony. This was followed by a list of pious bequests, especially foundations of masses, which could be said "in a low voice" or "in a loud voice and chanted," and could be either perpetual or for a limited period. The total number of masses and their distribution throughout the year varied widely from individual to individual. The purpose of the mass was also stipulated; sometimes it was exclusively for the repose of the donor's soul, but other times it included his "deceased relatives and friends." Again we find a selfish obsession with individual salvation, which reflected an important aspect of the clergy's teaching.

Individual Prayer

The primary means of demonstrating personal piety was through individual prayer. First in importance were morning and evening prayers, about which most seventeenth-century catechisms agreed: "Immediately upon awakening, you must lift your heart unto God, make the sign of the cross, dress promptly and modestly, take holy water, kneel before some pious image, and say the prayer in the following manner." According to the *Catechism of Nantes*, morning prayer consisted of a brief preamble followed by the "Pater, Ave, and Credo in Latin or French and the commandments of God and the Church." In the evening the same prayers were repeated, followed by an examination of conscience and the Confiteor. "Then you must undress in silence and go modestly to bed after making the sign of the cross with holy water; you must fall asleep thinking of death, eternal repose, and the sepulcher of Our Lord or other, similar things."

To facilitate individual prayer and meditation, many of the devout used personal prie-dieux, defined by Furetière in 1690 as "desklike stands for holding a prayer book." He adds, "people sometimes use the term prie-dieu to refer to small oratories in the bedroom or study." Although the Church approved the use of the prie-dieu, it stressed the value of family prayer, particularly in the evening, invoking the words of Christ: "For where two or three are gathered together in my name, there am I in the midst of them" (Matt. 18:20). In

Popular image, 18th century. A nobleman prays, having laid hat and sword on the ground. (Paris, Musée Carnavalet.)

the *Catechism of Agen* we read: "Question: How ought we to make the evening prayer? Answer: Together, the whole family should kneel down without bowing and taking care not to sit on the heels, with heads bare and hands joined." The *Catechism of Nantes* adds this comment for the benefit of the clergy: "You must do all that you can to exhort each family to gather in the morning and the evening for common prayer, with a member of the family reciting each prayer out loud."

Morning and evening prayers recited individually or as a family group were a minimum requirement. Good Christians were also expected to address God at other times. Toward that end, prayer anthologies became popular in the late sixteenth century. The first example of the genre is the *Treasury of Prayers, Orisons, and Christian Instructions for Invoking God at All Times*, published in 1585 by Jean de Ferrières, curé of the parish of Saint-Nicolas-des-Champs in Paris. The book contained chapters with such titles as "Orison for the Child to Say before Studying His Lesson," "Orison for Time of Plague," "Orison for Keeping a Good Reputation," and "Orison for a Woman Who Wishes to Marry." Other anthologies responded to the special needs of different "estates." One such was *Christian Instructions and Prayers for All Sorts of Persons*, published by Antoine Godeau in 1646, which contained prayers for married men, husbands mourning their wives, fathers and mothers mourning the death of an only child, children faced with deciding upon a career, financial officials, government ministers, merchants, and so on.

Apart from such specialized prayers, personal piety could be expressed through various kinds of individual and collective devotions. In the seventeenth and eighteenth centuries the eucharistic devotion became very popular. In *Practices of Piety*, Father Le Maistre wrote: "I want you to attend the benediction of the blessed sacrament two or three times daily, or, if you cannot go to church, I want you to go to your oratory to make a little prayer and a brief review." The Ave Maria became quite fashionable at court, as La Bruyère mockingly noted: "Neglect vespers as something old and outmoded; stay in your place for the Ave Maria." In many parishes pious individuals joined together for an hour during the day or night in the presence of the consecrated host, which thus became the object of uninterrupted adoration. Similarly, in the seventeenth century, the Infant Jesus became an object of devotion, as did, somewhat later, the Sacred Heart. Marguerite of the Blessed Sacrament, a Carmelite from Beaune influenced by

Crucifix (1764) of black wood and bone. This is a so-called Jansenist crucifix, with Christ's arms being close together in order to symbolize the small number of the elect. (Paris, Musée des Arts et Traditions populaires.)

Italian school, 17th century, an old woman saying her rosary, exemplifying the growing popularity of this form of worship in Catholic countries in the 17th and 18th centuries. (Nantes, Museum of Fine Arts.)

Pierre de Bérulle, became an ardent propagandist on behalf of the devotion of the Infant Jesus; the Carmelites and Oratorians successfully promoted the movement in the 1640s. At the end of the seventeenth century Marguerite-Marie Alacoque, a Visitant from Paray-le-Monial, after seeing visions in 1673, originated the new devotion of the Sacred Heart of Jesus.

The cult of Mary experienced an uncontestable revival in the seventeenth century, despite hostility from some quarters within the Church. Late in the century Louis-Marie Grignion de Montfort made himself the champion of the cause with his treatise on *The True Devotion to the Blessed Virgin*, which involved reciting the prayers of the rosary, a practice already popularized by the Dominicans and the Confraternities of the Rosary. If the curé of Sennely is to be believed, by 1700 "the devotion of simple folk who do not know how to read is limited to recitation of the rosary." Devotion to Mary was sometimes indicated by the wearing of a scapular, occasionally referred to as the "habit of the Virgin."

The cult of the saints remained vigorous. Evidence for this, apart from pilgrimages, can be found in the vogue for "saints' leaves," pages bearing pictures of the saints in vivid colors together with the stories of their lives and prayers to be recited regularly. Sold by hawkers of religious wares, they were pinned to bedroom walls.

Mystical Experiences

In mystical states we attain the ultimate degree of personal piety. Mysticism in the strict sense is the feeling of knowing God through intuition and of entering into direct communication with him, ecstasy being the supreme condition of such union. Compulsory religious practices were external and often collective, but mysticism, the highest form of spirituality, concerns relations with God of a most intimate and personal kind. In the first half of the seventeenth century Francis de Sales and Pierre de Bérulle were the two greatest representatives of what Henri Bremond has called the "French school of spirituality." The expression is misleading in some respects, in that the French authors, however original, have their place in a long tradition going back to the Flemish and German mystics of the fourteenth and fifteenth centuries and to the Spanish mystics of the sixteenth century. Francis de Sales's *Introduction to the Devout Life* (1608) moved mysticism out of the monasteries and into the world. "It is heresy," he wrote, "to wish to banish the devout life from the soldier's company, the artisan's shop, the prince's court, or the married couple's home. Wherever we are, we can and must aspire to a perfect life." He showed how performance of one's duties to the state could be as effective a means as prayer and contemplation for achieving perfection and attaining the highest levels of spirituality. He also expounded the idea that devotion and even mysticism do not belong to a separate part of life, to a few exalted moments, but rather that they should be nourished every day, even during working hours. Thus he responded to the needs of many Christians who, though engaged in the world, aspired to a perfection that hitherto had seemed reserved exclusively for men of the cloth.

By contrast, Pierre de Bérulle spoke primarily but not exclusively to those devoted to the religious life: priests, monks, nuns. In his *Discourse on the Condition and Grandeur of*

Francis de Sales, *Introduction to the Devout Life*, written in 1604, published in 1609, reprinted forty times in the author's lifetime, and translated into seventeen languages. Its success has continued to the present day. (Paris, Bibliothèque Nationale.)

Jesus (1623) he developed the idea that personal perfection consists in "adhering" to Christ. This adherence was to be achieved by imitating his various "conditions," the most significant episodes of his life on earth. Bérulle advocated not mere moral imitation but veritable spiritual annihilation in Christ. The furor over Quietism at the end of the seventeenth century provoked the Church not only to condemn the excesses to which mysticism could lead but also to acquire an enduring suspicion of mystics themselves. Nevertheless, the teachings of de Sales, Bérulle, and other spiritual writers helped strengthen a school of thought within Roman Catholicism according to which the ultimate perfection consists in personal union, in this life, of the soul with God.

The Communal Practices of the Protestant Reformation

Jean Calvin (1509–1564), the man of the book, in his study. This 17th-century painting is one of numerous portraits of the reformer showing him in three-quarter view, wearing a hat with ear flaps and a long beard. (Paris, Society for the History of Protestantism.)

Based on justification by faith, universal priesthood, and the exclusive authority of the Bible, the Protestant Reformation placed each believer in a direct relation with God and enjoined the faithful to read and question the Bible every day, since it contained the word of God. Luther said, "Everything is governed and ordained by the Gospel, baptism, and Sunday prayer; that is where Jesus Christ is found." Alphonse Dupront provides the following gloss: "This light but important baggage is enough to enable man to do what is necessary for salvation, and to do it by himself. The Lutheran soteriology demolishes the intellectual framework and instinctual basis of the communal soteriology which saw Christendom as the historical incarnation. Now man struggled alone with his eternal destiny." All intermediaries other than the Book were either eliminated or minimized: liturgy, clergy, sacraments, cult of the saints, prayers for the dead. Most had in fact lost their meaning, since the Christian was saved not by his own works or by any form of intercession but by faith alone, by his personal adherence to Christ the savior. Hence not only were all Christians priests, equal by baptism, but most of the communal forms of piety maintained and encouraged by the Roman Catholic Church no longer had any reason to exist. Emile G. Léonard describes the contrast between Protestantism and Catholicism: "The principle of Protestantism is salvation through faith. Not faith in itself, with no precise object, but faith in Jesus Christ as the only possible restorer of contact with the Father. That is the basis of all Christianity. In order to state this idea in Protestant terms, we must say 'through individual faith in Jesus Christ,' emphasizing the word *indi-*

Pieter Brueghel the Elder, *The Preaching of Saint John the Baptist*. This is a good representation of Calvinist preaching in the "wilderness," which was done wherever Protestants were in the minority and forced to worship in secret. (Private collection.)

vidual. In practice, Catholicism places before God not so much the individual as mankind, in the Christian form of the Church. The Church is saved because it has faith in Jesus Christ, and each Christian is saved because (and insofar as) he belongs to the Church. It is by contrast with this idea of salvation through the Church that the Protestant notion of direct and personal salvation through faith takes on its value and reveals its originality."[1]

It would be misleading to view the Protestant as a person left to confront God alone, in contrast to the Catholic, enveloped in a community tightly controlled by the clergy. In strict theology, belief in the communion of saints or in purgatory and the efficacy of prayer for the dead was unthinkable for a Protestant. Concretely, however, when it came to establishing the conditions of life in this world, both Luther and Calvin were too conscious of the realities of the age, as well as of the needs of men living in society in any age, not to have acquiesced in the establishment of a series of institutions and communal practices intended to help the just man maintain his faith without impinging upon his personal relation with God. Study of these practices reveals that the gap between Protestants and Catholics was not as wide as one might think.

Family Worship

Lutherans and Calvinists both engaged in individual daily prayer and Bible-reading, usually as a family group. There were several reasons for this. Until the end of the eighteenth century, notwithstanding the progress that had been made in education in Protestant countries, many of the lower classes still did not know how to read. Moreover, Bibles were quite expensive, and a family rarely owned more than one, which was piously preserved and passed from generation to generation. In 1620 Anne de Mornay, daughter of the celebrated Huguenot leader Philippe du Plessis-Mornay, wrote in her Bible: "This Bible was given to me by M. du Plessis, my much-honored father. After I am gone I want it to go to Philippe des Nouhes, my eldest son, so that he may read it carefully in order to learn to know and serve God in the Holy Trinity. To encourage him in this endeavor, let him think of the example of his grandfather, from whom he received nourishment, and let him constantly remember the wishes that I, his mother, have made for him." Finally, the reformers themselves stressed the value of family worship.

The father usually presided over the family Bible-reading. In the morning and the evening he assembled his wife, children, and servants and read a few verses. Then the family sang psalms, recited the *Our Father*, and read prayers which in Lutheran Alsace were drawn from Luther's *Catechism*. French Calvinists from Poitou to Languedoc and Lutherans in the Montbéliard region used French bibles printed in Geneva, Lausanne, or Neuchâtel. Alsatian Lutherans used German bi-

Abraham Bosse, *Blessing of the Table*, showing a Protestant family at dinner. On the wall, in a place of honor, is a reproduction of Exodus, chapter 20: "Thou shalt have no other gods before me."

This painting on wood represents a Quaker meeting in the United States at the end of the eighteenth or beginning of the nineteenth century. (Boston, Museum of Fine Arts, Karolik Collection.)

bles printed in Strasbourg, Basel, or Cologne. There were separate books of psalms, usually reproducing the hundred and fifty psalms of David adapted by Clément Marot and Théodore de Bèze. Singing played an important role; both Luther and Calvin praised the "virtues of song." In addition to the morning and evening prayers, the head of the family pronounced a blessing and said grace at the beginning and end of every meal. A good illustration can be seen in an engraving by Abraham Bosse, a Huguenot from Tours, of a Protestant family at the dinner table. The father's role extended far beyond presiding over family worship. He was also responsible for making sure that everyone in the family, including the servants, followed the path of righteousness. Olivier de Serres wrote: "The father shall exhort his servants, insofar as they are capable of understanding, to seek virtue and shun vice, so that, well instructed, they will live as they should without injuring anyone. He shall prohibit blasphemy, debauchery, thievery, and other vices, suffering none of these to proliferate in his home so that it may remain a house of honor."

Protestant piety did not flourish only at home. Calvinists and Lutherans were members of a parish and joined with others in communal religious practices. Even more than Luther, Calvin was convinced that individuals could not be left

"Catechism, that is, formulary for instructing children in Christianity, in the form of a dialogue, in which the Minister interrogates and the child responds, by Jean Calvin." (Paris, Bibliothèque Nationale.)

alone with their faith but required firm discipline. To be sure, every Christian was a "priest," and there was no question of reestablishing a priesthood limited to a few. But an "attenuated clerisy" was not incompatible with the universal priesthood. Each parish was headed by a pastor or minister, assisted by one or more schoolmasters and a consistory of elders. In the Lutheran principality of Montbéliard, with 28 parishes, there were, in 1725, 34 ministers, 97 schoolmasters, and 192 elders (not counting 87 mayors representing the prince). Thus, some 410 persons in all served a religious community of 15,000, a ratio of almost 1 to 40, which enabled the religious authorities to maintain strict discipline.

Preaching and Holy Communion

Discipline pertained first of all to communal religious practices, the most important of which was Sunday services. Services served three purposes: worship, conversion, and instruction. Prayer, Bible-reading, and singing were the instruments of worship and conversion. Instruction was achieved through the pastor's teaching. Article XII of the *Discipline of the Reformed Churches of France* (1675) states that pastors "shall not preach on any subject not based on a text from Holy Scripture, which ordinarily they will follow." After Sunday services adults generally attended catechism classes. In Montbéliard there was also an afternoon service, with sermon, on Wednesday or Friday, as well as daily morning prayer in church.

Lutherans and Calvinists celebrated the Lord's Supper four times a year—at Easter, at Pentecost, in early autumn, and at Christmas. Parish members received communion in the form of bread and wine. In offering the bread the pastor said: "The bread that we are breaking is the communion with the body of Our Lord Jesus Christ, who has died for our sins." When he offered the cup of wine, he added: "Remember that Christ spilled his blood on the cross for the remission of your sins." Before communicating, each parish member handed a crudely engraved token to an elder, thus enabling the consistory to determine if anyone failed to fulfill his duty. Having abolished private confession, the Protestant churches came up with a variety of substitutes to prevent avowed sinners from approaching the communion table. In Lutheran churches the pastor read a public confession of sins from the pulpit and then dispensed what was called "evangelical absolution" to the entire congregation. Calvin, concerned that "many people are

This engraving, taken from Bernard Picart, *Cérémonies et Coutumes religieuses de tous les peuples du monde*, published in Amsterdam in 1733, illustrates the Lutheran practice of granting collective evangelical absolution, which the pastor enunciates in the presence of the gathered faithful, men on one side, women on the other. (Paris, Bibliothèque Nationale.)

An engraving from the same work of Picart showing the Lord's Supper. The faithful, seated around a long table, take bread from a plate carried by one of the pastors, while a cup of wine is passed from hand to hand.

rushing without deliberation to holy communion," instituted the practice of "ecclesiastical discipline" in his churches: individuals were required to appear before the consistory for examination, and sinners were admonished or in some cases excommunicated, that is, forbidden to receive communion. Thus, admonition replaced confession, and public penance replaced private penance. Paradoxically, in this respect it was the Catholics rather than the Protestants who respected the sanctity of the inner life. The Protestants' concern with "evangelizing the church" took precedence over respect for the liberty of the individual Christian.

Collective Ceremonies

Major milestones in the lives of individuals were celebrated in church with the rest of the community. Protestants were less concerned with early baptism than were Catholics, whose attitudes toward salvation were different. Children born during the week were baptized together on Sunday, before the sermon. In his *Apology for Those of the Religion* (1647), Moise Amyraut described the baptism ceremony as practiced in his time: "After a solemn prayer, the child was offered to God, asking in the name of Our Lord Jesus Christ that he be made a participant in his salvation and that baptism produce in him his virtue, in remission of the original sin and in sanctification when he will have come of age. And, after a promise has been secured from those who present him that they will instruct him in the faith of the Gospel and the love of piety, water is poured over his head and the child is baptized in the name of the Father, the Son, and the Holy Ghost." A father could present his own child and choose its first name. Godparents, not mentioned in the Bible, were not obligatory; in practice, however, the custom of choosing godparents survived. Engagements and weddings were also celebrated in church. An engagement to marry was a solemn promise that could be broken only by the consistory "for great and legitimate cause." Marriage, which was not considered a sacrament, was normally celebrated six weeks later in the presence of a minister from either the bride's or the groom's parish.

By contrast, death and burial were private affairs, which should come as no surprise since neither Luther nor Calvin believed in Purgatory or in intercession on behalf of the dead. Burials were modest, with none of the pomp that marked some Catholic funerals. Among the Lutherans of Montbéliard, a short prayer was recited and the deceased was buried in the

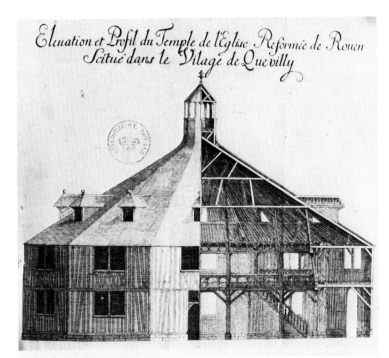

Eleuation et Profil du Temple de l'Eglise Reformée de Rouen Scitué dans le Vilage de Quevilly

Protestant church built in 1599 in Quevilly at the gates of the city of Rouen to serve approximately 5,000 worshipers, or 7 percent of the population of Rouen in 1602. Note the two-story construction and the interior staircase. (Taken from *History of the Persecution of the Church in Rouen*, 1704. Paris, Bibliothèque Nationale.)

presence of his family. Then relatives and friends gathered in church to hear the pastor deliver a sermon. Calvinist funerals were even simpler. Calvin himself had set an example by asking that his body be wrapped in rough cloth and carried to the cemetery without hymns or speeches and that no stone mark his grave. Such simplicity shocked Catholics and even Lutherans, like Elie Brackenhoffer of Strasbourg, who visited Geneva in 1643: "No funeral prayer, no song, no commemoration, much less any ringing of bells for the occasion. When a man dies, he dies. He is not given so much as a Paternoster for alms. The bereaved and others thus return home without consolation and without exhortation." The *Discipline of the Reformed Churches of France* forbids pastors to attend burials: "No prayer or preaching shall be made at burials to prevent any superstition." The deceased does not need the prayers of his friends and relatives, and they, sure of his election, need no consolation; salvation is a personal affair, and the hope of survivors is a certitude.

From family prayer to "ecclesiastical discipline," from baptism to Sunday services and holy communion, Protestant

Solidarities and Election

practices seem to have been at least as communal as Catholic ones. Yet there was a fundamental difference. For Catholics, the sacrifice of the mass, prayers for the dead, and pilgrimages to holy places derived meaning and justification from the communion of saints. The Christian did not seek salvation alone; working in his behalf were not only the merits of Christ but the suffrages of the saints and the prayers of the living. For Lutherans and other Protestants, the only purpose of communal religious practices was to sustain (and possibly to monitor) the faith of each individual.

The Protestant knew he was among God's chosen. But the certainty of numbering among the elect entailed a responsibility to the saving God. The Catholic, with the aid of grace, was supposed to merit salvation through good works. But the Protestant was supposed to live in accordance with the law without expecting any compensatory reward. Unlike the Catholic, he was freed from anxiety concerning death and judgment, but in return he was obliged to show by his conformity with the requirements of the Word that God had indeed chosen him. Thus, individualism and the inner life were at the heart of reformed theology. It is in this sense, and this sense only, that Claudel was correct when he wrote in *Les Souliers de Satin* that "the Protestant prays alone, but the Catholic prays in the communion of the Church." Both the Protestant Reformation and the Catholic Counter-Reformation played key roles in the internalization of piety. The Protestant churches attached as much importance to communal practices as did the Catholic Church, if not more. Philippe Ariès noted that the new forms of religion established in the sixteenth and seventeenth centuries played a major part in altering people's views of the world, particularly the idea of the self and its role in everyday life.

Painting on glass, Strasbourg, 1768. A Protestant marriage. The pastor, dressed in black with a white pleated collar, blesses the young couple, who clasp hands. The bride wears a black dress with a white collar and decorated bodice; on her head is a bridal crown. The legend beneath reads: "You are blessed, married couple, reach your hand out to me, I am ready." (Paris, Musée des Arts et Traditions populaires.)

Georges de La Tour (or his studio), *Saint Jerome*. Jerome was the reader most commonly portrayed in 17th-century painting. Alongside the open book are writing implements and a skull representing vanity. (Paris, Louvre.)

The Practical Impact of Writing

Roger Chartier

O NE of the most important developments of the modern era, according to Philippe Ariès, was the advent of written culture in Western society. The spread of literacy, the widespread circulation of written materials whether in printed or manuscript form, and the increasingly common practice of silent reading, which fostered a solitary and private relation between the reader and his book, were crucial changes, which redrew the boundary between the inner life and life in the community.

Between 1500 and 1800 man's altered relation to the written word helped to create a new private sphere into which the individual could retreat, seeking refuge from the community.

This development, however, as I will show, did not totally obliterate earlier practices, nor did it affect everyone who dealt with printed materials. Reading aloud, reading in groups for work or pleasure, did not cease with the arrival of silent and private reading. Different kinds of reading overlapped. But this should not cause us to lose sight of the fact that new models of behavior were being established, models that tell us a great deal about the process of privatization in the early modern period.

MEASURING LITERACY

Can the extent to which the written word penetrated Western societies in the early modern period be measured? Attempting to do so, historians have counted signatures on documents from parish records, notarial archives, the courts, and tax authorities; using these data they have estimated what proportion of the population consisted of people able to sign their own names. After lengthy debate, it is now widely accepted that, although this figure can be taken as a very rough estimate of a society's familiarity with writing, it cannot be interpreted directly as a measure of cultural advancement. In early modern societies, where the small fraction of children who attended school learned first to read and then to write, everyone who could sign his name could also read, but not everyone who knew how to read could sign his name.

Furthermore, not all signers could actually write. For some, instruction in writing never went beyond learning how to sign their names; for others writing was a skill lost for want of practice, and the ability to sign was merely a relic of that lost skill. Paradoxically, the signature is the mark of a population that knows how to read but not necessarily how to write. It is impossible to estimate what fraction of the signers could actually write, and some people who could read never learned to sign their names. This does not mean that all the data concerning percentages of signers at different times and in different places are worthless. The figures constitute a kind of rough, composite index, which does not precisely measure the diffusion of either writing skills (which the percentages exaggerate) or reading skills (which they underestimate).[1]

Numbers of Readers

With this caveat in mind, it is clear from all the data that between 1500 and 1800 the percentage of signers rose sharply throughout Europe. (For convenience, we may refer to this percentage as the "literacy rate," bearing in mind that it does not necessarily indicate the percentage of the population that could both read and write.) We possess sufficient data about three countries to permit generalizations on a national scale. In Scotland signatures collected for the National Covenant of 1638 (which affirmed the unity of the Presbyterian churches) and for the Solemn League and Covenant of 1643 (which promised Scottish support to the English Parliament, provided that it established the Presbyterian religion) reveal a literacy rate among males of 25 percent. A century later, signatures collected in the 1750s before the High Court of the Judiciary reveal rates of 78 percent for men and 23 percent for women; corrected to reflect differences between the social composition of the witness group and the general population, these figures suggest literacy rates of 65 and 15 percent, respectively.[2] In England signatures collected for the Protestation Oath of 1641 (an oath of allegiance to the "true religion, reformed and

Protestant"), for the Vow and Covenant of 1643 (an oath of loyalty to Parliament), and for the Solemn League and Covenant of 1644 (which introduced Presbyterianism) indicate a male literacy rate of 30 percent. In the second half of the eighteenth century the marriage registers of the Church of England, which after 1754 required the signatures of both bride and groom, reflect the progress of the written word: 60 percent of the men signed in 1755 and in 1790, compared with 35 percent of the women in 1755 and 40 percent in 1790.[3] In France, finally, signatures of brides and grooms in the parish registers (recorded in almost all départements by schoolteachers enlisted for the purpose by Rector Maggiolo in 1877) reflect a century of progress: in 1686–1690, only 29 percent of men and 14 percent of women signed; in 1786–1790, 48 percent of men and 27 percent of women did.[4] Thus, over a period of a century and a half, male literacy rates rose by 40 percent in Scotland, 30 percent in England, and 19 percent in France.

In other countries, for which we lack the data to determine the national literacy rate, we find evidence of similar progress in specific cities or regions. In Amsterdam, for example, notarized betrothal agreements were signed by 85 percent of men and 64 percent of women in 1780, compared with 57 percent of men and 32 percent of women in 1630.[5] In Turin 83 percent of husbands and 63 percent of wives signed their marriage contracts in 1790, compared with 70 and 43 percent, respectively, in 1710. And in the province of Turin—that is, in the rural region governed by the city—progress was even more spectacular: the percentage of male signatories rose from 21 to 65, and of female signatories from 6 to 30.[6] In New Castile, in the jurisdiction of the inquisitorial court of Toledo, witnesses and accused (eight out of ten of whom were men and nearly one out of two a notable), 49 percent could sign their names, more or less, between 1515 and 1600, 54 percent between 1651 and 1700, and 76 percent between 1751 and 1817. The nature of the sample precludes using these figures as an indication of the literacy of the Castilian population as a whole, but the rising percentages suggest that literacy was making steady progress.[7]

The trend was similar in the American colonies. In New England, 61 percent of men signed their wills in 1650–1670, 69 percent in 1705–1715, 84 percent in 1758–1762, and 88 percent in 1787–1795.[8] For women, the comparable figures for the first three dates were 31, 41, and 46 percent, respectively. In Virginia, 50 percent of men signed their wills be-

Throughout 18th-century Europe learning to write meant assimilating a complex repertoire of gestures and postures. To write well one had to learn to sit at a proper distance from the paper, place one's arm correctly on the table, and grasp the sharpened quill properly. Master writers were both the guardians and teachers of this technique, virtuosos of calligraphy. (Paris, Carnavalet Museum.)

tween 1640 and 1680, compared with 65 percent between 1705 and 1715 and 70 percent between 1787 and 1797.[9]

Thus, there was a widespread and often marked increase in the percentage of men and women able to sign their names, an increase that occurred regardless of the absolute level of literacy. In Protestant as well as Catholic countries, in countryside as well as cities, and in the New World as well as the Old, more and more people were familiar with writing. Large numbers of people acquired cultural skills that previously had been the exclusive possession of a minority. This is not to say that progress was uninterrupted. Although the literacy rate reveals a marked trend upward stretching over centuries, it was not without setbacks and recessions. In England the percentage of signers among witnesses before the ecclesiastical court of the diocese of Norwich shows temporary but significant declines. They affected those who reached their tenth year between 1580 and 1610, especially merchants, husbandmen, and yeomen; as well as the civil war generation, educated in the 1640s, where the decline among yeomen reached 20 percent; or in the period 1690–1710, which saw a particularly sharp decline in peasant literacy, especially among husbandmen.[10]

In Madrid the second half of the seventeenth century witnessed a similar decline in literacy: in 1650, 45 percent of testators signed their wills or declarations of poverty; between

1651 and 1700, this figure dropped to 37 percent.[11] The decline was more marked among men (68 to 54 percent) than among women (26 to 22 percent). Finally, in Provence the generations educated between 1690 and 1740 show no progress in literacy and in some areas suffered a sharp decline, to judge by the percentages of signatures on wills and marriage documents.[12] In general, literacy in Provence increased as it did everywhere else: between the end of the seventeenth century and the beginning of the nineteenth century, thirteen out of a sample of twenty communities doubled the percentage of signers. Yet this overall progress came in spite of lack of progress or even decline in the intervals between periods of significant advance, which in the case of Provence came between 1650 and 1680 and in the fifty or sixty years after 1740.

Reasons for the lack of progress, which varied from place to place, included deterioration of the schools, influx of less literate immigrants, or setbacks in the economy. The important point is that between 1500 and 1800 the progress of literacy was neither steady nor uninterrupted. It is this, perhaps, which distinguishes our period most sharply from the the nineteenth century, when the advent of mass education inaugurated an era of steady improvement.

Although familiarity with writing increased, it was not shared equally. Certain inequalities stand out, probably the most glaring of all being the inequality between men and women. Everywhere the male literacy rate is higher than the female, with a gap between the two as high as 25 or 30 percent. Obviously women had less of a role to play in the world of the written word. But the figures do not give an accurate idea of differences in reading ability. In early modern societies learning to read was long considered a part of a girl's education; learning to write was not, for writing was held to be a useless and dangerous skill for women to acquire. In Molière's *Ecole des femmes*, Arnolphe is eager for Agnès to read so that she can absorb his "Maxims for Marriage," but he succumbs to despair when he discovers that she knows how to write, especially to her beloved Horace. Thus, for women even more than for men, the percentage of signers is an inadequate measure of the percentage of readers (especially in the lower classes).

Inequalities existed between people in different occupations and estates. In seventeenth-century rural England the

Unequal Skills

Jean Puget de La Serre's *Le Secrétaire à la Mode*, published in 1640, was a best-selling anthology of sample letters. Initially intended for noble and bourgeois letter-writers, the secretaries soon became mass-market items. La Serre's book was included in the Blue Library of popular editions published in Troyes, along with the *Fleurs de bien dire*, a book that taught proper speech. Whether these learned models were really useful to lower-class readers is open to question, but owning such a book was a sign of cultural ennoblement. (Paris, Bibliothèque Nationale.)

ability to sign (measured by signatures of witnesses before the ecclesiastical courts) was closely correlated with work and social status. Nearly all clerics, notables, and important merchants knew how to write. Skilled artisans (goldsmiths, harness-makers, drapers) and yeomen could write in seven or eight out of ten cases. In most other trades, especially textiles and clothing, only about one in two could sign their names. Next came the village artisans and merchants (blacksmiths, carpenters, millers, butchers, and so forth), of whom only 30 to 40 percent could sign. At the bottom of the scale were building laborers, fishermen, shepherds, husbandmen, and agricultural workers, of whom at most one in four could sign their names.[13] With minor variations this example holds good throughout rural Europe, where the ability to sign one's name was largely determined by such factors as the degree of skill required by one's work and the degree of involvement in nonlocal markets.

In cities too the ability to write depended largely on occupation and status, but city dwellers were far in advance of their rural counterparts in absolute percentages. Consider early-nineteenth-century marriage records from the Emilia region of Italy.[14] In the five cities Piacenza, Parma, Reggio, Modena, and Bologna we find that 42 percent of grooms and 21 percent of brides were able to sign their names, whereas in the surrounding countryside the corresponding figures were, respectively, just 17 and 5 percent. The same is true in northern Europe: seventeenth-century London artisans and merchants were two to three times as literate as their rural counterparts, and domestic servants were two-and-a-half times as literate (in London, 69 percent signed, compared with only 24 percent in rural England).[15] This is one reason why the culture of the modern city was unique: large numbers of city dwellers knew how to write, and the ability to read and write was less unequally distributed than in the countryside.

All of these differences in access to the written word affected the process of privatization in the sixteenth, seventeenth, and eighteenth centuries. The ability to read was an essential prerequisite for certain new practices around which people built their private lives. Personal communion with a read or written text liberated the individual from the old mediators, freed him or her from the control of the group, and made it possible to cultivate an inner life. Solitary reading permitted the development of new forms of piety, which radically altered man's relation to the divine. The ability to

Jean-François de La Motte of Tournai, a specialist in trompe-l'oeil painting, here depicts a variety of writing implements and forms of writing. Next to the manuscript is a letter-opener, an inkwell, a stick of wax, a notebook, a portfolio, a letter and sealed envelope, and a sealed memoir. Next to the printed works is an engraving on copper (*AD fecit*) and an almanac (*Almanach for the year of Our Lord Jesus Christ MDCLXIX, calculated by M. André de La Porte*). (Saint-Omer, Municipal Museum.)

read and write enabled people to relate to others and to the authorities in new ways. The greater a person's familiarity with writing, the more emancipated he was from traditional ways of life, which bound the individual tightly to his community and made him dependent on others to read and interpret the divine word and the commandments of his sovereign.

Increasingly private ways of reading and relating changed the nature of European society, but at a different pace in each country. Broadly speaking, northern and northwestern Europe enjoyed higher rates of literacy than other areas. By the end of the eighteenth century 60 to 70 percent of the men in the more literate regions could sign their name: 71 percent in France north of the Saint-Malo–Geneva line, 61 percent in

The Geography of Literacy

Engraving from Bernard Picart, *Cérémonies et Coutumes religieuses de tous les peuples du monde* (Amsterdam, 1733). In the 17th and 18th centuries catechism in the Protestant countries made use of the book, which was read out loud and commented on by the pastor, while the pupils followed along, reading silently as they listened to the lesson. This was similar to teaching in medieval universities, where the master read aloud from his manuscript as students followed along in their books. (Paris, Bibliothèque Nationale.)

Austrian-dominated parts of the Low Countries,[16] 60 percent in England, 65 percent in Scotland. For women, the figures are 44 percent for northern and northeastern France, 37 percent in the Low Countries, and 40 percent in England. It is harder to gauge the literacy rate in other parts of Europe, where historians have done less research, but various signs indicate that it lagged well behind the rate of the more advanced regions. In Emilia, for instance, the *urban* signature rates were no higher than 45 percent for men and 26 percent for women in the early nineteenth century—a very late date. Hence there is every reason to believe that the literacy rate of the Italian population as a whole, counting peasants as well as city dwellers and the Mezzogiorno as well as the relatively advanced north, must have been lower, probably much lower, than that in northern Europe. In Hungary, in 1768, only 14 percent of the municipal magistrates in villages and towns could sign their names, and the percentage for the peasant population must have been even lower.[17] Finally, in Sweden, only 35 percent of conscripts in the 1870s knew how to write, which suggests that the literacy rate in the late eighteenth century must have been very low.

On the whole, however, northern and northwestern Europe was culturally more advanced than the rest of the continent: a crude contrast, but undoubtedly correct as far as it goes. Some corrections are called for, however. Between regions where the signature rate was as high as 30 percent in the late eighteenth century and regions where it was as low as 10 or 20 percent, there were transitional zones. Southern France, below the Saint-Malo–Geneva line, was one: on the eve of the Revolution, 44 percent of men and 17 percent of women signed their marriage papers.

Furthermore, even within the relatively backward zone, we can distinguish between areas where people could neither read nor write (as may have been the case in Italy and Hungary) and those where many people who could read were unable to write. In mid-eighteenth-century Sweden, for example, few people could write but 80 percent could read. With the promulgation of the Church Law of 1686, the Lutheran Church, backed by the state, had launched a campaign to teach people to read and see with their own eyes what God ordered and commanded through his sacred word. The parish clergy subsequently took charge of teaching reading. Periodically, parishioners were examined to test their reading skills and knowledge of the catechism, and those who could not read and did not know their catechism were prevented from receiving communion and marrying in the church. The campaign, which reached a peak of intensity between 1690 and 1720, left an enduring mark on the populations of Sweden and Finland, where everyone knew how to read (having been trained to do so by the clergy for religious purposes) but only a narrow elite knew how to write.[18]

Such a situation was probably not peculiar to Sweden. It may also have been true of Denmark, where the gap between reading and writing at the end of the eighteenth century seems to have been quite marked. It was surely true of Scotland, one of the most literate countries in Europe. According to evidence gathered in 1742 by the evangelical pastor of Cambuslang, a parish at the center of the religious revival then shaking the Church of Scotland, every man and woman in the parish claimed to be able to read, but only 60 percent of the men and 10 percent of the women said that they knew how to write.[19] Many said that they had learned to read in order to avoid the "shame" of not being able to participate fully in religious assemblies. Thus, in some Protestant countries, the ability to read was universal, regardless of the "literacy rate" measured by counting signatures.

Writing and the Reformation

A high rate of literacy was not a necessary effect of Protestantism, however. In Germany, as early as the third decade of the sixteenth century, Luther abandoned his insistence that every Christian should know how to read the Bible. Instead he emphasized the importance of preaching and catechism, that is, the role of the pastor as teacher and interpreter of the holy text. In Lutheran states there was a marked difference between the education offered to the pastoral and administrative elites and popular religious instruction, which, being mainly oral and based on memorization, was quite compatible with illiteracy.[20] In the Rhineland, in the second half of the sixteenth century, religious examiners found that many people could recite texts that they did not understand and that they responded to questions with answers learned by heart and not always appropriate, proving that catechism classes taught formulas by rote and did not seek to foster a personal interpretation of the Bible.[21]

It was not until the so-called Second Reformation initiated by Pietism at the end of the seventeenth century that all the faithful were expected to learn what was in the Bible and

Gérard Dou here portrays an old woman reading aloud to an old man. Reading interrupts the daily chores of these elderly peasants. In Calvinist areas, where many were literate, it was expected that the Bible would be read daily in every home. (Paris, Louvre.)

develop a personal interpretation. To that end, Protestants first taught one another in religious conventicles. Later the government issued ordinances governing the course of instruction to be offered in the elementary schools. This changed the very status of the Bible. In sixteenth-century Germany it had been a book for pastors, students studying for the ministry, and parish libraries; by the early eighteenth century it had become a book for everyone, mass-produced and sold at a low price. This may account for the steep increase of literacy among German Pietists: in eastern Prussia the percentage of peasants capable of signing their name rose from 10 percent in 1750 to 25 percent in 1756 and to 40 percent by the end of the century.[22] Pietism, not Lutheranism, spread the ability to read in Germany.

The progress of literacy and diffusion of reading were *Medieval Advances* major factors contributing to change in Western man's idea of himself and his relation to others. The magnitude of the phenomenon can be measured, however, only for the seventeenth and eighteenth centuries, because series of documents suitable for such techniques as counting signatures did not become available until the very end of the sixteenth century, and often much later. The cultural state of Europe in the late Middle Ages and even in the sixteenth century therefore remains largely unknown, and it is probably incorrect to assume that literacy rates were low everywhere and that only the clergy knew how to write. In Flanders, for example, various signs suggest that ordinary people could read, write, and count. In the cities "Latinless" schools taught the basics to common folk. There were probably more than twenty of them in Saint-Omer in 1468, and Valenciennes, a town of 10,000 inhabitants, had twenty-four such schools in 1497. Another sign is the presence of texts on church frescoes and paintings. Still another is the high percentage of signatures—on the order of 70 percent—found in receipts of all sorts (for rents, supplies, and labor) collected by the accountants of the aldermen and hospitals of Saint-Omer in the fifteenth century. Many merchants and artisans seem to have been literate, and only laborers and haulers appear in the majority to have been unable to sign their names. In the countryside the situation was no doubt different, but the keeping of poor-table records, community and charity registers, and tax rolls suggests that writing was a widely shared ability, and the posting of tax rates suggests that at least some people could read them.[23]

Medieval Flanders was by no means unique in its ability to read and write. In Italian cities, as early as the fourteenth century, many people, even among the lower orders, were able to write. In Florence, in 1340, 45 to 60 percent of children between the ages of six and thirteen attended city elementary schools; since far more boys than girls attended school, the percentage of boys receiving an elementary education must have been very high.[24] In some places the ability to write was an accomplished fact by the end of the Middle Ages. Accordingly, the spectacular and widespread advances that occurred in the period 1600–1800 should not be taken to indicate that only a very few people knew how to read and write between 1400 and 1500.

The Rejection of Writing   The progress made should not be allowed to obscure a persistent hostility to writing and its dissemination. Shakespeare dramatizes this resistance in *Henry VI*, Part 2 (whose quarto edition dates from 1594), in the treatment of Jack Cade's rebellion. In scene 2 of act 4 Cade and his men decide to kill "all the lawyers" and for their first victim choose the clerk of Chatham. Their social animosity is fed by a threefold rejection of writing. First, writing is the medium in which the decisions of the authorities are couched. Cade's reference to "parchment scribbled o'er" and sealed undoubtedly alludes to royal writs, which since the twelfth century had been used to record complaints submitted to the king and to convey decisions of the royal courts to local sheriffs. (Cade had been sentenced to having his hand burned for stealing livestock.) Second, writing was used to record the obligations of the poor, whence the reproach leveled against the clerk of Chatham: "He can make obligations and write court-hand," which is to say, he records debts in the cursive script used in notarized documents. Third, writing was thought to have magic and evil powers. The clerk of Chatham has "a book in his pocket with red letters in't," in other words, a book of witchcraft with rubrics or titles in red ink, possibly associated with his Jewishness, as indicated by his name, Emmanuel, whose epistolary significance is understood by Dick, one of the rebels: "They use to write it on top of the letters." The ability to write is thus a tool of the authorities, a method of domination, whether by law or magic, employed by the strong against the weak, hence the sign of a rejection of communal equality. Thus, Cade asks the clerk: "Dost thou use to write thy name, or hast thou a mark to thyself, like an honest plain-dealing man?" The mark, which anyone can make, is proof of respect for man's original equality, whereas the signature, which sets apart those who know how to write, indicates rejection of the common rule.

In scene 7 the rebels, having gained control of London, give free rein to their hatred of written culture. They attempt to destroy the places where that culture is transmitted ("others to th'Inns of Court: down with them all"), its ancient monuments ("burn all the records of the realm"), its techniques of reproduction (Lord Say is accused of having constructed a paper mill and introduced printing), and its lexicon of description (another charge against Lord Say being that he is surrounded by men "that usually talk of a noun and a verb, and

such abominable words"). Against these oppressive and corrupting innovations Cade sets forth the claims of a traditional
culture, based on speech and signs: "My mouth shall be the
parliament of England." He thus alludes to the ancient conception of law, according to which its force stems from its
oral proclamation. Instead of books and printed materials,
Cade prefers the ancient practice of recording private debts by
making notches on pieces of wood: "the score and the tally."
In fact, Jack Cade's rebellion took place in 1449, twenty-seven
years before the introduction of printing into England. In
writing about a rebellion that occurred a century and a half
earlier, Shakespeare was able to incorporate into his play the
fundamental tension between two cultures: one increasingly
based on recourse to the written word in both the public and
the private spheres; the other based on nostalgic and utopian
esteem for a society without writing, governed by words that
everyone could hear and signs that everyone could understand.
Whatever his intention in depicting a popular uprising as foolish and bloody and the rebels as dupes manipulated by others,
it is clear that the underlying cause of the rebellion is hostility
to writing, which is blamed for the upheavals that are transforming the society.

If Shakespeare depicted hostility to writing as a sentiment
of the lower classes, that sentiment had a more literate counterpart in the rejection by the educated of printed books, a
common reaction around the turn of the sixteenth century. In
Venice, for example, a Dominican named Filippo di Strata
proposed an argument against Gutenberg's invention that was
accepted by a large part of the Venetian Senate. Printing, he
maintained, was guilty on several counts: it corrupted texts,
which were circulated in hastily manufactured, faulty editions
composed solely for profit; it corrupted minds by making
available immoral and heterodox works over which the ecclesiastical authorities had no control; and it corrupted knowledge, which was debased by being divulged to the ignorant.
Whence the judgment: *"Est virgo hec penna, meretrix est stam-
pificata"* (The pen is a virgin, the printing press a whore).[25]

More than a century later echoes of di Strata's argument
can be heard in Lope de Vega's *Fuenteovejuna*, published in
Madrid in 1619. In act 2, lines 892-930, a peasant, Barrildo,
and a licentiate of the University of Salamanca, Leonelo, discuss the merits of printing. The learned Leonelo reveals his
doubts about the usefulness of Gutenberg's invention. To be
sure, it preserves valuable works and assures their wide dis-

In the 18th century, for Carmontelle and others, reading was primarily an act of solitude and silence, as indicated by the mouth closed with the fingertip. Here the Count of Schomberg has sat down to read in front of an open window, not behind a desk as for study but in a more relaxed posture, with his head resting on his hand. His book, *The Works of Voltaire*, has been set aside, and the reader is lost in thought. (Chantilly, Condé Museum.)

tribution, but it also causes errors and absurdities to circulate, allows those who would ruin an author's reputation to usurp his identity and distribute nonsense in his name, and confuses people's minds with an overabundance of texts. Far from contributing to the progress of knowledge, printing may well have added to the sum of ignorance. When Barrildo says that the growing number of printed books has made it possible for every man to think of himself as a scholar, Leonelo curtly replies: "*Antes que ignoran màs*" (No, they are more ignorant than before).

The advent of written culture in the West had to contend with the persistent notion that dissemination of knowledge was tantamount to profanation. The growing number of those who could read and write and the proliferation of printed matter caused disarray among "clerks" (lay as well as ecclesiastical), who had hitherto enjoyed a monopoly of the production and discussion of knowledge. In the Christian tradition, only clerics were authorized to interpret the secrets of God, nature, and the state. With the scientific revolution of the seventeenth century, the ancient taboos and limitations on access to knowledge were lifted, but only for a small minority, the *respublica litteratorum*, whose members were held to be the only people capable of pursuing knowledge without danger to religion, law, and order. At a time when Icarus and Prometheus became emblems of a knowledge without limits, people were also reminded that knowledge must remain the exclusive province of the new clerks: the intellectuals.[26]

Two motifs were indissolubly linked: the idea that the lower orders rejected written culture because they saw it as an instrument of domination and a threat to the social fabric, and the idea that the educated resisted appropriation by the vulgar of knowledge that had been theirs exclusively, hence also of the keys that gave access to that knowledge. Before the written word could find a place in Western society, it had to overcome both of these representations.

READING PRACTICES

Silent Reading

Between the sixteenth and eighteenth centuries, as growing numbers of people learned to read, new ways of reading became popular. The most novel of these, as Philippe Ariès has noted, was private reading in a quiet place away from other people, which allowed the reader to engage in solitary reflection on what he or she read. This "privatization" of reading is undeniably one of the major cultural developments of the early modern era.

What conditions made it possible? First of all, people needed to acquire a new skill: the ability to read without pronouncing the words as they were read. Otherwise the reader remained subject to communal contraints while reading in a library, say, or a room where others were present. Silent reading also made possible the immediate internalization of what the reader read. Reading aloud was slow, laborious, and externalized; silent reading was faster, easier, and more immediate in its impact on the inner self. Apparently, during the Middle Ages, one group of readers after another mastered the technique of silent reading. The first were the copyists working in the monastic scriptoria. Then, around the middle of the twelfth century, scholars in the universities acquired the ability. Two centuries later the lay aristocracy learned to read silently. By the fifteenth century silent reading was the norm, at least for readers who also knew how to write and who belonged to segments of society that had long been literate. For others, who belonged to groups that slowly learned to read and for whom books remained strange, rare objects, the old way of reading no doubt remained a necessity. As late as the nineteenth century, neophytes and maladroit readers could be identified by their inability to read silently. In Labiche's play *La Cagnotte* (1864), the farmer Colladan replies to a person who loses patience when he reads a very private letter out loud: "If I read out loud, it's not for you, it's for me . . . Whenever I don't read out loud . . . I don't understand what I'm reading."

Silent reading opened new horizons for those who mastered it. It radically transformed intellectual work, which in essence became an intimate activity, a personal confrontation with an ever-growing number of texts, a question of memorization and cross-referencing. It made possible a more personal form of piety, a more private devotion, a relation with the sacred not subject to the discipline and mediation of the Church. The spirituality of the mendicant orders, the *devotio moderna*, and even Protestantism, all of which presuppose a direct relation between the individual and God, relied heavily on silent reading, which enabled at least some people to nurture their faith on private reading of spiritual books or the Bible itself. Finally, silent, secret, private reading paved the way for previously unthinkable audacities. In the late Middle

Gérard Dou, painting of an old woman moving her lips as she reads the Bible. For a long time humble readers found it necessary to speak the words as they read in order to understand. (Leningrad, Hermitage.)

An almanac for 1681 in the form of a wall poster, entitled *Almanac of what is said, or the newsmongers of the Quai des Augustins.* In front of the book-shops and stalls along the quay, a man reads a gazette out loud to a group of impatient customers. The verse commentary mocks this enthusiasm for news, which could only be satisfied by an immediate public reading: "Gentlemen, the affairs of state are to divert your souls, and the affairs of your wives leave your foreheads in good shape. One of them may be happening now, while the Gazette is being read." (Paris, Bibliothèque Nationale.)

Ages, even before the invention of the printing press, heretical texts circulated in manuscript form, critical ideas were expressed, and erotic books, suitably illuminated, enjoyed considerable success.[27]

Although the invention of printing was indeed a "revolution" in that it made it possible to produce a large number of identical copies at a cost much lower than that of copying by hand (even at a time when print runs were small and printing costs quite high), it should not be credited with intellectual and psychological changes that were really the result of a new method of reading, regardless of whether the text was printed or manuscript. By the sixteenth century, the "other revolution"—the revolution in reading—was already accomplished, although it had only recently made its impact felt on laymen and remained incomplete, since large numbers of readers who had not yet mastered writing were incapable of reading silently. There seems to have been a clear division between those for whom reading was a private act and those for whom it remained a communal act, perhaps even an act of class solidarity.

Did silent reading result in greater familiarity with books and a more prominent place for them in the home? The evidence is unfortunately imperfect, incomplete, and much criticized; we must rely primarily on inventories, generally compiled after a death, which described (to a limited extent) and estimated the value of an individual's possessions, including his books. One problem is that the presence of a book in an estate inventory does not imply that the book was read or

More Books for More Readers

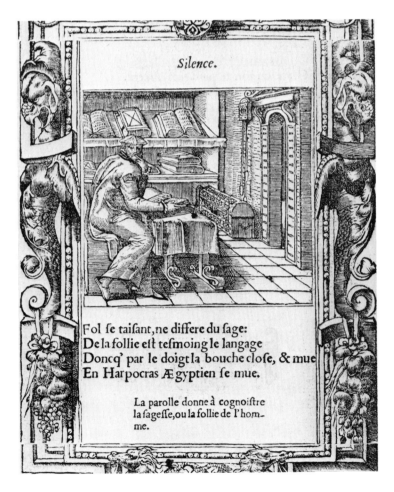

Silence.

Fol fe taifant, ne differe du fage:
De la follie eft tefmoing le langage
Doncq' par le doigt la bouche clofe, & mue
En Harpocras Ægyptien fe mue.

La parolle donne à cognoiftre
la fageffe, ou la follie de l'homme.

In contrast to humbler readers, the learned read silently and without moving their lips. In this emblem, taken from *Alciat's Emblems, newly translated into French* (Lyons, 1549), a reader in his study is shown closing his lips with his finger. (Paris, Bibliothèque Nationale.)

even purchased by the deceased. Inventories also failed to include printed materials of little value, even though these might constitute the bulk of a person's reading, and of course omitted any valuable or dangerous books that might have been removed from the library beforehand. Such evidence, therefore, should not be relied upon for anything more than very general indications concerning, for instance, the presence of a particular book in the libraries of a particular class of society. Even more than in the case of signature rates, we must be very cautious in comparing data from different places, for the figures may be influenced by differences in notarial practices and in the composition of the populations for which estate inventories were compiled.

By the sixteenth century the evidence suggests that private individuals owned more books than ever before. In some places the percentage of book owners, both overall and by social class, remained constant, but the number of books owned increased. In Valencia, for example, books are mentioned in one out of three inventories between 1474 and 1550. The hierarchy of ownership remained stable: nine out of ten clerics owned books, as did three out of four members of the liberal professions, one out of two nobles, one out of three merchants, and only one out of ten manual laborers. Within each group the number of books in the average library increased. Between the end of the fifteenth century and the second quarter of the sixteenth century, the average physician's collection increased from 26 to 62 books; the average jurist's from 25 to 55; and the average merchant's from 4 to 10. As for artisans in the textile trade, who had generally owned only one book, the average "library" now increased to 4 volumes.[28]

In sixteenth-century Florence the percentage of inventories compiled by the Magistrato de'pupilli in which books are mentioned remained quite low: 4.6 percent between 1531 and 1569, 5.2 percent between 1570 and 1608. (It had reached 3.3 percent between 1413 and 1453 but fell to 1.4 percent in the second half of the fifteenth century.) This percentage is much lower than that found in Valencia or Amiens (where, between 1503 and 1576, 20 percent of inventories mentioned books).[29] Was Italy backward in this respect? It is hard to say. We can, however, assert with confidence that, while the percentage of book owners increased very little, the proportion of books belonging to the largest libraries increased substantially. Libraries containing fewer than 6 volumes accounted for 55 percent of the total before 1570, but for only 31 percent after

that date. Conversely, libraries with 51 to 100 volumes increased from 4.5 to 9 percent, and those with 101 to 200 volumes from 1 to 8 percent. Libraries with from 6 to 50 volumes, which had accounted for 38 percent of the total before 1570, rose to 47 percent afterward.[30]

A third possibility was an increase in the percentage of the population that owned books. In Canterbury, around the turn of the seventeenth century, inventories of men's estates indicate ownership of books in one out of ten cases in 1560, one out of four cases in 1580, one out of three cases in 1590, and nearly one out of two cases in 1620. A similar pattern has been noted in two smaller cities in Kent: Faversham and Maidstone. Here again, ownership of books depends strongly on social rank: between 1620 and 1640 in Canterbury 90 percent of men in the professions and 73 percent of nobles owned books, compared with only 45 percent of textile artisans, 36 percent of construction workers, and 31 percent of the city's

Jacob de Gheyn the Younger, 1621(?), vanity. In this and many similar early-17th-century vanities, time and death vanquish the written word in all its bookish forms from the small format to the large folio, just as they vanquish military glory and artistic creation. In the face of a belief in the immortality of literary works reinforced by printing, which seemed to confer upon them an indestructible, perennial quality, the vanity painters issued a reminder that all things are ephemeral, even those born of the pen and recorded by the press. (New Haven, Yale University Art Gallery.)

Flemish school, 17th century, portrait of a young man, perhaps a student, with his back to the fireplace. In portrait art, books have always been one of the most reliable indicators of condition, estate, or practice. (Paris, Louvre.)

yeomen. With such high percentages the three cities in Kent are not typical of England as a whole. In rural parishes books remained rare, even in the seventeenth century. Only 13 percent of inventories in Bedfordshire at the end of the second decade of the century and 14 percent of those from Middlesex between 1630 and 1690 mention the presence of books.[31]

Did private ownership of books increase between 1500 and 1800? Did growing familiarity with books contribute to the privatization characteristic of the period? The answers to these questions depend on location. Leading Europe in book ownership were the cities of the Protestant countries. In the middle of the eighteenth century, in the German Lutheran cities of Tübingen, Spire, and Frankfurt, books are mentioned in, respectively, 89, 88, and 77 percent of all inventories.[32] Compare this with Catholic France, whether in Paris, where only 22 percent of inventories in the 1750s mention books, or in provincial cities. (In nine cities of western France, the figure for 1757–1758 was 36 percent, and in Lyons in the second half of the eighteenth century it was 35 percent.)[33] Other Protestant countries were more like Germany, even largely rural countries like the United States. At the end of the eighteenth century, 75 percent of the inventories in Worcester County, Massachusetts, 63 percent in Maryland, and 63 percent in Virginia mention the presence of books.[34] These figures indicate marked progress compared with the previous century, where the figure in these same regions was about 40 percent.

Protestant Reading

Religion established an important difference with respect to book ownership. There is no more striking proof of this than a comparison of Catholic and Protestant libraries in the same city. In Metz, between 1645 and 1672, 70 percent of Protestant inventories mention books, compared with only 25 percent of Catholic ones. The gap remains wide, regardless of occupation: 75 percent of Protestant nobles owned books compared with only 22 percent of Catholic nobles; in the legal professions the figures are 86 and 29 percent; in the medical professions, 88 and 50 percent; for minor officers, 100 and 18 percent; for merchants, 85 and 33 percent; for artisans, 52 and 17 percent; for "bourgeois," 73 and 5 percent; and for manual and agricultural laborers, 25 and 9 percent. Protestants owned more books than Catholics. Protestant professionals owned on the average three times as many books as their Catholic

counterparts, and the ratio was the same for merchants, aristans, and minor officers. As for those classed as "bourgeois," the libraries of the Calvinists were ten times as large as those of the Catholics.[35]

There were differences in the composition of libraries and in reading practices. In Lutheran countries all libraries, regardless of the social rank of the owner, were organized around a common set of religious books. In Rhenish cities this consisted of the Bible, pious books, manuals of preparation for communion and confession, and hymnals or *Gesangbücher*. The larger libraries had more titles and more different editions, but basically the same kinds of books. Differences in wealth and education were reflected not in these religious works but in the number and nature of profane books (which are found in just over a quarter of the libraries in the second half of the eighteenth century). Protestants thus developed a religious and cultural identity around a common set of books, used in connection with various religious exercises: Bible-reading, prayer, hymns, sermons, communion. Not all Protestant libraries were as homogeneous as these Lutheran ones, however. In seventeenth-century Metz, for example, apart from the Bible and psalms, titles and genres of books varied widely. The more puritanical Calvinist libraries resembled Lutheran ones, however, although they usually contained a smaller number of books.

In America reading and religion were inextricably intertwined, defining a culture based entirely on familiarity with the Bible.[36] Biblical stories were heard before they were read, since fathers or servants often read aloud to the entire family. In memoirs published in 1852, Joseph T. Buckingham, editor of Boston's first daily newspaper, recalls: "For a number of years . . . I read every day [in the presence of his master and mistress] at least one chapter, and often two or three chapters in the Bible . . . I have no doubt that I read the Bible through *in course* at least a dozen times before I was sixteen years old, with no other omissions than the jaw-breaking chapters of the Chronicles. The historical parts I had read much oftener, and the incidents and the language became almost as familiar as the grace . . . said before and after meals—neither of which ever varied a word during . . . nine years." In this culture the ability to read was taken for granted; from the moment the child first confronted the written word, he recognized texts that he had heard before and often memorized. Buckingham says: "I have no recollection of any time when I could not read . . . In December, 1784, the month in which I was five years old, I went to a master's school, and, on being asked if I could read, I said I could read in the Bible. The master placed me on his chair and presented a Bible opened at the fifth chapter of Acts. I read the story of Ananias and Sapphira falling down dead for telling a lie. He patted me on the head and commended my reading."

Reading meant returning again and again to the same books—the Bible and a few others—which were transmitted from generation to generation. This practice, sometimes termed "intensive" reading, had its radical exponents, such as the Quaker William Penn: "Keep but few books, well chosen and well read, whether concerned with religious or civil subjects. Reading many books only takes the mind away from meditation. Much reading is an oppression of the mind." The practice also had its methodological treatises. A sermon published in Boston in 1767 contains these recommendations: "Be diligent in reading holy scripture. Every morning and every evening you must read a chapter of your Bible or a passage from a pious sermon, and when you read you must not scan the text and then set it aside. Better not to read at all than to read in that way. When you read, you must pay close attention to what you are reading, and when you have finished you must mull over what you have just read."[37]

Samuel King, *Portrait of the Reverend Dr. Ezra Stiles*, minister of the Congregational Church, professor of ecclesiastical history, and president of Yale College—the very figure of the gentle Puritan. On the shelves, in identical bindings, are works of Plato, Livy, the *Ecclesiastical History* of Eusebius of Caesarea, Newton's *Principia*, a *History of China*, a book in Hebrew, and works of the Puritan preachers Isaac Watts and Cotton Mather. All knowledge is gathered here to make the point that encyclopedic erudition is necessary to faith in God, omnipotent and omnipresent in the heart of the believer. (New Haven, Yale University Art Gallery.)

Repeated reading of the same texts was the norm for American Protestants. In memoirs published in 1857, Samuel Goodrich, a writer and editor, says: "In our family Bible it is recorded that he [my father] thus read that holy book through, in course, thirteen times, in the space of about five and twenty years." The Bostonian Robert Keayne declared in his will: "As my special gift to him [my son] my little written book in my closet upon I Cor. 11, 27, 28, which is a treatise of the sacrament of the Lord's Supper . . . [It is] a little thin pocket book bound in leather, all written in my own hand, which I esteem more precious than gold, and which I have read over I think 100 and 100 times . . . I desire him and hope that he will never part with it as long as he lives." Read and reread, religious texts inhabited the minds of the faithful, who drew from them not only spiritual comfort but a manner of speaking and writing and ways of organizing individual and communal life in accordance with the divine word. Consider the experiences of Joseph Crosswell, an itinerant preacher born in 1712 and converted during the Great Awakening: "I know not when I have experienced greater consolation in reading the word of God. Blessed be its glorious and gracious Author. Sweetly regaled in the afternoon by the heavenly south breezes of the divine Spirit, whilst repeating scripture passages . . . I have this day repeated the whole book of Canticles by heart . . . Some enlivening about noon while passing through woods and repeating the last three chapters in the Canticles."

In America's Puritan culture we find the most radical privatization of reading. The book became the center of family life. People read for themselves and for others. They memorized passages, which by dint of frequent repetition became part of their everyday language. No doubt such diligence was quite rare, but practices were similar in other Protestant areas, even where the Calvinist and Puritan influence was small.[38]

The Library, Retreat from the World

The book thus became the companion of choice in a new kind of intimacy. And the library, for those who could afford one, became the ideal place for retreat, study, and meditation. Consider, as one of many possible examples, the case of Montaigne. In 1579 he sold his post as *conseiller* with the Bordeaux parlement and went to Paris to oversee the printing of the works of his friend Etienne de La Boétie. The following year, upon returning to his château, he had painted on the walls of his library, "a beauty among village libraries," this Latin inscription: "In the year of Christ 1571, at the age of thirty-eight, Michel de Montaigne, long since bored with the slavery of parlement and public office but still vigorous, withdrew to lay his head on the breast of the learned Virgins in calm and security; he shall pass the remaining days of his life there. Hoping that fate will allow him to perfect this dwelling, this sweet paternal retreat, he has consecrated it to his freedom, tranquillity, and leisure."

In the first place, then, the library was a retreat from the world, freedom enjoyed out of the public eye. Montaigne's description in the *Essays* (III:3) emphasizes its role as refuge: "When at home I turn aside a little more often to my library," the most exposed room in the castle, "which I like for being a little hard to reach and out of the way, for the benefit of the exercise as much as to keep the crowds away."[39] Separated from the main building by a courtyard, the library is where he engages in the best of the "three kinds of commerce," that of a man with his books, which is to say, with himself. Retreat does not mean seclusion or rejection of the world, however. Montaigne's library is a place from which one can see without

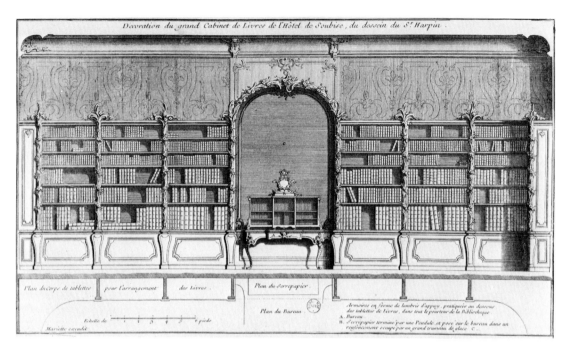

Decoration du grand Cabinet de Livres de l'Hôtel de Soubise, du dessein du S.ʳ Harpin.

being seen, which gives a kind of power to the person who retires there. Power over the household and its inhabitants: "I turn aside a little more often to my library, from which at one sweep I command a view of my household. I am over the entrance and see below me my garden, my farmyard, my courtyard, and into most of the parts of my house." Power over nature, which offers itself up to the eye: "It offers rich and free views in three directions." Power over the knowledge accumulated in the books that the eye takes in at a glance: "The shape of my library is round, the only flat side being the part needed for my table and chair; and curving round me it presents at a glance all my books, arranged in five rows of shelves on all sides." At a glance too Montaigne can take in the Greek and Latin sayings that have been painted on the beams, those taken from Stobaeus at the beginning of the retreat having been covered over later, in 1575 or 1576, by others taken from Sextus Empiricus and the Bible.

The tension between the desire to withdraw from the crowd while at the same time maintaining control over the world is probably symbolic of the absolute liberty made possible by commerce with books, hence of the possibility of complete self-mastery without constraint or supervision: "There is my throne. I try to make my authority over it

An engraving by Pierre-Jean Mariette from the *Decoration of the Great Library of the Hôtel de Soubise*, showing a most imposing set of shelves designed by Harpin. The classical arrangement of books was by decreasing size, with folio editions on the lowest shelves and the smallest formats (twelves and sixteens) on top. Under Louis XV sumptuousness turned into luxury, and libraries exhibited rank and provided comfort. (Paris, Bibliothèque Nationale.)

French school, 18th century. Harpin's design seems to have become a reality, at least on canvas. Reading has become an occasion for social intercourse, a time for young men and women to meet under the indulgent gaze of stone busts. (Private collection.)

absolute, and to withdraw this one corner from all society, conjugal, filial, and civil." The hours spent in the library are hours of withdrawal in two senses, which define the essence of privacy in the modern era: withdrawal from the public sphere, from civic responsibility, from the affairs of city and state; and withdrawal from the family, from the household, from the social responsibilities of domestic intimacy. In retreat, the individual is free, master of his time, of his leisure or study: "There I leaf through now one book, now another, without order and without plan, by disconnected fragments. One moment I muse, another moment I set down or dictate, walking back and forth, these fancies of mine that you see here." And dictate: note that the ancient method of composition, the writer speaking his words out loud as he walks and requiring the presence of a scribe, is not thought to be in contradiction with the sense of intimacy that comes from familiarity with the books of the library, which are close by and easy to leaf through.

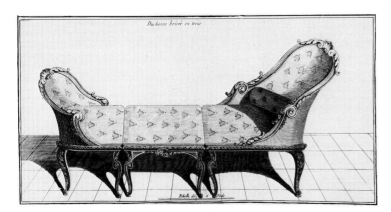

The sense of power conferred by withdrawal into a library is depicted in other texts, such as Shakespeare's *The Tempest*, probably written between 1610 and 1613. Like Montaigne, Prospero preferred the privacy of his study to public affairs: "Me, poor man, my library / Was dukedom large enough" (act 1, scene 2, ll. 109–110). In exile, he thanks the person who allowed him to take some of his precious books: "Knowing I lov'd my books, he furnish'd me, / From my own library, with volumes that / I prize above my dukedom" (act 1, scene 2, ll. 166–168). But these familiar, cherished books, companions in solitude and misery, are also the instruments of a secret power, feared and fearsome. Knowing this, Caliban thinks that Prospero's power can be destroyed if his books are seized and burned: "Remember, / First to possess his books; for without them / He's but a sot, as I am" (act 3, scene 2, ll. 83–85), and "Burn but his books" (l. 87). Prospero himself associates books with his power: "I'll to my book; / For yet, ere supper-time, I must perform / Much business appertaining" (act 3, scene 1, ll. 92–94). He also repudiates that power: "And, deeper than did ever plummet sound, / I'll drown my book" (act 5, scene 1, ll. 56–57).

Thus there emerges a strange alliance between reading, that most private and hidden practice, and true, effective power, power far more effective than that of public office. The reading of books of magic (such as the *Books of Experiments* in sixteenth-century England or *the* nameless book of magic widely read in rural Aragon and Languedoc in the nineteenth century) became the paradigm for all reading, which had to be done in secret and which conferred upon the reader a dangerous power.[40]

From François Boucher, *Interior Furnishing and Decoration (1760–1780)*. French readers in the 18th century preferred the straight-backed *bergère* (right) with its padded sides, sometimes lined with cushions, or the *duchesse* (left), in one or more pieces, upon which the reader could stretch out and abandon himself or herself to the pleasures of reading. (Paris, Musée des Arts décoratifs.)

This 17th-century satirical print mocks the preference of scholars and men of the robe for handsome bindings. The verse reads: "The greatest of all nature's fools is he who likes his books all gilt, well covered, well bound, nice and clean and dustfree, and who never looks at anything but the cover." Behind the caricature was the new reality of the bibliophile, whose relation to books was passionate and sensuous and involved more than just the text. (Paris, Bibliothèque Nationale.)

le Pautre Inuenit et fecit C.P.R.

Iollain excudit

C'est bien, le plus grand fou qui soit dans la nature
Que celui que se plaist aux Liures bien dorez
Bien couuers, bien reliez, bien nets, bien Epoudrez
Et ne les voit Jamais que par la couuerture

Reading Becomes Private

"Study: a place of retirement in ordinary homes where one can go to study or to find seclusion and where one keeps one's most precious goods. A room that contains a library is also called a study." This definition, from Furetière's *Dictionary*, reveals the library's new status. It is no longer, or at any rate not always, an ostentatious room for receiving visitors, for "show" as Pascal put it, but a place for keeping "one's most precious goods," not only useful and rare books but one's own self. Privately owned books and the place where they were kept and consulted therefore commanded special attention.

Consider two contemporaries, Samuel Pepys (1633–1703) and John Locke (1632–1704). In the diary he kept from 1660 to 1669, Pepys, then Clerk of the Acts of the Navy Board and living in an apartment adjoining the offices of the Royal Navy, tells of his efforts to acquire, bind, and store books.[41] An assiduous client of bookstores (and not only so as to make free with the bookseller's wife) as well as an avid reader ("I know not how in the world to abstain from reading," he wrote on 18 March 1668, at a time when his eyesight had already suffered serious deterioration), he took upon himself the task of arranging his books (13 October 1660: "Within all the afternoon, setting up shelfes in my study"), preparing a catalogue (4 February 1667: "A little to the office and then to my chamber and there finished my catalogue of my books with my own hand, and so to supper and to bed, and had a good night's rest"), until, his eyesight almost gone, he asked his brother to finish the job (24 May 1669: "To White Hall, and there all the morning, and thence home, and giving order for some business and setting my brother to making a catalogue of my books"). Wanting his books to look good, he made frequent trips to the binder (3 February 1665: "My bill for the rebinding of some old books to make them suit with my study cost me, besides other new books in the same bill, £3; but it will be very handsome"). Pepys kept his money in his study and did business there, suggesting that this was one of the most private rooms in his house. On 11 December 1660, having discussed at the tavern the best ways to invest his money, he wrote: "Up to my study, and there did make up an even 100l and sealed it to lie by. After that to bed." On 18 July 1664 he returned home with a man who owed him money, "and there he took occasion to owne his obligations to me, and did lay down twenty pieces in gold upon my shelf in my closett."

John Locke, collector and scholar, marked each of his books with his personal stamp and organized his library so as to facilitate research. In 1691, after years of exile in the United Provinces, Locke returned to England and installed his library in two rented rooms in Sir Francis Masham's castle at Otes in Essex, twenty miles from London. With the aid of an assistant, he numbered each work (with a tag glued to the back of the binding and reproduced on the top plate inside). He then marked each number on sheets inserted into the *Catalogus impressorum* of the Bodleian, published by Hyde, which served as both an annotated bibliography and a catalogue of his own library; later he pasted his numbers in two somewhat less cumbersome catalogues. This effort made his library more usable, the catalogue numbers facilitating the task of finding books on the shelves, where they were arranged according to size in two ranks, with no order by subject.

Every book that came into Locke's library was carefully marked as his personal property. He placed his signature on the top plate of the binding, alongside the book's number. He

A portrait of John Locke, book collector, one of several drawn by Godfrey Kneller and engraved in 1738. The image depicts the three-volume edition of the *Works of John Locke* (1st edition 1714, 4th edition 1740). (Paris, Bibliothèque Nationale.)

The bookplate was the usual way of indicating possession of a book. Here the treasurer of the Estates of Languedoc displays his coat of arms and his library, so that each work contains an image of the whole of which it is a part. (Paris, Bibliothèque Nationale.)

underlined the final figures of the date on the title page, placed a line over the page number on the final page, marked the price he had paid for the book, usually on the eleventh page, and recorded the number, date, and pagination in his catalogues. While reading he made additional marks in at least some of his books. Pages were noted on the lower plate of the binding, and notes were sometimes written on inserted sheets. Locke also made symbolic notations (letters in italics, dots, dashes, plus and minus signs, initials) whose meaning is for the most part unclear. (Some of these signs seem to refer to the merits of the edition or text or to the presence of a second copy in the library.)

Locke's commerce with his books was thus a time-consuming occupation. He respected them, never writing or underlining on pages that contained text. They were his most intimate possessions and therefore demanded to be passed on to someone who would know how to make good use of them. In his will, Locke specified what was to become of his books: some were to go to Dame Damaris Masham, his host's second wife ("four folios, eight quartos, and twenty small books which she may choose among the books of my library"); others to Mr. Anthony Collins of the Middle Temple, a freethinker and recent friend of Locke's; the bulk of the library, some 3,641 titles, was to be divided between his cousin Peter King and Francis C. Masham, Damaris Masham's only son, "when he shall have attained the age of twenty-one years."[42]

The presence of books became firmly linked to the habit of reading and privacy in seventeenth-century England. Estate inventories from Kentish towns show that they were less likely to be found in the hall, the most open room in the house, where guests were received, and more likely to be found in private areas such as the study (closet) or bedroom. (Between 1560 and 1600, 48 percent of books were found in the hall, compared with 39 percent between 1601 and 1640; the proportion of books found in more private rooms rose from 9 percent to 23 percent during the same interval.)

Books were found more often in the bedroom than in the "study" or "parlor," probably because it had become common to read before going to sleep. In Kent, for example, the wife of one yeoman in Otham was described by her maid in court documents as "reading her book as she often did before going to bed." This was Pepys's habit too, and in his diary we find frequent notations such as these from 1667: "and so after supper to read, and then to bed" (1 May), and "I to my book

again, and made an end of Mr. Hooker's Life, and so to bed"
(19 May).

Evening reading was not necessarily solitary. A couple
might read together or to each other: "I fell a-reading in
Fuller's *History of Abbys* and my wife in *Grand Cyrus* till 12 at
night; and so to bed" (7 December 1660). Sometimes they
read the same books (poems of Du Bartas on 2 November
1662, Aesop's *Fables* on 24 May 1663), and sometimes (as on
2 November 1660) one read aloud to the other: "In Paul's
church-yard I called at Kirton's, and there they had got a mass
book for me, which I bought and cost me twelve shillings;
and, when I came home, sat up late and read in it with great
pleasure to my wife, to hear that she was long ago so well
acquainted with." (Pepys's wife, Elisabeth Marchand, was the
daughter of an exiled Huguenot and for a time had been a
student at the Ursulines' school in Paris.)

Frequently Pepys ordered his valet to read to him, even
before his eyesight had begun to deteriorate: "I had the boy
up tonight for his sister to teach him to put me to bed, and I
heard him read, which he doth pretty well" (22 September
1660). Or again, on 9 September 1666: "Anon to Sir W. Pen's
to bed [after the London fire, Pepys had had to leave his
damaged apartment], and made my boy Tom to read me
asleep." And on 25 December 1668: "So home and to dinner
alone with my wife, who, poor wretch! sat undressed all day
till ten at night, altering and lacing of a noble petticoat: while
I by her, making the boy read to me the Life of Julius Caesar,
and Des Cartes' book of Musick, the latter of which I understand not . . . Then after supper I made the boy play upon
his lute, which I have not done twice before since he come to
me; and so, my mind in mighty content, we to bed." Like
the presence of the scribe in Montaigne's library, the presence
of the "boy" in Pepys's bedroom by no means spoils his
intimacy with his book; reading could be a private without
necessarily being a solitary pursuit.

By contrast, a person could enjoy a strictly private relation with his book outside the confines of the home. Pepys
read at home in the evening, but he also read a great deal in
various places around London. Sometimes he read while walking. On 18 November 1663: "And so I walked to Deptford,
where I have not been a very great while, and there paid off
the Milford in very good order . . . After dinner came Sir W.
Batten, and I left him to pay off another ship, and I walked
home again reading of a little book of new poems of Cowley's,

given my by his brother." On 9 May 1666 he again went to Deptford: "Walked back again reading of my Civill Law Book." Then, on 17 August 1666: "Down by water to Woolwich, I walking alone from Greenwich thither, making an end of the 'Adventures of Five Hours,' which when all is done is the best play that ever I read in my life." Reading whiled away the hours while traveling the Thames by boat, as on 1 May 1666: "Thence by water to Redriffe, reading a new French book by Lord Brouncker did give me today, *L'histoire amoureuse des Gaules*, being a pretty Libell against the amours of the Court of France." Or, on 10 June 1667, as Pepys returns from Gravesend: "So I homeward, as long as it was light reading Mr. Boyles book of *Hydrostatickes*, which is a most excellent book as ever I read . . . When it grew too dark to read, I lay down and took a nap, it being a most excellent fine evening."

Silent reading created an air of intimacy that separated the reader from the outside world. Thus, even in the middle of the city, in the presence of other people, he might be alone with his book and his thoughts. Certain kinds of reading demanded more privacy, however. On 13 January 1668 Pepys "stopped at Martins my bookseller, where I saw the French book which I did think to have had for my wife to translate, called *L'escholle des Filles* [attributed to Michel Millot and Jean l'Ange], but when I came to look into it, it is the most bawdy, lewd book that ever I saw, rather worse than *putana errante* [by Aretino], so that I was ashamed of reading in it." His shame seems not to have lasted very long, since on 8 February he revisited the bookshop "and bought that idle, roguish book, *L'escholle des Filles*; which I have bought in plain binding (avoiding the buying of a better bound) because I resolve, as soon as I have read it, to burn it, that it may not stand in the list of books, nor among them, to disgrace them if it should be found." The next day finds him impatient to read this promising work: "Up, and at my chamber all the morning and the office, doing business and also reading a little of *L'escholle des Filles*, which is a mighty lewd book, but yet not amiss for a sober man once to read over to inform himself in the villainy of the world." And that evening, after dinner and an afternoon spent with friends and well lubricated by drink, he says: "And then they parted and I to my chamber, where I did read through *L'escholle des Filles*; and after I had done it, I burned it, that it might not be among my books to my shame; and so at night to supper and then to bed." In the

Hubert Robert, *Mme Geoffrin's at Breakfast*. The lady is being read aloud to by a valet, who has set aside his broom and taken up a book. Reading was one of the duties of a servant, which accounts for the preference for educated domestics and the very high rate of literacy among manservants in the late 18th century. (Paris, Private collection.)

pidgin he reserves for such occasions, he describes the effects of his reading: "It did hazer my prick para stand all the while, and una vez to décharger." Licentious reading material cannot be exposed to public view.

The example of this seventeenth-century English reader shows that reading did indeed become a private activity, but in a variety of ways. By the eighteenth century the correlation of reading with privacy was firmly established, as though reading defined the limits of the inner life. Evidence for this can be seen in Chardin's painting *The Amusements of Private Life*. Commissioned in 1745 by Louise Ulrique of Sweden to paint two works, one on "Strict Education" and the other on "Gentle, Insinuating Education," Chardin chose to paint two different subjects: a women surprised while reading a book covered with colored paper resting on her knees, and a women recording her household expenses. The diptych thus contrasts leisure time with time spent in the chore of family adminis-tration. The second painting was called *The Administrator* and the first, *The Amusements of Private Life*. The latter name was acquired early in the history of the work, because the Swedish ambassador to Paris used it in a letter dated October 1746, after the work was shown at the Salon; an engraving made in 1747 used the same name.[43] This is, so to speak, a pictorial synecdoche: the part (reading) stands for the whole (private life). A single practice, that of reading, stands for the whole range of private pleasures in the time left free after family chores and obligations.

In this portrait of a woman reading, contemporaries rec-ognized a classic theme: the reading of romantic fiction. Con-sider two descriptions of the painting. In his *Reflections on Some Causes of the Present State of Painting in France* (1747), Lafont de Saint-Yenne saw it this way: "He [Chardin] has given this year a piece that represents a pleasant but idle woman in the guise of a lady casually if fashionably dressed, with a rather striking face wrapped in a white bonnet tied under the chin, which hides the sides of her face. One arm lies on her lap, and her hand casually holds a brochure. Beside her, a little to the rear, is a spinning wheel set on a little table." One year later, the painting, now referred to as *Amusements of the Tranquil Life*, was described in these terms in *Observations on the Arts and Some Paintings Shown at the Louvre in 1748*: "It represents a woman nonchalantly seated in an armchair and holding in one hand, which rests on her lap, a brochure. From a sort of languor in her eyes, which gaze out toward a corner of the painting, we divine that she is reading a novel, and that the tender impressions it has made on her have set her dreaming of someone whom she would like to see arrive at any moment."

Thus, Chardin's painted act of reading is characterized in two ways: in terms of objects and in terms of postures. The objects situate the reader in a comfortable apartment, a setting of some wealth. The reader's armchair is a high-backed bergère with a thick cushion and stuffed armrests, which allow the chair's occupant to relax with feet raised on a small footstool. Other styles of furniture—the chaise longue and the duchesse—permitted the reader to stretch out and relax even more. The casual if fashionable clothing worn by the woman

Jean-Baptiste Chardin, *Amusements of the Tranquil Life* (Stockholm, National Museum), and *The Administrator* (here in a 1754 engraving by Jean-Philippe Le Bas, Paris, Bibliothèque Nationale). These images, which contrast two roles of women, two moments of domestic life, and two uses of writing, were painted shortly after Chardin's marriage to Françoise-Marguerite Pouget.

Pierre-Antoine Baudoin, *Reading*. The artist depicts a comfortable, mellow interior, its privacy ensured by the closed door and screen. To the left, knowledge, symbolized by the large folio volumes, has been abandoned, left lying on the table or propped up on the floor. On the right are objects pleasing to a woman, including a guitar, a small dog, and a novel that has overwhelmed its reader, who has abandoned herself to sensuous imaginings. The painting carries a double message. Moralistically it warns against the dangers of romantic literature; lasciviously it violates the young woman's most intimate retreat. (Paris, Musée des Arts décoratifs.)

is a warm but lightweight indoor garment known as a *liseuse*—a dress for reading rather than for show or seduction. The book she holds in her hand is a "brochure," a book that is not bound but held together by a paper cover. On a low cabinet in a corner of the room, several bound books, larger in size than this brochure, are ranged against the wall.

For the commentators, the woman's posture is one of abandonment: she sits "nonchalantly" and "casually" holds the brochure; her gaze is languorous. These signs suggest that she is reading a novel, which fills her mind with disturbing images and sentiments and arouses her senses. From this description a modern spectator has some difficulty recognizing Chardin's painting, which shows, seated in a comfortable but austere room, a woman who is not languid at all and whose eyes by no means convey emotional turmoil. In fact, the descriptions seem to refer to other paintings, to Baudoin's *Reading*, for instance, which depicts, in a highly eroticized representation, a young woman in a state of total abandonment. The comments reveal the power of an association between female reading and idleness, sensual pleasure, and secret intimacy. More than the painting, which is deliberately estranged from the *topos*, the commentators' remarks reveal how eighteenth-century men imagined the act of reading by women, which by then had become the quintessence of private activity. Without the painter's intrusion it would have remained shrouded in silence.

The Spoken Text

In the eighteenth century the iconography of reading is exclusively female and secular, whereas previously it had been almost entirely male and religious—think of Rembrandt's readers, hermits and philosophers who have withdrawn from society in order to meditate over a book. Yet painting does not yield an exhaustive catalogue of early modern reading practices. Between 1500 and 1800 reading aloud, whether among friends or chance companions, was an essential ingredient of social life, even among the elite. Thus, the *corrector de la impresión* (editor of the revised edition) of *La Celestina*, published in Toledo in 1500 as *La Comedia de Calisto y Melibea*, specifies how it ought to be read in an octet that he appends to the work. It is entitled *Dice el modo que se ha de tener leyendo esta tragicomedia* (He indicates the manner in which this tragicomedy should be read). The *lector* (reader) to whom these instructions are addressed is advised to vary his tone, assume the part of every character, speak asides between clenched teeth (*cumple que sepas hablar entre dientes*), and make use of the *mil artes y modos*, the thousand ways and means of reading so as to capture the attention of his listeners, *los oyentes*.

Like the Latin and Humanist comedies, *La Celestina* was written to be read "theatrically" but by a single voice before a limited if select audience. In a prologue added to the Saragossa edition of 1507, which alludes to contradictory opinions about the work, the author accounts for the diversity of opinions by invoking the conditions under which the work was read: "So, when ten people gather to hear this comedy, in which, as is always the case, there are so many different humors, would anyone deny that there are grounds for disagreement about things that can be heard in so many different ways?" Ten listeners choose to come together to hear a text read aloud; the book becomes the center of a cultivated society of friends or acquaintances.

Along with *La Celestina*, other texts, particularly pastorals and novels, were favored for such gatherings, in which the written word was mediated by the spoken voice. Cervantes refers to this practice in *Don Quixote*, first by dramatizing, in chapter 32 of part 1, the reading of the *Curioso impertinente* by a priest to a small group of avid listeners gathered at an inn. And as title for chapter 66 of part 2 he chose: "Which treats of that which he who reads will see and that which he will hear who listens to a reading of it."[44]

In the seventeenth century people frequently listened to books read aloud. In the army in the field, such activity whiled away the time, strengthened friendships, and provided food for thought. As an ensign and, later, lieutenant in the Normandy Regiment between 1635 and 1642, Henri de Campion described in his *Memoirs* reading in the military: "I had my books, which took up a portion of my wagon's load, and frequently spent time with them, sometimes alone but most of the time with three friends from the regiment, intelligent and studious men. The Chevalier de Sévigné, a Breton and captain of the corps, was one. He was by nature a studious man, had read widely, and from birth had always been at war or at court. Le Breuil-Marcillac, a Gascon, brother of the lieutenant colonel and my captain, was the third member of our group. He had studied until the age of twenty-eight, his parents having destined him for the Church, which he quit in order to take up the sword, having spent well his time in school and later at the Sorbonne. He was a mild man, accommodating, with nothing of the rudeness of military men. D'Almivar, from Paris, a lieutenant and my close friend, was the fourth party to our studious commerce. He had a polished wit, was agreeable in conversations of all sorts, and quite sociable." Reading, listening to, and arguing about books established a strong and lasting friendship among the four men: "Those were the three men with whom I spent my hours of leisure. After reasoning together about the subjects that came up, without bitter dispute or desire on the part of one to shine at the expense of the others, one of us would read some good book aloud, and we would examine the finest passages in order to learn to live well and to die well, in accordance with morality, which was the principal subject of our study. Many people enjoyed listening to our discussions, which, I believe, were useful to them, for nothing was said that was not conducive to virtue. Since then I have found no society so comfortable or reasonable; it lasted seven years, during which I served in the Normandy Regiment."[45]

Thus, different ways of reading defined different but related social practices: solitary reading encouraged personal study and intellectual interchange; reading aloud, combined with interpretation and discussion of what was read, fostered friendship; and these friendly study groups could attract a wider audience, which benefited by hearing the texts read and discussed.

Similar "convenient" and "reasonable" societies existed in the cities. Before official academies came into being, people came together over books, which they lent to one another, discussed, examined, and read aloud. In 1700 a *petite académie* was founded in Lyons. Seven scholars and friends met in the home of one of their number: "The place where we hold our meetings is the study of one of our academicians. There we gather amid five or six thousand volumes, which constitute a library as choice as it is large. That alone provides ready and agreeable assistance to our scholarly conferences" (letter from Brossette, one of the founders and an *avocat* at the court known as the *présidial*, to Boileau, 16 July 1700). Sometimes a friendly visit could lead to discussion of books. Laurent Dugas, pres-

Joshua Reynolds, *The Conversation*. Men gather in the presence of the written word. The library, a natural meeting place, was painted for Horace Walpole. He received the painting in commemoration of three friends who, during the 1750s, spent Christmas and Easter with him at Strawberry Hill: George Selwyn, with book in hand; Richard, second Count Edgcumbe, drawing; and George James Williams, who looks on. (Bristol, Museum and Art Gallery.)

ident of the Cour des monnaies and one of the seven "acade-micians," gives a number of examples of this in his correspondence. On 12 January 1719: "Yesterday in my study I spent a good part of the evening with Father de Vitry and Father Follard, regent of rhetoric. I gave them chocolate. We spoke of M. de Cambrai and we argued about literature. Father de Vitry wanted to look at the new edition of Saint Clement of Alexandria, which the bishop of Oxford has pub-lished and which I own, to see if the editor remarked upon passages he had noted." 27 March 1731: "Cheinet spent the evening and had supper with me. We read some letters of Cicero and complained about the ignorance of the public, by which I mean the want of taste on the part of our young people, who amuse themselves reading new and often frivo-lous or superficial books and neglect the great models that might teach them to think well." 23 March 1733: "M. de La Font, gentleman-in-waiting to the queen, arrived and told me that he thought I would enjoy hearing a reading of a new work by M. de Voltaire entitled *The Temple of Taste*. If I were agreeable, however, we would await the return of my son, who had gone that morning to Brignais and was expected at any moment. He arrived a half-hour later and took the role of reader. The reading lasted an hour and a half. My wife, who came in at seven o'clock, heard three-quarters of it." Thus, people listened to readings, read to each other, talked about books, and conversed in their libraries: all were common practices, which depended on the existence of readers who often read alone but who sometimes used books as the basis of social occasions.[46]

Travel provided another opportunity for reading. On 26 May 1668 Samuel Pepys returned from Cambridge to London: "Up by 4 a-clock; and by the time we were ready and had eat, we were called to the coach; where about 6 a-clock we set out, there being a man and two women of one company, ordinary people, and one lady alone that is tolerable hand-some, but mighty well spoken, whom I took great pleasure in talking to, and did get her to read aloud in a book she was reading in the coach, being the King's Meditations [the med-itations of Charles I prior to his execution]; and the boy and I to sing." Here, reading is a way of establishing a temporary and friendly bond between traveling companions who had not known each other previously. An anonymous, ephemeral community is bound together by reading, conversation, and song, helping make the journey more agreeable for all. "We

Daniel Nicolaus Chodowiecki, engraving of women reading. One listens, another does not. (Paris, Bibliothèque Nationale.)

dining all together and pretty merry," Pepys notes, recording the felicitous consequence of his initiatives.

Reading influenced privatization in several ways. It contributed to the emergence of a sense of self, as the reader scrutinized his own thoughts and emotions in solitude and secrecy. It was also a group activity, which made it possible "to avoid both the boredom of solitude and the crush of the multitude," as Fortin de La Hoguette put it in his treatise *On Conversation*. There are numerous eighteenth-century images of these small groups bound together by reading. In 1728 Jean-François de Troy painted *Reading Molière*. In a rococo salon, at 3:30 according to the clock, five women and two men, comfortably seated on low armchairs, listen to one of the company reading a bound book, which he holds in his hands. The door is closed and a screen has been opened to protect the little group, gathered in a circle around the reader, from the rest of the world.

A year earlier Marivaux had written for the stage a play

Jean-François de Troy, *Reading Molière*, 1728. Salon reading gathered a select company but did not fully absorb everyone's attention, as is evident from the glances exchanged or avoided, signs of desire and complicity. The spectator, stared at by two of the women, is forced to spy upon this little group. (Collection of the Marquise de Cholmondeley.)

Diderot wrote of this popular engraving of a painting by Jean-Baptiste Greuze: "There is no man of taste who does not own this print." The image of reading here is opposed point-by-point to that of de Troy's *Reading Molière*: a peasant family versus a society gathering, a folio Bible rather than an unbound book in small format, absorbed listeners (only the infant's attention wanders) as opposed to the roving thoughts of the socialites, and a scene closed in upon itself rather than open to the regard of the spectator. (Private collection.)

entitled *Love's Second Surprise*. One of the characters, Hortensius, is presented as a "pedant" who has been hired by the marquise to direct her reading and read to her: "Two weeks ago I took on a man to whom I have entrusted my library. I do not flatter myself that I will become a scholar, but I am eager to occupy my time. He reads me something every evening. Our readings are serious and reasonable. He establishes an order that instructs as it amuses me" (act 1, scene 7). But Hortensius' readings are not reserved for his mistress alone. The marquise invites her visitors, such as the chevalier in scene 8 of act 2: "Chevalier, you are master if you wish to remain, if my reading pleases you." In both the painting and the play, listening together by no means precludes private sentiments. De Troy suggests them through the play of glances: eyes meet, glances are averted, people avoid looking at one another. Marivaux has the chevalier react strongly against what he hears being read, which is a way of stating his incipient love for the ironic and flirtatious marquise.

Family Reading

Reading aloud was a way of structuring family life. Husband and wife read to each other. On 22 December 1667 Pepys's wife had taken to her bed: "After dinner, up to my wife again, and who is in great pain still with her tooth and cheek; and there, they gone, I spent the most of the afternoon and night reading and talking to bear her company, and so to supper and to bed." Three days later, on Christmas Day, she does the reading: "And all the afternoon at home, my wife reading to me the history of the Drummer, of Mr. Monpesson, which is a strange story of spirits, and worth reading indeed." Fathers and sons read to each other. Dugas of Lyons gives several examples: "I spent considerable time with my son reading Greek and some odes of Horace" (22 July 1718); "I read with my eldest son Cicero's *Treatise on Laws*, and with my second son I read Sallust" (14 September 1719); "At night I play chess with my son. We start by reading a good book, that is, a book of piety, for half an hour" (19 December 1732).

Sometimes the entire family gathered around the reader, especially when the family was Protestant and the book the Bible. Protestant books of domestic instruction often described such compulsory reading. Justus Menius' *Oeconomia Christiana* shows, on the title page of the 1554 Regensburg edition, a father reading to his wife and children on his right and his servants in another corner of the room. On the table we see a heavy Bible, another, smaller book (perhaps the *Oeconomia* itself), a pair of eyeglasses, and a sandglass.[47] Although such Bible-reading was not always practiced in Protestant families, it is attested in a number of places from sixteenth-century Switzerland (where Felix Platter remembered from his youth that "my father was in the habit, before we went to church, of reading the holy Bible and preaching from it") to eighteenth-century New England.

Popular Customs

Conviviality, family and domestic intimacy, and individual retirement were the three aspects of life in which books and reading played a major role—and not only for the educated elite. Among the lower classes too printed materials fulfilled a variety of functions, but those materials were seldom books. Those who could read well usually read aloud to others who read less well or not at all. This was true in the cities and in the fields, at work and at leisure, among strangers or fellow workers. Reading matter ranged from "books of portraiture," that is, collections of models and patterns used in sixteenth-century workshops, to placards posted on city walls, from religious texts (as in Swabia, where peasants gathered in the late eighteenth century to listen to the reading of the Bible) to mass-circulation books such as those in France's "Bibliothèque bleue." or Blue Library, which were read in family gatherings or by people who shared a common life, such as

Shortly after the French Revolution the editors of *La Feuille villageoise*, a new periodical intended to serve rural readers, used a 1777 drawing by Marillier to represent their plans to educate and civilize readers: "It seems to us that wealthy Landlords, well-to-do Farmers, patriotic Curés, and Physicians and Surgeons . . . will be able to make themselves more useful to their Fellow Citizens, the Peasants, by buying and reading them this paper . . . These public readings will form a new Community, and small rural Clubs will spread truths and social virtues." In the picture a prominent personage gives a reading after Sunday mass concerning a fundamental art—baking. (Paris, Bibliothèque Nationale.)

early eighteenth-century shepherds in Lorraine, according to the testimony of Jamerey-Duval.[48]

In sixteenth- and seventeenth-century Spain, popular audiences gathered to hear a variety of works read aloud, novels of chivalry foremost among them. They were listened to by the common folk in the cities, according to Juan Arce de Otalora (1560): "In Seville they say that there are artisans who, on holidays and in the evening bring a book and read it on the *Gradas*," that is, in front of the cathedral.[49] Peasants also listened, at least in *Don Quixote*, according to the chapter cited earlier (part 1, chapter 32). In describing the novels of chivalry that he keeps in his inn, the innkeeper says: "As far as I can see, there is no better reading in the world. I myself have two or three of them along with some manuscripts, and they have been the very breath of life, not only to me, but to many others as well. For in harvest time the reapers gather here in

Ludolf de Jongh, *The Message*, 1657. A message is read aloud in a tavern by a professional, the town messenger or crier, who "with shouts and flourishes of trumpets" publicized official documents. The Dutch painter shows the figures, perhaps illiterate, in characteristic absorption, while treating the canvas in such a way as to close the painting in upon itself, without assuming the existence of a spectator. (Mainz, Mittelrheinisches Landesmuseum.)

In certain dioceses of southern France, including that of Lyons, it was part of the marriage ritual for the groom to give his bride a marriage charter along with the wedding ring. The charter contained, in calligraphy or print, the text of the wedding service, the names of the participants, and the date of the wedding and was signed by the curé. The iconography usually contained the four evangelists, frequently the Annunciation and the wedding of Mary, and more rarely the temptation of Eve. (Private collection.)

large numbers on feast days, and there are always some among them who can read. One of them will take a book in his hands and thirty or more of us will crowd around and listen to him with so much pleasure that we lose a thousand gray hairs."[50] Gathered to hear *Don Circongilio of Thrace* or *Felixmarte of Hircania*, the peasants and the innkeeper's family, including his daughters, never tire of listening: "We could go on listening day and night," says the master of the house. Other texts suitable for reading aloud included the *pliegos sueltos* or *pliegos de cordel*. Related by format (quarto volumes of two to sixteen sheets) and poetic form (generally octosyllabic, assonant *romances*), these plays were written to be read aloud. Their titles, always similar in structure, could be shouted out by those who sold them, usually blind hawkers who belonged to confraternities; the texts lent themselves to being spoken or sung to a public that related to the written word by way of the ear rather than the eye.

The common folk also had other access to written literature. Between 1500 and 1800 writing insinuated itself into the majority of households in the form of printed materials on which people set a high emotional value because they were associated with important moments in the life of the family or individual. In certain dioceses marriage charters were part of the marriage ritual; the husband handed the charter to the wife, and its text and images served as reminders of the ceremony. Certificates were distributed to pilgrims as proof that they had completed their journey and accomplished their religious duty. Confraternities gave certificates attesting to membership and fidelity to a heavenly protector. Whether displayed on a wall or kept in a safe place, such documents, which always included images along with the text, could be deciphered in a variety of ways. They played a fundamental role as aids to memory and self-affirmation, thus helping to constitute a private life that was at once intimate and on exhibit.

Some common folk used their ability to write to write about themselves. The practice may have been more widespread than is suggested by the few surviving autobiographies, such as Jacques-Louis Ménétra's *Journal of My Life* and the writings of Louis Simon.[51] Ménétra, a Parisian glazier, began writing his journal in 1802 or 1803, based on fragments he had been accumulating since 1764. Simon in 1809 began writing "the principal Events that happened in the Course of my life" in a "book" (that is, a handwritten journal) inherited twenty-one years earlier from an uncle by marriage. The book opens with the century-old accounts of the uncle's uncle, who had been a wine merchant at La Flèche.

From Reading to Writing

Ménétra and Simon had acquired the habit of writing long before beginning their memoirs. While touring France as a journeyman glazier, Ménétra used his writing skills for a variety of purposes, including keeping records for an organization of fellow journeymen known as the Devoir: "I was accepted as a companion of the Devoir, and my fellow members asked me to recopy the roll of what they call Maître Jacques or the Devoir, and I was named Parisien le Bienvenu" [companions called one another by secret names]. He wrote to his family in Paris, especially his grandmother, asking for financial assistance. He dealt with the correspondence and kept the books for the widows who hired him. And he acted as secretary for his comrades in a dispute with the intendant of Bordeaux over the drawing of lots for the militia: "They cast about for one of their number who could write. The Guyennois came looking for me, and I was the thirty-first companion [that is, he was added to the delegation of thirty chosen to negotiate with the authorities]. Thereafter I wrote the rules and counted up my fellow journeymen." Through frequent

The title page of Ménétra's *Memoirs*. (Paris, Historical Library of the City of Paris.)

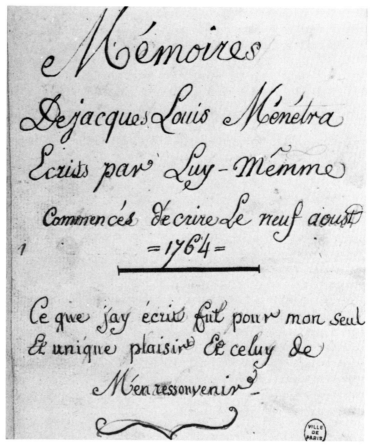

letters he nourished the hopes of the widow in Nîmes who expected that he would return to marry her when his tour of France was complete and who in the mean time treated him most generously.

Louis Simon, a clothmaker from the village of La Fontaine, was esteemed for his ability to write. He was called upon to keep the books of the fabric and the town government and to draft the parish's grievances against the government. For him, the French Revolution was time spent—and wasted—writing: "For I went three years without working because of the disturbances, and here they could only turn to me since I was the only one who knew how to write and who understood a little of affairs."

In writing their accounts of their lives, both men made perhaps unwitting use of books they had read in the past. Young Louis Simon came to know the books in the local

Gravestone. In highly literate colonial America, writing was found on objects of every kind, from "posy rings" given to a loved one to mourning rings worn in memory of the departed to tombstones, in this case that of Thomas Nichols, "who exchang'd worlds in the month of April 1765 / Aged almost 83 years." The words "Arise ye dead" express absolute confidence in the Last Judgment. (Wakefield, Massachusetts.)

priest's library as well as those (no doubt from the Blue Library) sold by a hawker who had returned to the area: "I spent my time enjoying the pleasure of playing instruments and reading all the books that I could obtain on ancient history, wars, geography, the lives of saints, the Old and New Testament, and other books sacred and profane. I also loved songs and psalms." His writing bears traces of this half-scholarly, half-popular background.

Ménétra mentions few books (only the Bible, the *Petit Albert* [a book of black magic], and the works of Rousseau), but his reading and knowledge of contemporary literary forms shaped the retelling of his life, part real and part imaginary. Erotic novels had provided him with a repertory of ribald plots and characters (the nun who violates her vows, the noblewoman whose lust is insatiable, the girl who succumbs against her will but to her great satisfaction, and so on). The theater, which he loved, had taught him how to arrange the players in his little dramas so as to give himself the leading role, as in his encounter with Rousseau. Stories borrowed from widely circulated books give relief to his more commonplace adventures. Though not cited in the *Journal*, these texts served as so many mirrors, or rather prisms, by means of which Ménétra observed at his own life and then recomposed it to suit his desires, creating an embellished, idealized version.

The two men were very different. Simon sought to recapture through writing his beloved wife, who had died five years earlier, whereas Ménétra gazed admiringly upon his own past and attempted to assert his own culture, reflected in his deliberate refusal to abide by the ordinary rules of punctuation and spelling. The writings of both show that ordinary folk were familiar with writing, the written word, and books.

J.-A. Larue, known as Mansion, *Bourgeois Interior*. (Nancy, Lorraine Historical Museum.)

ᴈ 2 ᴈ

Forms of Privatization

Jacques Revel
Orest Ranum
Jean-Louis Flandrin
Jacques Gélis
Madeleine Foisil
Jean Marie Goulemot

Introduction

by Roger Chartier

MANY innovations in architecture, literature, and emotional and physical life occurred between 1500 and 1800. As outlined by Philippe Ariès, the changes can be classed under six heads: manners, which promoted a new set of attitudes toward the body; self-knowledge, gained through private writing; solitude, prized not only for its ascetic value but as a kind of pleasure; friendship, cultivated in private; taste, valued as a means of self-presentation; and convenience, the result of improvements in daily living.

The contradictory relation between civility and intimacy is examined in this section. Prescriptions set forth by the many texts intended to govern social conduct are opposed, point by point, to the private passions and their physical and emotional consequences. Civility pertained to the space of communal existence, to the distinctive social life of the court and the salon, as well as to the domain of social ritual, whose norms apply to every individual regardless of status. By contrast, intimacy requires privacy, a space outside society that can provide solitude, secrecy, and silence. The garden, the bedroom (with its alcoves and recesses), the study, and the library filled the need, hiding what could not and should not be seen (care of the body, natural functions, the act of love) and offering a place for practices more than ever associated with isolation, such as prayer and reading.

The rules of civility, which governed the individual's behavior in society, established a protected zone around each individual. Prohibitions against physical contact became stricter as new social forms, particularly the court, established what Elias has called "the representation of rank by form," making the essence of the individual increasingly public and visible. People began to sleep alone. Physical contact, whether at play or in battle, was censured. Table manners no longer condoned eating from a common plate or with the fingers.

All of these things reflected a need for greater distance between one body and another, necessitated by the growing frequency of human contact and increased density of human relations. By contrast, intimacy—carnal or spiritual love or friendship—required proximity to another person's body, or at least an object capable of representing that body, of rendering it present even in its absence. From this need a new set of customs developed. Communion with another, so devoutly desired, was achieved by carrying an object that had once touched the beloved or preserving a memento of a departed loved one, or by contriving to sense the presence of God in one's own body. Certain behavior was prohibited in public but permitted, even required, by the proximity of loved ones; intimate gestures abolished absence, rendering present a body that could not be touched. This need, felt throughout the period dealt with in this book, may have grown stronger as the affections came to be concentrated on a few loved ones: the immediate family.

Civility and intimacy were opposed in another way. Civility was supposed to restrain the emotions, bridle the passions, dissimulate the impulses of heart and soul. Manners were rational, and rationality required that behavior toward another person take that person's rank and the desired effect into consideration. Manners could thus be used to create an image of oneself, to reveal only that identity by which one wished to be recognized. In solitude or in intimacy with another, this discipline ceased to be appropriate. Occasionally individuals were all but overwhelmed by the most immodest outpourings and the most extreme emotions. Civility did not stifle the passions entirely, as the words of the mystics or the occasional erotic confession reveals.

In courtly society all behavior was public and symbolic. Privatization undercut this public symbolism. It can be understood in terms of a shift from sumptuousness to luxury, to borrow a distinction first proposed by Jean Starobinski. In a monarchy the sumptuousness of the court is a kind of rhetoric, intended to make a point, to persuade others of the king's power: first the court, then the subjects. Monuments and rituals are emblems of public power—images that can be manipulated. Yet it was precisely in late-seventeenth-century France, where absolute monarchy attained its apogee, that this symbolic system began to crumble. Emancipated from the tyranny of the state, civil society conceived new aspirations, in which private expenditure, symbolized by aristocratic and bourgeois luxury, came to be associated with taste taken as a sign of distinction.

One chapter in this section deals with taste in food, for this was the area in which the primary modern sense of "good taste" emerged. A number of changes can be linked to the shift from sumptuousness to luxury. A centralized, theatrical manifestation of sovereign power gave way to a fragmented representation in which social differences were multiplied. Luxury emphasized the gulf between the happy few and the common herd. Display of wealth, including that of the prince, supplanted demonstration of power. At the same time good taste, evidence for which could be seen in refined manners, an aesthetic attitude toward life, and a keen interest in pleasures of the most delicate sort, justified the assertion of distinction, no longer through strict observance of the formalities of court etiquette but rather in private comfort and convenience. Small, well-appointed apartments, clothing and furniture designed for domestic intimacy, and a new culinary emphasis on the distinction between raw produce and cooked dishes are signs of a new way of life that no longer had to mark social distances on the public stage, satisfied as it was with a certitude of privately enjoyed and self-bestowed superiority.

In this way one of the many bonds linking forms of privatization with the new individual self-consciousness was constituted. Three manifestations of this new self-consciousness can be singled out: the emergence of a new image of the child as a unique person distinct from the family community, the prevalence of private writing in journals and diaries; and the change in the nature of literature, whose truth came to rest on exploration, exhibition, and exaltation of the self. To be sure, the history of private life should not be confused with the constitution of the individual as subject, whether in the philosophical, psychological, or political sense. But the new concept of the individual had an important influence on the definition of private space in the early modern era.

Away from the public eye people behaved in new ways. At home they played with their children; tenderness toward the young accompanied discovery of their individuality. In solitude writers recorded the details of daily life or explored the self by means of autobiography, confession, or fiction. These new habits of writing redrew the boundary between public and private. Literature based on self-dramatization offered the most private of secrets—about attachments, feelings, and even perversions—to the curiosity of readers, of whom it was hoped there would be a great many. Previously there had been a strict division between what could be written—for others, naturally—and what could not, a division based on the distinction between the universal, subject to public judgment, and the particular, which was suitable only for the author's eyes. Now the self was set up as sole guarantor of the text's veracity, and it became permissible to publicize in literature that which had to be concealed in society. As private space expanded, thanks to the triumph of intimacy over civility and of luxury over sumptuousness, the most innovative literature made the private world the primary object of its most public pronouncements, as if the definition of a sphere of existence not subject to the law of the prince or the gaze of others made intrusion legitimate and public confession possible.

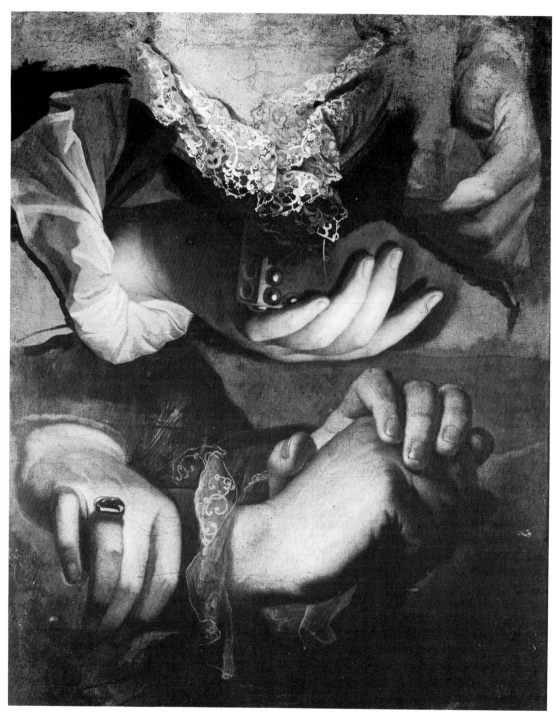

Study of Hands, 18th century. "Alphabets of the fingers and grammars of gesture": the iconography of the hand in the early modern era conveyed a complex characterology. The code was twofold: hands were expressive, but they also betrayed the dispositions of the soul. (Montpellier, Fabre Museum.)

The Uses of Civility

Jacques Revel

WHAT of the hands? We beg, we promise, call, dismiss, threaten, pray, entreat, deny, refuse, question, admire, count, confess, repent, fear, blush, doubt, instruct, command, incite, encourage, swear, testify, accuse, condemn, absolve, insult, despise, defy, vex, flatter, applaud, bless, humiliate, mock, reconcile, commend, exalt, entertain, rejoice, complain, grieve, mope, despair, wonder, exclaim, are silent, and what not?" Montaigne (*Essays* 2:12, Frame translation) was surely not the first to recognize that there is "no movement that does not speak both a language intelligible without instruction and a public language." Yet he does so at the end of a century that had passionately debated the nature and significance of nonverbal languages, particularly body language. His contemporaries were also interested in the function of such languages: movements of the body and face, bearing, and dress were taken as psychological and social signs, from which a vocabulary of recognition was created.

Montaigne was at odds with his contemporaries, however, in his praise for a language intelligible "without instruction." The sixteenth century was a time of intense effort to control social intercourse through rules of civility. Society insisted that a person's gestures be intelligible to others. Behavior was judged by the group. The rules of civility were in one sense a technique for limiting or even negating private life. The historian's task is to understand how, as manners changed over the course of three centuries, the boundary of privacy shifted.

There are two contradictory aspects to the evolution of manners in the period between 1500 and 1800. On the one hand, social control was intensified. Public behavior was subjected to strict regulation through education and various physical and spiritual disciplines. On the other hand, extracommunal refuges proliferated, the family foremost among them. Over the long run these two developments profoundly altered social experience.[1] Summarized in this way, the story is admirably simple, but unfortunately it takes for granted the dichotomy between public and private, which is precisely what I want to explain. A half-century ago Norbert Elias proposed looking at social and behavioral transformations as part of one social process.[2] By stressing discipline and the reproduction of social norms, his analysis restores unity to history. The rules of behavior became increasingly effective as they were internalized by individuals. Social constraints thus became subject to personal and private manipulation.

One way of evaluating Elias' interpretation is to turn to the literature of civility. The evidence is at best ambiguous. Social behavior is indeed minutely codified in the manuals of civility, but like all normative sources these raise a fundamental issue. To what extent were the rules they prescribe actually followed? It is possible to give at least a partial answer to this question. At times we can compare the prescription with the reality. Social representations, moreover, are no less "real" than their observable consequences. Treatises on civility were written for pedagogical purposes. All prescribed proper manners, but in a variety of ways that depended on the importance attached to rules, the intended audience, and the nature of the training suggested. By reading between the lines of the texts, we may be able to identify the audiences to which they were addressed and the private uses of manners which they proposed.

Erasmus: A Social Transparency

Changes in social behavior and imagery occur slowly and often in diffuse and contradictory fashion. We can rarely assign a precise date to a particular change or innovation. In the history of manners, however, one event does stand out, for the entire literature of civility derives from a single work, which was invoked as an authority if not mercilessly pillaged and deformed by subsequent writers. Erasmus' *Manners for Children (De civilitate morum puerilium)*, first published at Basel in 1530, met with enormous success.[3] Not only did this brief and didactic Latin treatise reformulate the very notion of civility; it set the tone for the whole "literature of manners" for the next three centuries.

At first glance there is nothing very impressive about the book. It was considered one of Erasmus' minor works, and Guillaume Budé reproached the elderly humanist for squandering his remaining powers and compromising his reputation with a "trivial book." It is a manual of a few dozen pages, in which Erasmus collects and puts into rough order observations and advice to children concerning the most important situations they are likely to meet in society. It discusses public demeanor and behavior in church, at table, in meetings, while gambling, and in going to bed. The same basic list can be found, with occasional additions, in the innumerable later treatises the book inspired. Yet Erasmus never intended to be original. He was in fact continuing an ancient tradition, knowledge of which was widely shared. He relied first of all on a vast classical literature on education and physiognomy, ranging from Aristotle to Cicero, from Plutarch to Quintilian. He knew something of the abundant medieval writing on these subjects, which since the twelfth century had attempted to regulate behavior. The medieval texts are diverse in origin and nature: anthologies for the instruction of monks, mirrors of princes, treatises on courtesy, advice to the young. Each type of work was addressed to a fairly specific audience, the size of which varied considerably. Yet works of different types borrowed from one other to such a degree that eventually a consensus was achieved. In addition to these scholarly and semischolarly sources, Erasmus did not disdain to incorporate folk wisdom into his text: proverbs, maxims, and fables, which he saw as a source of lost wisdom, of simple truths unaffected by changing fashions.

Thus, Erasmus' book was a composite of disparate materials reworked over a period of centuries, all making the same point: that physical signs—gestures, mimicry, postures—express a person's inner state in an intelligible fashion, revealing the disposition of the soul. *Manners for Children* begins with these words: "If a child's natural goodness is to reveal itself everywhere (and it glows especially in the face), his gaze should be gentle, respectful, and decent. Wild eyes are a sign of violence; a fixed stare is a sign of effrontery; wandering, distracted eyes are a sign of madness. The glance should not be sidelong, which is a sign of cunning, of a person contemplating a wicked deed. The eyes must not be opened too wide, for this is the mark of an imbecile. To lower and blink the eyelids is a sign of frivolousness. To hold the eyes steady is the stamp of a lazy mind, and Socrates was reproached for it.

One of the first Latin editions of *De Civilitate morum puerilium*, printed in Antwerp in 1530, the same year as the first publication in Basel. This particular book was well-traveled; a handwritten note indicates that it was used much later by the Parisian Oratorians. (Paris, Bibliothèque Nationale.)

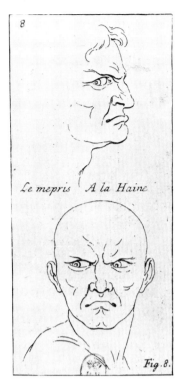

Le mepris   A la Haine

Fig. 8.

For Charles Le Brun and the physiognomic tradition that preceded him, the features of the face were an alphabet of the passions that everyone had to learn to read. He was fascinated by the similarities in the expressions of men and animals. (Paris, Bibliothèque Nationale.)

Piercing eyes signify irascibility. Too keen and eloquent eyes denote a lascivious temperament. It is important that the eyes signify a calm and respectfully affectionate spirit. It is no accident that the ancient sages said: the eyes are the seat of the soul." Psychological interpretation of the eyes is for us a commonplace. But every physical movement and gesture lends itself to similar interpretation, as does clothing. Gestures are signs and as such can be organized into a language, interpreted, and read as moral, psychological, and social markers. By such signs even the most intimate secrets are betrayed.

Conversely, if the body reveals a man's innermost secrets, it should be possible to influence and redress the dispositions of the soul by regulating the visible outward signs. Hence a literature came into being whose purpose was to define what was legitimate and to proscribe what was improper or wicked. The inner man was viewed solely as an object to be manipulated, to be brought into conformity with a model based on the notion of a happy medium, a rejection of all excess.

This view was widely shared, but Erasmus' treatise was innovative in three crucial ways. First, it was addressed to children, whereas previous texts generally purported to instruct both young people and adults. Along with piety, ethics, and the humanities, manners thus became part of the basic curriculum. The earlier in life lessons in civility were taught, the more effective they would presumably be, and humanists placed boundless confidence in such teaching. Embodying the simplicity and innocence of the gospel, the child not yet perverted by social life was held to be ripe for learning. He was also considered transparent, incapable of hiding any aspect of his being.

Second, *Morals for Children* was addressed to all children, without distinction. Late-medieval texts such as John Russel's *Book of Nature*, the *Babies Book*, the German *Hof-* and *Tischzuchten*, or the French books of courtesy and table manners were intended exclusively to teach the rudiments of aristocratic life to young members of the elite (and occasionally to their elders). True, Hugh of Saint-Victor's *Instructions for Novices* (twelfth century) did propose a "discipline," a model of behavior, to a wider class of people, namely, aspiring monks. But they were supposed to set an example for the rest of society, an example that most people lacked the means to emulate.[4] Admittedly, Erasmus' treatise was dedicated to a "child of great promise," the youngest offspring of a noble family that had long been the great humanist's protector. But the book was addressed to everyone: "It is shameful for the well-born not to have manners appropriate to their noble extraction. Those whom fortune has made plebeians, humble folk, or even peasants must strive even harder to compensate by means of good manners for what chance has denied them in the way of advantages. No one chooses his country or his father. Everyone can acquire virtues and manners."

Third, *Manners for Children* was innovative in that it aimed to teach a code of manners valid for everyone. Although Erasmus worked with traditional material (from which he occasionally distanced himself through ironic variation), he used it in a highly nontraditional way. Previously, the practices of a particular group or milieu had been held up as norms. By contrast, Erasmus sought to use a common code of manners as a basis for establishing social transparency, which he considered a necessary precondition for broader social intercourse. He did not often insist that particular forms of behavior were necessary. Rather, he was critical of any physical gesture (or habit of language) whose likely effect would be to make society opaque by inhibiting the free circulation of signs. He proscribed any gesture or posture that debased man to the level of the animals: a horselike laugh, a nasal voice reminiscent of the elephant, or a lopsided carriage like that of a stork. He censured anything likely to create confusion (between the sexes especially) or permit indiscreet expression of individual passions. But the primary target of his criticism was behavior typical of a particular group: a trade, a nation, or a social class.

G. B. della Porta, *Human Physiognomy, "Valde magni oculi"* (1586). To control one's expression, gestures, and attitudes was to affirm one's humanity against all that threatened it, latent animality above all. (Paris, Bibliothèque Nationale.)

From this point of view, the behavior of aristocrats was no better than that of common folk, although the aristocracy was granted greater collective license: "For princes everything is proper. We want to shape the child." True civility, whose sole purpose was to bring men closer together, meant ridding oneself of all idiosyncratic gestures and using only those recognized and accepted by the majority of people.

Contrary to what is often said, the novelty of Erasmus' treatise did not lie in the supposed shrewdness of its psychological and sociological observation. The author was largely content to repeat age-old commonplaces; he stated as his one principle that the child is naturally good. The work was innovative because it attempted to base social relations on a code of behavior learned by all. Erasmus was interested not so much in creating a science of the inner life as he was in fostering new social attitudes based on conscious efforts to transform the self and its relations to others. His last word is a plea on behalf of tolerance: "The most important rule of civility is this, that irreproachable as one may be, one must be ready to excuse the infractions of others . . . The rules we have just transcribed are not so essential that one cannot be a decent man without them." The goal is neither to bare the secret inner life nor to constrain the soul, but to prepare children for a better life.

Morals for Children became a best-seller by sixteenth-century standards. It was promptly reprinted in Basel, Paris, and Antwerp and a little later in Frankfurt, Leipzig, and Cracow. New editions adapted Erasmus' text in a relatively free manner: the humanist Gisbertus Longolius published an annotated edition in Cologne in 1531; Hadamarius recast the work in the form of questions and answers in 1537; and selected excerpts were published at various times. In each instance the book was recast so as to reach an audience that was suspected of being somehow different from the others. Translations came quickly: a German version appeared in 1531, an English-Latin bilingual edition in 1532, French and Czech versions in 1537, and a Dutch version in 1546. All in all, there were at least eighty editions and fourteen translations; by 1600 several tens of thousands of copies had been printed and distributed, for the most part in northern Europe, with an exceptionally high concentration in northern France, the Low Countries, and the Rhineland.[5]

That a humble manual, a peripheral product of the humanist renaissance, should have enjoyed such astonishing suc-

A French translation by Pierre Saliat (done in 1537) of Erasmus' book (published in Lyons in 1544). This elegant pocketbook edition was obviously not intended for children only. (Paris, Bibliothèque Nationale.)

cess is rather puzzling. Norbert Elias has proposed a convincing explanation: that Erasmus' book was not his alone but a collective work written in response to a need whose importance the success of the book reveals. The beginning of the modern era, Elias argues, was a moment of change and uncertainty between two ages of social glaciation. The unity of Catholicism had broken down, and the rigid hierarchies of the Middle Ages had suffered profound damage as courtly and chivalric society was called into question, but absolutism had not yet established its dominion. This was a period of social and cultural realignment. Social groups were more diverse than ever before, and relations among them more complex. Changing societies required a new common language and common points of reference. Even more than his specific teachings, Erasmus' project responded to these needs and gave them form.

Interest in manners survived well beyond this transition period. Erasmus' book became common property from the moment it was published. It was very quickly adapted for a variety of uses and purposes, for the most part before 1550, and its influence continued to be felt until the middle of the nineteenth century.

Manners for All

Although the book had been written from a humanist standpoint, it was quickly adopted by Lutheran and Calvinist reformers, as can be seen from the geography of its success: the book triumphed wherever the Reformation had succeeded or caused deep turmoil. This is not really surprising—although Erasmus had carefully steered a middle course between the two camps of Christianity—because the education of children was a central problem for the reformers. As Pastor Veit Dietrich of Nuremberg put it: "Is there anything on earth more precious, more dear, or more lovable than a pious, disciplined, obedient child ready to learn?"[6] This concern with education stemmed from two convictions. The first, diametrically opposed to Erasmus' belief, was that the child, like every other creature, is wicked, born with a propensity for evil. Only grace can save it, but a strict education can at least lay the groundwork for salvation and temporarily restrain the child's evil instincts and alarming spontaneity. The second conviction was more empirical: that, however sinful, children would grow up to be adults and would have to live together. Hence religious concern took on a political aspect. In most places

Cornelis de Vos, *Family*. Erasmus relied on the family to educate its children, but the future of civility lay in the schools. (Antwerp Museum.)

where the Reformation succeeded, schools were subjected to close supervision by the lay and ecclesiastical authorities, who examined rules, educational programs, and schedules.

Lessons in civility played a central role in this authoritarian program of education and discipline. The soul was disciplined by controlling the body, and all children were taught the same rules of social behavior. Children were trained to monitor their use of time, their occupations, and their attitudes. Five years before Erasmus, Otto Brunfels, a monk who had become a Protestant and been put in charge of the schools of Strasbourg, published *On the Discipline and Instruction of Children*, a treatise that, significantly, was published together with *Manners for Children* in several Protestant editions. The text sets forth in incredible detail the rules that were supposed to govern not only the child's religious exercise and schoolwork but his every action from morning till night.

The teaching of manners increasingly became the province of the schools. This was not the original intention. Erasmus favored education at home by the family or, failing that, by a carefully chosen tutor. At home the child could find examples of proper behavior: "If he does something inappropriate at table, he is chastised and thereupon learns to follow the example that is set for him. Taken to church, he learns to kneel down, to join his little hands, to remove his hat, and to assume the proper posture for prayer." Like the ancients, Erasmus was convinced that good manners were best learned by imitation, a social talent in which small children excelled. But Protestant pedagogues took a much more pessimistic view. None of them abandoned the idea that the family, under the authority of the father, was the place where a certain kind of education took place, but that by itself was no longer enough. Discipline was also needed, and the proper kind of discipline could be found only in the schools. More and more, instruction in civility was dispensed by the schools for civic as well as religious purposes.

Such instruction was destined primarily for children between the ages of seven (the "age of reason") and twelve (when puberty began), who were also taught reading, writing, and sometimes arithmetic. Throughout the sixteenth century school regulations, almost maniacal in their detail, prescribed lessons in civility for students in Germany from the Rhine to the Baltic as well as in England and the Netherlands; the Estates of Holland made such instruction compulsory in 1625, and it remained so throughout the seventeenth century.[7]

Learning the rules of civility was associated with the basic physical discipline of learning to write. (Paris, Bibliothèque Nationale.)

The manual of civility quickly became a manual of general knowledge and behavior. In this one we find a Gothic alphabet similar to 16th-century French handwriting. Manuals of civility would continue to be printed in this hard-to-read font down to the middle of the 19th century. (Paris, Bibliothèque Nationale.)

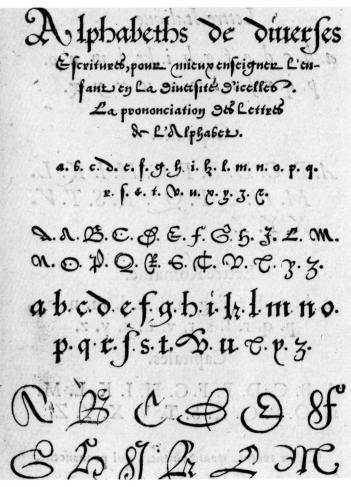

In addition to these decisions by the public authorities, there are many signs that treatises on civility became an essential element of elementary education in northern Europe. (This is not to say that they were not also used elsewhere. The Jesuits employed such treatises in their college at Cologne in 1574, and in 1578 François Hemme, professor at the capitulary school of Courtrai, produced a verse version of Erasmus' *Manners* which Nicolas Mercier, himself a teacher at the college of Navarre, republished in 1657 together with his own *De officiis scholasticorum*. It also inspired many seminary regulations.)

In smaller schools, treatises on civility were the culmination of the curriculum. After learning the alphabet and numbers, students were taught to read first Latin and then the vulgar tongue. After mastering printed materials, they were taught the art of deciphering manuscripts. After 1560 books on civility were increasingly printed in a new style invented by printers first in Lyons and then in Paris and based on the cursive script of the time.[8] Apart from their actual content, they were therefore convenient texts for teaching pupils how to read handwritten manuscripts.

The Counter-Reformation proposed a curriculum for the education of young girls that included lessons in civility. (Paris, Bibliothèque Nationale.)

So successful were the civility manuals as textbooks that by the final third of the sixteenth century their influence had spread beyond the confines of the Protestant world. As early as 1550 the University of Louvain recommended that such works be read, and the suspicions that surrounded Erasmus' text (often "corrected," it is true, by Protestant adaptors) were quickly dissipated. Instruction in manners became a part of the vast enterprise of Catholic Reformation. A telling sign is the use of a treatise on civility, now called *Instruction in Christian Manners and Modesty*, in the girls' schools that Pierre Fourier established in Lorraine in the early seventeenth century.[9] The change in title was not without significance. The reforming saint was careful to limit the aims of instruction. Mistresses "shall . . . take account of the reasonable desires and wishes of the father and mother and will refrain from including anything that is proper and peculiar to the religious life."

Such prudence did not last. In the final third of the century, Charles Démia and later the Christian Brothers (founded in 1679 by Jean-Baptiste de La Salle) organized charity schools in Lyons, based on the Erasmian model but authoritarian in their structure, intended for poor urban children. Children were not only taught manners but also kept under close surveillance. In 1703 La Salle published a weighty tome on *Rules of Propriety and Christian Civility*, which also enjoyed an impressive success. (At least 126 editions had been published by 1875.[10]) This was the culmination of a lengthy process, which for a century and a half had made the teaching of manners increasingly a matter for the schools.

These developments had important consequences. Erasmus' book had aimed primarily to make children aware of the need for a common code of social behavior, but in other respects it was by no means prescriptive, relying instead on lessons taught by the family on the virtues of imitation. But the first adaptations of the book show that a need for more disciplined instruction was felt. Responding to this, Hadamarius recast the book in the form of questions and answers, others rewrote it in verse, and Evaldus Gallus drew from it a set of authoritarian precepts (*Leges morales*, 1536). By the 1530s *Manners for Children* had been incorporated into Protestant texts which made no distinction between instruction in reading, morals, and religious indoctrination.[11] An example is the rough translation by the Protestant Claude Hours de Calviac entitled *Civil Decency for Children, With Lessons in Reading, Pronunciation, and Writing* (1559). The text began to incorporate alphabets and summaries of the rules of punctuation and spelling. It became nothing less than a textbook.

Two consequences flowed from this. First, there was a change in the way good manners were learned. Erasmus' book was designed to make the child aware of what his physical gestures revealed about his inner disposition; the real instruction took place at home, in the family. As the text evolved, however, so too did the practices for which it provided the rationale. The text acquired a value of its own. Many widely used seventeenth- and eighteenth-century textbooks of manners address the reader personally. The text had to be learned by heart, through dialogue like a catechism, or certain maxims had to be memorized regardless of the child's actual experience. Before long, the child's entire training in control of his physical gestures was obtained in school, where it was associated with arithmetic, writing, and prayer as part of a hierarchical program of education. The teacher read, the pupils repeated after him with their eyes on the book, and then they wrote down what they had read. Manners were learned as part of a lengthy educational process based on repetition and obedience. Instruction took place in a group, and teachers soon learned to make use of the possibilities of mutual surveillance

Dutch school, 18th century, and G. F. Cipper, known as Todeschini, *The Village Schoolteacher*. At school rules were inculcated by means of repeated exercises. The child listened to the teacher, repeated after him, wrote down the lesson, and recited it back.

offered by the classroom. The active invention of a new form of social life had given way to a coercive conformism.

Furthermore, as civility became a central element in the scholastic curriculum, its connections with the specific historical circumstances in which it had emerged as a subject were severed; it became a part of an enduring educational model. This was a period during which the school curriculum was a composite of disparate elements, particularly in smaller schools; civility, however, remained a central item well into the nineteenth century.[12] Textbooks, it is true, went through several metamorphoses. Still, given the wholesale social transformations that took place in the interim, the endurance of the original formula is impressive. In 1863 the Congregation of the Mission reprinted, in Latin, the *Rules of Civil and Christian Propriety*, first published in 1667.[13] This pedagogical conservatism was common to both Protestant and Catholic schools. In 1833 the Guizot Commission discovered that *Manners for Children* remained a basic text in French schools. Twenty years later school inspectors noted that it was still in use, and as late as 1882, Ferdinand Buisson's *Dictionary of Pedagogy*, a paean to the glory of the new French school system, circumspectly noted that certain of its rules "have remained popular."

This endurance of more than three centuries is puzzling. One reason for it was the very inflexibility of a pedagogical and cultural model that quickly achieved widespread dominance. Pierre Saliat, who was the first to translate Erasmus' treatise into French, was proud to announce in 1537 that "the French nation is second to none, and indeed surpasses all, in decency, countenance, gestures, and mores, and, in short, in all manner of gracious, human, and civil action and speech, which it seems by nature to possess." Similarly, seventeenth- and eighteenth-century texts referred to "the civility that is practiced in France." In fact, however, the rules remained the same in all countries, variations on an Erasmian theme.

Another reason for the endurance of the model was the invention of a new kind of book, small in size and low in price, which offered readers access to the same elementary wisdom. Erasmus' success was made possible by the extraordinary flourishing of the publishing industry in the Age of Humanism. His successors also benefited, and when the bookseller Richard Breton died in 1571 his estate was found to include 1,600 copies of Calviac's adaptation of Erasmus' book. When *Manners for Children* was included in the Blue Library, however, the scope of operations was dramatically increased.

The first edition published by Girardon of Troyes in 1600

was followed by several others in the second half of the seventeenth century. In the eighteenth and nineteenth centuries adaptations of Erasmus were joined by new editions, abridged and unabridged, of Jean-Baptiste de La Salle's *Rules*. In northern France, Normandy, the Loire Valley, and Flanders, publishers followed Girardon's lead, producing not tens but thousands of copies.[14] These books copied one another including even textual errors, and no canonical version was ever established. Most included lessons on manners, moral maxims (with Pibrac's *Quatrains* frequently added to the treatise on civility after the Oudot edition of 1649), reading and spelling exercises, and sometimes even "Pythagorean tables" to teach the rudiments of calculation, or a list of homonyms to help students distinguish between words that sound alike. The titles stressed the diverse resources offered by each text. An edition published by the widow Garnier of Troyes in 1714 bore this title: *Civil Decency for the Instruction of Children, in which is included at the beginning a way of learning to read, pronounce, and write properly; newly revised, and supplemented at the end by a very fine Treatise for learning how to Spell. Prepared by a Missionary. Together, fine Precepts and lessons for teaching the Young how to behave properly in all sorts of Company.* All this in eighty pages and a small format.

Abbé Morvan de Bellegarde,
The Perfect Education, 1713.
(Paris, Bibliothèque Nationale.)

We sense that in these mass-circulation editions the nature of civility has undergone a change, for the books are aimed at an audience outside the schools. Did not the very official Dictionary of the Academy record at the end of the seventeenth century that "one says proverbially of a man who fails to perform the most common duties that he has not read *Manners for Children?*" Aimed at the masses in all their diversity, the textbook became a compendium of knowledge of both a rudimentary and more individualized kind. Mme de Maintenon recalled having learned Pibrac's *Quatrains* when she was a young girl. The young bourgeois who proudly wrote on the first page of his text that "this book belongs to X" obviously came from a different milieu from the child who clumsily attempted to sign his name on the cover. For many if not most buyers, the treatise on manners, bought for little money but hard to read with its ancient and worn characters, served as a ready home reference, an encyclopedia of everything one needed to know in order to live in society. When it comes to cultural goods, possession is often tantamount to ownership. People acquired knowledge of manners well past childhood and outside the classroom in ways that we can only guess at.

Intimacy and Secrecy

Montaigne writes: "One French gentleman always used to blow his nose in his hand, a thing very repugnant to our practice. Defending his action against this reproach (and he was famous for his original remarks), he asked me what privilege this dirty excrement had that we should prepare a fine delicate piece of linen to receive it, and then, what is more, wrap it up and carry it carefully on us . . . I found that what he said was not entirely without reason; and habit had led me not to perceive the strangeness of this action, which nevertheless we find so hideous when it is told us about another country" (*Essays* 1:23, Frame translation, p. 80). Montaigne's amused irony is either too early or too late. Between 1500 and 1800 manners became stricter and more uniform. Elias was the first to show how group pressure influenced every individual in this direction and how individuals increasingly internalized social rules. Socialization was not a result of obedience to external constraint. The process was not complete until each individual sought, as so many ancient texts recommend, to become his own master, and thus came to regard social norms as a second nature, or, better yet, as the one true nature rediscovered at last.

Books of manners were intended to create conditions under which social intercourse would be easier and more in conformity with the heightened requirements of religion. Readers were exhorted to abide by ever more imperative and intrusive rules. Carrying the Erasmian logic to an extreme, they regarded every individual act as though it took place in public view. Yet the same textbooks invited each person to distinguish between what could be shown in public (what was "civil" and therefore good) and what was not fit to be seen even by the person himself. Individual space was thus invaded by communal controls, but at the same time a part of that space was hidden in silent shame; a part of the self, in other words, was repressed. It is misleading, however, to distinguish too sharply between these two aspects of the process, which were inextricably intertwined.

In one sense appearances triumphed. The traditional literature of manners had emphasized appearances for two reasons: self-presentation implied self-control, and it created the conditions necessary for social intercourse. But whereas the treatises on courtesy had regulated only certain kinds of public behavior, such as waiting on table or serving in the military, and whereas *Manners for Children* proceeded from the simple

Bronzino, *Eleonora of Toledo and Her Son*. A great lady and her son. The portrait reveals the importance of self-presentation: "Something grave and majestic." (Florence, Uffizi.)

principle that one should not do anything to offend or deceive others, later texts were quick to impose requirements on all aspects of daily life. Erasmus had little to recommend other than a happy medium, *aurea mediocritas*, equidistant from every form of excess and acceptable to the largest possible number of people. He prescribed nothing more than a "smiling and composed face, the sign of a clear conscience and an open mind," a "calm and frank" regard, a "gentle, serious voice," and, most important of all, discretion in all things. Almost two centuries later, La Salle devoted the entire first part of his book to "the modesty that one must exhibit in the carriage and bearing of the various parts of the body." The tone is set in the opening pages: "What contributes most to make a person look distinguished and set him apart by his modesty as a wise and well-behaved individual is when he holds all parts of his body as nature or custom has prescribed." Thus, La Salle's *Rules* turn modesty into a form of ostentation, with meticulous instructions for every pose: "Although there should be nothing studied about one's external appearance, one must learn to measure every action and attend to the carriage of every part of the body." Children were now expected to exhibit not Erasmian playfulness but "something grave and majestic," "a certain air of elevation and grandeur," "an air of gravity and sagacity."[15]

Eating in the company of others was one of the high points of the social ritual. A banquet was as disciplined as a ballet. (Paris, Bibliothèque Nationale.)

La Salle's recommendations did not end at generalities. Consider, for example, behavior at table, long a favorite of pedagogues, who since the mid-sixteenth century had counseled chiefly moderation, decency, and respect for one's fellow diners. Later texts reiterate these concerns, but the whole business is now complicated by a new attentiveness to the most minute details of gesture and bearing. Dining was but a pretext for a complex ritual and an occasion for social demonstration.[16] Table manners were delineated precisely. While Calviac, as late as 1559, could still be informed about the diversity of French table manners, his followers no longer had room for such ethnographic relativism, except to condemn it. Eating in company required self-control. A person had to forget about his body, with its indiscreet appetites, its functions, its noises, and its humors. But that alone was no longer enough. The diner had to learn how to conduct himself at table and how to consume his food. A meal became a kind of ballet, during which every gesture of every diner had to be controlled. The use of individual place settings and a variety of new utensils—plates, glasses, napkins, knives, forks—required training. Today all of this is so familiar as to seem natural. But it was only after the new rules had been learned that dining could fulfill its true function: to render visible the social relations among the diners.

Examples could be multiplied easily. All show that a high value was attached to whatever could be shown in public according to the rules. In a society undergoing reorganization, recomposing and reinforcing all its hierarchies, many things needed to be exposed to public view in order to be evaluated properly. Thus, manners were most essential in places where the social ritual was enacted in the open. Some were modest: the classroom, where the rules of the game were learned; the church; the street. One, however, enjoyed great prestige and in the second half of the seventeenth century came to function as a reference for all others: the court. Furthermore, these worldly models were bolstered by new religious requirements. Once manners had been for children and respectable men and women; now they applied to all Christians. Not that the duties of religion and the eminence of its practice had been ignored. But now these too had to conform to the rules of appearance. The pious Courtin, whose motives are scarcely open to suspicion, made this clear in an astonishing passage (1671): "If one were unfortunate enough to forget or neglect to kneel before God because of want of devotion, softness, or laziness, one must do it anyway for the sake of propriety and because in such a place one may encounter people of quality."[17] What matters is first of all what can be seen.

By the same logic, whatever was removed from the public eye, whether deliberately or not, tended to be seen as uncivil. Erasmus advised his pupil to avoid laughing in society for no apparent reason. "Nevertheless, it can happen. Politeness then requires you to state the reason for your hilarity. If you cannot do so, you must think of some pretext, lest one of the company think that you are laughing at him." The rule is still good will toward others. By the early eighteenth century, however, La Salle is ready to condemn even the most innocent action if it suggests a flagging of attention to social obligation: "When seated, you must not use a stick or cane to write on the ground or to draw pictures. To do so indicates that you are a dreamer or an ill-bred individual." Perhaps he meant a dreamer, *hence* ill-bred: any sign of inner life had become suspect. Here again, the Christian reference is fundamental. Children and adults do not have to show themselves as they really are, in the name of some sort of sincerity. We

Arthur Devis, *Day of Rest at Dr. Clyton's School in Salford.* The stiff bodies, fixed stares, and frozen gestures are alien to our concept of rest and leisure, but they demonstrate perfect self-control that was never relaxed for a moment. (London, Christie's.)

have come a long way from the Erasmian requirement of transparency. Rather, individuals are required to show by their gestures that they conform to proprieties that are at once civil *and* Christian. Forbidden is "anything which shows that a person has no virtue and is not striving to dominate his passions and that his manners are wholly human and not at all in accordance with the spirit of Christianity."

Clearly the constraints of civility affected the body most strictly of all.[18] Was not the body the source of the most shameful passions as well as the "temple of the Holy Spirit"? Tirelessly the moralists insisted that the body be forgotten but that the divine presence within it be respected. Between these contradictory imperatives the rules of civility steered a difficult course: "Sin has made it necessary for us to wear clothing and to cover our bodies." Hence clothing had to conform to moral and religious norms, and nudity was identified with original

Franz Hals, *Balthasar Coymans.*
Sumptuously austere, clothing
was invested with a dual function. It hid the misery of the
body, whose obligatory cleanliness was symbolized by the
whiteness of collar and cuffs.
At the same time it was a sign
of social position. (Washington,
National Gallery of Art, Mellon Collection.)

sin. Yet clothing could also become an object of unreasonable
zeal, of immodest passion. In order to avoid veering from one
sin to the other, it was necessary to "show contempt for what
appears without," while taking account of the exigencies of
life in society. La Salle's *Rules* insist on an uncompromising
middle course. Outside the realm of behavior fit for public
display, however, they insist on a strict elision of the body
(which "popular" versions of the text would state in even
stronger terms throughout the eighteenth century).

   In some respects this evolution began much earlier. Erasmus stressed the special prudence required by "parts of the
body which natural modesty causes us to hide." Yet he made
an exception for the excretory functions: "To retain one's urine
is injurious to health. It is proper to let it flow away from the
company." He further recommends respecting the privacy of
those who are responding to the call of nature. Thirty years
later Calviac is more severe: "It is most decent in a young
child not to handle his shameful parts, even when necessity

requires it and he is alone, except with shame and reluctance, for this indicates great modesty and decency." Fifty years later, in 1613, Claude Hardy, who purports to be a "Parisian aged nine," proposed yet another lesson in his adaptation of Erasmus' book: "To refrain from urinating is harmful to health. But to withdraw from the company before making water is worthy of the shame required of a child." Here, at the end of the process, the moral judgment is totally incorporated into the physical experience. The bodily function is still seen as a base and repugnant act. But the threat of spontaneity and sensuality is now dealt with, in the case of a routine need, by enforcing an obligatory distance, by relegating the function to a neutral zone defined by a technology.

We saw this previously in the case of table manners; not surprisingly we encounter it again in connection with the child's bed. While sleeping, the child is admonished not to allow the sheets to suggest the shape of his body, and "when you get out of bed, you must not leave it uncovered and you must not place your nightcap on a chair or in any other place where it might be seen." As Elias has shown, the logic of civility could go so far as to eliminate certain forms of behavior altogether. The texts for a long time discussed ways of blowing one's nose in public without inconveniencing one's neighbors. La Salle established rules in the name of both hygiene and morals; finally, in a late-eighteenth-century version of his book, the gesture was simply omitted.

Contemporaries were sometimes aware of the establishment of a network of constraints on behavior. Courtin observed that "in the past it was permissible to spit on the ground in the presence of persons of quality, and it was enough to place one's foot on the spot. Now this is indecent. In the past, one could yawn as long as one did not speak while yawning. Now a person of quality would be shocked by this." He thus attributes the changes to the growing self-control of a social elite, and in this he was not wrong. Nevertheless, in the diffusion of this elite model, religion—the Reformation and the Counter-Reformation—played a decisive role by stressing that even a person's innermost thoughts were not hidden from the eye of God. Erasmus had reminded his pupil of the constant if benevolent presence of guardian angels. By La Salle's time surveillance had become so strict that a person could no longer relate directly even to his own body: "Propriety demands that in going to bed you hide your body from your own eyes and refrain from even the least glance." All intimacy

At a time when many physical expressions of emotion were proscribed, tears were tolerated to a remarkable degree. At the turn of the 19th century they became a sign of private emotion. (Paris, Bibliothèque Nationale.)

was radically denied. On the eve of the Enlightenment a whole range of practices was rendered furtive, clandestine, shameful. The body was protected by layers of silence and secrecy.

These extraordinarily complex changes call for a few additional observations. Although the overall trend of behavioral change between 1500 and 1800 is clear, the pace of change varied depending on the nature of the behavior. Bodily functions soon ceased to be a question of civility. Although most expressions of emotional spontaneity soon came under surveillance, some were tolerated by the community for a long time. Consider crying.[19] Throughout the eighteenth century tears were permissible in public—at the theater, say, or while reading *La Nouvelle Héloïse* with a companion. Not until the beginning of the nineteenth century did this sign of sensibility give way to doleful melancholy, of which Senancour was the

Even in the bath the body remained hidden. This bather averts her eyes from her bare ankle. (Paris, Bibliothèque Nationale.)

precursor. The meaning of tears had changed. They had been tolerated over a long period of time because they were a public sign by which members of the elite experienced and made visible the privileged sensibility that united them.

The changes in mores that occurred in this period cannot all be related to civility, as Vigarello's work on the history of cleanliness shows.[20] From the end of the Middle Ages to the middle of the eighteenth century the manuals of civility reveal that cleanliness had little to do with water and was largely unconcerned with the body, except for the hands and the face, the only parts that showed. Concern was focused on what was visible: clothing and above all linen, whose freshness at collar and wrists was the true index of cleanliness. This accords well with what has been said thus far about civility. But it is also related to an idea of the body according to which water was to be shunned as a dangerous agent because it could penetrate everywhere. Cleaning was therefore "dry." It was a matter of wiping and perfuming rather than washing. Whence the importance of body linen, which was not simply a sign of social conformity. In the 1740s, water—first hot, then cold— made a spectacular comeback, and no doubt its use became a mark of new social distinctions. But again this use was associated with a new image of the body that went beyond mere propriety. Hygiene rehabilitated the body and bestowed legitimacy upon the search for better ways to use its resources. The object first of medical and later of pedagogical interest, the body became the focus of new methods of social control. Even though body care was strictly regulated, it could not be fully socialized solely by manuals of etiquette; several levels of representation were involved, extending well beyond the realm of civility.

Much routine behavior in the seventeenth and eighteenth centuries could not be discussed. Linen touched the naked body and metonymically revealed its cleanliness to all. Its function was to cover the surface, yet it simultaneously revealed what it hid. It separated the outside from the inside. But the body itself was thereby made an object of autonomous investments. It was not talked about, it was excluded from the realm of etiquette, yet dealing with it on a daily basis required close attention, special techniques, and, ultimately, a new sensibility which in the eighteenth century made possible new ideas about washing and hygiene. "Rules created a space" within which a lengthy process unfolded, ultimately calling the rules themselves into question. The history of cleanliness suggests that we ought to look at repressed activities for signs that another kind of intimacy was developing.

Aristocratic Privileges: Innate versus Acquired

The Erasmian tradition of civility was based on two implicit assumptions: that good behavior can be taught, and that it is the same for everyone. From the late sixteenth century on, these principles were modified in various ways, especially the second. As social hierarchies were revised and more precisely codified, manuals of etiquette began to pay more attention to questions of status and the proper distance between people of different classes. This was particularly true of La Salle's *Rules of Propriety and Christian Civility*, which dwelt at length on the question of recognizing social signs and gestures expressive of social differences. Nevertheless, even La Salle believed that the same general principles were valid for all.

At about this time, another series of texts approached the same problem in an entirely different way. These derived not from the books of courtesy of the thirteenth to fifteenth centuries but from the new court literature that first flourished in Italy in the first sixty years of the sixteenth century, exemplified most notably by Baldassare Castiglione's *Courtier*.[21] Published in 1528, two years before *Manners for Children*, this work too met with impressive success. It was translated into all the languages of Europe and, like Erasmus' work, was adapted, altered, and plagiarized. Similar works subsequently enjoyed successes of their own, such as Giovanni della Casa's *Galateo* (1558) and Stefano Guazzo's *Civil Conversazione* (1574). Yet *The Courtier*, which for two centuries became what A. Quondam has called "the basic grammar of court society," offered its readers a very different model from that of Erasmus.

The book is cast in the form of a conversation among aristocrats at the court of the Duke of Urbino, who in a light tone discuss the rules and values of social life. Thus, it presents itself not as a textbook but as the free improvisation of an elite, which is immediately recognized as such and which has no need to burden itself with "any kind of order, rule, or distinction of precepts." Furthermore, in drawing a portrait of their society, the book's characters do not seek to identify a model against which conformity can be measured. The perfect courtier can be recognized by two sets of criteria. The first is external, based on a simple social calculus: among the criteria included are the favor of the prince, the success that

Castiglione's *Courtier*, the breviary of court literature. The original Italian edition dates from 1528, the first French translation from 1537. This 1585 edition is bilingual, indicating that in the late 16th century the courtier model was still seen as partly foreign. (Paris, Arsenal Library.)

The true courtier affected nonchalance, but a nonchalance which, better than obvious effort, reflected true self-control, alleged to be an innate gift. (Paris, Bibliothèque Nationale.)

accompanies such favor, and the esteem of peers. The second consists of criteria that cannot be described, only affirmed: grace, birth, and talent. It follows that the excellence of the courtier is not something that can be learned; rather, it is obvious in his every action. The true gentleman demonstrates his merit by refusing to do anything that might indicate that his qualities are the result of effort. Grace consists in "always exhibiting a certain contempt and nonchalance [*sprezzatura*] that hides what is artificial and shows what one does as though it came easily and almost without thinking about it . . . True art is that which seems artless, and no effort should be spared to hide it, because if it is discovered it takes away all credit and esteem."

Thus, the courtier model contrasts point by point with the Erasmian model and its dream of social transparency. For

Antoine Watteau, *Costumes.*
(Paris, Ecole des Beaux-Arts.)
Fragonard, *Reading.* (Private
collection.) Grace versus effort.
Elegance becomes an index of
election.

Castiglione and his successors the rules of social behavior are distinctive; adherence to those rules depends on the cooperation of a closed group, which has set itself up as the sole judge of perfection. The courtier is one who aims to create a social role for himself, who seeks to please by the number and quality of his talents (in conversation, arms, dancing, gambling, and ordinary social intercourse). This image alone matters, and all signs of the inner man, of tension and effort, must be repressed. The function of "honest dissimulation" is to indicate through gesture, bearing, and attitude that social life takes precedence over the inner life. Seeming becomes a way of being.

Courtly literature exerted considerable influence for a long period and in many different social and cultural contexts. In Italy, *Galateo*, which in so many ways was inspired by Castiglione, ultimately came to be read, and read widely, as a manual of etiquette, contrary to its own initial logic. In France it was quickly classed among the manuals of civility and published as such.[22] The doctrine of aristocratic privilege and the primacy of appearances was received and interpreted differently in different cultures.

The range of interpretations in France was wider, perhaps, than in any other country and sheds more light on the social issues raised by the attempt to establish a code of behavior.[23] The courtier model was initially adopted in aristocratic and society circles, where in the 1620s and 1630s a theory and practice of *honnêteté*—refined, proper social behavior—were elaborated. The ideal of honnêteté was established in opposition to the king's court, which was reproached for its crassness, ostentation, and excess; it emphasized restraint and decorum in the social life of a closed elite consisting of a few noble Paris houses, the most celebrated of which was the hôtel de Rambouillet. The court was a public place, highly hierarchical and increasingly under the king's thumb; his courtiers were professionals. By contrast, the hôtel de Rambouillet received an elite that chose its own members, or, more precisely, whose members recognized one another's right to belong. When M. de Saint-Chartres made known his wish to be received in 1637, Chapelain advised him to wait patiently as required by the rules of the game: "I shall be glad to arrange things so that they will learn what you are worth and have no less desire for you than you have for them." This was a private hôtel, a place of intimacy ruled by a woman and in which commerce with women played a major role in civilizing man-

ners. Ostentation was out of the question, and the ordinary rules of civility did not govern daily interchange. Members of the group wrote and above all talked to one another. Conversation was a sacred art, the forum in which the group developed its taste. *L'Astrée* was staged as well as read; other reading included the historical novels of La Calprenède and Mlle de Scudéry, which held up a mirror of this microsociety. Commentary on such works was living theater.

Increasingly the word honnêteté was used instead of civility to denote the embodiment of what was both an individual virtue and a social need. It was a virtue that could not be taught or learned outside the closed circles in which it was practiced by those who already distinguished themselves by possessing it. There was no way of codifying it in a treatise. It was simply the group's amorphous commentary on itself in conversation, in correspondence, in the margins of *Cléopatre* or the *Grand Cyrus*, commentary which was the sole arbiter by which the rules of the group were established. What rules were there other than the exercise of judgment, the only social form of intelligence? Like the heroes of the novels they read, the select crowd that frequented the great Parisian salons continually questioned the grounds for the rules of civility and for the pleasure they took in one another's company. Interminable discussions ended with amazed recognition of the ineffable nature of honnêteté: "That talent must be a gift of birth, since it cannot be acquired by art . . . Judgment guides it . . . There must also be I know not what turn to an expression that finally makes it agreeable." The circle of complicity was thus closed. A unique gift, honnêteté flourished only in private.

This model had no future, however. In the second half of the seventeenth century it was supplanted by the strictly regulated social life of Louis XIV's court. The groundwork for this triumph had been laid over a long period of time. After 1630 steps were taken to control the public behavior of the nobility through the use of royal agents.[24] The king viewed the repression of excess and institution of civil norms as ways of curbing the nobility's claim to a privileged moral and political position and of eliminating private allegiances. The court was the culmination of these efforts, a visible symbol of their enduring success.[25] Nobles were granted the visible privilege of social eminence, but at the price of unconditional surrender to the supreme authority: the king. The court was ruled by appearances. From top to bottom of the hierarchy, behavior

Appearance, created in the mirror. Court dress was governed by laws, by a strict hierarchy as well as a system of mutual recognition that one had to know how to use to advantage in every situation. (Paris, Bibliothèque Nationale.)

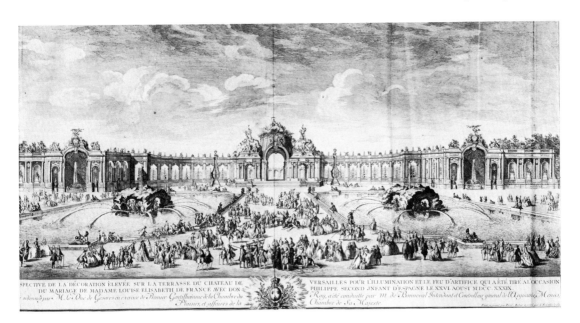

SPECTIVE DE LA DÉCORATION ÉLEVÉE SUR LA TERRASSE DU CHATEAU DE VERSAILLES POUR L'ILLUMINATION ET LE FEU D'ARTIFICE QUI A ÉTÉ TIRÉ AL OCCASION DU MARIAGE DE MADAME LOUISE ELISABETH DE FRANCE AVEC DON PHILIPPE SECOND INFANT D'ESPAGNE LE XXVI AOUST M.DCC. XXXIX

was governed by rank. Rules of etiquette spelled out this inegalitarian discipline in detail. At the same time, the rest of society contemplated the spectacle offered by the court, a model for all to admire and imitate.

The court, where everyone was watched by everyone else and by the nation at large. Appearance was the universal rule. (Paris, Bibliothèque Nationale.)

Court manners ceased to be a private affair and became eloquent signs of perfection, universally understood. "A king wants for nothing," wrote La Bruyère, "except the comforts of private life." This was even more true of his courtiers, whose every action was scrutinized by agents of the king and by one another. Appearances were everything. Etiquette, clothing, speech, and bearing were governed by the rules of rank. Perfume, powder, and wigs altered everyone's appearance to conform to the general expectation. The complete externalization of the rules of behavior is perhaps best illustrated by dancing. Through the codification of a rhetoric of gestures, this quintessential social art presented the individual body as part of a group, governed by its norms. No attempt was made to justify the superiority of the elite. Courtiers did not discuss the reasons for their election, as had been done in Parisian salons a generation earlier. They did not have to: they were perfect because they were at court and because the rules of the court required it.

Between the ethic of the salon and that of the court, between the belief in a birthright and the assumption of quality, lay a difficult middle ground. Absolutist society contained

At court dancing was perhaps the most polished and complex discipline of self-presentation. A social art, it showed the body only in order to demonstrate the dancer's control over it. (Paris, Bibliothèque Nationale.)

groups outside the court that aspired to emulate various models of perfection: lower-ranking nobles, provincials, and various elites who had linked their fate to that of the monarchy. Numerous treatises were published on such subjects as the "happiness of the court and true felicity of man" (Dampmartin, 1592), "the art of raising the nobility to virtue, knowledge, and other exercises appropriate to its condition" (Grenaille, 1642), and the "courtly spirit" (Bary, 1662). These works were addressed not to those who actually lived in proximity to the sovereign but to those who dreamed of gaining access. Among many other works, *The Courtier's Guide* (Nervèze, 1606) and the *Treatise on the Court* (Refuge, 1616) would have helped them find their bearings. Most of these texts drew on Italian works of the previous century, but the French court was part of a quite different system of social relations. If Castiglione's courtier felt that his talents were not duly recognized wherever he was, he could always move on to another court. In France, however, all power was concentrated in one place, and the court monopolized its symbols. Hence the apprenticeship required of the courtier was more stringent, because social success increasingly came to be identified with access to the king's graces. Aspiring courtiers differed from the "happy few" of the hôtel de Rambouillet, however, and had little in common with those already designated by royal election. Unlike the former, they had to believe that grace was not a birthright but something that could be learned. And unlike the latter, they had to invent qualities that would compensate for the deficiencies of their birth; while respecting the importance of social appearances, they somehow had to revive the notion of individual merit.

Consider two cases in point. In 1630, Nicolas Faret published *The Honnête Homme or the Art of Pleasing at Court*. The author himself was a living example of his preaching: son of a provincial artisan, he rose to a position of high responsibility in the king's entourage while also attaining a position of honor in literary society. As Sorel bitterly charged, he was a professional courtier. Accordingly, his treatise, dedicated to "Monsieur, the only brother of the King," was first of all a lengthy paean to the courtly ideal (at a time when its legitimacy was not yet firmly established). Anticipating Elias, Faret saw the court as the paradigm of a whole social order. He also saw it as a mirror of virtue and, relatedly, as a theater of individual success. Borrowing Castiglione's maxim, he restated it in more uncompromising form: success at court rewards the only merits that count. Where were those merits acquired? "I will say first that it seems to be very necessary that anyone who wishes to enter into the great commerce of the world be born a gentleman." Immediately, however, he corrects himself: "Not that I wish to banish those to whom nature has denied this good fortune. Virtue has no prescribed condition, and examples are fairly common of people who, though low-born, have raised themselves to heroic acts and grandeur." Thus it is *virtue* that equalizes opportunities unjustly distributed by birth. Virtue compensates for innate privilege, restores value to acquired graces, and bestows a role on the private individual: "Whoever feels that he possesses this treasure, the qualities that we have set forth, may boldly expose himself to the court and claim to be considered there with esteem and approbation."

Forty years later Antoine de Courtin's *New Treatise on Civility as Practiced in France among the Honnêtes Gens* (1671) espoused a similar view. But in the meantime things had changed. The court of Louis XIV had become the sole legitimate model and was viewed as such by a very much broader public. The very title of Courtin's *Treatise* reveals the change, for it treats as "civility" what had previously been the practices of an elite. Even the size and shape of the book resembled the size and shape of the widely read manuals of civility. And it enjoyed a similar success: by the middle of the eighteenth century, more than twenty French and foreign editions had been published. The fusion of two hitherto distinct literary genres makes it clear that Courtin's teaching was addressed not necessarily to readers who aspired to succeed at court but to people who wished to adopt courtly manners: young people of course, but also those who have not "the convenience or

Antoine de Courtin's *Treatise on Civility*, first published in 1671 and widely translated, proposed to teach its readers grace and to enable them to forget that their knowledge of the court was acquired rather than innate. (Paris, Bibliothèque Nationale.)

the means to come to Paris and to court to learn the fine points of politeness." With its mixed parentage, this text marks a crucial moment in the popularization of the courtly model.

Courtin forced his readers to enter into the rituals of a hierarchical society. The rules of etiquette vary according to a person's rank, prestige, and authority: "All conversation occurs either between equals, or from inferior to superior, or from superior to inferior." There are no absolute rules, and the first lesson is to recognize one's place in society and one's precise distance from people of every other rank. Courtin accepts without reservation the forms that the court held up as models to the rest of society. Yet he, and his readers along with him, probably believed that social preeminence was more than just a birthright. Like Faret, Courtin ascribed special roles to virtue and religion.[26] Discernment and manners were visible proof of a charitable attitude. What is more, Courtin was a teacher. His principle was that everything can be learned (which places him squarely in the tradition of Erasmus). Hence his book is filled with tension. As an optimistic educator, he places his confidence in the resources of the individual; yet he accepts the existing rigid hierarchy and teaches submission to its rules. Courtin walks a narrow line between contrary convictions, recommending that his readers convert the acquired into the innate, the lesson into the gift. When the earmarks of learning fade, nature can finally be revealed: "Civility must be entirely free, entirely natural, and not at all artificial or superstitious." Thus, the *Treatise* concludes by covering its own tracks.

Three years earlier Molière had painted a noticeably darker portrait of the contradiction between the rules and the individual in his play *Georges Dandin*, which was presented at court as well as in Paris in 1668. This farce is the story of an education in courtly manners gone awry.[27] The hero is a peasant who has made a lot of money and married the daughter of impoverished provincial nobles. But his social advancement is deceptive in two ways. The unfaithful Angélique makes a fool of him in his own home, while his hopes of being recognized as a true aristocrat are disappointed. His in-laws (who themselves conform to a rather old-fashioned code of conduct) refuse to accept his clumsy efforts to adapt (act 1, scene 3). Social distance can never be traversed: "Although you are our son-in-law, there is a great difference between you and us, and you must know yourself." Dandin consistently fails to live up to rules specifically designed to thwart his efforts. His failure makes the audience laugh, but it also destroys the inner man. Rejected by all the leading figures in the play, Dandin eventually ceases to believe what he sees and no longer knows what he is saying or who he is. The play ends with a fantasy of destruction which is at odds with its overall tone. In this case, the rules overwhelm the person, where the word "person" is intended in its most physical sense.

In the final third of the seventeenth century the values of civility were extended to an unprecedentedly broad and diversified portion of the French population, groups that differed considerably from one another. To accomplish this, the values were considerably altered. The purpose of the rules was changed, and the style of social life varied accordingly. The result was a family of different codes of manners: one for small schools, another for bourgeois *collèges*; one for the court, another for the city; one for the high aristocracy, another for the petty provincial nobility and the "bourgeois gentlemen." Yet despite the diversity of practices, the word "civility" continued to imply a common frame of reference. The impressive success of La Salle's *Rules* may be taken as a sign of this ambiguous triumph. This book, which set forth the canonical version of the rules of civility at the beginning of the eighteenth century, centrally embodied the contradiction between Erasmian universalism and social discrimination. Its success proves that a diverse audience was won over by its middle-of-the-road position.

The Revenge of Intimacy

Yet just when this compromise seemed secure, it began to be challenged in ways that led, after several decades, to a thorough reexamination of the whole question.[28] A process of disintegration was under way. The notion of civility began to fall apart, revealing underlying changes in society and in society's image of itself. One shrewd observer, Louis Sébastien Mercier, has nothing but contempt for "those foolish and ridiculous usages, so familiar to our ancestors, unhappy proselytes of a hampering and constraining custom." In his *Portrait of Paris* (2:62) he notes: "Only among the petty bourgeois are those tiresome ceremonies and pointless and eternal customs practiced, which they still take for *civilités*, and which are excessively tedious to people accustomed to society." At the end of the eighteenth century the old civility was seen as outmoded and formulaic.

At first this reversal may seem surprising. It was in the

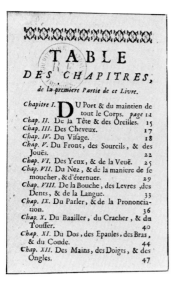

PREFACE.

C'EST une chose surprenante, que la plûpart des Chrétiens ne regardent la Bien-séance & la Civilité, que comme une qualité purement humaine & mondaine; & que ne pensant pas à élever leur esprit plus haut, ils ne la considerent pas comme une vertu, qui a raport à Dieu, au prochain, & à nous-mêmes; c'est ce qui fait bien connoître le peu de Christianisme qu'il y a dans le monde, & combien il y a peu de personnes qui vivent & se conduisent selon l'esprit de JESUS-CHRIST. C'est cependant ce seul esprit qui doit animer toutes nos actions, pour les rendre saintes, & agréables à Dieu; & c'est une obligation dont saint Paul nous avertit, en nous disant en la personne de premiers Chrétiens, que comme nous devons vivre par l'esprit de JESUS-CHRIST, nous devons aussi nous conduire en toutes choses par le même esprit.

Comme il n'y a aucune de nos actions, selon le même Apôtre, qui ne doive être sainte; il n'y en a aussi pas une qui ne doive

A ij

Initially intended for use by the pupils of the Christian Brothers, La Salle's text was widely used in the 18th and 19th centuries. It carried physical discipline to an extreme and made it a requirement of Christian morality as well as manners. (Paris, Bibliothèque Nationale.)

eighteenth century, and perhaps even more the first half of the nineteenth century, that the rules of civility enjoyed their widest social acceptance. Treatises on the subject were distributed in the remotest regions by printers specialized in mass circulation, and the rules remained more or less unchanged for a century and a half. What became of all those books? They were certainly used in the classroom, but that use probably became increasingly problematic. In the seventeenth century they were still used to teach handwriting, but as handwriting evolved toward simpler forms, closer to what we know today, the old "French art of the hand" became increasingly difficult to read, and there was less and less need for the ability to read it. At best, teachers continued to rely on the manuals as essential texts for teaching the rules of manners. They probably stopped reading pages that had become inaccessible to the majority. When Grimoux painted a young girl with a manual of civility in her hands (see color illustration in this book), was she really reading, or was she holding a badge of social conformity?[29] Whatever the answer may be, all signs are that the teaching of manners was becoming more remote from actual practice and increasingly old-fashioned. Reading the lessons required an effort at best, or mere lip-service to convention at worst. The old manners ceased to be regarded as "natural," at least by those who decided what natural meant.

The status of the civility concept was even more radically jeopardized by its very success. As we have seen, there was conflict over whether to define civility in terms of rules applicable to all or in terms of conformity with a model established by a small elite. By the late seventeenth century some of the elite concluded that the rules applied to too many people and began to distance themselves from a code that seemed likely to undermine their privileges. In 1693 F. de Callières, anxious to clarify the meaning of social distinctions, wrote *On the Good and Bad Use of Manners for Self-Expression. On Bourgeois Ways of Speaking; In What Respects They Differ from Those of the Court.* The treatise includes the advice that "*vous rendre des civilités* is a bourgeois way of speaking which must never be used under any circumstances." At almost the same time the abbé de Bellegarde, author of *Reflections on the Ridiculous and Ways to Avoid It* (1696), made this more general observation: "Bourgeois, provincials, and pedants are much given to flattery. They overwhelm people with their eternal compliments and embarrassing politeness. They encumber every doorway with interminable arguments about who shall enter last. The French have gradually ceased to pay heed to rules that seem inflexible." Here we are introduced to concentric circles of exclusion: foreigners are distinguished from Frenchmen, and commoners and provincials are distinguished from the aristocracy, which has rediscovered the advantage of being wellborn. Civility is a mark of vulgarity. In response to the danger of leveling through conformity to common rules, style—freedom to shape appearances independent of all authority—again becomes the arbiter of true propriety. Writing nearly a century later, Mercier has little to add. Himself a bourgeois, he is careful to note that it is only the "petty bourgeois" who lack familiarity with the ways of society. A few decades later only peasants continued to bear the unpardonable taint, still believing that the exterior equals the interior, that manners can be learned from books, and that correct behavior is the result of diligent effort. The cognoscenti sneer at these age-old delusions. Among them, other signs of distinction have taken hold.

Yet the fundamental crisis of confidence in civility cannot be explained simply by saying that broad acceptance of the rules of manners robbed them of value as social markers. The very values on which the whole enterprise of civilizing manners had been based were being questioned. One line of criticism was anthropological. What was a code of manners but one possible convention among many? What was the basis for belief in the correct gesture or for faith in a general semiology of behavior, unambiguous in its meaning and applicable to all? The most vigorous statement of this doubt comes of course from Montaigne: "Not only each country but each city has its particular forms of civility, and so has each occupation. I was brought up in this carefully enough in my youth, and have lived in good enough company, not to be ignorant of the laws of our French civility; I could run a school of it. I like to follow these laws, but not so timidly that my life would remain constrained" (*Essays* 1:13, Frame translation, p. 32). Thus, the Erasmian notion of civility is criticized on relativist grounds; eventually it was reduced to one system of manners among many.

The need to reinforce outward signs of social distinction now became more urgent. Courtin and later La Salle tried to preserve the idea of a general rule by detaching civility from its "purely human and worldly" aspects and reinterpreting it "as a virtue which pertains to God, to our neighbor, and to ourselves." Despite their immense success, they were waging

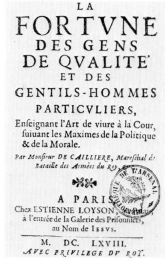

LA
FORTVNE
DES GENS
DE QVALITE'
ET DES
GENTILS-HOMMES
PARTICVLIERS,
Enseignant l'Art de viure à la Cour, suiuant les Maximes de la Politique & de la Morale.

Par Monsieur DE CAILLIERE, Mareschal de Bataille des Armées du Roy.

A PARIS,
Chez ESTIENNE LOYSON,
à l'entrée de la Galerie des Prisonniers, au Nom de IESVS.

M. DC. LXVIII.
AVEC PRIVILEGE DV ROY.

Appearance was challenged even as it was taking hold everywhere. What if it were nothing but falsehood, deception, vanity, or simply foolishness rather than the foundation of social intercourse? Too much civility was incompatible with civility. (Paris, Arsenal Library.)

"Ingenious lie," appearance was now denounced as artificial. Since it could be taken apart, it should be unmasked. (Paris, Library of Decorative Arts.)

a rear-guard action, for they addressed their teachings to the masses and therefore failed to reach the true elites, whose privilege it is to dictate proper behavior. In the French of the Age of Louis XIV civility became more or less synonymous with politeness. At best it was regarded as a strictly social exercise, a way of easing human intercourse. Listen to Mercier: "Without this ingenious falsehood, a circle would be an arena in which the petty and vile passions would appear with all their deformities." Frequently critics went further still. By the middle of the eighteenth century civility was seen as an impoverished form of politeness. Voltaire even drew a contrast between the two words in the dedication to *Zaire* (1736): "This politeness, unlike what is called civility, is not an arbitrary thing but a law of nature." Without going quite so far, the *Encyclopedia* limited the rules of civility to the most outward forms of social behavior, of interest only to "persons of inferior status."[30] In other words, because the rules applied to everyone, they lacked depth.

Another, more radical criticism denounced the deceptions of social parody. The sharpest expressions were heard just as the French elites exchanged real power for a mere semblance of power. At the height of the Fronde, after an attempt on the life of Condé, Retz gave this cynical assessment: "We were in conversation with one another, we paid each other *civilités*, and we were eight or ten times on the point of strangling one another." His contemporary Pascal denounced in darker terms the worldly vanities that subjected social life to so many evil illusions. Civility, he said, "must be accepted simply because it is a custom and not because it is reasonable or just." Although Pascal went further than anyone else in denouncing the falsehoods of this world, he was by no means alone. All the great seventeenth-century moralists, from La Rochefoucauld to Saint-Evremond, touched on the same theme, each in his own way. Even Courtin, that zealous propagandist for the new civility, was compelled to devote considerable space

Simplicity rediscovered: the natural and moral education of the individual. The child, under his father's watchful eye, learns the true values of work and mutual respect. (Paris, Bibliothèque Nationale.)

Return to the bosom of the family. In a Rousseauist setting, a child's first lessons are taught by its parents through love and example. (Paris, Bibliothèque Nationale.)

in his *Treatise* to the need to distinguish between true civility, which makes second nature the charitable disposition of the Christian soul, and false civility, which bears the stamp of affectation and calculation and aims to deceive.[31]

Not surprisingly, this antiworldly radicalism can be found a century later in the work of Rousseau. But here the intellectual and emotional context of the criticism is quite different. The theme is still denunciation of the conventions that constrain behavior and falsify the relations between man and man. But the order of values is reversed. Where Pascal saw nothing in the human heart but inconstancy and falsehood, Jean-Jacques in *Emile* pleads on behalf of man's essentially good and moral nature. Against the tyranny of custom he invokes the heart and reason, the forgotten resources of intimacy. Nor was he alone, even if he upset many by the incivility that he not only advocated but practiced aggressively. Emile was to be brought up outside society in order to prepare himself for life in society. At the same time, the French elite's educational ideal was changing. No longer was the emphasis on collective education, on training in the *collège*. Now it was the inner life that counted, the sensibility, the learning of values, the absorption of a morality. In the family or its extensions (especially the tutor's classroom) children were brought up in a new way. The principle of the new education was that lessons are best learned in the context of private and natural relations—blood relations. The child's nature and personality were best expressed and fostered at home.

Thus, intimacy had its revenge, more or less putting an end to the reign of civility. Yet treatises on the subject remained popular, and during the French Revolution "republican" manuals of civility attempted to bring about an impossible marriage between Rousseauist educational principles and a revised version of the Erasmian formula. The offspring of this unholy union were strange monsters, textbooks that combined the old gestures and the new values in a traditional framework that had scarcely changed at all. Voltaire's maxims replaced Pibrac's *Quatrains*, but the "simple ideas about God and Religion" as well as the "Precepts on Reason" were still being printed in ancient sixteenth-century fonts. The teaching, however, invoked the name of Rousseau and adjusted to the changed political climate: "In the days when men judged themselves and were judged according to their birth, their rank, and their wealth, much study was required to learn all the nuances of consideration and politeness to be observed in society. Today there is but one rule to follow in life's commerce, and that is to be free, modest, frank, and honest with everyone."[32] This is nothing but a reformulated version of the old dream of a perfectly comprehensible social order. Apart from these ringing introductory declarations, however, the body of the text remained more or less the same, although homage to the Supreme Being replaced La Salle's pious exercises. The formula had become fossilized, a victim of its own success, and could not be reworked or adapted. No sooner was the Revolution over, than France returned to its canonical textbooks of civility.

But even as these texts were adopted for use everywhere, they had lost much of their significance. A relic of the past, impoverished, outmoded, undermined by internal contradictions, the whole enterprise of constructing rules of social life was reduced to a set of authoritarian precepts, a farce in which only the simplest folk still believed. New social codes had yet to take hold; in the meantime civility cut a poor figure compared with the individualism and spontaneity, for the time being triumphant. Reduced to mere outwardness, civility became laughable. The shabby mid–nineteenth-century tutor described by Stanislas David was an ignoramus who had studied nothing and had no idea how to live. For this plebeian astray in the mansions of the wealthy, the all-purpose reference was a small treatise entitled *Civility.* "Oh! He studied it every day. It was his code, his rule of behavior, his store full of fine things. He thought about how to present himself. He studied himself, experimented with a thousand postures and a thousand turns of phrase. He delayed as long as he could the moment of his appearance, for he was singularly fearful of the new figures."[33] A textbook which for three centuries had been used to teach children about society had become an emblem of maladaptation. The dream of a "government of the soul" had degenerated into little more than ridiculous posturing. Civility remained where nothing else had been learned.

Attributed to François Clouet, *Diane de Poitiers*(?). Portraits of women included the objects that decorated her body and nourished her spirit: clothing, combs, flowers, jewels, mirrors, books, letters. (Worcester, Massachusetts, Art Museum.)

The Refuges of Intimacy

Orest Ranum

HOW can we get beyond the heroic histories of the individual and individualism of which traditional historians have been so fond?[1] In recent years historians have explored the social aspects of history in minute detail. Yet in studying the space of privacy—the imagination of self and intimate relations—they have not progressed much farther than the stage of edifying biography. In the history of the self and of intimacy, almost everything remains to be written.

European societies of the sixteenth, seventeenth, and eighteenth centuries differed markedly from one another, yet when compared to contemporary society they seem alike in at least one respect: individual development was hindered by family, communal, civic, and village ties. In old societies intimacy can never be taken for granted. Hidden behind coded behaviors and words, it must be ferreted out, reconstructed from the places and objects in which human emotions and feelings were embodied. To explore the sites where intimacy flourished and understand the significance of the relic-objects found there, we need to take an archaeological approach.

My hypothesis is this: in the past the individual identified most intimately with certain particular places—an identification effected by means of emotions, actions, prayers, and dreams. The souvenir-space (walled garden, bedroom, *ruelle*, study, or oratory) and the souvenir-object (book, flower, clothing, ring, ribbon, portrait, or letter) were quite private, having been possessed by an individual unique in time and space. Nevertheless, the significance of such spaces and objects was encoded and perfectly comprehensible to others. The source of meaning was social. The Metropolitan Museum of

An Archaeology of the Intimate

Jan van Eyck, *Timotheus*. The words inscribed on the frame confirm what is expressed by the expression and the message. (London, National Gallery.)

Art has a fifteenth-century boxwood comb covered with hearts and arrows and bearing the inscription *"Prenez plaisir"* (Take Pleasure)—a relic-object, which a woman might have given as a favor to her beloved. Thousands of similar objects must have existed over the centuries. Even if the historian cannot hope to discover the private thoughts of people who lived long ago, he can identify the places where they thought and the objects on which their thoughts centered. The significance of having clothing, a bed, or a rosary of one's own went beyond mere ownership. And even when belongings were shared, they might still lend themselves to intimate uses.

The intimate is also revealed in portraits, whether in paint or words. Such relic-objects have a special power. Not only do they speak to us in the language of smiles, expressions, and glances, but they also invite us to resume a never-ending dialogue. By inscribing the words *leal souvenir* at the bottom of his *Timotheus*, Van Eyck conveys the private significance of this portrait to the modern beholder. At first, these too-eloquent objects seem to betray their secrets rather than conceal them, but the closer we look, the more we realize that they may well be no more revealing than initials engraved on a sword or a silver locket or a cheap ring. The absence of private notations in the well-known memoirs of Turenne, d'Argenson, or Richelieu, for example, is a sign that one should not expect intimate revelations of a portrait by Nanteuil or the letters of Mme de Sévigné.

People expressed themselves by signing with a flourish, an emblematic device, or even an "X" duly attested before a notary. Just as men have always chosen nicknames or compared themselves with certain animals to assert their identities, so too have they distinguished themselves with secret signs engraved on rings, decorated writing desks, painted roof beams, tombstones, sculpted doors, and bookbindings. Even if we cannot always decipher the signs, all of these things are powerful relic-objects. Certain political and religious sects thrived on secrecy and mystery and seem to have made use of secret signs. Petrarch felt a deep affection for Saint Augustine. Rather like a schoolboy, he recorded in a special notebook—his *Secret*—the substance of inspired conversations with his venerable and holy friend. A divine force incarnate in mind and body, friendship encouraged dialogue with a man who had been dead for nearly a thousand years. Petrarch cherished this notebook as a relic-object, an intimate and precious possession. Other early modern diaries are often less religious than Petrarch's *Secret*, yet they reveal a need for intimate self-expression.

Sometime about 1660 Samuel Pepys, who suffered from gallstones, recovered from a bout with the disease at a critical moment in his family history and political life. Over the course of the next nine years he would write, in cipher, some 1,250,000 words about his intimate life.[2] Some of his compatriots wrote in Latin to prevent wives and relatives from reading what they had written. Pepys felt a deep need to preserve some memento of both his body's workings and life's pleasures. As if to enable himself to recapture at will the details of his inner life, he recorded memories of a pleasant tune, an agreeable stroll, the fragrance of the country in spring, feasts of oysters and wine, and a glimpse of a beautiful woman in church. He enjoyed writing. His amorous passions outstripped the evocative power of his words, and when Italian phrases proved insufficient to compensate for the deficiencies of English, he simply left a blank space on the page.

Intimate memoirs not infrequently evoke the ineffable. Accounts of mystical experiences, ecstatic moments at ancient ruins or in the depths of the forest, and sublime instants in which flesh and spirit were joined in love reveal a need to express to oneself or others an inner sense of transcendence.

The self-portrait, a relic-object that was preserved by the painter himself or given to a friend, shares many characteristics of the intimate diary. At age thirteen Dürer (1484) drew a picture of himself with the aid of a mirror, a prodigious accomplishment for such a young boy.[3] Even in Germany, where self-portraiture would flourish in the sixteenth century, it was still not quite a genre. According to Panofsky, the inspiration came from Dürer's father, a gold- and silversmith, who had earlier made a portrait of himself.[4]

Rembrandt went even further in developing the uses and symbolism of self-portraiture. Dürer had searched for his identity by painting himself in rather exotic costumes and elaborate hairdos. Rembrandt went beyond exoticism and exhibitionism to concentrate on physiognomy and expression, as if these expressed the self in its entirety. In innumerable self-portraits he recorded his most intimate thoughts in a gaze that gazes upon itself. Such concentration on things of the spirit is quite rare among early modern artists and artisans, whose chief means of expression is their manual dexterity. Rembrandt was

Rembrandt, *Self-Portrait*. The relation between the intimate and narcissistic pleasure is a historical question. (Florence, Pitti Palace.)

thus a forerunner of the narcissistic painters of the twentieth century; in his visual quest for the essence of the self, he had no direct disciple.

In studying the history of intimacy, then, we draw upon three kinds of evidence. We can study the kinds of places that lent themselves to private intercourse between two individuals. Second, we can examine the relic-objects which people used as mementos of love and friendship. And third, we have the evidence of painting and text: self-portraits, portraits, letters, autobiographies, diaries, and memoirs, which are just as much relic-objects as combs and rings. Every object speaks in its own way. Rather than allow one type of object to speak more than the others, we should note the diffusion and spread of intimate *imagines*. That they happen to appear in works of high art is no proof of their origin; obviously, relic-objects "of no artistic merit" are not preserved in museums. Nor did the sixteenth-century rosebud rosaries worn by the queens elected by youth groups in west-central France lend themselves to preservation for posterity as readily as did the painted roses that crowned the heads of Virgins.[5]

THE SCENE OF INTIMACY

Europeans at the end of the Middle Ages considered certain sites and spaces to be particularly propitious for communing with oneself or with another person. Few of these places exist today, but abundant iconographic sources tell us a great deal about them. Some small private gardens have survived adjacent to the private apartments of certain sixteenth-century English castles, such as Hampton Court. The closes of Oxford and Cambridge—small gardens surrounded by walls—still exist, as do the gardens of the English cathedral schools and the occasional Carthusian garden, used today for contemplation and intimate conversation. Although the decor of these gardens was modified between 1500 and 1800, none of their intimate significance was lost. The classical garden seems to have supplanted the small private of garden of old, but in fact the grove with its small gate cut into a box tree and its single bench hidden in the shadows fulfilled the same function as the walled garden.

In the early modern era architects created new private spaces in the homes of the well-to-do, or, rather, they increased the amount of private space by transforming into rooms what had previously been mere objects of furniture. In

Castle and garden of Idstein, 16th century. Only single men and couples are to be found in this space reserved for contemplation and amorous encounters. (Paris, Bibliothèque Nationale.)

Attributed to Robert Peake, *Henry, Prince of Wales* (detail), 1610. The walled garden, with its empty bench, enticed those seeking calm and repose. (London, National Portrait Gallery.)

the various languages of Europe, words such as study, *cabinet*, *bibliothèque* (shelf or library), and *écritoire* (writing desk or writing room) may still refer to items of furniture, but they also designate rooms serving a particular, often private, function. In French, even the word *cuisine* (kitchen), when distinct from the dining room, shares a similar ambiguity. It is not always clear whether one is talking about the room where the food is cooked or the food itself. The inclusion of distinctive rooms within the home is therefore not conclusive proof of privatization, except in the sense that a man who once kept a locked writing desk could now closet himself in his writing room and lock the door. From here it was but a short step to the nineteenth-century bourgeois home, with its accumulation of objets d'art, papers, books, and curiosities, always neatly ordered in glass cabinets and kept under lock and key.[6] The

Master of the Hansbuch, *Amorous Couple*. The presence of the small faithful dog and the vase of carnations reassures us: love does not transgress the bounds of friendship. (Paris, Bibliothèque Nationale.)

number of objects increased, they were more widely dispersed physically, and greater numbers of people enjoyed their use. But none of this necessarily implies privacy; the word still meant primarily "secrecy" and pertained to the realm of thought. The man who possessed a locked casket may have enjoyed the same level of privacy as the man who owned a vast house in which each room served a particular function.

The Walled Garden

With the help of fifteenth-century paintings, wood engravings, and tapestries we can not only describe the walled garden but almost smell its flowers and breathe its salubrious air. Low wooden enclosures, walls of espaliered fruit trees, or woven wicker fences enclosed beds of flowers or flowered lawns with low mounds to sit on. Fountains and pools, narrow lanes, and trellises covered with roses or grapevines completed the garden, the ideal place for an amorous, courtly, or religious encounter. Seldom was the garden depicted without young couples off to one side, absorbed in conversation or playing musical instruments. Often a solitary individual sat reading, or there might be a Virgin enthroned on a pedestal of wood or stone, surrounded by trees in blossom and garlands of roses. The walled garden was always an intimate place, except in Brueghel's drawings, in which we see gardeners at work. The presence of the Virgin, alone or with a patron saint, provided an occasion for anyone looking at the painting to kneel before her, as in the garden itself.

The air inside the garden was not the same as the air of city streets or country fields. It was saturated with fragrances of a superior kind—odors of roses, pure water, and sanctity, capable of healing the body and giving repose to the soul. The humanists and, later, the baroque literati stripped the garden of its rustic and Gothic trappings, substituting antique columns and benches as well as busts of philosophers for the edification of those who entered. But the potential intimate uses of the place remained. Flowers and grass were still providential messages, as in Henry Hawkins' *Parthenia sacra* (1633). Despite the symbolic tower of Babel erected by the poets, flowers retained their power to make man reflect upon himself:

Charles-Dominique-Joseph Eisen, *Love Scene in a Copse.* A mound of earth pillows the head of the sleeping woman, who has a coquettish smile on her lips. (Paris, Bibliothèque Nationale.)

"the Lillie of spotless and immaculate Chastitie,
the Rose of Shamfastness and bashful Modestie, the
Violet of Humilitie, the Gillsflower of Patience,
the Marygold of Charitie, the Hiacinth of Hope,
the Sun-flower of Contemplation, the Tulip of Beautie
and Gracefulness."[7]

And man reflected not only upon himself but, more profoundly, upon love and death. The garden inspired the poet. The beloved seemed nearer, and the poet himself decided when she would come and when, cruelly, she would disappear.

In Tasso the ultimate encounter of Armida with Renaldo takes place in a flowered garden. French opera would turn the garden into a magical place capable of melting hearts and confounding even the most sincere. In the paintings of Watteau, Boucher, and Fragonard, the garden became a park, but lost none of its almost magical power. The masked encounters enacted, two by two, by the denizens of Count Almaviva's household take place in a garden made particularly sensual by the dark of night. The solitude of the garden, the passage of time and season, and the fading of the flowers were reminders not only of life's fragility but of the death of Christ: "I walk the garden and there see / Ideas of his agonie."[8] In a print by

Engraving by Fernand de Launay after Jean-Honoré Fragonard, *Love's Cipher.* Like initials engraved with diamonds on window panes, letters carved into a living tree gave concrete embodiment to the union of souls. (Paris, Bibliothèque Nationale.)

Martin Schongauer, *Saint Mary Magdalene Meets the Resurrected Christ*, ca. 1480. Golgotha is depicted as a walled garden of death. (Paris, Bibliothèque Nationale.)

Martin Schongauer showing Christ's appearance to Saint Mary Magdalene, the desertlike quality of the garden is striking, with just one small, leafless tree and a few small mounds of bare earth. The single tree, with or without leaves, retained its power to evoke death.

After 1640 portraits of elderly couples began to appear in Holland. The favorite setting was the garden. Hoogstraten's paintings helped the bereaved widow or widower to imagine the departed spouse in a place of happiness by depicting the couple together in the garden. This kind of portrait gave concrete embodiment to a moment of thought, perhaps even of prayer and love. In Steen's painting of an elderly couple playing chess, the trellis evokes not only tranquil afternoons passed in its shadow but also weddings and baptisms, which were often celebrated in such places.

If, over the course of the seventeenth and eighteenth centuries, marriage for love and friendship gradually replaced marriage for interest and money, it was in the garden that love was expressed and thereupon recorded in portraits of young couples either alone or with their children. Donors, male and female, along with children and parents, were initially painted alongside the Virgin or a patron saint, frequently placed in a garden or in an oratory whose window opened onto a garden. They remained in the garden long after the intercessory saint had disappeared from the paintings. Double portraits on a single canvas became increasingly common in Protestant countries in the seventeenth and eighteenth centuries. In England and her colonies couples sought refuge in the intimacy of garden or park. Those of more modest means memorialized in writing the same activities that the wealthy immortalized in paint. Samuel Pepys, with lodgings at the Admiralty in London, had no garden to speak of, but the "leads" offered him the same enjoyments. On hot days he went there with his wife for a cool drink or to play his theorbo by moonlight. Only the threat of a Dutch invasion drove him to take refuge in his country house, where he buried his money in the garden.

Dutch painters transformed the walled garden into the common farmyard, but without eliminating its connotations of intimacy. The Virgin and saints have gone, but the image of two people absorbed in conversation remains, as does that

Rembrandt, *Portrait of the Mennonite Pastor Anslo and His Wife*, 1641. The word of God joins them. Is the pastor-husband trying to solidify his wife's faith? The inner meaning of the painting escapes us, for Rembrandt does not always use the iconographic elements (the handkerchief and empty candle-holder) according to the established codes. (Berlin, Dahlem Museum.)

of reading, no doubt of pious or romantic works. In reaction against conventional images of love and faith, certain simpler, coarser, but nonetheless intimate feelings were evoked. Young couples are shown playing chess or drinking (always with one glass for both), or, in a painting by Terborch in the Berlin Museum, a mother is seen searching for lice in her daughter's hair, an act that for centuries had been associated with thoughts of love.[9] An old woman seated alone in a small, shrubless courtyard or a dark corner of the house literally internalized these intimate acts, inciting the spectator to meditate upon his own death.

For those of melancholy temperament, gardens with their beds of flowers and colored sand were disorienting and upsetting. True repose lay in nature, untouched by the hand of man. The Puritans condemned geometrical gardens with shaped trees and shrubs, these being products of human reason, hence capable of impeding progress along the inner way. They systematically eradicated mazes of shrubbery.[10] Ruins were tolerated, however, since they helped the soul to concentrate on the hereafter. Thus, the new sensibility of inward-

Franz van Mieris, *Elderly Couple*, represented under the sign of friendship (carnations), with no indication of whether or not they are married. (Florence, Uffizi.)

ness, which regarded artifice as artificial, anticipated the eighteenth-century English garden and mystique of virgin forests, deep lakes, and ancient ruins.

The primary dwelling space (hall, *salle*, *Stube*, and so on) was the scene of varied activity. Here was the hearth or stove, along with kitchen utensils, a table, stands, benches, empty barrels, and bags of supplies, plus bedding, that is, some material to lie on but without a wooden bedstead or curtains. In one-room dwellings all activity took place in the hall, except those natural functions best performed in the fields or on the manure pile. When there was another room on the same level as the hall, separated from it by a door with a lock, it was variously called the *camera*, inner room, chamber, or borning room. In German the word *Zimmer* evokes the wooden panels that were attached to the wall, but otherwise the arrangement was the same. The chamber contained a large, curtained bed. In fourteenth- and fifteenth-century Florence the word *camera* was invested with dignity, and this may have been true of the French *chambre* as well. In fifteenth-century prints the matron of the house is always shown with keys attached to her belt. In large households in the city, the chamber was always kept locked. Seventeenth-century Dutch paintings show the relation of hall to chamber, the two being separated by a wall, with the street in the background.

When he was about thirty years old, Leon Battista Alberti, a wealthy Florentine merchant, wrote a book entitled *On the Family*. In it he describes the moment when a newly married husband shows his bride her new home. The visit ends in the chamber, where, having locked the door behind him, he shows her his riches—silver, tapestries, clothing, and jewels—which he keeps locked up in this private sanctum where he can enjoy the pleasure of looking at them in solitude. His books, *ricordi* (memoirs combined with accounts), and ancestors' papers were kept apart, in his study under lock and key, always hidden from his wife. The study described by Alberti could be either a separate room, the so-called *studiolo*, or a piece of furniture that could be locked. Ricordi were guarded, Alberti explains, "almost as if they were sacred and religious objects."

Having shown his treasures, Alberti requested that his bride never share her bed with another man and never admit anyone other than himself into the chamber. He insisted that

The Chamber

Israhel van Meckenem, *Amorous Couple*, ca. 1480. The woman's belt with its keys is undone; the boxes of makeup are the sign of the courtesan. (Paris, Bibliothèque Nationale.)

she behave modestly, shunning rouge and avoiding flirtation. Following these admonitions, husband and wife knelt and prayed God to help them and bless them with many children. As they prayed, their eyes were fixed on a saint "made of silver, with head and hands of ivory." Alberti did not record the name of the saint; the statue interested him primarily as a precious object. To his modern mind, little influenced by the theologies of the word emanating from the Sorbonne, noble and precious materials embodied the divine as such, without specific associations other than the form. If Alberti owned any paintings (none are included in his list of precious objects), they probably were of religious subjects and hung in the chamber rather than the hall.[11]

Such a division between secretly pleasurable activities and activities in the hall was characteristic of the great merchant class of the late Middle Ages. It tells us much about the division of space within the house, the classification of objects, and the role assigned to the wife. As time went on, these distinctions affected other classes as well.

When a family could afford a second room, it became the center of emotional life and intimate relations. Van Eyck's painting of the *Arnolfinis* (1439) seems to confirm Alberti's account that the newly married couple joined in the chamber in a ceremonious celebration of their new intimacy. And in Israhel van Meckenem's engraving of a couple seated on a bed, the chamber contains not only a large wooden bed with columns and panels but also a small table covered with a cloth on which have been placed a candlestick with two candles, boxes of powder, and a brush. A knife has been stuck into the lock on the door, preventing its being opened. The man has removed his sword and placed it on the dais. His left hand reaches around the woman's back and holds her below her left arm, an obvious sign of his desire to kiss her. Her arms are folded, but she seems to be removing her belt and keys. The bed curtains are parted. There is nothing religious about this scene.

The chamber also lent itself to use by wealthy men seeking the favors of "courtesans." Meckenem's engraving is the visible embodiment of a nightmare that Alberti sought to avoid by showing his riches to his new wife, praying with her, and in a sense keeping her locked up along with his other precious goods. The table with its boxes of powder, brushes, combs, and bottles of perfume symbolizes sexual intimacy out of wedlock. Boucher and Fragonard attempted to make the lady's dressing table a worthy and morally neutral subject, but this came later, at a time when the idea of marriage for love was making headway among the elite. In Fragonard's *Le Verrou* (The Lock), the chamber has become the place where the passions are vented. The man is shown locking the door while continuing his seduction. By contrast, *Le Placard* (The Closet), by the same artist, is an attempt at moralizing reflected in the painting's obvious academicism. Veering from the intimate to the theatrical, it reveals nothing about the nature of intimacy.

Seventeenth-century Dutch painting confirms the intimate nature of the chamber, depicting in even greater detail the physical acts that take place there. Women dress and undress, nurse their babies, and receive visits from female relatives and friends after giving birth. Canvases by de Hooch and Steen showing disheveled beds and women dressing alone attest to the fact that in the early modern period well-to-do males continued to fantasize about the bedroom. There is

Gabriel de Saint-Aubin, *L'Académie particulière*. The conceit of an artist with his model conceals an erotic chamber of the rococo period. A canvas turned toward the wall and a palette do not a studio make. (Paris, Bibliothèque Nationale.)

nothing ambiguous about the Rembrandt engraving entitled *Het Ledekant* which shows a man mounted atop a woman in a canopied bed. The surrounding space is obscure, as was customary with Rembrandt, but only the wealthy owned canopied beds.

The Ruelle *and the Alcove*

In sixteenth- and seventeenth-century France the *ruelle*, or space between the bed and the wall, was regarded as an especially intimate place. Think of Marguerite de Valois's *La Ruelle mal assortie*. Here too the lover in Tristan L'Hermite's *Le Page disgracié* felt shivers in his limbs and other physical reactions that threatened to transgress the bounds of propriety. Dumont de Bostaquet recounts in his *Memoirs* that, when a fire broke out in his house, "all my effort went to saving my papers: I had had a very proper alcove built in my chamber, and I had great closets in the ruelle of my bed, where my clothes were kept, and all that was most valuable, the deeds to my house."[12]

Like the ruelle, the alcove was a space beyond the bed, on the side away from the door leading to the hall (or antechamber in the homes of the elite). Thomas Jefferson had a compartment built around his bed, completely enclosing the little room beyond, to which he alone could gain access by getting out of bed on the side of the ruelle.

In the seventeenth and eighteenth centuries some felt a need for privacy greater than that offered by the chamber.

Rembrandt, *Het Ledekant* (often translated as "French-style bed"), 1646. The man has placed his hat on the bedpost as a sign of conquest. The couple has drunk wine from a single glass (as usual) before going to bed. The artist, who has not decided whether he wishes to portray the woman as simply lying back "asleep" or actively participating in the sexual act, has given her three arms. (London, British Museum.)

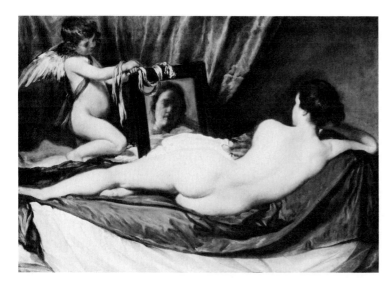

Diego Velázquez, *The Toilet of Venus*, ca. 1648–51. Does not the ribbon held by cupid indicate the presence of the man who commissioned the painting? The mirror here is not merely the symbol of vanity but an instrument for intensifying the amorous gaze. (London, National Gallery.)

Following the death of the Jansenist scholar Le Nain de Tillemont, a "belt covered with metal studs" was discovered in the ruelle of his bed. Mortification of the flesh, an ancient practice, was one purpose to which private space might be put.

In the eighteenth century the chamber lost none of its importance as a place of intimacy. Painters emphasized signs of intimacy and activities that took place nowhere else. In the previous century Abraham Bosse had been content to show a young woman fully clothed beneath the bedcovers, waiting for the handsome young doctor to administer the clyster while a maid stood by with a commode. In the eighteenth century, however, a painting of the same subject showed a woman lying naked on her alcove bed ready to receive the clyster, now administered, however, by the maid.

Watteau, Boucher, and Greuze provided more explicit versions of nearly all the intimate and erotic themes of seventeenth-century Dutch painting.[13] Watteau went well beyond the conventions in *The Lady at Her Toilette*. A young woman, her nightshirt open, sits on her bed, preparing to take a bath. A maid holding a basin passes her a sponge. The subject is quite banal, but the painting is so explicit that the observer, even in the twentieth century, feels like an intruder. This painting is quite small. To see it clearly, the observer must move quite close to the canvas, and he feels like a voyeur. The bather in the painting is doing nothing indecent, but the beholder is drawn into indecency.[14] Small statues and paintings

Tintoretto, *Susanna Bathing.* There is nothing intimate about this space. The female body is celebrated for a lover who may be lurking about in the person of one of the elderly gentlemen in the background. (Paris, Louvre.)

of pretty, naked women playing with dogs that hide between their legs compel the beholder to abandon his civilized detachment and confront his moral innocence or knowledge.

As early as the fifteenth century female grooming had become a commonplace of erotic art. Much of this grooming took place more or less "in public." Dürer invited the voyeuristic onlooker to gaze through a partially open shutter at six naked women in a public bath. Women at public baths and courtesans dressing alone in their rooms were subjects painted repeatedly over the centuries, but they were rarely evocative of inner lives, except in the imagination of the onlooker. Enforced proximity was an impediment to intimacy. In the eighteenth century the Rodez girl described by Prion d'Aubais in his *Autobiography* complained of the demands of the female relative for whom she worked: "Alas, she said to me, I cannot imagine a woman more difficult to serve. She so loves her precious body that she is entirely occupied with its convenience and comfort. The least disturbance in her health alarms her so much that she becomes perturbed. The slightest draft upsets her head. She is so afraid of the consequences that she is almost reduced to tears. Yet she nevers tires of preaching against the delicacy of those who are unwilling to suffer . . . I am always in a tizzy before I give her an enema, because she suspects that it will be too cold. And while I am giving it she complains that it is too hot . . . Since she insists that I try all her medicines and other drugs before she takes them, my bowels are always loose. She even wanted me to taste her enemas."

Titian's Venuses were both an idealization of the female body and pornography for the elite. Paintings by the School of Fontainebleau of women bathing embodied a particular human sensibility. These bathers did not emerge miraculously from the waters, nor did they relax like goddesses in the depths

François Boucher, *Madame Boucher*. With a purse, book, letter, and chinoiserie dear to her husband, Mme Boucher exhibits a respectable flirtatiousness. (New York, Frick Collection.)

of the forest. They were depicted in their chambers, amid servants, fireplaces, and furniture. Such paintings figured in the autoerotic fantasies of women as well as men, for the ladies in them seem quite happy to be painted nude, wearing only their jewels.

Similar in her female sensibility, but visibly modest for all her flirtatiousness, Mme Boucher stares at her husband, the painter. Lying fully dressed on her chaise longue among every-day objects arranged on distinctive eighteenth-century tables and shelves, she is not in a bedroom. Boucher was avoiding the iconography of the courtesan: his wife wears slippers and a bonnet; on the table lie a letter and a book; a purse hangs from the key to the drawer. There is not the slightest sign of religion, but that does not mean that a secularization of private space was under way. The early modern era always had a language of love free from religious sublimities. Adapted to the needs of consumer society, this secular discourse has contributed to the definition of the woman as a precious object possessed by her lover. We shall never know what hung on the walls of Boucher's bedroom, but it is not difficult to imagine a bust of Voltaire or of a Chinese on the mantelpiece of the study, as was common in eighteenth-century Paris, and a crucifix attached to the bed curtains.

Daniel Roche has observed that the location of the bed within the bedroom changed over the course of the eighteenth century, moving toward the corner of the room or into an alcove.[15] Bedrooms were furnished with minuscule shelves, small tables, dressers, and screens. After 1760 urban bedrooms became quite congested. Despite the installation of innumerable hallways, doors, antechambers, and partitions in old buildings, there may have been little increase in privacy before 1860. The wealthy naturally increased the amount of private space available to them, but for the rest of the population, the vast majority, the idea of privacy did not extend beyond the bedroom, and perhaps not beyond the bed curtains.

Jean-Baptiste Pater, *A Woman Bathing.* Adaptation of a genre scene known since the early 16th century. The man hidden behind the curtains or shutters always elicits pleasant surprise from the bather. (London, Wallace Collection.)

The *studiolo*, a tiny room or cell without fireplace or large window, first appeared in Italian Renaissance palaces, no doubt copied from monastic models. The two meanings of the word, which could refer either to a kind of writing desk or to a room used for the same purpose, tell us something about the way in which new private spaces were invented.[16]

The Study

Baccio Pontelli, paneling and marquetry from the study of Federico Montefeltro in Urbino, 1476. The images on the closed doors are a semiotic portrait of what lies behind, emphasizing the importance of the study in private life.

Lorenzo Lotto, *Study*. This young prelate is surrounded by everyday objects, including a canopied bed. He remains alone while reading. A bell is nearby for calling a servant. (London, British Museum.)

A retreat reserved for the master of the house, the study was sometimes equipped with sturdy locks and bolts. Reading, keeping accounts, and prayer required little furniture other than a small table and a chair. In less well-to-do homes, escritoires and small chests or coffers for storing letters, papers, and account books took the place of the study. Books were stored as in a monk's cell or hermitage, in niches in the wall of the study where rats could not reach them.

If fourteenth-, fifteenth-, and sixteenth-century portraits of Saint Jerome can be considered evidence for the transformation of the study, then it is clear that this room grew from an item of furniture to something like furniture in which one lived. The walls were covered with wooden panels and small cabinets with doors. The decor of surviving studies, especially in Urbino, is edifying, with iconography on the panels and marquetry depicting wisdom human and divine, mingled with the owner's blazons, devices, and initials.

Lawyers stored professional papers in their studies, alongside youthful verses and translations from the works of ancient authors. The proportion of bachelors in the liberal professions was much higher than in other elite groups; as a result, the study of a doctor or of a lawyer often contained his bed as well as books and equipment for scientific experiments.[17] Lorenzo Lotto's small drawing of a clergyman in his study is undoubtedly a more reliable source, or description, than are the portraits of Saint Jerome.

Love letters might also be kept in the study, especially if they were relic-objects of an extramarital liaison. The master went to his study alone or with a close friend, a son, or a nephew to discuss "in confidence" family business such as plans for marriage. The humanist synthesis of an active life in business and politics with love of literature and devout solitude had its focus there. Some studies sheltered collections of coins, medals, stones, or enamels. A collector like Pepys could live in his study among portraits, medals, and engravings of illustrious men.

In sixteenth-century France, châteaux and large urban houses also contained studies, often located in a tower or some other place at a distance from the hustle and bustle of daily life but almost always adjacent to the master's bedroom. At Tanlay the princely study is decorated with a very original program of iconography, proof that it was possible to combine royal politics with heroic mythology.

The Cabinet

The word *cabinet* referred both to a small item of furniture with a lockable door or drawers and to a small, wood-paneled room. Both were decorated with small paintings, frequently pious but even more often erotico-religious. The sober cabinet in the château de Beauregard was perfectly suited to a devoted servant of the state. At Vaux-le-Vicomte, the architect Le Vau and the painter-decorator Le Brun produced for Nicolas Fouquet (1615–1680), the man in charge of the king's finances, a veritable jewel: a cabinet lined with mirrors in which the master could contemplate himself. Louis XIV's great cabinet at Versailles (no longer extant) was also mirror-lined; the king's self-directed gaze was at once religious and narcissistic. During the seventeenth and eighteenth centuries these spaces were to some extent secularized and even eroticized, as the individual cast off the bonds that had attached him to venerable moral and religious values.

In England studies and cabinets served the same functions as in Italy and France. Robert Burton wrote *The Anatomy of Melancholy* (1621) in his study at Christ Church, Oxford. In the seventeenth century, however, the word closet (from the Latin *clausum*, closed) became increasingly common. In *King Lear* Shakespeare explained why the closet existed: "I have locked the letter in my closet" (Act III, Scene 3, line 12). Pepys and his wife, imitating a fashion borrowed from wealthy Italians, each had a bedroom and closet. Once, in return for a favor, Pepys received a cabinet as a gift. After carefully examining the operation of its secret drawers, he had it installed in his wife's closet. This story gives us pause. Did possession of furniture that could be locked really mean that privacy had increased? Pepys's wife could keep no secrets from prying Samuel's eyes.

Eighteenth-century novelists increasingly saw a woman's cabinet as endowed with erotic powers. Incapable of irony, Rousseau used all the commonplaces of sixteenth-century amorous discourse in describing Julie's private space, leaving us with a fine inventory of love's relic-objects: "How charming this mysterious place! Everything here gratifies and nourishes the ardor that devours me. O, Julie! It is full of you, and the flame of my desires touches every vestige of your presence. Yes, all my senses are intoxicated. I know not what almost indetectible fragrance, sweeter than rose and lighter than iris, emanates from every part. I think I hear the pleasing sound of your voice. The scattered items of your clothing fill my ardent imagination with images of the parts of yourself they

Nicolas Cochin, *The Lady's Tailor*. The conceit of the tailor conceals a nonintimate pornography. But this image might have inspired erotic dreams. (Paris, Bibliothèque Nationale.)

Abraham Bosse, *The Vision.*
A well-bred woman grooms
herself before a closed bed. Her
hair is curled and she wears a
coif. (Tours, Museum of Fine
Arts.)

once covered. This slight hairpiece that adorned your abundant blonde hair, pretending to cover it. This lovely scarf,
against which for once I shall not have to murmur. This
elegant and simple negligee so characteristic of the taste of the
woman who wears it. These slippers so dainty that a supple
foot fills them easily. This bodice so slender that touches and
embraces . . . what an enchanting waist . . . in front, two
delicate contours . . . O, voluptuous spectacle . . . the corset
has ceded to the force of the impression . . . delicious imprints,
I kiss you a thousand times! . . . God! God! What will it be
when . . . Ah, already I can feel that tender heart beating
beneath my happy hand! Julie! my charming Julie! I see you,
I feel you all over, I breathe the air that you have breathed.
You penetrate all my substance. How burning and painful
your room is for me!" (*La Nouvelle Héloïse*, part 1, letter 54).

From Black Robes to Dressing Gowns

Lorenzo Lotto, *Young Man in His Studio*. After 1420 it quickly became popular for well-to-do young men to have their portraits painted. The salamander can withstand fire, but why is it included here? (Venice, Accademia.)

If female clothing became more and more explicitly eroticized as time went on, some items were never mentioned. Male clothing continued to be associated with the study. In the sixteenth and seventeenth centuries men who repaired to their studies most commonly wore clerical garb—a veritable labyrinth of symbols linked to religious orders, universities, and the professions of law and medicine. Many young students in Italian Renaissance portraits are dressed in black. But in intimate portraits of men who were not scholars, courtly garb little by little supplanted the black gown. Given the current state of research, it is impossible to catalogue male costumes that were in some way "original," that is, invented to some extent by those who wore them. Consider Machiavelli, who, inspired by the Roman republican "model," was in the habit of wearing a toga while writing his books on politics and history. Montaigne thought deeply about the significance of clothing as an expression of the self, but was content to remain "modest" in his attire, even in his "library," a tower to which he retreated to muse in solitude.

After 1650 the dressing gown became fashionable among men. Made of brown satin and, in northern Europe, embroidered with flowers, it expressed a new pleasure in privacy that had nothing to do with religion. Pepys posed for a portrait in his. Dutch painters liked to depict two friends in dressing gowns playing chess. In the eighteenth century Diderot, echoing the ancient philosophers, sang the praises of his old dressing gown, which he said had molded itself to the shape of his body. It was marvelously in tune with all the objects in his room, accumulated over the years. When he acquired a beautiful new gown, the room had to be totally done over. The old furniture was replaced, and papers and brochures were stored behind the "glass doors of a fine bureau." The paintings and sculptures, previously placed carelessly about the room or pinned to the wall without frames, were rearranged to bring the whole cabinet into harmony with the taste of the age. Despite this great change, Diderot swore that he would remain the same, always ready to receive visitors. The revolution in his clothing and private space would not change the man.

Roger van der Weyden, *Saint Yves Executed*. This portrait attempts to portray the inner life. (London, National Gallery.)

The philosopher acknowledged that he was attached to the things that surrounded him, especially to the works that he had received from his artist friends, and, moreover, that a sense of a person's environment is an essential part not only of what others feel about him but also of what he feels about himself. In his epitaph he transferred this philosophy to his offspring: "He is long since dead, and his children are still looking for him in his armchair." Studies and cabinets increasingly became the expression of the individual as creator and intellectual, yet they continued to bear traces of their origins as a place for study, prayer, and seduction.

THINGS OF THE HEART

In the early modern era it was believed that behavior is determined by the quality and quantity of body heat. That heat was thought to come not from the liver or the spleen or the brain but from the heart. The idea of the self was therefore centered in the heart.

A man derives his unique identity from the passions of his heart, to which can be traced the darkest of crimes, the most heroic of deeds, the most violent of loves, and the most human or inhuman of sexual acts. Despite education, religious

The Ambiguities of the Heart

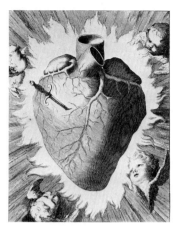

Anonymous print, 1685. A man's sins leave their mark on his heart, especially when he sins intentionally, that is, with all his heart. (Paris, Bibliothèque Nationale.)

faith, and fear of punishment or ostracism, reason cannot always control the heats that well up from the heart; men have great difficulty keeping them within accepted bounds. Excess is to be avoided. A man may be nothing without passion, but without control of the passions by reason he is lost.

Every individual sought to facilitate the process of deciphering his or her own behavior by creating an inner vocabulary, a veritable reckoning of passionate actions. In the fourteenth century signs of the existence of such reckonings begin to appear in the *ricordi*. One of the obligations of friendship was to allow new friends to see this record of passionate thoughts and actions—effects of the heat of the heart—for, after all, friendship itself was a thing of the heart.

In societies still marked by the spirit of chivalry, a triumph over an enemy celebrated for his courage did not go unnoticed. If through prayer a person came to see the Virgin or feel the body of Christ within himself, sooner or later that fact too became public. If his heart was moved by a woman's potent gaze, altering his behavior, or if he felt ill or listless, friends and relatives would want to know what had happened. In many cases the physical effects of the passions were apparent. Since the intensity of the heats was thought to vary enormously, the actions induced by those heats could also vary.[18]

Souvenirs

The passions left powerful impressions on the memory. In the vocabulary of intimacy, the word *souvenir*, though not limited to memories of the passions, became the preferred word for them in the eighteenth century. It even acquired a double meaning, denoting both a memory and/or a common object such as a ribbon or comb that belonged to a loved one or a gift that expressed the identity of the giver or recipient. Through the exchange of souvenirs the self became other and the other, the self. All souvenirs were unique and intimate yet immediately recognizable as such by society. A secret was a souvenir decipherable by someone else and therefore kept private by one or the other.

For centuries the heart remained a central symbol of intimacy and inwardness. It could be found everywhere, in engravings, sculpture, drawings, and paintings. As a symbol the heart is revealing of much that was ambiguous in the nature of intimacy. Was it a souvenir of religious faith? Of courage? Of love? In objects of aristocratic origin it was often explicitly a sign of love, either sacred or profane. But invari-

In this popular 16th-century woodcut François I offers his heart and Eleanor of Austria offers flowers to the Virgin and the Infant Jesus, asking their blessing for a marriage that for diplomatic reasons never took place. (Château de Panat, Aveyron.)

ably it was a sign of "inwardness," which expressed itself through passion or responded to the sensory impression made by another. Not everyone who carried the sign of the heart on his sword, ring, clothing, and books, or who lived in a house with a heart clumsily carved into the lintel of a door as a protective charm, was concerned about the symbolic significance of the object. They cared only about possessing a souvenir at once historic and present, capable of evoking some secret action or passion. As time went on, the search for self and others through the sight or feel of a souvenir become both increasingly common and increasingly complex.

Souvenir-collecting became prevalent just as a sort of "advanced technology" was making it possible literally to hold on to the man or woman with whom one had been on intimate terms. Private religious devotion had always depended on an intimacy made possible by the physical souvenirs known as relics. Churches were filled with relics that enabled the faithful to commune inwardly with the holy. Up to about 1700 it was common practice in princely and noble families to remove the

Relics

Heart of Jesus, taken from Joseph de Gallifet, *L'Excellence de la dévotion au coeur adorable* (Lyons, 1743). Anatomy lends support to religious imagery. (Paris, Bibliothèque Nationale.)

heart from a cadaver before it was laid to rest in the family vault or burial ground.

What was done with hearts thus removed from the bodies of the dead was determined by a strict hierarchy of sanctity. The Bourbons were quite scrupulous in such matters. When the Count de La Marche died in 1677 at the age of three years, three months, and twelve days, his heart was enclosed "in a small lead box in the shape of a heart" and placed in the coffin. But the heart of Mlle de Clermont, who died in 1680 when she was only fourteen months old and who had received not a formal but only an emergency private baptism (*ondoyée*), was not placed "in a small leaden heart as was customary."[19]

Affection for the body of the deceased was far more common than one might think from the prohibitions of the Church, which opposed it vigorously. Mme de La Guette recounts that at the death of her mother, "I was inconsolable; and in my painful emotion I even breathed into her mouth for a quarter of an hour, thinking that I could bring her back to life. I shed so many tears over her face, and I touched it so many times, that it became as smooth as glass . . . I conceived a desire to sever her head from her body so that I might put it in my cabinet and look at it in comfort and at my leisure. I found no occasion to do so, however, because the clergymen who watched over her told me that they would never give their consent."[20]

More familiar no doubt was the habit of keeping a lock of hair as a souvenir, and Mme de Sévigné regretted not having kept either the hair or a portrait of her late husband (even though the marriage had not been one of perfect love). Throughout this period the boundary line between the body literally preserved and its sign or souvenir was surprisingly fluid. No doubt Norbert Elias was right to stress man's growing estrangement from his body, but the body remained present in the intimate souvenir.

A brief inventory of the things of the heart will help show not only the ambiguities but also the elaborate and external nature of acts of passion. Fourteenth- and fifteenth-century houses, except perhaps for those of the high nobility, contained little furniture. Few objects were bequeathed by ancestors, and such rare souvenirs had market value. Intimate souvenirs were found only in churches, piled one on top of another. In the nineteenth century houses were filled with furniture and small mementos, many of no value yet capable of evoking the memory of an ancestor or a particularly moving incident. Between the time when homes were bare and the time when they were packed with souvenirs there was a long period during which the power of objects to serve as souvenirs of others and reminders of one's own passions was developed and elaborated.

I shall not catalogue the most public acts of passion— deeds of courage and valor—of which the principal souvenir was the sword. It is not surprising that swords were engraved with various signs to make them better fit to serve as reminders. In addition to colors, blazons, ciphers, rebuses, initials, devices, votive offerings, images of patron saints and the Virgin, and other signs that will never be deciphered because their creators took their secret with them to the grave, we find a variety of ancient motifs, names of comrades-at-arms, numbers and names of regiments, and dates of battles. Hearts often figured among these signs, but, of all the acts of passion, courage, being public, is perhaps the least ambiguous, which is not to say that acts of courage were not also occasions for self-examination.

The inner life of religion has always revolved around the figures of the holy. The question was how to achieve the repose of the saints in the presence of Almighty God. The fourteenth and fifteenth centuries saw an obvious humanization of the images not only of the Virgin and saints but of Christ himself. This took two forms. Artists in the Low Countries preceded their Italian and Spanish counterparts in depicting the divine body in ever greater physical detail. Christ's wounds and agony were realistically portrayed in small paintings, commissioned mainly by confraternities, and in books of hours. Meticulously detailed images of suffering and death were supposed to promote intimacy with God. Confusing human passions with Christ's passion, people identified with his suffering. Through the body he entered the spirit. People felt his wounds as their own, they shared his humiliation, his shame, and, most intimate of all, his pain without the mediation of theology. In rare but well-known cases, blood actually appeared on the hands, feet, and flanks of men and women who had sought intimate union with God. At times this realism of the passions went beyond the bounds of convention, as in the small painting of *Christ's Crucifixion* by van Eyck (Berlin): beneath the veil that surrounds Christ's loins, his "shameful parts" can be seen. This seems less sur-

Holy Figures

prising when we remember the collections of relics contained in the churches of that time. Christ's five wounds were often depicted without his body on a single sheet of parchment, the better to evoke his Passion (book of hours, Walters Art Gallery, Baltimore). In the seventeenth century the seven swords that pierce the heart of the Virgin (Saint-Amans-d'Escoudournac, Aveyron) reflect a desire to assess blessings and afflictions, much as stations of the cross and rosaries helped the faithful to comprehend the intensity of their individual quests for God. From the fifteenth to the eighteenth century this was probably the dominant theme in popular religion, perhaps in all religion.

The second aspect of the humanization of holy imagery was more social. People continued to observe the ancient tradition of attaching their own rings to a relic of a saint (as at Conques), dressing the relic as they believed it deserved. The nature of religious offerings is significant. Perhaps the most important was the small donation to a confraternity to pay for candles. Confraternal worship was far more intimate than weekly masses. Reciting the rosary before an image of the Virgin, lighted by a small candle,[21] recalled the biblical

Mortifement de Vaine Plaisance (Mortification of Idle Pleasure), 15th century. Quest for union with Christ through contemplation of his torment. (Metz, Municipal Library, ms 1486.)

Frans Hals, *Young Man Holding a Skull*. The theatrical look and gestures are not incompatible with either the inward expression or the "naturalism" of the 17th century. (London, National Gallery.)

exhortation to go pray "in thy closet" rather than call attention to oneself in the midst of a solemn service. Books of hours, made chiefly for the wives of wealthy merchants, encouraged an intimate, individualistic form of worship that involved reading and contemplation. Dutch genre painting evokes this feminine piety, for example, in the very popular *Old Woman Reading Alone*.

Religious paintings were filled with objects to assist worship: not only prayer books but also crucifixes and the ubiquitous skulls. Such objects were sometimes combined with the "signatures" of the saints, such as Saint Jerome's lion. El Greco's *Saint Francis* (Ottawa, Canada) shows the saint holding a skull, which he contemplates with attentive indulgence. Corpses spurred the emotions. Hamlet, seizing Yorick's skull, says to the gravedigger: "Alas, poor Yorick! I knew him . . . he hath borne me on his back a thousand times. And now, how abhorred in my imagination it is! My gorge rises at it. Here hung those lips that I have kiss'd I know not how oft" (Act V, Scene 1).

Small details of daily life were added to religious iconography. God left his house to be welcomed into the house
of everyman. In a painting of the birth of Saint John the
Baptist, angels seem to be making the bed of Saint Anne.
Bouts portrayed the Virgin feeding porridge to the Infant
Jesus. The more doctrinaire paintings were of course visual
embodiments of what began as mere words, but the results
were often entirely in keeping with the spirit of "passional"
painting. The Master of Erfurt (mid-fifteenth century) used
gold to indicate the presence of the divine fetus in the belly of
the Virgin (Berlin). A painting attributed to Witz, showing
the holy infants John the Baptist and Jesus at the location of
their holy mothers' hearts, embodied a whole tradition of
theology. It was only one step further for the artist to "remove" the heart of the Virgin or of Christ from the body in
order to present it by itself, wreathed in a crown of thorns,
inflamed and spewing forth the blood of Redemption.

Jan Steen, *Patient and Physician.*
The signs of illness on the face
are confirmed by the position
of the hand and legs. The physician need only decipher the
body's signs. (Prague, National
Gallery.)

Alain de La Roche (ca. 1465) preached that the Rosary had been established by the Virgin. Confraternity members were granted certain protections against "fire, thunder, thieves, murderers, pestilence, sudden death, and wicked assaults by the hellish enemy," provided they said a certain number of Ave Marias and paternosters. In addition to receiving God's protection, the obliging member experienced God's presence at his side: "By means of this psalter, with which he served the Virgin Mary, she marries him with a gold ring; and, more than that, she makes him feel most strongly her blessed son Jesus Christ, head against head, arm against arm, foot against foot."[22]

The Virgin and Christ are seen exhibiting their hearts in a walled garden. And the pious work *Les Quinze Joies de Notre-Dame* endowed flowers, books, rosaries, crucifixes, and religious paintings with personal significance for the multitude: "Sweet Lady, pray [Christ] that he may sway my heart and all my thoughts." In Jean Molinet's *Roman de la Rose moralisé* (1483) there is a rosary composed of paternosters. A "minor office" for private use in honor of the Sacred Heart was published in 1545 by Jean-Baptiste Anyès. The confraternities of the Sacred Heart spread throughout the world. The first church dedicated to the Sacred Heart of Jesus in the diocese of the Holy Spirit in Brazil dates from 1585. Veneration of the Sacred Heart made inroads even among Protestants, most notably in the seventeenth and eighteenth centuries among German Pietists, whose internalization of the faith went beyond church conventions to link up with the great mystical tradition.

Spiritual Passions

Our knowledge of encounters between the individual and the divine comes from narratives of the inner life. Some of these accounts inspired others, imitation being particularly prevalent among nuns. The stories of Catherine of Siena and Teresa of Avila induced thousands of nuns to follow their example. In their accounts of inner experience, the surroundings are almost devoid of devotional objects, yet pious objects with specific associations abound in the cells of nuns who venerate these saints.

Intimacy between God and those who seek him was not uniquely centered in either the body of the believer or the divine image. In the baroque era, confessors and spiritual directors were endowed by the Church with the power to aid

Flemish school, *Young Woman on Her Deathbed*, 17th century. The father or husband who commissioned this portrait sought to record the passage from life to death. (Rouen, Museum of Fine Arts.)

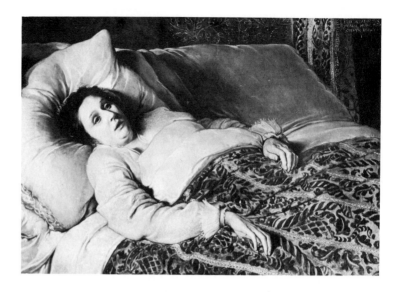

Christians in their search for fulfillment in God, while ensuring that the quest remained within prescribed bounds. Since the physical manifestations of sacred love were the same as those of profane love, a religious authority was needed to distinguish the spiritual from the carnal path. In the tradition of Virgil, to which Dante and Petrarch contributed greatly, union with God was pursued by means of an idealized woman, and it was hard to distinguish between sacred and profane love. A Roman "courtesan," upon hearing the sound of midnight bells signifying the Ave Maria, leapt from her companion's bed to kneel and recite her prayers. The "mother" of the house entered a room in "wrath and fury" to snatch a medallion of the Madonna from the neck of another courtesan, lest the medal be tainted by sin. These facts were recorded by Montaigne, good ethnographer that he was, during a sojourn in the capital of the Church. And the same Montaigne, because he believed deeply in the signs of divine love, caused to be placed in the famous rustic house of the Virgin at Loreto a shrine containing silver figures representing himself, his wife, and his daughter, all kneeling at the feet of the Virgin. He longed for pure love in an intimate, personal relationship with the mother of God.

Religious relics were not only possessions but also sources of miracles. In 1659 Mme de Beauvau told how a fall from a horse threatened the life of Prince Charles, only son of Duke François of Lorraine: "After six hours Mandra, his first gentleman-in-waiting, decided to go **and** fetch Our Lady of Foix, which the late Prince Ferdinand, his brother, used to pack with his wardrobe, and which had been given him by Father de Véroncourt, a Jesuit, because it had distinguished itself by sundry miracles. No sooner was it applied to the heart of the prince than he breathed, renewing hope for his life."[23] The provenance of the relic was noted in detail, in order to make its power both more irresistible and more specific.[24]

The relations between Mme de Mondonville and her spiritual director, Ciron, show that the quest for God via the heart could lead to passions of a quite carnal sort. When Ciron departed in the service of God, Mme de Mondonville was made feverish by his absence. In her letters to Ciron, she repeatedly indulges a need to reveal her inner life, and from his letters to her she draws divine sustenance: "Your letters are for me a torch, which reveals things in my heart about which I knew nothing."[25] With her director gone, she was often able to express her innermost thoughts with even greater intensity than usual: "Yes, Sir, you may speak to my heart, for it has true need of it, and I know not what it is, but it understands no other language . . . Having suffered a great barrenness at prayer, it suddenly seemed to me that I had some secret knowledge about both of us that God wanted . . . When that passed, I fell into a state of languor, which makes life tedious. You look without seeing, you eat without appetite, you live as if in a dream, and you love what you do not know. You wish there were someone to whom you could relate your pain, and you want to give air to the damped fire that seems to consume you."

Mme de Mondonville knows perfectly well that nothing can be hidden on the Day of Judgment. She has her secrets, her secret desires, and her concerns for Ciron's health—"horrible thoughts." Her need to learn from God what must be "circumcised" from her heart involves her in fasting, prayer, and the humiliations of mortifying charity. Her customary good work is to make the beds of female patients at the Saint-Jacques Hospital, but when workers are lacking she serves the male patients as well. A wounded young soldier "suffered greatly because his head was full of vermin." She cut his hair, "which at first made me sick to my stomach. But the thought I had, that it was for Jesus Christ that I was performing this service . . . led me to take the most vermin-laden locks and put them in my mouth." Ciron continued to guide his charge by letter and sent her a portrait of Saint Teresa, in which Mme de Mondonville apparently saw not only the saint's face but also her soul. She wrote Ciron that she had been praying mightily: "While looking at God in Himself in order to discover His will, it seemed to me that I was told that He wanted you to reveal that hidden fire that I then saw in you, as it seemed to me, and I have never been able to think differently."

She carried a cross "outside, but which penetrates deep within." When a nocturnal dream frightened her, she went to her cabinet to savor the peace afforded by the crucifix she kept there. And when, alone, she had difficulty breathing and feared death, Mme de Mondonville felt that she was in the heart of Jesus, or else experienced a vision of God. She could no longer express what was in her heart.

She sent Ciron a small reliquary, to be worn as a scapular. Oddly, however, she seems, like Alberti, to have forgotten the saint's name, which is left blank in the letter. Documents attesting to her progress toward divine peace follow one after another, an accounting of pietistic and theological dissertations written in the language of the notary. At prayer she forgot herself and, in 1660, soiled herself, but her director encouraged and supported her: "Since love dirtied itself by becoming flesh, you must not berate yourself." Objects of piety, such as the cross she wears around her neck, the crucifix in her cabinet, the portrait of Saint Teresa given her by Ciron, and especially his letters, help her to understand her passions and dominate them with the aid of divine love. These objects would remain powerful souvenirs throughout her life.

How typical was this case? Mme de Mondonville was certainly not an ordinary woman. What is interesting about her is her unwavering self-consciousness. A woman of the world, born into a pious and wealthy family, her sensibility was shaped by religion and by her decision to withdraw from social life. Her quest for intimacy with God through the agency of her spiritual director can only be interpreted as an especially intense and well-documented instance of a vast social and religious movement. In her *Memoirs*, written at a much later date, she describes her first meeting with her future confessor: "I saw in passing that M. de Ciron was giving communion . . . I informed him that I wished to confess . . . I therefore went to him with an extraordinary attraction . . . I was dressed in the fashion of the day and always had the most beautiful clothes . . . but after confessing to Father Lejeune . . . I had not shown my bosom and enjoyed a reputation for being highly modest." Ciron began his direction of her conscience by ordering her to wear "what people called Jansenist cuffs, which covered the arms." The path to reason and divine love was thus marked by exhortations to dominate the passions of the heart and objects intended to aid in that purpose.

In Joseph de Gallifet's erudite work on the life of Marguerite Alacoque, we find not only an ethnology of the devotion to the Sacred Heart of Jesus but also a science of its practice. Historical discussion is limited to the origins of the devotion of the Sacred Heart, with reference to the meditations of leading Church figures on the words "Create in me, O Lord, a new heart." Christ's inner suffering, that is, the suffering of his heart, was far crueler than his outward humiliation and wounds. Marguerite says: "I saw him, and I felt him very near me. I heard his voice. And I did so far better than if it had been through the physical senses. For I would have been able to distract myself from their impression and turn away, but I had no defense against these other sensations . . . After these words he [Jesus] asked for my heart. I begged him to take it. Which he did, and placed it inside his own venerable heart, and made me see that mine was like a tiny atom which was consumed in that ardent furnace. Then he drew it out, like a burning heart–shaped flame, and put it back in the spot from which he had taken it . . . The ardor [of the inflamed heart] did not die out, and you could find only a little cooling in bleeding."[26] This is still the physical world described by Lucretius. There is a close connection between the perfect light of the divine and the primordial heats of the human body as well as the cosmos. But the heart engraved and printed in the book also belongs to the anatomy of the century.

Love-Power

Physical beauty can arouse passions in bodies young and old. The merest glance can provoke a blush, a lowering of the eyes, a quickening of the pulse, even a swoon. Love is a kind of power, as the proverb (*Roman des deduis*, 1375) says:

> Amour a si très grant pouvoir
> Et par tout si grant seignorie
> Qu'Elle vaint tout

> Love has such very great power
> and such great dominion over all
> that it vanquishes everything.

Scalion de Virbluneau,
Legitimate and Modest Loves,
1599. Divine power manifests
itself by sending man love (the
heart) and death (the skulls).
(Paris, Bibliothèque Nationale.)

Love can so disturb the mind as to cause violent emotions, sickness, and even death. The person upon whom an amorous gaze has fallen may give a start or cry or talk nonsense or write verse. The power of love comes from outside the individual, from heaven or some more funereal place, and disturbs the equilibrium of the bodily fluids. All human beings are subject to love, but men and women react to it differently because of differences in their organs. Man is by nature colder than woman, hence less subject to love's great passions. In regard to women Rabelais wrote: "Nature has placed within their bodies, in a secret, intestine place, an animal, a member, which is not in men." The functions of the uterus, determined by the moon, can cause women to behave in terrifyingly deranged ways. Men are disturbed when a woman looks at them with love in her eyes. To be sure, what theologians have to say about the effects of love differs from and in some ways contradicts what physicians and jurists have to say, but the differences must be seen in the context of a broad consensus.

French law held that man is more subject to the effects of passion than woman, even if woman is the very incarnation of passion. The jurist Jean Chenu observes: "Experience, master of all things, shows that more husbands are passionately in love with their wives . . . and, in second marriages, second wives are more commonly favored by their husbands than are second husbands by their wives . . . And the reason for that is that man, as the Comic said, *cum ratione amare non potest* [cannot love with reason], so that in order to arrive at his ends he will spare nothing."[27]

The amorous gaze and the passions that it provoked resulted in a new attitude toward the body and clothing. Lovers, already careful about their grooming, became even more so. Until the aging King Henri IV fell in love with young Charlotte, he had been in the habit of neglecting his hair and beard and wearing worn, stained clothing. Suddenly he began to fix his hair, groom himself with great care, and dress in splendid new clothes.[28] Even before the rumors started, everyone at court knew perfectly well that the king was in love. His changed attitude stemmed from a new awareness of his outward appearance. Conversely, absence of the beloved could lead to neglect of the body and lack of appetite.

Passion also had inward effects, encouraging introspection. The presence of the beloved, her eyes, her gestures, her smile, her words, and above all objects that touched her body became sacred to the man who loved her. In profane as well as sacred love, a force, mysterious and divine, caused two

Jean-Baptiste Pater, *The Duo.*
Dressed as in the time of Henri
III, the man lifts his eyes up to
those of the "peasant girl." The
music is drawing to a close.
(Paris, Cailleux Collection.)

hearts to beat as one. The love poetry of Ovid, Virgil, Dante, Petrarch, and the troubadours found prosaic and rather physical embodiment among aristocrats in the sixteenth century and among other classes in the centuries that followed.

Poetry, for all its subtleties and contradictions, always centered on the scene of the amorous encounter and the beauty of the female body. Echoes of chivalry and pastoral can be found in intimate love letters. It was usual to use a word like "thing" or secret signs like the stars to refer to a part of the body or a sexual act while waxing ecstatic about imaginary cupids. Even those most secret and intimate diaries composed in cipher by Englishmen who wished to prevent their wives from reading what they had written were not entirely exempt from poetic flights.[29] Pepys wrote in Italian to describe his amorous adventures with London girls. While on a military expedition Henri IV, a king who in language and conduct belonged neither to the elite nor to the common, described for Corisande (the Countess of Gramont) islands near Marans, which he compared to love-nests. His erotic nature often expressed itself in descriptions of forests, especially the "delightful and lonely" woods near Fontainebleau. Young woman posed nude as Venus or Diana for portraits that were usually set in sylvan surroundings, with water nearby for bathing and perhaps a small hillock, as in the walled garden.

Earthenware plate, 16th century. The amorous gaze implies surveillance. The hand on the shoulder is a possessive gesture. (Paris, Louvre, Taillemas Collection.)

The Exchange of Objects

Pendant of a necklace designed by Hans Holbein. It became increasingly commonplace for people to distinguish themselves as individuals by wearing their own initials. (London, British Library, Sloane Collection.)

German midwife's sign, 16th century. The "vanities"—mirror and jewels—are for once relegated to a position of secondary importance, while the lady listens to three instructions for a good childbirth. (Château du Gué-Péan, Loir-et-Cher.)

Words of love were given concrete embodiment in certain relic-objects: notes, letters, perhaps even a single word in the handwriting of the beloved. In Dutch genre painting, an old woman reading a book signified piety and death, but a young man or woman reading a letter signified love. A lady who received a letter from her lover put it in her bodice, close to her heart. Love letters also could be placed in a small leather bag and worn around the neck as a charm. Such letters might be written in secret ciphers or in readily comprehensible signs such as "S," an enigmatic symbol of fidelity and love known since the fourteenth century but increasingly common after 1550; it occurs frequently in the love letters of Henri IV.[30]

Favorite love tokens included women's combs, ribbons, rings, bracelets, handkerchiefs, *gorgeoires* (bodice covers), mirrors, pearl necklaces, belts, and garters. A man gave his beloved a ring or a ribbon in exchange for a ribbon of hers or a handkerchief. In the sixteenth century it became increasingly popular to commission small portraits, and great artists such as Holbein and Hilliard supplied the needs of what might be called the market for intimate commodities.[31]

The fiction of the time described the exchange of love souvenirs in a style that was almost religious. Affected though it is and despite its picaresque inspiration, Tristan L'Hermite's *Le Page disgracié* is informative about the discourse of love, the sites of intimacy, and the objects exchanged by lovers. Tristan's heroine is sensitive, wealthy, and generous. For the French male she embodies an age-old fantasy: the beautiful English lady. He writes: "I felt a great emotion upon her arrival, and if someone had then touched my side, he would have recognized from the palpitation of my heart how much that object had moved me." When she is away, he kisses her dress and visits her private rooms, especially her cabinet. The lady touches his arm and begs him to keep, as a token of her love, "a small diamond . . . in exchange for a gold ring that he was wearing. His beloved gave him gifts such as paintings on marble with borders of lapis and gilded silver . . . candlesticks for the study, and small silver plates to keep in the ruelle of my bed."

Their meetings take place in her cabinet, where "at first she took my arm and, having sat in her chair . . . she asked me how I had spent the night." They talk about love novels, music, jealousy, abandonment, and death. Vows of fidelity follow, with "my heart stirred by my sobs and my eyes well-

Iron chest, 16th century, decorated with a painting of two persons in a garden. The lock is not to prevent theft but to protect intimate secrets: money, jewels, love letters. (Avignon, Calvet Museum.)

ing with tears." She gives him a bracelet made from her hair, with a clasp of "very beautiful table-cut emerald." These scenes from Tristan L'Hermite read like captions for Vermeer's paintings of amorous couples. Tristan then receives the ultimate gift: "A diamond-covered locket . . . and the portrait inside was covered with delicate paper, folded in four, on which I read the words, 'Wear these things for love of me, as I wish always to carry your image in my soul.' The note was unsigned, but there was a cipher [that she] had a hundred times in my presence engraved on the window glass with the point of a diamond."[32] Up to the end of the nineteenth century, intimate expressions engraved on glass would serve as the perfect symbol of the ambiguity of love and death. Tristan wears the locket over his heart. His beloved comes to him in her dressing gown, which moves him greatly. To avoid the heat of the English climate, she enters a grotto, one of those places where the dividing line between the divine, the human, and the animal was quite fluid.

Despite the faithful passion of the two lovers, the heroine's family intervenes to separate them. Tristan will forever keep secret the name of his beautiful lady, but he will never forget her. His *Memoirs* are the relics of an intimate relationship, real or imagined. Sick with plague and in a state of delirium, "they put an epithem over my heart to give me strength, and since my eyesight was as clouded as my judgment, I imagined that that huge black plaster was an opening in my body, through which the beautiful lady whom I had loved had removed my heart."[33]

Miniatures and Jewels

In the England of Queen Elizabeth I it became fashionable for people to have themselves painted "lonely and languishing" in the depths of the forest. Herbert of Cherbury, whom Tristan probably met, commissioned a portrait of himself in which he is shown lying in the woods. Such wilderness portraits were inspired by the absence of the beloved or by the spurning of a man's suit. A beautiful lady of the court went to Issac Oliver and asked for a miniature of Herbert's portrait. Later, while moving from chamber to chamber in the palace, Herbert saw with his own eyes, through partially drawn curtains, this same lady, alone in her bed, contemplating his portrait in miniature by the light of a candle.

Thousands of miniatures like the one given Tristan by his beautiful lady have survived the vagaries of time. Although

no comprehensive study has yet been done, it is clear that after 1500 the need for portrait painting became widespread among merchants, professionals, and nobles throughout Europe. About 60 percent of the surviving portraits bear no name and will remain anonymous, proof that the people who commissioned them did so to capture and exchange intimate feelings.

Miniature portraiture flourished, especially in Germany and England. Sixteenth-century portraits were rather like effigies on a blue background. In the art of Nicolas Hilliard we see evidence of increasing inwardness, a trend that culminated around 1660 in the miniatures of Samuel Cooper, which portray individuals staring into the distance. In one Hilliard portrait, of a young, anonymous courtier standing among wild roses with his right hand on his heart, the subject's look and pose convey a feeling of love and melancholy, insensible to time and space. Portraits of young men surrounded by flames are not rare. The flames make the passions of the heart visible to the beloved, who is supposed to think of the man's suffering when she sees the painting.

Miniatures were framed by jewels and hung around the

Isaac Oliver, *Lord Herbert of Cherbury*. The duelist describes how he spent the night alone in the woods before one of those duels whose notoriety and knightly aspect set many a female heart aflutter at the English court. (Print after a portrait from the collection of Count Powis.)

Nicolas Hilliard, *Young Man among the Roses*. He is surrounded by wild roses, a torment for this lover, separated from his beloved. (London, Victoria and Albert Museum.)

Isaac Oliver, *Portrait of a Child*. This baby is no temporary visitor in its parents' house. It will remain in their hearts forever. (Ham House, Surrey.)

neck on chains. Lockets with clasps became quite popular in the eighteenth century, as did locked diaries in the nineteenth. The portrait was often wreathed with a lock of hair, establishing a connection between the actual body of the beloved and the image. One remarkable example of a locket is three-quarters of an inch by one inch in size and contains miniatures of a mother and her daughter (or perhaps two sisters), with strands of both women's hair plaited together and fastened to the locket by two gold stars. Miniatures depicting just the eye of the beloved were fashionable in the eighteenth century. Often hidden in a locket or bracelet clasp, these eyes kept the passions alive when lovers were separated. Such contrivances reveal an obvious desire for intimacy, for bodily contact, no less significant than the desire to be buried along with the beloved.

A large cameo representing a woman "as the huntress Diana" (in the Bibliothèque Nationale) is designed to evoke the presence of the beloved not only by sight but also by touch. The sculpture's décolletage enabled the lover to mingle his pleasures. More familiar and no doubt more popular were small rings with clasped hands, and, even more widely represented, hearts from which knots or chains of flowers emerge. Gilles Legaré's book of designs (1663) indicates the models current at the time: knotted ropes, which, like drawings of knots of flowering plants in the closed garden, signified union, fidelity, and the souvenir of love between lovers or between husband and wife. Skulls, often present on these popular rings, were reminders of death, but they also betokened loyalty unto death to a lover, a spouse, or a friend.

In eighteenth-century popular jewelry heart-symbolism may have lost ground to other motifs, such as a pair of turtledoves or entwined garlands of oak leaves. The custom of engraving a brief saying or posy on either the outside or inside surface of a ring remained popular throughout the early modern period.

The often intimate relations between artists and artisans and their wealthy patrons encouraged self-expression in clothing, gifts, and furnishings. Petrus Christus' painting of Saint Eligius as a goldsmith portrays a young couple, most likely in the act of choosing a wedding ring. Rings for sale are displayed in a small casket. As the saint weighs one of them, the young woman makes a gesture of assent, and her fiancé encourages her with an embrace.

Erotic motifs were probably more common than one

Woman with jewels and belt in the form of a chain. The book suggests a fairly high social rank, as do the rings and the coat of arms. One wonders if she knows how to read, because she is holding the book closed with its clasps in place.

Samuel Cooper, *Miniature of a Lady*. The pearl necklace was a prestige item in northern Europe. Is this a love portrait or a death mask? With miniatures the question did not arise. The intimate did not allow itself to be differentiated. (London, Victoria and Albert Museum.)

would guess from the few vestiges of the genre that have survived successive periods of asceticism. Disguising women as goddesses fooled no one. Artists willing to make death masks no doubt were also prepared to use their talents to gratify the erotic fantasies of their patrons. The large size of paintings such as *The Woman with the Red Lily* (Atlanta), Titian's *Venus* (Prado), and the so-called *Diana in Her Bath* by Clouet (Washington) raises the question of where they were hung. They are far too large to have been hidden in a ruelle, even in a princely residence, or to have been hung behind a secret door in a cabinet. Henri IV kept an unframed portrait of his beautiful Charlotte rolled up in his private quarters. Large portraits celebrating the beauties of the female body were presumably exhibited in small, secret rooms, where no confessor or devout relative was likely to see them. The fact that some small cabinets with doors and drawers are decorated with erotic paintings supports this hypothesis. Were such paintings equipped with clasps and locks or "custodes" (doors and curtains that hid the picture beneath)?

Love and Friendship in Marriage

Love in marriage was expressed through the rhetoric of "perfect friendship," or the union on earth of two souls through divine love. Sexuality is often mentioned, but in friendship reason dominates the flesh, and reason is divine. In the seventeenth century the Vacherolles family lived nobly twenty-five miles from Le Puy. The young wife sent her husband genuine letters of love and friendship: "My very dear heart, I am pleased to have this opportunity, on the first day of the new year, to renew my vow to love you all my life and to cherish no one in the world but you. I beg you, my dear friend, to remember me, because whenever you think of me, you will find that my thought is in you, so that if our bodies are separated, our spirits are always together."[34] Individual and couple flourished in this union of souls. The husband's character adjusted to that of his wife and friend, and vice versa. The self was discovered in the other, and there was an end to the contradiction between passion and reason. In another letter the literary origins of Mme de Vacherolles words are more obvious, but her private thoughts lose none of their authenticity: "My very dear heart, I do not ask for more persuasive evidence of your love than you have given in the past. There is no need to sign in blood, because I believe in your love sufficiently without it, and I would be doubting that you love me were I to demand things of that kind."

School of Fontainebleau, *The Woman with the Red Lily*, 16th century, an intimate portrait made for the pleasure of her lover and no doubt commissioned by him from an artist whose talent was no better than average but who could reproduce the usual erotic signs—the head slightly lowered, the eyes upraised. (Atlanta, High Museum of Art.)

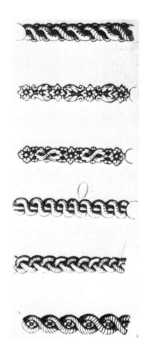

Gilles Legaré and Collet, *Drawings of Rings*. Knotted rings held hearts firmly together. They sold for modest prices. (Paris, Bibliothèque Nationale.)

Mme de La Guette, a sort of amazon born into a family belonging to the high *noblesse de robe*, tells the prosaic story of how she fell in love: "I saw in the princess' chamber a very well-built man, who looked at me a great deal. I returned to my father's house, but not as free as when I left, because that well-built man gratified my thoughts and troubled me without my being aware of the reason. I have discovered it since, for I loved him enough to make him my husband."[35] The man too had fallen in love. After several visits, "he spoke to me in the most gracious terms and assured me of his loyalty and fidelity, which were inviolable." They were subsequently separated by war, but "it was a great relief for me to receive his letters, and even at the time the great sorrow that was consuming me began to dissipate." Her father seems to have objected to the marriage plans for the simple reason that he had been deprived of his choice of son-in-law. But despite the opposition, with the help of aristocratic friends, the lovers married. A question of inheritance complicated matters. In a meeting in the presence of various august personages, the father and the husband "became so angry at each other . . . that I was taken aback to see plates being hurled at the tapestry . . . All the dignitaries fled, for those gentlemen are terrified of trouble and as a rule fight only with the pen . . . I saw my father and my husband within an inch of death . . . [And] I placed myself in front of my father as a shield and bared my breast. Then I said to my husband, who had unsheathed his sword: 'Pierce me here. You will have to kill me before you touch a hair on my father's head.'" Mme de La Guette was of the opinion that this gesture was dictated by nature, but surely it was influenced by memories of literature and the theater. Sometimes the colloquy between lovers exceeded the bounds of reason.[36]

Mme de La Guette was made jealous by her husband's visits to a fine lady: "I had no rest. I could not remain in one place. Everything became unbearable to me, including my bed. One night, in my husband's presence, I paced up and down a thousand times, and he asked, 'What is the matter with you? You keep moving around. Let's go to sleep, I beg you.' 'I can't sleep . . . I have a terrible headache . . . and you are the only one who can cure it.' He said: 'Explain what you mean.' 'All right, let's explain ourselves . . . What I have to say to you is this: if you continue to see a certain lady, I am determined to ruin you both. Make up your mind what you want.'"

Samuel Pepys was no doubt in love with the young Frenchwoman whom he married and who allowed him to think that she was a Huguenot refugee. He kept an obsessive eye on his wife's clothing and hairdo, yet he took genuine pleasure in accompanying her to town, to church, or to the theater. The almost religious nature of his love is evident in his efforts to avoid seeing the Queen of England except in the company of Mrs. Pepys. The sight of the queen was supposed to be an intimate act, full of amorous, sexual, religious, and political significance.

Mr. and Mrs. Pepys

One day, when Pepys returns home, he hears his wife and her dancing teacher practicing in *her* room. When the sound of their steps ceases, jealousy causes him to break out in a cold sweat. He has no reason to doubt his wife's fidelity, but, since he himself is so drawn to every skirt in London, he cannot help believing that his wife is deceiving him.

In town Pepys meets women of every station and always tries to slip his hand under their skirts or into their bodices. The number of women who allow him to have his way is remarkably high, an indication that behavior of this sort was part of the role of bar-girls and chambermaids. In church he always places himself where he can look at a beautiful woman during the sermon, and during the week he becomes aroused at the thought that on Sunday he will see this or that woman when he goes to pray. With certain women he is in the habit of "making love," but such occasions are infrequent, perhaps because the women in question are not particularly "fresh" or beautiful. His own servants provoke fatal passions in him. Pretty Deb combs her master's hair, and he cannot stop himself from slipping his hands under her skirt. Mrs. Pepys learns of this and forces him to show Deb the door. He walks the streets in hope of a chance encounter. Jealous and angry over her husband's passion for Deb, Mrs. Pepys approaches the bed with a hot poker hoping to intimidate him, but Samuel remains intrepid, even though he is being driven out of his mind by guilty passion. He reasons and he raves. Trying to get through to him, his wife confesses that she is not a Huguenot but a Catholic! This revelation troubles Pepys, not for the sake of his soul but on account of his political ambitions, for anti-Catholic sentiment ran high in England in the 1660s. Scientific observer that he was, however, Pepys recorded in his diary that his wife seemed to take more pleasure in sex when she was angry than when she was calm.

John Hayls, *Samuel Pepys*, 1666. Pepys had himself painted for his own pleasure. Here he is shown in a dressing gown, holding music that he had composed. (London, National Portrait Gallery.)

Pepys's house does not seem to have been filled with souvenirs of relatives or with inherited furniture. The couple chose their own new furniture with great care. Mrs. Pepys had nothing to say about major purchases, but she apparently exercised full powers when it came to selecting linen or curtains. A nursery was planned, but after a few years it became Mrs. Pepys's bedroom. At one point Pepys attempts to buy a child, but later he is glad not to have one.

He commissions portraits of his political protector, his wife, his father, and himself. In the last-named, instead of the conventional landscape, he asks the painter to leave the background obscure. He had himself painted in a dressing gown, holding a sheet of music that he had composed. Intended to record the face of a virtuoso in minute detail, the portrait was in no way meant to be a reflection upon death, despite the empty background. The music is a love song, insignificant when compared with the greatest examples of the genre but beautiful to Pepys because it was his own work. Pepys truly loved his wife and remained her sincere friend, but he fell easily into debauch. The portrait of his wife and his diary were his most cherished relic–objects.

A perfect melding of love and friendship was proposed in a broader religious context by certain Protestant radicals. The Lutherans and some British Protestants viewed marriage as a sacred fusion of divine love and friendship and as the "natural" bond between man and woman. For them, celibacy was not a superior state for men; the only true incarnation of divine love on earth, they held, was in marriage.

The Vacherolles were able to feel that they were always together in spirit, even after death, but for Protestants, who did not believe in the efficacy of prayer for a late spouse or in the power of the dead to serve as intercessors on behalf of the living, threats to the marriage bond were a more serious matter. Revolutionary individualism deeply affected the existing ambiguity between love and friendship. Daniel Defoe's *Conjugal Lewdness or Matrimonial Whoredom* (1727) was a God-centered philosophy of marriage that enumerated the various forms of selfishness to be avoided by the loving husband and wife. As an example of the rhetoric of love and friendship in marraige, listen to Sarah Goodhue, an American woman, who wrote: "O dear Husband, of all my dearest bosom friend, if by sudden Death I must part from thee, let not thy troubles and cares that are on thee, make thee turn aside from the right way. O dear heart, if I must leave thee and thine here behind, of my natural affection here 'tis my heart and hand."[37] Sarah Goodhue wrote what she could not say to her husband, who was concerned about her as she was about to begin the labor of childbirth. She seems not to have had the slightest worry about the fate of her own soul if she chanced to die, but the possibility that her husband might lose his apparently accounted for her writing this intimate note. The word *bosom* here has its biblical sense: the bosom of Abraham, a place of safety. The offer of her heart, symbolizing the inner self, and hand, symbolizing friendly loyalty, reflects the marriage vow. Her use of *thee* is another sign of her search for intimacy with her husband and with God.

In the early modern era, social and professional relationships were primarily friendships. Throughout Europe municipal political authorities, knightly orders, religious com-

Intimate Friendships

The inscription on the inside of this ring reads: "Gift of R. Sanders, 1744." This was a talisman given to a son, nephew, or friend to impart visible form to an intimate affection. (Worcester, Massachusetts, Art Museum.)

munities, confraternities, prominent families, and even scholarly organizations fostered friendly relations that formed the basis of emotional life. These friendships expressed themselves through strictly codified behavior. In the sixteenth century it was not unusual for the word "friend" to be used to refer to someone who belonged to one's own social *corps*.

An individual, it was believed, could be drawn into ever more intimate relations with another through the combined effect of heart, humors, and spirit. Close friendship was a form of love, a love whose affections and passions were held in check by reason, that is, by the spirit. For an individual of the early modern era, there could be no true friendship without such affection of one body for another. The iconography of friendship celebrated the union of bodies and minds.

Close friends cherished the memory of their first encounter. They gave each other presents, not to outdo one another socially but to give pleasure or show respect. Jewels, clothing, books, combs, mirrors, and pious objects were exchanged not as the calendar prompted but as the intensity of the friendship grew. A sick friend was a subject of much concern, even anxiety. In a great philosophical or religious friendship a part of one's self died along with the friend, as if a limb had been torn away. Friends exchanged portraits. Alberti liked to sketch the faces of his friends. His self-portrait in bronze sports a wingèd eye, Alberti's *impresa* and a sign that friendship is sustained by the gaze. A friend was quick to lend clothing and money when needed. Between friends of the same sex, the greatest physical affection, sexuality, was ruled out by reason, but erotic words and glances remained possible. Dark secrets were shared with one's friends, as were one's most terrible fears.

Marriage involved a mingling of bodies, if not out of passionate desire then at least out of duty. But sexual relations were not necessarily intimate or friendly. The sexual act required not intimacy, only privacy. When a couple married for profit rather than love, sex without spiritual intimacy was more like masturbation than lovemaking. When husband and wife did not confide in each other, or where the desire to reveal one's innermost self had been exhausted or never existed, their letters lacked the signs of friendship. Yet wives were usually referred to by their husbands as "friends," for it would have been almost an insult not to have done so. Nevertheless, it was not unheard of for a man to address his wife as "Madame." Even without intimacy, marital relations remained civil.

Lawrence Stone has observed that if intimate relations existed in English aristocratic families, they were between father and eldest son. This may be true of aristocratic families throughout Europe. In the ancient world male friendship had a language all its own. In France relations between fathers and sons such as the Pasquiers, Talons, Arnauld d'Andillys, and Lefebvre d'Ormessons were so close that the taboo against expressions of affection and strong emotions by males led to the creation of a literary genre: letters and wills in which fathers expressed their love for their sons and sons for their fathers. Even when father and son lived under the same roof, they wrote to each other.

When Olivier Lefebvre d'Ormesson's son André died, the father wrote, nostalgically no doubt but also with a jurist's knowledge of the depths of the heart, that "he loved me and

Father and Son

Gerard Terborch, *The Reading Lesson.* A genre painting showing a huge book, no mere primer. Intimacy thrived on pious and philosophical reading. (Paris, Louvre.)

I loved him very tenderly, and the names father and son served only to augment our reciprocal friendship and to make it stronger and more legitimate. This friendship, which was my joy during his lifetime, has been my affliction since his death . . . I have lost a son: that is not enough to express my pain, for the loss of a son is not always a great affliction for a father. But I have lost a loving son."[38]

Filial rebellion sometimes ended all possibility of close friendship. Arnauld d'Andilly built an entire philosophy of friendship around his warm relations with his father and father-in-law, perhaps to compensate for the bitter break between himself and his eldest son.

Among educated women we find little evidence of a similar concept of friendship with daughters. Of course there are far fewer sources to work with, perhaps because there were so few educated women. Mothers may have overcome their emotional inhibitions and discussed many things with beloved daughters. Mme de Sévigné is a shining example. Separated from her daughter for long years and by great distances, the marquise lived for her child and made herself a philosopher of intimate and creative friendship. She was driven toward intimacy not only by the warmth of her heart but also by the spirit, that human and religious force that keeps friends together forever.

Even more revealing of paternal friendships are the autobiographies of artists and artisans. Those of Benvenuto Cellini, Dupont de Nemours, and Jacques-Louis Ménétra,[39] different as they are by virtue of time and place, are linked by a common desire to relate to others an aging man's memories of youth. At the beginning of his account, Ménétra insists that he is writing solely for his own pleasure, but his story reflects throughout the importance of relations between master and apprentice.

Ménétra is overcome with emotion at the thought that his boy might be killed in the war. Among artisans and artists there was no sharp distinction between the image of the friendly apprentice and the beloved son. Ménétra is forced by his wife to sell his shop, however, before he is sure that his son has really decided not to follow him in the glazier's trade. Although his own father had not treated him kindly, he had taught him his trade and provided him with a shop. At the end of his life Ménétra is unable to do the same for his son.

Even sons who quarreled with their fathers over the choice of a career never doubted that they had inherited their

Anthony Van Dyck, *Portrait of Jean Grusset and His Son.* Nature, in the background, is neither menacing nor inviting. (Paris, Louvre.)

Continuing a 14th-century
Italian tradition, 17th-century
Dutch genre painting depicted
the ultimate physical pleasure.
From an illustrated French
translation of Boccaccio's *Deca-
meron* (Paris, 1757–1761).
(Paris, Bibliothèque Nationale.)

fathers' talents. Autobiographers from the lower classes
boasted of it, describing their fathers' appreciation of their
work as apprentices. After many years of conflict with his
father, Dupont de Nemours proved that he really could abide
by his father's rules. He made a magnificent watch upon which
he engraved his father's name. With this gift he finally escaped
his father's constant surveillance. To these artists and artisans,
the hands were endowed with gifts and even powers that were
neither entirely inherited nor entirely divine, but which they
believed had little to do with the intelligence.

Cellini felt a strong affection for a young apprentice, an
affection he likened to that of father for son. He played music
with the lad, and during the plague he risked his life because
he could not abandon a dying friend and fellow artist. Behavior of adults toward youths and vice versa was governed by
a generally accepted hierarchy of talent and professional skill.
Measuring an object, Cellini notes that it is "as long as the
hand of a twelve-year-old boy." Young apprentices preserved
their "freedom" by refusing to marry. Ménétra always preferred the intense social life of the shop coupled with amorous
adventures, travels, outings, and common meals shared with
his fellow journeymen. He did not worry much about money
or regular employment, even after his decision to "make an
end," by which he meant to marry.

Friends versus the Wife

The girl whom Cellini kept for "his pleasures" does not
appear to have been part of his intimate life. Apparently his
relations with her were simply carnal. Neither Cellini nor
Ménétra experienced love in marriage, but they knew that
such a thing did exist. While traveling in Languedoc, Ménétra
falls in love with a Huguenot widow, toward whom he is
quite affectionate. A sensitive woman, she corresponds perfectly to his idea of a loving wife. But her relatives have their
eye out for a husband who will be capable not only of running
the shop but also of assuming her late husband's place in
society and civic life. In the end, Ménétra decides that he is
not ready to give up the adventurous life or the companionship
of his fellow workers. For the rest of his life he looked back
on this lost idyll with regret. When he did marry, his wife
simply stepped into the role previously occupied by his stepmother. She took his money, ostensibly for household expenses but in reality to give to her nephews.

Ménétra's close friends are the people about whom he

feels most warmly. Each contributes a little money to pay for the services of a prostitute. With one friend Jacques-Louis commits what can only be called a rape. With another he arranges a rendezvous with a woman who, he discovers the next day, is his father's mistress. He maintains that the woman admitted that she had "more pleasure than she ever did with [his] father." Yet he foregoes the pleasure of a night with a friend's girlfriend out of consideration for him.

From novels, plays, or the opera, a simple glazier like Ménétra learned the rhetoric of love and friendship. A woman looking for a husband tells him: "I see from what you just said that you never loved me." And he concedes: "She was right, for no woman ever touched my heart except for the pleasure of the senses, and nothing else." He rents cheap rooms to see his women in, and in one eighth-story room in the Saint-Germain cloister he installed "a wall of small mirrors, which enabled me to see myself in bed from all sides." This secret place was not reserved exclusively for the pleasures of the flesh, it seems, but clearly such a bachelor's lair was a necessity for making new conquests. Yet even for Ménétra, intimate relationships—between young men or fathers and sons—were apparently one of life's basic needs.

Nicolas Lancret, *Lunch with Ham* (detail). (Chantilly, Condé Museum.)

✑ Distinction through Taste

Jean-Louis Flandrin

T HE first *History of French Private Life*, published in 1782 by Le Grand d'Aussy, dealt exclusively, and in three volumes, with customs pertaining to food and the table. This book cannot devote as much attention to the subject, so I shall omit the most familiar topics,[1] and focus on changes in taste in food in the seventeenth and eighteenth centuries and on the role of taste in social relations.

THE REFINEMENT OF TABLE MANNERS

Growing emphasis on a community of manners and tastes profoundly transformed the nature of the pleasure that people took in eating and drinking in company in the early modern era. Medieval manuals of civility (perhaps in speaking of this period one should say "manuals of courtesy"), when discussing table manners, condemned gluttony, fidgeting, filth, and lack of consideration toward other guests. These vices continued to be denounced in the seventeenth and eighteenth centuries, but new prescriptions were added. They usually pertained to matters of cleanliness. The use of individual plates, glasses, knives, spoons, and forks was recommended. Use of the fingers tended more and more to be forbidden, as did transferring food directly from the common plate to the mouth.

The changes reveal not only an obsession with cleanliness but also a growing individualism. Invisible walls went up around each diner. In the Middle Ages people served themselves from the common plate with their hands. Two or three

Utensils, Cleanliness, and Individuality

people sipped soup from the same bowl and ate meat from the same cutting board. Everyone drank from a single cup, which circulated around the table. Knives and spoons were passed from person to person. Bread and meat were dipped in the same saltcellars and sauceboats. By contrast, in the seventeenth and eighteenth centuries each person had his or her own plate, glass, knife, spoon, fork, napkin, and bread. Whatever was taken from common serving dishes, sauceboats, or saltcellars had to be served with utensils and placed on one's own plate before being transferred to the mouth. Thus, every diner was surrounded by an invisible cage. What was the

Nicolas Arnoult, *Feast Celebrating the Peace of Ryswick*, 1697. (Paris, Bibliothèque Nationale.)

At the end of the 17th century the spoon and the fork were permanently adopted by the social elite. Both utensils were still rather different from those we know, and they were used in somewhat different ways.

reason for these precautions, two centuries before Pasteur's discovery of bacteria? Of what uncleanliness were people so afraid? Perhaps their greatest fear was of contact with others.

The abundance of references to cleanliness in the seventeenth century is striking, particularly in works relating to food and the table. Georges Vigarello has shown how much our current notions of hygiene owe to this century, which in fact was one of the filthiest in history.[2] The ambiguity of seventeenth-century notions of cleanliness needs further emphasis, however. According to Robert's *Dictionary*, the French *propre* (clean) did not become an antonym for *dirty* until 1640. As late as 1704 the *Dictionnaire de Trévoux* defined the French *propre* as being synonymous with the Latin *ornatus* (ornate), *compositus* (carefully arranged), or *comptus* (adorned), and *propreté* as synonymous with *elegantia* and *concinnitas* (elegance). Elegance more than cleanliness was intended when one said: "Women are often affected and ridiculous in their *propreté*."

Anonymous engraving, *Noontime*, 1697. (Paris, Bibliothèque Nationale.)

It is true that the seventeenth-century French attached a great deal of importance to the "cleanliness" of the kitchen, plates and utensils, and eating habits, and that they denounced the "filthiness," "wretchedness," and other "disgusting ways of preparing and serving things" common in France in earlier periods and still current in other countries, especially outside Europe. But "cleanliness" and "filthiness" did not mean what they do today.

Furthermore, there was no obvious reason for some of the new table manners. Food was not to be placed in the mouth with the tip of the knife, but the tip of the knife could be used to pass well-cleaned pieces of cheese to one's neighbors. The fork was recommended for eating most foods, but olives were to be eaten with a spoon and green walnuts with the fingers. The napkin was not to be tied around the neck but smoothed against the chest. Ingenious explanations have been proposed for most of these prescriptions.[3] Whatever their value, they are less important than the role of table manners in creating social distinctions. This is especially clear in the case of rules that were replaced by their opposites as time went by. From the fifteenth to the seventeenth century all the manuals recommended cutting bread with a knife rather than breaking it with the hands, but from the eighteenth century to the present, the custom has been the opposite: bread must not be cut (in France at any rate) but broken with the hands. Table manners seem to be subject to fashion. What matters is not the rationality or morality of a practice but its conformity with the ways of the world.

In the 18th century forks took
on the shape that we know today. Spoons came in a bewildering variety of shapes: stew
spoons, coffee spoons, spoons
for entremets, and so on.
(Paris, Musée des Arts
décoratifs.)

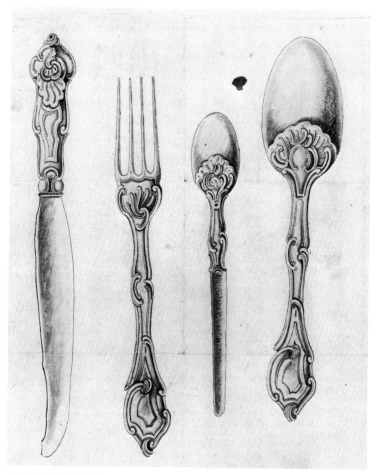

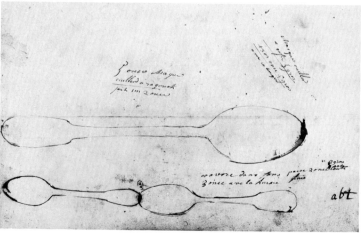

Fashions in manners were inaugurated by the entourage of the king and the leading nobles. They were not always accepted without resistance, however, and some were never accepted. Consider the question of how to hold oneself at the dinner table. In 1545 Guillaume Durand wrote in his French adaptation of Jean Sulpice's manual of civility (1483) that "the wealthy are accustomed to doing as they please and to more insolence than is reasonable. Whence it comes to pass that they are most insolent at table. They may be in the habit of resting their elbows on the table, but you shall not imitate them." In 1613 Claude Hardy is similarly reticent about the way in which certain courtiers break their bread: "Pressing the bread with one hand and breaking it with the nails and tips of the fingers is a pleasure that you must leave to a few people at court. For you it is proper to cut the bread decently with a knife." At the beginning of the seventeenth century Arthus Thomas, Sieur d'Embry, caricatured the affected manners of Henri III's entourage in his *Description of the Island of Hermaphrodites*. He mocks their reluctance to eat with the fingers and their use of the fork: "They never touch the meat with their hands but with forks which they raise to the mouth as they reach forward with their necks . . . They take the salad with forks, for it is forbidden in this country to touch food with the hands, however difficult it may be to pick up, and they would rather touch their mouths with this little forked instrument than with their hands . . . Some artichokes, asparagus, and shelled beans were brought in, and it was delightful to watch them eat these with their forks, for those who were not as adroit as the others let as many fall onto the serving dish or their plates or the ground as they placed in their mouths."[4] As the seventeenth century progressed, however, such opposition disappeared, and the most distinctive customs acquired the force of law at all levels of society.

Medieval literature, particularly in Italy, commonly used peasants to typify bad manners.[5] Although there is hardly an example of this in France before the end of the fifteenth century, by the sixteenth century it had become a commonplace. A custom was henceforth correct if practiced by respectable people, contemptible if typical of peasants and other common folk.

It is surely no accident that such sociological distinctions became increasingly common at about the same time that distinctive dining utensils came into use. The poor could not afford these utensils, possession of which became a convenient

Models of Letters, 18th century. To prevent servants and ungrateful guests from making off with the silver, spoons and other utensils were usually marked with the owner's initials. (Paris, Musée des Arts décoratifs.)

social marker. The new table manners, along with concomitant changes in language and literature, undoubtedly widened the gap between the social elites and the masses.

Segregation at the Dinner Table

A related development was segregation at the dinner table. Evidence for this can be found in remarks about how to avoid disgusting or annoying one's guests. *La Civilité nouvelle* (1667) recommends that plates removed from the table not be scraped clean in the presence of the guests, for "it will sicken those who see it." A few years later Antoine de Courtin warned that when truffles were served covered with ashes, they "must never be blown on," because "breath from the mouth is disgusting to some people." He also says that after eating with a spoon, it should be wiped before using it to serve, because "some people are so delicate that they would not want to eat soup in which you placed your spoon after it had been in your mouth." Furthermore, a napkin should never be so soiled that it resembled a kitchen rag, for that would "disgust anyone who saw you wipe your mouth with it."[6]

During the sixteenth century servants were forbidden to sit at their master's table in the dining rooms of noble Romans.[7] In the seventeenth century wealthy English nobles became increasingly reluctant to invite poor or modest neighbors to dinner in their country houses.[8] In the case of France, it is difficult to find proof that social heterogeneity at the dinner table existed in the Middle Ages. At banquets important personages were seated at different tables from the domestics. Few descriptions of ordinary meals have survived. Nevertheless, many signs suggest that social segregation increased at the table as it did in other areas of daily life.

Up to at least the beginning of the seventeenth century, being seated at the same table did not necessarily mean eating the same food or drinking the same drink. Olivier de Serre advised the country gentleman to stock wine of inferior quality for less illustrious guests, saving his best wine for their betters. Manuals of civility, cookbooks, handbooks on carving, and other literature pertaining to food were full of advice about what dishes to serve to the master of the house and the illustrious guests who honored his table with their presence.

Segregation increased in the eighteenth century as table manners became freer and more egalitarian. Intimate "libertine" suppers are a special but noteworthy case. No servants

Jean Michel Moreau the Younger, *The Refined Supper.* Libertinage and increased social segregation led to the development in the 18th century of wine coolers and other conveniences that made it possible to dispense with servants and their ever-present surveillance. (Paris, Bibliothèque Nationale.)

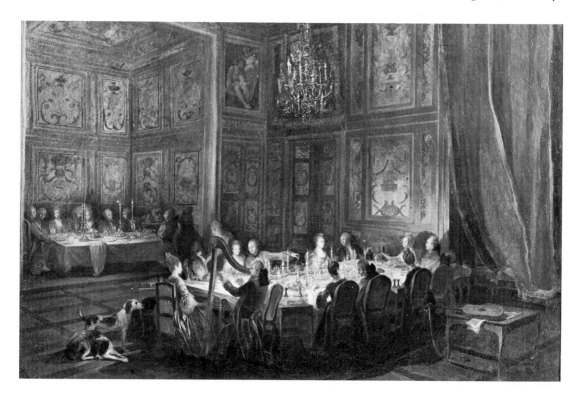

were present, and pleasures other than food and conversation were a part of the evening's entertainment. Guests at such suppers could not enjoy themselves unless the company was homogeneous.

Homogeneous in what sense? Wealth and social rank were not the only or even the most important criteria. Seventeenth- and eighteenth-century salons and tables saw nobles mingle with commoners and the rich with the not-so-rich. Already people were aiming for a homogeneity of culture, manners, and taste—taste in many things, not just food. Of course I am speaking of occasions where conviviality was essential. For ceremonious occasions, which still existed, good manners sufficed.

Like table manners, tastes in food changed in the seventeenth and eighteenth centuries. Even more than manners, it became an object of fashion and a creator of social distinctions, a pole around which new social groups were formed. In the seventeenth century and later the very idea of taste assumed a new importance.

Michel Barthélemy Ollivier, *Supper at the Prince of Conti's Residence at Temple*. Guests who are not conversing privately with their neighbors are lost in quiet reverie or read a paper or listen to a tune played on the harp. The large and sumptuous dining room, the number of guests, and the presence of a few servants did not prevent these 18th-century aristocratic diners from enjoying their meal in an intimate atmosphere. Even the dogs are calm. Their presence, traditional for centuries at noble tables, has become a deliberate sign of simplicity. (Versailles.)

THE TRANSFORMATION OF TASTE

Taste in food did change, to judge from travel literature and cookbooks. Relative to changes in table manners, however, the change in taste at first seems rather paradoxical, for rather than widen the gap between the elite and the lower classes, it narrowed that gap substantially.

In France and other European countries, one of the principal distinctive features of aristocratic cuisine in the fourteenth, fifteenth, and sixteenth centuries was the use of Oriental spices. In the seventeenth century, however, French travelers began to criticize the spicy dishes that were still being served in the rest of Europe. In France, meanwhile, cooks were actually using pepper, clove, and nutmeg more often than in the past but in smaller quantities, and they almost stopped using spices such as saffron, ginger, cinnamon, malaguetta pepper, hot pepper, galingale, and mace.[9]

The Decline of Spices

Native herbs and spices, not widely used in aristocratic kitchens in the Middle Ages, became much more prevalent in seventeenth- and eighteenth-century cooking: mint and hyssop lost favor to chervil, tarragon, basil, and especially thyme, laurel, and chive. Parsley, frequently mentioned in the Middle Ages, became even more popular. Shallots, scallions, and Spanish garlic were added to the medieval onion. Garlic, always regarded as a vulgar herb, was rejected by some cooks such as L.S.R. (the author of *L'Art de bien traiter*, The Art of Good Cooking), but prized by others such as Menon (who mentions it in his *Soupers de la cour*, Court Suppers). Such Provençal condiments as capers, anchovies, olives, lemons, and bitter oranges came into favor. Even more characteristic of French cooking in this period was the use of truffles and mushrooms of every variety. All of these ingredients were far more accessible to the common folk (in their native provinces at any rate) than were the exotic spices of the Orient. Thus class distinctions were apparently diminished.

The Choice of Meats

In the Middle Ages fowl and game furnished the noble meat courses; butchered meats, especially beef, were used primarily in stocks, minced meat dishes, and slowly cooked stews. As a result, chefs employed by the aristocracy seldom mention the different cuts of meat. Between 1400 and 1700, however, cooks began to discuss the characteristics of many

C E P A.

Franç. *Ciboulle,*
ou *Oignons.*

Ital. *Cipolla.*

Efp. *Cebolla.*

All. *Zvvifel.*
flam. ...

CEREFOLIVM
Cherephyllon
Matth.Caft.Lug.d.

Fr. *Cerfueil.*

It. *Cerefoglio.*

All. *Korffel kraut*
flam. Kërvël.

QVALITEZ
ch. & fech.

P E P O
Matth. Fuch.
Lugd. Caft.

Fr. *Melon.*

It. *Pepone.*

Efp. *Melon.*

All. *Meluon.*
flam. mëloën.

more cuts, and butchered meats were more often served as roasts as well as in stocks, stews, and pot roasts.

Surprisingly, most of these cuts were known to the butchers of the fourteenth century, and a number of them are mentioned in the *Ménagier de Paris*, a book intended for use in bourgeois households. Less well supplied with fowl and game than were the princely courts, more modest kitchens may have been obliged to make better use of butchered cuts. The chefs employed by the aristocracy in the seventeenth and eighteenth centuries seem to have followed the lead of bourgeois cooks, a development that cannot be explained in terms of an alleged improvement in the quality of the "gross meats."[10]

The location of an important social dividing line changed: the key distinction was no longer between aristocrats, who ate game and fowl, and bourgeois, who ate gross meats, but between the nobility and bourgeoisie, which ate the good cuts of meat, and the common people, who ate the *bas morceaux*, the low-grade cuts. Much could be said about precisely which cuts belonged to which category, because judgments varied with time and place. Cooking techniques were adapted to the specific qualities of each cut (or perhaps the cuts were selected with an eye to the dishes desired). Cuts with no particular qualities were rejected. The choice of cut took on a social character, dividing the vulgar from the distinguished. Consider pork, a "gross meat" from an impure animal. We can follow the changing list of rejected parts of the animal by studying contracts between the purveyors and the stewards employed by princes and other high nobles. Pigs' ears vanish from the contracts in 1659, pork chops in 1660, fry and lard in 1667, and feet, snout, belly, back, chitterlings, and *chair de porc* (byproducts of butchery) after 1670. Other nobles, including the king, ceased to buy any pork products other than

Scallion, chervil, and melon from the *History of the Plants of Europe* (Lyons, 1671). (Paris, Library of the National Museum of Natural History.)

Rembrandt, *Beef Carcass*, 1655. Beef was eaten by the lower classes and the bourgeoisie in the Middle Ages; it was especially popular in Flanders. In the 17th and 18th centuries the better cuts began to be served at aristocratic tables, stewed, braised, and sometimes even roasted. (Paris, Louvre.)

suckling pigs, ham, and lard, which long remained indispensable for cooking, despite the rising consumption of butter. Cookbooks confirm that there was a new squeamishness about eating pork. Ham gradually supplanted all other cuts of pork, which virtually disappear in the second half of the seventeenth century. Nor was this a passing fashion: twentieth-century writers on gastronomy still must contend with bourgeois contempt for other parts of the hog.

As the social elites became increasingly aware of the quality of different cuts of meat, the common folk resorted to piquant seasonings to make the less-than-choice cuts left to them palatable. In 1746 Menon remarks at the beginning of his chapter on beef in *La Cuisinière bourgeoise* (The Bourgeois Cook) that "in explaining the principal parts of the steer, I will not go into detail about what we call *basse boucherie* [the base cuts], which meat is used only by the *bas peuple* [the lower orders]. They prepare the meat with large quantities of salt, pepper, vinegar, garlic, and shallots to cover its insipid taste."

In the seventeenth and eighteenth centuries good cooks turned against many old practices that concealed the natural taste of food. Nicolas de Bonnefons wrote in his *Délices de la campagne* (Country Delights, 1654): "The subject . . . of this third book is the true taste to be given every food. . . . Try your best to diversify and distinguish by taste and appearance whatever you prepare. A good healthy soup should be a good bourgeois dish, well stocked with carefully selected, good-quality ingredients, cooked in a little stock, without chopped meats, mushrooms, vegetables, or other items. It should be simple, because it is called healthy. A cabbage soup should be flavored entirely with cabbage, a leek soup entirely with leeks, a turnip soup entirely with turnips, and so on . . . And you will see that your Masters will be healthier and have a better appetite and that you and the cooks will receive the praise. What I say about Soups holds true in general and is the law for whatever is eaten."

In order to preserve the characteristic taste of each food, chefs in aristocratic kitchens acquired the habit of cooking separately each ingredient of a complex dish. For instance, Menon gives one recipe for lamb stew in which the turnips are cooked with the mutton and another in which they are cooked separately and added to the meat at the last minute.[11]

Another technique of good cooks in the seventeenth and eighteenth centuries was to cook meat rather rare and serve it without sauce. In 1660 Pierre de Lune wrote in *Nouveau Cuis-inier* (New Cook): "Ducks and waterfowl should be drained and roasted on a spit without larding, and when half done they should be seared with lard and eaten quite rare, with salt and white pepper and orange juice or a natural poivrade" (p. 83). In 1674 L.S.R. went one step further. Of lamb roasted on the spit he wrote: "When it is almost cooked, sprinkle very fine salt on the top only, and pay no attention to those foolish petty-bourgeois recipes that use white bread, which only sucks up the substance and juice from the meat, or that recommend putting endless quantities of chopped parsley on lamb as well as veal and mutton" (p. 54). As for squab: "Such meat requires a vinaigrette or a poivrade, depending on your taste. But to tell the truth, the best and healthiest way to eat the roast is to take it straight from the spit in its natural juice and not too well done, without undue preparation which only destroys the true taste of things" (pp. 55–56). He then gives an example of an abominable old practice still in use in bourgeois kitchens: "Like those who, wanting to eat a good sirloin, after removing it from the spit cut it in pieces, place it in a mixture of water, vinegar, stock, and salt along with garlic, shallots, lemon and orange peels, nutmeg, capers, and a hodgepodge of other things which after a quarter an hour of boiling change the nature of the meat, making it tougher and more tasteless than

Etienne Jeaurat, *The Copper Pot*. In the 18th century the herbs and roots used in humble soups inspired painters of the simple life, but they were also used constantly in haute cuisine. (Auxerre, Museum of Art and History.)

wood. I maintain that the steak should be cooked according to its thickness on a slow fire to begin with, and that it should be eaten straightaway and enthusiastically in its own juice with nothing other than some salt and a little white pepper" (p. 56).

Quick cooking was recommended not only for roast meat but also for vegetables such as asparagus. L.S.R. writes: "Remember that asparagus should crunch when it is bitten and should retain all its green color, for otherwise it is just stringy . . . which you can tell easily by grasping the asparagus by the bottom. If it bends easily, that is a sign of overcooking, which is not appropriate and offensive to taste." More briefly, *Le Cuisinier français* warned in 1651: "Do not overcook them," and "get by with as little cooking as possible, that is the best." And Menon wrote: "A half of a quarter of an hour is enough cooking; they should be fairly crunchy."

To be sure, seventeenth- and eighteenth-century cooks did not carry this trend toward natural and proper cooking as far as they might have done. Some celebrated chefs like Massialot paid scarcely any attention to the question. The trend emerges only in comparison with medieval cooking, not in comparison with the twentieth century's *nouvelle cuisine*.

Many other trends were typical of this period: among them were the advent of meat-based sauces; the vastly increased use of butter in cooking (already important in the sixteenth century), despite the continued use of lard in haute cuisine; the tendency to separate sweet from salty dishes, still hesitant but already significant; a diminishing taste for acidic flavors, not unrelated to the moderation in the use of spices. But my purpose is simply to point out the changes that played a role in the transformation of social relations.

Gérard Dou, *The Vegetable Seller*. In the 17th century cabbages, onions, and various kinds of roots began to appear on aristocratic tables as well as those of the lower classes and the bourgeoisie. Asparagus, originally popular in southern France, began to be grown in other regions, where it was used in refined cooking. (Nîmes, Museum of Fine Arts.)

The Refinement of Taste

Historians of gastronomy make two related points. All agree that medieval Frenchmen were big eaters but not gourmets. "Ostentatious quantity of consumption was more important than quality."[12] Related to this is the idea that "for the medieval diner, the visual effect of food was as important as its taste, perhaps even more important."[13] The implication is that seventeenth- and eighteenth-century diners were more concerned with the taste of what they ate than were medieval diners. Yet neither of these assertions has been proved conclusively.

Quantity and Quality

The idea that medieval feasts were abundant but crude, whereas modern dinners were more modest in quantity but more refined in quality, was articulated as early as the seventeenth century. In the preface to *L'Art de bien traiter*, for instance, L.S.R. wrote: "Today there is not in good dining that prodigious superfluity of dishes, that abundance of ragouts and hashes, that extraordinary assemblage of meats, those bewildering heaps of diverse species, those mountains of meat . . . [these] are not the most prominent objects of the delicacy of our taste, but rather the exquisite choice of meats, the fineness of their seasoning, the politeness and propriety of their service, their quantity in proportion to the number of people, and finally the general order of things which contribute essentially to the quality and beauty of a meal that charms both the palate and the eye."

Abraham Bosse, *Seating Arrangement at the Feast Given by His Majesty to the Knights after Their Creation at Fontainebleau, 14 May 1633.* It was not in the Middle Ages but in the 17th century that tables disappeared beneath a carpet of dishes. (Paris, Bibliothèque Nationale.)

One troubling fact does not square well with this view of things: no medieval representation of a meal shows a table groaning beneath the weight of huge mounds of food. To be sure, the Duke of Berry's table in the *Très Riches Heures* is

well provided with dishes of every variety. But it was actually in the seventeenth and eighteenth centuries that tables began to disappear beneath a veritable carpet of dishes and we find roasting pans filled with meats of every description. Consider, for instance, Abraham Bosse's engraving of the banquet given by Louis XIII on 14 May 1633 for the knights of the Holy Spirit, or the dinner given by Louis XIV on 30 January 1687 at Paris's *hôtel de ville*. Note the pryamids of fruits and cakes that can be seen in every picture of a dessert, buffet, or supper. In comparison with these seventeenth- and eighteenth-century feasts, most medieval tables seem woefully bare. However unrealistic the artists may have been, it is clear that in the fourteenth and fifteenth centuries the aristocratic banquet was no gastronomic orgy.

The few surviving examples of medieval French menus, including the twenty-five recorded in *Le Ménagier de Paris*, are

François Alexandre Desportes, *Meat Lunch*. Meat days and meatless days continued to govern dinner menus in 18th-century France, but to a lesser degree than in the Middle Ages. Here fresh radishes and cherries are served along with the ham and pâté. (Paris, Private collection.)

LE DINE DV ROY A L'HOTEL DE VILLE DE PARIS

certainly lavish. But those published by Massialot in 1691, at the beginning of his *Cuisinier royal et bourgeois*, are no less so. On the contrary. The banquet given by the Duke of Aumont on 27 December 1690 included 16 soups, 13 entrées, and 28 hors d'oeuvres in the first course, and 16 meats, 13 side dishes, and 28 hors d'oeuvres in the second course. Add to that no fewer than 57 desserts, for a total of 171 dishes, some quite substantial, for 42 guests, as compared with no more than 36 dishes in the most lavish menu in *Le Ménagier*.

True, feasts of Rabelaisian proportions were not unknown in the Middle Ages. Consider the banquet given to honor the installation of George Neuvile, chancellor of England, as Archbishop of York in the sixth year of the reign of King Edward IV (1466–1467). The guests consumed 300 quarters or 4 tons of wheat, 300 barrels of ale, 100 barrels of wine, a cask of hippocras, 104 oxen, 6 wild bulls, 1,000 sheep, 304 calves, 304 hogs, 400 swans, 2,000 geese, 1,000 capons, 2,000 suckling pigs, 400 plovers, 1,200 quail, 2,400 rees (a kind of bird), 104 peacocks, 400 wild ducks and teals, 204 cranes, 204 kids, 2,000 chickens, 4,000 pigeons, 4,000 rabbits, 204 bitterns, 400 herons, 200 pheasants, 500 partridges, 400 woodcock, 100 curlews, 1,000 egrets, and 500 deer, as well as 4,000 cold venison pâtés, 1,000 dishes of many-colored jelly and 3,000 of single-colored jelly, 4,000 cold pies, 3,000 creamed dishes, 600 pike and 800 bream, 12 porpoises and seals, and quantities of gingerbread, sweets, and waffles.

Clearly the amount of food consumed here is impressive, and other accounts tell of banquets equally if not more grandiose. But these were public occasions, not unlike the civic banquets of the French Revolution, which must have consumed food on just as vast a scale. Attending the banquet honoring the Archbishop of York were most of the great lords and ladies of England, the high clergy, the leading officeholders and jurists, lay and religious notables, monks of the town, country squires and wealthy peasants of the region, 69 royal pages, more than 400 servants attending the various illustrious guests, plus 1,000 servants and waiters and a kitchen staff numbering at least 177. In all there were about 2,500 diners seated at innumerable tables in the hall, the chambers, the lower hall, the galleries, and kitchens of the castle, to which one should probably add the common folk of the city of York and the surrounding countryside, who were not seated inside but who surely must have feasted on what was not consumed by the 2,500 invited guests and servants.

Dinner Given by the King at the Hôtel de Ville of Paris, 30 January 1687. Note the many platters heaped with roasts and meats of every variety. Each guest has a fork, apparently used for serving meat from the platter. For putting the food into their mouths four of the guests are still using their fingers. (Paris, Bibliothèque Nationale.)

Banquets of this kind teach us less about the refinement or lack of it in the taste of the medieval elite than about the way in which social prestige was established in the Middle Ages. A great personage like the Archbishop of York had to feed immense crowds, seated hierarchically as far as the facilities allowed. In the seventeenth and eighteenth centuries, by contrast, the concern was not so much to please the crowd as to gratify the taste of the social elite, which was now increasingly cut off from the common folk. The dichotomy of quality and quantity refers to this change in social relations.

In the Middle Ages such magnificent repasts very likely enticed some guests into overindulgence. But there is no proof that such excesses were the rule around the head tables or in the dining rooms where the most notable guests were assembled, portrayed in medieval painting as dignified to an almost depressing degree.

Literature of the Kitchen

Treatises on cooking tell us something about the aims of those who staged banquets in medieval and early modern times. Historians of medieval cooking have called attention to some of the spectacular side-dishes that adorned the medieval table: pâtés of fowl which, when cut, released flocks of living birds; a "painted" dish that depicted the "knight on the swan" floating in a gondola, described in the second part of the *Viandier de Taillevent* in the Vatican Library; a dish that showed a Saracen tower attacked by a wild man, another that showed Saint George rescuing a maiden from the claws of a dragon, and yet another showing Saint Martha holding a dragon on a leash. Such spectacular dishes were typical of the fourteenth and fifteenth centuries, but examples from the seventeenth, and even the eighteenth and nineteenth centuries, are not unknown. No one was obliged to eat the figures of mincemeat and pastry or the scenes painted on canvas with wooden frames, and since the guests had already eaten their fill of other dishes, the pleasure they took in such showpieces in no way implies that they sacrificed their gastronomic pleasure.

A more significant change was the trend away from serving large birds complete with all their feathers. With great difficulty the bird's skin was removed without tearing it. Then the bird was roasted over a slow fire, after which it was put back inside its skin before being brought to the table, which probably did nothing to improve the already questionable gastronomic value of such species as the swan, stork, cormorant, crane, heron, or peacock. Unlike the decorative side dishes, these birds were intended to be eaten.

This fashion eventually passed, surviving only in the practice of decorating pâtés of pheasant and other handsome birds with feathered heads and tails. These unappetizing species gradually disappeared entirely from the cookbooks: the cormorant some time in the sixteenth century, followed by the swan, the stork, the crane, and the peacock between 1555 and 1650, and finally the heron, which *Le Cuisinier français* still included in its list of meats in 1651 but which vanished from later treatises for the kitchen. Instead of these large wildfowl, people began eating a wide variety of smaller birds, many of which are still prized by gastronomes today: snipe, the warbler of Provence, the *bénaris* or *vénaris* of Gascony, the bunting, the white-tail, the thrush, the lark, and so on. No doubt these birds were eaten in the Middle Ages in some regions of France, and they may have been served at the tables of the king and the high nobility. But cookbooks rarely mention them, and when they do it is simply under the head of "small birds." The substitution of tasty small birds for decorative large ones probably reinforced the idea that medieval eaters were inter-

Martin Engelbrecht, *The Cook*. To L.S.R., decorating a pâté with the head of the bird whose meat was used in the dish was "a grimace of the *patissier* . . . an ornament that strikes me as so bourgeois that I cannot tolerate the custom." Once considered elegant, this practice, like so many others, seems to have survived longer in Germany than in France, at least to judge by this engraving, which shows a pâté decorated not only with the bird's head but also with its tail and wings.

ested mainly in the visual spectacle, while modern ones are interested more in taste. The same conclusion might be drawn from the disappearance of whale, dolphin, and seal from the menu in the seventeenth century. Yet the whole argument seems rather ethnocentric, or perhaps one should say "chronocentric," given the impossiblity of proving objectively that swan, stork, crane, peacock, and heron or the great marine mammals are gastronomically inferior to snipe, bunting, and thrush.

The Lexicon of Flavors

Comparison of the words used in medieval and modern cookbooks is revealing. Three medieval manuscripts evince a concern for the quality of the dishes prepared. The word "good" (or "goodness") occurs 29 times, "better" 19 times, "tasty" 3 times, and "delicious" once. But four treatises from the seventeenth and eighteenth centuries refer more often and with a richer vocabulary to the quality of dishes: "good" ("goodness") occurs 56 times, "bad" 4 times, "better" 22 times, "delicate" ("delicacy") 14 times, "delicious" 2 times, "excellent" 10 times, "exquisite" 2 times, "refined" ("refinement") 7 times, "tasteless" once, "insipid" 3 times, and "tasty" 3 times. In all, more than 124 occurrences as compared with 52.

Nevertheless, if the modern vocabulary is more varied when evaluating different dishes, it is less precise in describing the diversity of flavors. The word *gout* (taste) does occur far more often in the modern treatises but generally in a vague sense and, in phrases such as "a good taste," more as a term of praise than a category of description.

Medieval treatises used the more technical term *saveur* (flavor), and a far wider range of flavors was evoked. To describe the sour flavor then so much in vogue, the sources used a range of words (*aigre, aigret, aigu, aiguiser, vert, verdeur*) and expressions (*saveur bien aigre, goût de verjus, assavourer de vinaigre*), whereas modern treatises yield only three terms (*aigrir, pointe, piquante*). The medieval sources all speak of saltiness, with words and expressions such as "to desalt," "oversalted," "too salty," "properly salted," and so on, whereas the modern sources seem unconcerned on this score. Again, medieval sources refer to "spiciness" in a variety of ways, while modern ones neglect it. On the other hand, bitterness is mentioned once in one of the seventeenth-century cookbooks but not at all in any of the medieval ones. Yet the medieval sources evoke bitterness indirectly in terms of green-ness, tartness, and *arsure* (a burnt taste). Sweetness is mentioned in both periods—ten times in the medieval sources and at least as often in the modern ones. But the word *doux* was used in the Middle Ages not only to refer to the sweetness of sugar but also to denote the absence of a salty taste.

In general, although taste was more highly valued in the seventeenth and eighteenth centuries, it seems to have been better analyzed in the fourteenth and fifteenth. Champions of medieval cooking might argue that modern cookbooks exhibit more rhetoric than discernment. To which proponents of classical French cuisine might retort that it was too complex and sophisticated to be analyzed with such simple terms as sour, salty, spicy, bitter, and sweet.

Change is also evident with regard to cooking techniques, consistency of sauces, cleanliness in the kitchen, and beliefs concerning the healthful qualities of different foods. Here again, however, there is no clear evidence that cooking became more sophisticated in the later period. Nor were aesthetic concerns more prevalent than before.

The truly significant changes are found in the details of cooking, particularly in the area of colors. Not that the medieval cookbooks mention more or different colors than modern ones. But medieval cooks were interested in color for its own sake or for the pleasure it gave the eyes, whereas seventeenth- and eighteenth-century chefs were interested in color for what it revealed about the nature and flavor of food.

In the Middle Ages many dishes were identified by their color as much as or even more than by the ingredients they contained. Examples include blancmange, green sauce, white garlic, green garlic, yellow sauce, yellow pepper, black pepper, red stew, green stew, green eel stew, white German stew, and so on. Furthermore, except for white, these colors were generally added to what we consider the essential ingredients of the dish.

We find such instructions as "add saffron for color," "mix in saffron to redden the blend," "add green coloring," "add a little saffron to the green," "burn the bread to give it color," and so on. Recipes for dishes such as "stuffed poultry," found in most of the cookbooks, are concerned primarily with the presentation of the food, and color is of central importance: "Decorate or cover with green and yellow: for yellow, take a great quantity of soft eggs and beat well with a little saffron,

The Value of Colors

and put the dressing in a plate or other vessel. And for a green dressing, chop greens into the eggs. And after your chicken is cooked . . . pour the dressing all over it and put it back on the fire two or three times until it takes, being careful not to overcook" (*Taillevent*, Vatican ms, pp. 92-93).

Various methods and substances were used for coloring dishes, starting with herbs used to add a green tinge, a list of which can be found at the end of *Le Viandier* (Vatican Library), after the spices: "Parsley. *Hearbe avens.* Sorrel. Grape leaves or buds. Currants. Green wheat in winter." Other more or less edible colorings included saffron for adding yellow or red; sunflowers for blue, violet, and red; alkanet for dark red; and red cedar for other shades of red and pink. But the effect of other colorants on the edibility of food is more dubious. The second part of *Le Viandier* lists fine azure (powdered lapis lazuli), gold leaf, silver, and for less noble repasts, "white, red, and green tin leaf." And the dishes in question were not decorative but intended to be eaten.

The medieval habit of selecting ingredients according to the desired color of the dish did not disappear all at once. Blancmange with green sauce is still eaten today. The seventeenth- and eighteenth-century sources mention white sausages as well as such artificially colored items as green base and red base, and green, red, yellow, and violet jelly, obtained by means of food coloring that could be purchased "from the grocer." Pierre de Lune made a "green cream" by mixing cream with an herbal juice.[14]

For the most part, however, the colors mentioned in the more modern sources were not artificially added. They were the "natural" colors of the food, or the colors that resulted after proper cooking. References to yellow and red carrots, to white and green chicory, to green and yellow peas, to green beans, green currants, green almonds, and green apricots served to distinguish particular varieties of these foods with their own special flavors and properties. Similarly, the white of the leek was quite different for culinary purposes than the green. The white meat of the chicken tasted different from the dark. The white of the egg was not the same as the yellow. All of this was perfectly obvious and taken for granted.

More interesting from the standpoint of the history of taste and cooking are the colors that result from cooking. White stock differed from brown stock in that the former was prepared by boiling raw meat, the latter by boiling meat that had been browned. White stock was used for "white soups" and for cooking "white meats," whereas brown stock was used for "brown soups," "brown entrées," and "brown meats." All these categories were eminently cultural products, but they are so fundamental to the structure of classic French cooking that they came to seem natural.

There was also "white butter," butter heated just to the melting point, and "brown butter," cooked longer and over a higher heat. Flavored with a variety of spices, these two butters provided the base for the two great classes of sauce in the seventeenth century: white sauce and brown sauce.

Today as in the seventeenth century color terms are used to describe cooking techniques. To blanch means not to whiten but to boil briefly in water. To brown means to cook (with or without butter or oil) until a piece of meat or vegetable begins to turn brown. Roasting or frying instructions often specify cooking until the meat takes on a "good color." And when Nicolas de Bonnefons says that a steak should be eaten "all bloody and red," he means not that it should be tinted with arkanet or red cedar but that it should not be overdone.

Thus, color was used to indicate both the quality of a food and the degree to which it should be cooked, and it is clear from the sources that seventeenth- and eighteenth-century cooks and diners were very attentive to such matters. Discussing "blue-cooked" pike, Bonnefons explains that it should be "well sprinkled with salt and doused with good vinegar" which "gives a very azure blue that is very pleasant to look at." Could this indicate a survival of the taste for blue that caused medieval cooks to add "powdered azure" to their dishes? But Bonnefons adds that "if the fish is alive, it takes on a much more beautiful blue than if it is dead." Clearly this is a fairly substantial reason for liking the blue of cooked fish and no doubt explains better than a supposed fondness for the color blue why people favored "blue-cooking."

To sum up, early modern cooks were not the first to concern themselves with the gastronomic quality of their dishes. Both medieval and modern cooks were also concerned about the visual appearance of food, as is shown by their words and their deeds. But the relation of aesthetics to gastronomy changed. Given our lack of knowledge about the tastes of the elite, it is hard to say just how much gastronomic pleasure fourteenth- and fifteenth-century chefs sacrificed to visual aesthetics, but it does seem clear that the two values were sufficiently independent that one could be pursued to the detriment of the other. By contrast, from the seventeenth

French school, *Banquet* (detail), 17th century. Fowl that were to be roasted were generally wrapped in bacon, because they were supposed to remain white and be covered with sauce. Roasts served dry, however, were supposed to take on a nice color in cooking. They were therefore laced with *lardons*, which provided enough grease to keep the meat from drying out or burning but not from browning. (Strasbourg, Museum of Fine Arts.)

Jean-Baptiste Lallemand, *The Bourgeois Kitchen*. The domain not only of the cook but also of the mistress of the house, old bourgeois kitchens were vast warehouses. Though well equipped with utensils, these were not arranged in any practical or pleasing manner, and the room seems quite cold despite the fire kept burning throughout the day. (Dijon, Museum of Fine Arts.)

century on the aesthetics of food became inextricably associated with its gastronomic qualities. The color of a dish was considered beautiful only because it augured well for the flavor. Signs of freshness were more enticing than realistic replicas of living animals.

Since we cannot ask those who dined how they felt about the pleasures of the dinner table, we must examine what contemporaries wrote on the subject. Hugh of Saint-Victor's twelfth-century *De institutione novitiarum* was translated into French in the fourteenth century. In it he reproaches gourmets not so much for their gluttony as for their overrefined tastes. There is no need to bother with food that is "overly precious and delicious" or "overly rare and out of the ordinary." He chides those whose gullets "cannot swallow anything that is not rich and delicious" and who excuse themselves if offered less exalted dishes, on the grounds that their stomachs are weak or their throats dry. Similarly reprehensible were those who totally shunned "the common run of dishes" and sent flocks of servants scouring "every crossroads" and hunting "in trackless mountain wastes" for certain roots, shrubs, or tiny fish. He condemned as too proud those who sought to distinguish themselves by the excellence of their diet, claiming to "be as unique in merit as they are in dining," as well as those gourmets who "took useless trouble in preparing their food" and invented "endless decoctions, fries, and flavorings." Or those who, like pregnant women, hanker after dishes "now soft, now hard, now cold, now hot, now boiled, now roasted, now with pepper, now with garlic, now with cumin, now with salt." To conclude his chapter on the oversophisticated palate, Hugh mocks wine-lovers who, "like tavernkeepers, raise the roof of the mouth with each mouthful of wine in order to savor the taste."

Gluttons and Epicures

Confronted with such evidence, how can anyone think that it was not until the seventeenth century that people began to care more about the quality of food and drink than about the quantity? What is striking about early modern texts on gourmet dining is that sophistication in taste is somewhat indulged, while gluttony is severely denounced.

In the best-known seventeenth- and eighteenth-century dictionaries, "gourmet" is simply a synonym for "glutton." Furetière's dictionary defines gourmet as a "ravenous eater, one who eats greedily and to excess." Between 1694 and 1798 the French Academy added the word "glutton" to this definition. And in 1611 Cotgrave's French-English dictionary defined *gourmand* as "a glutton," with "gormand" as a possible second translation.

Frequently using the same definitions, the same synonyms, and the same examples, French dictionaries gave a far less complex image of the *gourmand* and *gourmandise* than did the medieval texts. Alone among the major dictionaries, the *Encyclopedia* introduced a note of ambiguity and confusion with its unusually long and radically different article on *gourmandise*, which begins: "Refined and uncontrolled love of good food." Two columns of text elaborate on this definition with examples from antiquity: the excessive refinement of the imperial Romans and Sybarites is contrasted with the simpler gastronomic pleasures of Homer's heroes and with the frugality of the early Romans, the Spartans, and the ancient Persians. Gourmandise is portrayed as a consequence of luxury, which leads to decadence; the sophisticated gourmets of antiquity are denounced as a warning to the men of the eighteenth century.

Surprisingly, the Jesuits' *Dictionnaire de Trévoux* sharply rebuked this view in its 1771 edition: "GOURMANDISE: Not, as the *Encyclopedia* maintains, the refined and uncontrolled love of good food. The word does indeed encompass and denote the idea of excess, but not that of refinement in food. Gourmandise is the vice of the person who eats greedily and to excess. Gourmandise is one of the seven deadly sins." The reason for this reaction, apart from a consensus of the dictionary writers over two centuries, was probably that there existed another French word for sophisticated enjoyment of good food: *friandise*.

Richelet defined the *friand* as a person "who likes to eat something good." The Academy (1694–1798) defined him as one "who likes delicate and well-seasoned morsels." Similarly, *friandise* meant "passion, love for delicate or good-tasting food," according to Furetière and the *Dictionnaire de Trévoux*, and "love of good morsels" according to the Academy.

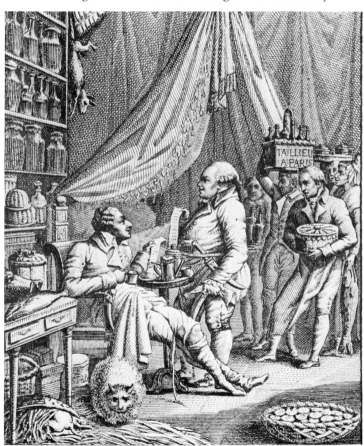

Engraving of Marriage in the manner of Charles. The image of the sophisticated gourmet launched in the mid-18th century by the *Encyclopedia* did not really catch on until the beginning of the 19th century with the publication of Grimod de La Reynière's *Gourmets' Almanac*. (Paris, Bibliothèque Nationale.)

Clearly this sensual passion was troubling to moralists. Richelet noted that it was "a rather uncontrolled appetite for things delicate and good to eat." But friandise was far less worrisome than gourmandise or gluttony, as the Jesuit authors of the *Dictionnaire de Trévoux* stated in no uncertain terms: "Friandise is a fault, but it is not as shameful as gourmandise." The Academy and Furetière said much the same thing.

Why such indulgence? If sophistication in taste was traditionally a form of gluttony, a capital sin, why was friandise considered less shameful than gourmandise? Furetière and the *Dictionnaire de Trévoux* observed that, in a derivative sense, "friandise is also said of things that are eaten for pleasure only and not for nourishment." This suggests that the friand eats for pleasure rather than out of natural need, in which respect he resembles those who use their conjugal rights "for pleasure" rather than for procreation. An age-old tradition held that it was worse to indulge in intercourse for pleasure than simply to indulge too often, that is, with a kind of gluttony. Why was it not the same, or no longer the same, when it came to eating? One possible interpretation is that both ecclesiastics and laymen in this period placed too high a value on sophistication in taste of every kind to condemn the epicure as severely as the glutton.

From G. F. Goez, *Exercises of Imagination of the Different Human Character and Forms* (Augsburg, 1784). In the 17th and 18th centuries gourmand was synonymous with glutton.

If in one sense friandise or epicureanism was a defect, in another sense it was a quality. The *Dictionnaire de Trévoux* puts it this way: "A good gourmet must have epicurean taste (*le goût friand*)." Here, the French word *gourmet* is used in its original sense, meaning a wine broker or taster employed by a wine dealer (Cotgrave, 1611). In 1679 Richelet defined a gourmet as "a person who tastes wine in the port of Paris to see if it is legitimate and marketable." But the meaning of the word was changing. A few years later, both Furetière and the *Dictionnaire de Trévoux* tell us that the word gourmet no longer applied only to certified professionals but to anyone capable of distinguishing between good and bad wine. This shift in meaning suggests that before the end of the seventeenth century a need was felt for a word denoting a connoisseur of wine, probably because connoisseurs existed outside the ranks of the professionals and were proud of their knowledge of wines, just as *friands* were proud of their knowledge of "good morsels."

To complicate matters even more, the word *friand* also applied to connoisseurs of wine. According to the Academy (1694–1717), "one says that a man is *friand* in wine in order to say that he has a refined taste and knows good wine." Between a *gourmet* and a *friand en vin* there were certain subtle distinctions, however. Nevertheless, the existence of two words with such similar meanings is yet another sign of heightened interest in sophisticated taste.

Tastes and Humors

Traditionally the rule was tolerance of the diversity of tastes, as evidenced by the Latin proverb "*De gustibus non est disputandum,*" which was included in the *Art de bien traiter* in 1674 and translated by the Academy in 1694: "Il ne faut point disputer des goûts" (or, as we say in English, There is no disputing taste). This tolerance was also manifest in the way food was served, what was known in the nineteenth century as the "French style of service." In the so-called Russian style that replaced it, and which is still in use today, the various courses of the meal are served one after another to each diner, and everyone is expected to taste all the dishes served. In the older French style of service, however, many dishes were simultaneously placed on the table, as in today's buffet or smorgasbord. For a dinner party of six to eight people, the *Nouveau cuisinier royal et bourgeois* (1742) proposed a menu of seven dishes per course. In good houses a dinner consisted of at least three courses. Hence a total of twenty-one dishes would have been served. For a party of twenty to twenty-five people the same book recommended serving twenty-seven dishes per course, for a total of eighty-one.

Not that the Frenchmen of old ate like pigs. Most guests were content simply to sample one dish that happened to be located near where they were seated. But their freedom of choice was far greater than ours today, and they saw nothing impolite about asking that a dish be passed from the opposite end of the table.

Old cookbooks and butler's manuals clearly state that the reason for the large number of dishes was to accommodate the diversity of tastes. The *Nouveau cuisinier* recommended arranging the dishes so that "each person can take whatever suits his appetite." It was important to "avoid placing two similarly prepared dishes close together, without another dish of a different kind in between. To do otherwise would be ungracious and might constrain the taste of some at table, different people liking different things."

Such indulgence of the variety of tastes, which is no longer the rule in private homes, accorded well with old the-

M. Desmaretz, *Banquet Given in Paris by the Duke of Alba for the Birth of the Prince of the Asturias,* 1707. With each course the table was covered with a variety of dishes among which the guests were free to choose. Here we see the last course: desserts and fruits. (Paris, Bibliothèque Nationale.)

Table de 24 Couverts, servie à 29, p. 9.

Diagram from Ménon, *New Treatise on Cooking* (Paris, 1739). Massialot, in his *New Royal Cook* (1742) wrote that "nothing is more disagreeable than confused and disorderly service." Cookbooks provided maîtres d'hôtel with table designs for various shapes of table and numbers of guests. (Paris, Bibliothèque Nationale.)

ories of diet, which attached the utmost importance to the diversity of temperaments and the different needs of each. Consider *L'Art de bien traiter* (1674): "People are often encountered who reject and condemn many good things to whose taste they have never been able to accustom themselves. It is a rare occasion when someone in the company does not object to something as antipathetic to his mild natural propensity, hence it is proper always to serve more than one sort of thing, so that the dominant humor can find what is most suited and in conformity with its desire." There was believed to be a basis in nature for the diversity of appetites. Taste was envisioned as a kind of sympathy between a person's nature and a particular food, and dislikes resulted from physiological aversion. Such sympathies and antipathies could be the result of habit, a second nature, but for the most part they were temperamental characteristics, that is, consequences of the relative importance of each of the four humors that constitute the temperament of every individual: blood, bile, phlegm, and melancholy. A person's taste could no more be changed than his temperament.

As time went on, however, these liberal attitudes were undermined by changes in the theory of diet and by the rise of gastronomy. In the Middle Ages physicians had recommended that the sick be fed very differently from the healthy. Disease was thought to consist in an excess of heat, cold,

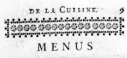

DE LA CUISINE. 9

MENUS

D'une Table de vingt-cinq couverts
fervie à vingt-neuf, à dîner
au mois de Janvier.

PREMIER SERVICE.

1. UN Surtout pour le milieu.
2. Deux Criftaux de profil à côté du Surtout.
3. Deux pots à fleurs à côté des deux criftaux.
4. *Deux pots à Ouille à côté des pots à fleurs.*
   Un d'un ris au blanc.
   Un d'une Ouille à l'Efpagnole.
5. *Deux Ouilles aux deux flancs.*
   Une d'une Jullienne aux pointes d'Af-perges.
   Une d'une Gendarme aux Racines.
6. *Quatre hors-d'œuvres de Pâtifferie à côté des flancs.*
   Un de Bouillans.

10 **NOUVEAU TRAITÉ**
Un de Riffoles.
Un de petits Pâtez à l'Efpagnole.
Un de petits Pâtez au coulis d'Ecre-viffes.

7. *Quatre hors-d'œuvres de Boudinailles à côté de la Pâtifferie.*
Deux de Boudins blancs.
Deux d'Andouilles & Sauciffes.

8. *Quatre moyens potages aux quatre coins des Boudinailles.*

Un d'une bifque de Pigeons au jus de Veau.
Un de Perdrix aux Marons.
Un de Sarcelles aux Navets.
Un de petits Poulets aux Choux-fleurs.

9. *Quatre hors-d'œuvres de grillades aux coins des potages.*

Un d'Aillerons à la Sainte-Menehould.
Un de cottelettes de Veau aux fines herbes.
Un de Poulets à la Tartare entiers.
Un de Pigeons en hattelets.

10. *Quatre caiffes pour renfermer les deux & troifiéme filets.*

Deux d'Allouettes.
Deux de queuës de Mouton aux petits oignons au Parmefan.

Once a table design was adopted, it had to be maintained throughout each course of the meal. Here is the first of four courses from a menu intended to go with the table design shown in the preceding illustration.

dryness, or humidity, and the patient's diet was supposed to correct this. If necessary, the sick might be given medicines that were poisonous if consumed by healthy individuals. By contrast, the "good health diet" was supposed to maintain a proper complexion, that is, a mix of humors suited to the temperament of the individual. Those who were warm by nature were advised to eat hot foods, to which they naturally found themselves drawn; those who were cold by nature ate cold foods; and so on. Such advice could be found, for example, in Aldebrandino of Siena's *Regime of the Body* in the thirteenth century or as late as the beginning of the sixteenth century in *Platine en françoys*.

By the late sixteenth and early seventeenth centuries, however, the principles of a healthy diet had changed completely. The *Trésor de santé* (1607) maintains that foods and drinks "that are humid and warm in quality" should be given "to those of melancholy humor" (that is, dry and cold). Drinks "that are cold and humid" should be given to the "choleric," by nature warm and dry. "Warm and dry" foods should be given to "phlegmatics," by nature cold and humid. And so on. After 1550 physician-dieticians began to treat temperaments as though they were diseases. They believed that good health was based on an equilibrium of the humors such that none dominated the rest, and that in order to attain such equilibrium a person was well advised to eat foods that would

From G. F. Goez, *Exercises of Imagination of the Different Human Character and Forms* (Augsburg, 1784). (Paris, Bibliothèque Nationale.)

compensate for his or her dominant humor. In other words, diet should counter rather than reinforce the peculiarities of the individual constitution.

After 1600 gastronomical principles were introduced into the kitchen. Nicolas de Bonnefons stressed "the true taste to be given to each food." Natural flavors were to be preserved rather than covered over by an endless variety of "mincemeats, mushrooms, herbs," and other superfluous ingredients. Bonnefons's aim is not simply to give specific recipes but to establish general culinary and gastronomic principles. In a less general but equally significant way L.S.R. set forth similar principles in *Art de bien traiter*, such as the instructions for roasting pigeon cited earlier.

Cooks were in no better position than other artists of the time to impose their personal tastes on their employers. By the seventeenth century, however, they had shed the submissive attitude characteristic of medieval cooks. In the fifteenth century the excellent Martino concluded his book of recipes with: "Make it sweet or sour according to the common taste or as your patron wishes." He never indulged in criticism of anyone's taste. Contrast this with L.S.R.'s attitude in 1674. Although he frequently allows his reader freedom to add or omit some ingredient or to serve or not to serve a particular sauce with a dish, habits such as pouring sweet sauce over meat strike him as evidence of a totally depraved taste. Of roast hare, for instance, he says: "Serve with a poivrade on the side. If anyone likes and asks for a sweet sauce, which strikes me as a highly impertinent and quite ridiculous thing to do, you may satisfy him by boiling red wine in a saucepan with sugar, clove, and cinnamon and reducing to the consistency of syrup."

Good Taste

By the middle of the seventeenth century cookbook writers had begun to discuss their art in terms of "good taste," which they took to be a universal principle, not specific to any time or place. They used that principle to criticize the gastronomic deviations not only of individuals but of entire nations.

In 1674 L.S.R. attacked his rival and predecessor La Varenne for what he considered to be ridiculous recipes, "wretched things with which one would put up more readily among Arabs and Levantines than in a pure climate such as ours, where cleanliness, refinement, and good taste are matters of utmost concern." And in 1691 Massialot defended the culinary art: "Man is not everywhere capable of such discernment, which is an emanation of his reason and intellect . . . Only in Europe do cleanliness, good taste, and skillful seasoning of meat prevail . . . while Europeans also rightly appreciate the marvelous gifts that we owe to the fortunate situation of other climates. Above all in France we can pride ourselves on our superiority in this regard to all other nations, as well as in manners and in a thousand other well-known advantages."

Not that good taste had been vouchsafed to the French

Attributed to Jan Brueghel the Elder, *Allegory of Taste*, 1618. The central figures are said to have been painted by Rubens. Meat, fish, and fruit of every variety figure in this early-17th-century Flemish allegory. Around the same time in France, Abraham Bosse treated the same subject in a very different way. His table contained artichokes, made fashionable by the Italians. Rather than a crude glutton, he showed a refined man and woman, the man holding a glass by its stem, the woman delicately eating a leaf of artichoke. Flemish gourmandise was thus contrasted with the delicacy of French taste.

for all eternity. Seventeenth- and eighteenth-century Frenchmen were aware that they had possessed it for only a few generations. Listen to the Jesuits Guillaume-Hyacinthe Bourgeant and Pierre Brumoy, who wrote the preface to *Dons de Comus* (1739): "The Italians taught manners to all Europe, and there is no denying that they taught us to eat . . . Meanwhile, France has been familiar with good cooking for two centuries, but without prejudice I can tell you that it has never been as refined as it is now, and that the job has never been done as expertly or with as sure a taste as it is now." Refined cuisine cannot exist without refined taste on the part of its consumers, and it is the good fortune of French culinary art that such taste exists in the eighteenth century: "We have in France several great lords who, to amuse themselves, do not disdain on occasion to discuss cooking, and whose exquisite taste greatly contributes to the formation of excellent officers."

For these reasons, culinary art has progressed with the other arts and with civilization itself: "Cooking, like all the other arts invented for need or pleasure, is perfected along with the spirit of the nation, and it has become more refined

as that spirit has become more polished . . . Progress in cooking . . . among the civilized nations has followed the progress of all the other arts." Although our two Jesuits feel obliged to refer to taste in food as a "corporeal taste," as opposed to the "spiritual tastes" that have developed in the plastic arts, music, and literature, they argue that one can "ascend from the corporeal taste to a very refined principle which it shares in some way with the purely spiritual taste." Their rather embarrassed treatment of the subject comes at the end of a century whose finest minds had been concerned with the nature of taste.

The ardor with which the reflection on taste was pursued can be gauged from the dictionaries. The articles in the dictionaries of Nicot (1607) and Cotgrave (1611) are brief and contain but one example not pertaining to taste in the culinary sense. Toward the end of the century, however, we find much more extensive articles in the dictionaries of Richelet, Furetière, and the French Academy as well as in the *Dictionnaire de Trévoux*, and these are primarily concerned with taste in the figurative sense.

People for a long time remained conscious of the fact that to use the word taste in other than a culinary sense was to use a metaphor. Listen to Voltaire in his *Dictionnaire philosophique* (1764): "Taste, the sense, the gift by which we distinguish what we eat, has yielded in all languages the metaphor whereby the word taste expresses the sentiment of beauties and defects in all the arts. It refers to a rapid discrimination like that of tongue and palate, and which similarly forestalls reflection. Like taste in the proper sense, it is sensitive and voluptuous with respect to the good. It too rejects the bad with disgust." This intellectual taste was credited with as authentic an existence as taste in the physical sense. Everyone agreed that its judgments were just as prompt. Indeed, the reason for the metaphor was to account for this type of intuitive, immediate judgment.

However philosophical and spiritual these reflections may have been, they indicate the importance of culinary taste in seventeenth- and eighteenth-century culture. It is scarcely conceivable that such a metaphor could have been elaborated to such a degree by a society indifferent to refined cooking and delicate discrimination in matters of food.

The metaphorical use may have encouraged the development of the idea of good taste in the culinary domain. The idea of taste dominated thinking about literature and art in the

Alexandre-François Desportes, *Still Life Showing Gold and Silver Pieces from the Royal Collection.* Sumptuousness and taste are combined in this still life from the reign of Louis XIV. The vessels are richly decorated but in perfect taste according to the standards of the time. The painter has attempted to show the succulence of the meats and fruits: note the plump ham and the creases in the figs, which are so ripe that they have split open. (J. Helft Collection.)

second half of the seventeenth century. According to Father Bouhours: "Good taste is a natural sentiment that derives from the soul. It is a kind of instinct of right reason." Voltaire develops in several works a parallel between good taste in food and good taste in literature and art: "Just as bad taste in the physical sense consists in being gratified only by overly piquant or exotic seasonings, so bad taste in the arts is a matter of being pleased only by affected ornament and of not responding to natural beauty" (*Dictionnaire philosophique*).

The question remains whether the related ideas of good and bad taste developed first in the culinary or in the artistic and literary domain. At the beginning of the seventeenth century they were to be found in neither one. But they were used in connection with cooking and gastronomy in the last quarter of the century. Although Father Bouhours and Saint-Evremond may have talked about good taste in literature and art at about the same time, Madeleine de Scudéry and the Chevalier de Méré did so even earlier.

But where did classical taste, which for Voltaire meant the same thing as good taste, first develop? It is natural to suppose that the authors of cookbooks followed in the wake of the great artists and writers who set forth its rules. Yet the purified taste that Voltaire championed, the taste for the natural, can be found as early as 1654 in Nicolas de Bonnefons's *Les Délices de la campagne,* long before the doctrine of classicism had been formulated in art and literature. Does this evidence weigh in favor of a materialist interpretation, according to which classicism in the arts derived from tendencies already evident in the kitchen?

Related to the concept of good taste was the notion of a "man of taste." Although the term *homme de goût* does not appear in the dictionary of the French Academy until 1932, Voltaire used it in his *Dictionnaire philosophique* as early as 1764: "The gourmet promptly senses and recognizes the mixing of two liquors. The man of taste, the connoisseur, will promptly notice the mixing of two styles. He will note the defect as well as the embellishment."

Ostentation and Taste

In the seventeenth century old aristocratic families felt threatened by the rise of parvenus, and indeed they really were threatened. They waged a political battle to hold onto part of their power. The program of aristocratic reaction, elaborated in the middle of the seventeenth century, was in large part

realized in the eighteenth century. The rivalry between nobility and wealthy bourgeoisie was played out in part symbolically, in terms of ostentation. In book five of *L'Histoire comique de Francion* (1623), for example, the hero organizes a group of "worthy and generous" nobles to humiliate the sons of merchants vain about their sumptuous clothing. To stem the insolent display of wealth by the bourgeoisie, kings had for centuries promulgated sumptuary laws, but to no avail. The bourgeoisie could not be prevented from dressing like great lords, buying offices, titles of nobility, estates, and châteaux, building luxurious hôtels, and staging ostentatious banquets. In such circumstances, was not good taste a weapon forged by the aristocracy to preserve some of its symbolic preeminence?

The new culture of the aristocratic salons enabled the aristocracy to look down its nose at even the most erudite of commoners. Similarly, new manners and new standards of taste, of which great nobles remained the arbiters, may have permitted the aristocracy to look down its nose at the ostentation of the newly rich.

Seventeenth-century literature is full of attacks on the bourgeoisie. Furetière in his *Romant comique* made fun of their way of being individual and natural, and Molière, in *Le Bourgeois gentilhomme* and *Les Précieuses ridicules*, ridiculed their efforts to imitate the aristocracy. Everywhere the tone was one of derision.

The tone of aristocratic cookbooks was similar. *L'Art de bien traiter* ascribes to the bourgeoisie or to even lower classes any taste the author wishes to discredit. From the very first page he attacks the "rusticity" of old ways of cooking and serving, which he castigates not for being too simple or poor but for yielding "useless and endless expenses, the utmost profusion without a semblance of order, and inappropriate excess that brings neither profit nor honor." Later he calls attention to the "baseness" and "shabbiness" of the *Cuisinier français* and expresses his dismay that such "disgusting lessons" had "lured and beguiled [not only] the foolish and ignorant populace" (which he subsequently calls the plebs) but also "some fairly enlightened people." In the chapter on roasts he makes fun of "vile petty-bourgeois recipes" that call for sprinkling lamb with breadcrumbs and chopped parsley. As for soups, he gives vent to a more traditional prejudice against the stinginess of the bourgeois: "To serve a soup naked, without any garnish or ornament: good God! What vileness for so small a saving! Away with bourgeois seasonings! Egg yolks mixed with verjuice on an important soup, and other ingredients of the same ilk: is there anything more mechanical and more egregious than such a method?" Later, discussing a pigeon stew, he is willing to countenance the use of the same garnish denounced so vehemently when applied to a soup, but the reference to the bourgeoisie is no more positive: "If you are lacking all the above . . . use the most common and bourgeois liaison, which you make by mixing egg yolk with verjuice."

To break bread with the hands rather than with a knife was an aristocratic way of affecting simplicity. So was the decision to eschew Oriental spices in favor of native herbs, as well as the use of butter, traditionally used in peasant cooking. The great birds with their magnificent plumage were sacrificed on the altar of sophisticated taste—another way of catching the parvenus off guard, just when they thought they could rival the old nobility in ostentatious display. In dress Bussy d'Amboise employed much the same gambit when he came to the Louvre, "dressed quite simply and modestly, but followed by six pages clad in gold-embroidered costumes, proclaiming loudly that the time had come when those of

André Bouys, *The Scourer.* (Paris, Musée des Arts décoratifs.)

least account would be the most gallant," that is, most richly dressed.[15]

Not all the new culinary fashions were as paradoxical or provocative, since many of the favored new foods, like truffles and first fruits, were rare and expensive. The crucial thing was that fashions in cooking changed constantly, and the power to launch new fashions in this and other areas remained with the great nobles—and their cooks.

Vincent de La Chapelle, chef to Lord Chesterfield and later to the Prince of Orange, tells, in *Cuisinier moderne*, of changing fashions: "The arts have general rules. Anyone who wants to practice them must abide by those rules. Yet the rules are not enough, and perfection requires constant effort to improve on methods that are established, yet, like all things, subject to the vicissitudes of the times. Therefore it is absolutely essential to follow today's rules. If a great lord's table were served today as it was twenty years ago, the guests would not be satisfied." But the ideology of progress quickly obscured the futility of fashion and the brutality of the mechanisms by which social prestige was ensured. In 1785 the author of the *London Art of Cookery* wrote: "Cookery, like every other Art, has been moving forward to Perfection by slow Degrees; and though the cooks of the last century boasted of having brought it to the highest Pitch it could bear, yet we find that daily Improvements are still making therein, which must be the case of every Art depending on Fancy and Taste." As we saw earlier, the preface to the *Dons de Comus* (1739) made a similar point, even though its authors were peculiarly aware of how much the art of cookery owed to the tastes of the great lords who employed the leading chefs.

The mechanisms of social distinction and class rivalry within the elite appear to have had some influence on the elaboration of the notion of taste and the ideology of progress in the arts. But they do not explain everything. For one thing, "men of taste" did not always come from the old aristocratic families, and not all blue-blooded aristocrats were renowned for their taste. For another, if the nouveaux riches were hateful and the bourgeois comical, minor nobles did not receive much better treatment at the hands of seventeenth- and eighteenth-century writers.

Furthermore, it is not at all clear that the notion of taste first emerged in connection with criticism of the nouveaux riches. It was not until 1932 that the Academy's dictionary drew a contrast between taste and wealth, and it was only in

Juste-Aurèle Meissonnier, *Book of Ornaments*. Serving dishes designed for table use. (Paris, Bibliothèque Nationale.)

1835 that it contrasted luxury with magnificence. There is no trace of such connotations in any of the major seventeenth- and eighteenth-century dictionaries.

Only a few individuals were blessed with taste. According to La Bruyère, "there are few men whose intellect is accompanied by a trustworthy taste." And the *Encyclopedia*, after noting that there are beauties "that affect only sensitive souls," concluded that "these kinds of beauties, made for a minority, are the proper object of taste."

Some writers held that taste was innate. For Saint-Evremond, "taste is a sentiment that cannot be learned or taught. It must be born within us." Similarly, Richelet wrote that "it is a part of ourselves that is born within us." The *Dictionnaire de Trévoux* (1752) developed the same idea at greater length: "Taste does not come from knowledge. One can know a great deal, be highly enlightened, and still have bad taste. Taste is a natural sentiment that derives from the soul and is independent of any learning that one may acquire. It is true that it can in some cases be perfected by knowledge, but in other cases knowledge can also spoil it . . . From which it follows that taste is the judgment of nature."

Yet no one in all these comments on taste suggests that it might be hereditary or the exclusive property of the well-born. In prerevolutionary France, where the nobility did not scruple to claim a monopoly on courage and the exclusive right to bear arms, this silence seems significant. Apparently others could have good taste.

Not only were seventeenth-century literary salons full of intelligent people of common birth, but the connoisseurs and patrons who encouraged the most celebrated artists and men of letters and supported them with their patronage were by no means all nobles of the oldest stock. Fouquet, who amassed a huge fortune through financial dealings as a royal official, discovered in the years that followed the Fronde most of the writers, painters, architects, and gardeners who were to bring luster to the age of Louis XIV. Somewhat later the banker Lambert had a hôtel built for himself on the Ile Saint-Louis that rivaled that of the Duke of Lauzun. Several men celebrated for the sophistication of their dinner tables were wealthy bourgeois or nobles of recent date: Grimod de La Reynière, the inventor of gastronomic literature, and his father, a royal tax farmer, are the best known. In the seventeenth century, however, there was the financier Bechameil, who gave his name to béchamel sauce, and Jacques Amelot, to whom Pierre de Lune dedicated his *Nouveau cuisinier* (1660) in gratitude for Amelot's having taught him to "please a difficult taste." Yet Amelot, *premier président* of the Cour des Aides, had not been Marquis of Mauregard for very long, his family having been ennobled in 1580. And the Marquise de Pompadour, daughter of a military supplier by the name of Poisson, showed herself to be particularly perspicacious in her choice of writers and artists as protégés. Many famous recipes took their names from her château de Bellevue.

Let us leave the eighteenth century, however, and turn once more to the *Histoire comique de Francion*. The hero is a minor Breton noble who detests royal officeholders and merchants. After becoming the protégé of a great lord, he exhibits this prejudice openly: "Gentlemen from the courts, finance, and commerce passed daily through my hands, and you cannot imagine what a pleasure it was for me to strike a few hard blows against their black satin gowns. Those who called themselves noble were not, nor did they find themselves exempt from the effects of my righteous wrath." Even before meeting his lord, Francion organized a gang of youths to prevent the sons of wealthy bourgeois from taking over the streets. Who belonged to this gang? "Everyone who was willing to abide by those ordinances . . . was accepted . . . no matter if he was the son of a merchant or a financier, provided he was willing to denounce commerce and finance. We paid attention not to breeding but only to merit."

Young men from a variety of social backgrounds chose to defend Francion's aristocratic ideal. The "gallant and generous" defended not their class interests or some religious ideal but a freely chosen way of life. As the seventeenth century progressed, a community of manners and tastes drew to the banquet table and salon people from very different backgrounds and walks of life, all of whom shared similar tastes in language, literature, music, painting, architecture, gardening, furniture, clothing, food, and so on. In all these areas the function of the arts was not only or even primarily to make life more agreeably pleasant for members of the elite but to enable them to exhibit their good taste, a new criterion of social distinction.

The criteria of distinction remained numerous, for social life was complex. Possession of political, economic, or military power did not necessarily imply a leading position in society, where birth, wealth, brilliance, and other qualities all contributed to distinction. Over the years it was in urbane society that the criteria of distinction proliferated. The Middle Ages had prized courtliness above all other qualities. In later years such criteria as civility, urbanity, and politeness came into vogue. Talking well was prized in the Renaissance and remained so thereafter. The seventeenth century invented good tase.

Good taste, partly a matter of what one was and partly of what one had, is the first of all these criteria to involve the individual as consumer. No doubt this had something to do with the fact that the great lords lost the major part of their old political and military powers in the seventeenth century; thus their primary role became that of great consumers. And the various classes that composed the social elite in the seventeenth and eighteenth centuries found it easiest to communicate with one another by means of consumption and luxury.

Good taste became the primary social virtue, a matter of inner being as well as outward appearance. Politeness and polished speech concerned only behavior toward others. But taste affected what a man was, what he felt about the world. The seventeenth century was greatly concerned with appearances, but it was not as cold and solemn as we might think. For it was also the time when people began to be concerned with what they felt, with what they were in their heart of hearts.

Nicolas Poussin, *Holy Family*. An attentive mother plays with her wide-eyed infant, while the father looks on. (Detroit, Institute of Art.)

✢ The Child: From Anonymity to Individuality

Jacques Gélis

FOR centuries a "naturalistic" view of life and time prevailed in western Europe, despite efforts by the Church to substitute a different, more theological view. In a society that remained fundamentally agricultural until the nineteenth century, Mother Earth was the origin of all life, an inexhaustible breeding ground that ensured the perpetuation of all the species, including *homo sapiens*. Year after year nature repeated the same spectacle. Season followed season without interruption, and everything else followed.

In a world where the old was constantly being replaced by the new, no affliction was more serious than sterility, which broke the cycle, disrupting the continuity of the family line. Dependent on the family, the individual alone was nothing. The bearing of children established a link between past and future, between humanity that was and humanity yet to come. To break the chain was unthinkable. Women played a special role, bearing and nursing the children on whom the future of the family and the race depended. They participated in fertility rites associated with "natural temples": stones or trees or springs thought to have special power to impart fertility, as though children sprang from seeds found in nature at certain designated sites.

The life of every individual was like a curve, its length varying from person to person. One sprang from the earth at conception and returned to it after death. The dead resided underground, where departed souls awaited reincarnation in their grandchildren. The custom of naming children after their grandparents persisted for a long time, as if the practice somehow ensured the family's survival.[1] Behind these beliefs and customs we can perceive a circular structure, a vital cycle,

Ex-voto, 18th century. Carrying twins to term was exceptional. Only a miraculous Virgin could grant such a favor. (Brabant, Our Lady of Hal.)

according to which the world was populated by an unvarying number of souls, some living, some dead. Souls departed this life and joined the world of the dead.

The Body: Self and Others

This view of life, this image of a series of generations following one after another, derived from an idea of the body very different from our own. People believed that each individual possessed a body of his or her own, yet the blood tie was so powerful that that body was not totally individual, totally independent of the family. My body was my own, but it also belonged to others, to the living members of my extended family as well as to my dead ancestors.

Consequently there was a contradiction between the collective destiny of the family and the right of the individual to savor life's pleasures, to "live his own life"—a right that today we consider perfectly legitimate. This contradiction was resolved in favor of that body whose survival had to be ensured at all costs: the family. The individual was master of his or her body only to the extent that his or her desires did not contradict family interests. In a sense, humans perpetuated life without really being allowed to live it. Their sole duty was to pass life on to the next generation.

Given these views of life and the body, the child was considered a scion of the family, an offshoot of the family tree. Individual branches might come and go; the tree endured. In the broad sense the child belonged to the family as much as to its own parents. It was, in this respect, a public child. Contradicting this interpretation, however, was the fact that the child was closely bound to its mother until the time of weaning. In fact, this privileged relationship reflected a necessity: born "incomplete," the child was incapable of providing for its own basic needs. The mother, having nourished it with her own blood during gestation, now nursed it with her milk, which was believed to be a bleached form of blood.[2] Weaned at twenty, twenty-four, or thirty months, the child embarked on a period of increasingly "public" education, although the father and mother would long remain the primary teachers.

The point is that the child was from birth the object of both public and private concern. It came into the world in a private place—its parents' bedroom—but its birth, witnessed by female relatives and neighbors, was a public occasion. It took its first steps in the cemetery where its ancestors were buried or in church during the elevation of the host, as a symbol of continuity, a public ritual marking the beginning of its existence as an independent individual. The first steps proved that the family line would endure.[3]

French school, *Little Girl with Doll*, 18th century. In the century of *Emile*, this portrait of a child with her toy attests to the newfound interest in children. (Grenoble, Museum of Painting and Sculpture.)

The common room of a country house. There was only one answer to the ever-present danger of death: a houseful of children. (Paris, Bibliothèque Nationale.)

Baptism, which was both a sacrament erasing original sin and a ritual of socialization, was also an opportunity to assure the soundness of the infant's body by magical means. After the ceremony, when the priest had departed, the child's body was rolled on the altar to strengthen its muscles and prevent rickets and lameness. To protect the child from stammering and muteness, the godfather and godmother were supposed to kiss as they passed under the belfry on their way out of church. Young people sometimes played an important role in the ritual. At Massiac in Auvergne at the beginning of the last century, the children of the village followed the procession after the baptism, raising a terrible racket with hammers and rattles in order to make sure that the child would not grow up deaf and dumb and, in the case of a girl, that she would have a pleasant speaking and singing voice.[4]

Early childhood was a time for learning. The toddler explored its home, its village, and the surrounding countryside. It learned to play with other children of the same age or with older children more knowledgeable and more daring. It

Marguerite Gérard, *The Child's First Steps*. A child takes its first steps, watched by its mother, nurse, and godmother. (Cambridge, Massachusetts, Fogg Art Museum, Harvard.)

Jan Steen, *The Painter and His Family*. In 17th-century Holland, a country ahead of its time, children were admired for their grace and talent. (The Hague, Royal Museum.)

learned to take care of itself, to abide by the rules of the community, to make its way in life. The child's father and mother played an important role in this early education. At the age of seven or eight young boys began to accompany their fathers into the fields to prepare them for "placement" with a neighbor or relative. Girls generally stayed home with their mothers, from whom they learned the rudiments of the wifely role that would one day be theirs. The experience of childhood and adolescence was supposed to strengthen the body, sharpen the senses, equip the child to deal with adversity, and above all prepare him or her in due course to become a parent. The influence of the community made every child a product of the group and equipped him or her to do what society expected. In such circumstances there was little intimacy, but a growing sense of belonging, for better or worse, to an extended family.

Early in the ninth decade of the sixteenth century, one of the sons of Scevole de Sainte-Marthe, mayor and comptroller of the town of Loudun, fell ill while still a nursling. The ablest

"I Will Not Let Her Die!"

physicians were called to his bedside, "but their efforts proved futile. They despaired of a cure." Scevole, however, was not ready to resign himself to his son's premature death. "Since he was a very good father and very learned," he rose to the challenge, sent the quacks packing, and "attempted to heal [his son] himself. To which end he diligently studied the most curious and learned works on the nature and complexion of children. A man of clever and lively mind, he penetrated the darkest secrets of nature and physics, and he put his knowledge to such good use that he snatched his son from the jaws of death." This exemplary father is known to us because, in response to subsequent urgings to "preserve his curious researches for posterity," he produced a poem in Latin, the *Paedotrophia*, concerning the feeding of young children.[5]

By the end of the fourteenth century signs had begun to appear of a new attitude toward children among wealthy urban families. The change affected not so much feelings toward children as it did the will to keep them alive. Scevole de Sainte-Marthe, who comes two centuries after these first signs of change appeared, may be taken as typical of the attitudes of the new Renaissance elite. The seventeenth century saw even greater determination to prevent premature death. Mme de Sévigné exemplifies the new unwillingness to accept the worst. When informed that her granddaughter was ill, she shouted: "I will not let her die!"

Anguished parents now did everything they could to cure sick children and save them from death. Make no mistake: at no time did parents willingly accept the death of a beloved child. But in years past a more cyclical view of life had made death somehow less final; resigned, parents who lost a child had no choice but to give birth to another. However hard the blow, the perpetuation of the family was essential. Thus, the refusal to accept death is one sign—an important one—of a new attitude toward life and time. There was nothing new about turning to doctors to prolong life and alleviate suffering. In the sixteenth century, however, the need for medical services manifested itself so forcefully that there can be no doubt of a fundamental change of outlook. Unfortunately, the medical profession, ill-prepared to assume its new role, remained incapable of meeting the need at the end of the seventeenth century, as Molière's plays make clear. John Locke's *Some Thoughts Concerning Education*, published in London in 1693 and translated into French by Pierre Coste in 1695, became one of the classics of European eighteenth-century pedagogy.

Gabriel Metsu, *Sick Child*. In the 16th century there was a new determination to save sick children from death, evidence of the emergence of a new sensibility. (The Hague, Private collection.)

Ex-voto, 18th century. Until the 18th century people were helpless in the face of disease. Death claimed its regular tribute of infants. (Upper Rhine, Our Lady of Kientzheim.)

Locke calls attention to the virtues of prevention as the best means of preserving a child's health: "The consideration I shall here have of health shall be not what a physician ought to do with a sick or crazy child but what the parents, without the help of physick, should do for the preservation and improvement of an healthy or at least not sickly constitution in their children."[6]

My Body, My Child

It was not easy to reconcile the demands of family with the growing desire on the part of individuals to live their own lives and choose their own careers. The man who worked exclusively to support his family and who saw himself as a link in the chain of generations had little reason to be concerned with himself. But now self-interest, present and future,

Avon studio, earthenware statuette, 17th century. (La Rochelle, Orbigny Museum.)

became a vital concern. Having learned to count, man knew that his days were numbered.

In an effort to resolve this contradiction, families changed their behavior. The calculating spirit, not limited to commerce, also affected family strategies. Was lending money at interest a sin? After much controversy the Church compromised on the usury issue, which led to new ways of doing business. Similarly, the contradiction between the family and the individual was resolved by a series of compromises as the family-centered mentality waned and the powers of the individual increased.

As the relation of individual to group changed, a new image of the body took shape. Increasingly it was seen as the property of the individual, not the family: "My body is mine," therefore I will try to spare it the agony of disease and suffering. Yet because I know it to be perishable, I will attempt to perpetuate it in the body of my child. This symbolic appropriation of the body, wrested from the family by the individual, is no doubt the key to much seventeenth- and eighteenth-century behavior. We can understand, for instance, why children came to occupy so important a place in their parents' concerns.

The cyclical image of time gradually gave way to a more linear, more segmented view of existence, a change that affected first the wealthy and then the poor, first the cities, then the larger towns, and finally rural villages. The individual, no longer in the shadow of the family, acquired a distinctive personality of his own.

A New Attitude toward Childhood

The change in the attitude toward children, a cultural change of profound importance, took place over a very long period of time, and its pace varied from place to place. Cities led the way, as the modern nuclear family began to emerge in fifteenth-century Europe. In the Renaissance city, man's once close relation to Mother Earth became more distant. Awareness of the changing seasons diminished. Concern with ancestors, once of primary importance, became less vital. There was less space in the cities to sacrifice to the dead, and less time to devote to them. Sterility was no longer seen as a problem to be resolved by "natural" magical means. In this new man-made environment, this Renaissance city increasingly "conceptualized in physical terms," the nuclear family withdrew into the intimacy of the private home.[7] Italian cities,

Florence in particular, led the way as early as the fourteenth century.[8] During the next two centuries cities in England, Flanders, and France would follow suit.

In France, however, these changes were halted if not actually reversed during part of the seventeenth century. The political and religious upheavals of the previous century, as well as the witch craze that affected much of Europe, had been symptoms of a profound crisis of values. In the early sixteenth century signs of a new attitude toward childhood had been evident. Literary and medical texts of the period discussed subjects that we usually associate with the eighteenth century. Consider swaddling. The child was born into a world of constraints, of which swaddling, which denied freedom of movement, became the symbol. Sixteenth-century physicians such as Simon de Vallambert argued that this lack of freedom could only be harmful to the child's health and development.[9]

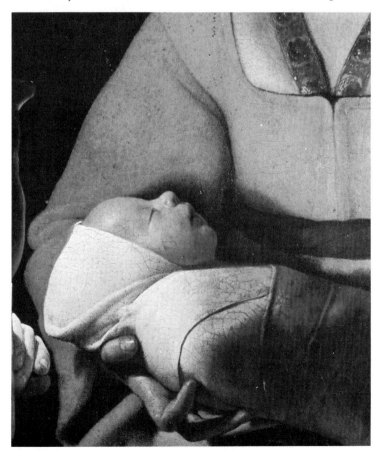

Georges de La Tour, *The Newborn*. (Rennes, Museum of Fine Arts.)

The child taking the nipple or resting after a long drink was the very image of happiness. The willingness to deprive a baby of its mother's breast and send it off to drink "mercenary milk" is evidence that new values had taken hold in urban society.

Joshua Reynolds, *George Clive(?) and His Family*. (Berlin, Stattliche Museen Preussischer Kulturbesitz.)

Wealthy families had few children, but they had their place at the center of the family.

Similar criticism was directed against the practice of using bonnets and caps to reshape the child's head in conformity with some aesthetic ideal.[10] The use of wet nurses was discouraged or even condemned. "Mercenary milk" was said to be dangerous; it was believed that "nurture transmits nature," hence that the "transfusion" of milk, affecting the spirit as well as the body, posed a threat to the very identity of the infant. Thus, the question of wet-nursing was situated in the context of a more general debate on the subject of nature versus nurture.[11]

The use of wet nurses was not a sixteenth-century innovation. In Florence the practice began in the late fourteenth century and became increasingly popular in the century that followed. The separation of mother and child, which all too often ended in the death of the latter, was strongly condemned by physicians and moralists. Even animals, they insisted, nurse their young.[12] But many parents ignored the criticism; new values were taking hold in the city, values different from those still prevalent in the rural environment in which infants lived with their nurses.[13] Hired wet nurses relieved the wives of the wealthy of a major burden. A woman might become pregnant again sooner because she did not nurse her child, but between pregnancies she had more free time for conversation, reading,

Cornelis de Vos, *Portrait of the Artist and His Family*. (Brussels, Royal Institute of Art.)

and ambling about. For the mother, however, the cost of this new attitude was high: estrangement from a beloved child and increased dependence on her husband. The separation of child-bearing from child-rearing changed the very way in which women were seen and altered woman's place in the cycle of life. It became easier to limit women to a reproductive role. Fertility was all that was expected of them. A woman carried her husband's child and gave it life, for in the city the child belonged to its father and to the paternal lineage.

But if some parents sent their children to wet nurses, others found "amusement and pleasure" in their company.[14] There was no contradiction between the two attitudes, only proof that choice was now possible. True, "nature" still argued in favor of the child's being raised by its mother. But a mother's life was no longer one of pure duty. Women claimed the right to lives of their own. Their husbands approved when they exhibited a desire to keep their bodies fresh and comely. The choice was never easy. The child's interests had to be weighed against the mother's. It is not surprising that the question attracted a variety of answers.

Parents, Children, and Education

The change in the relationship between parents and children affected the children's behavior. Sixteenth- and seventeenth-century writers championed the cause of the "new child." He was more alert, they said, and more mature. Sometimes the difference was noted with astonishment. Early in the seventeenth century Louise Bourgeois, midwife to the queen of France, Marie de Medici, noted in her *Instructions* for her daughter that "today's little children are remarkably fine."[15] Moralists became critical of parents who indulged their children. "For he that has been used to have his will in everything as long as he was in coats, why should we think it strange that he should desire it and contend for it still when he is in breeches."[16]

Moralists did not condemn the privatization of child care as such, but they did fear that parents would go too far. Indulgence fostered weakness. Some mothers behaved in truly deplorable ways, such as those who, still impure from having given birth, could not "refrain from indiscreet zeal in hugging and kissing their infant." So said physician Jacques Duval, who added that "indiscretion causes them to love like apes, who it is said squeeze their young so hard out of ardent affection that they suffocate them."[17]

Jan Steen, *Mixed School.*
(Edinburgh, National Gallery
of Scotland.)

To combat such excesses, a whole school of seventeenth-century writers sought to impose rules of proper behavior. Such repressive attitudes toward private education, alleged to be too tender and indulgent, may have contributed to the assumption of responsibility for education by church and state. Such innovations as the *collège* (roughly equivalent to our secondary school) quickly won the support of parents, who became convinced that their children were prey to elemental instincts that had to be repressed and that it was important to "subject one's desires to the government of Reason." To put a child in school was to wrest him from the grip of nature.[18]

The new schools were successful not for that reason but because they trained the mind while meeting the needs of an ever more exuberant individualism. There was no contradiction between private child-rearing in the nuclear family and public education. With the old extended family fallen into disrespect and with a new emphasis on individual fulfillment,

Needlework and pious reading turned model little girls into exemplary mothers. A good education was one that taught a child its proper place and position. (Paris, Bibliothèque Nationale.)

Were pupils in one-room schoolhouses really free? In reality, from the 17th century on, education was no longer a pleasurable amusement. Children were sent to school to protect them from nature and to train reason to curb the desires.

Gravelot inv.   L'ECOLE DES FILLES.   *Bachelier sculp.*
Avec Privilège du Roy.

it became necessary to turn to outsiders to impart to children the knowledge they could not obtain from their parents. Parents themselves recognized that education at home might well frustrate their children, since they were incapable of supplying what they themselves had received from the community.[19] Thus, as the extended family gave way to the nuclear family, the old open, communal form of public education and socialization was replaced by a system of public schools.[20]

Public Models, Private Uses

The change in the status of the child did not come about solely as the result of the evolution of family structures. Church and state undeniably played a part. The new attitude toward children that became evident around the middle of the sixteenth century was embodied in legislation responding to moral and political concerns.[21] The new laws, though not widely enforced, were the first sign of a determination on the part of the state to protect young children and, in a broader perspective, to intervene in matters of demography.

The most important role of church and state, however, was the elaboration of ideological models. The model child was a far cry from the ordinary child of the time, yet the model itself helped to alter the way in which people thought about children. The Church popularized two images of children: the child as mystic and the child as Jesus. By exalting those whose faith was strong enough to withstand the worst physical agonies, the mystics focused attention on the qualities of the individual. They created the model of the child saint: Peter of Luxemburg or Catherine of Siena, who from a very early age had no ambition other than to devote themselves to God. Their love of God led them to ignore the things of this world and neglect their still frail bodies. The exaltation of the child mystic was thus totally at odds with the "naturalistic" image of the family as a single body. The family did not tolerate behavior that threatened to interfere with the cycle of birth and death. But mysticism encouraged celibacy and looked with equanimity upon the prospect of a life without progeny; or, rather, it envisioned a posterity of a higher, more spiritual order.

Quentin Metsys, *Triptych of the Confraternity of Saint Anne at Louvain* (detail). (Brussels, Old Art Museum.)

Devotion to the Christ Child was popularized in seventeenth-century France by Cardinal de Bérulle, the Carmelites, and the Oratorian Fathers. Devotional manuals emphasized the human features of the "godly child," whose sweetness and innocence so touched those who gathered around the Christmas manger. Pierre Thureau, a priest in Orléans, reports in his *Saint Enfant-Jésus* (1665) that in the school at Châteauvieux, a bleak town in the diocese, there was "a large copper-plate engraving of the Infant Jesus, wrapped in swaddling clothes but holding out his hands to all who wish to be, like him, simple and small, and primarily to the children."[22] For three centuries the Church had preached against the dangers of the flesh, working on the fears of the faithful. Now the image of Jesus became the focal point of new and inward forms of piety.[23]

In a more secular vein was the image of the child prodigy. In 1613 a nine-year-old child by the name of Claude Hardy published a French translation of Erasmus' book on civility. In 1630 a child known as *le petit de Beauchasteau* was born. By the age of seven he was able to speak several languages, and at twelve he published a collection of poems.[24] And of course in the eighteenth century there was Mozart.

Training the mind sometimes required training the body. (Paris, Bibliothèque Nationale.)

A public personage from birth, the child of royal blood was not expected to prove himself at once. Kept under constant surveillance, a future king had no private life. His every gesture was observed and even recorded: witness the account of young Louis XIII left by Héroard, the royal physician. The heir apparent grew up under the watchful eyes of the court. Future father to his subjects, he had little contact with them.

His image was propagated by engravings, and especially by coins. In the second half of the seventeenth century and even more in the following century, the birth of a prince was often the pretext for striking a new coin, minting having become a royal privilege. "Populationist" theories being much in vogue, coins showing the royal couple flanked by its children were a good way of exhorting every family to follow the august example of the prince.

After Simon François of Tours, *The Adoration of the Word Incarnate.* The "godly child," image of innocence and sweetness, was quite popular in the 17th century. (Carmelite Collection.)

Children had always learned part of what they needed to know in public, outside the family, and part in private, from their parents. The two influences were often complementary. Over the course of the seventeenth and eighteenth centuries their relative importance changed. It is difficult to believe that there ever existed a period in which people were indifferent to their children and that, thanks to "progress" and "civilization," indifference gradually turned to enthusiasm. Enthusiasm and indifference coexist in any society, and at any given moment one may become dominant for cultural and social reasons that are not always easy to isolate.[25] The alleged medieval indifference to the child is a myth, and in the sixteenth century, as we have seen, parents were concerned about the health and welfare of their children.

Thus, the development in the eighteenth century of a new attitude toward children—*our* attitude—must be seen as a symptom of a profound upheaval in beliefs and structures of thought, a sign of an unprecedented change in Western attitudes toward life and the body. Life had been conceptualized in terms of clan and community; now those images gave way to the image of the nuclear family. The child had had a place in the public life of the community as well as in the private life of the family; now it became a possession of its mother and above all of its father. Increasingly, however, the spirit of the age was individualistic. In educating the child to realize its full potential, the couple, encouraged by church and state, delegated a portion of its powers and responsibilities to professional educators. A rural model gave way to an urban one, and men and women now had children not to ensure the continuation of a cycle but simply to love and to be loved in return.

Childhood: Enthusiasm and Indifference

French school, *Louis XIV as a Child,* 17th century. From birth the royal child was a public child who served as a model for his future subjects. (Beaune, Carmelite Convent.)

Charles Emmanuel Bizet d'Annonay, *Still Life with Books* (detail). Manuscript books, their pages disfigured by time, with parchment or leather covers. Kept by the master of the house, some contain only a few pages while others are voluminous. (Bourg-en-Bresse, Musée de l'Ain.)

❧ The Literature of Intimacy

Madeleine Foisil

I T IS not easy to penetrate the private or inner lives of people of the past. Private life was in part confounded with public life, and the inner life was hidden from view. The use of such sources as memoirs, diaries, and family record books (*livres de raison*) is intended not to glean anecdotes and miscellaneous facts but to shed light on how people conceived of their privacy. In other words, I am interested not in private life as such but in attitudes toward private life, hence not only in what people say but also in what they do not say.

DEFINITION OF A GENRE

Memoirs, diaries, and family record books were the main vehicles of private writing in the late seventeenth and eighteenth centuries. Contemporary dictionaries shed valuable light on the differences between these genres. Furetière's (1690) gives the following definition: "Memoirs, in the plural, refers to books by historians, written by those who took part in affairs or were eyewitnesses of events, or which contain accounts of the lives and principal actions of such people. This corresponds to what the Latins called 'commentaries.'"[1] This definition is followed by a list of examples: the memoirs of Sully, Villetory, Cardinal Richelieu, Marshals Thémines and Bassompierre, Brantôme, Montrésor, La Rochefoucauld, Pontis. By contrast, a *livre de raison* is "a book in which a good householder or merchant writes down what he receives and spends, keeping a systematic record of all affairs."

The contrast is clear. Memoirs are written by historians or eyewitnesses of political affairs and are concerned with important actions. Family records are kept by good householders and are concerned with receipts and expenditures.

Historical Memoirs

Seventeenth-century memoirs, individual works by public figures treating their glorious acts and describing men and events they witnessed at close range, were intended to be read. Without Louis XIV there could have been no *Memoirs* of Saint-Simon or *Journal* of Dangeau. Without Henri IV, Louis XIII, and a life filled with military exploits, there could have been no *Memoirs* of Bassompierre. Without Anne of Austria there could have been no *Memoirs* of Mme de Motteville. And without the renown earned by battlefield exploits there could have been no *Memoirs* of Villars.

Marc Fumaroli points out that late-sixteenth- and seventeenth-century memoirs were deliberately similar to historical narrative.[2] Memoir writers, having "devoted too much time to fashioning and playing a public 'persona,'" used what little time remained to them to put the finishing touches on the character they had created for themselves. Memoirs described the public lives of men who had had little or no private life.

Margaret MacGowan, relying particularly on the case of Bassompierre, has attempted to analyze the contents of the historical memoir. The author, she believes, writes as an observer or spectator of his own life or of the life of someone he has served as confidant, servant, or companion. He recounts what anyone else would have seen in his place; he does not confide, confess, or analyze. The memoir discloses the

Master of the Annunciation of Aix-en-Provence, *The Prophet Jeremiah* (detail). (Brussels, Royal Institute of Art.)

Wall painting on wood, 1705. Marriage in Brittany at the beginning of the 18th century. In the center the priest, wearing a surplice and stole, listens to the mutual vows of the bride and groom. On the left, the groom and his witness are dressed in the noble fashion of the day. On the right, the bride and her witnesses are all dressed modestly and wearing hoods. The inscription at the bottom probably reads: "Done in 1705 in the time of Yves Pulhasan, churchwarden." (Finistère, Chapel of Saint-Tugen-en-Primelin.)

Alexis Grimoux, *Girl Reading.* Is she actually reading? Or is she adopting a proper pose, with her book of manners in her lap on prominent display, attesting to her good breeding? (Toulouse, Musée des Augustins.)

Olof Fridsberg, *Ulla Tessin in Her Study*. This painting features a north European woman at a time when French styles were in fashion. An intimate setting filled with an overabundance of objects: bibelots of every sort and style, portraits of loved ones, boxes and chests, books, manuscripts. The woman's writing is interrupted for a moment by a thought or memory. (Stockholm, Nationalmuseum.)

Domenico Fetti, *Young Girl Sleeping*. With a slight smile on her lips, the young woman rests, adorned by flowers, jewels, a ring, and a handkerchief—almost a catalog of the items in favor. (Museum of Budapest.)

Ivory Dealer. Two young nobles cannot make up their minds about a gift for a lady: among the items to choose from are combs, spherical boxes, musical instruments, bracelets, and brushes. (Venice, Correr Museum.)

Jean-Baptiste Chardin, *The Serving Table*. Anything that did not have to be brought hot from the kitchen was placed on the serving table before the meal. A salad to be served with the roast is no doubt waiting in the earthenware bowl next to the silver-capped vials of oil and vinegar. The large cold pâté will be served after the entremets. For desert there are fruits, preserves in the three sandstone or glass jars, and cheese in a wooden container. A sugar loaf is wrapped in blue paper. The sugar bowl stands next to the cups. A spirit warmer is available to heat the coffee. (Paris, Louvre.)

Koedyck, *Weaver's Shop.* A Flemish family occupies a large, sunny room in a scene of domestic bliss, with mother and child, cat, work, and leisure mingled. (Lille, Museum of Fine Arts.)

William Hogarth, *Family Gathering*. At once an interior scene and family portrait illustrating the new way of life of the aristocracy and well-to-do bourgeoisie. Pomp is here supplanted by comfort. (London, Christie's.)

Pieter de Hooch, *Young Bourgeoise and Her Servant*. Summer in the Low Countries. The door is wide open, as is the window, through which we see a bridge arching over a canal. The bourgeoise is preparing cabbage; the servant is about to go out. (Lille, Museum of Fine Arts.)

Bruegel de Velours, *The Château de Mariemont* (detail), a vast rural estate. (Dijon, Museum of Fine Arts.)

Hubert Robert, *The Cenotaph of Jean-Jacques Rousseau in the Tuileries in 1794.* (Paris, Carnavalet Museum.)

Anonymous, *Louis XIV on Horseback Passing the Grotto of Thetis*, 17th century. The court of Louis XIV was a place where the crème de la crème crowded in, ostensibly to see the king but in fact to be seen by him. Courtiers became useless actors in a spectacle controlled by the king down to the minutest detail. (Château de Versailles.)

Etienne Jeaurat, *Carnival in the Streets of Paris* (detail), 1757. The center of this scene is a young man juggling kitchen implements. The woman beating the drum would be out of place in a more Mediterranean setting, where the drum was associated with the authorities. The painter shows how the carnival fostered brief communication between men and women, who are shown here in rather clearly differentiated groups. (Paris, Carnavalet Museum.)

Joseph Vernet, *View of the Port of Toulon* (detail). In the foreground a howitzer is being readied for action. The background, with its rows of cannonballs and cannon, resembles an industrial storage area. (Paris, Naval Museum.)

Joseph Vernet, *View of the Port of Toulon* (detail). Chained galley slaves arrive in port, whence they will sail for the prison colonies. Many young men later wrote home begging for their freedom. (Paris, Naval Museum.)

Nicolas Raguenet, *The Intersection of the Place de Grève and the Rue de la Mortellerie in 1751*. Whenever there was a public execution, windows on the place de Grève were filled with spectators. On hiring days the square was filled with job-seekers. (Paris, Carnavalet Museum.)

active self, which barely has time to reflect on events. Bassompierre "is a man surprised in the thick of action . . . He portrays himself to his sympathizers in technicolor, attending to the needs of war."[3]

To our way of thinking today, these seventeenth-century authors lacked awareness of the inner self. They were not so much autobiographers as authors of quasi-official portraits. In the words of Yves Coirault, "We have become accustomed to more intimate memoirs, to frank and indiscreet confessions . . . to unbuttoned autobiography and self-portraiture." Coirault goes on to distinguish, in his preface to Saint-Simon's *Memoirs*, between egocentrism and egotism: "Saint-Simon's extreme indulgence of the Duke de Saint-Simon, his extraordinary egocentrism, do not impart to his *Memoirs* that flavor of egotism that . . . delights us so much in the memoirs of our contemporaries . . . Some readers may be disappointed that Saint-Simon never appears in his dressing gown . . . [and] that the intimate scenes nearly always concern others."[4]

A systematic analysis of the series of memoirs investigated by Bourgeois and André[5] and by Cioranescu[6] would no doubt confirm the foregoing remarks. Even the titles are revealing. Many are short: Memoirs, or Memoirs of so and so. Longer titles add military, political, or diplomatic subjects, building on a variety of basic forms: Memoirs of, Memoirs for, Memoirs containing, Memoirs touching on, Memoirs for the purpose of, Memoirs to explain, Memoirs in which one sees. Some run as long as twenty or thirty words, which locate the work in history and justify its existence. Memoirs of private life do not exhibit such a profusion of titles, and it may be that historical memoirs are not private documents at all.

Any sweeping statement is likely to be misleading when applied to so profoundly individualistic a genre. Henri de Campion, for example, confesses his feelings for his little daughter Louise-Anne.[7] The abbé de Marolles writes about his childhood.[8] And Fontenay de Mareuil dedicates an account of his public life to his children.[9]

Historical memoirs should not be confused with autobiography. Autobiography, which appeared much later, is defined by Philippe Lejeune as "a retrospective account, in prose, of a person's own life, in which the main emphasis is on the life of the individual and especially the history of his or her personality."[10] By contrast, in the historical memoir personality is secondary to history.

Diaries and Family Records

Diaries and *livres de raison*—for simplicity call them journals—were often kept in the seventeenth and eighteenth centuries. Until recently widely dispersed and neglected by scholars, such humble writings were far more modest and less ambitious than historical memoirs. Originally the journal was simply a book of accounts, and even in more highly developed and elaborate examples of the genre the account remains the central element. Each day's happenings were recorded in the pages of the journal while they were still fresh in mind. The contents tend to be prosaic, the activities described of the most ordinary kind, recorded day after day in a formulaic and unsophisticated prose.

Journals divide time and action into a series of moments whose extent never exceeds a single day.[11] Perceived in this way, the action is fragmented. No literary form unifies its distinct moments. Narration, description, and other stylistic qualities are excluded. Hence the journal is not recognized as literature. Elisabeth Bourcier observes: "The problem of literary creation never arose for those who in the seventeenth century wrote daily in their journals. Authors were never tempted to submit their homely, monotonous notes to the curiosity of a wider public. Historical memoirs and, later, confessions and autobiographical journals were written to be published. Sometimes they were published immediately, sometimes after a delay, but they never remained anonymous. By contrast, journals and family records were consigned to oblivion until historians and ethnographers turned to them as sources."

What can be learned from such sources? They often yield an abundance of details from which it is possible to bring the past back to life. Gilles de Gouberville sits next to the sputtering kitchen fire. At dawn, even before the master of the house arises, people gather in his bedroom. One February night he takes a book from his library and reads it out loud to the family. The passage of time is recorded not only by the quarter-hour but also by the liturgical calendar—the saints' days, the major holy days—and even by the movements of the sun. We learn about the senses, about hearing and touch, if only sporadically, as well as about sickness and health, which are recorded not in the physician's arcane language but simply and directly.

The density, bulk, and duration of a few exceptional journals should not be allowed to conceal the fact that many were no more than a few pages long and had been soon neglected or abandoned. Others are not so much journals as village chronicles, recording baptisms, marriages, deaths, and local events but little or nothing of the inner life. Journals are by nature dry. Crisp in form, curt in expression, they lack narrative continuity as well as confidential confession. Comparison of French with English journals of the same period brings out these characteristics with even greater clarity.

Great care is required to read and interpret such sources correctly. Every family record is a distinctively individual work.[12] I shall concentrate on a few fairly typical examples of a vast genre: the journals kept by Gilles de Gouberville and a man whose style of life and writing was rather similar, Paul de Vendée; Charles Demaillasson, a prominent citizen of Montmorillon in the Poitou; Pierre Bourut, sieur des Pascauds and an *avocat* (attorney) in the parlement of Angoulême; and Trophime de Mandon and François de Merles, nobles from Nîmes and Avignon. In addition, a rare example of a journal kept by a woman, Marguerite Mercier, has been rescued from obscurity. Finally, the private life of a prominent citizen of Rheims, a contemporary and relative of Colbert, is revealed to us by the journal of a merchant, Jean Maillefer.[13]

Several more intimate memoirs are worth delving into. The dragonnades, or persecution of Huguenots in Poitou, had a profound impact on the life of Jean Migault, a schoolmaster from Mauzé. In exile he wrote and copied for each of his children a memoir of the trials he and his family had endured. Dumont de Bostaquet, another man who endured a lengthy exile, embellishes the past as he relives it in memory.[14] We also have what Bernard Beugnot has called the "retirement memoirs" of that pugnacious gentleman Henri de Campion, written after the death of his daughter, as well as the memoirs of Mme de La Guette, one of the few women to try her hand at the genre at a time when writing memoirs was a male monopoly.

Some journals, such as those kept by physicians and servants, reveal the private lives of people other than the writer. Physician's journals are rare, but surviving specimens are of the highest quality, such as Héroard's account of the health of Louis XIII[15] and the record of Louis XIV kept by his primary physicians, Vallot, Daquin, and Fagon.[16] These are rather episodic accounts, more summary than daily report, but they tell a great deal about the king's responses to illness. Servants' journals are rarer still, and I shall cite only two examples: that

Jan Josef Horemans, *The Gallant Concert* (detail). (Dijon, Museum of Fine Arts.)

Elisabeth Bourcier writes: "In closely examining these ancient and authentic documents, we would like to read beyond the yellowed pages and between the hastily written lines the state of mind in which each journal was written, for behind the document there lies the man."

of Dubois, valet to Louis XIII and Louis XIV, which was copied by the brothers Antoine, also valets;[17] and that of Mme de Motteville, maid and confidant to Anne of Austria.[18]

Héroard's Journal

The most fascinating but also the least well known of journals is that kept by Jean Héroard.[19] In form it is a monotonous, repetitious compendium of daily notes concerning not receipts and expenditures but the health of the king. Paradoxical as it may seem, it is similar in structure to the journal of the minor noble Gouberville, and the same methods may be used to study both.

Héroard's journal covers the period from the birth of Louis XIII through his twenty-seventh year. It is a banal compilation of information about the physical condition of the young prince in sickness and in health. We learn about the exercises intended to strengthen the royal child and the meals he was served four times a day: breakfast, dinner, snack, and supper. We learn about the little prince's gestures and words, recorded as they occurred, registered by the hour, the half-hour, and the quarter-hour. For a period of 10,000 days there are roughly 100,000 observations, a minimum of four per day. There is virtually no mention of public life—an occasional allusion, perhaps, but nothing like the continuous narratives contained in contemporary memoirs. Everything in the journal pertains directly to the private life of the prince.

Despite the scientific, professional rigor of the record, Héroard observed the child with the tender eye of a father. Each page quivers with emotion, bringing the young prince to life as he runs, plays, dances, and talks.

The most valuable information in Héroard's journal concerns the first ten years of Louis XIII's life, during which time the royal child was under the physician's constant scrutiny. As required by his office, Héroard attended the prince during meals. He watched him play. He kept the young lad at his side as he wrote his journal, as can be seen from the scribblings and drawings that litter its pages. He also accompanied little Louis on his strolls in the park, took part in some of the child's games, and followed him on the hunt.

A page from Héroard's *Journal*, a manuscript that puts us in direct contact with the author. We can see how he wrote— carefully or not, deliberately or hastily. We see what he crossed out and where he used the blotter. When his pen quivers with emotion, we are aware of it. (Paris, Bibliothèque Nationale, ms 4022, fol. 131.)

The wealth of information goes far beyond a mere medical record. We learn about the rhythm of the prince's day, about the interior of the old château at Saint-Germain, about the park that surrounds it, and about the new château whose appearance we are able to reconstruct. We meet the characters

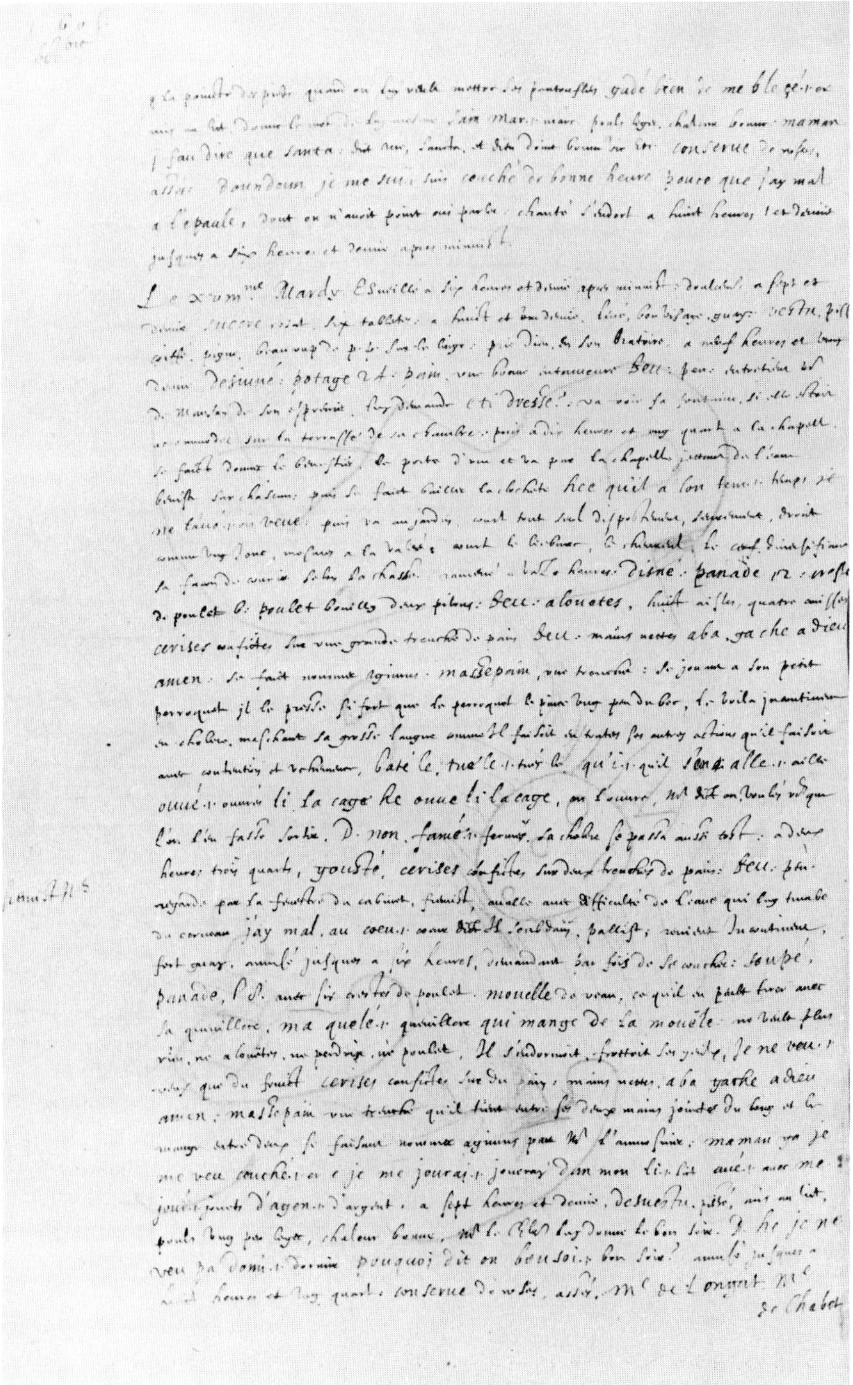

A native of Montpellier, where he studied medicine, physician to Kings Charles IX, Henri III, and Henri IV, Héroard was fifty when he assumed responsibility for the health of Louis XIII. He exercised that responsibility until his death at age seventy-eight. Evident in his gentle face is the tenderness of a father or a grandfather. (Paris, Bibliothèque Nationale.)

I HEROARD. S. D. VAVGRIGNEVSE. P. MEDECIN DV ROY LOVIS XIII.

who compose the royal entourage—not the lifeless lists that can be found in the papers of the royal household but the living court as revealed in conversation, recreation, argument, and conflict. We discover just how much time the king and queen spent with their son: from 1602 to 1606, the king spent 366 days, the queen 346. We learn how they behaved as parents. In the background we glimpse the other royal children and bastards, although Héroard's primary subject is always the dauphin. We are introduced to the cast of characters responsible for his welfare: governess, physician, and nurse, the future king's first teachers. We also meet the valets and chambermaids, the military officers and rank-and-file soldiers who wait on and protect him, as well as the workers and artisans who attend to the needs of his household. In all, an entourage of some fifty persons, a veritable social microcosm, in which the future king, treated always with the respect due his royal

Seated beside Héroard, the little prince practiced writing letters and drawing pictures. The physician carefully preserved all these sheets, dated them, and inserted them in his *Journal*. (Paris, Bibliothèque Nationale, ms 4022, fol. 481.)

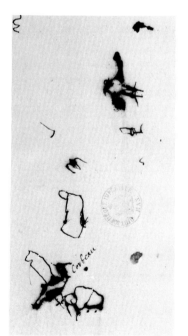

21 September 1606: "Amuses himself drawing on paper. Makes a crow, which he names thus." Louis would be five on 27 September. (Paris, Bibliothèque Nationale, ms 4022, fol. 320.)

Here, Fréminet, first court painter to Henri IV, guided the hand of young Louis XIII in his first drawing lesson, when the prince was four. (Paris, Bibliothèque Nationale, ms 4022, fol. 398.)

person but also as familiarly as any child, learns to relate to other people.

Finally, the journal tells us about the education of a royal prince. Young Louis learns manners and self-control. If Mme de Montglat raised the boy with a firm hand, threatening the whip more than she actually used it, Héroard intimates, if he never actually says, that his own methods relied far more on tenderness and affection.

Space does not allow me to explore Héroard's journal as fully as it deserves, so I shall limit myself to one aspect, the primary reason for its existence: the record of Louis's physical health.

PRIVATE SPACE

In his introductory remarks Philippe Ariès pointed out that private and public life in the late Middle Ages were closely intertwined. The record books of rural families in the period confirm his assertion, for they reveal no clear distinction, no dividing line, between public and private space. For all their valuable evidence, however, journals are not the best source for studying private living arrangements. Brief, episodic notations cannot compare with paintings, prints, and engravings. Estate inventories are far more instructive when it comes to interior decoration, furniture, objets d'art, tapestries, and fabrics. Such sources are far more useful than journals for discovering whether people's surroundings were bare or crowded, light or dark, comfortable or uncomfortable.[20]

What Elisabeth Bourcier says about autobiographers applies as well to journal writers: "They seem to have no home, no room, no bed and to notice nothing that goes on in the street." Although Bourcier studied English writers, the French were similiar in this regard. She continues: "The setting of family life is barely depicted. Houses were enlarged and modernised, but only the most recent are mentioned."[21] Nor do we find descriptions of the surrounding landscape.

In contemplating this perspective view of the park of Saint-Germain, Héroard's reader can note not only the imposing geometric design but also the lively, mobile figure of the young dauphin, as he learns to walk, exercises, and plays outdoors. (Paris, Bibliothèque Nationale.)

Private space is seen only as it relates directly to everyday experience. It must be read between the lines. We learn, for example, that one of Charles Demaillasson's daughters is born in the "lower hall" and another in the "russet" room. When repairs are made to Paul de Vendée's house, we learn the names of its various parts: hall, kitchen, pantry, upper-story bedrooms (reached via a staircase). Enhancements to comfort are mentioned occasionally: walls are whitewashed, floors tiled,

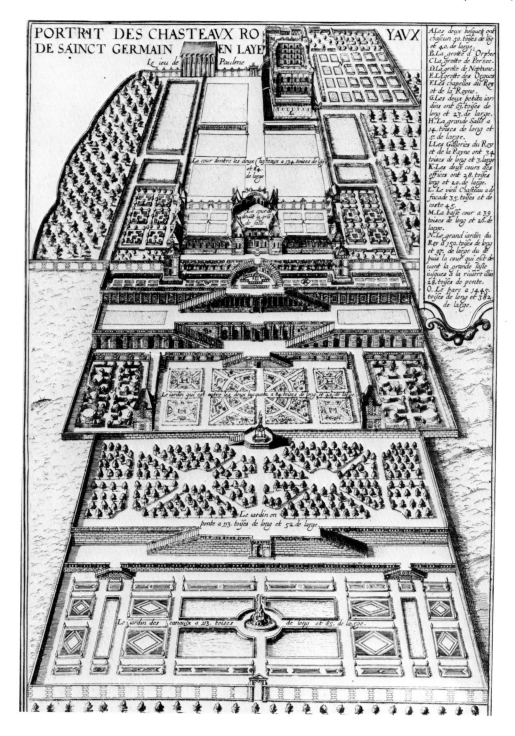

fireplaces made more efficient. When Gilles de Gouberville's floor begins to crumble into the cellar, he has it repaired. The kitchen floor and fireplace are refurbished. The mill is improved: walls are repaired, the roof is replaced, and new carts are constructed. No description is given, but as the work progresses over a period of three months, repeated notes enable us to visualize what the wood and stone building looked like—a perfect example of the kind of information that can be gleaned from family record books.[22]

Unexpected events reveal something about the nature of the place in which they occur. Dumont de Bostaquet, a Protestant compelled to write his memoirs in exile, devotes little space to the description of private residences.[23] But a fire on 31 August 1673 brings surroundings into sharp focus. The master's children share a room with a maid, separated from the master bedroom by a tapestry. Bostaquet's eldest daughters sleep in a room "full of beds and furniture under the peaked roof." The master bedroom, with its private alcoves and large armoires at the head of the bed, is decorated with portraits of the master and his wife. There is a beautiful wooden staircase and a fine roof of slate and lead. An estate inventory would yield a far more detailed description of the contents of the house, but the journal lets us experience the fire: the panic, the cries for help, the desperate race up the stairs to the smoke-filled bedroom, the furniture hurled out of windows, the children transported without clothes to the village.

The journals of Héroard and Gouberville are very revealing. Héroard gives us a feel for Saint-Germain, with its old and new châteaux and its terraces, grottoes, and fountains.[24] These are sketched in rapid strokes as the young prince moves about the premises. Interiors are mentioned but not described: the dauphin's bedroom, the nurse's room, the bedroom of Mme de Montglat, Héroard's office. Various other places are visited by the dauphin at certain times of day: the chapel, the oratory, the ballroom, the *palemail*, the king's and queen's apartments. Outside we explore the terraces and gardens in which the child plays and walks, diligently followed by his doctor. In passing we glimpse patios, herb gardens, walks, and the grottoes of Orpheus, Neptune, and Mercury, and we hear the splash of the fountains. The only places mentioned in the journal are those visited by the prince.

Gouberville's journal never describes the physical appearance of his estate, which can still be visited today. It included a manor, church, surrounding farms, enclosed pastureland, and cultivated plots. The surroundings figure in the journal only as they related to the writer's social life. He is the center of his world.

Gouberville's journal is a source of unrivaled richness on the subjects of familiarity and hospitality. Not a day went by when he did not record the most basic social gestures and acts. We discover, first of all, the familiarity that existed between the rural master and his servants, who lived nearby and whose families mingled constantly both at home and in the fields. Orders were given for each day's task, wages were paid by the master personally, and men and women worked together in fields, meadows, and woods.

Conversation was frequent and familiar. What was discussed is rarely indicated, but we can surmise: the weather, farm work, village news. There were frequent visits and encounters on the road or in the fields, of which Gouberville has left innumerable vignettes. Sunday mass was an important social occasion. It is not hard to picture what it must have been like in the village of Mesnil-au-Val, which has been preserved much as it was then. Around the church, in the cemetery, and on the roads into town peasants isolated all week long in their hamlets greeted one another. After mass the nobleman normally invited the curé to dine at the manor.

Hospitality was an important part of social life. Gouberville's valuable account tells us not just about great occasions but about the spontaneous, everyday forms of hospitality. Guests were received mainly in the manor's kitchen, occasionally in the hall, and rarely in the master's bedroom, where they arrived, we are told, "before I awoke," "with the rising sun," "in the early morning," "before I got out of bed." Here we touch on an important aspect of rural mores: no time and no place were reserved exclusively for private life. It was not considered an invasion of privacy to enter a man's bedroom at what we would consider an inappropriate hour.

In the ordinary course of the day guests who arrived at the manor kitchen close to mealtime were frequently invited to dine. Often they were asked to stay for supper and spend the night. When the day ended at Mesnil-au-Val—"at sunset," "as the sun faded," "as the cock crowed"—Gilles de Gouberville would invite his visitor to remain under his protective roof, safe from the dark and the dangers of the night, from

Familiarity and Hospitality

Gouberville's *Journal* helps us appreciate the intense social life that accompanied the summer chores of mowing and harvesting. (Paris, Bibliothèque Nationale.)

the immemorial fear of darkness. Those asked to stay included peasants, villagers, artisans, judges, and noblemen.

Illness and death were important social occasions, times when public and private life were confounded. Gouberville's journal makes it clear that sorrow, sadness, and outpourings of grief were not private emotions but a part of the common life of the village. The healthy hastened to the bedsides of the ill, the living to the homes of the dead, bearing gifts and offering assistance. With the nearest physician or barber miles away in the city, whichever villager was most competent did whatever he could to ease pain and suffering. The afflicted person was never alone.

Death occurred amongst family. The living pressed around the deathbed to pay their final respects, and a priest was called to hear the dying person's last words. Gouberville's brief notes and descriptions of deathbed scenes make us feel as if we were actually present in sixteenth-century Mesnil-au-Val.

Wolfgang Heimbach, *A Kitchen.* At the manor of Mesnil-au-Val the kitchen was the center of daily life and hospitality. (Nuremberg, Germanisches Nationalmuseum.)

The Loves of Gombault and Macée. Images of private life in an area not far from where Gouberville lived, here preserved in tapestry. (Museum of Saint-Lô.)

Assistance to the sick and dying was an essential part of private life, as Gouberville's *Journal* shows. (Paris, Bibliothèque Nationale.)

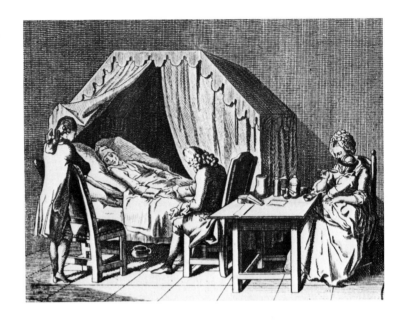

Families

The family was the center of social life. Gilles de Gouberville was not married. The family depicted in his journal consists of brothers, sisters, and servants. To learn more about family life we must consult other sources.

The *livres de raison* by their very nature contain no narrative and little evidence about family life as such. Their texts must be examined very closely to elicit whatever information can be read between the lines. Discretion was a part of the sensibility of the time. Writers were not effusive; they confided their feelings in few words. Furthermore, few journals were kept by women. Because things are depicted exclusively from the male point of view, we lack information about the crucial role of wife and mother.

The Wife

What do we learn, for instance, about Elisabeth Delavau from the journal of Pierre Bourut, lord of Les Pascauds? She was his companion for ten years, administrator of his household (as the text frequently intimates), and mother of numerous children. But how did the couple get along? When Jeanne Preverault, the woman he married four years after Elisabeth's death and who filled the same role of mistress of the household and fertile spouse, also died, Pierre wrote: "Ah, great God, our company was pleasant!" Did he love one more tenderly than the other? Was his second wife more diligent and competent in her domestic duties than the first? There is not the slightest hint of a distinction between the two.

Charles Demaillasson, a minor notable from Montmorillon, has very little to say about his wife, who is mentioned only twenty or so times in thirty-nine years. The author finds his good woman no more worthy of extended attention than himself. We never see her inside the home in her role as mistress of the house. At best there are a few allusions to her management of the female servants. When she experiences difficulty in childbirth, however, her husband delicately allows his anxiety to show: "That same day, at ten at night, my sister arrived from Lairat on account of my wife's illness, the labor having caused her much distress." Anxiety is also evident in the fact that Demaillasson, a great traveler, remained at his wife's side in the months that followed. When she becomes pregnant a second time, the journal entries again become briefer and more frequent.

At death the closeness of the couple is finally revealed: "On Friday died my dear wife Anne Clavetier, at two o'clock in the morning. She was a very worthy and virtuous person with whom I enjoyed a pleasant life during the time of our marriage."

In Arles, at the opposite end of France, Trophime de Mandon had little more to say about the woman with whom he shared his life. As Sylvie Fabarez observes, "he mentions

Gabriel Metsu, *Family*. Journals, by nature modest and reserved, reveal few details of family life, but the nature of family feelings can be read between the lines. (Berlin, Stattliche Museen Preussischer Kulturbesitz.)

his wife Marguerite on few occasions: when she brings a child into the world, when he calls upon her services, or when she assists him in the management of domestic affairs." In charge of the household, she administers her husband's fortune, manages his business, and raises his children. Yet he offers us no portrait; she is a faceless assistant. But he too is shaken by her death. The tenderness that a careful reader senses throughout the journal bursts into the open at the hour of her death: "On 5 January 1666, Wednesday morning, my very dear, most virtuous, honored, and lamented wife yielded up her noble soul to God."

From these varied texts, authored by men of very different social background and geographical location, a pattern typical of many similar journals emerges. The woman of the house is mentioned only briefly. We learn nothing about her appearance, her relations with her husband, her possible conflicts with him, or her behavior as a mother. Births, which occur almost annually, are discussed, especially when the difficulty of labor or postpartum complications elicit signs of the

French journals, almost all kept by men, have little to say about intimate matters such as childbirth. Paintings and engravings tell us much more about the appearance of the newborn and the care of the infant. (Paris, Bibliothèque Nationale.)

husband's devotion to or affection for his wife. The labor itself is rarely mentioned, nor the aftermath of a childbirth without complications. Only at death is the happiness of a long marriage evoked. Afterward the memory of the departed spouse is exalted and sublimated. The Huguenot schoolmaster Jean Migault saw his first wife die at the time of the persecution of Huguenots in the Poitou. In the memoirs he is writing for his children, their mother occupies an important role: "I knew sixteen or eighteen years of prosperity during the lifetime and with the delightful companionship of Elisabeth Fourestier, my beloved wife and your good mother. That is why, even though it was but a short time since God had called her to rest, I experienced such a profound pleasure in writing about the pains she had endured and suffered with me at the beginning of the persecution . . . This was so that the smallest of you might in this way come to know the woman who brought you into the world." These moving words are those of a man who remains bruised by the persecution, writing long after the events that he describes.

The Child

The years of early childhood, the most fragile years of life, are the very heart of private existence. Little is said in the journals about the presence of children. There are no stories of their activities, no portraits to tell us how they looked. Feelings toward them are seldom mentioned. Yet the *livre de raison* was not only a journal of household accounts but also a family record book—an essential if all too often elliptical family document. About children we find only brief notes, which must be read very carefully if we are to bring them back to life. Births were recorded, but in the manner of an official record with no note of congratulation. Baptism, which followed soon after birth, was also carefully recorded. The child was a creature of God, and in the infant one saw the future Christian: "May God grant that this child receive the Holy Ghost, preserve his baptismal innocence, live according to God's commandments, and die in holy fear and love of Him." More or less the same formula was repeated by Pierre Bourut at the birth of each of his children. Meanwhile, at the opposite end of the realm, Trophime de Mandon wrote: "God bless him in His holy grace" or "God bless the little girl."

Raising a child required the family to bear the cost of a wet nurse and, later, school tuition and board. These expenditures are recorded, but nothing is said about the child's looks

Aubry, *Family Scene.* The child's place in the home. The father's tenderness toward his child, about which journals tell us very little, is admirably rendered here. (Paris, Library of Decorative Arts.)

or behavior, physical prowess or character. But the absence of signs of affection does not indicate that parents were indifferent toward their children. Tenderness can sometimes be inferred from the use of diminutive nicknames: Trophime de Mandon writes of his Margot, Fanchon, and little Togne, whereas his eldest son, François, is already addressed by his last name, and severely, to remind him of his family responsibilities. Affectionate epithets are attached to his children's names by Eusèbe Renaudot, a Parisian physician and son of the celebrated Théophraste, who speaks of "Manon," "Cathaut," and "little François," also known as "Pépé." But the eldest boy is referred to with pride and severity as "my dear colleague."

Children were loved, but there was no sentiment about childhood. If a child died, little was said in the journal. It was not that people were insensible to the death, but that their sensibility differed from ours, as we gather from the fears of Jean Migault during the mortal illness of his "little René" or the distress of Charles Demaillasson when two of his grandsons die at the ages of five and seven. Yet his lament is modest and restrained: "He was 5 years, 4 months, and 22 days old, and as perfect in mind and body as one could wish." Of the second child he wrote: "He had a mind without equal." Renaudot describes the death of little François, nicknamed Pépé, as though it were predestined from birth: "His hands remained together" after his birth, in the attitude of a saint, which he became upon his death. The father's tender love and deep sorrow at the death of another child are transcribed in brief sentences in the journal: "We shall miss him for his beauty and his gentleness, which made us look upon him as another dear Pépé."

Family records were almost always kept by the father. There is little evidence of the woman's point of view. We do, however, have the journal of the Parisian bourgeoise Marguerite Mercier, into whose life came little Nanette. A month before the child's birth the family purchased a wicker cradle, a basket, a cover, and a small mattress. Shortly after the birth, which may have come sooner than expected, they bought "an *aune* [about a yard and a quarter] of serge for the little girl's cradle." Then the child was sent away to a wet nurse but continued to appear in the household accounts: at eight months she received a pair of shoes and two pair of stockings, and at one year another pair of shoes and "a pair of chamois gloves." At nine months she was also given a "child's chair" and at one year "children's toys." At eighteen months she received another toy.

When the little girl was almost two, she returned to her parents' home. At first Marguerite Mercier had referred to the

Slingelaudt, *Soap Bubbles*. With the exception of Héroard's remarkable work, private journals had little to say about childhood games and pranks. (Lille, Museum of Fine Arts.)

child as "our child." Then, during the time she was with the wet nurse, she became *la petite*, the little girl. Now that she is home again she becomes Nanette, and a new and more affectionate relationship develops between mother and child. But then Nanette falls ill. She is bled, a doctor is called, but no details of her illness are given. She seems to be doing better, because she receives another pair of shoes and stockings. Then silence. A single line in the household accounts alludes to her death: "6 l. to bury my poor child." The only sign of distress is the word "poor." But the handwriting in the manuscript is shaky and irregular, and the expression "forgot to write," which has never appeared before, occurs three times during the period of the child's illness.

This ambiguous document requires delicate interpretation. Does it indicate that Marguerite Mercier was a cold woman, one who lacked *tendreté* (the word used at the time)? A literal reading suggests that her daughter's death touched but did not really shake her. The *livre de raison*, basically a book of accounts, was not the place for an outpouring of sorrow; nevertheless, sorrow, unconsciously recorded, can be glimpsed in its lines. Elsewhere perhaps, in a letter or note, Marguerite Mercier gave vent to pain and love here betrayed by a word and a trembling hand.

Memoirs provided more ample scope for the expression of emotional turmoil. Witness Henri de Campion's obvious devotion to his daughter Louise-Anne: "I loved her with a tenderness that I cannot express," he writes after her death. "I spent my time at home very agreeably . . . playing with my daughter, who, despite her tender age, was so amusing to those who saw her." This was a rare confession at a time when people avoided mentioning "such things, which many people deem undignified." The little girl died on 10 May 1653, at the age of four. In defiance of convention, her father cannot contain his distress: "People say that such strong attachments may be excusable for grown persons but not for children." He rejects this view. The child, by her death, has entered his memory, filling it with "her luminous and sorrowful presence." In a similar vein, the Protestant Dumont de Bostaquet wrote: "Continuing my sorrows and chagrins, I suffered the pain of losing a son . . . This little boy was a handsome child."

English Private Diaries   Elisabeth Bourcier has analyzed English diaries contemporary with the French ones already discussed. As in France, the picture of family intimacy that emerges is quite different, not only from what we know today but also from what we see in private writings a few decades later. The diary-writers do not describe family life for its own sake, but they seem to have been less discreet than their French counterparts: the *livres de raison* say nothing about marital difficulties; the English diaries reveal differences of character and conflict between husband and wife. Adam Eyre recorded his wife's tantrums, rages, and oaths. Reverend Newcome, who advocated mutual affection and good relations between husband and wife, cannot hide his wife's rancor. And Sir Humphrey Midmay confided to his journal an account of his wife's abrupt changes of mood.[25]

Another difference between French and English journals is that the activities of women were better described on the English side of the channel. More Englishwomen seem to have kept diaries. In the sixteenth century both noblewoman and farmer's wife led full and active lives. Lady Clifford rose at three or four in the morning to inspect her estates on horseback: "I have spent most of my time working," she wrote. Left a widow, she filled her days with the management of her estates, supervising domestics, overseeing the work of seamstresses and cooks putting up preserves, and redecorating her house. No French journal tells us in as much detail about the activities of the mistress of a household like Lady Hoby: sewing, mending, cooking, putting up fruit and meat preserves, and manufacturing candles. The spinster Elisabeth Isham recorded the various kinds of needlework with which she occupied much of her time. Rural women visited the sick and helped women in labor to cope with fear, pain, and the dangers of childbirth. The diaries of both men and women yield poignant descriptions of interminable births.

If the diaries of Englishmen are less reserved about their wives' faults than are those of Frenchmen, in times of sickness or death both wax eloquent about the indispensable presence of a woman. Sir Thomas Mainwaring traces the development of his wife's illness day by day; when she finally recovers, he commissions a service of thanksgiving. Adam Eyre overlooks his wife's cantankerous character and takes her to London for treatment. Anthony Ashley describes the wife he has just lost as beautiful, chaste, affectionate, and an expert homemaker. And when Sir Henry Slingsby's wife dies after eleven years of marriage, he paints in his journal the portrait of a good and pious woman of the sweetest temperament.

English writers were also less reserved when it came to talking about their children. Reverend Josselin tells us that his little Thomas was climbing stairs by himself at the age of one, and that a month later he was trying to close doors by himself. John Greene worries that one of his son Alexander's shoulders is larger than the other and that he is slow to walk. At age two he is still walking in leading strings. Lady Cifford reports that her daughter Margaret fell several times while attempting her first steps. But childhood was short, and children were soon sent off to school where, deprived of the warmth of home, they prepared for the rigors of adult life.

The Diary of Samuel Pepys

Guybert, *The Charitable Physician*. "I have described to you in this little booklet the manner of preparing in your home the remedies used daily by good and faithful physicians for all sorts of diseases." (Paris, Ordre National des Pharmaciens, Bouvet Collection.)

Remarkable for its candor even among English diaries is that of Samuel Pepys, an exceptional document of English middle-class life covering the years 1660 to 1669.[26] Written in a richer, more narrative style than Gouberville's journal of the previous century, it takes us into the heart of private existence. Pepys casts a sharp eye on his marriage, his infidelities, even his own body. Where Gilles de Gouberville chose to remain silent, Pepys is voluble.

The spirited Pepys, in his thirties, writes of his marriage to a young Frenchwoman who claims to be a Huguenot émigrée: to bed, before going to bed, we went to bed early, to supper and then to bed are phrases that occur repeatedly. "We stayed in bed a long time," or "I stayed in bed with my wife and took my pleasure with her" or "Stayed in bed caressing my wife and gossiping." On another occasion he says that the couple made peace and went to bed together for the first time in four or five days. But the marriage does not remain calm for long. Despite the affection that husband and wife feel for each other, it is marked by jealousy and bitter quarrels. Disputes are followed by reconciliations. Jealous of her husband's infidelity, Elisabeth Marchand loses her temper. On 20 November 1668 we read: "But when I came home . . . I find my wife upon her bed in a horrible rage afresh, calling me all the bitter names; and rising, did fall to revile me in the bitterest manner in the world, and could not refrain to strike me and pull my hair." An even more violent scene occurs on 12 January 1669: "She silent, and I now and then praying her to come to bed, she fell out into a fury, that I was a rogue and false to her." Then, "about one a-clock, she came to my side of the bed and drow my curtaine open, and with the tongs,

red hot at the ends, made as if she did design to pinch me with them; at which in dismay I rose up, and with a few words she laid them down." What would become of this couple, its marriage shaken but still intact? The diary, which ends on 31 May 1669, does not say.

Anonymous, *Still Life with Books*, 17th century. Journals like Gouberville's and Pepys's were not intended to be read but by chance were preserved, the former in a private collection, the latter in Magdalene College, Cambridge. (Berlin, Staatliche Museen Preussischer Kulturbesitz.)

THE BODY

The body appears in writing in a variety of ways: in health, in exercise, in public—or in triumphant "spectacle," as Lucien Clare puts it in his study of the abbé de Pure's *L'Idée des spectacles*.[27] We also find a more intimate, more immodest view of the body in sickness rather than health.

In the *livre de raison* illness is recorded without details as a brief episode. The body is not only healthy but without sexual secrets. When sex is mentioned, the allusion is so obscure as to be all but impossible to decipher. Unconsciously, however, some writers moved toward a more intimate kind of diary, impelled perhaps by ill health or chronic disease. In this respect there is a world of difference between a Gilles de Gouberville and a Jean Maillefer.

Gouberville is often satisfied with a vague statement that someone is ill.[28] Occasionally, however, he names the illness: colds, headaches, upset stomachs coupled with vomiting, intestinal problems, and colic are among the milder maladies. Several times he is stricken with more serious diseases: "I was very sick and did not get out of bed." He suffers "a most violent toothache." Another time "I caught a chill, was obliged to vomit, and lay ill the rest of the day, suffering in my heart, my head, and my stomach." There is no analysis of the sickness, and no narrative. Though afflicted with syphilis, he never mentions the word; we divine the disease from his allusions to a variety of treatments, baths, fumigations, and purchases of mercury. Yet it is clear that Gouberville is more concerned with himself than with others. Words pertaining to sickness are used most often in connection with himself and those closest to him. His sister's illness upsets him so much that he drops everything and rushes to her bedside in the middle of winter. The frequency of illness is another indication of position in the social hierarchy: the persons most often afflicted are those who have the time and leisure to remain in bed. Servants and peasants are obliged to have better constitutions; in any case, they are rarely mentioned in Gouberville's journal. Nevertheless, if one of them "takes to bed," Gouberville is most solicitous.

Sexuality is no more prominently discussed than disease. Secrecy is the rule in regard to both the marriage bed and the brief encounter. The *livres de raison* paint a picture of untroubled marriage, private and undisturbed by temptation or transgression. Gouberville does break the silence, however, in a dozen notes written in Greek characters to foil prying eyes. This curious procedure may have been common practice. At about the same time the English alchemist and philosopher John Dee resorted to a similar subterfuge. "Probably in order to keep the contents of his journal secret," Elisabeth Bourcier recounts, "he even employed Greek characters to record certain details of his conjugal life." And we know that Gouberville was not indifferent to either alchemy or England.

We find the same dearth of confidences concerning illness and sexuality in journals of farmers and notables from around the same period or somewhat later, as well as in the journal of Marguerite Mercier, despite her agitation over her daughter's mortal disease. Journal-writers as a general rule are stingy with words, not much given to description or narrative.

Encyclopedia. "Few remedies are as widely used as bleeding." (Paris, Library of Decorative Arts.)

The one notable exception to this general rule is Jean Maillefer, a bourgeois of Rheims, who shows that in at least one instance the *livre de raison* evolved toward something more like what we would consider an intimate diary.[29]

Maillefer and Gouberville are poles apart. Gouberville's rural universe has little in common with the urban world of Maillefer, a man prominent in the textile trade and a distant cousin of Colbert. The two men approach ethics and culture in completely different ways. Gouberville reads books but does not identify with their authors. Maillefer, an assiduous reader of Montaigne, takes the author of the *Essays* as his teacher and model. In one section of his journal he compares himself to his favorite writer: "I share much of Montaigne's liking for the uniformity of a tranquil and ordinary life." Elsewhere he says: "Knowledge of ourselves is very necessary in order to govern our actions during the course of this life." Maillefer's journal is clearly a descendant of the discreet and

The Illness of Jean Maillefer

taciturn *livre de raison*, but he adds two new elements: autobiography and philosophical reflection in the manner of Montaigne. Patterned on a great model and composed in a skillful, supple style, his text combines the form of a *livre de raison* with the modernity of an intimate diary.

In an attempt to draw a portrait of himself entitled "Parallels with Montaigne," Maillefer reveals that he shares with his illustrious model a reluctance to spend too much time in bed or at table, a willingness to "let nature take its course in disease," and courage in adversity. The body's miseries become a subject for literature, effecting the transition from the *livre de raison* to the intimate diary with its quota of self-indulgence and immodesty. We learn of hearing problems, toothaches, and frequent falls on his back, but the information, brief and episodic, remains anecdotal. However, an intestinal hernia forces Maillefer to live with affliction and reveals the body in an intimate way. Frequent symptoms encourage frequent notes. Maillefer's vocabulary responds to his body's messages as he enumerates his ills: "My rupture, my hernia, my retention of urine, my intestines, my abrasions, my bandages [described in detail], my doctors." Some chapters are entirely given over to descriptions of this sort. In 1673, ten years after the hernia first developed, Maillefer devotes four full pages to his affliction: "I shall produce this chapter for the use of my children should they be stricken." A few years later he takes stock of his infirmities: "I shall speak of mine up to this day, 21 October 1678. I will be sixty-seven years old. . . . Sixteen years ago I had a rupture that has been herniated for twenty-seven months." Nothing else from the period compares with Maillefer's journal, which marks a major step toward a more intimate literature.

A much later example is the unpublished correspondence of Monseigneur de Saint-Simon, bishop of Agde. It deals in a most singular way with the bishop and the state of his body, which since youth has suffered from asthma as well as malaria contracted in the swamps of Languedoc.[30] In some letters, which concern the wretched state of his health, he describes at self-indulgent length his body's malfunctions and troubles. He relates his fear of summer nights, when a choking sensation sometimes drives him from his room. He discusses the state of his nerves: "You can see from my writing that my nerves are not in good shape." Full of self-pity, he describes the pains in his legs, his horrible insomnia, and his intimate diseases. He also discusses his meals, based on the finest recipes in the pharmacopoeia.

The letters of Monseigneur de Saint-Simon and the journal of Jean Maillefer both owe their intimate character to chronic illness. Had they not suffered, neither man would have been quite so frank in genres that were not intended to be literary but that would receive their literary patents of nobility in the centuries to come.

English diary-writers were much more aware of their bodies than their French counterparts.[31] The slightest illness is examined in minute detail. For months on end Geoffroy Starkey records his coughs, his spitting of blood, and his fever. Thomas Mainwaring is tormented by toothaches. Adam Smith records the duration of his bouts of colic. For John Greene the least chill was an occasion to note in incredible detail the evolution of his illness, reviewing in turn all the parts of his body: nose, mouth, throat, ears, head, stomach. Justinien Pagitt vigilantly observed every physical ailment: colds, sore throats, nosebleeds. The body was not viewed with the self-indulgent, narcissistic gaze that would become evident in later diaries, but rather with uncertainty and anxiety in the face of disease and death.[32] Health was not the principal preoccupation of Samuel Pepys, despite the fragile state in which he had been left by an operation for gallstones at the age of twenty-five (1658). He does, however, mention various afflictions: stomachaches, bowel troubles, extreme sensitivity to cold, and unbearable colic. On 14 May 1664 he screams with pain. The notation is brief and realistic but not at all self-indulgent. As soon as the pain has passed, he lauds the return of good health.

What better place to find a description of the body than in the journal of a physician? From the doctors we learn not only about diagnoses of disease but also about attitudes toward and images of the body. Louis XIII's physicians Héroard and Fagon offer unique evidence about the body of one man.

The Body of the Prince: Louis XIII

With a clinician's precision, Héroard provides daily readings of young Louis's pulse, temperature, urine, and stools. We also learn about the prince's meals, which are described daily. When this mass of information is finally indexed and catalogued, it will tell us more than any other source about the diet of the time.[33]

Héroard's only extended description of the infant Louis is the detailed professional account he gives of his examination of Marie de Médicis' newborn: "Large in body, stout in bone structure, highly muscular, well nourished, smooth skin, reddish in color, vigorous." The infant lies in its cradle sleeping or wailing. It chews its hands and takes the breast of its wet nurse.

But we also learn details that no other writer would have dared to state with as much sincerity as the physician. The child's body, especially its head and face, suffers from the nurse's mediocre milk. At an unusually early age Louis is given a porridge, the first time on 14 October, when he is seventeen days old. He is not being cleaned properly or sufficiently. Not a very pleasant child to look at or touch, according to Héroard's description: his eyelids are swollen, the skin of his face is marred by "red blotches" and "dry patches," there is oozing behind the ear and pimples on the face. In January his head is "circled with scabies like a crown." For seven months the same words, indicating the same state of ill health and the same unattractive appearance, occur again and again. Finally such notations become less and less frequent, and in August, Héroard finally writes: "The head is clearing up." The child grew, gained strength, recovered his health, and began to walk. On 19 September 1602 he "is beginning to walk with confidence, held by leading strings under the arms."[34] His childish grace finally reveals itself. Yet the prince's hygiene would remain inadequate. He was cleaned up, but when did he wash? When did he bathe? The words "washed" and "bathed" occur only once each in the first year. On 4 July "he is combed and for the first time enjoys it and offers his head." In subsequent years we read that the prince is "combed [and] dressed" every morning, but there is no mention of a more complete grooming. After every meal he washes his hands, as the words "clean hands" indicate. As Philippe Erlanger has written, "A prideful slovenliness reigned at court." Héroard's *Journal* bears him out.

Thus, our first portrait of Louis is not very flattering, but the royal physician feels bound by the obligations of his profession to record what he sees. This image is gradually effaced as the young prince comes into his own. He is a healthy child, and the words in which his good health is recorded by his physician are simple and invariable: "smiles, very nice, good face, gay." His progress, which can be followed in the pages of the *Journal*, amazed the members of his entourage. His first tooth arrives on 15 April, at the age of six and a half months. He is a vivacious child who recognizes the various people in his world. He babbles and gurgles his first barely

intelligible sounds, which Héroard eagerly records and interprets with astonishing naiveté. Aged one month, twelve days,
the child is asked "Who is that man?" With a perfectly straight
face, Héroard records that he answers, "incomprehensible to
all but the initiated but readily, 'Eoua.'" His hair grows longer
and more beautiful: "His hair makes him more radiant as it
turns blond" (27 March, six months). "His brown hair is
turning light chestnut" (4 May, seven and a half months). "His
hair is turning even lighter" (13 July, nearly ten months).

By this time Héroard has fallen under the child's spell; in
addition to his regular notes on hygiene, he dwells on little
Louis's antics, which enliven the pages of the journal. The
following passage, typical of numerous others, dates from 11
December 1602. It admirably captures the vigor and exuber-
ance of the healthy, fourteen-month-old prince and at the same
time reveals Héroard's style: "The eleventh, Wednesday, at
8:45. Annoyance and anger, quick and impatient. Strikes Mistress de Montglat on the fingers with an iron-clad stick. She
tries to take the stick away from him. He cries, strikes out,
writhes like a serpent, amused by the battle, comes charging
back, and lets loose with a good blow, striking the forehead
of de La Berge, his page, and causing a large lump. Resolute,
gay, babbling away, he goes strutting about."

Concerning the child's sexual initiation and activity, Héroard's *Journal* is an unparalleled source of information. Though
not an intimate diary, it takes us into the very heart of the
prince's private life. The sexual gestures, immodest teasing,
and questions whose answers are known in advance are all
well-known from one of the most novel chapters of Philippe
Ariès's influential *Centuries of Childhood*.[35]

It would be a mistake to think that the *Journal* is filled
with observations of Louis's sexual behavior. Such notes are
interspersed with all the rest, recorded in the same banal and
episodic style. Between 1601 and 1610 (3,285 days), there are
101 notes on sexual subjects, using a limited number of
words.[36] The actual frequency of sexual behavior was no doubt
much higher, and it is clear that Héroard placed no particular
emphasis on this type of observation. The first such note
occurs on 24 July 1602, when Louis, ten months old, is said
to have laughed "uproariously" when touched by his nurse.
Sexual notes are numerous up to 1606 (when Louis was five)
but almost totally absent after 1607; there are only two for all
of 1609 and 1610. In other words, particular attention was
paid to the prince's sexual behavior in early childhood.

Page from Héroard's *Journal*
containing a fragment of a letter from the six-year-old Prince
of Wales, the future Charles I,
to the dauphin, recopied and
signed by Héroard. (Paris,
Bibliothèque Nationale,
ms 4022, fol. 195.)

The child was not an inadvertent witness of gestures made and words spoken in his presence but the principal actor in the scene, urged on by members of his entourage who attached a high value to the royal genitals. The sexual games played were neither hidden nor shameful: "Asked for his penis to be kissed," "played with his penis," Héroard writes without a hint of prohibition or repression.

Young Louis's entourage included not only lackeys and maids but also those responsible for the prince's education. The king, the queen, and above all Héroard, author of the *Institution of the Prince*, insisted that "our little Prince, given by heaven to command . . . begin with himself, by learning that it is the duty of a King not to become the slave of desire and pleasure, that he must submit his vain and unbridled follies to the power of reason . . . and that he not think that perfect happiness lies in idleness and gratification of his desires." Héroard had an unusual feeling for childhood and respected it as a unique time of life. Indulgently, he drew Louis's attention to his genital organs on numerous occasions (12 December 1602, 12 August 1604, 27 August 1604, 2 April 1605, 1 July 1605, 19 August 1605, 17 October 1605) and provoked responses (17 September 1605, 21 July 1606, 30 November 1606). He observed what happened, scrupulously recorded the child's attitude, and stressed the laughter that accompanied sexual games. In a marginal note added on 15 May 1606, after a veritable exhibition, he wrote: "By nature will like pleasure."

The King's Suffering Body

Intimate images of a sick, suffering body were recorded by the physicians of Louis XIV in a journal whose original manuscript has survived. There is no splendor in this document, only the misery of an afflicted body and a record of the care that was provided and of the routine effects of that care.

The journal describes the various serious diseases from which the king suffered over the course of his life: smallpox in 1647, the "Calais disease" in 1658, measles in 1663, dental problems in 1684, and a major operation for a fistula in 1686. These afflictions were known to the public at large. But the king also suffered from a series of more minor ailments: vapors, fluxions of the stomach, colds, stomachaches, and so on. In the physicians' account we see the king off the public stage. We see his body in a way in which no other writers would have permitted themselves to portray it.

Here are a few images, as reported by Fagon. Suffering

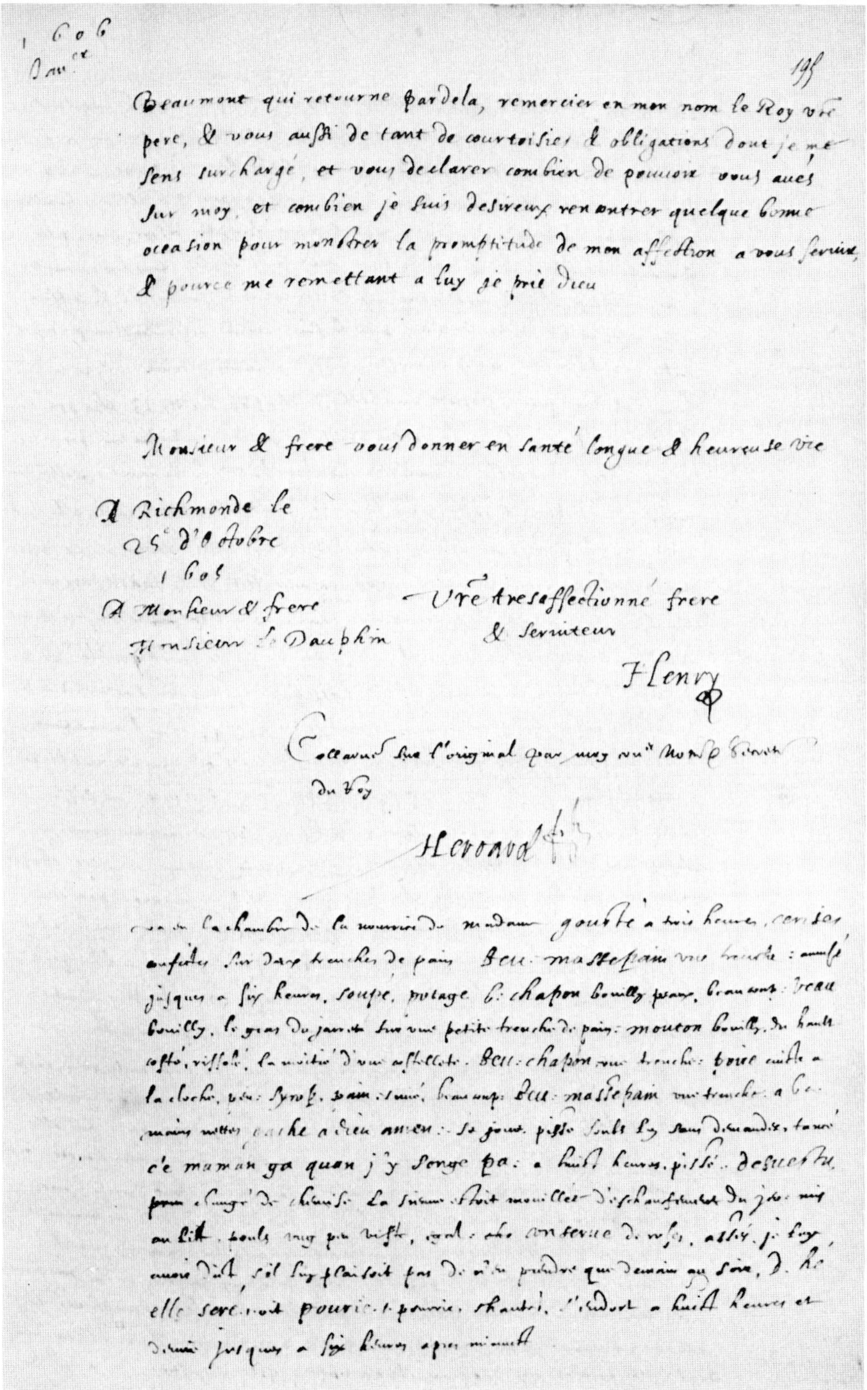

Beaumont qui retourne pardela, remercier en mon nom le Roy vre
pere, & vous aussi de tant de courtoisies & obligations dont je me
sens surchargé, et vous declarer combien de pouuoir vous aues
sur moy, et combien je suis desireux rencontrer quelque bonne
occasion pour monstrer la promptitude de mon affection a vous seruir,
& pource me remettant a luy je prie dieu

Monsieur & frere vous donner en santé longue & heureuse vie

A Richmonde le
25e d'Octobre
1606
A Monsieur & frere   — Vre treseffectionné frere
Monsieur le Dauphin   & Seruiteur

                                    Henry

Colleaué sur l'original par moy vre Monse Escuié
du Roy

            Heroard

en la chambre de la nourrice de madam goutté a trois heures, ce soir
ensuites sur deux tranches de pain. Beu: massepain vne tranche: ainsi
jusques a six heures, soupé, potage le chapon bouilly pean, beau coup, beau
bouilly, le gras du jambon sur vne petite tranche de pain: mouton bouilly, de haulte
costé, rissolé, la moitié d'vne assellete. Beu: chapon vne tranche: poire cuite a
la cloche, vne syrop, pain seué, beau coup. Beu: massepain vne tranche a be
moins mettes cache a dieu amen: se jour, pissé saoul & saus demandir, tourné
c'è maman ga quan j'y songe pa: a huit heures, pissé: deseuestu
pour changé de chemise. La sueur estoit mouillee d'eschauffement du jeu: mis
au lit, saoul, vng peu reste, egal: ahe conserue de vese, assis je loy,
auoir dict, sil luy plaisoit pas de n'en prendre que demain au soir, d'ké
elle seroit pourrie: pourrie, chanté, s'endort a huit heures et
demie jusques a six heures apres minuit.

from a paralyzing gout, the king could not sleep: "Gout in the left foot somewhat prevented him from sleeping" (21 November 1688). "Pain . . . interrupted his sleep for several hours during the night." "The nights were very bad, almost sleepless" (26 September 1694). "The pain . . . became quite violent and almost unbearable between eleven o'clock and midnight" (3 October 1694). Another cause of insomnia was a boil on the neck: "As the King put on his wig in the morning, he felt pain in the back of his neck . . . The King lay awake all Saturday night." Pain and suffering did not exempt the king from performance of his duties but obliged him to do what was necessary in unusual circumstances: "Gout prevents the King . . . from wearing his regular shoes" (May 1696). And he is forced to wear "galoshes" or to be carried in a sedan chair during a procession in cold, rainy weather at Marly on 6 May 1699. When the pain became unbearable, the king remained in bed, where he continued to attend to affairs of state. In January 1705 he experienced a gouty catarrh: "The pain that the King felt upon getting out of bed in the morning increased his suffering considerably . . . The King could not get out of bed . . . He heard mass in bed and since then has carried on in the same fashion, holding Council in bed, unable to stand on account of the pain."

The effects of the king's health were evident in 1685, the year of the Revocation of the Edict of Nantes. During that and the following year Louis suffered terrible jaw pains as a result of a tooth extraction in 1684. He also made the courageous decision to have his fistula operated on, and equally courageously bore the consequences.

Conversely, public events affected the king's health. Military campaigns were fatiguing: "The King spared no effort and did not rest day or night at Mardick, for the sieges of Dunkirk and Bergues," Vallot wrote in 1658, when Louis was twenty. And in 1691 Fagon wrote: "After his lengthy and difficult travails at the siege of Mons . . . he had gout in the foot."

His diligent attention to affairs of state brought Louis XIV the usual host of problems associated with the sedentary life: "Frequently, when H[is] M[ajesty] left the Council in the evening, his head was quite heavy and painful and filled with vapors" (1670). And in 1674 "air and movement do him a notable good, remedying the ills that his sedentary life and diligence in affairs cause to recur."

Private sorrows inevitably affected the king physically,

despite what Fagon called his "unshakeable courage in pain and peril." In 1711 came the "thunderbolt" (Fagon's word) of "the death of Monseigneur," which shook the king to his core. "H.M., arriving that night at Marly, fell into a general shivering of vapors caused by the violent shock to his heart . . . since then the constant recurrence of his sad and painful condition, perpetuated by the orders the King has been obliged to give in regard to this distressing subject, has left him to endure the unfortunate effects of an ever-present sorrow." For reasons we do not know, Fagon's journal ends a few days after this invaluable testimony. What would he have written about the torments of the year 1712, including the sudden deaths of the Duke and Duchess of Burgundy, which imperiled the continuity of the crown?

We have learned a great deal not only about the physical and emotional aspects of private life but also about people's attitudes toward their private existence. Private activities and intimate feelings (to which the public has no access) were not a subject of writing before the second half of the seventeenth century. The few examples that we possess should not be allowed to conceal this truth. What we learn about private life from Gouberville comes from the facts he relates despite his indifference to the subject. His journal is typical in its dryness, reticence, omissions, and absence of narrative. His reserve is extreme. These deficiences of the French journal emerge clearly from the comparison with contemporary English diaries, which are infinitely richer, freer, and denser—harbingers of things to come.

In France it is often to public figures that we owe the most revealing texts about private life. Not texts that they wrote themselves (as Louis II of Bavaria would do much later) but texts of which they were the principal subject, written by a relative, a physician, or a servant. The writers were not indiscreet; they were just doing their job. When it comes to writing on private life, Héroard, Fagon, Dubois, and Mme de Motteville are unrivaled in the seventeenth century.

Defrance de Liège, *At the Sign of Minerva*. As the activity of reading became increasingly private, the book became the primary instrument of cultural exchange. (Dijon, Museum of Fine Arts.)

✍ Literary Practices: Publicizing the Private

Jean Marie Goulemot

MEDIEVAL literature was oral and public. Genres such as the chansons de geste, chansons de toile [stories told by women while sewing or weaving], fabliaux, and works for the theater show that the consumption of literature was not yet conceived as a strictly individual act. This fact is related to the conditions under which the works were produced as well as to contemporary reading practices. Thematically too literary works dealt primarily with collective material, whether the defense of Christendom or fratricidal struggles among feudal lords or clergymen, to whom the arcane symbolism of the *Roman de la Rose* was familiar and legible. The bonds among the various Knights of the Round Table reflect the fundamentally collective nature of the Arthurian cycle.

Most medieval works are essentially religious; their religious character reflects the way in which the general subsumes the particular. Even François Villon, who since the nineteenth century has been seen as the originator of modern lyrical poetry, conveys not so much the inner life of the individual as the unhappy consciousness of having violated the rules of the community. Unhappiness is born of separation, and even a parody like Villon's *Testament* evoked, however unwillingly, a society in which the individual was caught up in a network of filiation and exchange. The passage of time so lamented by Villon is expressed in terms of common experience; his poems are all marked by a desire to reestablish communication with the other, the community: "Brother humans, who after us live on . . .," or "Tell me where, in what country . . ." The rhetorical overture of the ballads incorporates this anguished appeal, this desire for reunion.

Medieval literature was for the most part anonymous.

Forms of Privatization

Writers belonged to the community: jongleurs, clerics, authors of sacred mysteries and profane plays existed only because a community—a convent, confraternity, or city—"commissioned" their works. The community, in which specific cultural practices were embodied, was the writer's *raison d'être*; his work served its needs and brought it renown.

Private Space and Early Modern Literature

A tradition of sociological interpretation of literary works, still very much with us today, is based on content analysis. Evidence about private life allegedly can be gleaned from heroic adventures or from some detail of customs and habits. This approach denies that literature has anything to add to the historical record and reduces the literary text to the status of a historical document. No doubt it is interesting that in libertine novels by writers like Crébillon the action is generally situated in bedrooms, boudoirs, and alcoves. But other novels involved travel over long distances. The younger Crébillon's *Sopha*, *Egarements*, and *La Nuit et le Moment* may be contrasted with Diderot's *Jacques le Fataliste* or Abbé Prévost's *Manon Lescaut*, whose heroes roam widely.

One might of course resort to statistics. How many novels of travel were there, and how many intimate fictions? But the figures, at best suggestive of tendencies, would still require interpretation. If the libertine novel evokes private pleasures (the "follies" of the urban elite, savored in out-of-the-way *petites maisons*), it is rather paradoxical that such private pleasures were paraded in public. At a time when new forms of social intercourse were making love more private and secretive than in the past, the libertine novel broke the new rules by talking about what ought to have been kept quiet and transforming into a public act what ought to have been confined to an intimate and private setting. It is superficial and misleading to suggest that the exhibition of private activities violated the new rules. The reader, forced by the libertine novel to assume the role of a voyeur, spies in private upon ostensibly private acts.

Interpretation demands caution, so I shall concentrate on the presence of private space as mediated through new narrative forms and new literary ideologies and practices. I shall focus on the emergence of intimate journals, memoirs, first-person novels, and utopian tales, which evolved slowly as genres or at least categories of literature. I shall also consider the development of new ways of legitimating the literary statement. Authors will henceforth invoke their own moral authority as proof of the truth of their writing, as Rousseau does so strikingly in the *Dialogues of Rousseau with Jean-Jacques.* Literature also appropriated new subjects: self-knowledge, as in Rousseau's *Confessions*; autobiography; and pornography, which accounted for a major part of the literary output of the second half of the eighteenth century. All of these things are related: new themes, new narrative forms, and new means of legitimation (that is, a new ideology of writing and of the writer) are connected in complex ways. Intimate life is special, condemned to silence on pain of denying itself. It is necessarily separate from public life, yet it is also sought out as a retreat, and it is not always easy to distinguish which is which. The special status of private life does not provide grounds for a broad reinterpretation of early modern literature. The question to be asked of literature is what new things it had to offer writers and their readers.

RENAISSANCE CONTRADICTIONS

The sixteenth century was a period of transition during which the mutations and divisions so evident within the literary practices of the late Middle Ages were perpetuated. This is not the place to explore the inexhaustible riches of Renaissance literature, but three figures illustrate the way in which cultural habits were affected by the constitution of a private realm: Montaigne, Rabelais, and Ronsard.

Montaigne's *Essays* represent a mutation in the nature and status of knowledge. The work is in no way derivative of the medieval *summa*, or scholastic commentary. Where the summa is systematic, the *Essays* are fragmentary. Where the commentary refers to a unique work, of which it offers a gloss, the *Essays* are a compendium of many sources, a summary of wide reading. What makes them coherent is first of all Montaigne himself, sole master of his references and his queries and creator of his library. He characterizes his method of reading as plunder, as a rubbing of his mind against the minds of others. Perhaps the best statement of his method is this passage from "Of Idleness" (I:8, p. 21; Montaigne quotations are taken from the translation of Donald M. Frame): "Lately when I retired to my home, determined so far as possible to bother about nothing except spending the little life I have left

Montaigne, or the Mutation of Knowledge

French school, *Montaigne*, 16th century. "These are my fantasies, by which I try to give an idea not of things but of myself." (Chantilly, Condé Museum.)

in rest and seclusion, it seemed to me I could do my mind no greater favor than to let it entertain itself in full idleness and stay and settle in itself . . . But I find . . . that, on the contrary, like a runaway horse, it gives itself a hundred times more trouble than it took for others, and gives birth to so many chimeras and fantastic monsters, one after another, without order or purpose, that in order to contemplate their ineptitude and strangeness at my pleasure, I have begun to put them in writing, hoping in time to make my mind ashamed of itself."

Underneath the teasing style is a determination to be entirely free, an affirmation of the powers of the self and of the attention the self demands. Throughout the *Essays* Montaigne reiterates that knowledge and even wisdom are never external to the subject of inquiry, who chooses and orders. Knowledge being constituted by the subject, Montaigne rejects any knowledge that is preconstituted. He recognizes the existence of knowledge only in the process by which the self interrogates facts, established dogma, and wisdom institutionalized or revealed. Nothing is ever definitively acquired. Montaigne not only makes the reading and thinking self the foundation of all knowledge, he also transforms it into the primary object of his reflection. Textual support for these assertions is plentiful: "These are my fancies, by which I try to give knowledge not of things, but of myself" (II:10, "Of Books," p. 296). Or: "I dare not only to speak of myself, but to speak only of myself" (III:8, "Of the Art of Discussion"). The assertion, often repeated, is in the nature of a provocation.

Not that it was forbidden to speak of oneself, just that it was not yet acknowledged that the self could be the source of wisdom or knowledge. Did it even exist? To be interested in one's self was at best a foolish and frivolous waste of time, at worst a sin. Consider Saint Augustine. Montaigne was perfectly aware that he was altering the end of writing, yet he felt no guilt. "This book was written in good faith, reader. It warns you from the outset that in it I have set myself no goal but a domestic and private one. I have had no thought of serving either you or my own glory" ("To the Reader," p. 3). Montaigne's introduction is exemplary in its clarity. It states, in a striking mirror image, that not only is the act of writing private but so is the use to be made of it.

Rabelais Divided

François Rabelais and his work occupy a distinctive place in the literature of the Renaissance. Mikhail Bakhtin argues that he is heir to a burlesque tradition in medieval popular culture. Not only humanist polemics, *Gargantua* and *Pantagruel* are also vehicles for the popular culture of the Middle Ages. Evidence for this can be found in what Bakhtin calls the "vocabulary of the marketplace," part invented, part traditional, as well as in forms and images borrowed from the medieval feast, with its inversions, its giants, and its lunatics. In a broader sense, Rabelais's language creates a philosophy of existence out of a grotesque conception of the body, setting a "low," material style against a conception of man that is at once aristocratic, Christian, humanist, and courtly. Hence Rabelais, Bakhtin argues, is not the Renaissance man he is made out to be in traditional histories of literature. A Rabelais often judged to be in violation of the "canons and rules of the literary art" can only be explained as a product of the carnivalesque culture of the Middle Ages who has somehow survived into the Renaissance.

My own interpretation differs from Bakhtin's. What he interprets as a strict expression of a carnivalesque culture can equally well be read as a text that refers to a society that by its very nature excludes private space. Consider Rabelais's invocations of the organic: his discussion of wiping the behind (*Gargantua*, chap. 13) or the chapter in which Gargantua urinates on the Parisians who have come to admire him (*Gargantua*, chap. 17). These are merely verbal transcriptions of socially accepted and recognized practices. They were shocking in the second half of the sixteenth century only because new codes of civility had begun to take hold, imposing taboos on the exhibition of such basic physical acts. Similar anachronism is apparent in the verbal incontinence of Rabelais's characters, in his giants, in Gargamelle's delivery, and in a thousand other episodes of the Rabelaisian tetralogy.

Seen in this light, Rabelais's work bristles with contradictions. On the one hand it contains elements of feast and carnival, of the open, communal society of the Middle Ages. On the other hand, however, it contains a critique of religious and political authority and embraces antiauthoritarian social forms. Even Rabelais's encyclopedic knowledge is significant. Like that of Montaigne, it represents a choice, an affirmation of the individual's freedom to set his own standards, to reject received ideas and accepted beliefs, and to constitute a knowledge of his own. Yet in many respects the implicit goal of total knowledge betrays nothing less than a medieval summa in a new and modern guise.

Using the giant Gargantua's enormous body, prodigious physical and intellectual appetites, and mixture of the trivial with the spiritual, Rabelais dramatized the dualist Baroque conception of man and the world. (Paris, Bibliothèque Nationale.)

Ronsard: The Exhibition of the Singular

Excessive eating and drinking on the Ile de Crévepance leads to vomiting and drunkenness: the *Familiere description du tres vionporratimalvoisé et tres enuitaillegoulementé Royaume Panigonnois.* (Paris, Bibliothèque Nationale.)

Ronsard, and with him the group of poets known as La Pléiade, can be credited with originating lyric poetry as the Romantics would later define it: poetry that expresses private feelings and experiences. Much of Ronsard's poetry belonged to the still-flourishing genre of song, and many of his poems were set to music in his own time. He was not entirely un-influenced by collective (though no longer communal) forms of social and cultural exchange, to which we are indebted for his *Discourses on the Miseries of the Age* and *La Franciade* (an epic in the manner of Virgil). But he is no longer a poet who, like Villon, suffered from being separated from the community of believers and whose unhappy consciousness of his estrangement defined his inspiration. Ronsard's lyricism not only adopted new forms such as the ode and the sonnet but also concerned itself exclusively with the fate of a single individual. His reflection on time's flight takes the form of an exaltation of subjectivity, of individual desire, anguish, and love. The poems that Ronsard wrote on the eve of his death

illustrate to perfection his appropriation of a general theme in a particular discourse:

> Je n'ay plus que les os, un squelette je semble,
> Decharné, denervé, demusclé, depoulpé,
> Que le trait de la Mort sans pardon a frappé:
> Je n'ose voir mes bras de peur que je ne tremble.
> Apollon et son filz, deux grans maistres ensemble,
> Ne me sçauroient guerir; leur mestier m'a trompé,
> Adieu, plaisant Soleil! mon oeil est estoupé,
> Mon corps s'en va descendre où tout se desassemble.
> Quel amy me voyant en ce point despouillé
> Ne remporte au logis un oeil triste et mouillé,
> Me consolant au lict et me baisant la face,
> En essuiant mes yeux par la Mort endormis?
> Adieu, chers compaignons, adieu, mes chers amis!
> Je m'en vay le premier vous preparer la place.

> I have nothing left but my bones, I am like a skeleton
> Without flesh, nerves, muscles, or pulp,
> Struck by Death's unforgiving arrow:
> I dare not look at my arms lest I tremble.
> Apollo and his son, both great masters,
> Would not be able to heal me. Their profession
> has betrayed me,
> Farewell, pleasant Sunshine! My eye is stopped up,
> My body is falling apart.
> What friend, seeing me ravaged to this point,
> Does not come with eyes sad and moist,
> Consoling me in bed and kissing my face,
> While wiping my eyes, which Death has put to sleep?
> Farewell, dear companions, farewell, dear friends!
> I shall go ahead and make a place for you.

Unlike Villon's verses, these lines make no reference to the Christian community, which implies a radical change in the mode of address. Solitude is experienced as a misfortune and the imminence of death is rendered in terms of individual physical decline. A parade is made of the singular, the personal, and the intimate. Realistic descriptions of suffering and the body's ruin were a part of medieval communal discourse, as evidenced by church sculpture and charnel-house imagery. Here the same description is transposed to the first person, yet it continues to be presented in a public literary space. The situation is paradoxical, for given the new rules of civility

there is every reason for such images to be kept silent and secret.

Examination of three major sixteenth-century writers thus reveals a literature of transition, in which some old elements remain unchanged while new elements have begun to emerge. Rabelais is rife with contradictions, while Ronsard stands on the brink of a mutation in the nature of poetry that neoclassical poetry would conceal. With Montaigne and the poets of the Pléiade a new relation of the writer to the written literature is seen. The writer's subjectivity justifies and legitimates the writing, whether it be lyrical poetry or the knowledge-in-the-making that is the subject of the *Essays*. The self, its freedom and its history, has become the justification for the act of writing. The change is an opaque symptom of the constitution of a private space not yet under the seal of secrecy nor silenced by a taboo.

PRIVATE LIFE, HIDDEN AND REVEALED

It is logical to think that tendencies that first manifested themselves in the Renaissance would have been clarified and deepened in the age of neoclassicism (the seventeenth and eighteenth centuries), but this is far from the case. Although the baroque novels of Paul Scarron, Charles Sorel, and Antoine Furetière can be situated in the tradition of Rabelais, other literature of the period, whether lyrical poetry or the theater, is characterized by a dissimulation of private and intimate subjects.

The theater that came into being in the seventeenth century did not serve the same function as the medieval theater. One radical difference between the two lay in their relation to urban life. Unlike medieval mystery plays and comedies, neoclassical drama was not part of any civic or religious ritual. It did not engage either the Christian community or the group to which it was addressed, although it did represent the privileged leisure of the urban elite and cultivated courtiers. It was viewed as an art, constructed according to an aesthetic code, that is, referring to nothing outside itself except in a secondary way and fundamentally severed from everday life and the ordinary experience of time. Sacred tragedy became a separate genre, with its own authors: Boyer (*Judith*, 1696), Duché (*Jonathan*, 1699; *Absalom*, 1702), Nadal (*Saül*, 1705; *Hérode*, 1709).

During Racine's lifetime a careful distinction was made between his sacred and his profane plays. A play, whether religious or not, either pleased or displeased its audience. The public's attitude toward a play, its relation to the theater, was determined by pleasure or lack of it. There was the "theater of the fairground," lively plays in the Italian style, impressively catalogued by Lesage and d'Orneval in their *Theater of the Fairground, or Comic Opera, Containing the Best Plays Performed at the Saint-Germain and Saint-Laurent Fairs* (10 vols., 1721–1737). There were also the vulgar verbal fantasies of a Piron (1719–1730) and the so-called *parades*, plays written in a scatological argot for the private entertainment of important officials and judges. These genres bear nostalgic traces of a time when theater served another function.

In neoclassical theater per se a variety of rules served to exclude discussion of private space. Such theoretical treatises as La Mesnardière's *Poétique* (1639), d'Aubignac's *Pratique du théâtre* (1657), Pellisson's *Discours sur Sarrazin* (1656), and Rapin's *Réflexions sur la poétique* (1674) tell us at once that the theater, even when it treats individual destinies in particular situations, always speaks of man and his celebrated nature, and that the particular is only a means of expressing the general. Playwrights in their prefaces invariably made this maxim their own. They were able to do so because at that time people believed passions were timeless and universal.

The value of revealed feelings was essentially that of an example. Recourse to ancient or Oriental subjects, as in Racine's *Bajazet*, indicates a desire for distancing. Baring the heart was but a means of approaching a general truth. Various restrictions on the use of language (exclusion of low diction

Popular plays involving the crimes of Tabarin, performed on the Pont-Neuf or at the fairs of Paris, reflect a nostalgia for the communal theater of old.

French school, *The Gelosi*, 17th century. Italian comedians, like the Pont-Neuf players, were active, histrionic, and noisy. (Paris, Carnavalet Museum.)

and coarse or vulgar words) and other rules of theatrical propriety accentuated this tendency. At issue were the dignity and function of the theater. Everything was done to prevent the spectator from assuming the indiscreet posture of the concupiscent voyeur and to prevent him from identifying with the destinies of the characters, from sharing their inner doubts and transports. An impersonal model was enforced. In spite of appearances, comedy followed the same course. The vices condemned by Molière and Regnard are illustrated chiefly in terms of their social consequences. Religious hypocrisy, avarice, social pretension, misanthropy, and the passion for gambling are portrayed as a source of distortion and perversion in social relations.

One looks in vain for lyrical poetry in the neoclassical age. Apart from a few lines of La Fontaine, a few well-hidden confidences in Racine, a few verses that embody Abbé Bremond's definition of pure musicality, it does not exist. The lyricism of the Pléiade poets was abandoned. To measure the distance traveled, compare Ronsard's lines on the death of Helen or on his own anticipation of death with Malherbe's *Consolation to M. Du Perier, a Gentleman of Aix-en-Provence,*

Antoine Watteau, *At the Comédie Française*. (Private collection.)

Engraving by Sylvestre after Jean Le Pautre, *Entertainments at Versailles. Third Day. Le Malade imaginaire*. (Paris, Bibliothèque Nationale.)

In contrast to the popular theater and Italian comedy, the classical theater created a new kind of representation, a distant, glacial ritual.

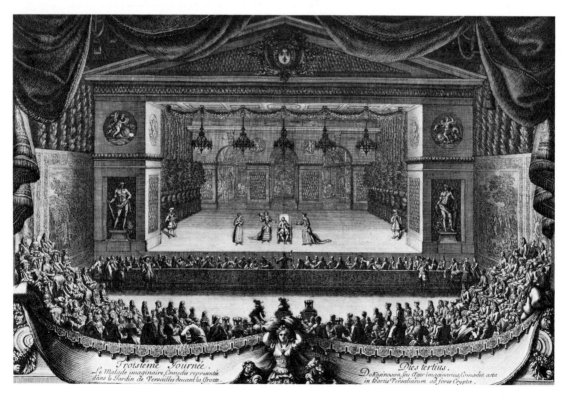

concerning His Daughter's Death. A lyricism based on experience as filtered through the subjectivity of the poet has been replaced by a poetry that proceeds directly to the universal, to a level of generality that has been called the lyricism of the impersonal. Private pain and suffering are dissimulated behind a veil of dignity and resignation. There is a refusal to expose what the men of the time believed ought to be borne not by the community at large but by the individual in private solitude, coupled with an exaltation of universality and generality.

It was no accident that the poet ceased to be regarded as either an accursed or an inspired figure and instead came to be seen as a fool, "no more useful to the state than a player of ninepins," Malherbe quipped. Molière transformed him into a grotesque pedant, a boor incapable of conforming to the rules of the new civility. Mathurin Régnier (*Satire II*) paints him as large of mouth and jaw, and Boileau and many others spun out caricature. The poet's image was degraded to the point where his private personality and history no longer sufficed as justification of his lyric.

Resistance

In various forms Pascal's stinging reproach to Montaigne—that "the self is hateful" and that his project of painting himself was "foolish"—was accepted as a general rule. Literature conformed to the tenets of the new civility, whose ideals were discretion, reserve, and conformity. The change did not come about without struggle or resistance, however. To be sure, the personal lyric produced no immediate offspring, but the limits of the apparent triumph of the new civility can be seen in the fact that farce survived even in the early plays of Molière (*La Jalousie du Barbouillé, l'Etourdi ou les Contretemps, le Dépit amoureux, le Docteur amoureux*) and obscene and scatological material flourished in the baroque novel. Scarron's *Romant comique* (published in 1651 and 1657) flouted the new taboos with its heterogeneous narrative and heavy reliance on scatological humor. Excrement—now private—was supposed to remain hidden, shameful, unspoken. Scarron's insistence on using the crudest verbs and portraying the natural bodily functions; his preference for the chamber pot, the privy, and the sweat of tennis-players over the aesthetic refinements of salon conversation; his exaltation of the bed and the table; and his fondness of drunkenness and vomiting were as much provocation as they were nostalgia. His vocabulary was equal to the occasion. Insults ("cuckold's beard," "daughter of a bitch")

Sil n'euſt eſté aſpre aux pots
Il fut party bien a propos

Il a trouué le pain
il ſeſt chargé de
vin.

Plein
iuſques
au collet

36
A PARIS.
Par Iacques Lagniet
au fort l'Euoſque

Lagniet, *Illustrated Proverbs*.
This picture of a man vomiting
is a survival of an archaic popular culture for which Quixote
reproached Sancho Panza.
(Paris, Bibliothèque Nationale.)

are dispensed with all the creative verve of a language untram-
meled by the strictures of a Vaugelas. Scarron's work, like
that of Sorel (*Francion*, 1623) and to a lesser degree Furetière
(*Roman bourgeois*, 1666) proved that old and already archaic
forms of sociability did survive. Because the dissimulation of
the body, that machine for producing secretions, sounds,
odors, and pleasures, accompanied that of the inner life, the
baroque novel can also be read as a nostalgic survival.

Throughout the eighteenth century there is a persistent
regret of the more joyous forms of community. Rousseau
gives vent to this nostalgia in evoking the delights of the
popular festival, whether in fiction, as in *La Nouvelle Héloïse*,
or, in more philosophical terms, in the *Letter to d'Alembert*
(1758): "What peoples have better grounds to assemble often,

*Nostalgia for Communal
Exchange*

Mayer, *Jean-Jacques Rousseau Gathering Herbs.* When Rousseau turned his back on a society filled with enemies, he gave himself up to the joys of solitary promenades and self-contained reverie. (Paris, Carnavalet Museum.)

and to form among themselves the sweet bonds of pleasure and joy, than those who have so many reasons for loving one another and remaining always united? . . . Let us not adopt those exclusive spectacles that sadly enclose a small number of people in a dark cavern . . . No, happy peoples, those are not your feasts! It is in the open air, beneath the sky, that you must gather and surrender to the sweet sentiments of happiness . . . But what will the objects of those spectacles be? What will they show? Nothing, if you like. With freedom, wherever affluence reigns, well-being also reigns. Set a post topped with flowers in the middle of a square, call the people together, and you will have a festival. Better yet, make a spectacle of the spectators. Make the people themselves the actors. Let each one see himself and love himself in the others, so that all may be united."

The idea of a citizenry transparent to itself continued to obsess Rousseau in the anguish of his final solitude (*Reveries of a Solitary Walker*, "Fifth Walk"). Although it is tempting to reduce the idea to nostalgia for a more primitive way of life, it is something more than that. It is also more than an idea only of Rousseau, first expressed in his *Discourse on the Sciences and the Arts* and *Discourse On the Origin of Inequality*, where he shows that man in a state of nature knows no social passions and that families in a presocial state promote communal exchange. The myth of the noble savage is not simply a convenient literary and philosophical device for judging contemporary society from the outside. It often represents nostalgia for a type of communal organization in which secrecy, isolation, and privacy are impossible. In Diderot's *Addendum to Bougainville's Travels* the dialogue between the two Europeans concerning the advantages of Tahitian society is unambiguous in this respect. Diderot shows that modesty and secrecy in regard to sexual practices are a product not of nature but of convention: "Man does not wish to be disturbed or distracted in his ecstasies. Those of love are followed by a feebleness that would leave him at the mercy of his enemy. That is all that could possibly be natural about modesty; the rest is convention . . . Once woman became man's property and furtive pleasure came to be regarded as a theft, the terms *modesty, reserve,* and *propriety* came into use and imaginary vices and virtues were invented. In short, barriers were erected between the sexes, which prevented them from inviting one another to violate the newly imposed laws, and which produced the opposite effect by warming the imagination and stimulating desire. When I see trees planted around our palaces, and an item of clothing covering a part of a woman's breast, I think I spy a secret return to the forest and a call to the liberty of our ancient dwelling place."

Do not be misled by the reference to the forest. The passage is really concerned with nostalgia for transparency. The same is true of Diderot's *Jacques le Fataliste*, in which the master, contemptuous of the respect that one is supposed to show for another person's privacy, insists upon questioning Jacques about his loves. The narrator engages in a long tirade against the hypocrisies of language and love: "And what has genital action, so natural, so necessary, and so just, done to you, that you exclude its sign from your conversations, and that you imagine that your mouth, your eyes, and your ears would be soiled by it?" Even more, in his *Letter on the Blind*

The Negro as There Are Few Whites, Paris, Year III. The noble savage was the white man's other, his historical precursor, whether naked or a king. He embodied an impossible compromise between nostalgia for the past and the constraints of the present.

for the Benefit of Those Who See, Diderot puts forth a materialist explanation of modesty. The etiquette of love was often questioned by the writers of the Enlightenment. With the exception of Voltaire, they took a paradisaical view of primitive society, which must be seen as a reflection upon the forms of social intercourse.

The debate on methods of education, so important at the time, also touched on the problem of modesty and reserve, as can be seen in Rousseau's *Emile*. (Bear in mind, however, that Rousseau admits in the *Confessions* to having been guilty of exhibitionism.) People were fond of educational experiments, real or imaginary, which allowed them to debate the issue of whether intimacy is natural. Du Laurens, in *Imirce, daughter of nature* (1766), took one side, while the *History of a savage girl found in the woods at the age of ten, published by Mme H...t* and attributed to La Condamine (1765) took the other. There was endless discussion of the basis for various amorous rituals.

Utopia

The theme of utopia met with considerable success in the eighteenth century. Between 1700 and 1789 some eighty new works on the subject were published. The utopian novel was an imaginative response to anxiety caused by the destruction of traditional political forms. Utopian literature was thus a response to absolutism, whose designs it publicized and fortified. The utopian city was a human invention, atemporal and ahistorical. Utopian discourse is concerned with the past. Utopia, it has been said, is the future of the past.

A utopia is created by a founding act: that of Utopus in More's *Utopia* (1516), of Sévarius in Vairasse d'Alais's *Histoire des Sévarambes* (1702), or of Vicorin in Rétif de La Bretonne's *La Découverte australe* (1781). The founding act determines the unique characteristics of each utopia and inaugurates its ahistorical existence. As a secondary sign of perfection, social relations in utopian societies are communal: meals are taken in common, education is collective, and festivals involve the entire community. The individual is never alone; each person lives under the scrutiny of all the others. The young Tahitians in Diderot's *Addendum* even copulate in public, urged on by spectators. In *Utopia* houses have neither doors nor windows, so that nothing can be concealed from onlookers. In Grivel's *Ile inconnue* (1783) incest symbolizes the fact that the inhabitants of the new world live in desirable proximity to one another: the society begins when a brother and sister are shipwrecked, and their offspring populate the island.

From a 1730 French edition of Thomas More's *Utopia.* In this astonishingly immodest scene we see how the reproduction of the community was managed.

Examples could easily be multiplied, some straightforward, others more in the nature of metaphors, to show that utopian literature was sustained by a peculiar paradox. In most utopias the state is extraordinarily powerful, indeed omnipresent to such a degree that some utopian literature has been called totalitarian. The state determines the forms of communal exchange. The inhabitant of utopia is a ward of the state. The transparency of hearts is revealed in public space, defined and controlled by the state, almost as if utopia were a way for the social imagination to reconcile the irreconcilable: dreams of bygone liberty with present-day institutional constraints. Privacy is lacking not because of the pervasive presence of communal relations but because everything is organized by the state. (In this respect it is perhaps true that utopia is totalitarian.) Privacy is not defined, as in Orwell's *1984*, in terms of an area of freedom preserved or wrested

From *La Découverte australe par un homme volant* (Paris, 1791), with illustrations by Binet. Utopia also provided room to dream. Rétif de La Bretonne's hero takes off on a solo flight of discovery. He will colonize the peoples he finds on his journey. (Paris, Bibliothèque Nationale.)

from the state. Instead it is conceived as the means by which one individual cuts himself off from others. Diderot, thinking perhaps of Rousseau, who had become his enemy, wrote that "the wicked man is always alone." The withdrawal of an individual was seen not as a form of opposition to the authorities' surveillance but as a kind of moral pathology. Paradoxically, in an age when the political rights of the individual were first established, he was judged morally and socially in terms of his openness to others.

This is illustrated in the new stagecraft, whose basic tenets were set forth by, among others, Diderot in his *De la poésie dramatique* (On Dramatic Poetry, 1759) and *Entretiens sur le Fils naturel* (Conversations on the Natural Son, 1757). Bourgeois drama as defined by Diderot, Sedaine, Louis Sébastien Mercier, or even Beaumarchais aimed to create a theater of conditions rather than of characters and individuals. Man was defined in terms not of his own nature but of his relation to various social roles, functions, and practices. Even more than neoclassical theater but in a different way, bourgeois drama avoided portraying man's inner life or secret self. Its heroes were identified by their most external characteristics. In a sense, bourgeois dramatists had learned their lesson from Pascal, who demonstrated the importance of dress, occupation, and appearances, but only in order to emphasize their futility. In translating this for the stage, however, the irony was eliminated. The habit truly made the monk. Social status alone determined what was moral and how people behaved.

In this neoclassical debate, this obscure clash which, properly interpreted, reveals so much about the constitution of private space, the theory and practice of the theater function as a valuable and often paradoxical proving ground. In his *Letter to d'Alembert* Rousseau attacked the theater as a corrupter of men, where women were exhibited and virtues held up to ridicule. For him the theater represented a degradation of family values and social intercourse. As a place where people were together yet separate, it was a caricature (perhaps tinged with nostalgia) of paradise lost. Rousseau contrasted the theater with the popular festival, in which the people were both actors and spectators. The claims made on behalf of private space were not initially seen as positive and progressive.

Memoirs and Diaries   Writing memoirs first became fashionable in the sixteenth century. Disruptive, contentious events such as the wars of religion, the regency of Anne of Austria, the Fronde, and the wars of Louis XIV yielded an abundant harvest of memoirs. As can be expected in an aristocratic society, most were written by prominent members of the social elite: generals, leaders of factions, eminent judges. Few people of humble or modest station left memoirs, even though they possessed the cultural equipment needed to write them. Even today it is surprising, as we cast our eyes over a list of eminent dignitaries and notables, to come upon such names as Mme de La Guette, the wife of a rather modest military officer, and Jean Marteilhe, who in 1757 penned the *Memoirs of a Protestant Condemned to the French Galleys for Reasons of Religion, Written by Himself.*

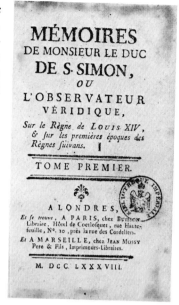

Ancien-régime memoirs were products of an aristocracy. (Paris, Bibliothèque Nationale.)

The sudden vogue for memoir-writing is significant. Leaving aside atypical cases, most memoirists abided by the implicit code of the genre. Writing as participants in known and recognized public events, they sought to describe and justify their own roles. The genre is an aristocratic one; the individual is reduced in it to his public acts. In a sense the memoir ends where private life begins. Anything not pertinent to public life was excluded. Indeed, memoirists often intimated that they had no private or inner life, or that, if they had, it was without interest and not a fit subject for public discussion. Readers of the memoirs of Cardinal de Retz learn nothing about his childhood, nor do readers of the memoirs of Saint-Simon, who begins with a genealogy of his house followed by his début in society. Never was such discretion combined with such prolixity. This is especially interesting in light of the fact that Saint-Simon has a great deal to say about the depravity of others. By their very construction his *Memoirs* embody the notion that what is not public is not sayable.

It would be more accurate, however, to say that the status of private life was ambiguous. The *Memoirs* suggest on the one hand that there is nothing to say about private life even out of public earshot, but on the other hand that there is an inner life which is not fit to be spoken or written about. In either case, positive value is ascribed only to public life.

When we look at the matter more closely, however, we find that even the notion of public life is frequently subject to serious distortion. The actions described may be generally known, but hidden motivations, or at any rate motivations unknown to most readers and generally kept silent, are revealed. This additional information can be interpreted as an expansion of the public domain or as a sign of its limits. The relation between memoirist and reader is problematical. A memoir is usually a plea on behalf of some action or a demonstration of the writer's satisfaction with his accomplishments. Implicit in this is the idea that the individual can fulfill his ambitions only through public life. Yet at the same time the memoir confirms the new importance attached to the individual subject at the expense of the collective subject. The reign of the hero, to which the production of memoirs bears witness, is thus contradictory in its consequences.

The emphasis of the individual at the expense of the collective is even clearer in diaries. To be sure, the diary-writer is not interested in magnifying his or her own role or in pleading a cause. Yet he is aware of having something to say that is beyond the reach of those who played a leading role in events. The diary-writer's view is unique because it is a common view, exterior to events. The writer rescues from oblivion what he himself has seen, heard, or inferred from the events of the day. Here we have the point of view of one who has deliberately set himself apart in order to provide an individual view of collective action. This is a less contradictory position than it seems, for diaries presumably were not intended for publication. If they were published, it was long after they were written, and almost by accident. This distinguishes the diary from the memoir, which was written from the outset to be read by a large public.

The popularity of diary-writing increased steadily

Ménétra's journal and Jamerey-Duval's memoirs marked the beginning of a new social practice: writing by autodidacts and social outcasts who created an identity for themselves through writing.

throughout the neoclassical period. Diaries were kept by city dwellers, travelers, and heads of family (expanding on the *livre de raison*). New importance was attached to the testimony of the individual. What each person saw and said now counted for something against the weight of public opinion. In fact, the development of private writing (not intended for publication) is not direct evidence for the constitution of private space. The diaries I am describing are not yet "intimate" diaries in which the writer is himself the object of his daily notations (such as the nineteenth-century diaries of a Benjamin Constant or Henri Amiel). What distinguishes the kind of diary I have in mind is the fact that the writer posits himself as the grounds for the truth of what he says. The guarantee of the private diary's veracity stems, paradoxically, from what is not public, from the private and intimate. Truth is not something to be proved. It has nothing to do with the subject's public actions. It is not the possession of a group, defined by the majority of public opinion. Rather, it is vested entirely in the individual gaze, marginal and almost secret, upon the things of this world. The diary-writer is conscious of this privilege from the moment he sits down to write.

THE NEW LEGITIMACY OF WRITING

The Credibility of Fiction

The diary should be viewed in relation to a broader range of literature, which established new standards of plausibility in fiction. Eighteenth-century novels often went to elaborate lengths to establish the credibility of the literary text. It was alleged, for example, that the manuscript of the work had been found in an attic or chest (*Robinson Crusoe, La Vie de Marianne*). The epistolary novel (*La Nouvelle Héloïse, Les Liaisons dangereuses*) was based on letters sent or discovered; the author presented himself in the role of a simple scribe. The novel could attempt to pass for truth because it was presented as the spontaneous testimony of a person who was not a writer and did not intend to publish his or her words. Throughout the century prologues and prefaces attempted to establish the private, intimate character of the work. This explains why the novel was so often attacked. Lenglet Dufresnoy compared it unfavorably to history, and other critics denounced its corrupting influence on feeble minds who took its pretensions literally.

First-person novels also became increasingly common.

Joseph Highmore, *Pamela*. It is impossible to exaggerate the importance of the novel in publicizing 18th-century private life. (London, Tate Gallery.)

One way of analyzing this is in terms of political ideology. How did the emphasis on the first-person subject of the novel figure in ideological conflict? What is interesting is the narrative appropriation of the new fictional practices by a subject who in effect vouches for the story's truth. Because the subject speaks directly to us, we believe what he or she says. The truth of what is said is grounded in the intimate and the private, in that which is hidden from public view. Hence it is worth taking a fresh look at the vogue for first-person novels. The seventeenth century had witnessed the emergence of a new ideology of merit, and the subject of the novel, in affirming himself, shared in that ideology. But at the same time truth was increasingly based upon individualized enunciations. The truth-effect of the first-person narrative derived from the intimate recognition of the writer by the reader. This helps to explain the success of the picaresque novel, both in translations from the Spanish (*Guzman d'Alfarache, Pícara Justina, Vida del*

Buscón) and in French adaptations and imitations, which became popular in the wake of Lesage's *Gil Blas de Santillane*.
The adaptations may have been popular because the first-
person narrative is so similar to the oral tale, capable of creating an illusion of direct communication without the aid of
the usual cultural mediations.

In a broader perspective, all literature of the late seventeenth and early eighteenth centuries is influenced by a similar
affirmation of private life, which is not easy to analyze. This
is obviously true of the genre to which contemporaries referred as "secret histories," based on the assumption that there
exists a hidden, hence truer, face of public events. Beyond the
apparent political causes of any revolution, for instance, there
are usually strictly private causes: jealousy, desire, uncontrolled and uncontrollable passions. Examples include not only
Mme Caumont de La Force's *Secret History of Mary of Burgundy*
(1694) and *Secret History of Henri IV of Castile* (1695) but also
Eustache Lenoble's *Idelgerte, Queen of Norway, or Magnanimous
Love* and *Abra Mulé or the History of the Overthrow of Mohammed
V* as well as Lesconvel's *Sire d'Aubigny* (1698). The method is
simple, as Lenoble indicates: "One treats in two different ways
the things about which one undertakes to impart knowledge
to those who wish to learn. The simplest and most common
is to reduce that knowledge to precepts presented in a didactic
order . . . But the more sublime way is to borrow the finesse
of Art in order to wrap those precepts in historical tales or
events, which teach lessons without appearing to do so, and
which, by diverting the mind, lead it imperceptibly to what
one wants it to know" (*Secret History of the Most Famous Conspiracies, Of the Conspiracy of the Pazzi against the Medici*).

In the late seventeenth century the private became an
essential element of fiction, the foundation of its truth as well
as the truth of historical causality. It is tempting to assume
that this evolution was relatively simple and clear-cut: that a
private space did emerge, that its emergence aroused resistance, and that it became a site of transference and investment
of new values. But evidence shows that the process was in
fact complex, and that the constitution of a private space and
the new value attached to the inner life went along with
exaltation of public man and of the social space of communication. Pascal was not alone in denouncing amusements that
estrange us from inner truth or in condemning Montaigne's
introspection. There is a disparity between the two objections,
however. For Pascal, denunciation of appearances and social

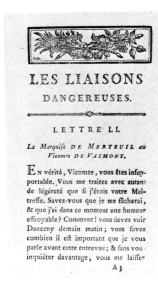

Pages from Choderlos de Laclos's novel *Les Liaisons dangereuses*. (Paris, Bibliothèque Nationale.)

signs of power does not imply wholesale acceptance of the inner life. He asks the believer to examine himself and reproaches him for preferring social diversions to necessary self-scrutiny, but he does not acknowledge the legitimacy of literature whose object is the self. Fearing that narcissistic self-indulgence will estrange man from God, he criticizes Montaigne for conceiving of "the foolish project of painting himself."

The epistolary novel, which enjoyed a peak of popularity in the eighteenth century, should be seen in light of the same evolution. Just as the first-person narrative creates an aura of truth because an individual narrator sets himself up as a guarantor of veracity, so the epistolary novel is authenticated by its intimate character. Its truth (or, more properly, truth-effect) derives in part from the fact that it presents itself as nonfiction and in part from the fact that letters are a strictly private, intimate medium. Jean-Jacques Rousseau in *La Nouvelle Héloïse*, Rétif de La Bretonne in *La Paysanne pervertie*, Crébillon the younger in *Lettres de la marquise de M. au comte de R.*, and Choderlos de Laclos in *Les Liaisons dangereuses* all insist on the authenticity of letters that they have been given for safekeeping and which they have subsequently edited. Not one claims to be the author, although Rousseau does offer his "Remarks on Novels" in a lengthy preface. The structure of the epistolary novel not only makes it possible to manipulate fictional time, to construct the narrative as a series of echoes, thus delegating the novelist's omniscience to the reader; at the same time it enhances the credibility of the fiction. In his "Editor's Preface" Laclos says: "This work, or, rather, this anthology, which readers may find too voluminous, contains but the smallest possible selection of the correspondence from which it is extracted." Yet the "Publisher's Notice" ironically underscores the fictional character of the correspondence: "We do not guarantee the authenticity of this anthology and . . . we even have strong reasons to believe that it is only a novel."

Thus we are told that here is a literary device to create an aura of truthfulness, whose deeper meaning we are obliged to analyze. The truth-effect undeniably depends on the dramatization of a private practice. Once again, however, the use of this device leaves the narrative in a paradoxical situation. Intimacy creates an impression of truth, but in doing so it becomes public. Literature presents itself as a violation. The private material warrants the truth of the fiction only because it is made public. Belying the public attitudes of Valmont and

Merteuil, the correspondence reveals their inner secrets. The correspondence tells the truth: it is the place where the characters surrender themselves. Even when a letter-writer lies in order to deceive the recipient, the reader knows where the truth lies. He is not deceived; at worst he is an accomplice. Reading places him in the position of the voyeur who glimpses the most intimate of secrets. The reader, who violates the sanctity of private space, always knows more than the protagonists who reveal themselves in their letters. The paradox is that the secrecy of private space produces its effect only by ceasing to be secret.

In a sense the Enlightenment was nothing more than an innovation in educational techniques: letters, dictionaries, and philosophical tales were all new ways of educating the public. Those who availed themselves of the new methods sought to establish their legitimacy. The writers of the Enlightenment continually asked what gave them the right to speak and repeatedly questioned their relation to truth. They frequently succumbed to the temptation to play the role of priest. Voltaire's allusions to the "new Church" were not innocent. Not that Voltaire was an unwitting believer. The problem is to establish the degree to which existing models influenced Enlightenment ideology and shaped writers' ideas of themselves and their struggle against "superstition." Revealingly, the philosophe saw himself as being in the world. The article "Philosophe" in the *Encyclopedia* states that for the philosopher "civil society is, so to speak, a divinity on earth." The truth of his propositions is grounded in reason, proof, and observation. He combines natural talent with method and diligence. He is a public figure: "Our philosopher does not think of himself as being in exile in this world. He does not think of himself as being in enemy territory. He wants to enjoy . . ." And later: "Reason requires that he know, study, and work to acquire the sociable qualities." He must participate in political debate: the people will be happy when the philosophers are kings, Antoninus reputedly said. The philosopher is granted a limited role in establishing the truth by means of his "natural talent." In many respects the Enlightenment philosopher continued to hold a religious view of his relation to truth. Some seem to have considered themselves inspired souls. In Diderot's *Essay by M. S... on Merit and Virtue*, a philosopher draws a parallel between himself and his brother, a canon, whom he sees as carrying out a comparable mission.

The Self as the Ground of Truth

The limits of illustration. The engraving on the right, by Moreau the Younger, for Rousseau's *La Nouvelle Héloïse* was rejected by the author. The reader is cast in the role of voyeur, surprising the couple in its rapture. The engraving below, by Gravelot, where the passion is just suggested, was accepted by Rousseau. (Paris, Bibliothèque Nationale.)

This view of the philosopher's relation to truth was transformed by the radical challenge of Jean-Jacques Rousseau. Rousseau did not believe that truth could be discovered by reason or that it was inspired by God. Instead he attempted to give a moral definition of the status of philosophical pronouncement. The philosopher, he said, is not a "bookman" or a "man of letters" or a "petty intriguer." Rather, he is a man who writes out of inner necessity. His frequently invoked description of his "illumination" on the road to Vincennes revealed to him the moral, political, and philosophical system that he would set forth in his two *Discourses* and in the *Social Contract*: "Suddenly I felt my mind dazzled by a thousand lights. Innumerable vivid ideas crowded in on me with such force and confusion that I was plunged into inexplicable turmoil" ("Letter to Malesherbes," 12 January 1762).

Those who merely "make books" seek worldly success. They act out of vanity and the desire for fame. They yield to fashion and cater to popular opinion. They are as servile valets to powerful men. They live and act only for the world. The public space that determines their character is also the source of their alienation. By contrast, the philosopher, as Rousseau

understood the term, exists only because he is free and independent. His liberty is fundamental, because without it he has no access to the truth. Being free, he is a stranger to worldly interests, and in particular to the interests of powerful and wealthy men. Hence he is able to choose for himself the stance from which he speaks.

Rousseau's "reformation" (which begins with his refusal to wear stockings, a wig, and a sword and continues with his determination to earn his living by working as a copyist, his withdrawal from Paris society, and his break with Diderot and the group around the *Encyclopedia*) was a deliberate decision, the beginning of his commitment to philosophy. The road to truth passes by way of social and moral asceticism. The truth is accessible to Jean-Jacques Rousseau because he is a moral person, free from compromise. In other words, freedom from social constraint is essential in order to know the truth. We may smile when Rousseau goes walking in the Saint-Germain forest in order to discover how men lived in a state of nature, yet his strolling is a significant part of his philosophical imagination. As a result of his antisocial attitudes, the Genevan misanthrope incurred the hatred of his fellow philosophes. It is oversimplifying, though perhaps reassuring, to see Rousseau's proud solitude as proof of neurosis. It is also an exaltation of privacy as the ground of philosophical truth. A man cannot speak the truth about the world unless he cuts himself off from it.

Rousseau's conversion experience on the road to Vincennes has often been compared to the ecstatic experience of a mystic. His vocabulary invites such comparison, for he describes the experience as one of revelation, as an unexpected and blinding vision of the truth, which is recognized as such by the force of inner conviction. Between this inner perception of truth and sentimental knowledge of God as developed in the *Profession of Faith of the Vicar of Savoy* there is no difference. Reasoning has little to do with either. Philosophy speaks to the heart rather than to the mind. This accounts for Rousseau's peculiar style of writing, which addresses the reader's feelings more than his intelligence (except perhaps in the *Social Contract*).

Rousseau steadfastly defends the morality of his behavior against the attacks of his critics. In the end he insists that it is the morality of his behavior alone (or at least in large part) that establishes the truth of his philosophical system. In *Rousseau, Judge of Jean-Jacques* he dramatizes an inquiry into his case

Engraving by N. Cochin for
Rousseau's *Confessions* (1793):
"I have laid bare my insides."
(Paris, Bibliothèque Nationale.)

designed to demonstrate that his behavior is virtuous, hence
that his philosophy is true. He has made the transition from
private life to the inner life. The dialogues focus on the philosopher's thoughts as well as his actions. Witnesses and judges
lay bare his innermost being. Morality is not so much a codification of relations between individuals as an inner conviction
of innocence.

The burden of proof is thus shifted from external criteria
such as valid reasoning and sound observation to inner criteria,
to inward conviction and self-knowledge. Much would be
made of the change in the nineteenth century, but in the
eighteenth it remained a minority view, strictly associated with
the name of Rousseau. Yet it was the first sign of discord
within the philosophy of the Enlightenment, marking a turn
away from the dominant ideology of literature of the seventeenth and eighteenth centuries. Ultimately this would lead to
the elaboration of a new ideology and image of the writer-
thinker totally at variance with the neoclassical ideal.

Necessary Autobiography

Quite apart from the usefulness of the *Confessions* in Rousseau's battles against his adversaries, it was a natural consequence of his philosophical views that he should have written
a book analyzing his inner self. His autobiography is not
concerned with the accidents of biography but with the essential logic of his approach to philosophy. Self-analysis is not
contingent but necessary for him, and he returned to it repeatedly. Rousseau's willingness to delve within was not simply a consequence of his "unhappy consciousness" but the
source of his entire philosophy.

He proclaims his ambition at the beginning of the *Confessions*: "This is the only portrait that exists or probably ever
will exist of a man painted exactly according to nature and in
all its truth." He proposes to give us a self-portrait without
embellishment or modesty, a book that will tell all from the
noblest of deeds to the most abject of vices. Truthfulness and
sincerity are set up as absolutes with which no compromise is
possible: "I want to show . . . a man in all the truth of nature.
And that man will be myself . . . I have shown myself as I
was, sometimes contemptible and vile, sometimes good, generous, and sublime. I have laid bare my insides" (*Confessions*,
book 1).

A decision is made at the outset to discuss what normally
was kept silent, bottled up within. Rousseau reveals his taste

for being spanked, his love affair with Mme de Warens, and his various temptations. The subject of his autobiography is the history of the self, with emphasis on the inner, hidden self. The barrier between public and private life has ceased to exist, as the private is exhibited in public. The reader is asked to understand the hidden self once the social cloak has been removed. Rousseau searches for the key events that explain his personality. He tears away masks and penetrates lies. He identifies the acts of foundation and records the continuities that have shaped his life. As Philippe Lejeune has noted, the key phrases in his style are "already at that time" and "still today." He compares past and present knowledge in order to know himself and recognize himself. The discontinuous chronology, repeatedly begun anew, is the price to be paid for inner knowledge.

The degree to which autobiographical writing marked a new departure in literature has to be appreciated. Those who practiced it in the eighteenth century were to some degree social misfits: not only Rousseau but also, somewhat earlier, Valentin Jamerey-Duval, a former peasant who became the imperial librarian in Vienna and who has left us a memoir of his peasant life. What is more, autobiography was defined in opposition to the traditionally aristocratic genre of the memoir. Whereas memoirs were concerned with the public realm, autobiography was concerned with the private and intimate. Memoirs dealt with having, autobiography with being.

The memoir was a coherent genre—a public document about public roles and actions. By contrast, autobiography was paradoxical in that it bared the writer's innermost secrets and exposed his private life to public view. The reader is pressed into service as witness. He becomes in a sense the negation of the secrecy that defines and gives value to the private and intimate. As a result of what Lejeune calls the "autobiographical pact," the reader takes the writer at his word and accepts as true his account of his own life; to doubt the writer's veracity would be to deny the work its status as autobiography. Hence the reader is necessary. A bond is established between writer and reader, who agrees to forgo proof and believe in the writer's sincerity. The result is a pale but nonetheless real reflection of that transparency of hearts which is for Rousseau the distinguishing characteristic of primitive and not-yet-corrupted societies. Autobiography thus makes reading a more private act than it properly ought to be, which may be the best reason for its existence.

Pornography was not very clearly defined. The word "obscene" was not widely used. "Pornographic," strictly speaking, meant writing about prostitution. The words *galant, érotique,* and *paillard* were more or less synonymous. In any case, erotic literature enjoyed tremendous success. The eighteenth century saw the publication of the classics of the genre: Gervaise de La Touche's *Histoire de Dom Bougre, portier des Chartreux* (1718), the Marquis d'Argens's *Thérèse philosophe* (1748), Mirabeau's *Erotika Biblion* (1783), and Rétif de La Bretonne's *Anti-Justine* (1793), all of which were reprinted innumerable times. Not one of the leading eighteenth-century writers escaped the temptation to try his hand at erotic fiction. Diderot wrote *Les Bijoux indiscrets* and Montesquieu *Le Temple de Gnide,* while Voltaire sprinkled his tales with erotic anecdotes, such as the story of the old woman in *Candide.* Even

Erotic Literature

From Rétif de La Bretonne, *Le Paysan perverti* (Paris, 1776), illustrated by Binet. In a fascinating mirror trick, the author (Rétif peers out from behind the curtain) and reader looking at the engraving are joined in the same voyeuristic position. (Paris, Bibliothèque Nationale.)

the virtuous Rousseau alludes to the febrile reading of his youth, done "with one hand." However poor some of these works undoubtedly were, erotic literature was an important eighteenth-century phenomenon, more important even than the revolutionary pamphlet. It also had a major influence on iconography. If Louis Sébastien Mercier is to be trusted, pornographic literature was everywhere. It circulated in the public marketplace as well as in workshops, boudoirs, and salons.

By the very nature of pornography, its setting was private. Sexual practices belonged to the realm of secrecy, and bodies were hidden beneath ample garments and ribbons. But pornographic literature, using a range of devices, exposed the most intimate acts. As in other novels, the reader was made to assume the position of voyeur, but here he was even more of an intruder. If heroes often began their careers by surprising a couple in the act of love, the purpose was to remind the reader how the book ought to be read.

Does pornography suggest a nostalgia for a time when bodies were more openly exhibited and sexual gestures were displayed with fewer inhibitions? Or does its popularity correspond to the individualization of reading? The phenomenon was complex. Pornography reflects not only changes in the nature of writing but also tensions engendered by new social practices. Hence it is worthy of serious attention.

Pornographic novels made use of all the new fictional devices: epistolary structure, first-person narrative, and dialogue form. The Marquis de Sade made abundant use of all three. The contradiction inherent in publicizing private and intimate behavior is even more striking in pornography than in autobiography, because reading pornography is by nature furtive and individual.

Sade's novels cannot be dismissed as simply pornographic or obscene. His work is not to be confused with the typical erotic tale. The difference, one feels, is evident even in the prohibitions that define his work, which may well have to do with the exhibition of the body. Sade extends sexual discourse to an intolerable degree, including the organic and the visceral. Ecstasy in his work involves the internal anatomy. Thus he violates what was undoubtedly an inviolable taboo.

Processes of Writing, Modes of Reading

One possible objection to my thesis is that I have confused the private with the intimate and the public with the communal, identifying the one with the individual, the other with the collective. I believe, however, that these necessary ambiguities accurately reflect the unique status of literature. Although literature is affected by social history, it does not reflect that history in any simple way. Literature scrambles social change, superimposing one thing upon another in such a way that it never strictly follows the evolution of society and can never be offered as straightforward illustration or proof of any historical proposition.

One question that has yet to be addressed concerns the production of modes of reading by literary texts themselves. Every text invents an imaginary reader, whom it addresses and calls to witness. In this process, the controversy between public and private in literary practice is clearly relevant. A more systematic study of the phenomenon is required, and the evolution of Rousseau's style may be a useful place to begin. His writing in the *Discourses* and the *Social Contract* is still social and public; subject and audience are simultaneously embraced. His later style is more contradictory. Its subject, Rousseau's private self, is distinct from his audience, the French public. Ultimately he restores unity to his style in the *Reveries of a Solitary Walker*, where writing is said to serve no other purpose than self-knowledge and the pleasure of commemoration: "My enterprise is the same as Montaigne's, but my aim is just the opposite, for he wrote his essays only for others, and I write my reveries only for myself. If, in my old age, on the eve of departure, I remain, as I hope I shall, in the same disposition as now, reading them will remind me of the sweet pleasure that I savor as I write, and by reviving times past will as it were double my existence" ("First Walk").

Once again, however, this evolution toward a literature that would abolish communication is a mirage. Reflecting the desires of a solitary man as well as his wish for revenge, the *Reveries* are a less than exemplary culmination, at best the trace of one individual. Even though much of nineteenth-century literary practice would follow Rousseau's example in concentrating upon the private, intimate subject, the *Reveries* exemplify but one kind of intimate writing, a tradition that would be continued in the diaries that became commonplace after the Revolution. For the most part literature would evolve first in a different direction, toward a discourse addressed to a unique and privileged recipient, creating an illusion of exchange modeled on the private confidence. Later, following its own dynamic as well as responding to further social and ideological change, an extraordinary range of contradictions would reemerge, contradictions whose problematic diversity was anticipated in the neoclassical age.

French school, *Place and Fountain of the Saints-Innocents* (detail), 18th century. (Paris, Carnavalet Museum.)

❧ 3 ❧

Community, State, and Family:
Trajectories and Tensions

Nicole Castan
Maurice Aymard
Alain Collomp
Daniel Fabre
Arlette Farge

Introduction

by Roger Chartier

ETWEEN 1500 and 1800 people began to imagine, experience, and protect private life in a new way; the change was neither smooth nor steady nor unambiguous. Philippe Ariès suggested one possible periodization, in three phases: first, a period of heightened individualism, as the individual set himself apart from the collectivity; second, a period during which individuals escaped their newly created solitude by joining together in small groups of their own choosing (smaller than the village or neighborhood, the class or guild, but larger than the family); and finally, a shrinking of the private sphere to coincide with the family unit, which became the primary if not the unique center of intimacy and emotional investment. In this section we make use of this periodization in order to bring out some of the fundamental conflicts and tensions in early modern private life. In some instances it has been necessary to abandon the comparative approach in favor of more detailed case studies. But whatever the method, the goal remains the same: to trace the history of private existence in all its complexity.

In order for private life to flourish, various obstacles had to be overcome. In particular, a clear boundary had to be drawn between the function of public representation and the private sphere of intimate retreat. Many people in the ancien régime held office and wielded authority; all of them, from the sovereign on down, had to divide time and space, roles and practices, between the public and private spheres. This was made possible by the transformation of the state, which imposed its laws and controls in domains hitherto governed (whether by tacit contract or through open conflict) by individuals, families, and client groups.

Because of the care taken to distinguish between the requirements of public office and the protected, secret commitments of private life, the exercise of public authority was thoroughly deprivatized (despite the persistently ambiguous status of ancien-régime administrative archives, which are considered to be both public documents and personal papers). Thus, the servants of the state led something of a double life, a situation accentuated and extended by the Revolution, which made obligatory an ostentatious civic commitment not always backed by similar private sentiments. This doubleness in a sense prefigures the antagonism that would develop in the nineteenth century between workplace and home, between professional conduct and behavior within the family. It affected not only public men but every individual in a society that required each to indicate his social status by appropriate gestures and codified appearances.

The opposition between intimacy and representation was perhaps most intense, in certain countries at any rate, when the state attempted to regulate all aspects of social life—not only the social life of its subjects but even more that of its administrators and rulers. France in the mid-seventeenth century is of course the prime example. A longer-term development was the effort to constitute a private life outside the constraints of the family. Although in the nineteenth century the family became almost synonymous with private life, earlier it had been one of the obstacles to an individual's freedom to live as he pleased among friends and confederates of his own choosing. Loyal friendships, repeated encounters, and voluntary or obligatory membership in various groups, some strictly regulated, others not, encouraged the development of especially close bonds among certain people. Such relations were free and pleasant, devoid of the formality required of public officials and of the discipline enforced by the family. Richelet (1679) defines the word *privé* as meaning not only "familiar" but also something like the English "at home": he is most *privé* here, he is most *privé* with Mr. So-and-so, are the examples he gives. Clearly there was a connection in people's minds between the familiarity of freely chosen social relations and the concept of privacy. Thus privacy did not require isolation, retreat, or protective walls. It was defined primarily by the ability to choose freely the company with whom one spent time not devoted to routine business and chores. Whether feminine or scholarly, amical or juvenile, secret or open, these freely chosen societies permitted a convivial intimacy that family life appears to have inhibited.

Thus, "the private" in the modern sense was defined by its distance from both the *res publica* and the family order. It was also defined by freedom from the collective constraints of custom. Custom in fact gave concrete form to the "anonymous sociability" that, according to Ariès, was slowly destroyed between 1500 and 1800 by the process of privatization. In this context, "anonymous" does not mean that people mingled with others whom they did not know but rather that custom established institutions, rituals, and penalties to enforce conformity with generally accepted norms. Social rules and roles were learned and internalized, and deviation from the norm was punished.

Every individual decision was subject to strict social controls, in some cases enforced by specific groups such as the "youth abbeys," in others embodied in ritual or applied by the entire community.

This collective surveillance gradually was repudiated, discredited, and denounced as an intolerable violation of the individual's freedom of choice or the family's sovereign right, an invasion of what came to be considered as privacy, the private sphere being that which was not subject to the jurisdiction of the community. In southern France collective restraints on the will of the individual were hotly contested in the eighteenth century. Elsewhere, especially in bourgeois milieus in large cities, precocious breeding grounds of individualist sentiment, the challenge probably came even earlier.

Among the now private prerogatives that the community had once tried to regulate were marriages, relations between husband and wife, and household life. The family became the focus of private life. For one thing, it occupied a space of its own. Most homes in this period sheltered a married couple and their children, but even if the house was occupied by several related families, each possessed its private space. Even in the cities, where the nature of housing made a certain promiscuity inevitable, individuals, couples, and families created what privacy they could in rented room, furnished apartment, or garret. The family became the center of emotional life. It was hardly novel in the eighteenth century for individual honor to be bound up with family honor, as many a seventeenth-century comedy proves. Also, friendships made at work, during youth, or by chance could rival familial and marital commitments. But, new attitudes toward children and a new respect for ancestors demonstrate that in the eighteenth century private life centered on the family.

Yet the privacy of the family was constantly threatened by community interference as well as by the imprudence of family members. To guard against scandal required reliable and powerful allies. Families were forced to turn to the public authorities, first and foremost to the authority of the king. It alone could ensure the secrecy required to maintain family honor while at the same time quelling the disorder that threatened to tear the family apart. It alone could protect the liberty of each individual from the collective constraints of custom. Endangered families could be helped in many ways, by the courts or the Church. But the principle was always the same: domestic troubles had to be disclosed to the public authorities, in return for which the authorities effected a discreet, private settlement without appeal to the customary organs of censure. Thus the construction of a modern state not only established the boundary line between the public and private realms but, more important, helped to sustain and defend the private authority thus constituted, whose influence over family life was becoming a force to be reckoned with.

Jacobus Vrel, *City Corner*. The doorway and window, principal observation points, marked the boundary of the family's territory. The street was part public, part private, a place for meetings, exchange of news, and commentary on current events. (Amsterdam, Private collection.)

❧ The Public and the Private

Nicole Castan

PUBLIC and private inevitably meet at a boundary. In Talleyrand's words, "the citizen's life must be walled off."[1] By the wall of private life, obviously. But what lay on either side of that wall? Today there is no ambiguity: on one side, a haven of peace, essentially a family refuge but also a place to invite friends and enjoy private pursuits; on the other side, the constraints of public life, the hierarchical discipline of work, and binding commitments of many kinds. Such a dichotomy heightens the value of the private preserve, which is portrayed as constantly menaced by fatally encroaching public demands.

This interpretation does not fit the seventeenth and eighteenth centuries, however. At that time the meaning of different spaces was subject to continual reinterpretation, and there was ambivalence about public and private roles. Throughout the period people stubbornly resolved to clarify the definition of both. Yet at first sight their lives were either entirely public or exclusively domestic. Who lived in a more kingly (at once noble and pleasurable) manner than Louis XIV? The king devoured the man, dispossessing him of privacy even in death. How easy it is to die in public! The same was true of the principal nobles until the seventeenth century. Teresa of Avila observed: "Nothing is private in the life of the great." Her friend Mme de La Cerda, an illustrious lady, "lives according to her rank and not according to what she loves, in a state of servitude that makes her the slave of a thousand things."[2]

Among more modest folk life was exclusively private. Bourgeois rentiers and relatively impecunious provincial nobles by their own admission devoted themselves entirely to the pleasures of the hunt and the delights of the dinner table. One Gascon squire confesses that he had nothing to occupy him except "idle fancies for little girls, no sooner conceived than satisfied." Perhaps the need to alternate between public and private roles and spaces is related to social rank. But then what are we to make of the poor of Naples, described in uncompromising terms by the French jurist de Brosses: "These people have no homes. They spend their lives in the streets."[3] From the king to the wretched of Naples, the rule seems to have been that life was either entirely public or entirely private. A rather less simple and conventional picture will emerge, however, from more detailed study of a variety of cases.

THE FAMILY TAMED

Liberty, like independence, is won first from the family. The family of the ancien régime was far from an affectionate haven. Regardless of rank, individuals were obliged to accept the dictates of the family and authoritarian assignment of tasks. Strict discipline protected the family honor and patrimony. Yet the overweening need for solidarity did not confine the individual. Escape from the group was possible without rebellion.

Childhood

As soon as they were old enough to be cut loose from women's apron strings, young boys, aged four to fourteen or fifteen, were largely on their own. At first it might seem that the opposite was more likely, for boys were sent to work in the fields, to learn a trade, or away to school. A gentleman from lower Languedoc does not hesitate to attribute the death of his three sons to the fact that they were sent away too early to boarding school at La Flèche. But many escaped this fate, attending school as day students and receiving supplementary private lessons at home. The journey from home to school offered important opportunities, as can be seen in the autobiography of the poet Tristan L'Hermite, raised at the court of Henri IV,[4] or in the childhood tales of Fonvielle, born in 1760 to an ennobled bourgeois family in Toulouse,[5] or of Guillaume Hérail, grandson of a wealthy merchant who had bought the Sérignac estate in the Agenais.[6] Though from different times, backgrounds, and education, all three men indulged in similar youthful escapades. They led double lives, appearing to be good students and pious children while enjoying secret pleasures in a world all their own. Tristan L'Her-

Louis Le Nain, *Young Card Players*. Hope for a miracle accounts for the passion for gambling in a society where wealth came slowly and amusements were monotonous. The model influenced even children. (Private collection.)

mite shared meals with a young prince of his own age, as well as lessons, games, exercises, and journeys from castle to castle. In return, he was obliged to wait on the prince from the "time his eyes opened until they closed," to amuse him, to cheer him up when he was sick. For this he employed his marvelous talents as a storyteller. His overflowing imagination soon captured the young prince's fancy: "Ah! Little page, I can tell that you are about to say that the wolf ate the lamb. I beg you to say that he did not eat him!" He thus earned his master's affection, a guarantee of freedom in a situation of constant servitude.

Unlike L'Hermite, Fonvielle and Hérail were raised at home. As the eldest sons in their families, their upbringing was carefully watched. Their schooling was ambitious and closely monitored. Educated initially by private tutors, they later received lessons at schools, supplemented by instruction from private coaches. Both were relieved when they finally escaped the constant surveillance of their families at age five or six, even if the reason was discord between the parents (a father involved with hunting and business, a mother caught up in the social whirl).

A boy had to know how to conceal his true feelings. In the confessional both Hérail and Fonvielle affected piety, and both carried religious tracts in their pockets whenever they

Drawing from the *Illustrated Land Register of Sadournin and Esparros* (Gascony, 1773), showing a child eagerly reaching for a tame magpie. Children often played with animals.

were home. Both boasted of their progress in Latin, arithmetic, and letters and with impunity held forth on what they had learned to the delight of women too ignorant to judge. Skillfully they copied their lessons with great haste. They were also prudent, always present for compositions and the award of grades. As "libertine" as ten-year-olds can be, they concealed their fondness for amusements, games, and good food.

The key to avoiding family discipline was to take advantage of the time spent passing from the jurisdiction of one authority to that of another. On the pretext of performing never precisely specified duties, L'Hermite wandered through the corridors and galleries of the palace. He mingled with valets, guards, young lords, and even actors who came to give performances. Since he was required to amuse his master, he had every excuse to scour Paris in search of a tame linnet or trained bear or other exotic creature. These expeditions were also excellent occasions to have a look about, meet people, and take part in games. At the end of the eighteenth century Fonvielle and Hérail took advantage of similar opportunities. Traveling between home and school offered chances to explore town and country in the company of other young rascals. Whatever time was left after school and family all three boys devoted to their "passions": reading (novels of chivalry, plays, Buffon), animals (birds and cats), flowers, but most of all cards and dice. Gluttons, they sampled little pâtés at age five, and Hérail boasts of having tasted a bottle alone at age eleven.

These pleasures had to be paid for. Clearly, private life began when a lad found himself with money in his pocket. Our three heroes admit that they were not short of cash and make no mystery about its provenance. The page L'Hermite took bribes from the purveyors of birds and other items to the prince. Hérail and Fonvielle simply stole, at first grain from the family stores that they resold for cash, then money itself. Hérail says that "his hands were glue" and that he convinced himself that "the money was not stolen as long as it did not come from the family." Stealing small amounts, 15 to 20 sous daily, he amassed a tidy sum, which he spent freely. Yet he was never short of cash. His father and grandfather provided him with "shiny new" gold louis to show in public, but he had to give an exact account of how he had spent the money, which was given as proof of the family's means and not for the child to squander.

Such free ways at a still tender age did not cause trouble, provided the child was shrewd enough to find protectors and accomplices at home. Young lords and actors hid the wayward page and protected him from the tutor's wrath. If worse came to worst, he could always find sure refuge in the arms of the prince: "For the price of a tear or two he obtained his pardon." Fonvielle and Hérail shamelessly took advantage of a mother's weakness for her firstborn. Actually they depended even more on the complicity of the servants. Fanchon, whose bed Fonvielle shared, concealed his absences and helped him sell stolen grain or exchange purloined cash.

Hérail says that he preferred the servants' company to that of his father and mother. The domestics encouraged his pranks, in which they found malicious amusement. In later years he judged them to be pernicious and corrupting, no doubt the better to praise nature for having restored his innocence.

Freedom was not limited solely to wealthy boys like the three on whose remembrances we have been relying until now. Ordinary village lads and artisans' sons and even the son of a Rouergue notary also knew how to grab life by the horns. For such youths the first priority was to serve the family business. But they knew how to enjoy themselves during breaks in the work and how to take advantage of familiar relations with maids, apprentices, clerks, and even clients. In short, they enjoyed a life of their own, more or less openly avowed, despite the usual constraints.[7]

The women of this period were so confined to the home that it may seem paradoxical to speak of their private life. They were excluded from public office and responsibilities outside the home, whether political, administrative, municipal, or corporative,[8] as Natalie Davis has shown in the case of Lyons.[9] It was acknowledged, though not without acrimony, that women could play an unofficial role, but certainly not an official one.

The Private Life of Women

A woman's occupations were essentially domestic. The household was her stage, and her calling was to embody the image of wife and mother sanctioned by the Church and civil society. Honor—a matter of saving face, loyalty to one's own, and good reputation—sums it up rather well. It was a woman's responsibility to serve those who shared her home and hearth: to feed them, raise them, attend to them in sickness, and assist them in death. Although women frequently contributed to production, it was not customary to praise them for their

Jacques Gamelin, *Interior Scene.* Home was the woman's dominion. To be sure, the man at table is being served, but here he was not on his own turf. (Carcassonne, Museum of Fine Arts.)

Pieter de Hooch, *Courtyard of a House in Delft.* A diptych juxtaposes two female roles. On the right a housewife in her private domain fondly guides her child's steps. On the left, standing in the corridor halfway between courtyard and street, another woman, scruples overcome by curiosity, spies and eavesdrops. (London, National Gallery.)

participation or to take note of it in one's will. Consider the devotion of Mme Acarie, future founder of the Carmelite Order in France, to her household and her daughters. She ruled them with a steady hand, calling them one by one to her side in order to establish "an amical communication that will instruct them and win their hearts." Her role is one of constant service.[10] Or Mme d'Ayne, mother-in-law of Baron d'Holbach. At her château de Grandval every summer she received, in addition to her children, numerous guests, including Diderot, who was a frequent visitor in the 1760s and who ascribed to her all the virtues of the perfect household mistress. Her constant concern, he tells us, was for the welfare and amusement of others: "If you showed interest in a dish, the next day you would have it, and so it was in all things."[11]

The woman was thus both servant and mistress of the household. The master delegated to her as much authority as she needed to carry out her tasks, demanding in return the virtues of modesty, devotion, and economy. She was not a strict subordinate of the family head, but one who shared in his powers and duties. Mme Phlipon, mother of Mme Roland, was the wife of a well-known master engraver in Paris. She reigned over the house, as he did over the shop, where journeymen and clients mingled. Mme Phlipon not only managed the household economy and directed the work of the maid

Pieter de Hooch, *The Linen Closet*. Linen, sumptuous closets, gleaming tiles—a utilitarian, harmonious setting for family life. (Amsterdam, Rijksmuseum.)

but also took charge of her daughter's education. She wanted to raise a finished, polished young lady, according to tradition. She handpicked the girl's tutors and supervised their work. The child received a smattering of all the arts and was dressed most fetchingly, above her station. Naturally she could not go to the market, to church, or to visit a relative without her mother's approval. On Sunday afternoons the family went walking in the King's Garden or, in summertime, at Soucy or Meudon.[12]

Mme Phlipon enjoyed many intimate and affectionate moments with her daughter, yet her attention to domestic matters never flagged. In the study of home life, the problem is to determine just how much freedom and privacy was possible. Women above the poverty line were not defenseless; for protection they had the marriage contract and the power to make a will. The contract was as fundamental to marriage as the sacrament; among the wealthy it was de rigueur. It protected the woman's dowry and gave her power over her own property, hence the means to adopt a personal strategy (usually shaped by family politics, however). Even Jeanne Fabre, a modest Nîmes housewife, was able to arrange her daughter's marriage with a gift of 36 livres and a few clothes. The Marquise de Lacapelle changed her will to settle a certain sum upon her granddaughter. In return, the girl was to be brought up by the Maltese nuns of Toulouse and to "pay court" to her benefactor. A woman could do as she pleased with her property, even at the risk of scandal. Mme de Pollastron, wife of a Gascon noble and of average wealth for her station, inherited some family property. Following her natural penchant and in the hope of securing a brilliant match, she added 3,000 écus to the dowry of a young cousin when 200 écus worth of clothing would have sufficed.[13] By so doing she betrayed not only her husband, who was kept in the dark, but also her children, who were robbed of a part of their inheritance. But legally she was perfectly within her rights.

Letters and court records suggest that women enjoyed a considerable degree of freedom, enough so that on occasion they could drop their masks and behave in unexpected ways. For instance, the choice of female servants was left to the lady of the house. One bourgeoise who lived in a noble manner in upper Languedoc in 1770 chose not only her maids but also her private lackey, all of whom she "insisted be comely and unmarried. Yet she closely monitored their expenditures and refused to allow them a free hand with her purse." She also administered punishment, ordering a servant who had stolen a hairpiece to be whipped in order to force her to confess and return the stolen goods. Apparently such behavior was normal for the wife of the prosecutor of Velay. Yet she not only supervised the work of her household staff but also lived with them on terms of familiarity, not to say complicity. Sophie

The Locus of Privacy

The signing of the marriage contract, at which the notary officiated, preceded the wedding, at which the priest officiated. The custom was widespread in southern France. The contract guaranteed the wife her dowry, other property, and widow's portion, which afforded her some independence in the family economy. (Toulouse, Paul-Dupuy Museum.)

Volland used her devoted maid to communicate with Diderot without her mother's knowledge. (Sophie was forty years old at the time.) And Mme de Pollastron was not unusual in the life she led in her country château or her house at Auch, which in the opinion of her spiritual director involved too much familiarity with her serving girls, whose company she preferred to that of her family. The mistress mocked her husband's rustic manners in the presence of her maids and said insulting things about her in-laws.

Women did not participate in the external economy unless they were widows or members of the upper classes. They made no deals in the marketplace. Administration of the patrimony, handling money, and making loans were not normally within their purview. One Toulouse woman even admitted that she was ashamed to ask her shopkeeper husband for money.

Nevertheless, money, supplies, clothing, and services did circulate among women, often without the knowledge of their men. Women's ventures were small-scale but significant. A worker's wife in Montauban borrows a few sous from a neighbor to buy her daughter ribbons, so that the girl can try her luck at attracting a man. Groups of three or four peasant women often left their villages in the early hours of morning to carry eggs and garden vegetables to the nearest market. Whatever they earned went into a private nestegg. A poor woman from Lavaur shows her confidence in a friend by revealing to her the existence of this secret stash (in this case, 12 sols kept in a bag stuffed into a hole in the fireplace). The two women swear to use the money for winding sheets. Private funds did not always go to the family. A maid from Montpellier entrusted three years of her wages to a friend. She had saved the money so that she might one day start a home of her own and did not wish to surrender her treasure to her family.

Women for the most part lived in a world of their own but not cut off from the outside. An open or closed door was both a symbol and a reality, whether in rich man's house or poor farmstead. In the country it was considered immoral for a man to enter another man's house when only women were home. When the door was closed at the end of the day, visits normally ceased—a surprising fact, which was remarked and commented on. But home was not a prison. Opportunities for independent relationships existed.[14] Friendship was not an empty word. To his beloved friend Sophie Volland, whom

Jean-Honoré Fragonard, *The Small Falls of Tivoli.* (Paris, Louvre.)

Jean-Honoré Fragonard, *Young Woman at the Fountain*. (Private collection.)

These two studies by Fragonard give evidence of a woman's world open to the outside. Ovens, washhouses, and shops were the province of women. A "chorus" of housewives made and unmade reputations and spread rumors. In the rural south, the cabaret, the center of male social life, was practically closed to women.

Grimm called a man and woman rolled into one, Diderot wrote in a somewhat ironic tone from the château de Grandval: "After dinner, the women returned, and we left them to their little confidences. When they have not seen each other for some time, this is an urgent need with them . . . [as are] the caresses they customarily bestow on one another."

For those who did not mingle in "society," friendship was limited to neighbors and kin. In crowded urban neighborhoods there were plenty of prospects. One three-story house in a Toulouse suburb accommodated the families of sixteen artisans. Lack of space and comfort forced people to leave home in search of water, warmth, and light. Women went to the washhouse, the fountain, the oven, and the mill. In the south of France they often traveled in groups of two or three and stayed for hours chatting with their neighbors.

What we have subsequently come to think of as indoor work and activities overflowed outdoors as well.[15] Doorways, streets, and even public squares were taken over by women. In the eighteenth century they were said to gather in Toulouse in "little platoons," sorting herbs and feeding their children. A barmaid naturally washed her glasses. In short, we see here a world that cannot be called strictly domestic but that has yet to be subdued by the public authorities. It would take many years of stubborn ordinances and renovations in housing to drive these private activities back into the home and its adjoining courtyard, garden, and staircase.

During the seventeenth and eighteenth centuries this is where the shifting boundary between public and private was located. There are many further indications of the appropriation of public streets for private purposes. When a woman in Bigorre is beaten by her husband, two neighbors bring her food in the street "out of friendship." And when a mother is informed of the death of her son, rather than take refuge in the bosom of her family she rushes into the street and collapses in tears in the arms of a neighbor.

Religion as Liberation

Feasts and holy days were opportunities to escape the family bastion. In the south of France girls were excluded from such youthful hijinks as charivaris, but traditionally they were allowed certain liberties, if only to exercise their charms in the hope of attracting a mate. Of course they were never allowed to be alone. At Saint-Antonin in Quercy girls walked arm-in-arm on the public square, Catholics and Protestants alike. In summertime they danced under an old elm "in groups so lovely, so bright, and so nimble" yet so difficult to approach, sighs Fonvielle, at that time an official in the royal salt monopoly. Feasts and other collective rituals were primarily occasions for the young, and girls took advantage of the opportunity.

Marriage marked a sharp break in a girl's life. Suddenly her role was changed. She became too old to celebrate along with the young. For compensation, she had religion. Like marketing chores, church provided an occasion to leave the house and meet friends, always under the watchful eye of the family and community. Religion necessitated not only attending services but also going to hear missionary preachers and setting out on seasonal pilgrimages. Women needed escape, and religion made escape legitimate. In the Albi suburb of Bout-du-Pont, in 1709, wives of wool-carders insisted that

nothing in the world could keep them from going to hear the Franciscan preachers after supper, while their husbands went to the taverns.

The Counter-Reformation unintentionally enlarged the scope of women's private lives. Saint Francis de Sales had managed to reconcile the requirements of salvation with those of society.[16] The influence of his *Introduction to the Devout Life* was profound. New pastoral techniques, involving particularly the use of missions, promoted a new model of feminine piety from the highest to the lowest ranks of society. Women were encouraged to experience with greater intensity than ever before the great truths of the Christian religion. Spurred on by missionaries and confessors, women arranged to include periods of retreat in their daily schedules. Consider the wife of a Toulouse surgeon in the 1750s. A diligent housekeeper, she rarely went out except occasionally to dine with friends or to attend church services with her neighbors. Usually alone but sometimes with a neighbor she also went to church every day at four o'clock for private prayer and to pay her respects to the Infant Jesus.

Antoine Watteau, *Fête champêtre*. Classes, sexes, and ages mingle on a river bank, with monuments in the background. (Agen, Municipal Museum.)

The Counter-Reformation encouraged private worship, especially devotion to the Infant Jesus or the Sacred Heart. Pilgrimages remained popular. (Drawing from the *Illustrated Land Register of Sadournin and Esparros*.)

Education, which had ceased to be strictly a family affair, obviously influenced these developments. Among the urban petty bourgeoisie girls often spent two or three years at a convent school, where their eyes were opened to hitherto unsuspected vistas. In the mid-seventeenth century in Auch, Mme Hérail discovered friendship in the convent, where she was drawn to a judge's daughter with a lively appetite for life by the name of Vavarette. Their friendship survived marriage, and the women invited each other for long stays at their respective country homes. For years they exchanged confidences, plotted together, and maintained an active correspondence, so active that it interfered with family life and disturbed their husbands. Manon Phlipon had a similar experience. At age twelve she asked her parents to send her to a convent school in the faubourg Saint-Marcel so that she might prepare for communion in a proper spiritual climate. Unexpectedly she befriended several girls unknown to her family, including two nuns who offered her the use of their cells, where she could read in peace and speak freely. In addition, she met another boarder, Sophie Cannet, who remained a loyal friend until her death: "My Sophie and I shared everything"—tastes, reading, thoughts. Thus, the convent school offered girls the same opportunity that the *collège* offered boys: an opportunity to sample life and to test themselves outside the family.[17]

The texture of private life became increasingly complex. For now, however, this seldom fostered a need for solitude or intimacy, which required a freedom and culture not often found. As a child Manon had fixed up her own alcove where, without telling anyone, she went at night to read books surreptitiously borrowed from her father's workmen. Her mother, who saw her reading, kept her secret but also kept a watchful eye on what she read. But few women, even those with a smattering of culture, reached this stage. In merchant families in Toulouse and Montpellier some women shared a taste for reading and in the interstices of domestic life found sufficient freedom to exchange books and to discuss their reading during late-afternoon visits.

From Rumor to Scandal

On the whole, however, women's lives remained largely unchanged. There was something contradictory about their role. Mistresses at home, they also shaped public opinion and spread rumors abroad. Such was their reputation, at any rate. Women allegedly knew nothing but how to talk, in particular about private matters, which, thanks to their conversations at the washhouse and in the doorway, they knew better than anyone else. They were said to be curious by nature. Women of the lower orders shamelessly admitted it. One confesses that she was "obliged" to follow the movements of a passerby, another that she could not help overhearing a conversation or lying in wait for a neighbor. And whatever they noticed was repeated. Not even thefts or secret births could remain unknown in this panoptic society, in which anonymity was so hard to come by. In Pézenas if a shop clerk paid attention to a young girl, a group of women immediately ran to inform her mother, but not before having calculated the probability of marriage and teasingly questioning the girl: "When can we expect to be eating sweetmeats?" Such rumors had no serious consequences, for their irresponsible nature was generally acknowledged. Responsible males, particularly court officials, were expected to be more sober.

It was an entirely different matter, however, when family secrets became a matter of public notoriety. The victim was

Constantin, *Landscape.* The doorway was an extension of domestic life into the outside world. (Marseilles, Longchamp Museum.)

si tu la cherche la voicy

Two images of woman. The headless figure confirms the popular saying: "Abyss of stupidity, seminary of misfortune, babbling mouth, cause of quarrels, and firebrand of hell." Below a woman is reading the life of a saint. Reading had become widespread, especially in the cities, where it figured in private devotional practices.

then obliged to seek reparation or forfeit his good name. Women played a decisive role in provoking scandal when norms were seriously violated. At Bédarieux, in 1780, a woman reputed to be a prostitute shared a one-room dwelling with the local physician. Pregnancies and miscarriages followed one after another. As long as the woman remained confined during her pregnancies, the talk remained muted. Scandal erupted only after the hussy *publicly* moved into a rented house with a maid to wait on her: "Rules, decency, modesty are no more!"

Women were important instruments of social control, often to their own detriment, since they were the primary target. Yet they were simply exercising their prerogative as guardians of the home and of family morality. For this purpose they wielded powerful weapons. By disclosing private scandals they aroused public opinion. They broke the law of silence that normally applied to domestic affairs, but only when the offense was grave. By revealing what they knew, they brought justice to their ever-changing domain.

A REDEFINITION OF ROLES

The Sun King reigned from 1643 to 1715, and for fifty-four of those years he reigned personally. Louis XIV established himself in magnificence at Versailles in 1683. The young court had grown to maturity. Now the difficult years began,

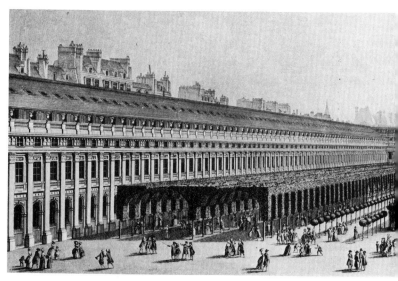

the years of crisis in the European consciousness. Man's view of the world and concept of life were transformed. The state extended its influence through the courts, the police, and the fiscal authorities. Meanwhile enlightened citizens longed to participate in government. People felt a need for clear distinctions between public, private, and family. Withdrawal from public life no longer implied retirement, to which Saint-Simon, speaking of the former chancellor, Pontchartrain, referred as "a wise and holy interval between life and death." Pontchartrain had devoted his life to king, country, and family. In old age, after the death of his wife, he left the court forever.[18] But in the eighteenth century men left the court not out of devotion to the king but in order to sample what Count de Brienne called the "delights of private life."

The first glimmerings of change could be seen while Louis XIV was still alive. At Versailles the prince and his courtiers occupied center stage, playing the complementary roles of sovereign and acolytes of monarchy. Amid the luxury of state chamber, salons, and royal park, all public places, the king lived a public life, inscrutable master of himself and his realm. There was little intimacy and still less family life; symbolism was everywhere. The king devoured the man. In return he expected a great deal of the grandees and nobles whom he held hostage at court because of their deserved reputation for

Ceremony and Leisure

The Palais Royal in Paris: a monumental verticality and a real-estate speculator's dream. The Duke of Orleans turned this palace in the very heart of Paris into a meeting place and crossroads of ideas. (Paris, Carnavalet Museum.)

The king receives the homage of the Duke of Lorraine. As in all public royal acts, the ceremony and speeches were governed by strict rules of etiquette, which emphasized the majesty of the sovereign. (Paris, Bibliothèque Nationale.)

sedition. The nobility surrendered not only its personal life but its political power. In exchange it received the favors of a ubiquitous master who knew the secrets of every family. The king made himself protector of the aristocracy. When a noblewoman to her chagrin discovered herself to be pregnant at an inopportune moment, it was to the king that she confessed in secret audience. In return the king protected her honor by packing her husband off to war.[19]

Hence all was grace for these aristocrats forced to live in foul-smelling, cramped quarters in the palace mezzanine and attics. Family and friends were sacrificed for the privilege of having to watch whatever one said. A century later Manon Phlipon was outraged to see the Archbishop of Paris living close to Versailles so he could "slink off every morning to the *levers* of those Majesties." Attendance being obligatory, the crowds were so large that it was almost impossible to see.

In the wings the actors permitted themselves a moment's relaxation. The monarch himself was in the habit of slipping off into private apartments into which few were invited. Anyone could address the king in public, but a private audience in his cabinet was a signal favor. In his private quarters, not often described, the king dropped his mask. The Venetian ambassador, Primo Visconti, noted that as soon as the king crossed the threshold, "he assumed a different expression, as though obliged to appear on stage." In private he lived with his intimates and much-envied valets. He saw his children and received his architects, whose plans he carefully scrutinized. Of course the jockeying for power never stopped, not even in Mme de Maintenon's apartment, where over the years the king became accustomed to a rather conjugal domestic life, much to the dismay of Saint-Simon, who was also irritated by the practice of granting audiences in the king's private cabinet. When the king came to work in private with one or two ministers or to receive a visitor, Mme de Maintenon was always there, the ever attentive confidante whom Louis called his "rock." She knew how to make him relax and divert himself at plays and concerts presented to a small circle of people away from the court. She also persuaded him to go to Marly, which Louis had envisioned as a place of "small scale and solitude," where the etiquette and protocol were less cumbersome, so much so that the Princess Palatine was scan-

Pierre Mignard, *Portrait of the Grand Dauphin and His Family* (detail). An official portrait of the royal child, whose education was entrusted to Bossuet. The pomp of the scene is counterbalanced by the presence of the small dog, the child's playmate. (Paris, Louvre.)

Before Marly, the Trianon was a relatively private place to which the king could retreat, at first for lunch, though later it was enlarged to allow the monarch and guests to stay for brief periods. (Paris, Bibliothèque Nationale.)

dalized: "The king is little in evidence. Everything is disorganized. The court is dispersed."

Thus, whenever there was a break in the ceremony, both king and court were quick to amuse themselves. The courtier regained his freedom—but not the same freedom he enjoyed at the beginning of the seventeenth century, for uprooted he was and uprooted he would remain. It was up to him to carve out a new role for himself, a new kind of liberty.[20]

The Height of Good Living

In the eighteenth century a new style of living took hold among the aristocracy, achieving a peak of dominance in the 1750s and 1760s. The court set the tone. The king set an example both in the exercise of power and in his determination not to allow his power to consume him entirely.

Unlike his predecessor, Louis XV did not relish his role. He distanced himself from the throne and spoke of state affairs as though he were not their master: "They thought it was best to do thus and so." As the monarchy became increasingly bureaucratic, the royal role became in some ways more remote. The rules of court ceremonial remained the same; but in return for submitting to them the king expected to be allowed a space of his own, first in his private cabinets and later in apartments concealed in the upper stories of the palace, where he could live free of the constraints of court etiquette. His inner sanctum included salons, galleries, a library, and even an aviary. To those who were granted the priceless privilege of entry, the king's apartments were a delightful retreat; to others they were a rat's nest. Family life bored the monarch, and the eighteenth century was hardly one to extol the domestic virtues. The king spent much of his time with his mistress and friends or alone in his library. To his celebrated suppers he invited a dozen or so frequent guests, who dined untroubled by the gaze of servants. The tone of these gatherings was free. The king, grim and silent in public, was gay, affable, and modest in private, where he laid aside the burdens of office in a setting that was much to his liking: small salons, decorated in discreet shades of gray and green and carefully arranged for comfort. Here the king lived the life of a great noble, a libertine to be sure but also a sedentary, a lover of cards, prints, cats, preserves, and coffee.

Grevenbroeck, *The Château de la Muette.* An old royal hunting lodge, La Muette was rebuilt in 1764 by Louis XV. Located on the edge of the Bois de Boulogne and surrounded by a charming park, it was one of those "follies," which expressed, in their simple yet refined comforts, the rural nostalgia of the aristocracy. Louis XVI often came here to flee the formality of the court. (Paris, Carnavalet Museum.)

Following the king's lead, the court emancipated itself even more fully from the constraints of protocol. At Versailles rival coteries still jockeyed for influence, but courtiers lived with one foot in the palace, the other in Paris. The aristocracy pursued its personal life in renovated urban hôtels or in smaller suburban houses in Passy or Auteuil, not to mention the anonymity, sometimes deliberately sought, that only Paris could offer. The city took revenge on the court. Public opinion was now shaped in Paris rather than Versailles, and Paris set the tone in manners.[21]

Greater intimacy was now de rigueur, indispensable for observation and analysis of a self no longer held to be hateful. Innumerable letter-writers did not wait for Jean-Jacques's *Confessions* to plumb the self's depths. But the Enlightenment also had its hidden aspects, lust not least among them. The voluptuary's epicurean indulgence required its secret gardens. Of these the best known was of course the convent favored by Sade, shut off from the world but open to a few initiates. The erotic novels that proliferated in the second half of the

Dogs and cats, refined by careful breeding, were treated like pampered children. Cats were particularly prized by the aristocracy, and Louis XV once became furious when his cat was mistreated by a page. The vogue for house pets reveals a new attitude toward nature and animals, which were no longer regarded as "wild." (Paris, Bibliothèque Nationale.)

eighteenth century observantly detailed the new topography of sex. Andréa de Nerciat, a contemporary of Choderlos de Laclos, recounted the career of a libertine in *Félicia ou mes fredaines* (Felicia or My Escapades).[22] Here architecture played a considerable role, ensuring the secrecy of pleasure. A counterweighted elevator moving in a padded shaft between the two floors of an apartment created a veritable labyrinth of lasciviousness. A gentleman furnished with the proper key could descend via the elevator and through a sliding panel enter the desired secret room, whose ordinary entrances had been blocked up. Thus anonymity was assured. Except that the operator of the premises, Sir Sydney, required for his own pleasure that he be able to keep an eye on the entire labyrinth. The architect had therefore provided him with a secret room between the two floors, connected to each bedroom by acoustic tubes and peepholes in the columns. Hidden in the shadows, the voyeur thus assured the principals the illusory security of secrecy.

Consider Diderot. The son of a cutler from Langres, by the age of fifty he had become one of the princes of the Republic of Letters and was received in many of the best-known salons, including that of Baron d'Holbach.[23] (The philosophes' most generous disciples were to be found among the high nobility.) Thus in many ways he was a "new man," which gave him the necessary lucidity to measure the extent to which styles of life had changed. "In the past people lived among their families, joined coteries, and frequented taverns. Young people were not received in good company. Girls were practically sequestered. Even their mothers were little in evidence. Men were on one side, women on the other. Nowadays people live pell-mell. Youths of eighteen are received. They gamble out of boredom. People live apart. Little children have twin beds, and grownups have separate apartments. Life is divided between two occupations: gallantry and business. A man is in either his office or his *petite maison*, with his clients or his mistress."

People of different age, sex, and status thus mingled more than ever before, but the gap between business and pleasure had widened. Diderot fits his own description. His family life was most sporadic. His home was hardly a peaceful haven. His marriage to a cantankerous linen maid, a moody, temperamental nag of a woman, was unfortunate and left him per-

The Triumphant Example of the Aristocracy

Portrait of Baron d'Holbach, who frequently entertained Diderot and Grimm at Grandval in the 1760s. The generous hospitality of the baron, himself a philosopher, earned him the epithet "maître d'hôtel to the philosophes." (Chantilly, Condé Museum.)

manently unsatisfied. His daughter Angélique had been surrendered, defenseless, to the shrew: "What health could have resisted?" Diderot returned home to comfort the girl and take charge of her education, but his real life was elsewhere: in his writing and, in those years, in the publication of the *Encyclopedia*. He spent his mornings in unavoidable discussions with authors, printers, booksellers, and engravers: "Using up my blood in writing and work . . . I wear out my eyes on plates bristling with figures and letters." The end of the day was taken up by friends, recreation, and lessons with Angélique. One day he dined with Grimm in the Tuileries, then strolled with him through Paris: "We talked." Sometimes he went to the theater, and often he spent his evenings in some salon. Vexing as his chores were, private life clearly offered rights, obligations, and liberties of its own.

One of the high points of his life came in the fall, when he left for a long stay with Baron d'Holbach at Grandval. There he found what made eighteenth-century life worth liv-

Carmontelle painted this portrait of the mother of Mme d'Epinay playing chess with her maid and daughter's tutor: an evening of bourgeois simplicity in casual attire. (Chantilly, Condé Museum.)

ing: comfort and freedom. He was given a quiet, cheerful, warm apartment, the most pleasant in the house, for he liked his comforts, and nowhere more than in the country. His hosts demanded nothing of him and left him free to read, write, or relax. Mornings and many afternoons were his own. But Grandval was no hermitage. The company relished the pleasures of the table as well as the mind: "Ice cream! O, my friends, what ice cream! It is so good you have to be here, you [Sophie] who love it so . . . Impossible to be sober here. I am becoming as round as a ball, my stomach touching the table and my back the fire." The charm of country living: all obligations forgotten, one moved from the labor of writing to the pleasures of society. In the afternoon or at supper friends of the baron's or neighbors like Mme d'Epinay gathered for half-teasing, half-serious talk about the dog Pouf or for speculation about anything under the sun, for an enlightened mind was supposed to be capable of comprehending the full range of human knowledge. In conversation the rule was anything goes, so long as it was witty and observed the proprieties. And when the guests were gone, the intimates remained to

French school, *Departure for the Hunt*, 18th century. Interior scenes were common in 18th-century painting. They reflect a less starchy atmosphere than interiors of the previous century and a greater willingness to enjoy the pleasures of nature and society. (Orleans, Museum of Fine Arts.)

savor even gayer moments. Diderot enjoyed fireside chats and long walks with Father d'Hoop over the slopes of the Marne valley. On nights when the women arranged to take supper in the salon, the men were free to converse in nightcap aned dressing gown. Too much solitude was to be avoided, according to Diderot, because it was a source of "spleen." This charming account of a vacation in the country reveals an age that refused to conceive of private life solely as a matter of exile, religion, and old age.

The Plurality of Roles: The Provinces

The court and the city led the way, the provinces followed. President de Maniban, born in Toulouse in 1686, reflects fairly well the changes in the life style of the provincial aristocracy.[24] As *premier président* of the *parlement* of Toulouse (the second most important parlement in France), he seems at first to have devoted his entire life to the service of the king. Duties of office and rank overwhelmed his private life. His family, of the high *noblesse de robe* [persons considered to be of noble rank because of their ownership of judicial office], was notoriously upper crust. Its substantial fortune, shrewdly managed, had, by the mid-seventeenth century, grown to approximately a million livres.

Maniban was destined to hold the highest offices, especially after he left Toulouse for a ten-year stint in Paris. Rather than take a bride from within the Toulouse aristocracy, he made a brilliant match in Paris, marrying in 1707 a Lamoignon, who brought him a dowry of 240,000 livres and contacts in one of the leading families in the Paris parlement. He became the brother-in-law of Chancellor de Lamoignon and the uncle of the director of the press, M. de Malesherbes. Frequent visits to Paris cemented the bonds with his in-laws, and he began a steady correspondence with the chancellor. In letters written "for you alone," he confided his opinions, his anguish, and his disillusionment. In 1722 Maniban was named premier président of the parlement of Toulouse, a post he held until his death in 1762. A devoted servant of the king, he was motivated by a spirit of justice and a desire for peace. Yet he also championed the cause of parlement, which was troubled by internal dissension over religion and politics. His heavy responsibilities denied him opportunities to pursue friendship and self-interest, and he never allowed pleasure to interfere with discipline and business. An exemplary official, he defended the interests of Toulouse at Versailles, while enforcing respect for the king's authority in his own jurisdiction. In September 1727, for example, he learned in Paris that a flash flood had inundated the Toulouse suburb of Saint-Cyprien. He hastened to the scene immediately. Unstinting in his efforts, he used a gift from the king of 95,000 livres to organize relief for the victims. Order was maintained, and the king was duly informed of his success.

Symbolism played an important part in Maniban's life. A court official could hardly do without ceremonial. Firmly he set the rules for young magistrates, who were advised to maintain an impassive face and to walk slowly: "He counted his steps and miraculously knew just how far to advance or retreat . . . He believed that the muscles of the face that produce laughter must never move in the physiognomy of a magistrate." And so he appears in his official portrait, playing his role to the hilt. Yet he has a sharp eye. He belonged, as it was the duty of a premier président to belong, to the aristocratic confraternity known as the Blue Penitents, and he served as godfather to a converted Jew.[25] His successors joined the Lodge of Perfect Friendship. He was a patron of scholars and a supporter of the Academy of Sciences. He was generous to the poor, who looked upon him as the "father of his people." Everyone was welcome in his hôtel. This too was a part of his service to His Majesty, for in fact he did not like the

Clubs, cafés, and philosophical societies were places where enlightened minds met, exchanged information, and conversed outside the home, fashioning the "public spirit" in a semiprivate setting. (Paris, Bibliothèque Nationale.)

sciences, the salons of Toulouse, or the theater. In return, from his people he expected respect and even veneration, which he received in abundance whenever he appeared in public.

For such a man sumptuous living was an official duty, and Maniban lived a life of unparalleled luxury. Everyone who was anyone in the province was welcome at his dinner table. He gave suppers every night at the hôtel des Pins and staged magnificent receptions for important guests. In 1754 Marshal de Richelieu, commander-in-chief of Languedoc, was guest of honor at a supper of four tables with twenty-five diners per table. Major events of the monarchy such as the king's marriage in 1725 and, in 1744, his recovery followed by the dauphin's marriage were celebrated with fireworks, illumination of the hôtel, fountains of wine, and so on.

All of this was only to be expected. A great noble had to maintain a magnificent household, particularly if he represented the king. His office, which provided an income of only 15,000 livres annually, would not have sufficed, but a personal income estimated at 60,000 livres permitted him to make ends meet. The required expenditure was all the more onerous because the provincial aristocracy customarily lived on the produce of its own estates. But those who symbolized the monarchy were forced to buy from Paris: fancy dress, liveries for the servants, lighting, fireworks, a four-seat coach and horses (six of which were ordered in 1751 at great expense). The chef was paid 120 livres per year. Barrels of sugar and

A hôtel in the neoclassical style, built in a century passionate about architecture with simple lines. (Toulouse, Paul-Dupuy Museum.)

spices were ordered from Bordeaux (331 livres in November 1741). Wine was shipped by sea from Burgundy in a variety unheard of in Paris. For this Maniban paid 525 livres in 1730, even though he owned numerous vineyards in Armagnac. He also employed seventeen servants (compared with six for the average parlement family), and three carriages and teams (compared with one carriage and a sedan chair for his colleagues). To top it off, he paid a confidential secretary to handle his correspondence. Accordingly, when he went over his books in 1752, he found that not much was left of his 60,000 livres: "No fortune is great that is not public."

Joseph Gaspard de Maniban paid dearly for the privilege of being premier président. There was no sharp distinction between official and private functions. Of course the king's service, demanding as it was, also brought favors and pensions. The more devoted the public servant, the more he expected of the king, and Maniban expected a great deal. He was disappointed, and said so bitterly in confidential letters written to his brother-in-law, the chancellor. He wrote because he had little opportunity to vent his frustrations at home. Fashionable marriage precluded conjugal intimacy, and correspondence, whether between Diderot and Sophie or Maniban and Lamoignon, served as a partial substitute.

Maniban lived alone in a hôtel that was open to all. He had no family life, probably as a consequence of his fashionable Parisian marriage. Despite a clause in the marriage contract, Mademoiselle de Lamoignon refused to live in the provinces. She could not do without the court and Paris, where, as the marquis noted with resentment, life was so expensive. As for children, she bore him only two daughters, so, to his great disappointment, his office and his fortune would pass at death to his cousin Campistron. The two girls were of course brought up in Paris and eventually made quite splendid matches at court (with the marquis of Malauze and of Livry); the king signed the marriage contracts. With the girls went dowries of 450,000 and 500,000 livres respectively, 50,000 of which was payable in cash. Maniban was forced to borrow from his friends, for his wife refused to contribute: "A man needs a good deal of patience," he exclaimed when the negotiations were concluded. Yet he felt real affection for his daughters.

Maniban's life was one of unremitting responsibilities, sporadic contact with his family, and little or no privacy. As compensation he bought himself a present, though not until

A rustic theater and a country château of the sort in which the members of the Toulouse parlement, extensive landowners, spent their judicial vacations without undue luxury. (From the *Illustrated Land Register of Sadournin and Esparros*.)

HAUT ET PUISSA
NT
SEIGNEUR M͂ᴿᴱ
BERNARD DE·
CARDAILLAC

1748: a retreat, a place of pleasure. He paid dearly for it: 48,000 initially and an additional 23,000 for renovations. The estate at Blagnac, three miles outside Toulouse, earned no income, but it was a place where Maniban could go "to relax and enjoy the country" in moments of discouragement. As a man who already owned several châteaux, he had no need for another, but this one pleased him. Everything, even the bed, was new, and there was no frivolous luxury in the renovations. Instead of Gobelins or other tapestries, Maniban preferred white-washed walls and sturdy furniture. His expenditures were prudent and aimed at providing genuine comfort. The style of life was modest compared to that of the hôtel des Pins, for here in the country symbolic ostentation was unnecessary. The staff was relatively small and very devoted. Maniban retained a private secretary and two gardeners, however, for even though he had no interest in making this property profitable, he did insist on a garden and a park as essential to the pleasures of country living. The garden of some two and a half acres provided his table with asparagus, artichokes, strawberries and other seasonal fruits and vegetables. He explicitly requested that a wall be erected around the twenty-five-acre park, but he did not care for geometrical designs or statues, savoring instead the quiet and the cool breezes from the Garonne.

Here Maniban lived unostentatiously, even frugally. Although he dressed casually, he was rarely alone, for solitude frightened him. He liked to invite his friends, who praised his taste: "I would die of boredom if I were there alone, but I always have many visitors because the city is so close." All in all, Maniban's life is quite typical of his time and rank: in compensation for his unremitting devotion to duty, he permitted himself a private refuge not with his family but with a select circle of friends. As old age and illness overtook him, he grew even more eager for retirement. The Lamoignons saw to it that he was treated for his maladies by the celebrated Dr. Fizes, who also treated Rousseau. Maniban's daughter the marquise de Livry comforted him with her presence; for the last three years of his life, she even came to live in Toulouse. In death, however, the magistrate triumphed over the private individual. In his will he had stated: "I want to be buried in the cemetery of the parish in which I die, without any pomp or funeral oration, which I expressly prohibit." But his funeral was in fact a grandiose affair, with all the magnificent ritual due a *président du parlement*, which Maniban was more than most. Twenty years later ideas had changed, and his successor, Puyvert, in accordance with his will, was buried simply.

The End of a Way of Life

By the end of the century people had clearly tired of incisive wit and dry rationalism, a style that inhibited the spontaneity of the civilized man.[26] Emotional enthusiasms were back in vogue: "Return, prodigal child, return to nature" (Holbach). After Bougainville, tales of travel in the Pacific and descriptions of primitive societies in Tahiti and elsewhere held out the promise of renewed happiness and innocence in the bosom of nature. It became fashionable among the high nobility to keep a place in the country not too far from Paris where homage could be paid to the illusion of wilderness; these were referred to as *folies* (follies). The supreme examples are the Petit Trianon at Versailles and Saint-Cloud: gifts of the king, fitted out for the retirement of a twenty-year-old queen. These were private properties in the strict sense of the word: no one, not even the king, was admitted without invitation. They were simple country houses, modest in size but exquisite in proportion and decor. Also at Versailles was the Hamlet, where the queen could play peasant in the midst of a cleverly constructed but apparently simple park.

There is abundant evidence that even those who occupied the throne desired a life free of the constrictions of the court: "I do not care for Court, I live as a private citizen." A life of freedom was one whose pleasures derived from friendship and shared tastes, with a minimum of obligations and protocol. Everyone did as he pleased. The queen strolled about in a white muslin gown, without a retinue. "She is no longer a queen," her enemies in Paris exclaimed, "she is a woman of fashion!" Do not imagine, however, that the monarchy was somehow at stake in the rules of the court at Versailles. As far as possible the queen lived in her own private apartments with servants and friends. She insisted that her dressmaker,

The queen's Hamlet was widely copied. Sensitive souls enjoyed solitary reverie and rustic labors. In fact, the "wilderness" was cleverly arranged to suit the convenience of an aristocracy in search of freedom and apparent simplicity. (Paris, Bibliothèque Nationale.)

Far from the menacing atmosphere of the gambling den, these aristocratic card players attend to their game but do not neglect other amusements in a setting made charming by noble architecure and abundant foliage. The Paris parlement deplored the popularity of gambling in good society and lamented its inability to punish, at this level of society, a vice that threatened so many families with ruin. (Paris, Bibliothèque Nationale.)

Bertin, and her hairdresser, Léonard, both retain private clients, so that they would not lose their touch.

Clearly the queen earnestly wished to escape the burdens of sovereignty and to live a more down-to-earth life. As a result, she cut the monarchy off from its natural environment. Elderly duchesses refused to call on her, for they never knew whether or not the queen would be available to receive their homage. She became the prisoner of her chosen circle, whose astonishingly free ways she tolerated, particularly those of her friend the Duchess de Polignac: "I think that just because Your Majesty wishes to come to my salon, that is no reason to wish to exclude my friends."[27] The queen gave in. Thus, a limitation on sovereign power was recognized: the private life of others, as respectable as one's own, was inviolable. The public was scandalized by such unprecedented expansion of the rights of privacy. At the same time the most enlightened citizens had no other aspiration but to escape the confines of civil society and participate at last in political decisionmaking.

REVOLUTIONARY CHANGES

We come to 1789 and the last generation of the Enlightenment, a time of widespread criticism of existing social institutions. Many, like Mme Roland, acquired the habit of "considering the relations between man and society." The problem was of the utmost importance at a time when the political system was being remade and the rights of man were being proclaimed. The old orders and the statutes that governed them had been abolished, and the field remained open for private initiative. Many people were therefore more concerned with the expansion of the individual citizen's prerogatives than with possible abuse of power by the state.[28]

With the aid of private papers we can follow the history of the Gounons, a family of provincial notables. In 1789 the family was headed by a wealthy merchant, Joseph Gounon. Born in Toulouse in 1725, he made a fortune in business, became a city magistrate, and acquired nobility by purchasing a seigneurie. He married the daughter of a family belonging to the *noblesse de robe* (whose members had also held municipal offices in Toulouse) and acquired the right to call himself Monsieur de Gounon, lord of Loubens—a classic ancien-régime career. Nevertheless, the fact that his wealth came from commerce is worth noting in a city dominated by its parlement and by landed wealth. It was more usual to obtain honors through office- and landholding than through trade.[29]

Throughout his relatively smooth rise to prominence Gounon's main interests were his family and the administration of his city. Joseph and his brothers continued to live much as they always had done. The youngest brother was sent to Paris to represent Toulouse in the offices of the royal administration, staffed by arrogant bureaucrats. The Gounons passively embraced Enlightenment ideas that had become common currency among the urban elite, but they never adopted aristocratic forms. Month after month they wrote letters to one another, some marked "confidential." Yet none have the nonchalant freedom of tone of a Julie de Lespinasse or a Diderot, nor are they very intimate. They simply express unshakable affection and solidarity in the face of all adversity, even lawsuits. Joseph makes this clear in a straightforward declaration: "I am always for our name."

As Philippe Ariès has pointed out, the Gounons were unusually attentive to and affectionate toward their children. After his wife died when quite young, Joseph never remarried,

and he devoted much of his free time to the education of his three children. Joseph's personality can be glimpsed in his taste for the natural sciences, an interest he shared and discussed with his brothers and friends. He ordered Buffon's *Natural History* from Paris and subscribed to various gazettes. And he was genuinely curious about agronomy, meteorology, and economics, all sciences with a direct bearing on his management of his wealth and his concerns as a public official.

Not surprisingly in view of his breadth of intellectual interests and demonstrated competence as a public administrator, Joseph de Gounon took a lively interest in public affairs, which were largely handled at Versailles. Thanks to his brother, he had a good sense of what was going on. He had served for a time as his city's deputy at the Estates of Languedoc, which met in Narbonne. Hence he knew better than most that the administration of a provincial capital like Toulouse depended in large part on measures taken by the intendant in Montpellier or on decrees issued by the King's Council or on a letter sent by a minister. This irritated him at times, yet neither brother presents himself as a reformer ready to put forward a specific program in order to enable others like themselves to have greater access to the political process. In keeping with tradition, they simply list their grievances. Be-

Family portraits. One is a classical representation of the magistrate adorned with symbols of his office. In private life he was an attentive father who did not remarry after the premature death of his wife, here pictured in the fashion of the time and in a most dignified pose. (Private collection.)

fore long, towns all over France would be filling books with similar grievances to lay before the king.

The Gounons are critical of the enormous waste at court. They disapprove of Admiral d'Estaing and favor the return of Necker. They are irritated by members of parlement, *ces grandes perruques* (bigwigs), and bitter about the despotic royal bureaucracy with its overpaid civil servants (who, they claimed, earned more than 1,000 écus annually and appeared at the office only to pick up their pay). There is nothing very original in all this criticism of the crushing burden of taxation on the poor or in these protestations of loyalty to the monarchy and support of Necker's reforms. The brothers favor moderate reform and, for themselves, greater participation in public life. In calling for a new society they are neither unduly optimistic nor utopian.

Yet Joseph de Gounon, a former city magistrate, was also a proud lord, who had recently had his land register straightened out by an expert in feudal law and who had brought suit to enforce his hunting rights. He viewed the coming of the first Revolution with the greatest of curiosity but with no wish for a sudden break with the past. The family drew closer together, as families do in times of uncertainty. Landowners worried about the abolition of feudal rights and later about the circulation of paper currency and overhaul of the tax sys-

Adepts of reading, as an activity not of solitary meditation but of passionate commentary. In the faces and attitudes we read expression ranging from mean and obtuse to pontificating and reverential. The picture undoubtedly was intended as a satire of a new social mode; it also reflects Foulquier's taste for compositions filled with contrasting physiognomies, each abandoned to its "unpunished vice." (Toulouse, Paul-Dupuy Museum.)

tem. Those who did not gain power through election reacted as best they could, seeking to continue to wield influence over the members of the National Assembly. They gathered information in Paris and passed it along to correspondents in Toulouse. Such information could be useful in responding to the rapidly changing situation. In fall 1790, for example, the Gounons did not hesitate to sign a declaration of loyalty to *both* the king *and* the Assembly in the face of a threat from the "enemies of the people." Actually they were gradually withdrawing from public life. Attentive observers, they nevertheless kept to themselves. Their greatest desire was to see a quick end to the Revolution.

The Break with the Past

In 1792 everything changed abruptly. War and the fall of the monarchy radicalized the Revolution. The new republic set out to build a society around the social contract. It was to be a community of citizens, each of whom desired only the good of all. A new world dawned, one of supposedly transparent and harmonious social relations accepted by all and prescribed by law.[30] Meanwhile, before the promise was fulfilled, the republic was in danger, threatened by enemies from without and traitors from within. All citizens were expected to join the nation, one and indivisible, in its hour of need.

For the Gounons and others like them, ignorant of Rousseau's political ideas, the change in the Revolution signaled an end to the world as they had known it. Building the ideal republic required destruction of the ancien régime, and the Gounons were inevitably suspect: "We have on our bodies three indelible marks: we are ex-nobles, we have an exaggerated reputation for wealth, and we are of such an age that we may be expected to be moderate . . . The people are in a blind rage against simply the name ex-noble or even ex-ennobled." They had to prove their loyalty in order to be accepted as citizens of the new nation. One way to do so was to purchase a certificate—a new *savonnette à vilain* [vulgarity remover, as royal offices were known under the ancien régime], indispensable for any suspect who wished to be recognized as a patriot. The Gounons did not know which way to turn. Accustomed to rendering unto Caesar what was customarily Caesar's, they were now obliged to confront the intrusive demands of a state that was "revolutionary even in peace." They were forced to deal with subsistence committees and bureaus responsible for issuing loyalty and residence certificates. In 1794 they had to fill every requisition for grain and hay or face the death penalty. They had to pay taxes and contribute to compulsory loans to the government, which were no longer paid back.

Citizen Gounon sought refuge on his estate at Fourque-vaux near Toulouse, where he spent much of his time. Fulfilling his obligations as a citizen became a full-time occupation—and a trying occupation it was, as all the things that had enabled the family to rise under the old regime became targets for the new. In letters to a cousin in Toulouse, Joseph vents the bitterness and astonishment of a well-born gentleman forced to confront the rigors of the new egalitarian society. Every journey, every application for a new certificate, required the presentation of papers and passports: "My documents must be more than in order." Thus the ex-noble was reduced to a status akin to that of a homeless vagabond under the ancien régime.

An even more onerous burden came in 1793 with the advent of mass conscription: national service and love of the fatherland required the sacrifice of all. Jean Mathias Gounon, the family's eldest son, was immediately dispatched to the Army of the Eastern Pyrenees, where he was horrified by the brutality of the generals and the rigors of war (rotten food, winter nights spent out-of-door, days spent digging trenches, epidemics). Only the peasants were equal to these harsh conditions, according to Jean, who was quite prepared to admire their fortitude: "But it is too much for us . . . How wonderful it will be to return home!"[31]

In such unpredictable circumstances it was not enough merely to observe all laws and regulations scrupulously. Loyalty had to be demonstrated in concrete ways. The Gounons quickly learned the new morality: "Christian virtues are good, but they cannot be applied at the present time." What was needed was a reputation for patriotism. It was essential that every act of loyalty be duly recorded. Give and give again, advised the cousin from Toulouse, who recommended a donation to the municipality (in 1794 an *assignat*, or paper bill issued by the revolutionary government, worth 400 livres) in exchange for a receipt or, better yet, an affidavit from the commune "declaring you to be a true, good, and useful republican." In the winter of 1793 the cousin himself had sent the republican club an "anonymous gift, delivered by a chair porter, of 130 pounds of bedsheets and tablecloths, along with a speech" (which he sent Joseph as a model, asking that it be returned promptly just in case); he had been certain, he confessed, that the right people would know who the donor was by the mark on the linen and the scientific expressions in the speech.

Revolutionary pressure intensified in 1794. The cousin had more advice than ever: put in an appearance at the Temple of Reason, he recommended, but avoid the two churches still open, since it was rumored that the municipality had decided to "record the names of the supposedly good patriots who attend mass . . . I myself shall behave as if I were in China. I shall hear my special mass, and I will not disturb the peace simply to see the priest at the altar." It was wise, however, to attend the celebrations organized in the various neighborhoods. At supper time everyone put a table out in the street and provided a dish or two. Patriotic songs were song, and people danced the farandole on the Place de la Liberté. "We shall make a good time of it. The whole family will be together, the children too despite the cold. We do not want to deprive them of this beautiful and brilliant feast." Here we see a first attempt at collective communion, intended to overcome traditional conflicts and private rancor.

The Gounons were not convinced supporters of the Revolution, despite their professions of public faith, which were merely propitiatory gestures. Never before had they so completely withdrawn from public life, one in a remote country house at Fourquevaux, the other cowering in his room in Toulouse. Apart from the occasional visit of a loyal friend, the latter's only pleasure was his scientific hobby: reading rain gauges. He lived in utter privacy, reduced to staring out the window through his spectacles and exclaiming, "What a sad life!"

Refuge

In reality it was a double life. Performing the required rituals ensured security; the underground life survived it. The family fell back upon proven allies, its clients and contacts. A member of the subsistence committee, "an intimate acquaintance of ours," was called upon to avoid a requisition or secure an exemption for Jean Mathias Gounon on grounds of poor eyesight. In Roussillon the family rented a room for the young man and paid for his meals at an inn so that he could escape the indiscriminate company of his fellow soldiers in the field. Survival was everything, and survival depended more than ever on connections. Obtaining food was a good test. Supplies

Toulouse le 10 fructidor l'an 2e. de la republique
francaise une et indivisible—

Bien persuadé de tes bontés cher concitoyen, tu
m'obligeras, de t'occuper le plutot qu'il te sera possible de
rediger le tableau de ma vie politique, que je suis dans
l'intention de faire imprimer, pour l'anvoyer dans
mon pays, quoique mes principes patriotiques y sont
bien connus, je desire leur rappeller les preuves que
j'anai données, par mon attachement constant à la
revolution, comme tout bon citoyen —

Si tes occupations, ne me privent pas que tu puisses
t'occuper de rediger le tableau de ma vie politique, tu
m'obligeras fort l'avoir fait d'ici a demain au soir je
l'en verrai chercher, marque de moi — Sois bien persuadé
de ma reconnoissance des soins que je te cause je
ne pouvois mieux m'adresser, et par la maniere
obligante que tu me l'offres; si je puis t'etre d'aucune
utilité disposé de moi — rappelle moi dans le souvenir
de tous les citoyens detenus — et du brave citoyen
Jerome le concierge, de sa femme, et de leurs fils
que j'estime infineament.

Je veux m'occuper, de ma santé bien delabrée et
faire des remedes en conséquence; a dieu cher concitoyen
sois toujours gay, et aimable tel naturel chez toi
Salut et fraternité — Villeneuve

were difficult to come by for a variety of reasons (The Gounons mention inflation, price ceilings, and requisitions for the army.) Toulouse experienced shortages. During the winter of 1793, people lined up in front of the butcher shops as early as six in the morning, often in vain.

As it happens, the cousin in Toulouse, though toothless as was to be expected at his age, was a gourmet and a glutton. He dreamed of juicy meat, crisp beans, and fine old wine, all but impossible to find since sale of wine by the glass at fixed prices had been instituted by the people. But our man could not countenance the acidic new wine, black bread, and tough meat. So he found a way. A sharp-witted young valet managed to find food in town, and additional supplies were sent from Fourquevaux on the carts used by the sharecroppers to deliver food to the subsistence committee. Joseph sent wood and dried vegetables to his overjoyed cousin: "With your shipment I am in heaven." Everything was scrupulously noted down for future repayment. The cousin himself played an active if occult role, relying on trusted friends. Like many others, he bartered hard-to-find luxury items such as tobacco (the finest available) and chocolate straight from Bayonne for capons and dancing shoes.

One could go on indefinitely about such double-dealing. The Gounons, who would have been suspect whatever they did, were simply trying to protect their kin and their property. Publicly they did what was expected of them and espoused the language of patriotism, following the example set by the announcement of the Ninth of Thermidor (which ended the Reign of Terror): "The terrible news that has so abruptly dispatched from the scene the most famous members of the Committee of Public Safety . . . Everyone is waiting in astonishment for what will happen next." The Gounons greet the event in noncommittal republican terms: "Never has the fatherland been more in need of concord and peace within and of a war to the death on its borders . . . We must be firm with the resolve of the sans-culottes." Their worries did not end with the demise of the Terror, however. In 1797, at a time of political and monetary crisis and new arrests, Joseph Gounon wrote: "Indeed it seems that the Revolution has only begun."

In the end their strategy paid off. Outwardly patriotic, they withdrew from the public scene and waited, attentive to news and rumors while remaining silent themselves, and writing nothing except in letters delivered by trustworthy couriers.

Conformity after the Revolution ceased to be a matter of attending church and became a question of projecting the private virtues into the public arena. Men made public profession of their political beliefs. (Private collection.)

Hierarchical gradation of figures relative to the Tables of the Law. The Tree of Liberty, as the earthly foundation of the supreme good of liberty as well as the legal apparatus erected by the sovereign people, juts from the pedestal itself. (Toulouse, Paul-Dupuy Museum.)

In 1794 a city official of their acquaintance said: "What are you complaining about? All the ex-nobles have been arrested. Stay in your home!" For those who through ambition and office had shared the hope of just and rational reforms, such behavior was hardly ideal. (A few, perhaps, persuaded themselves that in withdrawing from the world they were following Rousseau's ascetic example.) For the rest, the redistribution of power and freedom was difficult. They understood nothing of the aspiration to create, through the citizens' own commitment and even sacrifice, an ideal egalitarian nation. All they saw was the threat to the boundaries of private life.

What conclusions can be drawn from this overview of two centuries? Traditional society was in no sense homogeneous or unified, neither in what it was nor in what it aspired to become. It was dominated by a privileged minority capable of thinking in new ways about the division between the public and the private. For the favored few, protected by law and social institutions, access to private life was a sign of freedom. But for the rest, for those who lived humbly, and especially for the masses of peasants scattered throughout the countryside, there was no freedom. Family and work imposed constraints that left little room for innovation, except for those willing to risk uprooting themselves and enduring the attendant uncertainties.

Few who renounced the certainties of tradition survived.

When the controls were loosened there were of course opportunities for people to work together on common projects or to enjoy themselves in dancing, gambling, or hunting. There was no shortage of such occasions in a society that knew how to bide its time and cope with necessity. Private life was not conceived of in individual terms. It consisted of more or less open activities that filled the intervals between collective obligations. Not that intimacy (in marriage) or even secrecy was not sought at times. Perhaps the most intimate concern of all was money: hoarding it, hiding it, bequeathing it, and investing it after much patient deliberation.

In his book *The Wheelwright's Shop*, George Sturt asked whether private life could exist at all in traditional society. Thought, behavior, and exchanges of goods and services were so ritualized that each individual life reflected the underlying and animating common life. Yet each had his or her own jobs, responsibilities, and feelings. One person was much like another, yet everyone had personal attachments. Private life did exist, but it was inseparable from the indispensable community.

Robert de Tournières, *Lunch with Ham*. At a table set up for the occasion in an antechamber, the master receives unceremoniously. A certain disorder and freedom in attitudes and gestures suggests the new familiarity that prevailed in male company. (Versailles, Lambinet Museum.)

❦ Friends and Neighbors

Maurice Aymard

FOLLOWING the lead of anthropologists, historians of early modern Europe in the last twenty or thirty years have paid considerable (perhaps even too much) attention to the family. An abundance of sources has made this a rich vein to tap. Endless documents discuss daily living, domestic architecture, social relations, family law, and questions of household economy. The history of private life could perhaps be reduced to a history of the family organized around three major themes: the family's relation to larger structures defined by kinship and marriage; its relation to other families, with which it competed and compromised; and its relation to those ambitious and overweening institutions known as Church and state, which sought to regulate and control its behavior. Gradually the individual succeeded in establishing supposedly new rights, partly in opposition to the family, partly with its support.

Etymologically *privatus* means limited. The private realm can be defined in terms of concentric boundaries. Some of these have survived; others have been redrawn over the years, with certain ones assuming special importance. These changes occurred as the result of a series of significant and datable conflicts. The end result was that the "citizen's life must be walled off," a phrase that Stendhal, in a letter written on 31 October 1823, attributed to Talleyrand.[1]

Yet the interpretation of history as a question of the establishment and subsequent disintegration of a "family monopoly" is simplistic and misleading. Mediations, intermediaries, and arbitrators were never lacking between the family and the rest of society or between the individual and the family. Indeed, throughout the early modern era they were numerous and constantly changing. The family did not occupy

The mawkishness of mother and nurse and the bucolic setting mask the brutality of the practice of turning children over to wet nurses, which became popular in 18th-century cities. (Paris, Bibliothèque Nationale.)

the whole of the private sphere, nor was it the only theater of the emotions or the only school of personality. No child spent all his time within the family, which quickly learned to delegate some of its responsibilities. The old urban practice of giving the infant to a wet nurse became increasingly popular in large cities in the seventeenth and eighteenth centuries. The lower classes found it expedient to give up their children temporarily or permanently, for the costs were assumed by charitable institutions.[2] Older children were sent to school or apprenticed or placed in service (the frequency of which shocked seventeenth-century Italian visitors to England) or with guardians, who were not necessarily relatives. The education, occupational training, and socialization of the child involved people outside the family and places other than the home. And not only for boys: in England in the early seventeenth century "a stint in service was the usual method of preparing the daughters of the aristocracy for the only vocation open to them, marriage." Certain houses, such as that of the Countess of Huntingdon, "whose ability to educate [girls] . . . was as widely recognized as Lord Burghley's ability to educate their brothers," became widely known for receiving them.[3]

Individuals thus acquired a certain experience of the world. Some of this would be forgotten after they settled into lives of their own, and some early ties would be neglected, but others would blossom into lifelong friendships. The mere fact that friendships were not recorded in letters or intimate diaries does not make them any less real. Friendship combined with blood relations to create a network of horizontal and vertical ties around every individual, a mesh of symmetrical and asymmetrical relationships, some tranquil, others full of conflict. Each such relationship established certain rights and duties, for the interpretation of which a subtle casuistry was evolved. There was a rational, reasonable solution for every difficulty. Jaucourt's article on "Friendship" in the *Encyclopedia* is a model of the genre. In contrast to the Stoic tradition, which liked to pose these problems in all-or-nothing terms, here we find no single definition or code but rather "duties of friendship" that varied "according to degree and character."

For example, "the friend with whom one has nothing in common but simple literary amusements" or "whom one may have cultivated for the pleasure and charm of his conversation" was to be distinguished carefully from "the friend of good

S. de Bray. Before cafés and clubs, bookshops and print and painting galleries were favorite places for 17th-century meetings and discussions. (Amsterdam, Rijksmuseum.)

counsel," who himself had no right to the "confidence that one bestows only upon friends who are also family and kin." In every exchange based on gift, it was pointed out, there is a fundamental inequality: expect or demand "less rather than more," give "always more or less." There was also a desire for an equality that friendship had "to find or create." Yet friendship could "do no more . . . than blood relations," for between persons "of very different rank" neither friendship nor kinship authorized a change from "respect" to "familiarity." Yet friendship could be a source of "mutual satisfaction" and of the "pleasure" that comes from sharing thoughts, tastes, doubts, and difficulties—but always within prescribed limits. In other words, friendship is defined by the same elementary attitudes that A. R. Radcliffe-Brown analyzed in kinship (respect, humor, avoidance, and familiarity)[4] and that Claude Lévi-Strauss formalized in terms of reciprocity and mutuality, debt and credit.[5]

Nevertheless, no historian and few anthropologists before Robert Brain[6] have studied friendship for itself, whereas love, for obvious reasons linked to present-day concerns, has been the object of much curiosity. The issue has been confused by the fact that love borrowed the vocabulary of friendship. The Church referred to love as "carnal" friendship; more modestly it was called "tender" friendship. The word *love* was reserved for God alone. However much friendship may have been regulated and codified, it was never identified with any stable or visible institution of European society until the initially rather discreet emergence of "societies" based on "voluntary, optional, and flexible" individual membership of which Freemasonry was for a long time the prime example.[7] Yet friendship affected in overt or covert fashion the operation of most if not all social institutions, to the point of turning them against themselves. Families and communities, for instance, were at times divided into opposing factions cemented by ties of friendship. Friendship can also affect the very meaning of a social institution, as happens today when a political party or trade union or bureaucratic organization or even government is taken over by "friends of friends."[8]

Friendship is difficult to analyze because it can be viewed in two extreme and contradictory ways. On the one hand it is often confused with everyday social relations, while on the other hand it is seen as something exalted, which, like love, has only an individual history. The sources alternate freely between these two different interpretations.

In certain respects friendship was like an arranged marriage, whose success was guaranteed not by personal feelings but by objective factors such as status, wealth, family strategy, and parental approval. When Lorenzo Alberti, the father of Leon Battista, fell ill and became concerned about his children's future, his cousins Adovardo and Lionardo were able to reassure him without entering into competition with his brother Ricciardo: "We would like everyone to recognize that we are your good and very loyal relatives, and if friendship is stronger than kinship, we will do the same as true and just friends." Whereupon Lorenzo swore that he respected them as "dear relatives and true friends," individuals "who are tied to me by blood and whose ties to me I have tried throughout my life to increase through benevolence and love."[9]

Relatives, Neighbors, and Friends

Pieter de Hooch, *Family Gathering*. Courtyards and alleyways provided an intermediate gathering place between the home and the street. Families shared this space with friends and neighbors, with no apparent need to isolate themselves. (Vienna, Kunsthistorisches Museum.)

It would be interesting if this close affinity between kinship and friendship were somehow related to the existence (consecrated by law in certain regions of Italy and in the parts of France influenced by the tradition of Roman law) of a system in which a number of people resided together in a house (*ostal* or *casa*) under the absolute authority of a chief. In Tuscany this system was known as the *mezzadria*. It also existed in Montaillou, where Le Roy Ladurie has shown that the *domus* (house) was at the center of a "network of bonds" that "included not only kinship but also alliance between two different houses" as well as "friendship, born of intimacy and in some cases acknowledged through godparent relationships" and finally "proximity."[10] People helped one another in financial difficulty, in raising orphaned children, in providing apprenticeship and other occupational training, in resolving conflicts of interest, and of course in case of the inevitable vendetta.[11]

Yet the terms "relative" and "friend" were also associated in Normandy, which was governed by the tradition of customary rather than Roman law. In 1700 a marriage contract was drafted "in the presence and with the consent of the relatives and friends" of the future bride and groom.[12] A third term, "neighbors", is often found in conjunction with the other two. The phrase *parenti, vicini, e amici* (relatives, neighbors, and friends) is often found in Italian documents. The recurrence of this association reflects the endogamy that existed at the parish level and that still exists today; in some

David Téniers, *Country Revel.* A rustic version of a gathering place, as idealized by an urban painter. After the summer's labor is over, people gather outdoors with relatives and friends and the entire village for drink, dance, and conversation. (Madrid, Prado.)

parts of France all the inhabitants of a village consider themselves to be related.[13] But there may be more to it than that,
as is suggested by the requests of peasants in the Alpine valleys
of the Como diocese, who in the sixteenth and seventeenth
centuries asked church authorities for dispensation from the
rules of consanguinity.[14]

In their letters they emphasized the need to renew old
alliances upon which the maintenance of friendly, neighborly
relations depended. Friendship was not a luxury but an essential component of the necessary social bond among these peasant families. Such friendship was fragile: "It needs constant
or, rather, periodic proof, made concrete by the exchange of
women." Friendship bound families more than individuals,
or, rather, it bound individuals through their families. Calculated friendship of this kind confirmed and reinforced kinship and marriage ties, translating them into practical terms,
reciprocal obligations extending over two or three generations. Hence people sought to replenish and accumulate this
essential capital of friendship. Consanguine marriage not only
allowed "closer unity through kinship" but also "renewed" or
"increased" the friendship between "always good friends." It
also permitted an end to hostilities or, as in Normandy, prevented possible conflict.[15] Danger, always lurking, had to be
avoided, and in villages of a few dozen hearths local marriage
was an ideal way of doing so: "We do not go elsewhere
looking for wives, and the people from neighboring villages
do not come here."[16] But this endogamy was itself a source
of division, which only friendship could overcome. Also of
course there were many degrees of friendship, ranging from
nodding acquaintance to intimate familiarity.

Friendship was ubiquitous, commonplace, and necessary.
It took many forms and was a part of the fabric of social
relations, which it helped to shape. It kept the social machinery
running smoothly. Yet friendship, when it involved two people who chose each other freely and with no end in mind but
themselves, was also exceptional and unique, setting the
friends apart from the rest of society. Such friendship was so
rare that Montaigne, boasting of his with Etienne de La Boétie,
reckoned its probability at "once in three centuries." Personal
friendship was defined by contrast with ordinary social friendships. It took its model from the Stoics and adapted it to the
realities of the age.

Friendship and Friendships

Jan Vermeer, *The Lesson.* From father to son or tutor to pupil, the teaching of reading was a masculine business, which stressed the hierarchy of knowledge and prepared young boys to assume adult responsibilities and occupations. (London, National Gallery.)

Did the family foster natural friendship? Toward fathers, Montaigne tells us, children felt not friendship but respect, for they were separated by "the greatest disparity," and it would have been improper for fathers to communicate "their secret thoughts" to their children lest they "engender a private misunderstanding," just as it would have been improper for children to offer "advice and correction, which is one of the first offices of friendship." And brotherly love—though "truly the name of brother is a beautiful name and full of affection"—was hard put to survive in an atmosphere of competition and conflict created by "the confusion of ownership, the dividing, and the fact that the wealth of one is the poverty of the other." The family, a hierarchy, was based on and reproduced inequality. It dramatized what it sought to quell.

"Affection for women," Montaigne says, "is the result of our choice," which gives it a decisive advantage over family ties, for "father and son may be of entirely different dispositions, and brothers also." Nevertheless, love "is an impetuous and fickle flame, undulating and variable." Unlike friendship, "enjoyment destroys it, as having a fleshly end, subject to satiety." "As soon as it enters the boundaries of friendship . . . it grows faint and languid," unless it incites vengeance, like that of Mme de La Pommeraye against M. des Arcis in *Jacques le Fataliste.* And marriage "is a bargain to which only the entrance is free . . . and . . . ordinarily made for other ends," which makes it susceptible to external influences. "And indeed, but for that, if such a relationship, free and voluntary, could be built up, in which not only would the souls have this complete enjoyment, but the bodies would also share in the alliance, so that the entire man would be engaged, it is certain that the resulting friendship would be fuller and more complete." But for Montaigne, who definitely does not believe in equality between the sexes, women are incapable of true friendship: "their soul [does not] seem firm enough to endure the strain of so tight and durable a knot."

(From Rétif de La Bretonne, *Le Paysan perverti.*) The ambiguity of relations between men was nothing new, but the 18th century, imagining homosexuality everywhere, both encouraged and condemned close male friendships. (Paris, Bibliothèque Nationale.)

As for "licentious Greek love," though "justly abhorred by our morality," Montaigne finds more promise in it than in love between man and woman, despite the "disparity in age and difference in the lovers' functions." But success depends on overcoming these initial disparities and transcending "external" in favor of "internal" spiritual beauty in a relationship of education, imitation, and mutual perfection. It too can become "a love ending in friendship."[17]

It is tempting to contrast Montaigne's "modernity" with

François Chauveau, *The Pleasures of the Spirit.* A change of style and sensibility: the Roman costumes are perfectly appropriate to the purity of disinterested speculation, further enhanced by the silence of the rural surroundings. The Stoic virtues were taken over by the noble souls who cried over Rousseau. (Paris, Bibliothèque Nationale.)

the more "traditional" forms of friendship associated with kinship and proximity of residence. It might seem plausible that the evolution from the latter to the former was a straightforward matter, that the cultivated elite led the way in insisting upon and practicing a new form of friendship based on freedom of choice and absence of self-interested motives. According to this view, exercise of freedom in friendship would have preceded its exercise in love, since free choice of friends did not necessarily imply conflict with the family and might easily be reconciled with family obligations. Thus, the ability to choose one's friends prepared the way for the ability to choose one's spouse.

But this interpretation is misleading. Montaigne's friendship with La Boétie derived directly from ancient Stoic tradition. Montaigne contrasts it with "acquaintanceships and familiarities formed by some chance or convenience," but these had nothing to do with his family. They too were based on the preferences and decisions of a mature man involved in the political life of his time. They bear the mark of a temperament "quite capable of acquiring and maintaining rare and exquisite friendships" and which "fastens so avidly on acquaintances that are to its taste," but "common friendships . . . [are] by no means sterile and cold." Nor does friendship prevent him from appreciating the "gentle commerce . . . of beautiful and respectable women."[18] Montaigne envisions a "soul of many stories . . . which is comfortable wherever fortune takes it" and capable of easy and correct social intercourse of every degree. In many ways he thus anticipates the dissolution of friendship in the diffuse, undifferentiated, and indiscriminate social relations characteristic, according to anthropologists, of contemporary society, composed of a "diaspora of individuals."[19]

It is best to avoid the pitfalls that lurk in the various theories of friendship (whether modernizing or pessimistic, literary or scientific). In every era and every society such a theory has been proposed, and no doubt we can find in all of them the tension between friendship in the singular and friend-

Hyacinthe Rigaud, *Arch of Triumph.* Amid the geometrical order of the French garden, games of amusement and recreation exacerbated the tension between the strict rules of politeness and the individual's need to protect his privacy. Everyone lived in public, scrutinized by everyone else including the king, but all wore masks. (Paris, Library of Decorative Arts.)

ships in the plural. Change is most likely to be found at the level of specific, concrete social practices, which determine the rules of friendship: where it takes place, at what age, according to what rituals, and involving what rights and duties. Between 1500 and 1800 these practices, which orient the behavior and strategy of individuals and groups, evolved slowly. The family had obtained the upper hand long before. By persuasion, domestication, and/or coercion it sought to socialize its members to assume roles and perform tasks necessary for its own perpetuation and for maintaining relations with other families as well as larger groups such as the community or the state.

Both rural and urban society pretended to ignore or at best to tolerate any peer friendship not sanctioned by society. Conceptualized as a relation of perfect reciprocity, friendship was something "extra," something distinct from normal social relations. It existed outside the family, often in institutions that replaced the family on a temporary or permanent basis: the school, youth cohorts, the army. The existence of such friendships implies the existence of a sphere of freedom. Friends were not chosen at birth by a child's parents or relatives or by the chance of being born on a certain day, as is the case in some non-European societies studied by anthropologists. Yet two men could decide from birth that their children would marry. In 1698 Dreux and Chamillart, both *conseillers* in Parlement and "intimate friends," decided, when their wives gave birth "at the same time to a son and a daughter," that the two children would marry in twenty years. But they could not decree that the son and daughter should like each other. Dreux's son grew up to be a "very brave man but stupid, gloomy, and brutal . . . and his wife was not happy either through him or with him as she so richly deserved to be."[20]

Saint-Simon: Polyglot, Strategist, and Hero of Friendship

The best portrait of friendship in all its many guises and languages is probably the *Mémoires* of Saint-Simon. To appreciate the full grandeur of the work, one must look beyond Saint-Simon's attempt to marry one of the daughters of the Duke de Beauvillier, the failure of which elicited from him the lament "that it was not his wealth that drew me to him nor even his daughter, whom I had never seen, but he himself who charmed me and whom I wanted to marry along with Mme de Beauvillier" (I, 116). The beginning and end of this attraction must be borne in mind. Beauvillier "had always remembered that my father and his father had been friends, and that he himself had lived on such terms with my father, insofar as the difference in their ages, situations, and lives had permitted, and he had already been most attentive to me" (I, 114-115).

Beauvillier, married to one of Colbert's daughters, was a minister of state, head of the Council of Finances, and first gentleman of the chamber. For Saint-Simon, the result of the attempt to marry his daughter was the same as if the marriage had actually taken place: "The conversation ended in the most tender protestations of undying and intimate concern and friendship. He said that he would serve me in everything and for everything with all his counsel and credit, in small things as well as grand, and that he would henceforth consider us as father-in-law and son-in-law and as linked by an indissoluble bond" (I, 121). In addition to this spiritual marriage, Saint-Simon enjoyed all the benefits of a real marriage with the daughter of Marshal de Lorge. Yet his marriage did not prevent a partial break with his widowed mother-in-law, who refused to facilitate a friendship between Saint-Simon and his brother-in-law.

Thus, Saint-Simon, just starting out in life at age eighteen soon after the death of his father and mother, after many years of preparation scored a double victory. Born in 1675 of a father nearly seventy years old and a mother not yet thirty, he had heard his mother "repeat continually" that he had better find someone to whom he could prove his worth, since he was "a young man entering society on his own, the son of a favorite of Louis XIII all of whose friends were either dead or no longer in a position to be of any help, and of a mother who had been raised from childhood by a relative, the elderly Duchess of Angoulême, and who, having married an elderly man, saw only their old friends and had never had an opportunity to make friends of her own age" (I, 16). She had, moreover, lost all her close relatives except for "two obscure brothers, the elder ruined." To make one's way in the world, no fortune was sufficient, because wealth could do its work only if it was lavishly and ostentatiously spent; one's friends were as important as one's kin and connections through marriage. Friendship defined a wider circle than kinship or marriage and was complementary to them. In a system based on exchange, such relations were important. Friends could be bequeathed almost like personal property: the friends of Saint-Simon's father and mother were supposed to protect him even after the parents themselves were gone. Friendship was therefore capital, partly inherited, partly accumulated over the course of a lifetime; managed accordingly, its fruits were transmitted to one's heirs at death.

As with any capital investment, it was prudent to diversify. Among his friends a man needed not only peers and superiors but also inferiors. In fact the latter made the best friends, for provided they were properly grateful they were eternally in one's debt. Saint-Simon's grandfather, nearly ruined, had made his two sons pages of Louis XIII, "where people with the greatest names placed their sons in those days" (I, 56). The younger boy was clever enough as a page to make himself "quite the favorite," thereby securing his fortune. Nor did he forget his duty toward his elder brother. He was also "fortunate in several kinds of domestics, who made considerable fortunes" (I, 63): Tourville, father of the future marshal and sailor, was "one of his gentlemen"; his secretary had a son, Du Fresnoy, who became a high official under Louvois; two "domestic surgeons" enjoyed brilliant careers; and two valets, one the father of the celebrated Bontemps, "owed their fortune" to him. Hence early in the morning on the day after his father's death, Saint-Simon went to see Bontemps and Beauvillier, who arranged for him to be received by the king that very afternoon so that he could be confirmed as his father's successor as governor of Blaye, a position sought by the brother of Mme de Maintenon, and of Senlis, which the Prince de Condé wanted for himself. Quick action saved the day.

In 1698 Saint-Simon courted another minister of state, this time Pontchartrain, who became chancellor the following year. If the result "does him too much honor not to be embarrassed to report" it, his approach was necessarily quite passive. Unlike Beauvillier, Pontchartrain was not an old friend of Saint-Simon's father, so any direct initiative would have been seen as an intrigue. The overtures had to come from Pontchartrain. In 1697 Pontchartrain's son had married a first cousin of Mme de Saint-Simon, a marriage that the Saint-Simons had desired "only for the contacts . . . and they did all that was necessary to take advantage of them." The second step was to establish a friendship between the two cousins. "Sympathy of virtue, taste, and spirit soon formed [between the two women] a friendship that ultimately became extremely intimate, with as little reserve between them as between two sisters." At the same time Mme de Saint-Simon fostered a close friendship with the Duchess of Lesdiguières, the two "living together less as cousins than as sisters" (II, 374). Next, Pontchartrain "urgently" requested of Saint-Simon "the honor of [his] friendship." Once over his surprise, owing to "the disproportion of age and employment," Saint-Simon understood that he had to choose sides: "I told him that . . . I had one friendship that would always take precedence over all others, and that this was my intimate relationship with M. de Beauvillier, with whom I knew he was not friendly, but that if he still wanted my friendship on that condition, I would be delighted to give it to him, and overjoyed to have his." This declaration is followed by expressions of emotion and an exchange of embraces and promises: "We pledged ourselves to each other. We both fully kept our word until his death, in the greatest of intimacy and the fullest of confidence." Informed straightaway, Beauvillier also "tenderly" embraced the young duke and approved his actions. The secret was confided to no one else: "What is unusual is that Pontchartrain said nothing about it to his son or daughter-in-law, nor did I, and for a long time no one at court suspected that so singular a thing had occurred, namely, an intimate friendship between two men so unequal in everything" (I, 559–560).

"No salvation without reconciliation." The public kiss sealed a new friendship or repaired a breach in an old one before God and in the eyes of "Christian morality." (Paris, Library of Decorative Arts.)

For Montaigne, friendship spoke the language of passion. For Saint-Simon, it spoke the language of a carefully calculated marriage, one that, like his own, created a profound and durable understanding. The affair was begun by the search for an alliance. It was furthered by fostering an "intimate friendship" between two women, cousins who became like sisters. And it ended with an unwritten but scrupulously observed contract between two men, as a result of which they agreed to overlook their inequality of rank and to share confidences and secrets.

The same pattern can be found in Saint-Simon's relations with still another minister, Chamillart, who became comptroller general of finances in 1699. The king accepted Chamillart as a friend because he was a good billiards player. (Saint-Simon's father had won the good graces of Louis XIII because, while hunting, he had alertly presented the king with a fresh horse onto which he could leap from his old one without having to dismount.) Chamillart also enjoyed friendly relations with the Duke of Chevreuse and his brother-in-law Beauvillier owing to his diligent efforts concerning the sale of certain properties. Again the first step was a marriage: Saint-Simon's brother-in-law married Chamillart's third daughter.

The marriage had been arranged by Chamillart's mother-in-law at the behest of Lauzun, her other son-in-law, without Chamillart's knowledge and at a time when he was openly advocating a different marriage.

Saint-Simon, who knew of Chamillart's distaste for the marriage but otherwise knew the man only "as one knows people in official positions," called on him to offer his congratulations. "Never was there an initial conversation so full of confidence on both sides, though first encouraged by that of Chamillart, between two men who knew each other so little and whose employments were so different." Next, Chamillart asked for Saint-Simon's friendship. "I behaved with him as I had in similar circumstances with the chancellor [Pontchartrain]. I naturally confessed to him my intimacy with the father, my connection with the son, that of Mme de Saint-Simon and of Mme de Pontchartrain, cousins-german but more closely united than two true sisters, and I told him that if, under those conditions, he desired my friendship, I should give it to him with all my heart. This frankness touched him . . . We made promises to each other, and until his death we tenderly and loyally kept them." Saint-Simon then informed Pontchartrain and his son, who received him as Beauvillier had done four years earlier. The results were as expected: the brother-in-law's career and marriage failed, and Mme de Lorge, wife of the marshal, withdrew from society in frustration. Saint-Simon, moreover, enjoyed "the pleasure of Chamillart's confidence and of the services I was able to render my friends and to obtain for myself," to say nothing of an abundance of information "about the court and the state."

Unabashedly and passionately curious, Saint-Simon found himself at the center of a prodigious intelligence network, which he supplemented with news gleaned from his many female friends: Chamillart's daughters, the ladies of the palace, the Duchess of Villeroy, and various others, who "kept him informed of a thousand feminine bagatelles often more important than they themselves believed" (II, 146-150). He lacked only the friendship of Torcy, the fourth minister but a nephew of Colbert. Despite the fact that the Castries were their common friends, friendship between the two men would have to wait until conflict erupted in 1721 between Torcy and Cardinal Dubois, which enabled Saint-Simon to act as mediator and by the elegance of his intervention make up for his former hostility to the secretaries of state. "Torcy was most grateful for my contribution and to his death we lived on

Engraving by Saint-Igny after Abraham Bosse, *Young People Strolling*. A century earlier the castle garden was the scene of amorous encounters that but for a miracle never resulted in marriage. (Paris, Bibliothèque Nationale.)

terms of the utmost intimacy" (VI, 714-718). In return Saint-Simon was shown Torcy's memoirs and copies of letters opened by postal officials at his behest, an invaluable source of information.

That frankness and confidence should so effectively negate inequalities of age, status, and power is somewhat surprising and might lead one to doubt Saint-Simon's sincerity. Yet his account reveals the precise rules that governed the closed, hierarchical society of the court and of the families and client networks that revolved around it. Calculation was the key to success, but prudence sometimes required taking great risks in the hope of reaping great rewards. That is the meaning of Saint-Simon's frankness. But one also had to know when to say no, as Saint-Simon did to the Duke of Maine. His behavior is remarkably consistent, and the whole detailed ritual of passionate declarations, requests, compliments, and lifelong pledges is to be taken literally. This was the essence of friendship.

The patiently constituted network to which Saint-Simon owed his influence at court did not include all of his friends. He maintained other personal contacts far from rumor-ridden Versailles. One, who had been a friend of his father, was the celebrated Rancé, reformer of the Trappist monastery located five leagues from Saint-Simon's property at La Ferté-Vidame, to which he made periodic retreats. The Bishop of Chartres, Saint-Simon's "diocesan," also came to see him "with an old friend of [his] father's": "Little by little friendship grew up among us, as did trust." At the same monastery he also met the count of Le Charmel, who had renounced society for the sake of his soul (I, 560-561).

At the other extreme, Saint-Simon enjoyed special relationships with the Duke of Chartres (later the Duke of Orleans), who would become regent after the death of Louis XIV. The two men shared a common background and had played together as children at the Palais-Royal: "Eight months younger, I had practically been raised with him, and if age permits such an expression to be used between two youths of such unequal rank, friendship united us." After both had married, however, the libertine behavior of young Chartres cast a cloud over their friendship: "My life suited him as little as his suited me, so great had the distance between us become" (II, 77). It took the mediation of common friends, acting at the express wish of the Duke of Orleans, to revive the youthful friendship: "The revival of the old friendship on my part was

Joseph Vernet, *The Port of Bordeaux Seen from Château Trompette,* 1759. Esplanades on either side of fortified walls lost their military usefulness over the course of the 18th century and became fashionable places to stroll. The predictable hazards of encounter gave opportunities to exchange greetings and winks, bows and empty formulas, or to engage in more intimate conversation. (Paris, Naval Museum.)

the result of the many advances with which he honored me, and it was quickly sealed by total confidence between us, which lasted without interruption until the end of his life" (II, 78). This despite a lessening of the intimacy between the two men at a time when Cardinal Dubois's power was at its peak. Saint-Simon made a symbolic gesture of friendship in 1712, when the duke, rumored to have poisoned the dauphin and dauphine, was abandoned by the entire court: "I was the only—the unique—person who continued to see the Duke of Orleans at my regular hour and in his apartments as well as in the king's, the only one to approach him and to sit with him in a corner of the salon." Despite the advice of Beauvillier, Pontchartrain, and all his other "friends, male and female," who told him that he risked his downfall "by conduct so opposed to the universal judgment . . . I remained firm. I felt that in case of such rare misfortune it was proper not only not to abandon one's friends when one did not believe them to be guilty but also to draw even closer to them" (III, 1224).

Like Montaigne, Saint-Simon chose his friends outside the circle of relatives and neighbors. Of course he relied heavily on his father's friends, but to that inherited circle he added new friends of his own, whom he chose deliberately for their usefulness in furthering his objectives. Friendship ties sometimes coincided with bonds of kinship and marriage, but the three were not identical. Excluded for reasons that are not difficult to imagine was Louise de Crussol, wife of Saint-Simon's paternal uncle, a "proud and nasty woman who had never forgiven my father for remarrying" and for having had a male heir, and "who had done everything she could to drive a wedge between him and his brother" (I, 232) and who had found "the means to transfer most of my uncle's property to the Dukes of Uzès" (her brother and nephew) "and to make my father and me pay a large part of his debts, while leaving the rest unpaid" (I, 56). Also excluded was his brother-in-law, the Duke of Brissac, who, being "too Italian" a husband, quickly separated from Saint-Simon's half-sister. Upon her death in 1684 her nephew inherited the bulk of her estate. Also excluded, as we saw earlier, was his brother-in-law de Lorge and his widowed mother. And Lauzun, his brother-in-law by marriage, was never really included either. His ties to Colbert's two sons-in-law, Beauvillier and Chevreuse, did not give him access to the nephew of the minister Torcy, though he was their cousin by marriage. His friendship with Pontchartrain does not appear to have resulted from the good offices of Jerome Bignon, a member of the council of state and a good "friend of his father," who had agreed, "though not related," to be the executor of the Brissac will and who had married the chancellor's sister. Friendship might depend on or grow out of marriage, but it was always deliberately sought by individuals who coveted its advantages and accepted its constraints and obligations.

Family and Friendship: Spiritual Kinship

In combining ostentatious disinterest with the profits of friendship anticipated and hoarded, Saint-Simon was not unique at the court of Versailles, where everyone was obliged to develop personal bonds of trust, intimacy, and privacy. The court, with its many constants and single variable, was like a scientific laboratory. The constants were the hierarchies of rank and fortune, marriages and titles, which remained stable but for the accidents of birth and death. The variable was the king, the powerful master who manipulated all the stakes and who could be approached only through intermediaries: his children, both legitimate and illegitimate; his ministers; his "domestics"; and his favorites, male and female. Individuals had no choice but to gamble on friendship for their own sake and for the sake of their families. The rules of the game had long been established; it was up to each courtier to make the best of the cards he was dealt.

Change the variable—the riveting, artificial presence of a single center of power—and the rules remained the same. The point of the game still was to control a vast segment of society as completely as possible. The social structure centered of course not on the individual but on the family. In the eleventh and twelfth centuries the lineage had attempted to arrogate the power of social control to itself. At that time true friends, so-called friends by blood,[21] could be acquired only through kinship or marriage. But only a few feudal lineages were powerful enough to enforce their claims, so the attempt was doomed to failure. Other answers needed to be found quickly. The most robust and general solution was to combine kinship, proximity, and friendship. Yet an earlier response was the systematic development of spiritual kinships. In fourteenth- and fifteenth-century Genoa families were incorporated into larger structures known as *alberghi*, whose names they adopted. Members were obliged to come to the aid of their neighbors in specific ways and circumstances that were spelled out in detail before a notary. Such formalization, however, was extreme.

By "spiritual kinship" anthropologists mean a set of institutions and formalized practices modeled on the family, whose vocabulary, rights, and obligations they borrow. Normally these institutions incorporate individuals and/or groups from outside the family, however broadly it may be conceived, and in one way or another complement or compete with its functions. Adoption, godparentage, blood brotherhood, and adoptive brotherhood share similar features. Individuals or groups enter into a commitment voluntarily, or at any rate their commitment is ritually enacted as though it were voluntary (like marriage, once it is held to depend upon mutual consent of husband and wife). By so doing they assume certain reciprocal obligations, even if they are not equals and even if the definition of their relationship implies differences of age, social status, prestige, and so forth. The function of spiritual kinship is to do what the family cannot: take care of children, orphaned or not; provide religious or professional education; and prepare children for adult life. It also serves as a defensive bulwark against external threats. Finally, real or symbolic sanctions are provided in case the obligations of spiritual kinship are not met. To emphasize the total life-or-death nature of the commitment, those sanctions were as severe as any in the realm of interpersonal relations. The state sometimes tolerated them, but it never assumed any responsibility for enforcement.

Spiritual kinship exists in many forms and for a variety of purposes, sometimes explicit, sometimes quite vague. It can serve family interests, but it can also conflict with those interests, since it is difficult for the family to accept that the life or property of one of its members is subject to the power of an outsider. The nature of spiritual kinship depends on whether or not the partners are equals. Although most of the work on spiritual kinship pertains to non-European societies, all the practices identified elsewhere are well-attested in antiquity and the Middle Ages. After the sixteenth century they did not disappear, but they did lose their institutional support. Absorbed by the private sphere, the practices no longer appeared in written records; they increasingly came to seem like anomalous vestiges of a lost tradition ultimately destined to disappear wherever the new social and political rules took hold. Families attempted to assert control over surviving practices for their own purposes, and the Church and the state attempted to eradicate them. Yet they continued to influence individual as well as collective behavior. Under these conditions the symbolic character of spiritual kinship practices was reinforced. The terminology ("blood pact," "friendship in life and death") was increasingly divorced from immediate and practical ends. Practices that survived this routinization acquired a greater and more personal emotional charge; individuals seized upon them as a means of free expression.

Adoption, for example, disappeared from French law and did not reemerge until the Revolution, at which time the laws, which now envisioned adoption only in the case of the death of both parents, were designed to protect the adopted child, who was placed in the hands of guardians. Nevertheless, it remained a common practice to entrust the education of a child, orphaned or not, to a relative—a grandmother, uncle, aunt, or cousin—or even to a person or couple not related to the child's parents. Relations with the adoptive parents or foster parents were not governed by legal statute.

Blood brotherhood was sealed by a blood pact: the partners drank each other's blood either from a deliberately made wound or from a glass. It has been said that such a pact joined the blood brothers "more intensely than consanguinity itself." The practice, attested in early medieval legends from Germany, Scandinavia, and Ireland, is repeated in the literature of chivalry.[22] Subsequently it seems to have disappeared, whether in spite of or because of the implicit allusion to the Last Supper, and we find only a few surviving traces, as in the western Highlands in the seventeenth century.[23] In the nineteenth century it was found to exist in Bulgaria, where the blood brother was "not just a brother but more than a brother"[24] and in Albania, Serbia, and Montenegro, where it was associated with communal sharing of property and women.[25]

Other practices survived more successfully. Adoptive brotherhood, the traditional basis of interfamilial solidarity

The Church prohibited adoption, which did not become legal under French law until the Revolution. But a guardian had all the rights, duties, and responsibilities of a father. (Paris, Bibliothèque Nationale.)

among both peasants and nobles, was aided by the demographic crisis of the fourteenth and fifteenth centuries: "Brotherhood in fifteenth-century Cévenne . . . ultimately became an essential part of social life."[26] Relatives, spouses, and friends commonly signed contracts of mutual support. The practice declined slowly, succumbing to the increasing demands of the nuclear family. The vendetta, or private war, which in the thirteenth and fourteenth centuries was legal everywhere and in some cases compulsory,[27] survived for a long time in spite of the state's new claim to a monopoly of violence. And so did godparentage, which established spiritual kinship between unrelated families, with the result that members of the baptized child's family were not allowed to marry members of the godparent's family or even the family of the priest who celebrated the baptism. The practice existed throughout Europe. The French *compérage* was equivalent to the Spanish *compadrazgo*; in English we have the word *godsib(ling)*, from which *gossip* derives. Italian has *compare, commare,* German *Gevatter, Gevatterin,* and Slavic *Kum, Kuma* for godfather and godmother.[28]

The high and low points of the institution of godparentage are significant. Luther rejected "spiritual relations" as "superstitions . . . limiting the Christian's freedom" and "traps intended to enrich the Pope."[29] Catholic dogma soon followed suit. The Council of Trent did not go as far as Luther had, but it did limit spiritual kinship to the parents, godparents, and child. The political authorities of central Europe, from the German Princes to Joseph II, issued regulations modeled on the sumptuary laws limiting the number of godparents a person could have and placing restrictions on their geographical and social origin. At about the same time godparentage became extraordinarily popular in Spanish America, while in Europe it all but disappeared outside of Spain, Italy, and the Balkans.

Jesuit missionaries to Albania discovered an extreme form in 1890: spiritual kinship was acquired at baptism and extended indefinitely, whereas the Church had never asked for more than four degrees of kinship and settled for much less. Furthermore, the godparent was not permitted to be related to the child. In tribes practicing systematic exogamy, many things seem to have been pretexts for identifying a new form of spiritual kinship: blood pacts, baptism, and even a ritual associated with the child's first haircut, for which "they chose the person with whom they were most friendly or with whom

The workshop opened into both house and street, creating solidarities that could be hard to distinguish from family ties. (Florence, Uffizi, ceiling by Poccetti.)

they desired closer relations. They subsequently enjoyed with that person and his or her parents a relationship of total confidence, as if they were members of the family." Marriage witnesses also "joined the broad group of *kumar* [spiritual kin] with whom they enjoyed a special fraternity and friendship and who would come to their aid in case of *sangue* [vendetta] as well as in other circumstances." The friend whose aid was enlisted in a vendetta was not allowed to take the initiative in granting pardon or offering financial compensation. Disillusioned, the Jesuit missionaries concluded that "these false kinships . . . are held in much higher esteem than the Church admits" and that it would do no good "to condemn such prejudices repeatedly, [for] it would take time for them to disappear."[30]

Missionaries and anthropologists realized that the practices they were studying were no longer familiar. Often they justified even the more extreme practices on the grounds that they were necessary or useful. Yet they failed to observe the parallel decline of the godparent's role as religious educator, protector, and provider. Later of course the godfather would become the principal figure in criminal organizations that also required initiation, instruction, respect, and obedience.

Children continued to maintain a special relation with their godparents, further strengthened by a tendency to exclude the child's parents. In 1845 in Franche-Comté the residents of Broye had created "a kind of religious kinship through baptism of their children. Everyone was a godfather or godmother."[31] But the decline in the importance of such spiritual solidarities was well under way by the fifteenth or sixteenth century. This was related to the gradual pruning back of the lineage to the more narrowly defined family, traditionally favored by the Church but also encouraged by the growing power of the state. As this process continued, a new, more inward and autonomous view of the individual gained prominence, opening the way toward new forms of friendship.

Forms of Association: From Brotherhood to Friendly Societies

First to occupy the newly abandoned terrain were various kinds of associations. Ostensibly composed of voluntary members, these established a model of what the family ought to be but was not. Yet many faced similar constraints and risked similar failure.

An early example was the *compagnonnage*, composed of journeymen, or *compagnons*, employed in a particular trade.

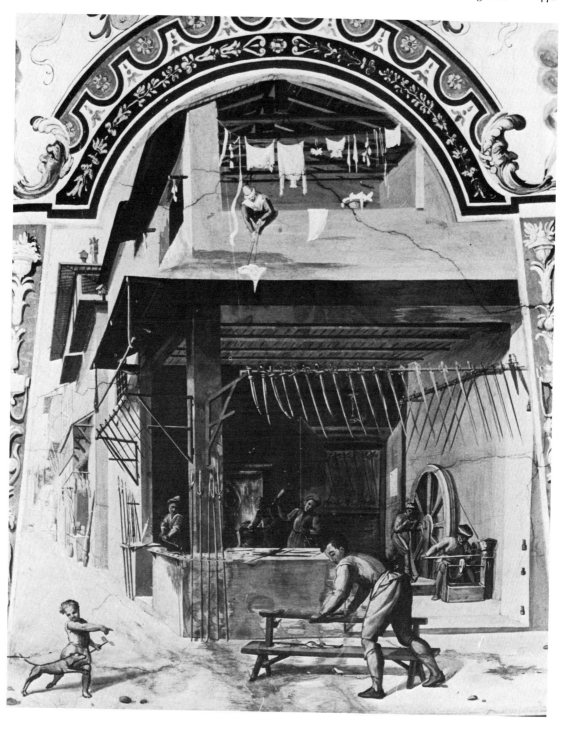

Engraving by Galle after Stradan. The workshop brought together workers of all ages, from children to the elderly. Far from fostering equality, however, it underscored and accentuated hierarchies of knowledge, age, and status. (Paris, Bibliothèque Nationale.)

Their terminology was borrowed from the family. Each compagnonnage was headed by a "mother." Members were obliged to support one another in conflicts with the masters who employed them and with compagnonnages representing other trades. The compagnonnages borrowed initiation procedures and secret oaths from rituals associated with friendship. Their purpose was to establish order in the crucial period of apprenticeship. The status of master craftsman was not strictly hereditary; frequently some hurdle had to be overcome. The compagnonnages also maintained discipline among skilled craftsmen who often had no hope of acquiring the status of master. Many journeymen traveled about the country in search of work, cut off from parents and family and unable to start families of their own. The more fortunate ones lived in their master's house and ate at his table; in return they were expected to submit to his paternal authority. Hence the compagnonnage was intended to be a family of a different kind, based on perfect equality among its members. In a memoir published in Lyons in 1572 that included "phrases from journeymen briefs in Lyon in 1539-40," journeymen printers wrote that in their trade, "above all the other Arts, the Masters and Journeymen are and should be only one body together, like a family and fraternity."[32]

A constant in the language of associations, whether religious or nonreligious, professional or nonprofessional, the reference to fraternity, confraternity, and brotherhood has survived to this day in union programs and party platforms. Men have long dreamed of rebuilding the world on the basis of universal brotherhood. This is merely the egalitarian version of the family terminology favored by these early voluntary associations. Such a choice could turn out to be tenuous and misleading, however, if the words masked competition within a hierarchy (as between masters and journeymen) or between individuals ("my dear colleague, yet still my friend") over the very purposes of the organization (such as problems of wages and clients) or access to positions within it. The compagnonnages reveal that unmarried journeymen, who possessed a strong sense of their dignity and skill, experienced a real need to establish a personal and professional identity for themselves. This need was particularly strong among the journeymen printers of Lyons: although their masters maintained that they were *levissime literis tinti*, barely tinged with letters, their ability to read and write led them to define themselves "as free men working voluntarily at an excellent and noble calling"—a definition in which every word is important.[33] Again, the compagnonnage aroused hopes that it could not fulfill.

The Masonic lodges, established two centuries later, are often seen as a new form of association, whose aim was to establish a civil society based on free choice and total absence of state control. The secrecy upon which the Masons insisted

Masonic Lodge in Paris, 1740. Initiation into the secrets of Freemasonry provided access to a society of equals, joined together by shared knowledge and common ideals. (Paris, Bibliothèque Nationale.)

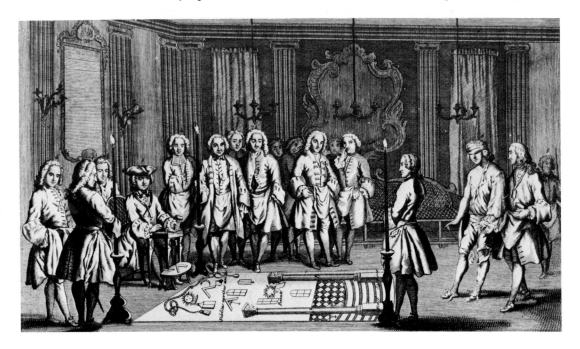

was that of private (that is, nonpublic) assemblies. Freemasonry rejected "a discipline based on age-old and unalterable solidarities: family, parish, corporation, order."[34] Lodges were based on the principle of social equality. Rank and promotion were to be determined by "true personal merit," a combination of virtue and talent. The Masonic lodges were an innovation but not a radical break with the past, for their only avowed goal was one of faith and morals and their only claims were universal. They were actually a locus of sensibility rather than an instrument of private interests. Hence even a government as nervous as the French monarchy did not see the Masons as an organized corps that had to be regulated or abolished. By contrast, the state much earlier felt a need to exert control over such institutions as the family, the village, and the guild or corporation. These posed a greater threat to it, because they were more fundamental and more fully integrated into society, whose reproduction they accomplished by purusing their own private and concrete goals.

As long as the Masonic lodges did not become political "academies," the state could regard them as neutral and leave them alone. Members included both unmarried men (soldiers and clergy) and married ones. Officeholders and merchants played a major role in establishing Masonry, which suggests that the lodges helped such men escape the confines of their local environment, meeting the needs of more mobile members of society whose work required them to move from place to place. But the lodges were not a substitute for the family, nor did they serve family interests. They existed outside the family and were indifferent to it. Masons were not required to renounce other commitments; the lodges operated on another level. A rather vague ideology served as a basis for moderate, limited social relations among individuals who had freely chosen one another. That ideology incorporated certain practices and obligations of friendship, but these were routinized, and the individual's newly won freedom was submerged in the harmony of egalitarian interpersonal relations. The "fraternal friendship" of lodge brothers was functional and enforced by statute. The organization's identity was bolstered more than that of its members, enabling it to evolve as they did without major conflict.

Freemasonry was not simply a byproduct of the Enlightenment but also a manifestation of a more long-term change in the nature of social relations, at least among males. (According to the terms of Ramsay's *Discourse* [1736-37] women

Introduction de l'Apprentif maçon dans le Temple de la Vertu.

Introduction of the Apprentice Mason into the Temple of Virtue. Along with the knowledge of Masonic secrets went new duties and a new code of conduct. (Paris, Bibliothèque Nationale.)

A London coffeehouse at the end of the 17th century. Coffee, a new drink, was drunk by men who wished to escape the low company of the taverns. (London, British Museum.)

were excluded from membership "for the sake of the purity of our maxims and mores.")[35] Men had begun to gather in regular assemblies, in some cases institutionalized. These groups shared common interests, whether scientific or intellectual, religious or secular, perhaps even political or merely a liking for "honest commerce" or plain conversation.

Renaissance princes like the Medicis and Farneses had led the way by hosting gatherings of humanists, artists, courtiers, and friends who were distinguished from the rest of the entourage because they were received on intimate terms by the prince. Louis XIV used invitations to Marly as a tool for controlling the nobles who crowded the court at Versailles. A new situation was created in the seventeenth and eighteenth centuries, however, by the proliferation of public meeting places such as taverns, coffeehouses, and chocolate houses.

The authorities became alarmed. The Church kept a watchful eye and increased the number of penitential confraternities, over which it exercised influence.[36] The state was prepared, as always, to offer support in exchange for submission to its control. Richelieu created the Académie française out of the circle of men of letters that in 1629 had begun to meet once a week at the home of Valentin Conrart. Napoleon acted in a much more discreet manner vis-à-vis the Société d'Arcueil that formed around Berthollet and Laplace.[37]

Richelieu's action combined two traditions. There was, first of all, a long tradition of royal control over "assemblies" and "corps," which the king exercised by asserting his right to issue letters patent authorizing such bodies. Colbert systematically pursued a policy of creating a culture that would contribute to the king's glory.[38] Second, there was a tradition of aristocratic patronage, a good example of which can be seen in the efforts of young Federico Cesi in the early seventeenth century to create the Academy of the Lincei in Rome: "Nepotism and diplomatic objectives counted more heavily in the recruitment of members than did strictly scientific criteria."[39] And municipal authorities in eighteenth-century Provence kept a wary eye on theater audiences.

Even more than Italy, England provided the model of free associations with its clubs, which date back as far as the fifteenth century (the Court de Bone Compagnie) and the sixteenth century (Friday Street or Bread Street, which was founded by Sir Walter Raleigh and met at the Mermaid Tavern). Over the next two centuries the number of clubs increased dramatically. Samuel Pepys and his friends went to Wood's in Pall Mall "for clubbing." During the Enlightenment the French imitated this English habit, but the experience of the Revolution compelled them after 1815 to create a substitute for the club known as the circle, a name chosen to underscore its nonpolitical nature. Rules for such meetings, quite simple, were quickly established. Members were all male. Club members decided who could and could not join on the basis of social and cultural criteria.

Clubs always met outside private homes; in this they were distinct from salons. Meetings originally were held in public places, usually a tavern or café. In the nineteenth century many clubs obtained their own premises, access to which was limited to members. Their purpose was simply to foster social relations in a very general sense. Some clubs favored discussion of political or literary subjects, but many more simply catered

"Establishment of the new philosophy. Our cradle was a café." Cafés imitated the décor of aristocratic salons, and the philosophes who congregated in them aped the dress and manners of the aristocracy, the better to change the world. (Paris, Bibliothèque Nationale.)

to the leisure-time tastes of the wealthy. Ignoring the family, the club established a new model of private relations, without secret rituals, initiations, or programs. Gone were all references to brotherhood and all commitments to mutual support. Members merely agreed to abide by a common code of conduct, which neither forbade nor required any preferential treatment of particular individuals. Conviviality was liberated from the constraints of friendship and family: "English life—that death of the heart—the life of clubs and circles," wrote Baudelaire.[40]

In one respect these new types of social relation bore the mark of their origin: they were almost exclusively masculine. Unlike the salons, the clubs were not simply microsocieties. Members deliberately sought isolation and segregation not

Masculine-Feminine

Reception of Women at the Lodge of the Mopses. In the mid-18th century people mocked the Masons for segregating men and women. Abbé G.-L. Calabre Pérau followed the fashion with his books *The Secret of the Freemasons* (1744), *The Freemasons Crushed* (1747), and *The Secret of the Mopses Revealed.* (Paris, Bibliothèque Nationale.)

only from the family but also from the mingling of sexes and ages that occurred in the ordinary course of life. Not only women but also children and adolescents were excluded from club membership. A young man's admission into the tavern marked his arrival at adulthood and acceptance of responsibility for his own decisions and livelihood. Women had been the spirit behind the first "circles." Saint-Simon tells us that Louis XIII missed the "majesty of the circles of his mother the queen" (II, 412). Under Louis XIV circles formed around the dauphine and later around the Duchess of Burgundy. Women continued to be the animating spirit behind this form of social life down to Madame Bonaparte.[41] But after that the very word was stolen from them by men. To be sure, women subsequently had their own lodges and clubs, but these were kept scrupulously separate from the men's groups. This systematic exclusion of women suggests another aspect of the club's significance.

There is no shortage of explanations for this state of affairs. For the sake of morality men had to be kept safe from temptation: this was the reason invoked by the Masons, whose membership at the time included a large proportion of un-married males and men traveling alone.[42] A strict division of labor and territory confined women to the home and denied them access to the "public" places in which men met. Women in any case enjoyed less liberty than men, for they were subject to the authority of father or husband. They also lacked skills, and those who worked were denied access to the trades or-ganized in the form of compagnonnages.

None of these arguments applies to women of the wealth-ier classes, who were served by numerous servants and who enjoyed comparative freedom of movement and even, in the eighteenth century at least, of morals. Mme de Saint-Simon was frequently invited to Marly without her captious husband, who never dreamed of complaining—quite the contrary. The fact that the exclusion of women was an object of derision confirms that it was indeed a basic principle and perceived as such. President de Maniban grasped this point when he wrote to Cardinal de Fleury from Toulouse on 18 April 1742: "on the eighth of this month an order was established at a supper attended by a few ladies and gentlemen of mature age, which was at first to be named the Order of Free Friendship but whose name was changed to the Gallant Knights . . . as a joke . . . directed at the Freemasons, whose secret is a mystery and who do not admit women."[43]

The primary danger obviously was the mingling of the sexes, not the establishment by women of an alternative set of institutions. It is clear that men wished to be alone with other men, at leisure as well as work. The sexes continued to be separated at work, but the growing number of leisure activities might have brought them together. Over a very long period this determination to keep the sexes apart was typical of the various youth associations (referred to as "kingdoms," "abbeys," and youth corps) that were formed as early as the twelfth or thirteenth century outside of, but patterned after, the Church. These appear to have been the earliest form of association, although some doubt remains in regard to Eng-land and Spain.[44] In other respects, however, the youth asso-ciations were quite different from adult clubs: age of membership, freedom of entry, duration of participation, and geographical range of recruitment. They were "temporary" but obligatory associations of the youths of a village or neighborhood.[45] They remained exclusively male; girls were called upon only for those activities that required their presence, and their participation was always of secondary concern.

Traditionally youth associations were active in four areas. They monitored morals, and especially marriages. For this, they relied primarily on charivaris, or noisy mock serenades, to deride adulterers of both sexes, battered husbands and wives, and widows and widowers who remarried persons younger than themselves. Second, they acted as a kind of militia. In the eighteenth century a well-armed royal militia made the youth abbey's military function superfluous, though it remained a colorful part of local folklore.[46] In seventeenth-century Brabant, however, constantly traversed by troops of every stripe, youth militias frequently battled one another yet paraded side by side on Saint Michael's Day. When a group of drunken soldiers aimed their muskets at the bourgeois of Nivelles in October 1695, townspeople called upon the youth brigade, which arrested two of the offenders.[47] None of this is surprising, given the large number of "young" men in the population, almost as many as there were able-bodied heads of household. Well-organized and disciplined, they were more accustomed to fighting than their elders and always ready to cross swords.

The third function of the youth abbeys was to organize festivals, which in the eighteenth century became more common as they became increasingly secularized. But the fourth function, that of exercising political opposition through derision in carnivals and other ritual forms of social inversion, was subject to increasingly strict surveillance after the sixteenth century. The youth abbey acted as the voice and the right arm of the entire community.[48] It had all the appearances, if not the powers, of an institution.

Because the youth abbey was actually an organized age cohort, it played a key part in shaping the personalities of its members. It disciplined young men during the period between puberty and marriage (or emigration). For men marriage was delayed even longer than it was for women, and the period of "youth" could last a good ten years—from age fifteen to twenty-five. Thus the youth organization assumed responsibility for the years after a boy had ceased to be fully a part of his family but before he was reintegrated into adult society as the head of a household. Here, in other words, we have a severance of ties followed by a reintegration: the two classic phases of the rite of passage.[49] In the interim the youth group was a haven recognized by peers and accepted or tolerated by adults.

The function of the youth group was shaped by contemporary educational practices. Boys and girls were raised together by women until they reached the age of nine or ten. Boys then passed into the hands of men, either their fathers or other adults to whom authority over them was delegated. Meanwhile, at home or in another household, girls continued to learn domestic chores and responsibilities. The two sexes were most separate during this period, which lasted from age ten to twenty or twenty-five.

In addition to activities assigned or tolerated by the community, the youth abbey intervened in two kinds of conflicts. Young men, deprived of power, wives, and property, often found themselves in conflict with their fathers, who were everywhere masters (and, in those parts of France governed by written law, absolute masters) over their sons. The father decided when a boy was ready to marry, what the material conditions of his marriage would be, and who his partner would be. In view of the functions assigned to the youth abbey, it seems that fathers preferred to allow youths to participate in the life of the community rather than relinquish power in this area. In addition to conflict between fathers and sons there was conflict between families, in which youths could potentially act as mediators. Literature from *Romeo and Juliet* to Roger Martin du Gard's twentieth-century novel *Les Thibault* has depicted such mediation exercised by a pair of young people (through love or friendship).

Last but not least, youth abbeys were at least tacitly assigned the crucial role of teaching young men how to behave sexually in accordance with the "well-defined and institutionalized masculine status" assigned them by society.[50] Emphasis was therefore placed on the difference between males and females and occasionally on aggressiveness toward women. Individuals could of course be as aggressive toward women as groups: in his fifteenth year Valentin Jamerey-Duval told his successive masters—farmers, shepherds, millers, and others—that he would obey them but not their wives, but his protestations were of no avail and he was regularly obliged to leave his employment: "Without knowing [the other sex] I had imagined that a defensive league of men would protect me from its attacks."[51]

When hostility toward women was expressed by a group rather than an individual, its range was wider and its attacks

Jean-Baptiste Chardin, *The Toiling Mother*. (Paris, Louvre.)

"The husband holds the distaff." Throughout the early modern period, reversal of male and female roles provided the theme for innumerable engravings. (Paris, Carnavalet Museum.)

La femme a le mousquet la quenoüil l'Epoux
Et berce pour surcrois l'enfant sur ses jenoux.

were more effective. Individuals who might hesitate to be so bold on their own were obliged to conform by group pressure. The choice of victims in charivaris is revealing of the group's underlying intentions. Why attack the widow or widower who remarried a younger single person, given the fact that for most young people marrying a rich widow was a coveted means of rising socially? This was especially true of journeyman artisans, who could aspire to marry the widow of a master craftsman. Why the indiscriminate attack on adultery, when male adultery affected young males only if committed with a single woman and when female adultery could be to their advantage? Why single out couples in which wives beat their husbands? It is quite plausible of course that there should have been a wish to punish any attempt by women to "wear the pants" in the family.[52] Yet male submissiveness was also denounced, as was masochistic pleasure in being beaten. Engravings showing men with their breeches lowered being flogged by their wives are all too reminiscent of Jean-Jacques's spanking at the hands of Mlle Lambercier: "After the spanking I found the trial less terrible than the anticipation had been, and what is even more bizarre is that this punishment made me feel even more affection than before for the woman who had administered it . . . For I had found mingled with the pain, and even the shame, a sensual pleasure that had left me feeling more desire than fear to feel it administered again at once by the same hand . . . Mlle Lambercier, no doubt having detected some sign that the punishment was not achieving its desired end, declared that she would not go on . . . Until then we had slept in her bedroom . . . Two days later we were made to sleep in another room, and from then on I enjoyed the honor, which I willingly would have done without, of being treated as a grown youth. Who would have thought that this punishment, received by a child of eight from a woman of thirty, would have determined my tastes, my desires, my passions, and my self for the rest of my life?"[53]

Jamerey-Duval and Rousseau were both exceptional individuals who insisted upon their unique status as "social bastards."[54] They taught the eighteenth century to say out loud (or rather, to write—which is at once more and less) what had previously gone unsaid. And the unspeakable was particularly so for groups that were by definition conservative. The youth abbey naturally dispersed when its members married, and we

"'Down with your breeches, you deserve a whipping' . . . 'That's enough, my backside is all bloody.'" The woman who beats her husband is the ultimate target of derision. But the engravings often suggest that the male victims feel a curious mixture of pleasure and pain and that they accept a status which is really that of a child more than a woman. (Paris, Bibliothèque Nationale.)

do not know whether the youthful bonds that it created proved durable. The organization and hierarchy of the abbey, the discontinuous nature and occasional brutality of its activities, were hardly conducive to the development of intimate, emotional relations between two or more individuals. The abbey in fact functioned as an instrument of socialization, and as such it was challenged by adults and reduced to a marginal position.

The authorities, who equipped themselves with police forces of their own, no longer required the assistance of youth associations. The government, from Louis XIV's militia to the introduction of mass conscription, asserted the right to call upon young men for military service and imposed its own recruitment procedures, organization, and discipline, though not without resistance from young men and their families. Municipal and ecclesiastical authorities increasingly frowned upon charivaris and "other masquerades," which were denounced as "disorders." At best only festivals escaped the ban on youth group activities.

New groups, drawn from the ranks of a trade, a social class, or a neighborhood, imitated certain aspects of the youth abbeys but began to accept married members. At a deeper level, the youth groups lost their educational and socializing role as they were replaced by new institutions whose avowed objective was to instill discipline. These included, in order of emergence, apprenticeship, preparatory school, and the army. Adults assumed control over the education of children and adolescents, limiting what autonomy and spontaneity had been left to the young. The new discipline was not only powerful and coercive but technically sophisticated and effective. As a result, the nature and purpose of friendship was profoundly altered.

Adolescence

Philippe Ariès, responding to Natalie Davis' critique of his view that the notion of adolescence was a creation of the eighteenth century, called attention to the change in "education, that is, in the transmission of knowledge and values," that had been brought about since the Middle Ages by the system of apprenticeship, whose spread "tended . . . to destroy . . . the system of age cohorts" and "obliged children to live among adults, who conveyed to them both know-how and manners."[55] And Alan MacFarlane has explained what he believes to be a feeble sense of family continuity and weak emotional bonds between parents and children at all levels of society in medieval and early modern England as the result of "fostering out" young children to families other than their own as servants, farmhands, apprentices, pupils, or pages.[56]

In both France and England, however, education continued at home. The father's authority was strengthened at the expense of ties between members of the same generation, though not enough to prevent young boys from forming bonds with other boys of the same age. The fact that boys often found themselves among others in similar situations, far from their own families, encouraged this. Jean-Jacques's friendship with his cousin Bernard ("who did not take undue advantage of the fondness that people in the house felt for him as the son of my tutor") dates from the time that both were boarders in the home of the Lamberciers: "In no time at all I felt more affectionate toward him than toward my own brother, and that affection has never disappeared."[57]

School created an even deeper rift between the child and his or her family. Over the past thirty years the history of education in the early modern period has been thoroughly studied, from its inception in response to a strong demand on the part of families to its development in a climate of intense competition among cities, states, religions, and lay and religious orders.[58] Research has shed much light on the geographical distribution of educational institutions, the recruitment of students, the organization of schools, and the development of a variety of specialized educational institutions. Here I am mainly interested in the new discipline of children and adolescents. Children were sent to schools that offered courses roughly corresponding to our secondary-school curriculum, including logic and physics. They were divided into classes as the needs of the curriculum dictated and subjected to unremitting discipline, day and night. The discipline of boarding students set the model for the discipline imposed on day students. The curriculum emphasized modernity of content, efficiency of method, and quality of the final result in every sense—religious and moral as well as intellectual. Graduates were equipped to make their way in the world, to obtain (and perform well in) positions that their families desired for them and to which they enjoyed access owing to rank, wealth, connections, or simple good fortune.

As one might expect, the reality was a long way from the theory, especially in the less prestigious schools. Only the best institutions offered quality courses in all subjects. Until

Engraving by Engelbrecht. Adolescence was a long period of waiting, not fully justified by the time required to learn a trade, that ended with the death of the father. In the meantime the young man could only play at being an adult and ape adult occupations and games. (Paris, Bibliothèque Nationale.)

the eighteenth century there was a fairly wide disparity of ages within each class, and despite the discipline there was much violence in the schools, ranging from daily brawls to outright rebellion requiring the intervention of troops. This situation persisted longer in England than in France.[59]

The very ambition of the school was contradictory and a source of great tension. On the one hand, formal education institutionalized the notion of a homogeneous age cohort, thus emphasizing age rather than family ties or even social rank as a unifying principle. The cohort became a more cohesive group than it ever was in ordinary life. In this respect schooling was like knighthood, but on a much broader scale involving a wider spectrum of social groups and affecting men whose later careers were far more diverse. On the other hand, the school sought to destroy solidarity among its students through competition, constant surveillance, encouragement of tattling, and corporal punishment administered by the students themselves. The aim was to eliminate all horizontal ties, leaving only one vertical tie between student and master.

The *collège* of La Flèche, a model boarding school of the first half of the 17th century. The school was patterned after the model of the aristocratic monastery. (Paris, Bibliothèque Nationale.)

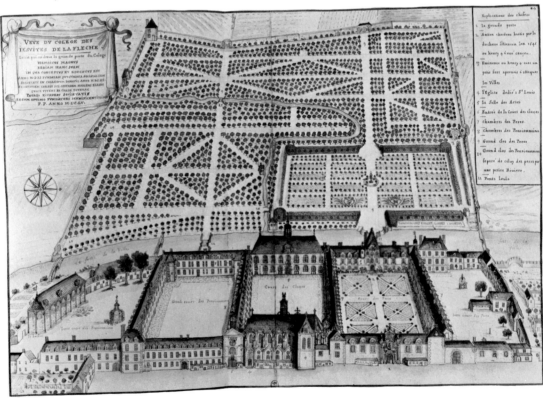

In the 17th century the wealthiest students had rooms of their own and servants. In this dormitory at the Collège de Navarre, the precursor of that of the Ecole Polytechnique, the rows of cells kept students isolated and facilitated round-the-clock surveillance. (Paris, Bibliothèque Nationale.)

As always, students' families took a middle-of-the-road position, anxious in the short run, self-interested in the long. They supported scholastic discipline, which they felt guaranteed the profitability of their substantial investment in education. They also expected the child's education to reap long-run benefits, which depended on the formation of lasting ties to other students. At school French children made what P. Coustel in 1687 called "advantageous acquaintances and friendships that often lasted until the end of their lives."[60] The sentiments of Italian parents were similar, although with an indifference to the location of the child's future career that is to be expected in a politically fragmented country. In a letter dated 7 October 1705 to his son Marco Antonio, a student in Parma, Vincenzo Ferdinando Ranuzzi Cospi, a Bolognese senator, writes: "Keep in mind that if you make friends at school with others who will graduate along with you, and if God grants you the long life that I desire for you . . . [your fellow graduates will become] prelates, cardinals, ambassadors, and generals, men of such importance that, thanks to your friendship with them, they will be in a position to make the fortune of the house into which God has caused you to be born."[61]

The compromise struck between the rebelliousness of the young and the obedience to schoolmasters advocated by parents (who had swallowed the advertising claims of school officials) tended to promote close relations among classmates, which did not end with adolescence but continued, even with-

The French monarchy set up specialized schools to train military officers, taking over educational responsibility from the students' families. Future officers were taught to march and obey orders in much the same manner as the soldiers they would one day be called upon to command. (Paris, Bibliothèque Nationale.)

out institutional support, to influence careers in later life. This became even more pronounced as religious and secular schools were established that offered specialized training beyond the secondary level: seminaries and novitiates, after the end of the sixteenth century; naval colleges and companies of cadets, after the end of the seventeenth century; and military schools after the middle of the eighteenth century. The Ecole militaire of Paris, patterned after the academies of Saint Petersburg and Berlin, was founded in 1751; it followed the School of Engineers of Mézières, which was established in 1748, and preceded the School of Artillery of La Fère, founded in 1756. Combining academic and technical training with a discipline designed to make youths from different backgrounds conform to a common mold, the military academies were the first of a series of highly selective institutions whose purpose was to train state functionaries.

Up to this point only an elite was affected. Even among the wealthy, many people still favored traditional methods such as education by tutors or on-the-job training. Statistics show that in 1627–1629 there were 40,000 students in Jesuit secondary schools in France and that in 1789 there were some 48,000 students in secondary schools of all kinds. But figures can be misleading. Like English universities in the early seventeenth century, the schools accepted students of two sorts: elder sons and younger sons.[62] The former often completed only a part of the curriculum and were content to receive a general education in the liberal arts. Barring misfortune, their positions were assured, for as elder sons they would in due course assume leadership of their families. Younger sons, however, had to make their own way in the church, the army, or the government, in France, and in England, in trade or liberal professions as well. Many remained bachelors and pursued careers that permitted them to maintain their friendships with those they had met at school. With luck they might benefit from contacts with both elder and younger sons of families wealthier than their own.

The very discipline of the school created a climate favorable to strong and passionate friendships. By isolating adolescents from the rest of society, it made adolescence the age of friendship. The nature and vocabulary of friendship may have remained the same as before (it is difficult to be certain), but its social, spatial, and temporal environment changed profoundly. Friendship, or at any rate its origin, was isolated from the family. It could be disinterested, but it could also mask attractions that schoolmasters found disturbing. It might endure beyond the school years, though this was by no means assured. Chronologically prior to love, friendship was the child's first discovery of the "other." Hence it played a central role in the definition of identity.

Still another novelty was the education of the daughters of the elite in convent schools and by sisters of the new teaching orders such as the Ursulines, Visitandines, and Sisters of Saint-Louis and Saint-Cyr, which were established in the sixteenth and seventeenth centuries. For the first time the sexes shared similar experiences. We read, for example, that "the Countess de La Marck, . . . daughter of the Duke de Rohan, was a close friend of Mme de Saint-Simon and her sister Mme de Lauzun, her former companions in the convent." When the former died in 1706, a good dozen years after the three had left the convent, the tears of the two sisters did not please the king, "who knew little of the laws of nature and the movements of the heart." Saint-Simon, for his part, was "deeply touched" by his wife's bitter tears (II, 554-555).

All these changes had just begun, and the nineteenth century would prove to have much more to say on the subject of school and convent friendships than did the eighteenth. Yet we can already see that things are moving toward a broadening of the social horizons. Through friendship, whether freely contracted as in the case of Montaigne and La Boétie or sought for mutual interest as in the case of Saint-Simon and his friends at court, the adult asserted his independence from the family and from the superficial relations of ordinary social intercourse. As for the latter, the same adult males attempted to organize, codify, and institutionalize it, to make it comfortable and peaceful, in England in the seventeenth and in France in the eighteenth century. In others words, they tried to create a setting outside the home where they could be themselves on a footing of equality with others.

Family networks did not disappear. For the majority of the population, especially in the country, they remained a necessity. Spiritual kinship was on the decline, however. The family's main support now came not from other families but

Saint-Cyr. Like their brothers at the military school, the poor girls of good family who were admitted to Saint-Cyr learned skills that would equip them for the duties of adulthood. One had to know how things were done in order to see to it that they were done properly by others. (Paris, Carnavalet Museum.)

from the state, which in exchange for protection obliged the family to withdraw into itself and to sever some of the many ties that surrounded it. The interval between childhood and adulthood became the age of friendship, a time of protracted adolescence, of anticipation and learning, of choice and personal commitment. Some adolescent friendships endured in later life. It was up to individuals to decide.

In character, morals, and style of life, no two men could have been more dissimilar than Boswell and the Reverend William Johnson Temple. But having met at the University of Edinburgh, they continued to write and confide in one another for thirty years. Boswell named Temple as his executor, and, on 24 June 1767, Temple wrote: "Your friendship is, I believe, the only happiness in my life. For the members of my family are in truth my worst enemies: a cruel father, a wretched brother . . . O Boswell! Believe me, I love you as myself, and when I die I shall thank God above all else for having given me your friendship."[63]

Michel-François Dandré Bardon, *The Hearth*. The narrow window provides less light than the fire in the hearth. The furniture is rudimentary. This composition, with two young women and six young children, is more a genre painting of filth and disorder than a portrayal of a family group. (Marseilles, Museum of Fine Arts.)

✑ Families: Habitations and Cohabitations

Alain Collomp

A LBRECHT Dürer left a number of drawings and watercolors of houses in rural villages and urban neighborhoods in Germany, Austria, and Italy in the late fifteenth or early sixteenth century. They are precious not only for their artistic qualities but also for the acuity of Dürer's observation, whether of houses, trees, rabbits, or fading peonies. The drawings give an accurate idea of the building materials used at the time. Bricks were sometimes left exposed, sometimes covered with a protective coating, as in the beautiful half-timbered houses with sloping tiled roofs of Nuremberg's Saint John's quarter.[1] Houses in the village of Kalchreut were large and well spaced, with immense thatched roofs, and tucked away in a vale in the shade of hundred-year-old trees.[2] In Italy's fortified town of Arco stone houses with slightly sloping tile roofs were packed tightly inside the ramparts.[3] This last watercolor suggests the northern artist's amazement at the bluish leaves of the olive trees and the novel light of the southern countryside. Dürer sometimes reused his sketches of houses in engravings such as the *Prodigal Son*. The biblical scene serves as a pretext for showing a German farmyard surrounded by buildings with a few windows or small openings for light and low doorways but all topped by immense thatched roofs.

Representations: From the House to the Domestic Interior

In shape, size, and construction material, sixteenth-century houses in the Nuremberg region closely resemble houses built in German and Alsatian villages two or three centuries

Albrecht Dürer, *The Prodigal Son*, ca. 1498. This engraving of the biblical scene shows a south German town of the early 16th century, with its church, high thatched roofs, cob or brick walls, and tiny windows. (Paris, Bibliothèque Nationale.)

later. And the Italian houses sketched by Dürer on his first trip to Venice share many of the characteristic features of eighteenth-century southern French and Italian construction. Thus the main types of regional domestic dwellings (which are today being catalogued in Italy, France,[4] and England on the basis of surviving examples, many of relatively recent construction) are well-represented in early-sixteenth-century German and Flemish painting. Construction techniques endure for centuries, and, despite the changes and improvements that occurred between 1500 and 1800, residential housing exhibits fairly stable regional characteristics of a cultural as well as material order. Unfortunately, Dürer's drawings permit no access to the interiors of homes whose exteriors he so carefully observed.

Brueghel and the Flemish Farm

Somewhat later than Dürer, Pieter Brueghel the Elder painted detailed portraits of Flemish villages showing buildings with wood-framed cob walls and high thatched roofs. A few large houses were all brick, with a gable atop a staircase on the facade. Brueghel occasionally allows us to penetrate into the interior of the house. The *Farm Visit* is known to us from two copies of what was probably a pencil-sketch original, one (a polychrome on wood) by Pieter Brueghel the Younger, the other by Jan Brueghel.[5] The copies by the two sons, quite similar, depict a large room inside a farmhouse. We see the contents of a late-sixteenth-century peasant's home: a large bench cum storage chest with back and arm rests, a child's low chair and armchair, a cradle in the foreground with a dog asleep in it, a round table covered with a white tablecloth (the same white tablecloth found in peasant interiors by the brothers Le Nain) upon which are bowls filled with some kind of cream soup (the farm clearly has cows, because a man and a woman in the background are churning butter). The most surprising feature is the central hearth, at floor level, above which a huge cauldron hangs suspended from an enormous pothook. The father, as master of the house, receives three visitors. In the background, behind what seems to be a nuclear family—a couple and three children—we can make out five other persons, who appear to be part of the household. A man seated on the bench, another drinking soup at the table, a young man and woman churning butter, and, not obviously coming or going, a young woman in the doorway, with a wooden door topped by a transom of leaded glass.

Jan Brueghel the Elder, *Farm Visit*. Three bourgeois visit a Flemish peasant home in the late 16th century. The table is set for the seven people of the household. In the foreground are the three children, the youngest in the arms of the mother, who warms herself from the central hearth, above which hangs an enormous cauldron. (Vienna, Kunsthistorisches Museum.)

We are inside a Flemish farmhouse at mealtime. The adults are absorbed in their occupations with the exception of the eldest, who, like the bare-legged eldest child, is facing two of the visitors. We have no idea of the relation among the various figures in the painting. Are they related? The picture probably was painted not as an inventory of a peasant interior but as an allegory illustrating for moralistic purposes some proverb or scene from the Bible, as was common in sixteenth-century Flemish painting. The visitors, to judge from their dress, are wealthy bourgeois. Are they paying a call on a woman about to give birth, or, as some critics have suggested, have they perhaps come to see the eldest child, who seems to be conversing with the lady in the foreground and who may be her son or a young relative put out to nurse in this peasant home?

Genre paintings were in great demand by Flemish art buyers in the sixteenth and seventeenth centuries, and in them the documentary interest is usually secondary. Behind the depiction of routine bourgeois or peasant life in Vermeer's interiors or Brueghel's *Farm Visit* usually lay a gnomic significance of some sort, expressed in a sort of code understood by all who studied art. Commonplace objects are present for precise symbolic reasons; the same was true of contemporary still lifes, often "vanity paintings." It would be a mistake to ascribe too much documentary significance to such objects and to consider these representations of peasant and bourgeois interiors as authentic snapshots of the daily life of Flemish merchants and peasants.

The Le Nain brothers' paintings of seventeenth-century French peasant interiors lend themselves to similar errors of interpretation. The celebrated *Peasant Meal* (1642) and *Peasant Family*, both in the Louvre, are not accurate portraits of family groups.[6] The Le Nains were too great as painters and too shrewd as salesmen to have painted mere sociological documents. The *Peasant Family*, which depicts a thin old woman with a wry smile and men in the prime of life together with a younger man and several grave children playing the violin and the flageolet, evokes the theme of the ages of life, a favorite of Italian painters from Titian to the imitators of Caravaggio, rather than a family group.

Peasant Interiors by the Le Nain Brothers

Neither painting reveals much about the order of the meal. The Le Nains avoided overloading their canvases with relatively trivial culinary detail, preferring a more open composition with an air of timeless irreality contributing to the symbolic meaning of the work. In the *Peasant Meal* we see a tablecloth but not a set table. The cloth is too large for the bench over which it has been thrown, and the table contains only a wine pitcher, a loaf of bread, and a knife that has begun to cut the loaf. The other painting contains only a tin bowl on a plate and a single spoon.

The setting of the Le Nains's peasant interiors is always the same: the ceiling is peculiarly high, the fireplace huge. The room seems vast, more like a stage setting than an accurate portrayal of a poor peasant's smoky cottage. There is little furniture: one or two benches, a few chairs and stools. The bed or beds, which in peasant homes were always located in the *salle* (hall, or living-dining room), seldom appear, although the canopy of a bed with velvet curtains can be seen in one corner of the *Peasant Meal*.

Flemish and Dutch interior paintings from the same period provide more accurate depictions of household furnishings and architecture. Pieter de Hooch shows us urban interiors and even suites of apartments. The northern light, admitted through high windows, is reflected by gleaming checkerboard floors and brings out the furniture's high polish. An alcove is hidden in a dark corner of the room. Luxury, order, calm, and a certain feeling for comfort and convenience are evident. Other Flemish painters such as Adriaen Brouwer and David Teniers inclined toward the popular and picturesque. Their interiors are dirty and disorderly, with nothing but a half-barrel for a table and a stump for a seat.

Brouwer's hastily painted genre scenes, Dürer's travel sketches, Brueghel's illustrated proverbs, and the tranquil compositions of the Le Nains recorded an instant of time for all eternity. Fascinating as such works are to the historian, they do not help us discover how Flemish and German farmers

Le Nain brothers, *Peasant Meal*, 1642. The Le Nains painted several groups of peasants at the dinner table. Here the woman is standing and the men are seated, sharing, almost symbolically, bread and wine. (Paris, Louvre.)

or Laonnois peasants lived in the sixteenth and seventeenth centuries. We must turn to other sources, primarily written documents.

WAYS OF LIVING

How many persons lived in the low houses built of wood, cob, and thatch in the villages of Auge and Sologne? How many occupied the large, half-timbered houses with gallery and interior courtyard found in the Alsatian plain? And how many inhabited the tall, narrow stone houses tightly packed together in the villages of Provence? Ideally we would like to know not only how many people lived together but what relations existed among them. Was the structure of the peasant family always the same? Did nuclear families live alone, or did several families share a single house presided over by a patriarch? We would like to know how these family systems functioned. How were they affected by laws and economic conditions? The size and structure of households must have been influenced by variations in what Jean Yver has called "the geography of customs," regional variations in the laws of inheritance.[7]

Pieter Elinga Janssens, *The Sweeper* (detail). A servant, whose face can be seen reflected in the mirror, sweeps the gleaming marble tiles of this well-to-do Flemish house. (Paris, Louvre.)

Pieter de Hooch, *Woman Picking Lice*. This Flemish interior is simpler. The floor is of terra-cotta tile. A mother picks lice from her daughter's head in front of a bed entirely enclosed by curtains. De Hooch used this same interior in other kinds of scenes. (Amsterdam, Rijksmuseum.)

A peasant house was not simply a building inhabited by a family. Usually it also sheltered the family's livestock, its reserves of food, its unsold harvest, and its farm implements. The *domus* of southern France,[8] the *ousta* or *ostal* of northern France, the *Hof* of Alsace and Germany were factories as well as residences, identified by a patronymic or, in Alsace, a family insignia. The words *domus, ousta,* and *Hof* referred not only to buildings but also to lands, to the whole of the property owned by a family, as distinct from the common lands and possessions shared by all the inhabitants of the village: passageways, common pasture, and even, in Provence and Languedoc where the available space was quite limited, common threshing grounds.

A Changing Habitat

What a family owned was not immutable. The uses to which different buildings and lands were put changed over the generations in response to changing needs. In the seventeenth century just as today, a part of the barn might be fixed up as an extra bedroom. Or a house might be divided in two to be shared by parents and children or by two brothers. New homes were constructed around an existing courtyard to house retired parents or to provide space for a newly married son and his family. In 1788 the Jargots, laborers in the village of Courcelles (Burgundy), shared their house with their eldest son after his marriage. The marriage contract specified that "a newly constructed house" would be provided for their second son, Jean. And for their youngest boy, Simon, the parents reserved "a small space for building a hayloft adjoining another area located in the aforesaid Courcelles and provided him in dower, on which he may build a house."[9] Thus the parents' house was joined by two new dwellings, and the three younger Jargots evidently planned to live as close neighbors.

Similarly, at Azereix, a village in the Pyrenees in which large houses were built inside walled family compounds, Anne Zinck has noted that the number of hearths increased from 116 in 1636 to 171 in 1792, although the amount of developed space in the village did not increase: "Sons, brothers, and sons-in-law built new houses within the existing family compounds."[10]

Villages in France and Germany were constantly changing as old houses were abandoned and new ones were built. There were several reasons for this. Economic and demographic factors were important. The wars of the early seventeenth

century had a major impact on housing in Lorraine, but so did meteorological conditions. Less obvious factors were also at work. Practices pertaining to the division of family property upon inheritance and to the establishment of children at marriage played a crucial role. The availability of resources dictated the choice of building materials. The social composition of the village influenced the nature of the houses built there, for relatively wealthy plowmen and merchants lived differently from ordinary farm laborers.

Before going to Italy, a very young Dürer painted several watercolors of his native Nuremberg. The houses of the Saint John's quarter are minutely detailed, with their tiled roofs and half-timbered walls. (Bremen, Kunsthalle.)

The Homes of the Poor

In the seventeenth century and even less in the eighteenth century, not all peasant houses were smoky cottages with walls of dried mud mixed with straw or heather and roofs of rye straw or reeds or other local vegetation. Such crude cottages were poorly insulated and vulnerable to the elements. "These cob-wall buildings had to be repaired annually. A new cottage required repairs the year after it was built."[11] Fire could destroy them in a matter of hours. They were small dwellings with only one room fit for human habitation and small openings for light. Toward the end of Louis XIV's reign the prior of the village of Sennely (Sologne) remarked on the discomforts of his parishioners' homes. They "do not like high ceilings," he said. "They like to touch the beams with their heads." As for light, "they ought to have large windows for ventilation, but instead their houses are dark, more suitable as dungeons for criminals than as homes for free men."[12]

Single-room dwellings were fit to house only small families: a husband and wife (or a widow) together with their younger children. Older children had to rent space in the homes of wealthier neighbors or move elsewhere to earn their livings. Such small huts simply could not accommodate more than two generations or large numbers of children. Apart from

Hans Van Dalem, *Farmyard with Beggars*. This farmyard contains a house and several barns. (Paris, Louvre.)

lack of space, small cottages implied small means. Common between 1500 and 1800 in many parts of Europe, their number increased in the wake of war, pillage, and famine. Wretched huts coexisted with much more spacious homes, reflecting the inequalities of rural society. In some localities the huts of the poor were scattered about here and there, while in others they were concentrated in a particular location. In eighteenth-century Auvergne there were "slums" of laborers' huts ranged in long lines, each with a door and small window and access to the loft in the rear.[13] In late-eighteenth-century Corsica, "certain peasants have no place to live except for a single-room hut with drystone walls."[14]

Archaeological research in Brucato, Sicily, has shown that *bracciante*, poor agricultural laborers, lived with their families in single-room huts from the fourteenth to the nineteenth century, as did the vast majority of Sicilian villagers. Auvergne slum dwellings consisted of a single room divided into two parts. People and possibly animals slept in the darker portion, farthest from the street. The other portion contained the hearth and kitchen area. Both archaeological and documentary evidence suggest that the space in front of each house was also appropriated for domestic activities.[15]

At still lower levels of poverty in sixteenth- and seventeenth-century England and France, particularly western France, housing was even worse. In 1649 the people of Saint-Christophe-en-Roc in Poitou outlined their wretched living conditions in an affidavit to the Estates General: "There are only about ninety hearths, and most are begging and scraping for their bread . . . Nowadays one sees nothing but crowds of paupers . . . and all sleep on straw and have been forced to build small huts in the fields for want of other lodging."[16] Cabins at the forest's edge, huts in the fields, dilapidated hovels on village outskirts—these were not suitable dwellings for stable family groups. Of course the residents of Saint-Christophe drafted their petition in troubled times: the Fronde was then agitating all of France. But, to judge from surviving tax records, even in calmer periods beggars were a common sight in many regions as late as the end of the eighteenth century. Crippled husbands shared shabby huts with sickly wives, and blind fathers lived with working sons, depending in part on local charities to see them through. When famine threatened, many fled, either alone or in groups, with or without their families, to other parts of the country and especially to the cities, where they were imprisoned.

Higher up the social scale we find farmers in Ile-de-France, Flanders, and Lorraine, peasant landowners in Languedoc and Provence, rural master craftsmen, and vine-growers in Burgundy and the Loire Valley. Their homes were more spacious than those of laborers, with more than one room for habitation plus outbuildings such as barns, stables, and storage sheds.

The Homes of the Wealthy

In the villages and towns of eastern France as well as in some parts of southern France where houses are entered directly from the street one finds richly decorated doorways with coats of arms, owners' initials, mottoes, and pious images.

In Villejuif, not far from Paris, the contents of a farmer's house were inventoried in 1647. The house consisted of "a lower kitchen on the street, adjacent to a staircase, with a wagon entrance on the other side, two large bedrooms above, and a small bedroom with an attic above it, and another lower hall at the end of the kitchen."[17] In other words, this was a two-story house with attic, made of stone as was common in Ile-de-France, with a tile roof covering both the house and its dependencies connoting a certain level of wealth, thatched roofs being far more common than tile in most northern French villages in the seventeenth century.

Broadly speaking, houses were constructed of earth and wood in the northern countries (northern France, Flanders, England, Germany) and of stone in the south (southern France, Spain, Italy). But this general statement needs to be qualified. Granite was used in Brittany and Cornwall, limestone in Burgundy, and quarry stone in Ile-de-France. The choice of materials was dictated by their availability, and stone was not always preferred to earth and wood. Not all stone houses were opulent, as the stone huts of Corsica and Sicily indicate. Conversely, the cob-and-wood construction found in Kochersberg (Alsace) as well as in certain Norman manors was used to build spacious and even sumptuous homes that accommodated the substantial households of wealthy farmers and nobles.

How did farmers and rural artisans live? Guy Cabourdin has studied three farmhouses in the village of Anthelupt near Lunéville. In the villages of Lorraine houses were built close together along both sides of the main street. All three peasant houses in question had two wings; ordinary laborers' houses had only one. One roof covered not only space for human habitation but also storage area and barn. In the mid-eighteenth century these three peasant families had two inhabitable rooms: "In front, next to the street, was a room referred to as the *belle chambre* or *grande chambre* or *poêle* [stove], and in

Anonymous, *A Farm in Autumn* (detail), 18th century. This prosperous farm includes several buildings, one of which contains two stories. The walls are carefully built and the roofs are covered with tile. (Rheims, Saint-Denis Museum.)

This sketch, from Barthélemy Faujas de Saint-Fond, *Study of the Extinct Volcanoes of the Vivarais and Velay* (Paris, 1778), shows a group of peasant houses in central France, a so-called *barriade*, often a hamlet of several houses occupied by related families. (Paris, Bibliothèque Nationale.)

In eastern France, Germany, and Switzerland, where winters are cold, stoves of glazed tile (*Stübe*) provided warmth and gave their name to the room in which they were placed. (Paris, Bibliothèque Nationale.)

back, the kitchen."[18] The French *poêle* was the equivalent of the German *Stüb*, used in Alsace and other German-speaking regions. Montaigne, in his *Journal de voyage en Italie* (1580), expressed amazement at the heating systems he encountered in Lorraine, Alsace, Germany, and the Swiss cantons, a system well adapted to the harsh winters in these regions: "Is there anything more perfect than their stoves, which are made of pottery?" The system was indeed ingenious: the stove was placed between the two rooms, it heated both and could also be used for cooking. This allowed full use to be made of both rooms, whereas in other regions the only fireplace was located in the hall, and in winter people tended to crowd into that room to sleep.

Beds in the three farmhouses at Anthelupt were located in both the *belle chambre* and the kitchen, sometimes in alcoves. In Alsace twin beds were placed in a large alcove, almost a separate room carved out of the vast *Stüb*, in which the master of the house and his wife slept. Elsewhere beds were usually placed in dark corners of the room, seldom in the middle. Between 1500 and 1800 the bed, like other furniture, evolved considerably. The first beds, called *châlits*, were quite rudimentary affairs, little more than boards covered with straw mattresses. Gradually they became more elaborate and costly. By the end of the eighteenth century beds had columns of turned wood, canopies, curtains of Bergamo tapestry or serge in vivid colors, most often green, wool-stuffed mattresses, down pillows, blankets, and bedspreads.

Estate inventories from the second half of the eighteenth century show that people attached considerable importance to the quality of their bed. The beds of the poor were amazingly expensive, as Gérard Bouchard noted in the poor Sologne villages he studied: "In a sample of fifty hired laborers, the bed accounted for forty percent of the total value of their property."[19] Beds were constructed differently in different countries, reflecting different needs and tastes. Sleeping customs, characteristic of any culture, persisted for centuries. Montaigne observed: "You make a German ill by putting him to sleep on a mattress, or an Italian on feathers, or a Frenchman without curtain and fire" (*Essays* III:13).

How were beds distributed about the house? In single-room dwellings the answer is simple: one or more beds were placed in the only room, which was used not only for sleeping but also for eating and other waking activities. Among poor peasants the whole family often shared a single bed. In 1683 the Count de Forbin, a Provençal nobleman of high rank, traveled by post from Blois to Poitiers. Having "strayed from the trail in a fog at night" in the marshes of Poitou, he came to a peasant's house: "Upon entering, I asked him if he could make us a fire and take us in for the evening. 'Alas, Monsieur, as you can see, I have only this wretched bed for myself, my wife, and my children.'"[20]

Even in larger houses with several rooms, owned by wealthier farmers and bourgeois, the bed or beds were always located in the room in which people lived, kept a fire going, and prepared and ate food. This was true in Lorraine, Provence, and Burgundy, as well as in the large houses of Béarn and the valleys of the Pyrenees, as Frédéric Le Play noted in 1850 of the Mélouga family.[21] When people did sleep in different rooms, it is clear that sleeping in the room with the fireplace or stove was the privilege of the head of household and his wife. Evidence of this has been found in Kochersberg as well as in four-room dwellings in upper Provençal villages. In Varzy (Burgundy) seventeenth-century estate inventories

Sleeping Arrangements

leave no doubt: "The utensils used for preparing and cooking food were listed in the inventory as having been in the room in which the deceased had passed away. This appears to have been the room ordinarily used for family activities, an all-purpose room, the poor man's calfectory."[22] A traveler from Paris, employed as a salt-tax inspector, recorded the disgust he felt at the smell of the *Stübe* in poor Alsatian homes: "It is almost impossible to stay in the room, because they sleep in it, eat in it, dry their laundry in it, and store fruit in it, which gives rise to a repulsive stench."[23]

The number of beds depended on the number of people living in the house. Of the three farm families from Anthelupt, one consisted of a couple and young child, the second of a couple and four children between the ages of eight and twenty-two, and the third of a couple and eight children between the ages of ten months and twenty years. But all three houses had two rooms. It is not hard to imagine the crowding in that of Jean Homand and his wife Anne Damien, whose youngest children had to sleep in the parents' bedroom while the older children used the other room. And they slept not in canopied beds but on simple boards with straw mattresses.

Adriaen van Ostade, *Farm Interior*. Van Ostade has left a number of quick sketches of everyday life, such as this one showing a family gathered around the hearth. The curtained bed and the rod on which clothes were hung to dry are located near the fire. (Paris, Museum of the Ecole supérieure des Beaux-Arts.)

Single-room dwellings were often quite large and filled with a good deal of furniture. In a village in the Mâconnais, the estate inventory of a cooper who died in 1674 indicates that the main and only habitable room of the house contained a fireplace, four beds with curtains, five chests with locks, and two kneading troughs.[24] We do not know the composition of the family that occupied the four beds, however.

The widow of a former military official died in the Mâconnais in 1780, having slept, according to her estate inventory, in a four-poster bed in one bedroom of the house, which also contained another bed "in which the shepherdess sleeps." (The latter may have been employed as a nurse to watch over the elderly woman in her last days.) The woman's two unmarried daughters slept in another bedroom, each in a four-poster bed. This house had no bed in the kitchen—a hallmark of bourgeois status, but also a consequence of the fact that several grown children had already left home. As late as the end of the eighteenth century not everyone slept alone. In this bourgeois home, however, privacy was a symbol of status. The notary is careful to point out that the mother, elder daughter, and younger daughter each had separate closets, or, rather, locked armoires, which in the 1600s and 1700s replaced locked chests for the storage of clothing, personal effects, and linen. When a woman married, her chest or armoire was moved to her husband's house on the wedding day; its contents accounted for a substantial share of her dowry.

In boarding houses and inns many beds were often crowded into every room. Montaigne praised the quality of German inns, some of which offered heated rooms with single beds and hallways allowing access without having to pass through other rooms. The Count de Forbin recounts in his *Memoirs* (1677) a night spent in an inn at Montargis: "It was time to go to bed. They put all four of us in one room with three beds." The other three were travelers whom the count had met on the road: a canon from Chartres, originally from Provence, and two unknown "gentlemen" wearing officers' uniforms, who turned out to be highway robbers, one of whom would later be executed on the place de Grève in Paris.

In rural houses many people may have been forced to share a single room, but at least they were close relatives. In the cities virtual strangers were forced to live in close proximity owing to poverty and a shortage of housing. In eighteenth century Rouen a "lady" was obliged to "place her bed" in a sublet corner of a room already occupied by a married couple.[25]

After Baudoin, *The Sleeping Guard*. The closeness of the beds is a pretext for a rather spicy scene of a sort quite popular in the 18th century. (Paris, Bibliothèque Nationale.)

RESIDENTIAL GROUPS AND FAMILY STRUCTURES

In Anthelupt the three farmhouses already described accommodated nuclear families. In other parts of France, Italy, and Germany residential groups were more complex. Joseph Baret's house in the Provençal village of Saint-Léger in the Var Valley was home to ten people. In 1782 Baret was fifty-three years old. His wife, slightly older, lived with him, along with their five children, all boys, aged fourteen to thirty. In addition, Baret's mother lived with her son, as did Marianne Genesy, the wife of Baret's eldest son Claude, and one-year-old Joseph Baret, son of Claude and Marianne, who, if God spared him, would as eldest son of the eldest son one day become the head of the household.

Two Family Systems

The differences between Jean Homand's household in Lorraine, with its nuclear family of ten, and Joseph Baret's household in Provence reflect two different family systems, which affected the apportionment and use of living space. When a married son lived with his parents, the division of roles was different, social relations were more ritualized and hierarchical than if he lived in a house of his own. The son was subordinate to the father and the daughter-in-law to the mother-in-law, complicating the usual subordination of wife to husband.

Inheritances were also divided differently in the two systems. Where nuclear families predominated, laws were different from those in regions where trigenerational households were in the majority. In the former the law usually enforced an equal division of property among the children, or at least among the sons. In the latter it was customary to choose a single heir, who remained in the parents' home. The law sanctioned such discrimination in favor of the chosen heir at the expense of his brothers and sisters. Although laws varied considerably from region to region until the adoption of the Code civil, there were regional patterns in regard to inheritance and division of property.[26] In France most provinces south of the Loire favored the single heir and unequal division of property, whereas most provinces to the north favored a more egalitarian system. The detailed picture is considerably more complex than this bald summary suggests, however. There was a transitional zone in the center of the country, and there were provinces in the north and east that adopted the inegalitarian system. Note too that this entire analysis is based

Le Nain brothers, *Preparations for the Dance*. This is one of several paintings the brothers made of children who are dancing to the sound of the flageolet, watched over by an elderly woman. (Private collection.)

on legal documents. But the laws of each province were not always in accord with the practical realities. The situation was equally complex in Germany, Italy, and Spain, where the problems of interpretation are similar.

The family strategies that governed social and biological reproduction in the old agricultural societies were complex responses to economic, material, cultural, and ideological conditions. In Great Britain before the sixteenth century and in many parts of France, including Normandy, Anjou, and the open-field regions of the Paris basin, all the children left the home in which they were raised. Some left home when quite young, either for positions with other families or to seek their fortune. Others moved into new houses built close to their parents' homes, maintaining close ties and even working together. Yet it would have been considered improper for a son to bring his bride home to his father's house. Young men

Le Nain brothers, *Interior Portraits*. Here, despite the presence of a musician, the children are not dancing but posing for a family portrait. The group includes two couples, one older than the other, perhaps the parents with their younger daughter, while the older daughter stands next to her husband. (Paris, Louvre.)

preferred to delay marriage until they could afford to establish an independent household. Mother-in-law and daughter-in-law preferred not to cook their soup over the same fire.

In other parts of France, Italy, and Germany, more extensive than is generally believed, one child continued to live with the parents. The purpose of this arrangement was to promote continuity in the management of patrimonial property, whether an ancestral fief, an office in parlement, a farm, or an artisan's shop. This system is often referred to as that of the stem family.

The Stem Family: Places and Roles

When a daughter-in-law came to live with her husband's family (or, more rarely, when a son-in-law married a woman in line to inherit her family's property and went to live with them), inevitable problems of integration arose. Where should the couple sleep? Certainly not in the room where the parents slept, and not in the room or rooms where the other siblings had their beds. There had to be a vacant room ready to receive the young bride and whatever trunks she brought with her, containing her trousseau.

The two couples (parents and newlyweds) could if necessary coexist in a two-room dwelling provided that the son was the only child who remained at home. In reality, in most regions where the stem-family model prevailed, houses were large enough to accommodate at least three and often four inhabitable rooms.

More than half of the hundred or so houses in Saint-André-les-Alpes in Provence's Verdon Valley contained four inhabitable rooms in the mid-eighteenth century.[27] Houses were tall and narrow, usually with four stories, and contiguous with one another. On the ground floor were a barn and storage area. Above it were two occupied floors, "hall and chamber on the second floor, hall and chamber above," as the notaries put it, with a hayloft at the very top. Four rooms to live in—a substantial amount of space for a modest family of peasants or artisans, indeed a luxurious amount at times in the family cycle when the house was occupied only by parents and children. But at other times the head of household and his wife occupied the alcove of the second-story hall, where the fire was kept, while the unmarried children slept in the adjacent hall. In some cases daughters might share a room with a widowed grandmother. The son and his wife usually slept in the hall above the son's parents, and the son's children slept in the adjacent chamber. Eighteenth-century estate inventories as well as more recent oral testimony suggest that people in Provence intensely disliked having older children sleep in the same room they slept in. While nursing, however, children did sleep in the same room as their parents. Eighteenth-century inventories frequently mention the presence of a cradle along with a child's covers and sheets.

In both the semidetached houses of Provençal villages and the large detached houses of the Pyrenees, the existence of complex residential groups comprising three or even four generations meant that rooms were assigned in a ritualized, hierarchical manner. The head of household and his wife were given the best room. In Saint-André-les-Alpes this was the second-floor hall, which had a view of the street and contained the fireplace, in which a fire was always kept burning. The priorities were the same in the villages of Provence and Languedoc as well as in the Alsatian plain with its large houses.

Eventually, when the father died, the son and his wife would claim the prized bed in the alcove of the main hall (or Alsatian *Stüb*). If the son's mother survived her husband, she would move to another chamber, which she might share with her unmarried daughters or granddaughters. The son inherited the best bed along with the right to govern the household.

The stem-family system (whether practiced in Provence or Italy or Japan) implies a division of labor between two generations: father/son and mother-in-law/daughter-in-law. Roles were differentiated at home, in the fields, and at church.

Ritualized distinctions made cohabitation less difficult and reduced the opportunity for conflict. In every household there
was a hierarchical assignment of female roles. The mother-in-
law ran the kitchen, and the daughter-in-law minded the children and worked in the fields. The family ate in the same hall
in which the mother and father slept, with seating and service
of the meal dictated by tradition.

The seating hierarchy in Kochersberg was as follows:
"The master of the house has the best place, which is left
empty when he is absent: namely, the corner of the bench,
from which he can keep an eye on the street, the courtyard,
and the family papers, kept under lock and key in God's
corner." At meals "the master is at the head of the table, his
wife at his right, his sons at his left, his daughters alongside
their mother, and then the domestics."[28] An almost identical

Illustration by Binet from
Nicolas Rétif de La Bretonne,
La Paysanne pervertie (The
Hague, 1784). The family meal
described by Rétif is depicted
in this celebrated engraving in a
naive, idealized manner. The
ancestral portrait dominates the
scene. (Paris, Bibliothèque
Nationale.)

description of the seating arrangements in the houses of northern Burgundy can be found in Nicolas Rétif de La Bretonne's *La Paysanne pervertie*, early editions of which contained an engraving of a family meal.

No doubt this portrait was somewhat idealized, not only by Rétif but also by the ethnographers who studied Alsatian customs in the late nineteenth century. It pertains essentially to large family farms, rarely encountered in practice. There is abundant evidence that even among the wealthier peasants women rarely sat at the table while the men ate. Instead they served. Lazare de La Salle de L'Hermine writes in his *Memoirs* of a journey through Alsace: "Whatever the nature of the feast, the mother never sits down except for dessert. In other words, when she joins the company, everyone knows that there is nothing more to be ordered or brought from the kitchen." The father cut the bread, poured the wine, served himself first (no doubt taking the best pieces), and then distributed what remained to the other guests.

An Alsatian baker has identified his house with his initals and the symbol of his profession. (Paris, Bibliothèque Nationale.)

The Father's House

Not only room assignment and the ritual of dining but also teaching children correct attitudes, gestures, and forms of speech (such as the use of the formal *vous* with parents, common in many regions) served to instill in the young a proper respect for their elders. The younger sons—and the daughter-in-law—were taught to accept the preferential treatment of the eldest son. The private correspondence of Provençal merchants and householders is full of marks of respect and deference of children toward parents and younger toward older brothers. Census records for villages like Saint-Léger list the members of each household in hierarchical order: first the head of the family, next his wife, next his eldest son. If the son was married, his wife's name usually followed those of his younger brothers. Then came the sisters of the heir-apparent, followed by the children, that is, the grandchildren of the head of household.

In Provence, Languedoc, and Aquitaine the laws of inheritance contributed to the maintenance of paternal authority. The father had full control of the family patrimony. By will or gift he was free to favor one child over the others. What is more, he had the option of retaining the usufruct of any property whose ownership was granted by marriage contract to the son who remained with him. This was prudent insurance against being left with nothing of his own, a way of keeping a tight grip on the household reins and enforcing continued respect. The prospective heir, whom his father and mother had "promised to feed and maintain," could hardly complain about being obliged to work "for the benefit of the estate," since ultimately the patrimony would fall to him—but only after the death of his father. Fathers agreed to emancipate only those sons who left the paternal home and established themselves elsewhere. The heir-apparent, often referred to in French as the *fils de famille*, the family son, was deprived of the right to make decisions, sell property, or draft a will—even as a married man in his forties—as long as his father remained alive.

Evidence shows that heirs tolerated their father's authority over themselves, their wives, and their children even as late as the eighteenth century. "Community contracts," signed when an heir married, always included an escape clause: "in case the parties prove incompatible" or "incapable of tolerating one another" or "in case of incompatibility," as the notaries put it. In Saint-André-les-Alpes, however, elder sons seldom left their parents' home. When a split did occur, it was almost always in the months following a son's marriage. It soon became apparent whether mother-in-law and daughter-in-law could or could not get along. If they could not, the son established a separate household, supporting himself by working land that his father had promised to give him immediately in case of *rupture de la communauté*, severance of community relations. The young couple might occupy the upper part of the house, now divided in two, or they might move into a nearby house owned by the family. After the eldest son had claimed his share of the inheritance, the father, if family finances still permitted, would take in one of his younger sons and attempt to establish a new "community."

The stem-family system could not function without a minimum level of prosperity. In addition to a fairly large house, it required an income from shop or farm sufficient to support two families. After the daughters had received their dowries and the younger sons their portions, the *force de l'héritage*, or strength of the legacy, as the notaries put it, had to be great enough to feed five to ten people. The system flourished in regions where peasants owned their own land. There were exceptions to this rule, however. In Berry and Limousin, where sharecropping was common, so were extended families. The stem-family system was also prevalent in regions where master craftsmen and merchants possessed substantial reserves

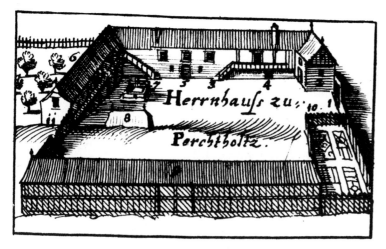

This view of a farm, from Merian, *Topographia provinciarum austriacarum*, is placed in the upper corner of an engraving that represents an Austrian village of the mid-17th century. The use of each building is carefully noted.

of cash, land, and livestock. The Englishman Arthur Young, who traveled in France in the late eighteenth century, remarked that peasant smallholders were far more common in France than in England. In Flanders, Alsace, on the banks of the Garonne, and in Béarn, small landowners struck Young as being so prosperous that they deserved to be called farmers rather than cottagers. As it happens, these regions were precisely those in which the stem family was most common.

In a variant of the stem-family system, the parents retired from active management of the household when the heir-apparent took a wife. This system was found in Germany, Austria, and Ireland. When the parents retired, they moved into a separate house. Sometimes this was located nearby (within the enclosure of the *Hof* in Germany). Sometimes a small addition was built onto the main house, as in certain Austrian villages. In Alsace a new room was added, called a *Kleinstüb*; in Ireland it was called a "west room."

The parents not only lived separately but also had their own budget. When they relinquished control over the bulk of the farm and the main house, they drew up a contract specifying which fields were reserved for their use and what items would constitute their "survival pension": grain and other supplies, clothing, fuel, and money to be paid by the heir.

This modified stem-family system was a compromise between the pure system (found in Provence and the Pyrenees) and the system of equipartition practiced in Lorraine, Normandy, and England. Like the stem family, the compromise solution tended to concentrate the bulk of the patrimony in the hands of a single heir at the expense of his brothers and sisters, but parents and child lived separately and the parents relinquished much of their authority, as in the more egalitarian system of equipartition.

The Egalitarian System and Lineage Solidarity

The fact that there were compromise solutions between the stem-family and egalitarian systems suggests that the dichotomy should not be interpreted too strictly. We must also be wary of anachronism. In the ancien régime the separation of parents and children at the time of marriage (or even earlier among poorer peasants, and commonly in regions of equipartition) may indicate not individualism or a desire for independence on the part of the younger generation but simply a response to economic necessity. Different systems of inheritance and residential group structure essentially are different ways of answering a single question: How can a society whose primary resource and means of subsistence is land reproduce itself generation after generation?

In all cases, regardless of the manner in which the soil was farmed, the land—ancient manses, parishes, or fiefs—was divided among family units, whose members lived together. However different the various systems of inheritance were, all derived from a common principle. Some favored one heir over the others, giving precedence to the vertical transmission of property within household units (*maison, oustal, domus*). Others, more egalitarian, required a new division of ownership or land rights with every generation. Such division posed problems for the survival of family farms, but the dangerous division was compensated by purchase or exchange of parcels, which reconstituted parcels fragmented by inheritance. In open-field regions, where equipartition was practiced, law and custom reflect strong solidarity within lineages. There were restraints, both moral and legal, on the sale of land to nonkin, such as the *retrait lignager*, a right of first refusal accorded to members of the lineage. In the plains communal customs strengthened the solidity of the lineage.

Solidarity within the lineage was not simply economic; it extended to social and affective life as well. Even though people in equipartition regions lived in separate small households, feelings of allegiance and solidarity were not lacking within larger kinship groups. Small residential units were part of a larger network of relations between parents and children, brothers and sisters, and in-laws, who shared or exchanged

parcels of land. In Ile-de-France nuclear households remained grouped together in courtyards; in Normandy they were grouped inside farm enclosures; and in Lorraine they were lined up along the main street. Endogamy was just as much a force among vintners in the Paris basin or artisans in Norman villages as it was in regions where inegalitarian inheritance prevailed. In potters' villages in eighteenth-century Auge, "family structures were confined within a tightly closed endogamic circle. The potters' children, themselves potters, shared a central courtyard. Divisions of property gave rise to numerous rights and obligations."[29]

What became of widows and widowers once the family patrimony was divided among the children? If their children refused to pay their pensions, did they end their days living alone on handouts? Some parents certainly did implore their children for help. In 1730 the widow of a laborer from Avenières "in view of her advanced age and infirmity, begs

Jean-Baptiste Greuze, *Village Betrothal.* "Be joined, my children, may love keep you together." La Fontaine's verses are illustrated in this painting of an engagement in a rural village, with all the pathos characteristic of the painter and the period. (Paris, Louvre.)

After Jacques Callot, *The Fair at Gondreville*. The long rows of houses in this Lorraine village stretch into the distance in this flat region. (Paris, Bibliothèque Nationale.)

Jean Heaume, farmer, her son, to kindly take her into his home along with her few possessions and see to it that she is given room, board, bed, and washing, given that she is unable to earn her living."[30]

One hopes that other widows did not need to issue such public appeals to stir their sons' filial feelings. Judging from eighteenth-century census data, there were few single-person households in regions of equipartition. At Longuenesse (Artois) in 1778 there was only one out of sixty-six hearths, compared with eleven households in which a married couple lived with one or both of the husband's parents. Two demographic factors inflated the proportion of nuclear households: people died young and married late.

In the regions of equipartition, and just as we saw earlier in the stem-family regions, no fundamental challenge was raised to the authority of parents in such matters as the choice of spouse or division of the patrimony. Even where newly married couples established their own households, the parents' good will was essential. If the parents delayed in dividing their property, a son might have to wait until he was thirty or more before he could marry and start his own household. Young plowmen and vintners continued to live and work with their parents until they reached that age.

Although there were undeniable regional differences in construction, use of space, and legal codes, the daily life of a farmer in Ile-de-France may not have been very different from that of a peasant in Provence. Housing had to suit the environment (soil, climate, and agricultural methods). Although very ancient legal principles played a part in determining the rules of inheritance and coresidence, the different systems were also responses to natural and socioeconomic conditions.

Hence it was possible for more than one system to coexist in a single province or in two neighboring provinces. In Galicia, a province of northwestern Spain, we find three distinct systems. In the hills, the stem-family system was common. In the valleys close to the sea and in fishing villages along the coast, a different type of inegalitarian system was found: a daughter was chosen to inherit the parents' house. (In many parts of southwestern Europe male heirs were not preferred to females.) And in the plains of southern Galicia equipartition was the rule, parents and their married children seldom occupied the same house.[31]

Family Systems: Similarities

Anonymous drawing, *View of the City and Castle of Sisteron*, showing the stone houses of the upper Provençal town squeezed between the cliffs and the Durance. (Paris, Bibliothèque Nationale.)

In both stem-family and equipartition regions, households were relatively small. In seventeenth- and eighteenth-century France, Italy, and Great Britain, the number of related individuals living under one roof in peasant homes was never very high. In equipartition regions the reason for this is clear: at marriage the young couple established its own household and subsequently lived alone with its children and possibly a parent. Yet the numbers of inhabitants were not very different in stem-family houses, because economic conditions set a ceiling to the number of people who could inhabit one house. The marriage of the eldest son was delayed in order to make sure that no daughter-in-law would arrive until a requisite number of sons and daughters had moved out. In some regions people preferred to settle the elder children in new homes and to keep the youngest son at home as heir, to support his parents in their old age.

In stem-family regions it was highly unusual for two married brothers to share a house, even after their parents had died. Multiple households of this kind, known as *frérèches*, did not exist in seventeenth- and eighteenth-century Provence, Alsace, or the Pyrenean valleys. Such an arrangement would have been contrary to the ideology of the stem family, which favored a single heir, as well as dangerous for the economic and affective equilibrium of the household. Younger brothers seldom remained in their parents' homes to the end of their lives. Lifelong celibacy was rare in rural areas during the ancien régime, and even rarer for males than for females.

A Survival: Extended-Family Communities

Thus, households were quite small even in stem-family regions. As numerous historians have found, the notion of a "great patriarchal family," a single household accommodating grandparents (and perhaps great-uncles and great-aunts), several of their children, all married, and numerous grandchildren, is a myth. After the sixteenth century in western Europe there is no tangible reality to which it might correspond. For a long time the only known example of such a patriarchal family was the Yugoslav *zadruga*, believed to be an aberrant survival from antediluvian times. In fact, however, similar extended-family communities were widely spread throughout many regions of central and eastern Europe—in Hungary, Romania, and especially Russia—in the eighteenth and nineteenth centuries.

Indeed, if we look carefully, it is not impossible to find

very large households in France as late as the eighteenth century: in Auvergne and Berry as well as some parts of Burgundy, the Jura, and the Bourbonnais. They are mentioned by travelers in the sixteenth, seventeenth, and eighteenth centuries. François de Belleforest had this to say about the Limousin in his *Cosmographie* (1575): "The inhabitants . . . are healthy, bright, ready, and strong and, what is more, such good housekeepers that for fear that their houses might be ruined, you will see in the villages families in which an old man takes in his offspring down to the fourth generation, who without dispensation will marry among themselves, never dividing any of their property. And I have seen such families in which more than a hundred related persons lived in common as at a boarding school."[32] Two centuries later the Breton Le Quinio, in *Journey in the Jura,* described family communities in much the same terms: "Father, mother, children, grandchildren, great-grandchildren, cousins, and grandcousins all live together. It is a genealogical tree whose branches divide only after a very long time, and the venerable patriarch, who thanks to pure air and a simple life almost always remains quite healthy at the end of a long career, has long held command over a large army of offspring."[33]

Agricultural communes in the ancien régime were defined as groups of people generally related by blood or marriage and "making residence and common life in the same pot, salt, and purse." Contemporary texts called them *communs, communes, parsonniers,* or *coparsonniers.* The customaries of central and to some extent western France called them "tacit communes" or "silent communes," as did sixteenth- and seventeenth-century legal commentaries, particularly that of the well-known Nivernais Guy Coquille. Here "tacit" and "silent" are intended to imply that these family corporations were valid even in the absence of a written contract, simply by virtue of "common residence and life for a year and a day." This sufficed until the middle of the seventeenth century. Later, however, under pressure from royal edicts requiring the registration of deeds, notaries prepared formal documents covering the constitution of these family corporations as well as changes to that constitution (such as admission of new members, departure of old ones, and dissolution).

The form of the agricultural commune varied from time to time and region to region. In size communes ranged from four or five persons to more than forty. Some were composed of individual smallholders, others of sharecroppers. The nature of housing varied widely. Most common were the communes of smallholders, which were known by the family name, a patronymic of the founding ancestor: the Jault community in the Nivernais, for example, or the Quittard-Pinon in Thiers (Auvergne), which became famous in the late eighteenth century because of the philosophes' interest in it. Also in Auvergne were the Garnier, Pradel, and Anglade-Tarenteix communities, along with others too numerous to mention.

The symbol and physical embodiment of the commune was a particular kind of dwelling. A commune like the Quittard or Pradel could not have functioned without its communal house or *hostel*, any more than a monastery could have functioned without a refectory and dormitory. The communal house was a large building, usually a blockhouse, with a large, often enormous, common room: 79 by 26 feet in the Jault commune and 82 by 33 feet in the Légaré commune, also in the Nivernais—in other words, about ten times the size of a farmhouse in Ile-de-France. The hall contained either an immense central fireplace or a number of wall fireplaces. All members of the commune gathered for meals in this heated room. Much of social life took place here. But the common room also contained beds for the master of the community, chosen by election, and his family, who, like the head of a stem family, was given the privilege of sleeping in a heated room. The master, called a *mouistre* in Auvergne, enjoyed extensive powers; his word was law. In large communes there was also a mistress, usually not the master's wife. Her main role was to tend the children of commune members.

In addition to the common room with its monumental fireplaces, the big house contained any number of small rooms in which commune members lived with their wives and children. In some very large communes other nearby buildings provided additional housing. Some big houses had long corridors giving access to these rooms, while others offered direct access to each room from the courtyard. Built of stone or half-timbered, the blockhouses of central and western French communes are in some respects reminiscent of the great wooden houses found in eastern European communes, such as the Palots and Matyos communities in nineteenth-century Hungary.[34]

In France communal houses came in many forms. In the large communes of the Nivernais large blockhouses typically conformed to a basilica plan. Elsewhere there were long houses with multiple bays, possibly reflecting a polynuclear family organization. In Quercy there were even multistory communal houses. Like other houses, communal buildings were subject to renovation, addition, subdivision, abandonment, and reconstruction.

In other communes the rules of communal life were less strict. Rather than living together in one large house, commune members occupied several separate dwellings. "This was the case at Boischaut in the early sixteenth century and at Chippaudière, where the Chippault commune resided with its thirty-three members, twenty-four of them children. Two families lived in old buildings, another in a 'newly built' house, and a fourth in a house and barn built 'for the purpose of lodging.'"[35]

Constitution and Dissolution of Tacit Communes

Were these less disciplined communes stable? Perhaps not. A statistical study has been done of land use in the provinces of central France. The results show that in regions such as Auvergne, communal living was the most common form of residence. Many of the communes were small, including just a few brothers or brothers-in-law or parents and children. During the fifteenth century, when frérèche arrangements were most in vogue, perhaps 60 to 90 percent of all inhabitants lived in a commune of some sort. The phenomenon was still current in the sixteenth century. But then, as in all periods, many communes fell apart (as a result of poverty or seizure of property), while others formed. It now seems certain that the celebrated Quittard-Pinon commune, which in the late eighteenth century was believed to be at least five centuries old, had actually been founded at the end of the sixteenth century by three brothers, sons of Jean Quittard, plowman in the village of Pinon.

In the sixteenth century or later hamlets were created when family communes dissolved. J. Chiffre cites an example: "In Autunois, the Chèze commune collapsed some time between 1500 and 1514, leading to the creation of two hamlets, one called Bas de la Chèze and the other called Haut de la Chèze. Some years later these took the names Bonnards and Pelletiers, respectively, names that they have kept to this day."

No doubt traces remain of old communes in hamlets with patronymic names, often that of the founder preceded by the word Chez, such as Chez-Fiataud and Chez-Blanchet in Limousin, Chez-Piffetaud and Chez-Gentet in Charente, and Chez-Gagnat and Chez-Bariou in Thiers. In other instances,

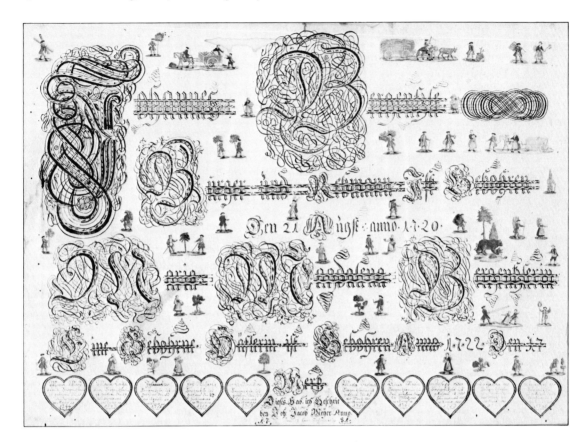

This genealogical reconstitution of the Bergentzle family of Alsace gives free reign to the arabesque lettering of a baroque writer with a taste for the old-fashioned. (Strasbourg, Alsatian Museum.)

often in the same regions, the hamlet is designated simply by the patronymic preceded by the plural definite article: Les Mondaniaux, Les Ferriers, and Les Garniers are three hamlets in Thiers, still inhabited today. The Garnier commune was close to the Quittard, and, in the eighteenth century, the two frequently intermarried. However, the existence of patronymic hamlet names, quite common in some Provençal valleys, while it may honor the memory of a founding ancestor, is not proof that communal residence ever existed. In Provence and many other parts of southern France there were never either small frérèches or extended-family communes. The patronymic hamlets of Provence were inhabited by kin, but they lived in separate houses.

It is tempting to relate the presence or absence of tacit communes to the different legal status of peasants in central and southern France. Southern peasants had long since freed themselves from certain feudal constraints that still bound peasants in eighteenth-century Auvergne, Bourbonnais, and Burgundy. In those last-named regions peasants had only limited rights to the land they tilled, and in the absence of a direct male heir residing in his father's house there was a danger that the plot would revert to the landlord upon the father's death. One way to avoid the risk of mortmain, as this reversion was called, was to enter into "communal life for a year and a day," even with remote kin. Thus, wherever mortmain existed, tacit communes flourished. Many authors, starting in the eighteenth century, have noticed this, but it was probably just one reason among others—economic, social, and affective—for the formation of communes.

Like the stem family and the egalitarian family, the extended-family commune was a fundamental social model. Its complex organization is highly instructive. In some respects the family commune resembles the stem family, in others the egalitarian family. For economic and demographic reasons, even extended-family communes could not keep all children of all branches together. With each new generation some number of children had to be excluded. Joachim Faiguet, writing on "Moravians and united brothers" in volume 10 of the *Encyclopedia* noted: "Each of these families forms different branches, which live in a common house and whose children intermarry, but in such a way that each of the consorts settles just one son in the community, who will one day, after the death of his father, represent the branch within the community." The children who leave the commune "are excluded by law" from sharing in the common property, in compensation for which they receive a fixed sum of money. This system is highly reminiscent of the stem-family system in southern France, in which younger sons are forced to leave their parents' home.

However, unlike the stem-family system, which is based on the father's authority over the married son and heir who shares his home, tacit communes were organized as corporations. Each member owned a certain number of shares, which he either acquired upon joining the commune or inherited from his parents. Marriage added to the general fund of property, hence scarcely affected the operation of the commune. Formally at least, the system was egalitarian. In reality things were more complicated: a woman who married a commune member brought both a communal dowry and a personal dowry.

Authority in the communes was not wielded in a patriarchal manner. The master of the commune, though elected for life, was chosen by the other members. From notarized documents we know something about the personalities chosen to head the Quittard-Pinon commune in the eighteenth century. In 1705 Annet Quittard was elected master. He was only thirty-seven years old and succeeded not his father but his uncle Blaise Quittard, who had sons of the same age in the commune. Thus in this one commune at any rate, authority was neither vested in the old nor transmitted hereditarily from father to eldest son.

The Myth of Utopia

Joachim Faiguet de Villeneuve was the first intellectual to discover the great communes of Thiers. He first wrote about the Quittard-Pinon commune in the *Journal économique* in 1755, and ten years later contributed his article "Moravians and United Brothers" to the *Encyclopedia*. Drawing on the book *Rustic Socrates* by the Swiss physician H. C. Hirzel, the Marquis de Mirabeau and other physiocrats advocated the commune as a model of social and family organization. Toward the end of the eighteenth century a mythical image of the commune as an organization at once patriarchal and democratic was propagated in France and survived the Revolution.

Nicolas Rétif de La Bretonne described in *Le Paysan perverti* (1776) the fictitious "statutes of the town of Oudun, compiled by the R. family, living communally." He imagined a utopian commune, a collective farm explicitly modeled on the communes of Auvergne. He advocated "total equality among our children," while recommending that they remain "subject to the eldest sons of the eldest male in our family." The author of *La vie de mon père (My Father's Life)* imagined the construction of a building that would contain not only the communal oven but also a "great hall capable of holding a thousand persons: this will be the communal refectory."

Twenty years later Legrand d'Aussy in his *Journey in 1787 and 1788 through the former Upper and Lower Auvergne* (1795) gave a lyrical account of the Quittard-Pinon, who were described as the direct descendants, blond and hirsute, of the ancient Arvernes. In an age of progress and growing individualism, economists, philosophers, and essayists gave specious luster to archaic and confining communal structures in the very moment of their decline.

The stem family, solidly implanted in parts of France, Germany, Italy, and Spain, proved better able to withstand the increasingly individualistic and egalitarian tendencies of the nineteenth century. The stem family frequently coincided with the small family farm, and by keeping the property intact it could be preserved over several generations. The old custom of choosing a single son as heir remained workable, despite the leveling tendencies of the Code civil. Younger sons, content to accept cash payments, did not demand a share of the inheritance. Intergenerational bonds and lineage solidarities in equipartition regions remained intact even longer. The changes in family structure that occurred during the nineteenth century were as much the results of social and economic upheaval as of cultural evolution.

Attributed to Quentin Matsys. The signing of the marriage contract was a decisive moment. The future bride shown here appears to have brought nothing to the marriage but her personal belongings and jewelry, but she will enjoy the use of her husband's hard cash. In the background an innocent hails with a wide-open mouth the addition of a new member to the fraternity of ridiculed husbands. (São Paulo, Museum of Fine Arts.)

Families: Privacy versus Custom

Daniel Fabre

I N RURAL villages and urban neighborhoods everything having to do with marriage was for a long time subject to the closest scrutiny. The moment of domestic reproduction was of concern not only to close relatives but also to neighbors and especially to young people of the same age group as the prospective bride and groom. Scrutiny of the marriage arrangements was extended to scrutiny of the marriage itself, with censure if necessary of any infraction of the unwritten rules of propriety. Rumor and slander, sometimes discreet, sometimes public, were prevalent, as were outbursts of invective against offenders. Until the last century of the ancien régime, however, in many segments of society the most common way of publicizing and punishing infractions of custom was part and parcel of the ritual of social transition itself. At those times in an individual's life when he or she moved from one social status to another, self-identity was entirely dependent on collective recognition. The rite of passage bestowed a new role and at the same time reflected a judgment of conformity, the obligatory counterpart of its integrative function. Hence those who experienced the rite experienced not only the anxiety of the neophyte but also the nervous anticipation of public judgment, for charivari accompanied marriage as its shadow.

Between 1300 and 1800 charivaris incurred the censure of both religious and civil authorities, which after 1650 agreed that order and decency required the prohibition of the "insulting commotions" sometimes provoked by marriages and marital disputes. Even more significant, in France after 1740 the number of complaints and court cases associated with charivaris began to rise as the targets of derision fought back.

Clearly this mechanism of social control was in the process of being rejected, but the change, which did not come about without resistance, led to the invention of new controls.

THE RITES OF UNVEILING

Maypoles

When a girl reached marriageable age, her change in status was recognized in one or more ceremonies celebrated at fixed times of the year. On the night of 30 April a maypole was erected in front of the house of any nubile girl. By so doing, young men as a group not only paid homage to the girl but also rendered a judgment on her behavior. The symbolism was known to all: prickly plants denoted the ambiguous quality of pride; elder, which not only stank but was also easy to "drill," proclaimed debauch for all to see. If feelings ran particularly high, a wider spectrum of defamatory signs was brought into play, including smelly cade oil, urine, and manure. Worse yet, in early May 1717 an ironmonger in Carcassonne found "bones and carcasses of horses and other animals" in front of his shop; ox horns had been nailed to the facade. In the morning his neighbors were upset to find their street "filled and infected" with carrion. Five or six young men from the same neighborhood and milieu (sons of artisans) had taken their revenge against Catin, the shopowner's daughter. After nine at night they had loaded up with supplies at the rubbish dump outside the walls of the lower city, dragged their booty back into town, and left it under the girl's window. They were paying her a *ramade*, they said, using a term which in the local Occitanian dialect referred to the setting of a maypole. They also sang songs whose "insulting and defamatory words" denounced a scandal about which we know nothing more.[1]

Papillon, *Rejoicing*. An official, public maypole is planted on a promenade outside of town, hailed by the authorities and a military band, while in the background people dance the farandole. (Paris, Bibliothèque Nationale.)

Every year in early May a code of olfactory signs was used to categorize and classify nubile girls. At carnival time in Mediterranean regions another kind of code, even more comprehensive and ostentatious, was used. In Carcassonne again, this time in the City, the "mad virgin" of the year, represented by a grotesque marionette bearing her name, was the subject of a song that detailed her adventures in the crudest terms. Males, ranging from young boys to adults, met throughout the winter in an out-of-the-way cabin to rehearse the song before singing it in the church square on Palm Sunday.

For young girls the only question was honor. It was not simply a question of virginity but rather a judgment of all her qualities: dress, language, and above all resistance to male overtures, tact in distributing tokens of love, and constancy of choice.

The emphasis shifted at the time of marriage. It was important to make a good match, and many considerations came into play. The first requirement was of course that both parties be free to marry. If either party was widowed, the community might object to the marriage despite the approval of the Church. The result was a so-called charivari, or concert of bells, horns, drums, tongs, and cauldrons alternating with shouts and catcalls. A plausible argument has been made that this ritual commotion was intended primarily to secure the separation of the surviving partner from his or her late spouse.[2] According to this view, the explosion of cacophony, a perversion of the harmonious wedding music, amplified by the raucous oaths of the young males, made possible the union of the new couple.

But at least in part the charivari was intended as a denunciation of the impending marriage. For a widower to marry a virgin violated a rule whose essential tenet was expressed in 1818 by Captain Deville: "In seeking the possible causes of this custom, I have been obliged to settle on this: at a time when women were no doubt less numerous than they are today, men stimulated by the desire to bind their destiny to a woman must have found it difficult to watch one of their number, who had already claimed his tribute from the fairer sex, aspire to take another at the expense of those still animated by this fond hope. Unable to thwart his will without violating the law, they sought, by holding him up to public mockery, at least to inspire fear in anyone who might dare imitate the action" (*Annales de Bigorre*, Tarbes, 1818). In other words, remarriage improperly deprives some male of a possible mate.[3]

There were other grounds for charivaris. A great disparity in age between bride and groom might provoke an outburst. So might a glaring difference in social rank, or the fact that the husband was regarded as a "stranger"—not necessarily a foreigner but perhaps from a nearby village or district. Charivaris thus stigmatized marriages in which bride and groom (or their families) failed to maintain a "proper distance."

By noisily publicizing the discordances in an impending

Charivaris

The early-18th-century "horn merchant" belongs to a popular genre that ridiculed cuckoldry. Young bourgeois and other literate people participated in this written and figurative form of carnival. A "Diploma of Cuckoldry" was printed in Toulouse in 1746. In Bordeaux, Bernadau, future correspondent of Abbé Grégoire, wrote one of many "Dissertations on Horns." The function of these rituals was ambivalent: they affirmed man's symbolic fate but they also censured real excesses. (Paris, Bibliothèque Nationale.)

Mariette, *Springtime*. This maypole, which represents the season, may have had a more personal purpose as well. Two young women look on attentively as young men raise the leafy, beribboned tree. The children in the foreground are carrying a basket that probably contains eggs for an egg hunt and food for a picnic. (Paris, Bibliothèque Nationale.)

marriage, the charivari implicitly restored harmony. The couple about to marry were offered a chance to reduce the intensity of the disturbance by paying a certain sum of money to the potential demonstrators. In some cases this sum was fixed by custom, but in the eighteenth century it was usually determined by private negotiation. The scope, duration, and aggressiveness of the ritual were determined by this transaction. If the couple were evasive or niggardly or refused to enter into negotiations, the charivari could easily turn violent. In early February 1787 a small group of young artisans from Varages, a pottery-making town in lower Provence, harassed Jean Eissautier, a weaver their own age, and Victoire Roux, his intended spouse, a widow of sixty. When the banns were read the youths ran through the streets ringing cow bells. They seized the old widow and paraded her about on a wagon. A week later they waited for the couple outside the offices of the notary where they signed their marriage contract and

pitched them into the mud. Finally, on the day of the benediction, they serenaded them in front of the church.[4]

Sometimes entire communities became involved in the
derision, which could reach spectacular heights. Prion, clerk
in the seigneurial court of Aubais, in his *Chronologiette* tells of
one memorable charivari: "On Thursday, 4 February 1745,
one Baudran, tanner of the city of Sommières, aged 64, married in Aubais Miss Thérèse Batifort, aged 44, their two ages
together totaling 109 years [*sic*]. The lady claimed to have 22
teeth, canines and molars; the groom had only 14, age having
claimed those that might have been serviceable. The groom
in this wedding couple being a widower, the youth of Aubais
performed the most extraordinary charivari in the world. The
groom had not been as generous as he should have been.
Offended by his stinginess, the young people, 117 in number,
assembled and formed a barricade so that the newlyweds could
not leave the village. They removed the wheels . . . from
Venus' wagon. His honor the Judge, flanked by his shepherds,
went in person to try to raise the barriers that had been placed
in the way of the nuptial cortege. The oldest people in Aubais
swore that never had there been as great a commotion as that

Engraving after a drawing by
Brueghel the Elder of the wedding of Mopsus and Nisa, a
subject treated in his *Combat
between Carnival and Lent*, in
which the wedding party is
included in the train of King
Carnival. Although the two
heroes take their names from
Virgil's Eighth Eclogue, they
actually represent the burlesque
marriage of a wild woman,
played here by a coarse-
featured male wearing a sieve
for a crown. As the players go
from place to place, a young
man collects money from the
crowd.

which greeted this elderly couple. All the people of Aubais came out of their homes to enjoy the spectacle of insults. When the members of the nuptial cortege mounted their beasts of burden, they were warned that all passages were blocked. The nymph and nymphet and members of the company took a different route, but the young men and children involved in the charivari headed them off. The charivari frightened the horses, and the riders were pelted with mudballs. The bride was riding with another girl or woman in a wagon ill disguised as a carriage. Ten or twelve of the malcontents climbed on the back of the wagon, with the result that the traces lifted up and the horses pawed at the air . . . On the road from Aubais to Sommières are . . . two castles called Gavernes and Grestin. Carters had barricaded the road with their carts, and shepherds had gathered with cowbells. With these and other similar instruments they made a charivari that could be heard as far away as Aubais. People shouted with all their might. When they drew near Sommières they were greeted by the entire populace with horrible jeers and an equally tumultuous charivari. Tombs along the way were decorated with lighted candles. Never had this city seen such a tumultuous uproar. The soldiers of the garrison fired upon those responsible for the charivari. But the soldiers were found to be at fault and imprisoned on the spot to expiate their crime . . . The leaders of the charivari tied the arms of Baudran, the groom, whom they placed at the head of the cavalcade for the entry into the city, in which posture he was exposed to the laughter and jeers of the people."[5]

The Asouade

When charivari reached such paroxysms, it set aside its furtive, masked, nocturnal aspect. In disrupting the nuptial cortege and turning the groom into the protagonist of a grotesque cavalcade, the riotous crowd was drawing upon the symbolism of another ceremony of sanction, often visited upon married couples involved in some kind of disagreement. The most ostentatious public punishment was reserved for the husband who was dominated or beaten by his wife, or, much more rarely, for the wife beaten by her husband. This was the *asouade*, a public parade in which the victim was mounted on an ass. It occurred only when a marital dispute extended outside the house. In becoming an affair of the street and marketplace it became fair game for public censure.

In Béarn on 19 April 1762 Raymond Blasy, "responsible

for marking the fabric" manufactured in the textile town of Coarraze, entered a cabaret there to have a drink. He sat down for a game of cards with three partners, including the taverner. A short while later his wife, Ménine, arrived and, on the pretext that someone wanted to speak to him, attempted to persuade her husband to quit the game. Seeing that nothing was happening, she hurled herself on the players, tore up their cards, and dragged her husband home. Onlookers, scandalized by Blasy's passivity, immediately threatened to make him "run the ass," and a decision was reached soon after his departure. Two days later, the town crier of Coarraze announced to the entire village that "on the 24th, Sunday next, the ass would be run for Labadie de Magouber [the Abbey of Misrule] and that anyone who wished to attend the spectacle was invited." The announcement was repeated the following day, and on Sunday night the parade began. Two drummers and a group of boys preceded a tip-cart filled with singers who chanted a rhymed commentary on the events. They were followed by two figures "dressed in capes and hats, one riding an ass, the other a horse." The pantomime, which would be repeated until midnight, was always the same: the woman—played of course by a boy—grabbed her partner by the hair and threw

William Hogarth, *Skimmington*. A cavalcade of cuckolds. Some wear horns, others carry distaffs or kitchen utensils, while marching to the sound of horns and the rhythm of a cauldron. (Paris, Bibliothèque Nationale.)

William Hogarth. This charivari is directed against a tailor,
who no doubt had been beaten
by his wife, to judge by the
participants' beating of sticks,
bones, and butcher blocks.
Tailors, who worked indoors
at tasks considered feminine,
were generally believed to be
weak and easily dominated.
(Paris, Bibliothèque Nationale.)

This Florentine woodcut juxtaposes two successive phases in the story of the carnival king: the judicial procession and the hanging. At one time violators of sexual and marital norms were exhibited on parade. (Florence, National Library.)

him from his ass, then beat him with a distaff that she carried with a flourish. Later there was another episode: a card game was simulated on the back of the ass, but once again the wife arrived, disrupted the game with her distaff, and tore up all the cards.[6]

In addition to the use of masks and the performance of a farce, another detail illustrates the ceremonial nature of this Béarnais rite. The crier had mentioned Labadie de Magouber, the Abbey of Misrule, a reference to the raucous confraternities that organized carnival festivities in such sixteenth-century cities as Dijon, Mâcon, Lyons, and Rouen. And after 1750 in the region of Toulouse and northern Catalonia, the carnival culminated on Ash Wednesday in a ritual of derision against the foolish husband organized by a variety of mock organizations known variously as *cours cornuelles, sociétés asiniennes,* and *tribunaux carnivores.*

Rituals of Death

Continuing along life's course, we reach the ultimate rite of passage: the passage from this world to the next. Since the central Middle Ages the Church had sought to gain control over it. The three aspects of the death ritual that were disputed especially bitterly were the vigil over the body, the lament for the dead, and the meal following the burial. There were opportunities in the ritual for public judgment to be expressed. In southern Europe funeral monologues such as the Béarnais *aurost* and the Corsican *vocero* were occasions for nothing less than posthumous indictments, formulated by women who specialized in the genre.[7] There is also oral evidence from various locations, particularly western France, supporting the claim that funeral rites from the vigil to the cortege were sometimes interrupted by charivarilike demonstrations. In these no doubt extreme cases the community wished to express disapproval of the deceased.

Code and Intentions

After 1640 the authorities prohibited not only matrimonial charivaris but all "nocturnal assemblies," "disreputable songs," and "indecent actions" associated with a variety of rites of passage. Thus they began to apply the still obscure notion that ceremonies of this sort should be coherent and homogeneous.

In what respects do these various kinds of disruption seem similar? First, they obviously shared a common language. A similar code (olfactory, musical, and theatrical) applied to a variety of rituals despite obvious differences between them: for example, the charivari took place at night, the asouade in the daytime; the strewing of branches was done in silence, while other demonstrations were accompanied by much tumult. This festive language marked the rite of passage and the arrival of carnival and Mayday. By relating private judgments to regular rituals, it established a link between the linear time of human life and the cyclical time of the calendar.

In all these rituals the intention and dynamic were the same. They registered a protest against some indignity about which local people were in agreement, including even those who took no part in the action. This unanimity of judgment, evidence for which can be seen in the absence of internal conflict over the demonstrations, stemmed from the transparent nature of social relations. The ritual merely manifested what everyone already knew. Implicit, discreet knowledge was transformed into spectacle, not in order to change the course of events but simply to take public note of an individual's reputation. There was a subtle gradation in the means of derision: the items strewn about in the May ritual, the intensity of the charivari, the duration and repetition of the asouade, and the possibility of combining more than one form of insult all depended on the magnitude of the scandal and the way in which the ritual was received.

Those cases that have been recorded for posterity were singular events. In the first place, there was nothing automatic about the decision to stage a charivari or other disruption. Not all flirtatious girls or remarriages or henpecked husbands elicited a punitive ceremony. Judgment was merited only in

cases where a variety of grievances had accumulated against an individual and his or her family. Hence there is an obvious disparity between the alleged pretext—an inappropriately exogamous marriage, say—and the charges formulated in bawdy songs and jeers, which in their comprehensive hostility always went far beyond the mere offense to custom. In Montréal (Aude) in 1769 a violent charivari smashed the door and set fire to the hedge of a modest peasant, apparently in protest against his daughter's impending marriage to a "stranger," a native of Lézignan, fifteen leagues away. But the protesters, shouting their lungs out, told another story: the prospective groom had left a girl with child in his native village. He had swindled a second out of 80 livres. His mere presence in Montréal had transformed his father-in-law's house into nothing less than a "public bordello."[8]

The first order of business in a charivari was to paint a portrait of the victim that justified the intervention of the populace. Once a charivari had been planned, the victim was informed, sometimes by an official delegation. At this stage

The Torture of the Cuckolds, with Seville in the background, portrays a scene earlier described in *La Celestina* (1494). While the judge looks on, three people are whipped by an attendant and jeered by onlookers, some of whom mimic horns with their hands. We see the illicit lovers and, probably hidden beneath the thick false beard, the procuress. The man wears deer's antlers adorned with flowers, which are naturally yellow, probably Spanish broom. The young woman rides in front, covered with honey, which attracts a swarm of insects. Taken from Georges Bruin, *Theater of Maps of the World* (Brussels, 1594).

This Italian woodcut depicts the "wagon of death," known in southern Europe since at least the early 14th century. There are aspects of charivari in the conceit: the dead come noisily to welcome the new arrival. The band of masked youths recurs frequently in rituals of derision. (Florence, National Library.)

the criticism still could be toned down. The victim could pay off the demonstrators or offer them a drink or even play along in the hope of becoming the hero of a triumphant burlesque. In the 1740s we read in official reports that "no one reported to me that the new husband complained" or "the young people made a charivari, which the newlyweds bore gracefully." But those who, like the elderly couple in Aubais, decided to defy their tormentors laid themselves open to every kind of offense. This negotiable gradation—typical of the charivari but in fact omnipresent—added to the fear inspired by the ritual of unveiling and reinforced its authority. Since censors were traditionally conciliatory, it was the victim himself who by refusing to compromise knowingly chose to incur their wrath. Thus, as late as the eighteenth century some courts were concerned not so much with the legitimacy of the ritual as with the proper price to be paid for their moderation.

THE MOCKERS

With their broad field of action, protean forms of expression, and striking effectiveness, all these rituals can be interpreted as aspects of a strict mechanism of social control. In areas ranging from the honor of girls to the authority of husbands it laid down the law in the centrally important realm of authorized sexual behavior. But how extensive were these practices in ancien régime societies? If the orders of clergy and police prohibiting them can be taken literally, they concerned only the lower orders, the *bas peuple* of town and countryside. Certain evidence, however, makes us hesitate to accept such an interpretation. Because of its spectacular drama, we know of the so-called *bal des ardents*, or ball of the burning dancers, in which courtiers disguised as savages burst into flames before the panicky eyes of the future Charles VI. Two centuries later Bassompierre reports that a charivari at the court of Louis XIII was directed against an officer who had married a widow and that it was witnessed by Gaston d'Orléans.

No doubt such ceremonies were devoid of punitive intent and were seen simply as friendly entertainments to enliven otherwise dull weddings. Town dwellers of the best society had long celebrated in this way, occasionally being interrupted by overzealous police. In Toulouse on the night of 27 June 1750 a number of youths and two officers rented instruments with which to "serenade" a widow who was about to remarry. The lieutenant of the watch threatened to arrest the demonstrators and, returning later, collared a number of them. But this was a well-to-do neighborhood, and the ruckus brought a magistrate, several officers, and a number of ladies into the street from a nearby house, all of whom began jeering the lieutenant. The military commandant quickly put an end to what had become an ugly affair: "I had the opportunity . . . to speak with the prosecutor, who told me that according to the letter and spirit of the law the assembly of instruments used here did not constitute a charivari and who assured me that the lieutenant of the watch had erred in his judgment and by his imprudence caused the disturbance. I am not aware that the newly married husband had filed any complaint or that he had called this officer, which is a clear sign of his imprudence."[9]

Thus, in eighteenth-century towns there were charivaris and charivaris. The ritual and the reasons for a demonstration might be known to all, but there were distinct ways of going about it and normally only common folk paraded in the streets. There were also sharp differences between rural and

In Town and Village

urban charivaris. Many examples are known of ritualized social controls in nineteenth-century villages. In addition to the charivari and the funeral demonstration, there were other rituals, less frequent and more cautious in their expression. The annual judgment of girls at carnival time was never as aggressive in rural villages as it was in larger towns, where it was relatively easy to single out a servingwoman who slept with her master or a linen maid whose independent ways earned the scrutiny of her neighbors. By contrast, in the village ritual the social relations subject to censure were at once more egalitarian, more permanent, and more complex. Seldom did an unmarried woman lack relatives to defend her, so disapproval took more furtive forms. Hence in the eighteenth century punitive rituals were most fully developed and most regularly practiced among urban artisans, shopkeepers, and clerks.

Keeping these distinctions in mind, we can examine the social nature of these rituals. Although the tacit consent of a fairly extensive community was always required, the actual participants were drawn from a much narrower group. Who were they? What relation existed between their role as enforcers of norms of personal and family conduct and their position in local society?

An Exception: Groups of Women

At Castelnaudary in 1735 a group of fifteen women pursued a woman known as Mélix, who was accused of acting as a procuress for her daughter while her son-in-law was serving with the hussars. "They chanted songs in the faubourg and distributed copies in which they referred to the aforesaid Mélix as a whore and a drunk and a woman incapable of holding her wine . . . They incited the Bourrel children to insult her." The only couplets mentioned in the indictment are in Occitanian. They describe Mélix's fondness for the bottle and portray her husband as a fixture at the local tavern and as a man dominated by his wife, to whom he spoke in the meekest of voices. The six women accused are young, ranging in age from twenty-five to forty. Several are shopkeepers, and all but one can sign her name. When interrogated about the songs, the leader of the group even claimed the supreme distinction of not understanding patois.[10]

We know of similar occurrences in nineteenth-century Vaud. Women, often assisted by children, placed horns in doorways and scrawled insulting slogans on walls. Such punishment was meted out to a clerk who impregnated another man's fiancée, to a widow and daughter of a physician accused of loose morals, and to the wife of an elderly man who took young mistresses. To be sure, it was unusual for women to assume the role of symbolic censure, but the very rarity of examples makes these even more significant. They indicate, first of all, that women in the communes of Vaud and the commercial streets of Languedocian cities enjoyed a substantial degree of economic and cultural autonomy, so much so that they were able to assume full charge of these rituals rather than merely designating victims and bringing charges. More important, there is in all these affairs a notable congruity between the principles of the women involved and their punitive intentions. Whether defending a pregant girl or chastising another woman's debauch they behave as though by defending the honor of all women they were giving proof of their own integrity. The ritual not only denounces the im-

Mariette, *March. Celebrations of the Popinjay.* "Shooting the popinjay" here represents the month of March, though it more commonly occurred at the beginning of May or at Ascension or Pentecost. In this 18th-century scene it has become almost a military exercise, with the men carrying muskets. The game connotes both virility and youth. In the name of youth's ancient prerogatives young men in the cities defended the right to shoot birds and name an annual king. (Paris, Bibliothèque Nationale.)

morality of some scandalous act but at the same time upholds the morality of the participating women. The value judgment involved was so unanimous that a pastor from Mézières (Vaud), though in principle hostile to demonstrations of this kind, wrote the court in 1817 that he was in favor of charivaris conducted by women.[11]

The Rule: Youths

As a rule, however, the principal actors in eighteenth-century charivaris were young men, and the contrast with female-led demonstrations is striking. Here unanimity was unthinkable, for the youths involved were often at odds with official morality. They were the principal actors in a ritual of social control, which they claimed as their right.

Let us focus attention on the Youth (the capital was always used in contemporary reports) of Limoux, a small town in Languedoc at the head of the Aude valley. Limoux in 1786 was a textile center with some 6,500 inhabitants as well as a market town serving a region in which a variety of crops were grown. It had a diverse, hierarchical social structure, primarily industrial and mercantile. In this period these characteristics suggest that it would have possessed an ebullient youthful population. And in fact, between 1740 and 1789, in consular affidavits, political council minutes, instructions to the seneschal, and private complaints to the provincial commandant at Montpellier give evidence of more than a hundred cases, some minor, others serious, some unique, others recurrent, involving young people.[12]

A gentleman by the name of Terrier, salt-tax collector, gives some idea of the general tenor of the charges in his *Memoir in Complaint against the Youth of Limoux* (November 1746), which rehearses in conventional terms the usual litany of accusations. "The town of Limoux possesses a very libertine and uneducated Youth, which day and night insults men and women in the streets. In the eight years that I have been there I have seen all sorts of disorders, usually committed by a troop of a dozen who assemble in one particular house, where they decide what disturbance they will create each night. They are indeed of a rather mature age, and most of them have neither father nor mother and have consumed all their inheritance, so that it is dangerous to meet them. For besides the insults that one receives from them, they knock at doors in such a way as to break them down, not even sparing the religious communities of both sexes; not long ago they broke down the

door of the hospital sisters and shattered it. They remove door
knockers; block up the pipes leading to the fountain that supplies the entire city with water, causing them to break; climb
the walls of courtyards and gardens to steal chickens and
anything else they can find; demolish the stone benches alongside houses and around the square; break windows; and engage
in every kind of excess. For nearly two years I have been the
target of their whims without being associated with them in
any way. There is no insult that I have not received. My wife
and daughters are continually jeered. My windows are broken
by stones. A bench by my door was demolished. My door
lock has been blocked up with small iron nails. And they are
constantly knocking at my door saying that the whole town
is on fire."

These young men were not disciplined by any youth
organization, such as those that still survived in Provence and
Poitou under the aegis of the consular or seigneurial authorities.[13] Limoux's youths regained their corporate identity only
when a solemn entry required the population to form up in
battalions for a procession. Their accusers simply pointed out
"certain young people" or a "troop of youths" or "young
libertines," generally of mixed social origins. The gang that
persecuted the salt-tax collector with a charivari whose reasons
are not obvious was by his account composed of homeless
orphans. Yet one of them, named Poulhariez, protested in a
lengthy petition that he was an honorable merchant; admittedly he had made some bad business deals, but he was no
criminal. As for the companions with whom he liked to "fool
around," some came "from the best families in the town."
Another merchant joined him in denouncing the slander. In
1757 "prominent young men in the town" rebelled against the
consuls and escorted two young prostitutes to prison. In 1772
an inspector of public works for the diocese, serenaded
throughout the carnival as a cuckold, one night "recognized
the voices . . . of youths of good family."

No gang could do without a few relatively well-to-do
youths, who gathered around them a group that reflected the
familiar allegiances of urban society, the interrelated speciali-
ties of the leather and wool trades, of manufacturing and
commerce. In the early 1770s, when Youth bitterly defended
its carnival rights, bold young laborers reinforced the gangs
of young men who jeered, insulted, and mocked the town
consuls. To be sure, social divisions among youths did emerge
from time to time. At one carnival lower-class lads who

danced to drums and oboes clashed with the children of the wealthy, who danced to the sound of violins. But neighborhood and clientage bonds tended to mask or efface class differences. At any rate, as far as the rest of society was concerned, Youth was defined by a style of behavior, a set of shared customs.

Circumventing Established Order

Youthful customs were associated with certain places. The outskirts of Limoux belonged to the young. Youths claimed the esplanade outside the town walls, which was closed in 1765 and again in 1767 because of frequent brawls. In the moat beyond the esplanade, prostitutes serviced their clients in broad daylight. Inside the walls, not far from the gates, young people congregated on the streets alongside the convents of the Augustinians and Franciscans, whose windowless walls provided protection against curious onlookers. Gambling dens and meeting places were perpetually on the move from neighborhood to neighborhood; when one closed down, another opened up. When night fell the entire city became fair game. A baker, a midwife, and a bourgeois returning from a reception testified to gatherings glimpsed from afar and carefully avoided, for the city by night belonged to Youth. This nocturnal rule enabled the young to circumvent the order that even the smallest eighteenth-century cities had managed to establish.

Little by little the streets became public property. The consuls of Limoux prohibited their use as chicken yards or parking lots for haycarts. Pigs were banished beyond the city walls. Garbage could no longer be emptied in the street. Monuments were erected in the heart of town. The central square of Limoux was the object of the city fathers' attention. Bordered on three sides by arcades topped by balconies, it was a bustling center of activities whose aspect varied with the season. During the summer action centered on the fountain, whereas in wintertime the covered arcades offered protection against bad weather. Shops lined the square. A weekly market was held. Every day during the summer day laborers gathered in the square for hiring. On Sundays worshipers from the nearby Church of Saint Martin paused to chat with their neighbors. After a terrible fire in 1693 stone gradually replaced the wooden pillars, floors, and facades, and the public fountain was restored and enlarged.

In this showcase of urban order the young, performing

their usual rituals, annually struck fear into the hearts of the populace. On the night of 28 January 1771 the carnival was officially begun. A frightened woman testified as to what occurred: "The town square was illuminated by flames, which she believed emanated from the surrounding arcades. Approaching the square, she allegedly saw a fire and a brazier under two of the roofs, which are built partly of stone and partly of wood and mostly covered by the wooden floors of houses."

In August 1748 another gang scandalized a local merchant. "We have in the middle of the town square a large and beautiful fountain, the water from which accumulates in a substantial basin. This always remains filled with water for use in case of fire. The water flows along a small channel, overflowing occasionally but without bothering anyone. These young libertines amused themselves, however, by diverting the ordinary stream. After channeling it beyond a

Van Nieulant, *Carnival Scene before the Walls of Antwerp.* Beyond ramparts, moats, and lists were the winter sports arena and the carnival area. This was the city's wilderness, a disreputable zone ruled by card sharps and young libertines. Here in Antwerp bourgeois men and women have come by carriage to watch a masked parade on the slippery, frozen ground. (Brussels, Old Art Museum.)

small lot next to the arcade, they funneled it over a steep incline toward the door of my house, where there is an iron grille to allow light into the courtyard. To that spot they channeled a large amount of water from the aforementioned fountain by making a large hole between two of the stones of which the aforesaid basin was constructed."

The implicit rule governing the nighttime activities of youths was that everything in the streets belonged to them. They destroyed the benches of wood and stone that lined the facades of buildings. They smashed merchants' stalls in the marketplace, overturned butchers' tables, and used ladders to climb up and knock over a vase of flowers in a window and to remove a bird cage that was then tossed into a hastily improvised fire.

Because of these routine disturbances, people closed up their houses and property more tightly than before, inciting even more destructive violence. Doors—symbolic as well as physical barriers—were forced open, stoned, or smashed by rampaging youths. A barber complained that one gang repeatedly forced his door and smashed the water pitcher that was kept nearby. And in 1747 the following confrontation occurred: "Sieur Bernard Reverdy, master tailor, stated that around 11 o'clock at night, while he was at work in his shop, a gang of youths that had been kicking all the doors on the street came to his and broke it down, damaging the lock, catch, and hinges . . . When he went into the street to see who had committed the crime, the younger Roques boy accosted him and said, 'You scoundrel, how dare you venture out against so large a gang! I thumb my nose at you and the whole town.' And then he hurled several stones at him, which [Reverdy] avoided only by hastening back to his shop and barricading himself inside."

Vegetable gardens, farmyards, and rabbit hutches near cities, villages, and noble residences were periodically visited: "They are suspected of having robbed the Château de la Tourzelle and several other nearby châteaux of all its chickens, turkeys, and so forth during the carnival" (1760).

Unstinting Expenditure   Young bourgeois shared with young laborers an ethic of free expenditure, which contributed to their disdain for law and order. The main occasions for this expenditure were the lengthy carnival and other festivities. The carnival began on January 1 with a tour of the village and ended on Ash Wednes-

day. Extravagant costumes were not yet a necessary part of the ritual, but householders were expected at the very least to pay for the music that accompanied street-dancing. Rival gangs fought over the services of musicians who were summoned from long distances. In 1763 three hautbois players—from Villardebelle, Saint-Hilaire, and Espéraza—earned a total of 27 livres for the evening of Mardi gras and 19 during the day of Ash Wednesday. The more prestigious violinists probably earned twice as much. Spending money for musical entertainment became the sine qua non of youth festivities. Throughout the year for occasions of every kind—a serenade for prostitutes, a charivari, a masked attack on well-to-do strangers walking the streets, a New Year's party in the consular prison—musicians were hired to play the hautbois and violin.

During the long winter months another popular entertainment was gambling. Games of chance sprang up in private homes and out-of-the-way gardens as quickly as the authori-

Mariette, *February. Masquerade.* During carnival houses had to open their doors to masked revelers. To the music of violin and hautbois they presented a short play and solicited food for the pre-Lenten feast: a ham and a strip of lard hang from the rafters. The girls, who were often serenaded on these occasions, exhibit a mixture of fear and interest. (Paris, Bibliothèque Nationale.)

Flemish school, *Carnival Scene,* 17th century. This nocturnal revel takes place out of doors. Groups of skaters glide along the frozen canal. The musicians, in the center, are preceded by a small boy wearing a crown who beats a friction drum, a child's instrument, which establishes a link between the carnival and the charivari. (Evreux, Municipal Museum.)

ties could stamp them out. Associated with taverns and sometimes with prostitution, brelan and lansquenet tables attracted the cash of young bourgeois as well as craftsmen. In the midst of the carnival of 1769 an anonymous letter denounced the situation to the councils: "It is shameful for an honest man to write an anonymous letter, but I am forced to do so in spite of myself for fear that otherwise some harm might befall me. As a father I am pleased to beg you to put an end to a game of chance that has long existed in our town. My children are ruining me, to say nothing of other families that have also been ruined. The guilty party is Sieur Balada, a stranger to these parts, who was driven out of Pamiers for having operated a card game there. He has a house near the Franciscans, which is used only for gambling. I know that M. Andrieu [the first consul] has warned him not to operate this game, but in spite of that he continues to do so night and day. This is a scandalous thing near a church . . . from which they can be heard shouting and fighting."

Those who operated gambling dens were often accused of inducing their habitués to commit robbery: "Youths dishonor themselves to cover their considerable losses." Raids were ineffective. When the authorities knocked, those within doused the lights and in the darkness smashed the lanterns carried by the consuls and their lackeys, allowing the gamblers to make their getaway. According to neighbors compelled by the courts to talk, the young gamblers "plotted to destroy houses" and set out out to wander about the city amidst "a frightful din."[14]

Young men were equally profligate in their relations with prostitutes. In eighteenth-century Limoux no house of prostitution was tolerated, so prostitution was a family affair, a business carried on by a widow and her daughter, two sisters, and the daughters of a bankrupt miller. Married men and wealthy bourgeois were discreet about their visits. They could be seen, according to neighbors, creeping along the walls at daybreak, hiding their faces. By contrast, young bachelors paid public homage to the ladies of the night. They kissed them in the street, serenaded them, danced the farandole with them during carnival, and bestowed gifts that the ladies wore with pride. The sisters Anne and Marguerite Pascal, notorious for their behavior in the years from 1752 to 1758, "wore very

William Hogarth, *The Rake's Progress*. At the gaming table hopes of fortune go up in smoke, hatreds are unleashed, youth is corrupted, and families are ruined. (Paris, Bibliothèque Nationale.)

proper clothing, hairpieces, and lace, very expensive items, beyond what the ladies and damsels of this town can afford." They also wore "silver buckles on their pumps." Their young admirers were fervently devoted. In 1754 an apprentice goldsmith stole some scrap silver and a Spanish pistole from his master to give to the elder of the two sisters, Anne. He also bought her, on his father's account, a fine piece of muslin, which she had made into an apron. Other prostitutes received silver dishes and gold rings from their clients.

Social Conformity and Orderly Disorder

Nocturnal mischief and expenditure as pleasure were the rules by which youths lived, according to their neighbors and victims, who described what they had seen and endured. And yet the young insisted on punishing others for supposed misdeeds. Private individuals, bourgeois visitors, and young women were targets, for reasons that we cannot always grasp, of jeers, songs, stonings, and displays of carrion, while their young assailants hid in the dark, protected by masks, bonfires, and the music of violins. In 1773 youths directed the customary charivari against a widow of good family who, though in mourning for her father, persisted with plans to remarry. Because the groom refused to pay, the couple became the target of the usual clamor, stench, and stones.

Starting about 1770, however, these youthful protests seem to have assumed a rather theatrical dimension. Demonstrations continued throughout the year, culminating at carnival time. A case that went to the courts in 1772 furnishes useful details. Since August of the preceding year Jean-Pierre Amans Dufour, inspector of public works, had been the subject of a song sung by more than a hundred youths. It could be heard in the first hours of darkness beneath Dufour's windows. On at least one occasion the youths had attempted to enter his house, probably to negotiate with their victim or to abduct him. As carnival drew near, the youths chose two lesser victims to accompany the inspector—the bakers Fregoli and L'Auzino—and went from house to house dancing and "singing the aforementioned songs, occasionally shouting *Couioul! Couioul!*"—patois for cuckold. For cuckoldry was indeed the misfortune said to have befallen the three heroes of a farce related in fifteen couplets set to fifteen well-known tunes and entitled the *Noubel Opera de Cournanel* (New Opera of Cournanel). Deceived by a wife who prefers younger men, and himself impotent, as evidenced by five years of childless marriage, the cuckold was asked to accept his lot and inscribe his name in golden letters in a book preserved in the "Archives of Cournanel."

Apparently the parodied text changed each year. An opera in 1772, in 1775 it appears to have been a political constitution, to judge from the title, which is all that has survived: *Las Leis del Grand Cornelius, ame le discours dal general das couiouls* (The Laws of the Great Cornelius, with the Speech of the General of Cuckolds). The skit was written, rehearsed, and staged by a whole army of youths. After New Year's its tone became sharper. The whole thing was written down and copied by the most literate of the youths, perhaps a clerk or a student— yet another reason for broad social recruitment. This particular skit was composed in Occitan, a language that had been little used for writing for two centuries and whose oral tradition licensed the crudest turns of phrase. The young made this dialect their own. In music and writing it became their most incisive and fearsome weapon.

This portrait of youth culture in a small town at the end of the ancien régime reveals an interesting paradox. On the one hand, it is tempting to see the youths of the town as enforcers of the common morality, for their condemnation of bad marriages, impudent girls, and indulgent husbands seems to have been widely shared. Yet they themselves were accused not only by the authorities but by the community at large of being dissolute troublemakers, always ready to sow disorder. The edifying intent of their rituals seems to have become no more than a pretext for mischief.

For a long time social conformity appears to have been enforced by those who temporarily found themselves on the margins of the social order. In this instance the object of control was marriage, and it was those who had not yet married and who did not yet bear responsibility for a family who were accorded the right and the duty to eradicate disharmony by exposing it. To that end they used a language of dissonance: cacophonous noises, obscene words, and incongruous objects. In a broader sense, it was incumbent upon the young to reveal the dissonance in the social order by testing the limits of the tolerable. In rural villages the natural settings for their activities were the forests and marshes, where disruptive savagery could be observed from a safe distance. In town the same experiments took place in areas in which, in the eighteenth century, law and order reigned by day but debauch reasserted itself by night. In both town and country

Louis Sébastien Mercier, Paris "at nine at night." The perversion of public order, or, rather, the assertion of another order. In the second half of the 18th century municipal authorities throughout France took steps to install street lighting in order to maintain order in the streets at night. (Paris, Bibliothèque Nationale.)

every house contributed, through voluntary gifts, extorted contributions, or tolerated pillage, to the expenditures of the young for gambling and reveling, youthful activities in which the cardinal values were extravagance, chance, and contempt for thrift. That such temporary, codified disorder could give rise to a durable order is exemplified by the life of the former bachelor who, upon taking a wife and becoming a father, renounced his youthful ways. In eighteenth-century Languedoc the married men of the village did not fail to make the new head of household pay for his innocence.

Owing to this implicit logic of juvenile social control, men tolerated a custom they had once practiced themselves. They may have cursed, but they did not fight very hard. Even the authorities tolerated the mischief, "because Youth must pass." But the paradox inherent in the system became increasingly apparent. Achieving order through disorder became an intolerable contradiction. The rites of derision revealed nothing but the uncivilized behavior of those who participated in them.

The Despair of the Ladies of the Night. (Paris, Bibliothèque Nationale.)

PUBLIC ORDER AND THE PRIVATE SPHERE

Leading the way, the Church for reasons of liturgical discipline condemned charivaris against widows. A second marriage was no less sacred than a first. Charivaris, which mocked the sacrament of the second marriage, were therefore sacrilegious. The Council of Compiègne had proposed this argument as early as 1329–30, and it would be repeated verbatim by dozens of synods and bishops in France and Italy down to the middle of the eighteenth century.[15] True, the Church itself had for a long time deprived the second marriage of solemnity. In the first place, a widow retained ties of kinship to her late husband's lineage, so that many who might have been convenient marriage partners were ruled out—down to the fourth canonical degree. Second, moralists had painted a rather dark portrait of the widow, casting doubt on her character and suggesting that she was a poor choice for a mate. More important, the theology of the marriage sacrament excluded benediction of second marriages in many dioceses. (It is still not known how these were distributed geographically.) Yet the Church opposed, vehemently but ineffectively, all the parallel and rival rituals that apparently resulted from its own adherence to a sacrament without a rite.

Condemnation by Church and Parlement

Although the civil authorities initially borrowed the vocabulary of the prelates, their intention was different. During the fourteenth and fifteenth centuries the police and the courts never dealt with charivaris and similar rituals as such unless they led to some bloody incident such as a riot or murder, particularly since local customs, whether urban or seigneurial, sometimes legitimated the control of marriages by young unmarried males. The authorities even claimed a portion of the customary charivari fine paid by the groom. But when order became an end in itself, made all the more urgent by religious and social antagonisms, explicit prohibitions began to appear. The very Catholic parlement of Toulouse prohibited charivaris in 1538, and it repeated the ban four more times in the sixteenth century. The prohibition became familiar: the parlements of Burgundy in 1606, Bordeaux in 1639, and Aix-en-Provence in 1640 issued reminders of a prohibition that applied throughout the kingdom. Yet in view of the fact that the civil authorities were defending not a holy sacrament but "public tranquillity," it is surprising that none of the proclamations mentioned cited by name any disturbance other than the chari-

ARREST
DE LA COUR
DE PARLEMENT,

Qui fait défenses à toutes perfonnes, de quelqu'état & condition qu'elles puiffent être, de s'affembler & de s'attrouper, fous aucun prétexte, & dans aucun temps de l'année; de fimuler les fonctions de la Juftice; de courir mafquées ou déguifées dans la ville & fauxbourgs de Verberie; porter ou repréfenter aucune effigie; faire aucuns charivaris, parades, cavalcades, ou autres jeux tumultueux, infulter aucuns particuliers de quelqu'état & condition qu'ils foient, par défignations directes ou indirectes, fous les peines portées audit Arrêt.

EXTRAIT DES REGISTRES DU PARLEMENT.

Du fix Février mil fept cent quatre-vingt-trois.

VU par la Cour la Requête préfentée par le Procureur Général du Roi, contenant qu'il a été informé que, dans la ville de Verberie, plufieurs particuliers s'affemblent, au nombre de trente ou quarante, le Mercredi des Cendres, pour faire le procès à quelques habitans de ladite ville, fous le prétexte qu'il aura été frappé par fa femme, ou qu'il aura rempli quelques fonctions intérieures du ménage;

ARREST
DE LA COUR
DE PARLEMENT

PORTANT DEFENCES
de faire aucunes Affemblées appellées Charivary, à peine de mille
livres d'amende.

Donné le premier jour d'Avril 1681.

A TOULOUSE,
Par JEAN BOUDE, Imprimeur du Roy, des Eftats Generaux
de la Province de Languedoc, de l'Université de Touloufe,
& de la Cour, près le College de Foix. 1681.

Parlementary decrees condemning charivaris. (Above: Paris,
Musée des Arts et Traditions
populaires; right: Paris, Bibliothèque Nationale.)

EXTRAIT DES REGISTRE
de Parlement.

LOUIS par la grace de Dieu, Roy de France &
Navarre, au premier noftre Huiffier ou Sergent fur ce
quis, comme fur les requifitions verbalement faites à Noft
Cour de Parlement de Touloufe, par DE MANIBAN, pour r
ftre Procureur General, difant que par un abus tres-contraire a
bonnes mœurs, & à la Police generale de noftre Royaume, o
accouftumé de faire dans la prefente Ville, & autres du Reff
de noftre dite Cour, des Affemblées nocturnes, qu'on nom
de Charivary, à l'occafion des feconds Mariages d'un hom
veuf avec une Fille, ou d'une Veuve avec un Garçon; & com
ces Affemblées font toûjours pleines de diffolution & de deb
che, l'on fe donne auffi prefque toufiours la licence de décrié
Reputation des gens, & de divulguer le fecret des familles;
qui peut non feulement produire des inimitiez implacables, n
encore favorifer les reffentimens & les vengeances, exciter
émotions, & troubler le repos & la tranquillité publique; a
quels inconveniens, auffi-bien qu'à la diffolution des mœr
eftant tres-important de remedier, requeroit noftredite Co
de faire tres-expreffes inhibitions & deffenfes à toute forte
perfonnes d'entreprendre de faire à l'avenir aucune de ces Affe
blées nocturnes appellées Charivary, foit dans la prefente V
le, que dans les autres du Reffort, à peine de mille livres
mende, & des contreventions en eftre enquis par le pren
noftre Iuge ou Magiftrat requis, pour l'information faite & r
portée, eftre decerné contre les coupables tel decret que

vari. Why this long silence concerning other rites of derision such as the asouade, which were even more disruptive of law and order?

The discreet silence of the decrees calls attention to a latent tension between local customs and the penal code elaborated in the courts. We learn from a court document that in 1375 in Senlis the customary rule that "husbands who allow themselves to be beaten by their wives shall be obliged and condemned to ride an ass, with their face in the direction of said ass's tail" had been applied. In 1404 a similar article was contained in the *Customs* of Saintonge. And as late as 1593 the bailiff of Hombourg decided that, "in accordance with ancient custom," a woman who had beaten her husband should be made to ride backward on an ass whose bridle was held by her feeble spouse. In England under the Tudors and Stuarts the courts sentenced both men and women to ride backward on a horse while wearing the clothes of the opposite sex, sometimes to the accompaniment of "rough music."[16] Three decrees of the Paris parlement between 1729 and 1756, as well as a custom of Toulouse attested as late as 1775, held that a notorious procuress should be made to ride backward on a female ass, while her husband, if she had one, followed on a

Ritual Penalties and Judicial Punishments

The Promenade of Procuresses. Prostitution was practiced in two forms: discreetly in private apartments or publicly in the streets, with rates officially set by the authorities. The former required the services of procuresses. If an entremetteuse was denounced, she was punished, as late as the 18th century in both Paris and Toulouse, by being paraded backward on an ass. (Paris, Bibliothèque Nationale.)

mule. In Toulouse the asses were equipped with bells. A common threat in eighteenth-century Languedoc was that of being forced to "ride through town with feathers and a basket," reminiscent of the feathering of prostitutes and adulteresses. The women were first covered with honey, then rolled in feathers, and baskets were placed over their heads; then they were paraded through town on the back of a donkey. Fernando de Rojas' Celestina was subjected to this ignominy. (See illustration on page 541.) Other punishments, including removal of the roof, smashing of doors and windows, dismantling of wagons, spoiling of wells, and immersion in water, which figured in "popular" rituals of censure in various parts of Germanic and Latin Europe, were also part of the official penal code until the seventeenth or eighteenth century.[17]

In all these punishments the public was supposed to serve not as passive onlookers to be edified by example but as active participants. Indeed, the severity of the punishment was determined by the intensity of the laughter, jests, and satiric improvisations of the public. Judges and crowd shared a conviction that the punishment must fit the crime. With time, however, the scene of punishment became increasingly restricted. The penal code insisted upon a more solemn spectacle, on breaking the symbolic link between the crime and the punishment and establishing in its place an abstract schedule of penalties. With the adoption of the French Penal Code and similar codes in other countries, a formal system of punishments triumphed throughout Europe. But this product of the Enlightenment was a long time coming. Burning at the stake was outlawed by the end of the seventeenth century. Thereafter, little by little the ritual punishments were gradually discredited, freeing judges who came upon rites of derision to declare firmly and unequivocally that they were unquestionably illegal.

In 1610 the parlement of Bordeaux condemned those responsible for a "ceremony called running or riding the ass, because of hatred of a man . . . who had allowed himself to be beaten by his wife"—but only after a memorable trial in which the attorney for the defense argued doggedly that the ritual was not only lawful but morally justified.[18] In 1655 the aldermen of Bayonne issued a writ against individuals who "boast of running the animal that they call an ass." Other prohibited rituals included "defamatory verses" (Bayonne, 1655) and "obscene and insulting songs" (Toulouse, 1762). Judges classified these offenses together with illicit nocturnal assemblies, extortions, libels, and the like. Statutes were occasionally directed against specific situations, such as the one created by "the youths of several towns and places who . . . frequently congregate, especially on Sundays and holidays, run through the streets at night singing wicked songs of all sorts, and create various disturbances and disorders" (Montpellier, 1737).

Repression became broader and stricter than in the past. It was aimed at a style of conduct rather than a particular offense, and in this respect it had much in common with the concerns of Counter-Reformation clerics, who used similar language. But it took most of the eighteenth century to persuade authorities at lower levels of the hierarchy, particularly in the villages, of the wisdom of this approach. The elites felt that the village authorities were sometimes too apt either to compromise with custom or to impose unduly harsh penalties upon their local enemies.

These new laws and penalties, developed for a variety of reasons, answered a growing need. Throughout the eighteenth century the courts heard growing numbers of cases involving every conceivable form of ritual derision. Between 1700 and 1790 the criminal chamber of the parlement of Navarre judged forty-seven charivaris. During the second half of the century, in the vast jurisdiction of the parlement of Toulouse, courts at all levels heard more than five hundred such cases. In Provence the frequency was no doubt similar, and investigation will probably yield equivalent results in other regions.[19] Although the authorities sometimes acted on their own, most cases originated with the filing of a complaint by a private individual. The strength of custom had established a necessary accord among those involved in the ritual. But when the custom ceased to be uniformly accepted, some victims did not hesitate to counterattack, even at the risk of aggravating hostilities. What were the points of dispute? And what were the social causes of what can be only be considered the revolt of the victims?

The Victims' Resistance

For one thing, there was increased resistance to the extortion of money by youth gangs, for which derisive rituals provided the most lucrative pretext. For any marriage a bribe had to be paid: in Mediterranean France the *pelote*, in the Vaud the so-called *vin des mariés*, or newlyweds' wine. The fee was increased for exogamous marriages, and it cost even more to mute a charivari. But those who could most easily have paid began to resist. They protested against demands that increased insatiably with the victim's ability to pay. A bourgeois from Saint-Victor (Uzège) decided after two months to petition the military commandant in regard to "horrible noise" and "vulgar songs." He notes: "At first I employed the most decent means of putting an end to this persecution, inviting them for food and drink and handing out a substantial sum of money." In order to prevent the ante from being raised, the first consul of Paulhan in 1780 heroically chose to turn a deaf ear to the *toutoures*, clay horns that were sounded on the night of May 1: "Since I had just married for the second time, and since I knew the malice that certain people bore me, I understood that this was a charivari and was prudent enough not to get up."

More often than not, however, a dispute ensued. When the youths of Saint-Hippolyte-du-Fort presented their demands during the engagement banquet of a widower who happened to be a fairly wealthy merchant, his fiancée's outraged parents drove them away, provoking a monster charivari. Subsequently they refused to end the derision in the face of demands for payment that reached 50 livres.[20] "Remember that they are attacking me and that I owe them nothing!" exclaimed a remarried young widower to witnesses of an attack by youths who assailed him in broad daylight on the streets of his village. Against the ritual he asserts the law, which justifies his refusal while protecting his money.

Eighteenth-century property owners reacted agressively against youths who attempted to take what belonged to them. In small Languedocian towns such as Limoux contributions to youthful festivities, whether freely given or coerced, became increasingly rare after 1750. Anyone who wished to make a celebration had to pay out of his own pocket. Inevitably youths of the "better ranks" took the lead in rituals and games that required music.

The nature of the search for money changed. For some gangs New Year's Day rounds became an occasion for theft and pillage. Youths broke into the homes of helpless artisans, emptied their pantries and cellars, manhandled and threatened the occupants. The customary nocturnal pilfering by young males, which had been condoned as long as it was kept within certain limits, now got out of hand. Those who robbed gardens and farmyards were punished. In Pézenas "young artisans, farm laborers, and gardeners [who] mischievously pick grapes at night and, not content with thievery, do considerable damage by destroying vines were attacked." Any derisive ritual, from mocking a fornicator with bells to a full-scale charivari, came to be regarded as a major crime if it was accompanied by damage to property. Any action that destroyed, damaged, or dislocated property was punished. Such actions became the leading forms of protest against the established order. Defying the bourgeois in one quarter of Castelnaudary, youths in October 1729 smashed all the doors on one street. People felt an almost physical attachment to their private property, and, certain that they were in the right to protect it, protested against symbolic attacks as well as extortion.

By thus rebelling against youthful male traditions, property owners not only exacerbated the violence but helped to transform into common crimes what once had been considered rituals of derision. That at least, is the impression given by the endless charges and affidavits, signs of an ongoing war between youths and their elders in the towns and small cities of France in the years prior to the Revolution. The bourgeois of the time made free use of the word "libertine" to describe any disruption to law and order as defined by people of established families: idleness, keeping low company, squandering of patrimony through gambling and frequenting prostitutes, spendthrift street festivities, and contempt for authority.[21]

Youths who wielded the weapon of derision posed an even greater threat to the new order. They would have been no less offensive had they done little damage to property and little to disrupt law and order, because, in claiming to influence the institution of marriage, the nexus of family history, they crossed an increasingly impregnable line. Their worst offense was no longer attacking the "sacrament of marriage" or "public tranquillity" but, as the parlement of Navarre put it in a 1769 decree outlawing charivaris, against "freedom within families." Faced with growing numbers of recalcitrant victims, judges around the middle of the eighteenth century began to question the justification for the ritual itself. The charivari, wrote the prefect of the Hautes-Pyrénées in the Year XII, was a relic "worthy of the ancient savages who lived in these parts." In other words, it was a ritual in which the community presumed to judge and to punish the actions of families. But the property-owning bourgeoisie, whose members sat on the courts and filed charges before them, had gradually been won over to the view that these were matters for families themselves to decide and that no outside agency ought to influence their decisions. And the law unambiguously favored the right to throw a veil of secrecy around private life.

A great deal of evidence supports this interpretation, as does the language itself, which reflects growing awareness of the change. Yet among the thousands of cases recorded in the archives, some interesting anomalies remain to be explained. In Limoux in the period 1740–1790 the leading targets of derision included an official of the slat monopoly, a specialist in feudal law, a prosecutor in the court of the seneschal, and an inspector of public works for the diocese. All reacted vehemently against the attempt to censure their private behavior as husbands or fathers. All owned property, but primarily they were men who wielded paper and quill. Embodying the external legality of the state and accordingly well-versed in the use of the courts, they precipitated a debate between tradition and ritual on the one hand and legal and bureaucratic modernity on the other. And just as, in the past, every family sooner or later encountered the charivari, now every family eventually ran afoul of the new state apparatus.

The Powers of the Curé

In rural villages tension focused even more significantly on another very important personage: the curé. Trained in the seminaries of the Counter-Reformation, which brought uniformity to priests' views on religion and morals, the curé naturally opposed all traditional forms of derision. In the name of "family peace" he condemned the charivari and the carnival judgment. In Vivarais priests denounced the practice of setting maypoles with phallic symbols in front of girls' homes. In Burzet a priest in 1780 went so far as to protect a couple threatened with charivari by dispensing them from two of the three readings of the banns and celebrating their marriage secretly in the middle of the night. Denouncing the traditional customs of youth, the curé refused to allow young men to collect what they considered their due at occasions like weddings: "Whenever anyone marries, [the youths] make them pay for food and drink. If the newlyweds refuse, they immediately repair to some tavern and order quantities of food at the couple's expense, while harassing and insulting them until they pay up" (Saint-André, Lodève, 1749).

Priests kept a detailed record of the "exactions," "scandals," "disorders," and "sacrileges" perpetrated by youths. "They counterfeit the ceremonies and pay no heed to remon-

strances. They run through the village in disguise, dancing, displaying carnival on Ash Wednesday. They enter the sanctuary during services, station themselves between the cross and the priest in processions as though they were clergy, turn their backs to the altar, laugh and talk during services, pound on the benches, fire pistols in church or in front of it on wedding days and holy days, dance in front of the church on the pedestal of the cross, even before catechism and during Advent, and sing obscene songs" (Neffiès, Béziers, 1769).

To be sure, in opposing such unorthodox practices, the curé was faithfully reflecting a religious ideal. But his social ambitions and de facto position in the community more or less obliged him to oppose the right to scrutinize morals that youths claimed to exercise on behalf of the community as a whole. Since the end of the seventeenth century the curé had filled two equally important roles. He now possessed the cultural equipment to discharge his pastoral role more effectively than ever before, and his hand was strengthened by his control over the elementary school. In addition, the monarchy had

Mural painting on wood, 1705. The authority of the curé over his flock was reinforced by periodic visits of the bishop, who made sure that the local priest was maintaining good order and strict discipline. During this visit the bishop is confirming the newest communicants. (Finistère, Chapel of Saint-Tugen-en-Primelin.)

chosen him as its representative at the village level.[22] From 1667 on he was empowered to record baptisms, marriages, and deaths; in 1737 a new regulation required him to make copies of these records, establishing the keeping of vital statistics as a universal practice. He was also called upon to provide other data. In Protestant areas, for example, the curé monitored the behavior of new converts and, if need be, denounced miscreants to the authorities. In southern France, where municipal authorities were often illiterate, he assessed taxes and from the pulpit at the end of mass read decrees and ordinances received from the provincial governor.

Because he fulfilled a dual role, at once religious and political, the curé was able to keep a close watch on family morals and denounce such transgressions as adultery, concubinage, and illegitimate pregnancy. He acted as an intermediary, facilitating certain marriages, and was often called upon to give advice in marital matters. He could refuse communion to the dissolute or refuse burial in the church cemetery to a "libertine." And he could personally hear the confessions of girls whom he knew to be tempted by dancing or flirtation. Every priest aspired to direct the consciences of the women of his village, especially those from the wealthiest families. Some asked probing, intimate questions about the "lamentable secrets" that enabled women to avoid pregancy. Nicole Castan tells of one priest who compelled his eighteen-year-old penitent, daughter of the local castellan, to leave for the convent the very night after she had spent three hours in his confessional accusing her family, for he believed her to be in jeopardy owing to the untoward affections of an elderly and jealous father.

A disproportion of urban victims of charivari consisted of officials and bureaucrats. The conclusion to be drawn from that fact is confirmed by evidence from rural villages: that ritual censure in the eighteenth century was directed primarily against its most outspoken opponents, foremost among whom was the village curé. Himself a long-time resident of the village, the curé headed a family of sisters, brothers, nieces, and nephews, whose education he watched closely and whose futures he sought to assure. His own life was quiet and meditative, and he pointedly contrasted his demeanor with the disorderly conduct of others, especially youths. "Sunday last, the holy day of Pentecost, they appeared as usual, beating their drums and dancing their farandole. At that time I was busy on the ground floor of my house, rereading my breviary.

It was impossible to concentrate. I went out to apprise them of the sanctity of my occupation, but in response to my prayers and warnings, they told me to address their behinds, and they accompanied their words with gestures of the hand" (Estesargues, Uzès, 1774).

By upholding public order and family freedom, the curé acquired a discreet power of his own. By exercising bureaucratic authority as well as spiritual persuasion, he defined a sphere that was private, to be sure, but also transparent to his gaze alone.

Custom's Revenge

This evolution did not go unopposed. In the first place, families seem to have misunderstood its significance. Among townfolk and rural merchants the aspiration to greater autonomy was coupled with nostalgia for the paternal authority of old. In southern France the father retained absolute power over family affairs and choice of heir. As late as the eighteenth century notaries in Lodévois were still recording solemn emancipation rituals. To combat "libertinage," even to go as far as to have a wayward son imprisoned by lettre de cachet, was to join in the Church's moral struggle but without necessarily submitting to the authority of the curé, whose power frequently provoked factional disputes or led to insidious charges of sexual misconduct, fairly common in the eighteenth century, which saw numerous parish priests accused in diocesan courts.

The youths whose rituals were condemned replied in more obvious ways, persecuting the curé with all the means at their disposal: banging on his door at night, pilfering the presbytery garden, singing insulting songs, and stoning, sometimes accompanied by more serious threats. At Aramon on the right bank of the Rhône young men were particularly unruly in the 1790s. During one carnival they staged a charivari against a newly married couple, singing a song in which they promised to parade the husband on an ass. The curé condemned the agitators, but when they reacted he did not persist, having been made prudent by a terrible mishap that had befallen his predecessor, who had taken the bold step of entering the cabaret, that ineradicable den of iniquity, to continue his sermon against the town's youth: "Three or four youths grabbed him, tied him up, and carried him on their shoulders to the Rhône, into which they proposed to throw him. But one of them was moved by his shouts, and he was untied . . . They made him swear that he would never name them, and he kept his promise."

These challenges to tradition were not without effect on the rituals themselves, and changes in them reveal the strength of the protest. The customary right of scrutiny was strictly limited to relations between the sexes at the time of marriage. Communal censure was permissible only when a violation of the norms became public. Infractions before or after marriage were protected as long as they were discreet. Only the wedding itself was fair game for public scrutiny and judgment. The Church's oversight went much further, and since the Church set itself up as the rival as well as the adversary of traditional forms of censure, traditionalists were obliged to broaden their field of view. In Aramon a 1781 charivari, which provoked strong opposition from both the husband and the curé, led to increasingly detailed revelations. The gentleman in question had "attempted to violate the honor of several women, who brought charges against him." A song was composed which recounted in detail his misadventures with a neighbor woman and a laundress. His wife, a servingwoman who "did not earn her living by crossing her legs," had given birth to a stillborn child fathered by her late master; it was further intimated that she had somehow misappropriated a part of his estate. In Limoux that same year more than one hundred persons, led by "eight or nine youths, law clerks and manufacturers' and retailers' boys, aged fifteen to twenty," had serenaded a notary's daughter from carnival time until midsummer. The girl was accused of seeing too much of a female friend, the daughter of a dealer in animal feed.

Thus, the most private of matters became grist for the mills of public morality as well as the Church. This trend continued in the nineteenth century. In Germany, according to E. Hinrichs, the scope of the charivari, or *Haberfeldtreiben*, expanded: "In addition to the usual charges of immorality, adultery, and forbidden love, now homosexuality, incest, concubinage, and polygamy were added to the list. After 1870 sodomy was also included." In Gascony as well as Germany, the sex lives of the two representatives of political and moral authority, the curé and the schoolteacher, were subjected to close scrutiny.[23] Primarily for their benefit a new ritual of derision was invented: ivy, feathers, sawdust, and weevil-gnawed beans were strewn between the doors of the illicit lovers by night. This was an offense that the lawmakers had not foreseen, a derivation from the defamatory rituals of May and an inversion of the custom of honoring newlyweds by throwing rice at them or strewing flowers on the ground. It was a way of revealing the secrets of those who knew and manipulated the secrets of everyone else.

Jan van Hoogstraten, *Slippers*. An open door with the keys left in the lock. There was little distinction between inside and outside in 18th-century Paris apartments. News was exchanged at the threshold, and noise filtered in from outside. (Paris, Louvre.)

❧ The Honor and Secrecy of Families

Arlette Farge

PARIS was a city that worked like a mirage. Attracting people whom the countryside could no longer support, it simultaneously expelled those who could not adapt, who could not accommodate themselves to the illusion. It encouraged a constant circulation, as people came to the city in winter and returned to the fields in summer. Thus its population was a mobile one, not made stable by either housing or work. Paris was a city at the boil; as such it fascinated contemporary chroniclers and memoir-writers, who recorded events in full awareness that they were at the tumultuous center of the world. "Must the capital be destroyed in order to populate the countryside?" asked Louis Sébastien Mercier in his celebrated *Tableau de Paris*, in which he enthusiastically described an active, eloquent urban population, a people from whom flowed an "unstanchable deluge of words."[1]

Those who moved to the city came from the lowest strata of society; the homeless and penniless. It was not the wealthy peasants who left the land but laborers, hired hands, and youths from Savoy and elsewhere—what Abel Poitrineau has called "migrant flocks."[2] Families were divided: some left, others remained. Some returned to the country, but most envisioned sending for family members left behind. In the meantime, those who went made their lives in the city. They encountered others who had come, perhaps from the same village, and to make life easier a man and woman sometimes shared a room without benefit of wedlock. The numbers of abandoned children reached impressive heights, and the Foundlings' Hospital was a most dismaying refuge, ravaged by disease and death.[3] Putting children out to wet-nurse far from Paris was a necessity: of 21,000 children born each year,

20,000 were dispatched on a bizarre and dangerous journey, hauled away in wagons by hired agents to be delivered to wet nurses over whom the parents had no control.[4]

In view of the precariousness and harshness of urban conditions, it might seem that among the common folk no such thing as family existed. But that was far from the case. Even a brief glimpse at police archives reveals a life not more benign but more complex than is usually described. This complexity created some unusual interactions between public and private.

The Urban Family

The family did indeed exist, although not always under one roof.[5] Grandparents and grandchildren might live in different places, but they were aware of one another's existence, as police records show. Even among the poorest segments of

Abandoned children were a common sight. The child quickly had to be turned over to the Foundlings Hospital. Abandonment was from necessity, not choice, and occasionally a child would be left with a baptismal name and recommendations. (Paris, Bibliothèque Nationale.)

Etienne Jeaurat, *The Arrival of the Wet Nurses*. Parents who awaited the convoy's arrival sometimes were able to recognize their child only by its clothing. (Laon, Municipal Museum.)

the populace very few people claimed to have no nearby relative. A major event about which we happen to be particularly well informed is revealing in this respect. On 30 May 1770 the dauphin's marriage was celebrated in Paris with royal pomp and popular revels.[6] Responding to the king's appeal, people crowded the streets around the Place Louis XV, where they hoped to see a display of fireworks larger than that planned for the Hôtel-de-Ville. Despite the tremendous crowds, carriages insisted on crossing the square, with disastrous results. One hundred thirty-two people died, some trampled but most standing up, simply unable to breathe because of the pressure of the crowd. The dead were laid out in the Cemetery of La Madeleine La Ville-l'Evêque for identification by friends, neighbors, or family. Three-quarters of the bodies were claimed by relatives. Few people were truly alone in Paris.

Another event gives similar indications of the presence of family. When execution dates were set for persons condemned to death by the revolutionary tribunal, they wrote letters of farewell. These were intercepted by Fouquier-Tinville [the revolutionary prosecutor] and can be found today among his

30 May 1770: the marriage of the dauphin to Marie-Antoinette. At the height of the celebration, disaster struck: 132 died on Rue Royale, crushed in a panic that probably could have been avoided. (Paris, Bibliothèque Nationale.)

papers in the National Archives.[7] Some were written by humble folk who ran afoul of the revolutionary authorities for shady dealings that had nothing to do with ideology or politics. Nearly all were addressed to a family member: wife, brother, sister, or child.

The life of the family was not withdrawn or self-centered. It was dispersed yet connected. Exposed to the world, it knew no intimacy in the current sense of the word. It was open to the outside to the extent that it could not sustain itself otherwise. Among the nobility of court and robe family was a matter of lineage, title, landed property, inheritance, primogeniture, and blood. The common folk lived a different kind of life, open to the scrutiny of others. Family was but one of many networks of relations on which they relied to make a life for themselves not only in the present but in the uncertain future as well.

The typical family was permeated, if not in fact constituted, by a network of external dependencies. Its essence was living in day-to-day confrontation with other people, in solidarity with some, in antagonism with others.

Housing, a powerful constraint on its occupants, established a uniquely Parisian way of life. Tenements were hemmed in by narrow, muddy, ill-smelling streets. Buildings were densely populated, as owners sought to turn a profit on every square inch. They were full of passageways, attics, alleyways linking ateliers to courtyards, and *quarrés*, exterior balconies surrounding the courtyard and sometimes equipped with a source of water. Latrines were located on staircase landings. Inhabitants were mercilessly on display.

In the eighteenth century it was still usual for the bourgeoisie to mingle with the common folk. The well-to-do had not yet decamped toward the west end of the city or retreated into splendid hôtels; they still occupied the "noble floors" of ordinary buildings, generally the apartments on the second through fifth floors. Above and below, ordinary workers were housed wherever space was available. The ground floor usually contained a workshop or boutique with an entry from the street, sometimes with displays extending into the street itself. A mezzanine just above the work space contained a storage area as well as bedrooms for apprentices and journeymen, linked to the shop space via a ladder. Next to the shop was an alleyway, closed at night, through which residents passed to gain access to the inner courtyard and upper stories of the building; pedestrians also used the alley to pass from the street to other buildings located off the courtyard. One or more staircases with windows served the upper stories, with access from landings to the apartments, whose rents varied. Some rooms on the landings were connected with others, and custom required doors to landings and to other apartments to be kept open much of the time. It was possible to go from room to room, or perhaps to another staircase or passageway. At the very top were garrets and attics: cold in winter, hot in summer, they sheltered a working population as large as it was mobile. If the artisan or merchant who owned the ground-floor shop was wealthy enough, he would sublet this space to his employees. Otherwise garrets and furnished rooms were rented to lodgers for two or three sous a night. The poor lived several to a room, sleeping on mattresses or straw, usually placed on the floor, and wrapping their meager belongings in the sheets.[8]

An apartment building was a public theater. Some held forth, others squabbled, but no one had any privacy. Marital

The Apartment House: A Public Theater

disputes, illicit love affairs, noisy tenants, restless children—nothing could be concealed and everything could be heard. Behavior and habits were shaped by inescapable promiscuity.

Street and Shop

Work space was no better protected. Innumerable street businesses gave Paris a unique look often described by writers and sketched by artists. Many carried their businesses on their backs: tinkers, pastry-makers, dentists, florists, ironmongers. For them visibility was the key to survival. People in certain trades wore distinctive clothing so as to be easily recognized. They made their way through the streets, shouting to announce their presence, and customers hailed them from their windows. Known in the neighborhood, they attracted a regular clientele; sometimes, for greater security, they set up shop temporarily at a crossroads or under a porch. Handymen, street porters, and chimney sweeps also did business this way.

The atelier, traditional workshop of artisans, journeymen, and apprentices, was a space intermediate between public and private. Stalls and workbenches extended out into the street. Clients and journeymen conversed throughout the day. Far from being confined, workers rapidly learned what was happening in the neighborhood, and this encouraged exchanges with passersby and feelings of solidarity. If the master got into a dispute with his workers, everyone knew about it, and anyone could tell at a glance which shops were well run and which were not. In such circumstances competition was fierce, and masters did not hesitate to set their apprentices to spying on the neighbor's clientele so that they could be drawn in as they passed by.

Children were a familiar sight around the shop as well as in the apartments above. Between the ages of ten and sixteen they lived an adult existence, while clinging to the pleasures and games of childhood. Apprenticed early or obliged to help their parents with routine chores, children knew the rhythms, constraints, and rigors of working life. Not yet independent from the family, the child served as a link among the various areas in which individuals moved. Belonging as much to the neighborhood as to his parents, he carried messages, ran errands, or struggled as an apprentice under the watchful eye of his master. He roamed throughout the city with astonishing freedom and played a genuine part in public as well as private life. Neighbors, artisans, merchants, curates, and deacons all kept an eye on youngsters growing up.

The Cries of Paris. Hawkers and street vendors cried their wares. (Paris, Carnavalet Museum.)

Pieter Brueghel, *Market.* Stalls and workshops encroached upon the street, and a merchant was more likely to sell his wares if he obtained a good location at a street corner. (Aix-en-Provence, Museum of Fine Arts.)

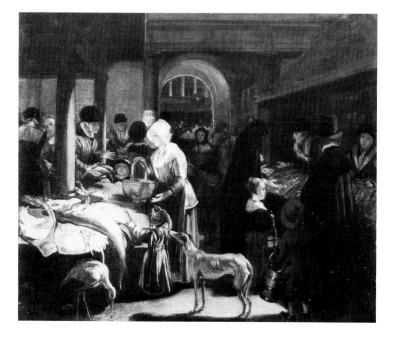

Emanuel de Witte, *The Amsterdam Fish Market.* At stalls there was as much discussion as there was buying. Cities facilitated many kinds of exchange, allegiance, and conflict. (Lugano, Thyssen-Bornemisza Collection.)

A neighborhood was a place where everyone kept an eye on everyone else. (Paris, Bibliothèque Nationale.)

A neighborhood was much more than a section of the city. It was an autonomous environment with rules and laws of its own, a place where everyone was watched by everyone else. Various authorities kept all under surveillance: the chief constable (*commissaire*) and his associates along with the parish priest and his acolytes and deacons.[9] Moral figures of the utmost importance, these were the guarantors of order and charity. People sought them out when they needed authority or understanding, severity or indulgence. They were visible presences, well-informed and available to all. In some cases they worked together. The constable often turned to the priest for information about a suspect neighborhood resident. People were aware of this, and the police archives contain numerous certificates of clean living issued by the parish priest.

The constables were the eyes and ears of the neighborhood, and the lieutenant general of police made sure that they did their job, that they went everywhere and knew everything. The slightest incident brought them running. Constables and informers kept them apprised of rumors and plots discussed in the streets, inns, and cabarets and around the fountains.

In such turbulent conditions, where public life and private life were mingled, where people lived outside as much as inside, and where rules were enforced by the scrutiny of others, honor was a most important possession, an indispensable necessity.

HONOR

Honor had long been considered an essential good, almost as essential as life itself, and to be defended in every possible way. Early in the sixteenth century Jean de Mille, provost of Paris and a leading figure in legal circles under François I, wrote a long text entitled *Criminal Practice*, addressed to the members of his profession. In his dedication to the king he wrote: "I have in the past had to deal with cases that came to me as the occasion arose, both in the city . . . and in the provinces. Upon returning home I attempted to assemble these cases in due form in a single corpus. I have been particularly interested in crimes against persons. A loss of property or patrimony is always reparable in one way or another, but never a loss of *honor* or *life*."[10]

The Honor of the Poor

Dishonor, a fate comparable with death, was a familiar theme in seventeenth- and eighteenth-century treatises on civility. Honor, Courtin wrote in his *Treatise on the Point of Honor*, "is what makes men prized and esteemed. It is the foundation of all good faith, upon which one swears. It is that which triumphs over all the insults of fortune and all the attacks of the world. It is that alone which brings happiness. It is that which, in the end, men prefer to life itself, what men hold most dear, most precious, and most sacred."[11]

Far from being a monopoly of the great, honor was a good to which common folk vehemently laid claim: "Ask anyone what it means to possess honor, and he will tell you that it means to have heart. Ask what it means to have heart, and he will tell you that it is to die rather than suffer a wrong" (Courtin). Being wronged was more than an idea or notion, it was a feeling, a conviction with which ordinary men and women lived and struggled. In the eighteenth century Lenoir, the lieutenant general of police, wrote about the common

A poor man had little but his honor to protect. (Paris, Bibliothèque Nationale.)

man's jealous regard for honor: "Administering the police force of a large city, in which societies of all kinds mingle and men and women live in one another's almost constant presence . . . gives one a good idea of the power of slander and calumny. Charges of insult and libel were frequent in Paris. Some people sought to recover damages in the ordinary courts. But the greater number of Parisians importuned the police with their domestic disputes and their points of honor."[12]

Here we sense police irritation at the growing number of complaints involving honor and reputation. Lenoir had a good grasp of the source of the problem: when men and women "live in one another's almost constant presence," as in an eighteenth-century city, words carried tremendous power. Slander and calumny could do grave harm and provoke serious conflict.

One source of honor was the constant interaction between families and communities in a situation in which there was no clear distinction between public and private. This continuous scrutiny yielded knowledge of others and justified discussion of their behavior. Police reports often begin, significantly, with the words: "I knew him to be . . ." Everyone, moreover, knew and shared the hazards of daily life. Risk was a part of everyday experience. Cities were dangerous and sometimes threatening. Sickness, accidents, loss of employment, and death were daily occurrences of which all were aware. Attitudes toward risk affected behavior. Some people were overwhelmed, others coped, and still others defied the odds or attempted to shift the burden. In a situation of shared danger one person could get ahead at the expense of others.

Ordinary people continually tested their equality in the face of physical and economic insecurity. Unable to rise socially, they strove not to fall below what they considered their proper level. Conditions were precarious, and everyone was vulnerable to neighbors and onlookers. People were careful not to say too much or to show themselves lest they become the victims of the moment. In a society of "equals," one needed the esteem of one's neighbors.

Woman Picking Lice. (Strasbourg, Museum of Fine Arts.)

People were also acutely aware that as subjects of the king they belonged to an indistinct mass. They were *le peuple*, the common crowd, upon which the sacred power of the king rested. Within this mass, however, honor made a man stand out. But his singular status could evaporate very quickly, for it depended on the opinion of others and on every man's desire to distinguish himself from the crowd. Honor and dishonor marked the destiny of the individual within the solidarity of

A meal, and alms being given to the poor. (Paris, Bibliothèque Nationale.)

the community. The logic of honor permitted collective actions taken in self-defense against the authorities to coexist with personal challenges to one's neighbor, by means of which each person defined his or her place.[13]

Words and Insults

"Words are dangerous intruders, which breach established defenses."[14] In neighborhoods where social life outside the home revolved around talk, a man's words established his identity in the community. Conversation created society, but it could also endanger members of that society.

Louis Sébastien Mercier has left a marvelous description of urban talk: "In the merest marketplace or shop one engages in conversation on any number of irrelevant topics. Making the smallest purchase requires endless verbiage, and lowering the price a few sous wears out the lungs of both parties. Even extensive conversation in a room is not enough. It is customary to continue conversing in the doorway, on the landing, and all the way down the stairs. . . . Listen to the noisy, loquacious, and foolish disputes in the cafés. Petulance of language is familiar to Parisians, for every café table has its talker. If he is alone, he talks to the busy waiter or to the

Richard Brakenburg, *Interior of an Inn.* A place for relaxation and discussion but also for work (where shopboys and apprentices were hired and the wages of journeymen were paid). Women were also welcome. (Paris, Louvre.)

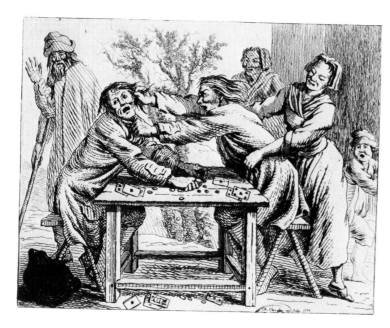

Since people lived outdoors, arguments did not lack for an audience, always ready to lend a hand. (Paris, Library of Decorative Arts.)

owner's wife and cashier, or, failing that, he looks around for anybody willing to listen. Coachmen and carters swear at one other with well-known oaths before falling into a crude war of insults. They come to blows only after much talk, and the talk resumes once the blows have ceased. On passenger barges there is such a constant hubbub that you cannot hear at all. The sailors find it difficult to exchange the words necessary for maneuvering the boat. When two barges meet, a loud voice rises from the deck of each, exciting the passengers and unleashing a broadside of rapid insults, as each person attempts to get the better of his neighbor. Sharp and thunderous voices argue back and forth. Even if the barges lay two hundred fathoms deep, one could still hear the din of a protracted clamor and the particular tone in which some foolish oath was uttered."[15]

People established their own position in society through conversation with others. The social hierarchy was subtle enough that a person had to worry constantly about how he was seen by others. Where talk is supreme, there is always the danger that some day one will fall victim to it. This was compounded by the obligatory proximity to one's neighbors and the impossibility of concealing one's habits.

Any insinuating, provocative, or even evasive remark about a person's reputation had immediate consequences.

Tanzio da Varallo and Giovanni d'Errico, *Christ Appearing before Herod* (detail). A word whispered in an ear can make or break a reputation. (Varallo, Sacro Monte, Chapel 28.)

Doubts about an individual affected all who had considered themselves his peers, all with whom he had been involved in relations of reciprocal esteem (or assent). The egalitarian relationship was ended, replaced by a hierarchy. The offending individual was excluded. Yet this cessation or modification of relations with a particular individual leaves the larger system of social relations intact, for that larger system is itself composed of rival alliances, accustomed to competing with one another.

Insulting words thus threatened a social order founded on reason and nature. Both the social elites and the police wished to maintain a society based on dependency: "This society can endure only through subordination, which is naturally the soul of every society." So said Courtin, here explaining "precisely what an insult is." Once this principle is accepted, if follows that everyone must honor not only parents and sovereign but also hierarchical institutions of any kind. With such a view of society it is a simple matter to define "insult." One must not assault a person's life or bed, Courtin says, for to lose "the honor of modesty is a loss as irreparable as that of life." Marriage is the bedrock of society, a sacred and natural principle. Attacking a person's property or reputation is also an unforgiveable insult. It is also impermissible to impair in any way the welfare or tranquillity of civil society.

This definition of insult reveals where families and communities are most vulnerable, hence where insult is most damaging and destructive. Insult destroys values, because slander and calumny undermine the natural consensus that individuals develop through their relations of dependency. A review of cases involving insults in the police archives makes it clear that conflict arises wherever there is subordination.

It is not surprising that the most popular way of insulting an individual or a family was to draw upon the age-old arsenal of conflict between men and women. The commonest form of insult was to question the virtue of a woman. Insults of this sort have a peculiar universality, but their effects were nonetheless real. Lenoir, in a chapter of his memoirs entitled "On the difficulty of stamping out false rumors once they have become established" (ms 1422, fol. 302), alludes to this perpetual problem: "Nothing was more common in Paris than to cast doubt on the virtue of women, even those women whose behavior gave no real or apparent grounds for reproach." This tactic was used to defame both the woman herself and the men related to her. It was often used in situations other than marital dispute or emotional conflict. A journeyman, for instance, might seek to ruin his master's reputation by casting doubt on the behavior of the master's wife. Much less frequent than sexual insults were slanders on the traditional themes of honesty, sobriety, industriousness, thrift, friendship, and so on.

The social effects of insults were compounded by the grave economic consequences of a bad reputation. The socially discredited individual stood to lose profits, employment, and lodging. Given the instability of the population, this was a serious matter. An artisan taunted for drunkenness, laziness, boastfulness, or an ill-behaved wife could lose clients. An apprentice about whom neighbors gossiped might never find a new job. A man or woman whose marital affairs were criticized might lose a job or get into difficulties with a landlord. A woman seduced and abandoned had little hope of finding a place to live with her child.

Honor had economic value. Insults were aimed squarely at vulnerable spots. The artisan was vulnerable socially and economically. The couple, no matter how secure economically, was vulnerable to sexual innuendo against the wife. And women were vulnerable in their very existence, not only to direct attacks but also to casual insinuations made simply to spice up a conversation. Anyone who brought charges of slander knew that they faced economic risks. Hence they sought to reestablish, as one put it, "the honor on which their bread depends," by appearing before the constable and if necessary subpoenaing witnesses.

Recourse to the authorities was a necessity. A family whose reputation was besmirched had to prove its innocence. If a member had in fact violated one of the traditional norms, a way to erase the sin or cause it to be forgotten had to be found in order to restore normal relations with the community.[16]

The constable, as the local representative of the lieutenant general of police, was a key figure in the neighborhood. After 1738 there were forty-eight constables in Paris, each with the title of *conseiller du roi*, councilor to the king. They were exempt from tallage and enjoyed certain other privileges. Their responsibilities were vast, modeled on those of their immediate superior, the lieutenant general. Their civil duties included supervising the seizure of property and the affixing

Restoring Lost Honor

Nothing happened without the knowledge of the police constable, the best-informed person in the neighborhood. (Paris, Bibliothèque Nationale.)

of seals, which provided the bulk of their legitimate income; when an estate was divided, they made the necessary inquiries and notified relatives. Their responsibilities in the area of criminal justice were no less important. All charges and complaints were made to them, and they prepared affidavits and subpoenaed witnesses. In case of flagrant crime, they were obliged to act swiftly—to arrest the perpetrator, interrogate him, hold him in prison, conduct an investigation, and gather evidence. In addition they performed ordinary police duties, hearing the complaints of people involved in lawsuits or disputes.

The constable's office, usually his residence, was easy to locate, because its walls were covered with printed notices, police ordinances, royal edicts, notices of sentence, and announcements of public punishments. People posted items of news and notices of lost property there. Sometimes hastily scribbled denunciations were posted by private individuals. Thus the constable's house was a center for news and information, a meeting place, in some cases a haven, in others a scene of wrath.

Among his other duties the constable was expected to keep the lieutenant general of police informed of everything that happened in the quarter. He was obliged to report on any unusual occurrence: carriage accidents, marketplace brawls, fires, large gatherings, suicides. So, besides maintaining a permanent headquarters, he was obliged to be constantly on the move throughout his quarter, and he was constantly exhorted by his superior not to neglect duty. Finally, he was expected to supervise necessary public works for the maintenance of sewers, public sanitation, and roads.

"Close" to the common folk, the constable knew their hopes and concerns. He learned what angered them or outraged their sense of decency, and he discovered in what areas they felt they needed protection. He was a unique figure precisely because his responsibilities were so broadly defined. Well-informed, he could plausibly pose as the representative of royal authority. He was also seen as something of a father-figure, now reproachful, now conciliatory, and he used this to his advantage. He was both loved and hated, at once repellent and fascinating. Authors who wrote treatises on the police function perpetuated this image and commented on the constable's functions, symbolic as well as real: "I regard the constable's house as a kind of civil temple, to which people go to seek help against misfortune." Here the soothing vocabulary (house, help) accords well with the socialization of the function (civil temple). Despite the public nature of the constable's authority, he was clearly an intermediary figure in whom public and private easily mingled.

A person who heard slander spoken of himself could come to the constable to complain and if possible to put all suspicion to rest. Witnesses were sometimes called, and the constable moved quickly to calm tempers and admonish the party guilty of spreading the ill-founded gossip. Some constables kept notebooks in which on occasion they recorded the advice they gave about protecting honor and reputation.

When a family's honor was seriously jeopardized by the flagrant misbehavior of one of its own (a prodigal son, a libertine wife, a drunken husband who regularly slept away from home, a child living as a concubine) and the constable's admonitions were to no avail, the family could file a formal complaint against its wayward member requesting judgment and public punishment. The purpose of punishment was to

The police made arrests day and night. Their haste sometimes led them to commit errors. (Paris, Police Museum.)

sever the offending member from the family and to discourage him (or her) from continuing his wicked ways.

One situation that arose frequently was a woman's demanding that her husband be imprisoned because his behavior was condemned by all his neighbors. His offense might be squandering the family's resources, spending too much time at the cabaret and neglecting his noisy or unruly children, or carrying on with women in a disreputable manner. Women who filed such complaints generally got what they wanted. Neighbors were questioned, the husband was interrogated, and ultimately he was thrown into prison. But not for long: many women needed their husbands to support them and quickly dropped charges until the next incident.

These were rather traditional problems. For some families the public judicial process was as scandalous as the transgression it punished. They considered themselves twice dishonored, once by the fault and again by its public punishment. Justice was public: the sentence was posted and the victim was pilloried at a busy corner or, if a juvenile, whipped. Thus honor was not truly restored. The mark of justice was an enduring blemish on a family's reputation, and appealing to the authorities was a double-edged sword.

The Lettre de Cachet

For families in the mid-eighteenth century faced with dishonor because of the behavior of a family member yet unwilling to turn for help to the usual authorities, the *lettre de cachet* proved to be a great boon. This was a letter granted by the king that could be used to order imprisonment without public proceedings; it became a means of restoring honor without violating family secrets.

A curious appeal to an early-eighteenth-century order of Chancellor Philipeaux, Count de Pontchartrain, sheds a great deal of light on the principles and purposes of the lettre de cachet. In 1709 Pontchartrain became embroiled in a prickly affair with M. de Brilhac, premier président of the parlement of Rennes. A young woman by the name of du Colombier had been abducted by soldiers acting on orders of Brilhac as she left mass at midday. She was taken to a convent that housed women of ill-repute on the sole grounds that she had had an affair with one Martiny, a président of the parlement of Rennes. Her abduction was ordered without judicial proceedings of any kind, in the manner of an arrest based on a lettre de cachet. When Pontchartrain learned of the case, he wrote two sharp letters, one to M. de La Bédoyère, président général of the parlement of Rennes, and one to M. de Brilhac.[17] In these letters he stated his views on the proper form of arrest orders and the manner in which the king wished them to be used.

He objected first of all to Brilhac's acting on his own initiative: "You cannot give any order on your authority alone. Otherwise justice would become arbitrary and would reside entirely in your person. Only the king can act in this way, and he does so only with much circumspection on extraordinary occasions and by way of lettres de cachet." No one but the king was entitled to arrogate to himself the privilege of direct judgment, not even a président of parlement. High judges were simply not allowed to dispense with the normal judicial procedures. If the lady in question was the cause of some disorder, then an indictment should have been obtained from the royal prosecutor. The case could not be heard by a président of parlement until a lower court had issued its judgment and that judgment had been appealed. In other words, the lettre de cachet was not to be abused even by those who wielded great power, as was of course the case with a premier président.

In his second letter, to the président général, Pontchartrain emphasized the secrecy necessary in affairs of this kind, demonstrating that one of the principal reasons for use of the lettre de cachet was clandestinity: lettres de cachet "can be executed only after precautions of every sort have been taken in order to avoid notoriety and scandal." In the case of the young women abducted upon leaving mass, the action had been so public that the entire city of Rennes and indeed all Brittany knew the facts. "Could one imagine a more notorious way of proceeding, or one that would have done more to dishonor this officer in society, than that which was taken?" Pontchartrain continued: "Even if the premier président believed that it was his right to proceed in this way, he should at least have taken measures to prevent scandal, and he did the opposite."

Pontchartrain probably would have pardoned the offense had secrecy been maintained. And secrecy was the essence, the supreme justification, of the lettre de cachet. By a single royal act a person could be arrested quietly and without scandal. Both the offense and the guilty party could be buried without a word. M. de Brilhac had bungled the affair in every

No one knew how to write a letter to the king better than the public writer. Before taking up his pen, he listens to the complaints of a woman who wants to have one of her sons imprisoned by lettre de cachet. Illustrations from Louis Sébastien Mercier's *Tableau of Paris.* (Paris, Bibliothèque Nationale.)

An arrest on royal orders saved a man from dishonor, for there was no noisy commotion, no "public clamor." (Paris, Bibliothèque Nationale.)

respect. Not only had he claimed a right that was not his, but he had acted with such notoriety as to provoke immediate scandal and dishonor.

Pontchartrain's letters give us the strict interpretation of the lettre de cachet as it was understood in 1709. By midcentury royal orders were probably easier to obtain, and they were certainly used more often. In Paris the lieutenant general of police possessed the exclusive privilege of executing royal orders, and he had the right to use them as he deemed necessary for the maintenance of public safety and tranquillity. The lettre de cachet became a tool for cleaning up the capital. Families not only assented to the use of the letters, but sought to obtain them on their own initiative.

SECRECY PRESERVED

For a family without rank or position, to maintain honor in the face of violence, aggression, theft, bad faith, and deception was a way of life, a way of battling the evil words of others. When a blemish on the family escutcheon became an object of public notoriety, one way to clear the family name was to denounce the offending member to the police, who would investigate the matter and, if warranted, jail the transgressor. Honor was safe so long as the king's order to imprison the offender remained a secret, private act and did not involve the regular courts. With dishonor removed from public view, the family's purity was restored, its public face unblemished.

By proceeding in this way a family concealed what could not normally be concealed owing to the lack of a clear dividing line between private life and public life. Thus, in order to maintain secrecy and a kind of intimacy, families made use of the most arbitrary of all royal institutions, that which made the monarchy seem most absolute. There is a surprising paradox in this. The lettre de cachet served the interests of ordinary families in at least two ways: it made them feel that they were just as much royal subjects as bourgeois and noble families, and it enabled them to preserve their honor while avoiding the degradation of a public judicial process.

Family Demand

Families internalized this process. It never occurred to them that recourse to this institutionalized royal power might be an excessive response to the threat of lost honor. Families sometimes were in no hurry to see their prisoner released for

Les pillards de St lazare parcoururent le fauxbourg montmartre,
et se porterent a cinq heures du matin rue de la tour
d'auvergne, autour de ma maison, le
C'est ici! disoit une jeune poissarde. on nous a dit qu'il demeuroit à la
maison peinte en brique.
nous voulons Christophe mort ou vif, crioit un vieux fort de la halle,
c'est un accapareur de bled!
et y a des houzards dans sa maison, ajoutoient des brigands
armés de piques et de bâtons.
je descendis, presque en chemise, et leur dis avec calme, je ne suis
point monsieur christophe, je suis officier dans la garde nationale,
mon chien s'appelle houzard, mais il n'y a pas d'autre houzard que lui
dans la maison, entrez plutot, il n'y a que Madame, son fils et sa
femme de chambre! c'est un bon patriote! dit l'un d'eux!
madame lescot effrayée, appelloit madame st jean notre voisine et
d'autres voisins au secours! je lui dis d'etre tranquille, puisque ces
messieurs et ces dames demandoient Mr christophe, que nous ne connoissons pas,
ils furent effectivement chez lui a l'autre bout de la rue, mais il s'etait caché
dans une fosse recouverte de gazon et leur echappa.

A good marriage had to be pleasing to the parents. It was an economic and social as well as emotional bond.

fear that honor would again be compromised by further escapades. Prisoners' files are highly illuminating in this regard. Petitions addressed to their families often drew severe rebukes from relatives unwilling to countenance release.

Letters of the governor of the Ile de la Désirade are quite instructive. From 1763 to 1789 he prepared lists of "subjects whom he considered to be ready to return to society." In almost every instance he noted that the family was unwilling to agree to the prisoner's release, even though the young man was prepared to submit to any decision they might make. One said he would consent to the marriage his father desired. Another said that despite his "miserable countenance," he would no longer refuse to become a monk, as his family wished. Many of the prisoners named in these odd lists suffered tragic ends, racked by sickness, misery, and exhaustion.

In 1765 a prisoner by the name of Alliot wrote a particularly poignant letter to his father: "Deign at least to alleviate my suffering. Am I not punished enough by the pain in my leg and the separation from my wife and son without having to be 2,000 leagues from home, more miserable than the Negroes who inhabit this country?"[18]

Men and women held closer to home, in Parisian jails, also maintained curious relations with their relatives. Families were regularly informed of the behavior of their prisoners and offered their advice about whether or not the person should remain in prison. It was not uncommon for prisoners to ask to remain in prison despite their good conduct, but the reports are so laconic that it is impossible to know the reasons for their decisions.[19] It is not implausible that some people may have preferred the certainty of three prison meals a day to the harshness of the seasons, the hazards of a difficult family life, and the suspicions and slanders of others. In any case, the degree to which families accepted the imprisonment of one of their members as a means of preserving honor and secrecy and of compensating for the failure of their authority is truly remarkable.

The Response of the Authorities

Initially the royal administration met the families' demands for imprisonment unhesitatingly. It held that the practice was entirely justified, on grounds of public order and tranquillity. Maintaining the latter was one of the reasons for which the post of lieutenant general of police had been created in 1665. Treatises on the police point out that public tranquillity depends on family harmony and the happiness of all. Des Essarts wrote: "Police is the science of governing men and doing good for them, the art of making them happy as far as possible and to the extent that they ought to be in the general interest of society."[20] To promote happiness and contribute to the general welfare or, better still, to promote the general welfare by making men happy: that was the philosophy of "police." So defined, the task was immense. With such a conception of the general welfare, it made sense to exclude from society potential causes of serious disruption likely to lead to tumultuous judicial action. Thus, imprisonment could both protect family honor and maintain public order. This led to the elaboration of a "civic" conception of honor, defined in terms of respect for order in general, a far cry from the conception of honor as a manifestation of caste superiority.

It is not surprising that a police based on a philosophy of happiness and order should have taken an interest in the well-being of families. Its jurisdiction, accordingly, was vast, as Duchesne indicated in his *Code of Police* (1757), described by its author as an abridgment of Delamare's great *Treatise*: "The object of police is the public general interest, hence the objects that it embraces are in a sense unlimited." Here the idea of public interest is akin to that of "civilization," or reasonableness of manners and customs, and civilization itself was often confused with such notions as politeness, gentleness, and civility. Norbert Elias points out that the word "civilized," more or less synonymous with "cultivated," "polite," and *policé*, was used by people at court to characterize the specificity of their behavior and to contrast their high standards with those of humbler, less socially advanced folk.[21] The elder Mirabeau was not mistaken when he wrote: "If I were to ask, 'What is the nature of civilization?' someone would answer: 'The civilization of a people is the amelioration of its mores, urbanity, and politeness.'"

The nobility and the bourgeoisie always believed themselves to be in possession of civility and politeness, which visibly distinguished them from their inferiors. In the eighteenth century, however, it became necessary to promote an idea of civility distinct from the traditions of court and robe—in other words, to transform civility into a social norm. No longer was civility embodied in a social class or group; now it was represented by the state itself. A process of civilization was begun: whatever seemed barbaric, violent, or unreasonable had to be refined or eliminated. The police became one of the most reliable means of obtaining a minimum of civilization where there had been only confusion, especially since the authorities were able to exercise power by altering the equilibrium between social groups. Nobility and bourgeoisie canceled each other out: between them there was enough common ground to keep the social system intact but enough conflict to prevent their joining forces against the king. The people, still too weak to govern, became the target of efforts of pacification, sanitation, and civilization. Civility and harmony were to reign everywhere. The royal police (including the Paris police) embodied an eighteenth-century dream: to achieve happiness through civilization without disturbing the established order. King and people were to be forever joined through the exercise of personalized forms of authority.

Militiaman, 1736. (Paris, Bibliothèque Nationale.)

The mission of the police was to know the people and to intervene in its everyday affairs and family relations in order to encourage orderly behavior. The police, which reflected the personal power of the king, became as much an instrument of vision as an instrument of order. Its deep involvement with families was one aspect of utopia; the families' assent to that involvement was the other. And that utopia was nothing less than the fusion of the people with its king.

Authority and Secrecy

The lieutenant general of police was the official in the best position to exercise personal power and to embody the royal presence. Through his lieutenant the king named the unnameable disease and cured it through imprisonment, which the family in its tragedy experienced as both symbolic and real. If the lieutenant general deigned to consider a family's case, he simultaneously acknowledged that family's existence and granted it pardon, thereby personalizing its relations with the king. Families therefore submitted to examination of their most intimate secrets. In exchange for their gift of privacy they expected the king to eradicate forever whatever scandal might attach to their name.

Thus, a temporary equilibrium was established between arbitrary royal power and ordinary people who used that power to protect their honor and assure normal relations with others. The various lieutenants general used and abused their powers as their personalities dictated: Berryer, Sartine, and Lenoir (to name a few) often expressed satisfaction at having averted scandal, saving the names of certain families. The lieutenant general operated with quite a free hand. In addition to heading the police, he was, in Marc Chassaigne's phrase, "the king's newsman."[22] He kept himself informed of everything that was said and done, becoming the king's eyes and ears. The qualities needed for the job were more curiosity and cunning than knowledge of the law. Des Essarts was correct in saying that the lieutenant general needed "unflagging attention, exact vigilance, rare energy often and great wisdom always."[23] He made up his job as he went along, for it was his responsibility not to enforce an existing code of laws (although he did enforce royal edicts) but to create rules, customs, procedures, and orders wherever he believed that none existed.

At times, however, the people did attempt to limit these

Pieter de Hooch, *Card Players* (detail). Family honor was at stake, and one way of protecting it was to turn to the king. (Paris, Louvre.)

extraordinary powers. Families accepted the principle of imprisonment by lettre de cachet unless the implicit principle of equal exchange—royal favor in return for submission to scrutiny by the authorities—was violated. A single example will suffice: the rebellion that erupted in May 1750 to protest the mass arrest of artisans' children on the streets of Paris.[24] Youths caught gambling (and called libertines) were arrested in broad daylight on orders of the lieutenant general by police inspectors and informers, some of whom wore disguises. Many of the children were hauled away in windowless police vans. Outrage mounted. People gathered and rioted, chased constables and police officers, and murdered several of them. As soon as a family discovered the whereabouts of its arrested son, it hastened to the jail and obtained his release. The disturbances worried the Paris parlement. An investigation was begun, and numerous witnesses were heard. The police were interrogated about their activities and asked where their orders had come from and how they had gone about carrying them out. They were astonished to find themselves the target of widespread enmity, forced to bear the shame of accusation. Did they not respond daily to the complaints of parents unable to control their own offspring? Were their offices not besieged by parents requesting imprisonment of their own offspring? Why, then, was it suddenly so scandalous that they had arrested these young gamblers and roughnecks? And why were parents who normally requested the help of the police this time driven to rebellion?

The event is revealing. Requests for imprisonment were normally private acts for purposes of private repression. They were used to avoid publicity and keep an arrest private. The matter took on an entirely different complexion when the state acted on its own initiative through the lieutenant general of police. The act became public, and the royal gift of imprisonment was no longer a favor but a formal and public punishment. The lettre de cachet and arrest warrant became arbitrary and despotic.

The curious history of the lettre de cachet cannot be understood unless this difference between private and public initiative is kept in mind. When the police usurped the initiative, the delicately balanced system fell apart. "The lettre de cachet was the consecration of paternal authority by royal power . . . Here royal power is merely a counterpoint to domestic authority."[25]

TENSIONS AND DEBATES

The brief alliance between domestic peace and public order eventually broke down in the face or rising demands, freedom of thought, proliferating notions of individualism, and hostility to despotism.

The constables had so much work to do in so many areas (roads, traffic, provision of supplies, criminal justice, and so on) that by 1760 the responsibility for family disputes had become burdensome. Were disputes between husband and wife or parents and children really a matter for the police? Questions were raised about the propriety of making the private sphere a prime target of the police. At about the same time liberal writers were attacking the use of royal orders.

A Challenge to Arbitrariness

Illustration from Louis Sébastien Mercier's *Tableau of Paris*. The prisons, insalubrious and dangerous, were certainly not places to educate children or young men. Lenoir, lieutenant general of police in 1774, expressed outrage that prisoners emerged as sick, hardened men. (Paris, Bibliothèque Nationale.)

The king was criticized for becoming an accomplice to parental tyranny, as well as for allowing a sacred power to be used
in ridiculous, petty disputes. There was debate about the need
for laws and the infringement of freedom. Some demanded
that power be restored to judges, who were bypassed in the
recourse to authoritarian methods. Furthermore, as Malesherbes was quick to point out, no one could fail to be struck
by the fact that low-ranking police officials had become the
real masters of royal orders. Remonstrances were regularly
made to the king on this score, but the monarch invariably
invoked the close connection between domestic tranquillity
and public tranquillity (Louis XV, for example, used this argument in 1759.) But no one was convinced. Eventually even
the lieutenant general came to doubt the efficacy of the lettre
de cachet in settling family disputes. Sounding quite modern,
Lenoir wrote to the constables' syndics in October 1774: "It
is dangerous to use, in regard to children not subject to penal
servitude, a punishment [prison] that throws them together
with older individuals who cannot but serve as bad examples
. . . Prison, which is inflicted upon them as punishment, does
not cure them of vice but teaches them new ways of being
vicious . . . Except in cases of grave offense, they should be
returned to their parents rather than sent to the school of
vice."[26]

Lenoir's letter contains three distinct themes: the prison
as school of vice; children as vulnerable and best protected
from exposure to adults; and parents as the primary educators
of their offspring. The last-named stands out as particularly
important. Once public, the responsibility for education was
in the process of being shifted from the state to private families. Little by little a line was being drawn between public
order and domestic harmony.

The idea was in the air. There was concern about the
legitimacy of family demands for lettres de cachet, which
could be used for private intrigue and manipulation of inheritances or in other ways that were flagrant abuses of power.
It became increasingly difficult to understand how family
honor could be saved by a mere procedural device. Did not
the cause of dishonor lie in the punishment rather than in the
offense? So argued Mirabeau in his book *On Lettres de Cachet
and State Prisons* (1782). What is more, lettres de cachet were
in daily use in ways that had nothing to do with protecting
family honor. The growing numbers of victims included people ranging from thieves to priests, libertines to prostitutes.

No one knew any longer what offenses fell within the jurisdiction of the ordinary courts. The arrest records of the police show that an extraordinarily high proportion of those arrested were imprisoned on royal orders, without judgment, yet it was impossible to say why a particular criminal was treated in this way rather than by the regular procedures of justice.

The lettre de cachet became the focal point of a storm of protest. It symbolized the most odious and intolerable aspects of royal power. The king's power to judge privately was challenged. Judgment, many felt, ought to be public. The problems of families were not problems of state.

Malesherbes and Mirabeau unleashed fierce attacks on the lettre de cachet. A memorandum drafted in 1784 by Breteuil, minister of the king's household, attempted to establish rules where arbitrariness alone had prevailed.[27] Obvious abuses had to be eliminated at once. Families were by nature emotional, hence given to disproportion and exaggeration. Restraints had to be placed on the parents' will: "One can at least make a few rules, which will cover the majority of cases." Lunatics and "imbeciles" were no problem: society had to be protected against them, and they had to be protected against themselves. As for libertines, who, except in extreme cases, posed no threat to public order, reason required only that they be subjected to a brief period of "correction," not to exceed one or two years. A great deal of mischief could be ascribed simply to the passions of youth. Of course the "weaknesses of women and girls" had to be dealt with. And marital disputes demanded great vigilance: these were the cases where abuses were greatest and excesses most harmful. In any case, families should be aware that discredit attached not to them but to the guilty individual and that the intervention of the public authorities was not required in every case.

This text is important because its tone is one of embarrassment. Breteuil does not for a moment contemplate simply rejecting the families' demands out of hand. His only purpose is to establish stricter rules. Yet he does question the reality of the dishonor to a family caused by a member who is a debauchee or libertine. And he asks whether it really ought to be an affair of state. He also calls attention to problems that would not be eliminated by the abolition of the lettre de cachet in 1790, problems that would be much debated in revolutionary assemblies.

The parlement of Paris made remonstrances to the king, reiterating its criticisms of royal authority. Louis XVI stood firm. For him, domestic order and public order were one and the same. On 21 November 1787 he answered: "I will not suffer my parlement to raise its voice in protest against a power that family interest and the tranquillity of the state often demand."[28] On 11 March 1788 parlement resolutely renewed its attack, charging that lettres de cachet were "lamentable errors."[29] The opinions of the king's advisers varied. Maupeou, for example, argued that the letters were valid when required for reasons of state but that abuse of the practice by families should be curbed. By contrast, the *cahiers de doléances*, compilations of grievances submitted by communities throughout France, were unanimous: the lettre de cachet was the symbol of tyranny.

Law versus King

The Declaration of the Rights of Man states that no man may be deprived of liberty except by due process of law. The era of the lettre de cachet was definitively over. Yet Louis XVI declared in June 1789 that a way had to be found to reconcile the suppression of royal orders with "the maintenance of public safety." Public safety, the king argued, depended on the absence of rebellion, the absence of criminal collusion with foreign powers, *and* family honor. A committee, with Mirabeau among its members, was established to look into the problem. The National Assembly debated the issue extensively before voting, in March 1790, to abolish the lettre de cachet. The following August, however, a law was passed establishing a system of family tribunals.

Why could the government not allow families to take care of their own honor? The question debated was at once clear and obscure. Initially we encounter very definite convictions, based firmly on ideological and philosophical certitudes. The people, it was proclaimed, are no longer the property of the king. The will of the nation determines the law. It is degrading to be subject to royal authority and liberating to live under a government of laws. The inversion, both real and symbolic, is complete. No longer did one feel "touched" by the goodness of the king and protected from the public punishment of the regular courts, for the holy union of king with people was a thing of the past. The king's proven tyranny had put an end to a thousand-year-old accord and inaugurated the reign of liberty. "It is a degrading privilege to be judged by the king rather than by the law!" exclaimed the Count de

Castellane, deputy, at a session of the National Assembly in October 1789.[30]

Castellane continued: "No one speaks any longer of family honor, which they once said could be preserved only by arbitrary orders. Now that well-worn phrase is nothing but a mask for the secret proponents of slavery!" It was barbarous for the king to take charge of matters of family honor, particularly in light of a tenacious prejudice according to which the relatives of a criminal are somehow tainted by the infamy of his crimes. Such a notion of collective honor must be eradicated, Castellane maintained; crime is an individual matter, and its shame attaches only to the individual, not to those close to him. On 21 January 1790 Abbé Papin expressed his views on the subject in the strongest of terms: "Give in to the cries of reason. Reproach what sound philosophy condemns. In a wise nation crimes should be exclusively individual affairs . . . It is a barbarous prejudice to allow the guilty man's dishonor to affect an innocent family down to the most recent generations."[31]

The very architecture of the Bastille embodied the tyranny of the lettres de cachet. The dank spaces, heavy grilles, thick iron rings, bars, and chains speak for themselves, shouting that it was a "degrading privilege to be judged by the king rather than by the law." (Paris, Carnavalet Museum.)

In order to combat this prejudice people's attitudes must be changed. Error that has been deeply rooted for centuries must be eradicated. Guillotin, who spoke on the same day as Papin, predictably observed that the difficulty of the task was compounded by the fact that this was a prejudice rooted in the archaic superstitions of common folk. Whether in the ancien régime or at the height of the Revolution, error was the province of the common man: "It is in the people above all that [error] has established itself. The nobility had already freed itself from this belief. Moral truths are not readily grasped by a people that has been misled, which out of habit respects everything that it has inherited from its forebears and religiously worships even the falsehoods that it heard repeated in its cradle. It is to be hoped that the people will hasten to educate itself."

Laws existed in order to establish truth, hence the legislature should act at once to alter opinion by not confiscating the property of condemned criminals: "It is admirable to govern opinion" and undermine archaic beliefs. Two proposals were made in the course of the debate. First, when a man was executed, it was proposed that the judge rehabilitate his memory at the site of the execution. Second, anyone criticizing the condemned man's relatives should be punished. "No one should be allowed to reproach a citizen on the grounds that a

Abolition of privileges, 4 August 1789. Seven months later the lettres de cachet were also abolished. But the legislators immediately began debate on another way of preserving family honor. (Paris, Bibliothèque Nationale.)

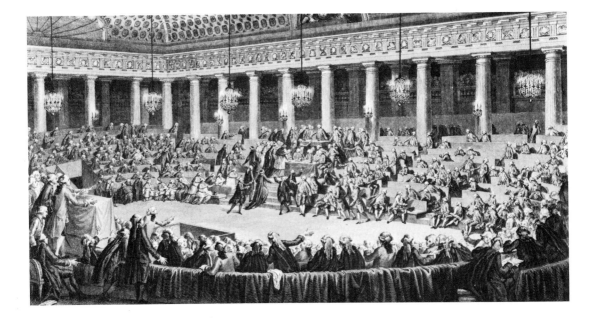

relative was executed or convicted of disgraceful crimes. Anyone who dares to do so shall be reprimanded publicly by the judge. Do not doubt for a moment that the prejudice persists. This revolution will take time to accomplish. Nothing is more difficult than to destroy a foolish notion that has attached itself to the imposing pretext of honor" (Guillotin).

Initially, then, family honor was linked to the superstition, barbarousness, backwardness, and credulity of the lower orders. The law was to be written so as to rescue the notion of honor from the confusion in which tyranny had been careful to leave it shrouded. The condemnation is harsh and firm. The common people are dismissed as backward and superstitious. Nothing at all is said about the equilibrium that had come to exist between families and authorities. Originally families at least had had recourse to the arbitrary power of the king on their own initiative and for their own purposes, at times unjust. The sovereignty of the people, though ostensibly based on the national will, called for laws whose purpose was to educate a people that had allegedly been misled. To quote Guillotin once more: "Being universal, the revolution will strike at the moral fallacy that has the innocent sharing the punishment for a crime or misdemeanor."

While legislators argued about the individuality of guilt and the scope of feudal barbarism, discussion also turned to other questions. It seemed impossible to separate the notion of family difficulties from that of security. The need for preventive detention, protection of family secrecy, and preservation of paternal power channeled debate toward the idea of establishing a family tribunal. It was with this prospect in view that the lettre de cachet was abolished. Only a few months later, in August 1790, the tribunal became a reality.

The problem of preventive detention was raised on 7 February 1790 by Voidel, deputy for Sarreguemines, in connection with a specific case. The twenty-four-year-old son of an officer of the parlement of Nancy was a particularly dissolute and unstable character, in debt up to his ears. One night, after a series of escapades, he feigned suicide, and when the national guard broke down his door he fired three shots from a pistol, wounding one of the guardsmen. But after the young man was taken into custody, the prosecutor of Nancy made plans to release him, even though the prisoner repeatedly stated that he intended to kill his father. Thus the immediate

Family Tribunals and Paternal Authority

problem facing the legislators was that to prevent a parricide, a man would have to be held in prison on orders of the prosecutor and at the behest of his family. The deputies' answer was immediate. An order from the prosecutor would be a lettre de cachet, which they wanted no part of. The answer was simple. In Mirabeau's words: "Let us hasten to establish a family tribunal. Prevent crimes by justice, never by arbitrariness."[32]

Looking beyond this case, the deputies were concerned about prisoners already held under lettres de cachet. To free all of them at once, on the grounds that the lettre de cachet had been abolished, would pose a danger to society. Debate on the question was acrimonious, and Robespierre, voicing his opinion on the articles of a law about to be voted by the assembly, expressed astonishment: "You will not free these wretches from the dungeons of despotism only to transfer them into the prisons of justice." Despite such reservations, the family tribunal was seen as an institution necessary to cope with the dangerous and slippery domain of family relations.

In this period, when every established truth was open to question, it was well and good to be convinced that family honor was an archaic concept and that every individual was responsible for his own actions. Family difficulties still caused real worry, and scandal continued to be something that prudent people took precautions to avoid. Avoiding publicity was still the rule, just as it had been under the ancien régime. Family honor and secrecy remained public questions, and thinking about the issue remained contradictory: the protection of privacy required the assistance of public authorities, while private scandal was supposed to be kept secret.

In this connection the session of the National Assembly on 5 August 1790 is quite revealing: "The purpose of the family tribunal is to control by legal means youths still under the authority of their fathers or guardians who ignore that authority and who give cause for alarm concerning the abuse they are likely to make of their freedom. It is also necessary to quell without notoriety disputes between husband and wife or close relatives, which otherwise may not only scandalize society but bring an entire family to ruin."[33]

Once it became clear that a family tribunal would be established, people began considering the question of paternal authority. One deputy, Gossin, stated: "After the Declaration of the Rights of Man and of the Citizen, it is appropriate to make a Declaration of the Rights of Spouses, Fathers, Sons,

and Relatives, as it were."[34] On 16 August 1790 the law establishing family tribunals was passed. Each party to a dispute was to name two arbiters. In case of a tie vote, an outside judge could be called in to decide. A party displeased with the judgment could appeal to the district court.

Not surprisingly, difficulties were encountered immediately. Families could not always find members objective enough to act as judges. It was then decided that arbiters did not have to be close relatives, whereupon the family tribunal ceased to be a family tribunal and became a public institution. The Constitution of Year III did away with the family tribunal. Families were no longer obliged to settle disputes internally.

But that did not end the debate. In 1796 the Council of Five Hundred, meeting on 29 Pluviôse, discussed the issue in an animated session. (The Revolution had adopted a new calendar, which was used for several years.) It raised the question whether the Constitution of Year III had in fact abolished the family tribunal. Some deputies argued that the abolition was implicit; others insisted that a law be passed; still others refused to accept abolition. Renaud, the deputy for Orne, summed up the debate in a lyrical speech in which he argued that a family tribunal was necessary to protect morals and preserve family harmony and secrecy: "How is it possible that the Constituent Assembly wished to destroy so beautiful, touching, and useful an institution as this? An institution whose primary purpose is to protect morals and preserve family harmony. An institution whose aim is to reconcile son with father, wife with husband, brother with brother. Nothing in the world is more vital than an institution of this kind. Nothing is more important for the Republic than these tribunals, responsible for calming domestic animosities and hatreds, restoring family peace and happiness, and avoiding the odious and scandalous public spectacle of a son pleading in court against the man who gave him life, forced to end his career by relentlessly persecuting his own flesh and blood; or of a wife dishonoring her husband in the eyes of the nation, overwhelming him with humiliation and suffering and, contemptuous of all modesty, striving to heap upon him opprobrium and infamy. And they talk of abolishing these tribunals!"[35]

As work progressed on the Civil Code, the debates over paternal and marital authority had a familiar sound. For some, "the errors of children should be smothered in the bosom of the family, without judicial formalities or written records."

For others, "the father has the right to imprison a child of twelve, but a constable must give his authorization for the imprisonment of a child over sixteen." Still others argued that excessive power breeds barbarism and that the law of nature requires that the authority of parents be protected and that children show "proper respect." Ultimately, articles 375-383 of the Civil Code of 1803 resolved the problem by establishing laws governing paternal (not parental) correction. Imprisonment was abolished. In its place fathers were granted certain rights over their minor children and husbands over their wives. The Penal Code added the possibility of prison terms for miscreant women, and in 1838 a law was passed establishing insane asylums in each département to deal with the traditional problem of "imbeciles and lunatics."

The law gave men the right to punish those who were the source of domestic woe. The rights of fathers and husbands were private rights publicly recognized. The family was an authoritarian realm within which women's rights were nonexistent. Families were able to satisfy the need for secrecy while meeting the conditions established by the law. Once "named" in law, the private and public spheres took on a life of their own. Men alone wielded authority and bore civic responsibility.

⌘ Epilogue

Roger Chartier

THIS cannot be considered a conclusion, because the evidence and analyses collected in this volume are but the first fragments of a new kind of history, which has yet to be written. Still, at the end of this collective effort, I would like to say a word or two about our choices, our decisions, and our limitation of the subject, particularly with regard to time and place. The history of private life, like that of attitudes toward childhood and death, is not a national phenomenon. Its natural setting is that of an entire civilization, the Western world. It would have been impossible to examine the various topics considered here on so broad a scale. Hence we deliberately chose to deal with each topic on a different scale. In some cases we consider the West in its entirety, but in others we focus on specific, homogeneous societies—a province, a city, even a nation.

When our focus is national, France is our country of choice, as is only natural in a book written by French historians and others who are specialists in French history. Contingent though it is, this choice can also be justified on historical grounds. France during the ancien régime was deeply affected by the three evolutionary processes that redrew the boundary between public and private in the early modern era. Of all European states the French monarchy provides the purest, most fully realized model of absolutist government: government which arrogates to itself the right to judge and to tax and which imposes its own order upon society, based upon the model of the court. Furthermore, France was a country of divided religious allegiances; it experienced the effects of both Reformation and Counter-Reformation, admittedly to unequal degrees. Finally, between 1500 and 1800 French society was introduced to the culture of the written word. Within its boundaries the cultural dichotomy of the West as a whole is reproduced: northern and northwestern Europe—England, Holland, Flanders, the Rhineland, and northern France—had highly literate populations quite early, while southern Europe remained largely illiterate for a much longer time. Thus, it is legitimate to approach the history of private life in the early modern era through France, because all the major factors influencing that history can be observed there.

The French slant to this volume has affected its chronology. Some chapters have been extended down to the time of the Revolution (which will be examined in its entirety in the next volume of this series). In some areas, such as the tension between public behavior and private isolation or the relation between family secrecy and the jurisdiction of the state, the Revolution merely continued what the monarchy had begun.

The emphasis on France has given particular prominence to the second half of the seventeenth century, to the reign of Louis XIV, a period that emerges as a turning point. A private life based on sumptuousness, civility, and ostentation and dominated by the new ambitions of the state began to yield to a new concept of personal privacy, sustained by an increasingly individualized notion of piety. People learned to read, discovered the seductions of the self, and retreated into domestic intimacy.

The limits of this volume reflect certain explicit decisions. We did not wish to separate the spaces, habitats, or objects of intimacy from the affective investments that they reflected or allowed. Hence primary importance was accorded to sentiments and values rather than to the history of material culture—to housing, decoration, furniture, or dress. To the extent that material culture does figure in our work, it is always as it relates to social and individual practices. Also we have sought to relate three concurrent or overlapping aspects of privatization: friends and associates, family, and individual retreat. This was necessary because there is no single or universal definition of privacy. The relations among these distinct components of privacy change over time, and a given social form (the family, for instance) can be at times a refuge, at other times a trap. Kindred, lineage, nuclear family, friends, and associates—all are now foci of an individual's most intimate and secret affections, now intolerable constraints on his freedom. Accordingly, we cannot avoid looking into conflicts between friendship and marriage, family and community, individual freedom and family discipline. Related to this is a further intention of our work, which is to use the history of private life as a means of understanding the different definitions of public space: village or neighborhood, jurisdiction of the sovereign, or realm subject to criticism by what is held to be public opinion.

In all these areas our work calls for further study, and for evidence culled from witnesses other than those so often invoked in this volume: Montaigne and Pepys, Henri de Campion and Saint-Simon, Jamerey-Duval and Ménétra. The crucial, and difficult, question is to evaluate the extent to which the model of privatization as revealed by study of France can be applied to other countries where religious divisions were less pronounced, where absolutism did not exist, and perhaps where the progress of literacy was less dramatic. The speed with which a private sphere was constituted varied from country to country. To unravel the complexity of the phenomenon we have proposed a number of hypotheses, interpretations, and models. By doing so we have tried to keep faith with the intentions of the man whose idea this series was—Philippe Ariès.

Notes

Bibliography

Credits

Index

Notes

Introduction

1. The first part of this Introduction was written to introduce a seminar on The History of Private Space, organized in May 1983 by the Wissenschaftskolleg of Berlin.

2. The editor of this volume and various contributors to it have here appended their recollections of the thoughts that the seminar inspired in Philippe Ariès.

3. Some of the ideas expressed in this Introduction, particularly those concerning the state, were inspired by conversations with Maurice Aymard, Nicole and Yves Castan, and Jean-Louis Flandrin.

I. Figures of Modernity

POLITICS AND PRIVATE LIFE (YVES CASTAN)

1. Etienne de La Boétie, *Discours de la servitude volontaire,* ed. Gayard-Fabre (Paris: Flammarion, 1983).

2. Henri de Campion, *Mémoires,* ed. Marc Fumaroli (Paris: Mercure de France, 1967).

3. Tallemant des Réaux, *Historiettes,* ed. G. Mongrédien (Paris: Garnier, 1932).

4. Louis Gabriel Ambroise de Bonald, *Théorie du pouvoir politique et religieux,* ed. C. Capitan (Paris: Union Générale de l'Edition, 1965).

5. Unpublished letters.

6. R. Bonald, *Le Cours de théologie morale* (Toulouse, 1651).

7. Uncatalogued records of criminal trials in the parlement of Toulouse.

8. Ibid.

9. Abbé Fabre, *Histoira dé Jean l'an prés,* an Occitanian tale of the eighteenth century, examined by Emmanuel Le Roy Ladurie in *L'Argent, l'amour, la mort en pays d'Oc* (Paris: Seuil, 1980).

10. Madame de Maintenon, *Extrait de ses lettres, avis, conversations et proverbes* (Paris: Hachette, 1884).

11. Turgot, *Lettres à la Péruvienne,* ed. Bray-Landy (Paris: Flammarion, 1983).

12. Roger Chartier, "Norbert Elias, interprète de l'histoire occidentale," *Le Débat* 5 (1980): 138–143.

13. Benjamin Constant, *De la liberté chez les Modernes,* ed. Marcel Gauchet (Paris: Actuels, 1984).

THE TWO REFORMATIONS (FRANÇOIS LEBRUN)

1. Emile G. Léonard, *Le Protestant français* (Paris: Presses Universitaires de France, 1953), p. 138.

THE PRACTICAL IMPACT OF WRITING (ROGER CHARTIER)

1. My interpretation of signature rates therefore differs from that of François Furet and Jacques Ozouf, *Lire et Ecrire. L'alphabétisation des Français de Calvin à Jules Ferry* (Paris: Minuit, 1977), I, 27. After examining, for 1866, signatures on marriage documents, conscripts' educational documents, and cultural data, they conclude that "the ability to sign one's name corresponds to what we now call literacy, meaning the ability to read and write" and that "there is a presumption in favor" of the hypothesis that the correlation between ability to sign and complete literacy is valid "for earlier periods."

2. Robert Allan Houston, "The Literacy Myth? Illiteracy in Scotland, 1630–1760," *Past and Present* 96 (1982): 81–102.

3. See David Cressy, *Literacy and the Social Order. Reading and Writing in Tudor and Stuart England* (Cambridge: Cambridge University Press, 1980), pp. 62–103, for the oaths of 1641–1644, and R. S. Schofield, "Dimensions of Illiteracy, 1750–1850," *Explorations in Economic History* 10 (1973): 437–454.

4. Michel Fleury and Pierre Valmary, "Les progrès de l'instruction élémentaire de Louis XIV à Napoléon III d'après l'enquête de Louis Maggiolo (1877–1879)," *Population* 12 (1957): 71–93, and Furet and Ozouf, *Lire et Ecrire.*

5. Simon Hart, "Onderzoek naar de samenstelling van de bevolking van Amsterdam in de 17e en 18e eeuw, op grond van gegevnes over migratie, huwelijk, beroep en alfabetisme," *Geschrift ien Getal. Een keuze uit de demografisch-economisch en sociall-historische studiën op grond van Amsterdamse en Azzanse archivalia, 1600–1800* (Dordrecht, 1976), pp. 130–132.

6. M. R. Duglion, "Alfabetismo e società a Torino nel secolo XVIII," *Quaderni Storici* 17 (May–August 1971): 485–509.

7. M.-C. Rodriguez and Bartolomé Bennassar, "Signatures et niveau culturel des témoins et accusés dans les procès d'Inquisition du ressort du tribunal de Tolède (1525–1817) et du ressort du tribunal de Cordoue (1595–1632)," *Caravelle* 31 (1978): 19–46.

8. Kenneth A. Lockridge, *Literacy in Colonial New England: An Inquiry into the Social Context of Literacy in the Early Modern West* (New York: Norton, 1974).

9. Kenneth A. Lockridge, "L'alphabétisation en Amérique, 1650–1800," *Annales ESC*, 1977, pp. 503–518.

10. Cressy, *Literacy*, pp. 157–174.

11. André Larquié, "L'alphabétisation à Madrid en 1680," *Revue d'histoire moderne et contemporaine*, 1981, pp. 132–157, and "L'alphabétisation des Madrilènes dans la seconde moitié du XVIIe siècle: stagnation ou évolution?" *Colloque "Instruction, lecture, écriture en Espagne (XVIe–XIXe siècle)"* (Colloquium on Teaching, Reading, and Writing in Spain [16th–19th century]), Toulouse, 1982, mimeographed.

12. Michel Vovelle, "Y a-t-il eu une révolution culturelle au XVIIIe siècle? A propos de l'éducation en Provence," *Revue d'histoire moderne et contemporaine*, 1975, pp. 89–141.

13. Cressy, *Literacy*, pp. 130–137, esp. table 6.8, p. 136.

14. Daniele Marchesini, "La fatica di scrivere. Alfabetismo e sottoscrizioni matrimoniali in Emilia, Sette et Ottocento," in Gian-Paolo Brizzi, *Il Catechismo e la Grammatica* (Bologna: Il Mulino, 1985), II, 83–169.

15. Cressy, *Literacy*, pp. 124–125, 128.

16. Joseph Ruwet and Yves Wellemans, *L'Analphabétisme en Belgique (XVIII-XIXe siècle)* (Louvain, 1978), p. 22.

17. Kalman Benda, "Les Lumières et la culture paysanne dans la Hongrie du XVIIIe siècle," *Les Lumières en Hongrie, en Europe centrale et en Europe orientale*, proceedings of the 3rd Colloquium of Matrafüred (1975) (Budapest, 1977), pp. 97–109.

18. Egil Johansson, "The History of Literacy in Sweden," in H. J. Graff, ed., *Literacy and Social Development in the West: A Reader* (Cambridge: Cambridge University Press, 1981), pp. 151–182.

19. T. C. Smout, "Born Again at Cambuslang: New Evidence on Popular Religion and Literacy in Eighteenth-Century Scotland," *Past and Present* 97 (1982): 114–127 (which cites Markussen and Skovgaard-Petersen's study on Denmark).

20. Richard Gawthrop and Gerald Strauss, "Protestantism and Literacy in Early Modern Germany," *Past and Present* 104 (1984): 31–35.

21. Bernard Vogler, *Vie religieuse en pays rhénan dans la seconde moitié du XVIe siècle (1556–1619)* (Lille, 1974), II, 796–799.

22. Rolf Engelsing, *Analphabetentum und Lektüre. Zur Sozialgeschichte des Lesens in Deutschland zwischen feudaler und industrieller Gesellschaft* (Stuttgart, 1973), p. 62.

23. André Derville, "L'analphabétisation du peuple à la fin du Moyen Age," *Revue du Nord*, special issue, *Liber amicorum. Mélanges offerts à Louis Trénard*, nos. 261–262, April–September 1984, pp. 761–776.

24. Christiane Klapisch-Zuber, "Le chiavi fiorentine di Barbalù: l'apprendimento della lettura a Firenze nel XV secolo," *Quaderni Storici* 57 (1984): 765–792. The reason for the variation in the percentage of children in school has to do with varying estimates of the Florentine population in the period 1330–1340.

25. M. J. Lowry, *The World of Aldus Manutius. Business and Scholarship in Renaissance Venice* (Oxford: Basil Blackwell, 1979), pp. 26–41.

26. Carlo Ginzburg, "High and Low: The Theme of Forbidden Knowledge in the Sixteenth and Seventeenth Centuries," *Past and Present* 73 (1976): 28–41.

27. Paul Saenger, "Silent Reading: Its Impact on Late Medieval Script and Society," *Viator. Medieval and Renaissance Studies*, 13 (1982): 367–414.

28. Philippe Berger, "La lecture à Valence de 1747 à 1560. Evolution des comportements en fonction des milieux sociaux," *Livre et Lecture en Espagne et en France sous l'Ancien Régime*, colloquium of the Casa de Velázquez, ADPF, 1981, pp. 97–107.

29. André Labarre, *Le Livre dans la vie amiénoise du XVIe siècle. L'Enseignement des inventaires après décès, 1503–1576.* (Paris-Louvain: Nauwelaerts, 1971).

30. Christian Bec, *Les Livres des Florentins (1413–1608)*, ed. Leo S. Olschki (Florence, 1984), esp. pp. 91–96.

31. Peter Clark, "The Ownership of Books in England, 1560–1640: The Example of Some Kentish Townfolk," in Lawrence Stone, ed., *Schooling and Society. Studies in the History of Education* (Baltimore: Johns Hopkins University Press, 1976), pp. 95–111.

32. Etienne François, "Livre, confession, et société urbaine en Allemagne au XVIIIe siècle: l'exemple de Spire," *Revue d'histoire moderne et contemporaine*, July–September 1982, p. 353–375.

33. For an overview of the French data, see

Roger Chartier and Daniel Roche, "Les pratiques urbaines de l'imprimé," in H.-J. Martin and Roger Chartier, eds., *Histoire de l'édition française* (Paris: Promodis, 1984), vol. 2, *Le Livre triomphant, 1660–1830*, pp. 402–429, which uses, among other things, the work of Jean Quéniart on the cities of western France and that of Michel Marion on Paris.

34. R. A. Gross, "The Authority of the Word: Print and Social Change in America, 1607–1880," paper presented to the colloquium Needs and Opportunities in the History of the Book in American Culture, Worcester, Mass., 1984, mimeographed.

35. Philip Benedict, "Bibliothèques protestantes et catholiques à Metz au XVIIe siècle," *Annales ESC*, 1985, pp. 343–370.

36. David D. Hall, "Introduction: The Uses of Literacy in New England, 1600–1850," in William L. Joyce et al., eds., *Printing and Society in Early America* (Worcester, Mass.: American Antiquarian Society, 1983), pp. 1–47, from which the quotations that follow are taken.

37. The quotations in this paragraph have been retranslated from the French.

38. Rolf Engelsing, "Die Perioden der Lesforschung in der Neuzeit. Das statistische Ausmass und die soziokulturelle Bedeutung der Lektüre," *Archiv für Geschichte des Buchwesens* 10 (1969): 945–1002, and *Der Bürger als Leser. Lesergeschichte in Deutschland, 1500–1800* (Stuttgart, 1974).

39. Michel Eyquem de Montaigne, *The Complete Essays of Montaigne*, trans. Donald M. Frame (Stanford: Stanford University Press, 1957), p. 629.

40. Daniel Fabre, "Le livre et sa magie," in Roger Chartier, ed., *Pratiques de la lecture* (Marseilles: Rivages, 1985), pp. 182–206.

41. *The Diary of Samuel Pepys*, ed. Robert C. Latham and William Matthews, 9 vols. (Berkeley: University of California Press, 1970–1976).

42. John Harrison and Peter Laslett, *The Library of John Locke* (Oxford: Clarendon, 1971), 2nd ed., esp. Laslett, "John Locke and His Books," pp. 1–65.

43. Concerning these two paintings, see the notices in the catalogue *Chardin, 1699–1779* (Paris: Editions de la Réunion des Musées Nationaux, 1979), pp. 278–283.

44. Miguel de Cervantes Saavedra, *Don Quixote de la Mancha*, trans. Samuel Putnam (New York: Modern Library, 1949), p. 943.

45. *Mémoires d'Henri de Campion* (Paris: Mercure de France, 1967), pp. 95–96.

46. See *Correspondance littéraire et anecdotique entre M. de Saint-Fonds et le président Dugas* (Lyons, 1900), and Roger Chartier, "Une académie avant les lettres patentes. Une approche de la sociabilité des notables lyonnais à la fin du règne de Louis XIV," *Marseille*, no. 101, *Les Provinciaux sous Louis XIV*, 1975, pp. 115–120.

47. Gerald Strauss, *Luther's House of Learning: Indoctrination of the Young in the German Reformation* (Baltimore: Johns Hopkins University Press, 1979), pp. 108–131, engraving p. 114.

48. David Sabean, "Small Peasant Agriculture in Germany at the Beginning of the Nineteenth Century: Changing Work Patterns," *Peasant Studies* 7 (1978): 222–223. Valentin Jamerey-Duval, *Mémoires. Enfance et Education d'un paysan au XVIIIe siècle* (Paris: Le Sycomore, 1981), pp. 191–193. On the reading of Blue books, see Roger Chartier, "Livres bleus et lectures populaires," *Histoire de l'édition française*, II, 498–511.

49. Cited by Maxime Chevalier, *Lectura y Lectores en la España de los siglos XVI y XVII* (Madrid: Turner, 1976), p. 91.

50. Cervantes, *Don Quixote*, trans. Putnam, p. 275.

51. Jacques-Louis Ménétra, *Journal de ma vie* (Paris: Montalba, 1982); trans. by Arthur Goldhammer as *Journal of My Life* (New York: Columbia University Press, 1986). Anne Fillon, "Louis Simon, étaminier 1741–1820 dans son village du haut Maine au siècle des Lumières," thesis, Université du Maine, 1982.

2. Forms of Privatization

THE USES OF CIVILITY (JACQUES REVEL)

1. Philippe Ariès, *L'Enfant et la vie familiale sous l'Ancien Régime* (Paris: Seuil, 1961).

2. Norbert Elias, *The Civilizing Process*, trans. E. Jephcott (New York: Pantheon, 1982). A study of variations on the notions of civility and its values may be found in Roger Chartier, "From Text to Manners. A Concept and Its Books: *Civilité* between Aristocratic Distinction and Popular Appropriation," in *The Cultural Uses of Print in Early Modern France*, trans. Lydia G. Cochrane (Princeton: Princeton University Press, 1987), pp. 71–109.

3. *De civilitate morum puerilium libellus* (Basel: Froben, 1530). The most recent French translation is that of A. Bonneau (1877), republished in 1977 with an introduction by Philippe Ariès. [The author used this for the quotations in his text; the English versions are translated from his French. Trans. by Robert Whytington as *A Lytell Boke of Good Manners for Children* (1563); and by Thomas Paynell as *The Civilitie of Childhode* (1560).

4. Cf. Jean-Claude Schmitt, "Gestures," *History and Anthropology* 1 (1984): 1–18.

5. Henri de La Fontaine Verwey, "The First 'Book of Etiquette' for Children," *Quaerendo* 1 (1971): 19–30; on sixteenth-century editions, see Roger Chartier, Dominique Julia, and Marie-Madeleine Compère, *L'Education en France du XVIe au XVIIIe siècle* (Paris: SEDES, 1976), pp. 139–140.

6. Gerald Strauss, *Luther's House of Learning: Indoctrination of the Young in the German Reformation* (Baltimore: Johns Hopkins University Press, 1979); Steven Ozment, *When Fathers Ruled: Family Life in Reformation Europe* (Cambridge, Mass.: Harvard University Press, 1983).

7. Franz Bierlaire, "Erasmus at School: The *De civilitate morum puerilium libellus*," in R. L. De Malen, ed., *Essays on the Works of Erasmus* (New Haven: Yale University Press, 1978), pp. 239–251.

8. Harry Graham Carter and Hendrik D. L. Vervliet, *Civilité Types* (Oxford, 1966); Henri de La Fontaine Verwey, "Les caractères de civilité et la propagande religieuse," *Bibliothèque d'humanisme et Renaissance* 16 (1964): 7–27.

9. Alix de Rohan-Chabot, *Les Ecoles de campagne en Lorraine au XVIIIe siècle* (Paris, 1967), p. 167.

10. Presentation of the *Règles de la bienséance et de la civilité chrétienne* by Brother Marucie-Auguste, *Cahiers lassalliens,* no. 19 (Rome, 1964). As early as 1722 an edition for use in Christian girls' schools was published.

11. Rodolphe Peter, "L'abécédaire genevois ou catéchisme élémentaire de Calvin," *Revue d'histoire et philosophie religieuses* 1 (1965): 11–45.

12. Dominique Julia, "Livres de classe et usages pédagogiques," *Histoire de l'édition française,* II, 468–497.

13. *Praeceptiones ad vitam inter homines ex decoro eoque christiano instituendam* (Paris, 1863). The text is by Jacques Carborand de La Fosse. I am indebted to Dominique Julia for this document.

14. Cf. Claude Lanette-Claverie, "La Librairie française en 1700," *Revue française d'histoire du livre,* 1972, pp. 3–44.

15. Georges Vigarello, *Le Corps redressé: Histoire d'un pouvoir pedagogique* (Paris: Jean-Pierre Delarge, 1978).

16. Elias, *The Civilizing Process,* chap. 4; J.-C. Bonnet, "La table dans les civilités," in *La Qualité de la vie au XVIIe siècle,* special issue of the review *Marseille,* 1977, pp. 99–104.

17. Antoine de Courtin, *Nouveau traité de la civilité qui se pratique en France et ailleurs, parmy les honnestes gens* (Paris, 1671); 1675 Brussels edition cited here, p. 87.

18. Michel Foucault, *Surveiller et punir: Naissance de la prison* (Paris, 1975).

19. Anne Vincent-Buffault, *Histoire des larmes* (Paris: Rivages, 1986).

20. Georges Vigarello, *Le Propre et le sale. L'Hygiène du corps depuis le Moyen Age* (Paris: Seuil, 1985).

21. *Il libro del Cortegiano* (Venice, 1528). On this central text, see the collection edited by Adriano Prosperi, *La Corte e il cortegiano* (Rome: Centro di studi sull'Europa delle Corti, 1980).

22. The French translation published in 1598 by Jean de Tourny used the so-called civility font.

23. The fundamental work remains Maurice Magendie, *La Politesse mondaine. Les Théories de l'honnêteté en France au XVIIe siècle, de 1600 à 1650,* 2 vols. (Paris, 1925).

24. Orest Ranum, "Courtesy, Absolutism, and the Rise of the French State, 1630–1660," *Journal of Modern History* 52 (1980): 426–451. Although extreme, the French case was not unique; cf. J. A. Vann, *The Making of a State: Württemberg, 1593–1793* (Ithaca: Cornell University Press, 1984), pp. 128–132.

25. Norbert Elias, *La Société de cour* (Paris, 1974; rev. ed., 1985).

26. A whole series of treatises, many of Jansenist leaning, gave a "Christian" interpretation to the concept of civility. Notable among them was that of Pierre Nicole, whose *Civilité chrétienne* (1668) was mentioned by Courtin. These texts laid the groundwork for La Salle's synthesis, which combined "propriety and Christian civility."

27. Roger Chartier, *Le Social en représentation. Lectures de George Dandin,* forthcoming.

28. See Elias, *The Civilizing Process,* chap. 6, and Chartier, "Civilité."

29. Grimoux's painting is in the Museum of the Augustins in Toulouse. It was discussed by Ariès in *L'Enfant et la vie familiale,* p. 432.

30. *Encyclopédie ou dictionnaire raisonné des sciences, des arts et des métiers,* vol. 3 (Paris, 1753). The article on "Civility, politeness, affability" is by the Chevalier de Jaucourt.

31. Courtin, *Nouveau Traité,* chap. 21.

32. Chemin, *Civilité républicaine contenant les principes de la morale, de la bienséance et autres instructions utiles à la jeunesse. Imprimé en différentes sortes de caractères, propres à accoutumer les enfants à lire tous les genres d'écritures* (Paris, Year III), pp. 14–15.

33. Cited in *Les Enseignants vus au XIXe siècle* (Paris, 1984).

THE REFUGES OF INTIMACY (OREST RANUM)

1. Warm thanks to Roger Chartier, Georges Dethan, Gérard Defaux, Robert and Elborg Forster, Josué Harari, Pierre Lançon, the Count de Panat, Patricia M. Ranum, and Mack Walker for their help in writing this chapter, which Philippe Ariès had requested, but which I hesitated to submit to his scrutiny.

2. *The Diary of Samuel Pepys,* ed. Robert C. Latham and William Matthews, 9 vols. (Berkeley: University of California Press, 1970–1976).

3. There was nothing very original about the act itself. For self-portraits of Marcia (ca. 1400), see Millard Meiss, *French Painting in the Time of Jean de Berry: The Limbourgs and Their Contemporaries,* 2 vols. (London, 1967; New York: Braziller, 1975), ills., pp. 287ff.

4. Erwin Panofsky, *Albrecht Dürer,* 3rd ed. (Princeton: Princeton University Press, 1948), vol. 1.

5. Nicole Pellegrin, *Les Bachelleries. Organisation et Fêtes de la jeunesse dans le Centre-Ouest* (Poitiers, 1982), p. 94.

6. See Peter Thornton, *Seventeenth-Century Interior Decoration in England, France and Holland* (New Haven: Yale University Press, 1978).

7. Sir Roy Strong, *The Renaissance Garden in England* (London, 1979), p. 210 (quotation from Henry Hawkins).

8. Ibid., p. 206 (Henry Vaughan quotation).

9. Emmanuel Le Roy Ladurie, *Montaillou, village occitan de 1294 à 1324* (Paris: Gallimard, 1975), p. 204. Trans. by Barbara Bray as *The Promised Land of Error* (New York: Braziller, 1978).

10. Janet Bord, *Mazes and Labyrinths of the World* (New York: Dutton, 1975), p. 46.

11. Kent Lydecker, "Domestic Setting of the Arts in Renaissance Florence," PhD thesis, Johns Hopkins University, 1987. See also Robert Wheaton, "Iconography of the Family Portrait," *Journal of Family History,* forthcoming.

12. Dumont de Bostaquet, *Mémoires,* ed. M. Richard (Paris, 1968), p. 77.

13. Elise Goodman-Soellner, "Poetic Interpretations of the 'Lady at Her Toilette,'" *Sixteenth Century Journal* 14 (1983): 426.

14. Watteau himself confirms this hypothesis with the "voyeur" who creeps up on his knees to look at the naked women in *L'Enseigne de Gersaint* (Berlin, Charlottenburg Castle). On intimacy in eighteenth-century painting, see Michael Fried, *Absorption and Theatricality: Painting and the Beholder in the Age of Diderot* (Berkeley: University of California Press, 1980).

15. Daniel Roche, *Le Peuple de Paris* (Paris: Aubier, 1981), p. 135. Trans. by Marie Evans as *The People of Paris: An Essay in Popular Culture in the Eighteenth Century* (Berkeley: University of California Press, 1981).

16. W. Liebenwein, *Studiolo: Die Entstehung eines Raumtyps und seine Entwicklung bis zum 1600* (Berlin: Mann, 1977).

17. Françoise Lehoux, *Le Cadre de vie des médecins parisiens au XVIe au XVIIe siècle* (Paris, 1978), p. 135.

18. Janet Todd, *Women's Friendship in Literature* (New York: Columbia University Press, 1980), p. 109. I disagree with Todd's interpretation that the nosebleed in *Clarissa* is a "simulacrum for the rape." Since men also bled from the nose (including the statue in *The Castle of Otranto,* IV), a nosebleed is rather an "effect of the passions."

19. Sainctot, Chantilly, ms 113B27, fol. 26.

20. Mme de La Guette, *Mémoires,* ed. M. Cuénin (Paris: Mercure de France, 1982), p. 67.

21. Pierre Lançon, "L'Ordre des Dominicains dans la ville de Rodez depuis leur fondation à la Révolution," MA thesis, University of Toulouse.

22. A. Wilmart, "Comment Alain de La Roche prêchait le Rosaire," *La Vie et les arts liturgiques* 11 (1924): 112.

23. Mme de Beauvau, *Memoirs* (Cologne, 1688), p. 170.

24. Krzysztof Pomian, "Entre le visible et l'invisible: la collection," *Libre* 3 (1978): 3–56.

25. Mme de Mondonville, *Lettres inédites,* ed. Léon Dutil (Paris, 1911), *passim.* See also A. Auguste, "Gabriel de Ciron et Mme de Mondonville," *Revue historique de Toulouse* 25 (1914).

26. Joseph de Gallifet, *L'Excellence de la dévotion au coeur adorable de Jésus-Christ* (Lyons, 1743), p. 43.

27. Jean Chenu, *Cent notables et singulières questions de droit,* 4th ed. (Paris, 1611), p. 268.

28. André Lamandé, ed., *Les Lettres d'amour d'Henri IV* (Paris, 1932).

29. Elisabeth Bourcier, *Les Journaux privés en Angleterre de 1600 à 1660* (Paris, 1976).

30. Claude Dulong, "Les signes cryptiques dans la correspondance d'Anne d'Autriche avec Mazarin," *Bibliothèque de l'Ecole des Chartes* 140 (1982): 61–83.

31. John Murdoch et al., *The English Miniature* (New Haven: Yale University Press, 1981); Anne Ward et al., *Rings Through the Ages* (New York, 1981).

32. Tristan L'Hermite, *Le Page disgracié,* ed. M. Arland (Paris: Stock, 1946), p. 147.

33. Ibid., p. 38.

34. Jean Torrilhon, ed. *Le Maître de Craponne* (Puy-de-Dôme: Nonette, 1980), p. 75.

35. La Guette, *Mémoires,* p. 44.

36. Her behavior on the night following her husband's death is also worth noting: "When everyone had retired, and the priests had gone off to eat something . . . I got up quietly to fetch my dear husband's body, with the intention of hiding it in my bed. As I lifted him up onto my shoulders, which was very difficult to do because he was already cold, I made some noise, which those good priests, supping in the room below his bedroom, heard" (p. 159). Thus, the same priests who prevented Mme de La Guette from doing as she wished with her mother's body now intervened again to protect the body of her husband.

37. Gordon E. Geddes, *Welcome Joy: Death in Puritan New England,* ed. Robert Berkhofer (Ann Arbor: UMI Research Press, 1981), p. 51.

38. Olivier Lefebvre d'Ormesson, *Réflexions d'un père sur la mort de son fils,* ed. A. Chéruel (Paris, 1860–1861), I, lvii.

39. Jacques-Louis Ménétra, *Journal de ma vie,* with commentary by Daniel Roche (Paris: Montalba, 1982), p. 197; trans. by Arthur Goldhammer as *Journal of My Life.* (New York: Columbia University Press, 1986).

Distinction through Taste (Jean-Louis Flandrin)

1. See Barbara K. Wheaton, *Savoring the Past: The French Kitchen and Table from 1300 to 1789* (Philadelphia: University of Pennsylvania Press, 1983).

2. Georges Vigarello, *Le Propre et le sale. L'hygiène du corps depuis le Moyen Age* (Paris: Seuil, 1985).

3. Norbert Elias, *La Civilisation des moeurs* (Paris: Calmann-Lévy, 1973), pp. 173–183.

4. Alfred Franklin, *La Vie privée d'autrefois. Arts et métiers, modes, moeurs, usages des Parisiens du XIIe au XVIIIe siécle,* vol. 6, *Les Repas* (Paris: Plon, 1889), pp. 181, 206, 104–105, 107.

5. J. Dauphiné, "Bonsevin de la Riva: De quinquaginta curialitatibus ad mensam," *Manger et boire au Moyen Age,* colloquium proceedings, Nice, 15–17 October 1982 (Paris: Les Belles Lettres, 1984), II, 7–20.

6. Franklin, *La Vie privée,* pp. 218, 231, 232–233, 234.

7. Cf. Francesco Priscianese, *Il Governo delle corte di un signore in Roma* (1543), and Cesare Evitascandolo, *Il Dialogo del maestro di casa* (Rome, 1598), cited by Lucinda Byatt in a seminar at the Institut universitaire européen.

8. Felicity Heal, "The Idea of Hospitality in Early Modern England," *Past and Present* 102 (1984): 66–93.

9. Philippe Gillet, *Par mets et par vins. Voyages et gastronomie en Europe. XVIe–XVIIIe siècle* (Paris: Payot, 1985), pp. 157–167; Jean-Louis Flandrin, "La diversité des goûts et des pratiques alimentaires en Europe du XVIe au XVIIe siècle," *Revue d'histoire moderne et contemporaine* 30 (January–March 1983): 66–83; Jean-Louis Flandrin, Mary and Philip Hyman, *Le Cuisinier françois* (Paris: Montalba, 1983), pp. 14–17.

10. The common people generally ate older oxen and cows. But the monks of Charité-sur-Loire consumed a young ox in the Middle Ages. Cf. Frédérique Audouin, "Les ossements animaux dans les fouilles médiévales de La Charité-sur-Loire," *Comptes rendus de l'Académie des inscriptions et belles-lettres,* January–March 1984, p. 213.

11. Menon, *La Cuisinière bourgeoise* (Brussels, 1777), p. 62.

12. Fernand Braudel, *Civilisation matérielle et capitalisme* (Paris: Armand Colin, 1966), p. 139.

13. Wheaton, *Savoring the Past,* p. 15.

14. None of the ingredients of blancmange was found in the 37 recipes studied. Cf. Jean-Louis Flandrin, "Internationalisme, nationalisme et régionalisme dans la cuisine des XIVe et XVe siècles," *Manger et boire au Moyen Age,* II, 75–91.

15. Bussy d'Amboise, *Journal de l'Estoile pour le règne d'Henri III,* 6 January 1578.

The Child: From Anonymity to Individuality (Jacques Gélis)

1. The custom also ensured the perpetuation of the first name, a symbolic possession highly prized by families. In England the first two or three sons were sometimes given the same name. If the eldest died, his younger brother filled the breach. See Lawrence Stone, *The Family, Sex and Marriage in England, 1500–1800* (London, 1973), p. 409.

2. The theory probably dates back to Hippocrates. See Marie-France Morel, "Théories et pratiques de l'allaitement en France au XVIIIe siècle," *Annales de démographie historique,* 1976, p. 395.

3. Folklorists report evidence of such rituals of the first steps from the late nineteenth century. See Jacques Gélis, *L'Arbre et le fruit* (Paris: Fayard, 1984), pp. 472–473.

4. Arnold Van Gennep, *Le Folklore de l'Auvergne et du Velay* (Paris, 1942), p. 22.

5. Scevole de Sainte-Marthe, *Paedotrophia ou la*

manière de nourrir les enfans à la mamelle, translated from the Latin (Paris, 1698).

6. John Locke, *The Educational Writings of John Locke,* ed. James Axtell (Cambridge: Cambridge University Press, 1968), p. 115.

7. Françoise Choay, "La ville et le domaine bâti comme corps dans les textes des architectes-théoriciens de la première Renaissance italienne," *Nouvelle Revue de Psychanalyse* 9 (Spring 1974): 239–251.

8. Christiane Klapisch-Zuber, "Parents de sang, parents de lait: la mise en nourrice à Florence, 1300–1530," *Annales de démographie historique,* 1983, pp. 33–64; *Women, Family and Ritual in Renaissance Italy* (Chicago: University of Chicago Press, 1985).

9. Simon de Vallambert, *De la manière de nourrir et gouverner les enfans* (Paris, 1565), chap. X. See also Scevole de Sainte-Marthe, *Paedotrophia.*

10. Gélis, *L'Arbre et le fruit,* pp. 434–457.

11. See Scevole de Sainte-Marthe, *Paedotrophia.* His criteria for choosing a wet nurse prefigure those of the eighteenth century: neither young nor old, neither stout nor thin, gay, with a good complexion, a broad chest, and large, round breasts. She should not have had a miscarriage.

12. Klapisch-Zuber, "Parents de sang," p. 60.

13. We do not know how rural wet nurses viewed the parents who entrusted to them the responsibility of nursing. Given what we know of their view of the world, they must have regarded these city folk as unnatural creatures, indifferent to the fate of their offspring. But why would they have cared about what became of these children rejected by their own parents?

14. See Philippe Ariès, "Les deux sentiments de l'enfance," *L'Enfant et la Vie familiale sous l'Ancien Régime* (Paris: Seuil, 1973), pp. 134–142.

15. Louis Bourgeois, *Instructions à ma fille* (Paris, 1626), pp. 218–219.

16. Locke, *Educational Writings,* p. 139.

17. Jacques Duval, *Des hermaphrodits, acouchemens des femmes* (Rouen, 1612), pp. 260–262.

18. On this debate, see the discussion between J.-B. Pontalis and Philippe Ariès, "L'Enfant," *Nouvelle Revue de psychanalyse* 19 (Spring 1979): 13–25. See also the excellent survey of sixteenth- and seventeenth-century educational doctrines in Jean Molino, "L'éducation vue à travers l'Examen des esprits du Dr Huarte," *Marseille* (Spring 1971), pp. 105–115.

19. See Eugenio Garin, *L'educazione in Europa, 1400–1600: Problemi e Programmi* (Bari: Laterza, 1957).

20. Philippe Ariès sees a relation between the increased attention paid to children and education in the schools; see his review essay "L'enfant à travers les siècles," *L'Histoire* 19 (January 1980). Lawrence Stone, however, believes that the school was a result of the destruction of the old family structure, certain of whose functions were assumed by public institutions.

21. Examples cited by François Lebrun, *La Vie conjugale sous l'Ancien Régime* (Paris: Armand Colin, 1975), pp. 153–154.

22. Ibid., pp. 66–67.

23. See Jean Delumeau, *Le Péché et la peur* (Paris: Fayard, 1983).

24. François-Mathieu Chastelet, known as de Beauchasteau, *La Lyre du jeune Apollon ou la Muse naissante du petit du Beauchasteau* (Paris, 1657).

25. Daniel Teysseyre, *Pédiatrie des Lumières* (Paris: Vrin, 1982), pp. 7–8.

THE LITERATURE OF INTIMACY (MADELEINE FOISIL)

1. Furetière, *Dictionnaire universel,* 1690. This is our best source concerning seventeenth-century French language.

2. Marc Fumaroli, "Le Dilemme de l'historiographie humaniste au XVIIe siècle," in the proceedings of the Strasbourg and Metz colloquium, 18–20 May 1978, in Noémi Hepp and Jacques Hennequin, eds., *Les Valeurs chez les mémorialistes français du XVIIe siècle* (Paris: Klincksieck, 1979), pp. 21–45.

3. Margaret MacGowan, "Découverte de soi ou poursuite de la gloire? Le Dessein ambigu des mémorialistes," in Hepp and Hennequin, eds., *Les Valeurs chez les mémorialistes français,* pp. 211–222.

4. Yves Coirault, introduction to Saint-Simon, *Mémoires de Saint-Simon* (Paris: Gallimard, 1983).

5. Emile Bourgeois and Louis André, *Sources historiques, 1610–1715,* vol. 2, *Mémoires et lettres* (Paris, 1913).

6. Alexandre Cioranescu, *Bibliographie de la littérature française du XVIIe siècle,* 3 vols. (Paris: CNRS, 1969).

7. Henri de Campion, *Mémoires* (Paris: Mercure de France, 1967); "Les Valeurs"; Bernard Beugnot, "Livre de raison, livre de retraite. Interférences des points de vue chez les mémorialistes," in Hepp and Hennequin, eds., *Les Valeurs chez les mémorialistes français,* pp. 47–64.

8. Michel de Marolles, *Mémoires,* 2 vols. (Paris, 1656–57).

9. Fontenay de Mareuil, *Mémoires* (Paris: Michaud et Poujoulat, 1837).

10. Philippe Lejeune, *L'Autobiographie en France* (Paris: Aubier, 1985).

11. Madeleine Foisil, *Le Sire de Gouberville, un gentilhomme normand au XVIe siècle* (Paris: Aubier, 1981).

12. Christian Jouhaud, *Mazarinades, la fronde des mots* (Paris: Aubier, 1985), is a stimulating study, with interesting methodological remarks.

13. The texts mentioned are treated in the following monographs: Sylvie Fontaine, "Le Livre de raison de Paul de Vendée d'après le Journal de Messire Paul de Vendée, seigneur de Vendée et de Bois-Chapeleau, publié par l'abbé Drochon, Société de statistique des Deux-Sèvres, 1879," master's thesis, Paris—Sorbonne, 1981; Vincent Boyenval, "Le Livre de raison de Charles Demaillasson, 1653–1694, publié par V. Baldet, Archives historiques du Poitou, t. XXXV–XXXVI, 1907–1908," master's thesis, Paris—Sorbonne, 1981; "Pierre Bourut, sieur des Pascauds, papier de raison publié par A. Mazière," *Bulletin de la société archéologique de la Charente* 3 (1902–03): 1–177; Sylvie Noelle Fabarez, "Les Livres de raison de Trophime Mandon d'après les manuscrits conservés aux Archives nationales," master's thesis, Paris—Sorbonne, 1983–84; Corine Bouquin, "Beauchamp, vie d'une seigneurie du comtat Venaissin au XVIIe siècle, d'après le livre de raison de François du Merles, seigneur de Beauchamp," master's thesis, Paris—Sorbonne, 1983–84; Patricia Moutet, "Le Vécu quotidien professionel, familial et social du XVIIe siècle, d'après les livres de raison d'Eusèbe Renaudot, médecin parisien, 1646–1679, et de Mathieu François Geoffroy, maître apothicaire parisien, 1670–1702," master's thesis, Paris—Sorbonne, 1984; Christine Wautier, "Le Foyer et la sociabilité au XVIIe siècle, d'après le livre de raison de Marguerite Mercie conservé à la Bibliothèque d'histoire du protestantisme français," master's thesis, Paris—Sorbonne, 1981; Florence Terrien-Duquesne, "Mémoires, Œuvres morales et Journal de Jean Maillefer d'après les Mémoires de Jean Maillefer, marchand bourgeois de Reims (1611–1684), publiés par Jadart, Reims," master's thesis, Paris—Sorbonne, 1979–80; Nadine Meaupoux, "Etude structurelle thématique de journaux et Mémoires protestants: le foyer et la famille, en particulier d'après le *Journal* de Jean Migault publié d'après le texte original par N. Weiss, reprints, 1978, 307 pp.," master's thesis, Paris—Sorbonne, 1982.

14. Dumont de Bostaquet, *Mémoires* (Paris: Mercure de France, 1968).

15. Jean Héroard, *Journal de Louis XIII*, Bibliothèque nationale, ms Fr. 4022–4027. The only published edition is mediocre and gives a false idea of the text: Soulié and Barthélemy, *Le Journal de J. Héroard,* 2 vols. (Paris, 1868).

16. Vallot, Daquin, and Fagon, *Journal de la santé du roi Louis XIV de l'année 1647 à l'année 1711* (Paris: J. A. Le Roi, 1862).

17. Dubois de Lestourmière, *Mémoires publiés par L. de Grandmaison,* Bulletin de la Société archéologique, scientifique et littéraire du Vendômois, 1932–1935.

18. Mme de Motteville, *Mémoires* (Paris: Michaud et Poujoulat, 1838).

19. Madeleine Foisil, "Le *Journal* d'Héroard, médecin de Louis XIII," *Etudes sur l'Hérault* 15 (May–June 1984): 47–51; "Et soudain Louis, neuf ans, devint roi," *Historama,* April 1985. These brief articles summarize a number of theses devoted to Héroard's *Journal,* a critical edition of which is currently being prepared by the Centre de recherche sur la civilisation de l'Europe moderne. The theses in question were written by Monique Beynes-Jauffret, Sylvain Bihoreau, Thierry Bornet, Pascal Busson, Marie-Christine Cecillon, Patrick Coville, Valérie Desnoyers, Catherine Dufils, Christian Dupin, Michel Flament, Isabelle Flandrois, Didier Lamy, Laurence Leport, Francis Montécot, Bruno Nguyen, and Marie-Christine Varachaud.

20. Annik Pardailhé-Galabrun, *La Naissance de l'intime. 3000 foyers parisiens XVIIe–XVIIIe siècles* (Paris: P.U.F., 1988); Daniel Roche, *Le Peuple de Paris* (Paris: Aubier, 1981).

21. Elisabeth Bourcier, *Les Journaux privés en Angleterre* (Paris, 1976).

22. Foisil, *Le Sire de Gouberville,* "Bâtir et réparer," pp. 128–135.

23. See Jean-Marie Constant, *La Vie quotidienne de la noblesse française au XVIIe siècle* (Paris: Hachette, 1985), pp. 222–223.

24. Georges Houdard, *Les Châteaux royaux de Saint-Germain-en-Laye* (Paris, 1911).

25. Bourcier, *Les Journaux privés,* pp. 221 ff.

26. Samuel Pepys, *Diary.*

27. Lucien Clare, "Les triomphes du corps ou la noblesse dans la paix, XVIIe siècle," *Histoire, Economie, Société,* no. 3, 1984.

28. Foisil, *Le Sire de Gouberville,* vol. 4, part 2: "Maladie et mort," pp. 209–218.

29. Maillefer, *Mémoires,* pp. 270 ff.

30. Xavier Azema, "Un prélat valétudinaire, Mgr de Saint-Simon, évêque d'Agde," *Etudes sur l'Hérault,* 1985.

31. Bourcier, *Les Journaux privés,* part 2, chap. 4.

32. Ibid. Subsequent examples are from the same chapter.

33. My study is based on unpublished work on diaries done at the Centre de recherche sur la civilisation de l'Europe moderne.

34. Jacques Gélis, Mireille Laget, and M.-F. Morel, *Entrer dans la vie: naissance et enfance dans la France traditionnelle* (Paris: Archives, 1978). Héroard's *Journal* confirms the authors' remarks on early childhood, based on much more theoretical sources.

35. Philippe Ariès, *L'Enfant et la vie familiale sous l'Ancien Régime* (Paris: Seuil, 1973). See also Hélène Himmelfarb, "Un journal peu ordinaire," *Nouvelle Revue de psychanalyse* 19 (Spring 1979), "L'Enfant." Pierre Debray-Ritzen, *La Sexualité infantile* (Paris, 1982), has related the subject to more general questions of pediatrics and medicine.

36. See Isabelle Flandrois's introduction to the forthcoming critical edition of Héroard's *Journal*.

3. Community, State, and Family

The Public and the Private (Nicole Castan)

1. The expression occurs in an 1823 letter written by Stendhal. Compare successive definitions given by the dictionaries of Furetière, Trévoux, the *Encyclopedia,* and Larousse.

2. Teresa of Avila, *Autobiography.*

3. Letter from President de Brosses to M. de Neuilly, *Epistoliers du XVIIIe siècle* (Paris: La Renaissance du Livre, n.d.).

4. Tristan L'Hermite, *Le Page disgracié* (Grenoble: Presses Universitaires de Grenoble, 1980).

5. Chevalier de Fonvielle, *Mémoires historiques* (Paris, 1820).

6. Guillaume Hérail, *Mémoires,* manuscript copy in the municipal library of Toulouse. Hérail and Fonvielle grew up in the last twenty years of the ancien régime but wrote their memoirs later, one at the beginning of the Restoration, the other in 1793, under the influence of Rousseau's *Confessions* and of a change in values associated with the Revolution.

7. Compare the adventures of the young Count de Losse-Valence, who was twelve years old in 1778 when seen in Paris on the arm of a streetwalker. On his school vacation he deceived his family and found freedom. Departmental Archives of Haute-Garonne, series E, 182.

8. Unclassified criminal court records.

9. Natalie Zemon Davis, *Society and Culture in Early Modern France* (Stanford: Stanford University Press, 1965). For Languedoc, see Nicole Castan, *Justice et répression en Languedoc à l'époque des Lumières* (Paris: Flammarion, 1980).

10. Mme de Maintenon, *Lettres, avis et entretiens sur l'éducation* (Paris: Hachette, 1885).

11. Diderot, *Lettres à Sophie Volland* (Paris: Gallimard, 1938); Mme de Charrière, *Caliste, lettres écrites de Lausanne* (Paris: Editions des Femmes, 1979).

12. Mme Roland, *Mémoires* (Paris, 1821).

13. Fonds Pollastron, Departmental Archives of Haute-Garonne, series E.

14. Hérail, *Mémoires:* "My mother was happy to have a woman friend, which allowed her to go out occasionally and enjoy herself."

15. Arlette Farge, *Vivre dans la rue à Paris au XVIIIe siècle* (Paris: Gallimard, 1979).

16. François de Sales, *Œuvres* (Paris: Gallimard, 1969).

17. Mme Roland, *Mémoires.* George Sand enjoyed similar friendships in a convent in the early nineteenth century but regretted that social boundaries were not transgressed more often; *Histoire de ma vie.*

18. As did Mme Louvois. See André Corvisier, *Louvois* (Paris: Fayard, 1983).

19. Duc de Saint-Simon, *Mémoires* (Paris: Gallimard, 1983–1985); Louis XIV, *Mémoires et lettres* (Paris: Taillandier, 1927); Georges Mongrédien, *Louis XIV* (Paris: Albin Michel, 1962).

20. Norbert Elias, *The Court Society,* trans. E. Jephcott (Oxford: Basil Blackwell, 1983).

21. Daniel Roche, *Le Peuple de Paris. Essai sur la culture populaire* (Paris: Aubier, 1981).

22. See also the numerous works of Mirabeau.

23. He considered the proliferation of furniture with secret compartments a sign of the century's corruption.

24. Departmental archives of Haute-Garonne, subseries J, Maniban; S. Clair, "Joseph Gaspard de Maniban, premier président du parlement de Toulouse," thesis of the Ecole des Chartes, ms 306 on deposit at the Departmental archives of Haute-Garonne.

25. Michel Taillefer, *La Franc-Maçonnerie toulousaine, 1741–1799,* Commission on the Economic History of the French Revolution, 1984; Robert Forster, *The Nobility of Toulouse in the Eighteenth Century: A Social and Economic Study* (Baltimore: Johns Hopkins University Press, 1960).

26. Cf. J.-F. Marmontel, *Mémoires d'un père pour servir à l'instruction de ses enfants,* 4 vols. (Paris, 1807):

"I cannot express how charming and pleasurable life was for us until the time of the Revolution."

27. Mme Campan, *Mémoires,* ed. Jean Chalon (1979); Prince de Ligne, *Mémoires et lettres* (Paris, 1923); Count de Tilly, *Mémoires,* ed. Melchior-Bonnet (1965).

28. Marmontel, *Mémoires:* "Soon the interests of the republic and worries about the fate of the state took hold of my spirit, and my private life necessarily changed."

29. I wish to thank M. Charles-Louis d'Orgeix, who kindly allowed me to consult his personal archives, which contain the private records and correspondence of the Gounon-Loubens family.

30. Jean-Jacques Rousseau, *The Social Contract;* Saint-Just, *L'Esprit de la Révolution* (Paris: Plon, 1963).

31. The letters of Jean Mathias de Gounon from the Army of the Eastern Pyrenees are filled with observations on the progress of the revolutionary war as seen by an admittedly not very enthusiastic citizen soldier.

FRIENDS AND NEIGHBORS (MAURICE AYMARD)

1. Emile Littré, *Dictionnaire de la langue française,* article "Privé."

2. Volker Hunecke, "Les enfants trouvés: contexte européen et cas milanais, XVIIIe–XIXe siècle," *Revue d'histoire moderne et contemporaine* 32 (1985): 3–29. For more on family roles, see Esther N. Goody, *Parenthood and Social Reproduction: Fostering and Occupational Roles in West Africa* (Cambridge: Cambridge University Press, 1982).

3. Ivy Pinchbeck and Margaret Hewitt, *Children in English Society,* vol. 1, *From Tudor Times to the Eighteenth Century* (London: Routledge and Kegan Paul, 1969), p. 28.

4. Alfred R. Radcliffe-Brown, *Structure and Function in Primitive Society* (London, 1952).

5. Claude Lévi-Strauss, "L'analyse structurale en linguistique et en anthropologie" in *Anthropologie structurale* (Paris: Plon, 1958), pp. 37–62; trans. by Monique Layton as *Structural Anthropology* (New York: Basic Books, 1963, 1976).

6. Robert Brain, *Friends and Lovers* (London: Hart-Davis-MacGibbon, 1976).

7. Meyer Fortes, *Kinship and the Social Order: The Legacy of Lewis Henry Morgan* (London, 1969), p. 63, cited in N. Sindzingre, "Amis, parents et alliés: les formes de l'amitié chez les Senufo (Côte-d'Ivoire)," paper delivered to the colloquium "Amicizia e le Amicizie," Palermo, November 1983, pp. 24–26, to appear in the colloquium proceedings and in the journal *Cultures.*

8. Jeremy Boissevain, *Friends of Friends. Networks, Manipulations and Coalitions* (Oxford: Basil Blackwell, 1974).

9. Leon Battista Alberti, *I Libri della famiglia,* intro. by Ruggiero Romano and Alberto Tenenti (Turin: Einaudi, 1969).

10. Emmanuel Le Roy Ladurie, *Montaillou, village occitan de 1294 à 1324* (Paris: Gallimard, 1975), p. 83; trans. by Barbara Bray as *Montaillou: The Promised Land of Error* (New York: Braziller, 1978).

11. Ibid., pp. 84–85, and Charles de La Roncière, "Une famille florentine au XIVe siècle: les Velluti," *Famille et Parenté dans l'Occident médiéval* (Rome: Ecole française de Rome, 1987), pp. 228–248.

12. J.-M. Gouesse, "Parenté, famille et mariage en Normandie aux XVIIe et XVIIIe siècles. Présentation d'une source et d'une enquête," *Annales ESC* 27 (4–5): July–October 1972, p. 1145.

13. Jean-Louis Flandrin, *Familles, parenté, maison, sexualité dans l'ancienne société,* 2nd. ed. (Paris: Seuil, 1984), p. 40.

14. R. Merzario, *Il Paese stretto. Strategie matrimoniali nella diocesi di Como. Secoli XVI–XVIII* (Turin: Einaudi, 1981), pp. 23–26.

15. Gouesse, "Parenté," p. 1146.

16. Merzario, *Il Paese,* p. 105.

17. All quotations in the preceding paragraphs are from Montaigne, "On Friendship," *Essays,* I, 28; Frame translation, pp. 136–138.

18. Ibid., III, 3, "On the Three Commerces."

19. Brain, *Friends and Lovers,* pp. 301–302.

20. Saint-Simon, *Mémoires* (Paris: Gallimard, 1953–1958), I, 659–660. Further references to these memoirs are found in the text.

21. Marc Bloch, *La Société féodale,* 2nd ed. (Paris: Albin Michel, 1949); trans. by L. A. Manyon as *Feudal Society,* 2 vols. (London: Routledge & Kegan Paul, 1961).

22. L. Hellmuth, *Die germanische Blutsbruderschaft,* Wiener Arbeiten zur Germanischen Altertumskunde und Philologie, 7, Vienna, 1975.

23. H. Tegnaeus, *La Fraternité de sang. Etude ethno-sociologique des rites de la fraternité de sang, notamment en Afrique* (Paris: Payot, 1954), p. 25.

24. S. Ciszewski, *Künstliche Verwandschaft bei den Südslaven* (Leipzig, 1981), p. 47.

25. Hellmuth, *Die germanische Blutsbruderschaft.*

26. Emmanuel Le Roy Ladurie, *Les Paysans de Languedoc* (Paris: SEVPEN, 1966), I, 166; trans. by John Day as *The Peasants of Languedoc* (Champaign: University of Illinois Press, 1974).

27. Bloch, *La Société féodale,* I, 215.

28. S. W. Mintz and E. R. Wolf, "An Analysis

of Ritual Co-parenthood (compadrazgo)," *Southwestern Journal of Anthropology* 6 (1950): 341ff., and Shmuel N. Eisenstadt, "Ritualized Personal Relations: Blood Brotherhood, Best Friends, Compadre, etc. Some Comparative Hypotheses and Suggestions," *Man* 96 (July 1958): 90–95.

29. Luther, "Tischreden: Anton Lauterbach's Tagebuch aufs Jahr 1539," *D. Martin Luther's Werke, Kritische Gesamtausgabe,* vol. 4, 1916; Weimar cited by Mintz and Wolf in the article cited on p. 349, n. 28.

30. G. Valentini, *La Legge delle montagne albanesi nelle relazioni della missione volante, 1880–1932* (Florence, "Studi Albanesi, Studi e testi, 3," 1969), p. 25.

31. Arnold Van Gennep, *Manuel de folklore français contemporain,* vol. 1, *Du berceau à la tombe* (Paris: Picard, 1943), p. 233.

32. Natalie Zemon Davis, *Society and Culture in Early Modern France,* 4th ed. (Stanford: Stanford University Press, 1975), p. 3.

33. Ibid., p. 5.

34. Ran Halévi, *Les Loges maçonniques dans la France d'Ancien Régime. Aux origines de la sociabilité démocratique* (Paris: Armand Colin, 1984), p. 11.

35. Gérard Gayot, *La Franc-Maçonnerie française. Textes et Pratiques* (Paris: Gallimard/Julliard, 1980), p. 69.

36. Maurice Agulhon, *Pénitents et Francs-Maçons de l'ancienne Provence* (Paris: Fayard, 1968).

37. Maurice Agulhon, *Le Cercle dans la France bourgeoise, 1810–1848. Etude d'une mutation de sociabilité* (Paris: Armand Colin, 1977), pp. 19–20.

38. Daniel Roche, *Le Siècle des lumières en province. Académies et Académiciens provinciaux, 1680–1789* (Paris and The Hague: EHESS-Mouton, 1978), p. 18.

39. J.-M. Gardair, "I Liucei: i soggetti, i luoghi, le attività," *Quaderni storici* 16 (December 1981): 768.

40. Baudelaire, *La Fanfarlo,* 1847, cited by Agulhon, *Le Cercle,* p. 52.

41. Agulhon, *Le Cercle,* p. 23.

42. Gayot, *La Franc-Maçonnerie,* p. 69.

43. Ibid., p. 123.

44. Davis, *Society and Culture,* pp. 166–172.

45. Robert Mandrou, *Introduction à la France moderne. Essai de psychologie historique, 1500–1640* (Paris: Albin Michel, 1961), pp. 184–187.

46. Agulhon, *Pénitents et Francs-Maçons,* pp. 947–950.

47. X. Rousseaux, "Criminalité et répression en milieu rural et urbain. Le cas du Brabant wallon au XVIIe siècle," paper presented to the meeting of the International Research Group on the History of Justice and Criminality, 11–12 January 1985, Paris, Maison des Sciences de l'homme, p. 13.

48. Davis, *Society and Culture,* p. 171.

49. B. Bernardi, *I Sistemi delle classi di età. Ordinamenti sociali e politici fondati sull'età* (Turin: Loescher, 1984), p. 20.

50. Frank W. Young, *Initiation Ceremonies: A Cross-Cultural Society of Status Dramatization* (Indianapolis: Bobbs-Merrill, 1965), p. 30.

51. Valentin Jamerey-Duval, *Mémoires. Enfance et éducation d'un paysan au XVIIIe siècle* (Paris: Le Sycomore, 1981), p. 150.

52. O. Niccoli, "Lotte per le brache. La Donna indisciplinata nelle stampe popolari d'*Ancien Régime,*" *Memoria,* 2 October 1981, pp. 49–63.

53. Jean-Jacques Rousseau, *Les Confessions,* in *Oeuvres complètes* (Paris: Gallimard, 1959), p. 15.

54. Jamerey-Duval, *Mémoires.*

55. Philippe Ariès, *L'Enfant et la vie familiale sous l'Ancien Régime* (Paris: Seuil, 1973), p. viii.

56. Alan MacFarlane, *The Origin of English Individualism: The Family, Property, and Social Transition* (Oxford: Basil Blackwell, 1978).

57. Rousseau, *Confessions,* p. 13.

58. Ariès, *L'Enfant*; G. P. Brizzi, *La Formazione della classe dirigente nel Sei-Settecento. I seminaria nobilium nell'Italia centro-settentrionale* (Bologna: Il Mulino, 1976); F. de Dainville, "Collèges et fréquentation scolaire au XVIIe siècle," *Population* 12 (July–September 1957): 476–494.

59. Ariès, *L'Enfant,* p. 356.

60. P. Coustel, *Règles de l'éducation des enfants* (Paris, 1687), cited by Ariès, *L'Enfant,* p. 422.

61. Brizzi, *La Formazione,* p. 165.

62. Lawrence Stone, *The Crisis of the Aristocracy, 1558–1641* (Oxford: Clarendon, 1965), p. 689.

63. James Boswell, *Boswell veut se marier, 1766–1769* (Paris: Hachette, 1959).

FAMILIES: HABITATIONS AND COHABITATIONS (ALAIN COLLOMP)

1. Albrecht Dürer, *Saint John's Chapel at Nuremberg,* ca. 1494, watercolor and gouache (Bremen, Kunsthalle).

2. Albrecht Dürer, *The Village of Kalchreut,* ca. 1500, watercolor (Bremen, Kunsthalle).

3. Albrecht Dürer, *Arco,* 1495, watercolor and gouache (Paris, Louvre).

4. A series of volumes on French rural architecture, classified by region, is currently being published by the Musée National des Arts et Traditions populaires (Paris: Berger-Levrault).

5. Pieter Brueghel the Younger, *Farm Visit,*

painting on wood, 1620 (private collection); reproduced in catalogue to the Brueghel exhibition (Brussels, 1980), no. 90. Jan Brueghel, *Farm Visit,* copper engraving (Vienna, Kunsthistorisches Museum), no. 118 in the Brueghel catalogue.

6. Le Nain, *The Peasant Meal,* also called *The Benevolent Women* and *The Topers,* and *The Peasant Family* (Paris, Louvre).

7. Jean Yver, *Essai de géographie coutumière* (Paris, 1966).

8. Emmanuel Le Roy Ladurie, *Montaillou, village occitan, de 1294 à 1324* (Paris: Gallimard, 1975); trans. by Barbara Bray as *Montaillou: The Promised Land of Error* (New York: Braziller, 1978).

9. G. Gudin de Vallerin, "Habitat et communautés de famille en Bourgogne (XVIIe–XIXe siècle)," *Etudes rurales* 85 (January–March 1982): 33–47.

10. Anne Zinck, *Azereix, une communauté rurale à la fin du XVIIIe siècle* (Paris, 1969).

11. Gérard Bouchard, *Le Village immobile: Sennely-en-Sologne au XVIIIe siècle* (Paris, 1972), p. 95; cahier de doléances of the inhabitants of Vouzon in 1789.

12. Ibid., p. 94, n. 32.

13. Abel Poitrineau, *La Vie rurale en basse Auvergne au XVIIIe siècle* (Paris, 1970).

14. Paul Arrighi, *La Vie quotidienne en Corse au XVIIIe siècle* (Paris, 1970).

15. J.-M. Poisson, "La Maison paysanne dans les bourgs siciliens (XIVe–XIXe siècle). Permanence d'un type?" *Archeologia medievale* (Geneva) 7 (1980): 83–94.

16. Louis Merle. *La Métairie et l'Evolution de la Gâtne poitevine, de la fin du Moyen Age à la Révolution* (Paris, 1959).

17. Jean Jacquart, "L'habitat rural en Ile-de-France au XVIe siècle," proceedings of the colloquium on the "Quality of Life in the Seventeenth Century," *Marseille* 109 (1977): 69–73.

18. Guy Cabourdin, *Quand Stanislas régnait en Lorraine* (Paris, 1980), p. 317.

19. Bouchard, *Le Village immobile,* p. 98.

20. Count de Forbin, *Mémoires,* 2 vols., 1729.

21. Frédéric Le Play, *L'Organisation de la famille selon le vrai modèle* (1871), 5th ed. (Tours, 1907), p. 143.

22. Romain Baron, "La bourgeoisie de Varzy au XVIIe siècle," *Annales de Bourgogne* (June–September 1964), pp. 161–208.

23. Lazare de La Salle de L'Hermine, *Mémoires de deux voyages et séjours en Alsace, 1674–1676 and 1681* (Mulhouse, 1886).

24. Suzanne Tardieu, *La Vie domestique dans le Mâconnais rural préindustriel* (Paris, 1964).

25. J.-P. Bardet, *Rouen aux XVIIe et XVIIIe siècles* (Paris, 1983).

26. Yver, *Essai.*

27. Alain Collomp, *La Maison du père. Famille et village en haute Provence aux XVIIe et XVIIIe siècles* (Paris, 1983).

28. M.-N. Denis and M.-C. Grohens, *L'Architecture rurale française, Alsace* (Paris, 1978).

29. Florence Colin-Goguel, "Les potiers et tuiliers de Manerbe et du Pré d'Auge au XVIIIe siècle," *Annales de Normandie* 25 (June 1975): 99–111.

30. François Lebrun, *La Vie conjugale sous l'Ancien Régime* (Paris: Armand Colin, 1975), p. 64.

31. Carmelo Lison-Tolosana, "The Ethics of Inheritance," in J. G. Peristiany, ed., *Mediterranean Family Structure* (Cambridge: Cambridge University Press, 1976).

32. François de Belleforest, *Cosmographie universelle de tout le Monde,* 1575.

33. J. Le Quinio de Kerblay, *Voyage dans le Jura,* 2 vols. (Paris, 1800).

34. B. Gunda, "The Ethnosociological Structure of the Hungarian Extended Family," *Journal of Family History* (Spring 1982), pp. 40–52.

35. Jean Chiffre, "La maison commune et les différents bâtiments de la communauté familiale," special issue, "Avec les Parsonniers," Clermont-Fernand colloquium, 1981, *Revue d'Auvergne* 95 (1981): 273.

FAMILIES: PRIVACY VERSUS CUSTOM (DANIEL FABRE)

1. Archives cantonales, hereafter abbreviated as A.C., Carcassonne, FF1.

2. Claude Karnoouh, "Le charivari et l'hypothèse de la monogamie," in Jacques Le Goff and Jean-Claude Schmitt, eds., *Le Charivari* (Paris: Mouton-EHESS, 1981), pp. 33–44.

3. The "matrimonial economy" figures in the analysis of charivari by Claude Lévi-Strauss in *Le Cru et le cuit* (Paris: Plon, 1964), pp. 343–344.

4. Archives départementales, hereafter abbreviated as A.D., Var, Justice seigneuriale de Varages, May 1788.

5. Private archives; excerpts from the *Chronologiette* were published in E. G. Léonard, *Mon village sous Louis XV* (Paris: Presses Universitaires de France, 1940).

6. C. Daugé, "Une azoade à Coarraze en 1762," *Bulletin de la société de Borda* (Dax) 45 (1921): 107–115.

7. On Marie Blanque, see M.-C. Salles, *La Poésie populaire en vallée d'Aspe* (Orthez, 1980), pp. 96–106; and E. de Martino, *Morte e pianto rituale* (Boringhieri, 1975).

8. A.D., Aude, B 1210.

9. A.D., Hérault, C 6851.

10. A.D., Aude, B 2641.

11. L. Junod, "Le Charivari au pays de Vaud dans le premier tiers du XIXe siècle," *Schweizerisches Archiv für Volkskunde* (Basel) 47 (1951): 114–129.

12. All the cases cited are taken from the communal archives of Limoux, which were examined systematically for the period 1740 to 1790, along with complaints and petitions to the military command of the province (A.D., Hérault). In addition, I examined an extensive sample of unclassified documents for the seneschal's court (A.D., Aude).

13. Maurice Agulhon has noted a disparity between the role of youth as a municipal institution and the actual behavior of youths, based on his examination of the police archives of Toulon (1774–1779); see his *Pénitents et Francs-Maçons de l'ancienne Provence* (Paris: Fayard, 1968), p. 62. For the case of Poitou, see N. Pellegrin, *Les Bachelleries dans le Centre-Ouest* (Poitiers, 1983).

14. See *Le Jeu au XVIIIe siècle* (Aix-en-Provence: Edisud, 1976).

15. See André Burguière, "Pratique du charivari et répression religieuse," in Le Goff and Schmitt, *Le Charivari,* pp. 179–196. No catalogue of civil sentences has yet been compiled. For some observations on the question, see J.-L. Sourioux, "Le Charivari. Etude de sociologie criminelle," *L'Année sociologique* (Paris: Presses Universitaires de France, 1962), pp. 410–414.

16. M. Ingram, in Le Goff and Schmitt, *Le Charivari,* p. 253.

17. On these penal rituals, see P. Saintyves, "Le Charivari de l'adultère et les courses à corps nus," *L'Ethnographie* (Paris, 1935), pp. 7–36, and R. Pinon, "Qu'est-ce qu'un charivari?" *Kontakte und Grenzen,* Festschrift for Gerhard Heilfurth (Göttingen, 1969), pp. 393–405.

18. The plea is reprinted in *Plaidoyers et actions graves et éloquentes de plusieurs fameux avocats du parlement de Bordeaux* (Bordeaux, 1646), pp. 197–208.

19. For Béarn, see Christian Desplat, *Charivaris en Gascogne* (Paris: Berger-Levrault, 1982), p. 103. Nicole Castan examines fifty cases from Languedoc in Le Goff and Schmitt, *Le Charivari,* pp. 197–206.

20. For these three cases see A.D., Hérault, C 6864, 6666, 1778.

21. On libertinage, see C. Nicod, "Les 'Séditieux' en Languedoc à la fin du XVIIIe siècle," *Droit pénal et Société méridionale. Mémoires et Travaux publiés par la Société d'histoire du droit* (Montpellier, 1971), pp. 145–165. Remarkable portraits of libertines imprisoned by lettres de cachet at the fort of Brescou near Agde can be found in G. Sarret de Coussergues, *Une Prison d'état au milieu du XVIIIe siècle* (Paris: Les Presses Continentales, 1950). A portrait of a rural libertine, the abbé Fabre's *Jean l'an prés,* is examined in Emmanuel Le Roy Ladurie, *L'Argent, l'amour, la mort en pays d'Oc* (Paris: Seuil, 1980).

22. On the curé at the end of the ancien régime, see Nicole Castan, *Les Criminels de Languedoc* (Toulouse: Université de Toulouse—Mirail, 1980), pp. 127–128, 145–158, and the continuing research of A. Molinier, described in "En Languedoc: Le Curé de village (XVII–XVIIIe siècle)," *Etudes sur Pézenas et l'Hérault* 11 (1980–1983): 59–65.

23. For Germany, E. Hinrichs has found a similar redefinition of the boundary of social control in Le Goff and Schmitt, *Le Charivari,* pp. 297–306; for Gascony, see Daniel Fabre and Bernard Traimond, ibid., pp. 23–32.

THE HONOR AND SECRECY OF FAMILIES (ARLETTE FARGE)

1. Louis Sébastien Mercier, *Tableau de Paris* (Amsterdam, 1781–1788; Babil ed., Paris: Maspero, 1979).

2. Abel Poitrineau, *Remues d'hommes. Les Migrations montagnardes en France, XVIIe–XVIIIe siècle* (Paris: Aubier, 1983).

3. Lenoir, "Mémoires," Municipal Library of Orléans, ms 1422.

4. Georges Duby, ed., *Histoire de la France urbaine* (Paris: Seuil, 1981), III, 316.

5. Daniel Roche, *Le Peuple de Paris au XVIIIe siècle* (Paris: Aubier, 1981).

6. Arlette Farge, *Vivre dans la rue à Paris au XVIIIe siècle* (Paris: Gallimard, 1979), p. 82.

7. Olivier Blanc, *La Dernière lettre. Prisons et condamnés de la Révolution 1793–1794* (Paris: Laffont, 1984).

8. Thefts of money, handkerchiefs, snuffboxes, and watches occurred frequently. Complaints to constables describe the space assigned to each person and how personal affairs were stored.

9. There were twenty quarters in Paris and forty-eight constables.

10. Jean de Mille, *Pratique criminelle,* intro. by Arlette Lebigre (Paris: Les Marmousets, 1983), p. 37.

11. A. de Courtin, *Traité du point d'honneur et*

des règles pour converser et se conduire sagement avec les civils et les fâcheux (Paris, 1675).

12. Lenoir, "Mémoires," fol. 302.

13. Julian Pitt-Rivers, *The Fate of Shechem or the Politics of Sex* (Cambridge: Cambridge University Press, 1977).

14. Michel Maffesoli and Alain Pessin, *La Violence fondatrice* (Paris: Le Champ urbain, 1978), p. 69.

15. Mercier, *Tableau de Paris,* p. 37.

16. This question is examined at length in Arlette Farge and Michel Foucault, *Le Désordre des familles. Lettres de cachet des Archives de la Bastille* (Paris: Gallimard, 1982).

17. Paris, Bibliothèque Nationale, ms fr. 21129, fols. 174–178, collection of letters written by Pontchartrain, 1699–1714 (reference thanks to Dominique Julia).

18. Archives nationales, C10D2, Archives of La Désirade, July 1765.

19. Archives of the Bastille, ms 12690, 1740, state of persons imprisoned at Sainte-Pélagie in accordance with royal orders.

20. N. T. des Essarts, *Dictionnaire de police,* vol. 7, 1786–1789, p. 343.

21. Norbert Elias, *La Civilisation des moeurs* (Paris, 1973), p. 67; trans. by E. Jephcott as *The Civilizing Process* (New York: Pantheon, 1982).

22. Marc Chassaigne, *La Lieutenance générale de police à Paris* (Paris, 1906).

23. Des Essarts, *Dictionnaire,* 7, 343.

24. Jean Nicolas, "La rumeur de Paris: rapts d'enfants en 1750," *L'Histoire* 40 (1981): 48–57; Charles Romon, "L'affaire des enlèvements d'enfants dans les archives du Châtelet, 1749–1750," *Revue historique* 170 (1983): 55–95; Arlette Farge and Jacques Revel, "Les Règles de l'émeute: l'affaire des enlèvements d'enfants, Paris, mai 1750," *Mouvements populaires et Conscience sociales, XVIe-XIXe siècle,* 1985, pp. 635–646.

25. Franz Funck-Brentano, "Origines du pouvoir royal en France," *Revue du foyer,* 1 February 1912.

26. Archives nationales, Y 11262, 4 October 1774, letter to syndics in archives of Constable Thierry.

27. Breteuil's memorandum to the intendants of the kingdom and to the lieutenant general of police in Paris concerning prisoners held by lettres de cachet, March 1784; Franz Funck-Brentano, ed., *Les lettres de cachet à Paris,* 1926, p. xlii.

28. Flammermont, *Remontrances au parlement de Paris, 1787,* III, 713.

29. Archives nationales, X1B8979, cited by Monin, *L'Etat de Paris en 1789* (Paris, 1889).

30. Archives parlementaires, 1790, 9, 413–414.

31. Ibid., 11, 279.

32. Ibid., 11, 488.

33. Ibid., 17, 617.

34. Ibid.

35. *Le Moniteur universel,* 27, 523–524.

Bibliography

Adams, W. H. *Les Jardins en France. Le Rêve et le Pouvoir.* Paris: Equerre, 1980.

Agulhon, Maurice. *Pénitents et Francs-Maçons de l'ancienne Provence.* Paris: Fayard, 1968.

Aimer en France. University of Clermont—II, 1980.

Amussen, S. D. "Féminin/masculin. Le genre dans l'Angleterre de l'époque moderne," *Annales ESC,* pp. 269–287.

Aragon, H. *Les Lois somptuaires en France.* Perpignan, 1921.

Ariès, Philippe. *L'Enfant et la vie familiale sous l'Ancien Régime.* Paris: Plon, 1960; Seuil, 1973. Trans. by Robert Baldick as *Centuries of Childhood: A Social History of Family Life.* New York: Knopf, 1962.

——— *Images de l'homme devant la mort.* Paris: Seuil, 1983. Trans. by Janet Lloyd as *Images of Man and Death.* Cambridge, Mass.: Harvard University Press, 1985.

——— *L'Homme devant la mort.* Paris: Seuil, 1983.

"Avec les parsonniers," special issue of *Revue d'Auvergne,* no. 486, 1981.

Babelon, J.-P. *Demeures parisiennes sous Henri IV et Louis XIII.* Paris: Le Temps, 1965.

——— "Du Grand Ferrare à Carnavalet. Naissance de l'hôtel classique," *Revue de l'Art* 40–41 (1978).

Baczko, B. *Rousseau. Solitude et Communauté.* Paris and The Hague: Mouton, 1974.

——— *Lumières de l'Utopie.* Paris: Payot, 1978.

Bakhtin, Mikhail. *Rabelais and His World,* trans. Hélène Iswolsky. Cambridge, Mass.: MIT Press, 1968.

Bardet, J.-P. *Rouen aux XVIIe et XVIIIe siècles.* Paris: SEDES, 1983.

——— et al. *Le Bâtiment. Enquête d'histoire économique, XIVe–XIXe siècle,* vol. 1, *Maisons rurales et urbaines dans la France traditionnelle.* Paris and The Hague: Mouton, 1971.

Bénichou, Paul. *Le Sacre de l'écrivain.* Paris, 1973.

Bercé, Y.-M. *Fête et Révolte. Des mentalités populaires du XVIe au XVIIIe siècle.* Paris: Hachette, 1976.

Berkner, Lutz K. "The Stem-Family and the Development of the Peasant Household: An Eighteenth-Century Austrian Example," *The American Historical Review* 77 (1972): 398–418.

Bertelli, S., and G. Crifo, eds. *Rituale, Ceremoniale, Etichetta.* Milan: Bompiani, 1985.

Bouchard, G. *Le Village immobile, Sennely-en-Sologne au XVIIIe siècle.* Paris: Plon, 1972.

Bourcier, Elisabeth. *Les Journaux privés en Angleterre de 1600 à 1660.* Paris, 1976.

Brizzi, G. P. *La Formazione della classe dirigente nel Sei-Settecento. I Seminaria nobilium nell'Italia centro-settentrionale.* Bologna: Il Mulino, 1976.

Campion, Henri de. *Mémoires.* Paris: Mercure de France, 1967.

Camporesi, P. *Il Paese della fame.* Bologna: Il Mulino, 1980.

——— *Alimentazione, Folclore a Società.* Parma: Pratiche, 1980.

Caro Baroja, J. *Las Formas complejas de la vida religiosa. Religión, sociedad y carácter en la España de los siglos XVI y XVII.* Madrid: Alkal, 1979.

Castan, Nicole. *Justice et répression en Languedoc à l'époque des Lumières.* Paris: Flammarion, 1980.

——— *Les Criminels de Languedoc. Les Exigences d'ordre et les voies du ressentiment dans une société prérévolutionnaire (1750–1790).* Toulouse, 1980.

Castan, Yves. *Honnêteté et Relations sociales en Languedoc, 1750–1780.* Paris: Plon, 1974.

Certeau, Michel de. "La formalité des pratiques. Du système religieux à l'éthique des Lumières (XVIIe–XVIIIe siècle)," *L'Ecriture de l'histoire.* Paris: Gallimard, 1975, pp. 152–214.

——— *La Fable mystique XVIe–XVIIe siècle.* Paris: Gallimard, 1982.

Chartier, Roger. "From Text to Manners, A Concept and Its Books: *Civilité* between Aristocratic Distinction and Popular Appropriation," in *The Cultural Uses of Print in Early Modern France.* Trans. Lydia Cochrane. Princeton: Princeton University Press, 1987.

——— "Livres bleus et lectures populaires," in H.-J. Martin and Roger Chartier, eds., *Histoire de l'édition française.* 2 vols. Paris: Promodis, 1982, II, 498–511.

——— ed. *Pratiques de la lecture.* Marseilles: Rivages, 1985.

——— "Stratégies éditoriales et lectures populaires," in Martin and Chartier, eds., *Histoire de l'édition française*, I, 585–608.

——— and Daniel Roche. "Les pratiques urbaines de l'imprimé," in Martin and Chartier, eds., *Histoire de l'édition française*, II, 402–429.

——— Dominique Julia, and Marie-Madeleine Compère. *L'Education en France du XVIe au XVIIIe siècle*. Paris: SEDES, 1976.

Chaunu, Pierre. *Le Temps des réformes. Histoire religieuse et système de civilisation*. Paris: Fayard, 1975.

Chevalier, Maxime. *Lectura y Lectores en la España de los siglos XVI y XVII*. Madrid: Turner, 1976.

Claverie, E., and P. Lamaison, *L'Impossible mariage. Violence et parenté en Gévaudan, XVIIe, XVIIIe, et XIXe siècles*. Paris: Hachette, 1982.

Collomp, Alain. *La Maison du père. Famille et village en haute Provence aux XVIIe et XVIIIe siècles*. Paris: Presses Universitaires de France, 1983.

Compagnon, Antoine *Nous, Michel de Montaigne*. Paris: Seuil, 1980.

Compère, Marie-Madeleine. *Du collège au lycée (1500–1900). Généalogie de l'enseignement secondaire français*. Paris: Gallimard/Julliard, 1985.

Corpus de l'architecture rurale française. Paris: Berger-Levrault, 1977.

Curtin, Michael. "A Question of Manners: Status and Gender in Etiquette and Courtesy," *Journal of Modern History* 57 (1985): 395–423.

Dann, O., ed. *Lesegesellschaften und bürgerliche Emanzipation*. Munich, 1981.

Darnton, Robert. *The Literary Underground of the Old Regime*. Cambridge, Mass.: Harvard University Press, 1982.

——— *Mesmerism and the End of the Enlightenment in France*. Cambridge, Mass.: Harvard University Press, 1968.

Davis, Natalie Zemon. *The Return of Martin Guerre*. Cambridge, Mass.: Harvard University Press, 1983.

——— *Society and Culture in Early Modern France*. Stanford: Stanford University Press, 1975.

Delany, Paul. *British Autobiography in the Seventeenth Century*. New York: Columbia University Press, 1969.

Dellile, G. "Dot des filles et circulation des biens dans les Pouilles aux XVIe et XVIIe siècles," *Mélanges de l'Ecole française de Rome* 96 (1983).

Delumeau, Jean. *La Peur en Occident (XIVe–XVIIIe siècle). Une cité assiégée*. Paris: Fayard, 1978.

——— *Le Péché et la Peur. La Culpabilisation en Occident (XIIIe–XVIIIe siècle)*. Paris: Fayard, 1983.

Demoris, R. *Le Roman à la première personne*. Paris, 1975.

Dickens, A. G., ed. *The Courts of Europe: Politics, Patronage, and Royalty, 1400–1800*. New York, 1977.

Dumont de Bostaquet. *Mémoires*. Paris: Mercure de France, 1968.

Dupront, Alphonse. "Réformes et 'modernité,'" *Annales ESC*, 1984, pp. 747–767.

Ebner, D. *Autobiography in Seventeenth-Century England*. The Hague, 1971.

Elias, Norbert. *Über den Prozess der Zivilisation. Soziogenetische und Psychogenetische Untersuchungen*. Basel, 1939; Berne: Francke AG, 1969. Trans. by E. Jephcott as *The Civilizing Process: The History of Manners*. New York: Urizen, 1978; Pantheon, 1982.

——— *Die höfische Gesellschaft. Untersuchungen zur Soziologie des Königstums und der höfischen Aristokratie*. Neuwied and Berlin: Hermann Luchterhand, 1969. Trans. by E. Jephcott, as *The Court Society*. Oxford: Basil Blackwell, 1983.

Engelsing, Rolf. *Analphabetentum und Lektüre. Zur Sozialgeschichte des Lesens in Deutschland zwischen feudaler und industrieller Gesellschaft*. Stuttgart, 1973.

——— *Der Bürger als Leser. Lesergeschichte in Deutschland 1500–1800*. Stuttgart, 1974.

——— "Die Perioden der Lesergeschichte in der Neuzeit," in *Zur Sozialgeschichte deutscher Mittel- und Unterschichten*. Göttingen: Vandenhoeck and Ruprecht, 1978.

Fairchilds, Cissi. *Domestic Enemies. Servants and their Masters in Old Regime France*. Baltimore: Johns Hopkins University Press, 1984.

"Famiglia e comunità. Storia sociale della famiglia nell'Europa moderna," *Quaderni Storici* 38, 1976.

Farge, Arlette. *Vivre dans la rue à Paris au XVIIIe siècle*. Paris: Gallimard/Julliard, 1979.

——— *La Vie fragile. Violence, pouvoir, et solidarités à Paris au XVIIIe siècle*. Paris: Hachette, 1986.

——— and Michel Foucault. *Le Désordre des familles. Lettres de cachet des Archives de la Bastille*. Paris: Gallimard/Julliard, 1972.

Fillon, A. *Louis Simon, étaminier 1741–1820 dans son village du haut Maine au siècle des Lumières*. University of the Maine, 1982.

Flandrin, Jean-Louis. "La diversité des goûts et des pratiques alimentaires en Europe du XVIe au XVIIIe siècle," *Revue d'histoire moderne et contemporaine*, 1983, pp. 66–83.

——— *Familles. Parenté, maison, sexualité dans l'ancienne France*. Paris: Hachette, 1976; rev. ed. Paris: Seuil, 1984.

——— *Les Amours paysannes. Amour et sexualité dans les campagnes de l'ancienne France (XVIe–XIXe siè-*

cle). Paris: Gallimard/Julliard, 1975.

——— *Le Sexe et l'Occident. Evolution des attitudes et des comportements*. Paris: Seuil, 1981.

Foisil, Madeleine. *Le Sire de Gouberville. Un gentilhomme normand au XVIe siècle*. Paris: Aubier, 1981.

Forestier, H. "Le 'droit des garçons' dans la communauté villageoise aux XVIIe et XVIIIe siècles," *Annales de Bourgogne* (1941): 109–114.

Foucault, Michel. *Surveiller et punir. Naissance de la prison*. Paris: Gallimard, 1975. Trans. by Alan Sheridan as *Discipline and Punishment: The Birth of the Prison*. New York: Random House, 1979.

Franklin, Alfred. *La Vie privée d'autrefois. Arts et métiers, modes, moeurs, usages des Parisiens du XIIe au XVIIIe siècle*. Paris, 1888–1901.

Frigo, D. *Il Padre di famiglia. Amministrazione privata e Pubblico Governo nell'Italia moderna*. Rome, 1985.

Frijhoff, W. *La Société néerlandaise et ses gradués, 1575–1814. Une recherche sérielle sur le statut des intellectuels*. Amsterdam, 1981.

Gayot, G. *La Franc-Maçonnerie française. Textes et Pratiques*. Paris: Gallimard/Julliard, 1980.

Gélis, Jacques. *L'Arbre et le fruit. La naissance dans l'Occident moderne, XVIe–XIXe siècle*. Paris: Fayard, 1981.

——— M. Laget, and M.-F. Morel. *Entrer dans la vie. Naissances et enfances dans la France traditionnelle*. Paris: Gallimard/Julliard, 1978.

Gillet, P. *Par mets et par vins. Voyages et gastronomie en Europe, XVIe–XVIIIe siècle*. Paris: Payot, 1985.

Gillis, John R. *Youth and History*. New York: Academic Press, 1974.

Ginzburg, Carlo. *I Benandanti. Stregoneria e Culti agrari tra Cinquecento e Seicento*. Turin: Einaudi, 1966.

——— *Il Formaggio e i Vermi. Il Cosmo di un mugnaio del '500*. Turin: Einaudi, 1976. Trans. by John and Anne Tedeschi as *The Cheese and the Worms: The Cosmos of a Sixteenth-Century Miller*. New York: Penguin, 1982.

Gloton, J. *Renaissance et Baroque à Aix-en-Provence. Essai sur la culture architecturale dans le midi de la France*. Paris, 1979.

Goody, Jack. *The Development of the Family and Marriage in Europe*. Cambridge: Cambridge University Press, 1983.

——— Joan Thirsk and E. P. Thompson, eds. *Family and Inheritance. Rural Society in Western Europe, 1200–1800*. Cambridge: Cambridge University Press, 1976.

Gough, R. *The History of Myddle*, ed. J. Hey, 1834. London: Penguin, 1981.

Goulemot, J.-M. "Démons, merveilles et philosophie à l'âge classique," *Annales ESC* (1980): 1223–1250.

——— "Pourquoi écrire? Devoir et plaisir dans l'écriture de Jean-Jacques Rousseau," *Romanistische Zeitschrift für Literaturgeschichte* 4 (1980).

——— "Le lecteur-voyeur et la mise en scène de l'imaginaire viril," *Laclos et le Libertinage*. Paris, 1982.

Groethuysen, Bernard. *Origines de l'esprit bourgeois en France*, vol. 1, *L'Eglise et la bourgeoisie*. Paris: Gallimard, 1927.

Grussi, O. *La Vie quotidienne des joueurs sous l'Ancien Régime à Paris et à la cour*. Paris: Hachette, 1985.

Gunda, B. "The Ethnosociological Structure of the Hungarian Extended Family," *Journal of Family History* (1982): 40–52.

Gutton, J.-P. *Domestiques et Serviteurs dans la France de l'Ancien Régime*. Paris: Aubier, 1981.

——— *La Sociabilité villageoise dans l'ancienne France. Solidarités et voisinages du XVIe au XVIIIe siècle*. Paris: Hachette, 1971.

Habermas, Jürgen. *Strukturwandel der Offentlichkeit*. Neuwied and Berlin: Hermann Luchterhand, 1962.

Halévi, R. *Les Loges maçonniques dans la France d'Ancien Régime. Aux origines de la sociabilité démocratique*. Paris: Armand Colin, 1984.

Heal, F. "The Idea of Hospitality in Early Modern England," *Past and Present* 102 (1984): 66–93.

Hepp, Noémi, and Jacques Hennequin, eds. *Les Valeurs chez les mémorialistes français du XVIIe siècle*. Paris: Klincksieck, 1979.

Jamerey-Duval, Valentin. *Mémoires. Enfance et éducation d'un paysan au XVIIIe siècle*. Paris: Le Sycomore, 1981.

Le Jeu au XVIIIe siècle. Aix-en-Provence: Edisud, 1971.

Joyce, William L., David D. Hall, Richard D. Brown, and John B. Hench. *Printing and Society in Early America*. Worcester, Mass.: American Antiquarian Society, 1983.

Jurgens, M., and P. Couperie. "Le logement à Paris aux XVIe et XVIIe siècles: une source, les inventaires après décès," *Annales ESC* (1962): 488–500.

Kagan, Richard L. *Students and Society in Early Modern Spain*. Baltimore: Johns Hopkins University Press, 1974.

Klapisch-Zuber, Christiane. *Women, Family and Ritual in Renaissance Italy*. Chicago: University of Chicago Press, 1985.

Kniebiehler, Y., and C. Fouquet. *L'Histoire des mères du Moyen Age à nos jours*. Paris: Montalba, 1980.

Kolakowski, Leszek. *Chrétiens sans Eglise. La Con-

science religieuse et le Lien confessionnel au XVIIe siècle. Paris: Gallimard, 1966.

La Fontaine-Verwey, H. "The First 'Book of Etiquette' for Children: Erasmus' *De civilitate morum puerilium*," *Quaerendo* I (1971): 19–30.

Lafon, J. *Régimes matrimoniaux et mutations sociales. Les époux bordelais (1450–1550)*. Paris and The Hague: Mouton, 1973.

Laget, M. *Naissances. L'Accouchement avant l'âge de la clinique*. Paris: Seuil, 1982.

Laslett, Peter. *Family Life and Illicit Love in Earlier Generations*. Cambridge: Cambridge University Press, 1977.

———— Karla Oosterven, and Richard M. Smith. *Bastardy and Its Comparative History*. London: Edward Arnold, 1980.

———— R. Wall, and J. Robin, eds. *Family Forms in Historical Europe*. Cambridge: Cambridge University Press, 1983.

Lebrun, François. *La Vie conjugale sous l'Ancien Régime*. Paris: Armand Colin, 1975.

Le Goff, Jacques, and Jean-Claude Schmitt, eds. *Le Charivari*. Paris and The Hague: Mouton, 1981.

Lehoux, F. *Le Cadre de vie des médecins parisiens au XVIe et au XVIIe siècle*. Paris: Picard, 1978.

Lejeune, Philippe. *L'Autobiographie en France*. Paris: Armand Colin, 1973.

———— *Le Pacte autobiographique*. Paris: Seuil, 1975.

Le Roy Ladurie, Emmanuel. *L'Argent, l'amour, et la mort en pays d'Oc*. Paris: Seuil, 1980.

———— *Le Carnaval de Romans. De la Chandeleur au mercredi des Cendres, 1579–1580*. Paris: Gallimard, 1979.

———— and Orest Ranum. *Pierre Prion, scribe. Mémoires d'un écrivain de campagne au XVIIIe siècle*. Paris: Gallimard/Julliard, 1985.

Levi, G. *L'Eredità immateriale. Carriera di un esorcista nel Piemonte del Seicento*. Turin: Einaudi, 1985.

Liebenwein, W. *Studiolo: Die Entstehung eines Raumtyps und seine Entwicklung bis zum 1600*. Berlin, 1977.

Livre et Lecture en Espagne et en France sous l'Ancien Régime. Paris: ADPF, 1981.

Lottin, A. *Chavatte, ouvrier lillois. Un contemporain de Louis XIV*. Paris: Flammarion, 1979.

———— et al. *La Désunion du couple sous l'Ancien Régime. L'exemple du Nord*. University of Lille—III, 1975.

Lougee, C. *Le Paradis des femmes. Women, Salons and Social Stratification in Seventeenth-Century France*. Princeton: Princeton University Press, 1976.

MacFarlane, Alan. *The Family Life of Ralph Josselin,*

a Seventeenth-Century Clergyman. An Essay in Historical Anthropology. Cambridge: Cambridge University Press, 1970.

———— *The Origins of English Individualism. The Family Property and Social Transition*. Oxford: Basil Blackwell, 1978.

McKendrick, Neil, John Brewer, and J. H. Plumb. *The Birth of a Consumer Society. The Commercialization of Eighteenth-Century England*. Bloomington: Indiana University Press, 1985.

Magendie, M. *La Politesse mondaine et les Théories de l'honnêteté en France au XVIIe siècle, de 1600 à 1650*. Paris, 1925.

La Maison de ville à la Renaissance. Paris: Picard, 1984.

Malgeri, F., and C. Russo, eds. *La Società religiosa nell'età moderna*. Naples, 1973.

Manger et Boire au Moyen Age. Paris: Les Belles Lettres, 1984.

Maza, Sarah. *Servants and Masters in Eighteenth-Century France. The Uses of Loyalty*. Princeton: Princeton University Press, 1983.

Ménétra, Jacques-Louis. *Journal de ma vie. Jacques-Louis Ménétra, compagnon vitrier parisien au XVIIIe siècle*. Paris: Montalba, 1982. Trans. by Arthur Goldhammer as *Journal of My Life*. New York: Columbia University Press, 1986.

Merzario, R. *Il Paese stretto. Strategie matrimoniali nello diocesi di Como, secoli XVI–XVIII*. Turin: Einaudi, 1981.

Milstein, Barney M. *Eight Eighteenth-Century Reading Societies. A Sociological Contribution to the History of German Literature*. New York: Peter Lang, 1972.

Montaigne, Michel Eyquem de. *The Complete Essays of Montaigne*, trans. Donald M. Frame. Stanford: Stanford University Press, 1957.

Morgan, Edmund S. *The Puritan Family. Religion and Domestic Relations in Seventeenth-Century New England*, rev. ed. New York: Harper and Row, 1966.

Muir, Edward. *Civic Ritual in Renaissance Venice*. Princeton: Princeton University Press, 1981.

Pellegrin, N. *Les Bachelleries. Organisation et fêtes de la jeunesse dans le Centre-Ouest, XVe–XVIIIe siècle*. Poitiers: Société des Antiquaires de l'Ouest, 1982.

Pepys, Samuel. *The Diary of Samuel Pepys*, ed. Robert Latham and William Matthews. Berkeley: University of California Press, 1985.

Peristiany, J. G., ed. *Mediterranean Family Structure*. Cambridge: Cambridge University Press, 1976.

Pinchbeck, Ivy, and Margaret Hewitt. *Children in English Society*, vol. 1, *From Tudor Times to the Eighteenth Century*. London: Routledge and Kegan Paul, 1969, and Toronto: University of Toronto Press, 1970.

Plumb, J. H. "The New World of Children in Eighteenth-Century England," *Past and Present* 67 (1975): 64–95.

Poisson, J.-M. "La Maison paysanne dans les bourgs siciliens (XIVe–XIXe siècle). Permanence d'un type?" *Archeologia medievale* 7 (1980): 83–94.

Pratiques de la confession. Des pères du dessert à Vatican II. Quinze Etudes d'histoire. Paris: Cerf, 1983.

Prosperi, A., ed. *La Corte e il "Corteggiano."* Rome, 1980.

Prüsener, M. "Lesegesellschaften im 18 Jahrhundert. Ein Beitrag zur Lesergeschichte," *Archiv für Geschichte des Buchwesens* 13 (1973): 396–594.

Ranum, Orest. "Courtesy, Absolutism, and the Rise of the French State, 1630–1660," *Journal of Modern History* 52 (1980): 426–451.

—— "Inventing Private Space. Samuel and Mrs. Pepys at Home, 1660–1669," *Wissenschaftskolleg zu Berlin, Jahrbuch 1982/83*, pp. 259–276.

Les Rites de passage. Neuchâtel: Museum of Ethnology, 1981.

Roche, Daniel. *Le Peuple de Paris. Essai sur la culture populaire.* Paris: Aubier, 1981.

—— *Le Siècle des Lumières en province. Académies et Académiciens provinciaux, 1680–1789.* Paris and The Hague: Mouton, 1978. Trans. by Marie Evans and Gwynne Lewis as *The People of Paris: An Essay in Popular Culture in the 18th Century.* New York: St. Martin's, 1986.

Rossiaud, J. "Prostitution, jeunesse et société dans les villes du Sud-Est au XVe siècle," *Annales ESC* (1976): 289–325.

—— "Les fraternités de jeunesse dans les villes du Sud-Est au XVe siècle," *Cahiers d'histoire* (1976): 67–102.

Roux, S. *La Maison dans l'histoire.* Paris: Albin Michel, 1976.

Saenger, Paul. "Silent Reading: Its Impact on Late Medieval Script and Society," *Viator, Medieval and Renaissance Studies* 13 (1982): 367–414.

Saint-Simon. *Mémoires.* Paris: Gallimard, 1953–1958.

Scala, G. *Illuminismo e Reforme nell'Italia del Settecento.* Bologna: Zanichelli, 1970.

Segalen, M. *Mari et Femme dans la société paysanne.* Paris: Flammarion, 1980. Trans. by Sarah Matthews as *Love and Power in the Peasant Family.* Chicago: University of Chicago Press, 1983.

Shorter, Edmund. *The Making of the Modern Family.* New York: Basic Books, 1975.

Smith, S. R. "The London Apprentices as Seventeenth-Century Adolescents," *Past and Present* 61 (1973): 149–161.

Solé, J. *L'Amour en Occident à l'époque moderne.* Paris: Albin Michel, 1976.

Starobinski, Jean. *L'Invention de la liberté, 1700–1789.* Geneva: Skira, 1964.

Stone, Lawrence. *Family, Sex, and Marriage in England, 1500–1800.* New York: Harper and Row, 1977.

Strauss, Gerald. *Luther's House of Learning: Indoctrination of the Young in the German Reformation.* Baltimore: Johns Hopkins University Press, 1979.

Strong, Roy. *The Renaissance Garden in England.* London: Thames Hudson, 1979.

Tardieu, Suzanne. *La Vie domestique dans le Mâconnais rural préindustriel.* Paris, 1964.

Thomas, Keith. *Man and the Natural World.* London: Penguin, 1983.

—— *Religion and the Decline of Magic. Studies in Popular Beliefs in Sixteenth- and Seventeenth-Century England.* London: Penguin, 1973.

Thornton, Peter. *Seventeenth-Century Interior Decoration in England, France, and Holland.* New Haven: Yale University Press, 1978.

Todd, Janet. *Women's Friendship in Literature.* New York: Columbia University Press, 1980.

Trexler, Richard C. *Public Life in Renaissance Florence.* New York: Academic Press, 1980.

Versini, L. *Le Roman épistolaire.* Paris, 1979.

Vigarello, Georges. *Le Corps redressé. Histoire d'un pouvoir pédagogique.* Paris: Jean-Pierre Delarge, 1978.

—— *Le Propre et le sale. L'hygiène du corps depuis le Moyen Age.* Paris: Seuil, 1985.

Vogler, Bernard. *Vie religieuse en pays rhénan dans la seconde moitié du XVIe siècle (1556–1619).* University of Lille—III, 1974.

Vovelle, Michel. *La Mort et l'Occident de 1300 à nos jours.* Paris: Gallimard, 1983.

Watkins, O. C. *The Puritan Experience: Studies in Spiritual Autobiography.* New York: Schocken, 1972.

Watt, Ian. *The Rise of the Novel. Studies in Defoe, Richardson, and Fielding.* Berkeley: University of California Press, 1965.

Weissman, Ronald F. E. *Ritual Brotherhood in Renaissance Florence.* New York: Academic Press, 1982.

Wheaton, Barbara K. *Savoring the Past.* Philadelphia: University of Pennsylvania Press, 1983.

Yver, J. *Essai de géographie coutumière.* Paris, 1966.

Zapperi, R. *L'Uomo incinto. La Donna, l'Uomo e il Potere.* Cosenza: Lerici, 1979.

Credits

The objects illustrated in this book (on the pages noted) are found in various locations, as follows: Accademia, Venice, 230; Alsatian Museum, Strasbourg, 526; Antwerp Museum, 175; Arsenal Library, Paris, 190, 201; Bibliothèque Nationale, Paris, 23, 26a, 28a, 29, 30, 31a, 34ab, 36b, 43, 54, 56abc, 61, 72, 73, 74, 78, 80ab, 81, 82, 84b, 87, 90, 91, 92, 94, 99, 103b, 105ab, 107, 116, 118, 126, 127, 135, 138, 139, 140, 145b, 150, 155, 169, 170, 171, 172, 176ab, 177, 181, 183, 187, 188, 191, 194, 195, 196, 197, 200ab, 203, 204, 210, 211b, 212, 213, 214, 218, 219, 228, 232, 234, 244ab, 254, 262, 266, 267, 270, 278, 280, 290, 291, 293, 294, 295ab, 296abcd, 305ab, 311b, 322, 323b, 333, 334, 335abc, 337, 339, 342, 344, 359, 367, 368, 370, 373b, 375, 380, 381, 386ab, 388ab, 391, 393, 420, 422, 424, 429, 434, 435, 448, 454, 456, 462, 468, 472, 473, 474, 477, 478, 483, 485, 486, 487, 488, 495, 505b, 506, 509, 514, 515, 520, 521, 532, 533, 534, 537, 538, 545, 551, 553, 555, 556, 558c, 559, 572, 574ab, 578, 580, 581b, 586, 589ab, 591, 594, 597, 602; Boymans-van-Beuningen Museum, Rotterdam, 58; Bristol Museum and Art Gallery, 149; British Library, London, 246a (Sloane Collection); British Museum, London, 220, 226b, 475; Cailleux Collection, Paris, 245a; Calvet Museum, Avignon, 248; Carmelite Collection, 324, 325; Carnavalet Museum, Paris, 41, 96, 114, 372, 376, 396, 418–419, 423, 482, 490, 576, 601, 605; Chapel of Saint-Tugen-en-Primelin, Finistère, 565; Marquise de Cholmondeley, collection of, 151 (photo A. Kurt); Christie's, London, 185; Conde Museum, Chantilly, 124, 264, 366, 426ab; Correr Museum, Venice, 46; Dahlem Museum, Berlin, 215; Dunkirk Museum, 88; Ecole des Beaux-Arts, Paris, 192; Fabre Museum, Montpellier, 166; Fogg Art Museum, Cambridge, Massachusetts, 312; Frick Collection, New York, 223; Gemaldegalerie, Dresden, 84a; Germanisches Nationalmuseum, Nuremberg, 341; Château du Gué-Péan, Loir-et-Cher, 247; Ham House, Surrey, 250b; J. Helft Collection, 300; Henri Dupuis Museum, Saint-Omer, 59; The Hermitage, Leningrad, 125; High Museum of Art, Atlanta, 253; Historical Library of the City of Paris, 158; Hôtel Jacques-Coeur, 28b; Institute of Art, Detroit, 308; Kunsthalle, Bremen, 501; Kunsthistoriches Museum, Vienna, 451, 496; Lambinet Museum, Ver-

sailles, 446; Library of Decorative Arts, Paris, 202, 346, 353, 457, 461, 583; Library of the National Museum of Natural History, Paris, 273abc; Longchamp Museum, Marseilles, 417; Lorraine Historical Museum, Nancy, 160; Louvre, Paris, 35, 65, 110, 120, 131, 222, 245b (Taillemas Collection), 259, 260, 274, 412, 421, 481, 498, 499a, 502, 512, 519, 570, 582, 596; Mittelrheinisches Landesmuseum, Mainz, 154; Municipal Library, Lille, 70; Municipal Library, Metz, 236; Municipal Museum, Agen, 415; Municipal Museum, Cambrai, 45; Municipal Museum, Evreux, 552; Municipal Museum, Laon, 573; Municipal Museum, Saint-Omer, 117; Musée de l'Ain, Bourg-en-Bresse, 326; Musée des Arts décoratifs, Paris, 137ab, 146, 268ab, 269, 303; Musée des Arts et Traditions populaires, Paris, 93, 97, 108, 558ab; Museum of Art and History, Auxerre, 275; Museum of the Ecole supérieure des Beaux-Arts, Paris, 508; Museum of Fine Arts, Aix-en-Provence, 577a; Museum of Fine Arts, Béziers, 26b; Museum of Fine Arts, Boston, 103 (Karolik Collection); Museum of Fine Arts, Caen, 32; Museum of Fine Arts, Carcassonne, 408; Museum of Fine Arts, Dijon, 288, 331, 362; Museum of Fine Arts, Lille, 25, 347; Museum of Fine Arts, Marseilles, 492; Museum of Fine Arts, Nantes, 98; Museum of Fine Arts, Nîmes, 277; Museum of Fine Arts, Orleans, 79, 427; Museum of Fine Arts, Rennes, 317; Museum of Fine Arts, Rouen, 240; Museum of Fine Arts, São Paulo, 530; Museum of Fine Arts, Strasbourg, 287, 581a; Museum of Fine Arts, Tours, 229; Museum of Painting and Sculpture, Grenoble, 311a; Museum of Saint-Lô, 340; National Gallery, London, 208, 221, 231, 237, 409, 455; National Gallery, Prague, 238; National Gallery of Art, Washington, 186 (Mellon Collection); National Gallery of Scotland, Edinburgh, 321; National Library, Florence, 539, 542; National Portrait Gallery, London, 211a, 256; Naval Museum, Paris, 464; Old Art Museum, Brussels, 323a, 549; Orbigny Museum, La Rochelle, 316; Ordre National des Parmaciens, Paris, 350 (Bouvet Collection); Our Lady of Hal, Brabant, 310; Our Lady of Kientzheim, Upper Rhine, 315ab; Château de Panat, Aveyron, 233; Paul-Dupuy Museum, Toulouse, 411, 418ab, 430, 438, 444; Petti Palace, Florence, 209; Picardy Museum, Amiens, 33; Police Museum, Paris, 587;

Count Powis, collection of, 249; Prado, Madrid, 298, 452; Querini Stampalia Gallery, Venice, 68, 83, 85; Rijksmuseum, Amsterdam, 410, 449, 499b; Royal Institute of Art, Brussels, 319, 328; Royal Museum, The Hague, 313; Sabauda Gallery, Turin, 77; Sacro Monte, Chapel 28, Varallo, 584; Saint-Denis Museum, Rheims, 505a; Society for the History of Protestantism, Paris, 100; Stattliche Museen Preussischer Kulturbesitz, Berlin, 318, 343, 351; Stockholm Museum, 36a, 145a; Tate Gallery, London, 384; Teesside Museum, Middlesborough, 31b; Thyssen-Bornemisza Collection, Lugano, 577b; Uffizi, Florence, 182, 216, 471; Château de Versailles, 20; Victoria and Albert Museum, London, 250a, 251b; Wallace Collection, London, 224; Worcester Art Museum, Massachusetts, 159, 206, 258; Yale University Art Gallery, New Haven, 129, 133; P. de Zoer Gallery, Amsterdam, 12.

Photographs were supplied by the following agencies and individuals: ACL, Brussels, 319, 323a, 328; Anderson-Giraudon, 216; Archives photographiques, 455, 582; J. Bernard, Aix-en-Provence, 417, 492; Bridgeman Art Library, London, 250b, 251ab; Bridgeman-Giraudon, 185, 321, 477; Bruckmann-Giraudon, 84a, 314; Bulloz, 28a, 36a, 65, 88, 100, 102, 110, 136, 192, 193, 230, 260, 264, 266, 275, 311, 372, 373a, 376, 396, 405, 412, 413, 415, 446, 451, 457, 490, 511, 552, 576, 601, 602, 605; CDDP des Hautes-Pyrénées, Tarbes, 406, 416, 432; Carmel de Beaune, 325; Carmélitaine Collection, 324; J.-L. Charmet, 41, 54, 61, 96, 156, 158, 169, 190, 201, 202, 333, 335abc, 350, 353, 359, 382, 461, 473, 482, 533, 541, 583, 587; Fabre Collection, 535; G. Dagli Orti, 46, 160, 182, 247, 326, 346, 452, 464, 472, 530, 584; Goulemot Collection, 377, 379; M. Feronato, 68, 83; H. Fillipetti, 504, 517; Fotografia Chomon-Perino, 77; Frequin-Photos, 58; J. Gélis, 310, 315ab;

Giraudon, 12, 20, 25, 28b, 31b, 33, 45, 86–87, 117, 124, 125, 142, 152, 166, 238, 245b, 248, 271, 274, 279, 287, 301, 308, 316, 317, 339, 366, 402, 421, 426ab, 495, 505a, 508; Hanfstaengl-Giraudon, 549; Cl. Inventaire Centre/J.-C. Jacques and R. Malnoury, 427; Inventaire général-SPADEM-1978, 565; Kunstfoto Speltdoorn, Brussels, 101; Lauros-Giraudon, 26, 32, 59, 79, 98, 114, 229, 240, 245, 276, 362, 423, 481, 519, 573; Mary Evans Picture Library, London, 249; Private collections, 37, 101, 136, 142 (Paris), 152, 156, 193, 279, 314 (The Hague), 373a, 402, 405, 413, 437, 442, 511; Réunion des Musées nationaux, 35, 120, 131, 222, 259, 498, 499a, 502, 512, 570, 582, 596; Roger-Viollet, 175, 179ab, 209 (photo Anderson-Viollet); 213, 223, 246, 283, 313, 592; Scala, Florence, 85; Seuil Archives, 99, 103b, 107, 116, 155, 177, 181, 187, 196, 197, 200ab, 290, 291, 294, 295ab, 296abcd, 322, 323b, 339, 342, 375, 381, 386b, 474, 478, 515, 537, 538, 553, 558abc, 581b; Yan, 408, 444.

Credits for color plates, in order of appearance, are: Chapel of Saint-Tugen-en-Primelin, Finistère, Inventaire général-SPADEM-1978; Musée des Augustins, Toulouse, Yan; Nationalmuseum, Stockholm, Statens Konstmuseer, Stockholm; Museum of Budapest, Lauros-Giraudon; Correr Museum, Venice, G. Dagli Orti; Louvre, Paris, Lauros-Giraudon; Museum of Fine Arts, Lille, G. Dagli Orti; Christie's, London, Bridgeman-Giraudon; Museum of Fine Arts, Lille, Lauros-Giraudon; Museum of Fine Arts, Dijon, G. Dagli Orti; Carnavalet Museum, Paris, Lauros-Giraudon; Château de Versailles, G. Dagli Orti; Carnavalet Museum, Paris, G. Dagli Orti; Naval Museum, Paris, G. Dagli Orti; Naval Museum, Paris, G. Dagli Orti; Carnavalet Museum, Paris, G. Dagli Orti.

Index

solidarity, 518–519; extended family communities, 522–528; urban families, 572–574. *See also* Family life

Houses, 6, 7, 49, 499; fireplaces, 7, *492;* the chamber, 217–220, 221; alcove, 220; ruelle, 220; bedrooms, 225, 507–509; the study, 225–227; the cabinet, 228–229, 246; in family record books, 336, 338; kitchens, *341;* Durer's drawings of, 493–494, *495, 501;* Brueghel's paintings of, 494, 496–497; farmhouse, 494, 496, *502,* 504, *505,* 517; Le Nain Brothers' paintings of, 497–499; peasant houses, 497–503; changing uses, 500–501; construction materials, 504; rural artisans' houses, 504; barricade, *505;* and the stem-family system, 513; communal house, 524–525; apartment buildings, 575–576; shops located in, 575

Huchon, Jean, *Flambeau des chrétiens,* 71

Hugh of Saint-Victor, *De institutione novitiarum,* 170, 288, 289

Huguenots, 331, 345

Hygiene, 186, 187, 189, 267

Individualism, 7, 265

Inns, *582,* 509

Insane asylums, 607

Insults, 580, 582, 584, 585

Intellectual societies, 8

Intellectuals, rise of, 124–125

Intimacy, 163, 164, 207, 400; and secrecy, 182–199; civility and, 199–206; archaeology of the intimate, 207–210; architecture of, 210–229; with God, 239–243; sexual relations and, 262–263

Isham, Elisabeth, 349

Jamerey-Duval, Valentin, 391, 481

Jansenism, 73, 80

Janssens, Pieter Elinga, *The Sweeper,* 499

Jeauart, Etienne: *The Copper Pot,* 275; *The Arrival of the Wet Nurses,* 573

Jefferson, Thomas, 220

Jewelry, 246, 248–252, *254, 258*

Journals. *See* Diaries and journals

Justice, 42–44, 47, 48

Kant, Immanuel, 17

Keayne, Robert, 133

King, Samuel: *Portrait of the Reverend the Dr. Ezra Stiles, 133*

L'Hermite, Tristan, 404, 405, 406; *Le Page disgracié,* 246, 248

L.S.R., *L'Art de bien traiter,* 272, 275, 277, 278, 294, 297, 302

La Bruyère, Jean de, 78, 97, 195, 305

La Hoguette, Fortin de, *On Conversation,* 151

La Motte of Tournai, Jean-François de, *117*

La Salle, Jean-Baptiste de, 177, 181, 183, 184, 190, 200

La Serre, Jean Puget de, *Le Secrétaire à la Mode,* 116

Labiche, *La Cagnotte,* 125

Laclos, Choderlos de: *Les Liaisons dangereuses,* 386; *Félicia ou mes fredaines,* 425

Lagniet, *Illustrated Proverbs,* 375

Lallemand, Jean-Baptiste, *The Bourgeois Kitchen,* 288

Lancret, Nicolas, *Lunch with Ham,* *264*

Largillière, Nicolas de, *The Aldermen of Paris, 33*

Larue, J.-A., *160*

La Tour, Georges de: *Dice Players,* *31; Saint Jerome, 111*

Launay, Fernand de, *213*

Law, 44, 602; family complicity, 44; rights of property owners, 47, 48, 515, 562; protection of the person, 47–48; secrecy in the law, 48, 54; of theft, 53–54; criminal trials, 55–56; witnesses' behavior, 56–57; litigiousness, 58; effect of passion, 244; property rights of women, 411–413; Tables of the Law, *444;* of inheritance, 510–511, 515–516, 518; local customs and, 559–561; punishment, 559–560; charivaris and, 560–561, 563–564; French Penal Code, 560; loss of honor and, 579–580; 584, 587–588; lettre de cachet, 588–600; family tribunals, 600, 604, 606

Le Brun, Charles, 228; School of, *Establissement de l'Académie des sciences, 20*

Le Grand d'Aussy, *History of French Private Life,* 265

Le Nain Brothers, 497–499; *Young Card Players, 405; Preparations for the Dance, 511; Interior Portraits, 512*

Le Nain de Tillemont, 221

Le Play, Frédéric, 507

Le Quinio, *Journey in the Jura,* 523

Le Roy Ladurie, Emmanuel, 51, 452

Le Vau, Louis (architect), 228

Legaré, Gilles, 250

Lejeune, Philippe, 391

Lejeune, Pierre, 329

Léonard, Emile G., 100

Lepautre, Jean, 72

Lettre de cachet, 588–600

Lévi-Strauss, Claude, 450

Libraries, 128, 129, 132, 134–144

Liège, Defrance de, *At the Sign of Minerva,* 362

Lighting, street, 555

Literacy, 4, 18, 19, 111, 121; religious tracts and, 74; national literacy rates, 112–115, 117–119; class differences in, 115–116; rural-urban differences, 116; and the Reformation, 119–120; hostility to writing, 122–124; among servants, 142. *See also* Books; Libraries

Literary salons, 8, 305–306

Literary societies, 17

Literature. *See* Books

Little societies, 8

Livre de raison. *See* Family record books

Lobineau (Dom), 91

Locke, John, 138–139; *Some Thoughts Concerning Education,* 314–315

Longhi, Pietro, *68, 83,* 85

Longolius, Gisbertus, 172

Lotto, Lorenzo: *Study, 226,* 227; *Young Man in His Studio, 230*

Louis XIII, 323, 332, 355–358, 461, 478

Louis XIV, 10, 15, 279, *280, 325,* 358, 360, 361, 403, 418, 419, 475, 478

Louis XV, 422, 423, 598

Louis XVI, 599, 600

Love, 7, 243–245; courtship, *35;* garden scenes, 212–215; letters, 227, 246; in marriage, 244, 252, 254; exchange of objects, 246–248, *258;* miniature portraits, 248–252; friendship compared to, 454

Loyalty, *36*

Lune, Pierre de, *Nouveau cuisinier,* 275, 286, 306

Luther, Martin, 100

Lutheranism, 102–104, 109, 118, 173